TAPESTRY OF THE GODS

VOLUME II

Psychospiritual Transformation and the Seven Rays

by

MICHAEL D. ROBBINS, Ph.D.

FIRST EDITION

COPYRIGHT 1988 © BY MICHAEL D. ROBBINS, PH.D.

ALL RIGHTS RESERVED
INCLUDING THE RIGHT OF REPRODUCTION
IN WHOLE OR IN PART IN ANY FORM

PUBLISHED BY THE UNIVERSITY OF THE SEVEN RAYS PUBLISHING HOUSE
A DIVISION OF THE SEVEN RAY INSTITUTE
A NON–PROFIT, TAX–EXEMPT EDUCATIONAL CORPORATION
128 MANHATTAN AVENUE
JERSEY CITY HEIGHTS, NEW JERSEY 07307
(201) 659-6638

COVER DESIGNED BY IRIS SPELLINGS

LIBRARY OF CONGRESS CATALOG CARD NUMBER: 88-51065
ISBN NUMBER 0-9621869-0-2   VOLUME I
ISBN NUMBER 0-9621869-1-0   VOLUME II
ISBN NUMBER O-9621869-2-9   TWO VOLUME SET

MANUFACTURED IN THE UNITED STATES OF AMERICA

TABLE OF CONTENTS
VOLUME I

THE SEVEN RAYS: AN ESOTERIC KEY TO UNDERSTANDING HUMAN NATURE

Dedication i
Acknowledgements iii
Commentary, by Robert Gerard, Ph.D. v
Table of Contents xxiii

INTRODUCTORY THOUGHTS

I. The Purpose of *Tapestry of the Gods* xxxix
II. Format for *Tapestry of the Gods*, Volumes I and II xl
III. The *Tapestry of the Gods* Series xliv
IV. A General Introduction to the Science of the Seven Rays xlvi
   A. The Nature of Individual Purpose xlvi
   B. The Nature of Energy xlvii
   C. Energy and Human Identity xlviii
   D. Quality as a Key to Identity il
   E. The Purposeful Approach to Living l
   F. Entities and Emanations within our Local Cosmosystem li
   G. The Seven Rays lv
V. The Names of the Seven Rays lvi
VI. How to Use this Book lvii

SECTION I
AN EXAMINATION OF THE POSITIVE AND NEGATIVE TRAITS OF THOSE WHO ARE STRONGLY INFLUENCED BY A PARTICULAR RAY ENERGY

I. Ray I: The Ray of Will and Power 5
   A. Some Strengths Characteristic of Those upon the First Ray 5
   B. Some Weaknesses Characteristic of Those upon the First Ray 12
II. Ray II: The Ray of Love–Wisdom 19
   A. Some Strengths Characteristic of Those upon the Second Ray 19

B. Some Weaknesses Characteristic of Those upon the Second Ray 29
III. Ray III: The Ray of Active Intelligence 36
    A. Some Strengths Characteristic of Those upon the Third Ray 36
    B. Some Weaknesses Characteristic of Those upon the Third Ray 50
IV. Ray IV: The Ray of Harmony Through Conflict 59
    A. Some Strengths Characteristic of Those upon the Fourth Ray 59
    B. Some Weaknesses Characteristic of Those upon the Fourth Ray 77
V. Ray V: The Ray of Concrete Knowledge and Science 89
    A. Some Strengths Characteristic of Those upon the Fifth Ray 89
    B. Some Weaknesses Characteristic of Those upon the Fifth Ray 102
VI. Ray VI: The Ray of Devotion and Abstract Idealism 109
    A. Some Strengths Characteristic of Those upon the Sixth Ray 109
    B. Some Weaknesses Characteristic of Those upon the Sixth Ray 118
VII: Ray VII: The Ray of Order and Ceremonial Magic 128
    A. Some Strengths Characteristic of Those upon the Seventh Ray 128
    B. Some Weaknesses Characteristic of Those upon the Seventh Ray 141
VIII. Ray Types 150
    A. Types (1A) and (1B) 152
    B. Types (2A), (2B) and (2C) 152
    C. Types (3A) and (3B) 153
    D. Types (4A) and (4B) 154
    E. Types (5A) and (5B) 155
    F. Types (6A) and (6B) 156
    G. Types (7A), (7B) and (7C) 157

SECTION II
AN ANALYSIS OF THE DIFFERENCES
AND SIMILARITIES IN RAY QUALITIES

I. General Contrasts Between Ray 1 and Ray 2 165
    A. Major Ray 1 and Ray 2 Differences 166
    B. Major Ray 1 and Ray 2 Similarities 166
II. General Contrasts Between Ray 1 and Ray 3 168
    A. Major Ray 1 and Ray 3 Differences 169
    B. Major Ray 1 and Ray 3 Similarities 169
III. General Contrasts Between Ray 1 and Ray 4 170
    A. Major Ray 1 and Ray 4 Differences 171
    B. Major Ray 1 and Ray 4 Similarities 172

- IV. General Contrasts Between Ray 1 and Ray 5 173
  - A. Major Ray 1 and Ray 5 Differences 174
  - B. Major Ray 1 and Ray 5 Similarities 174
- V. General Contrasts Between Ray 1 and Ray 6 175
  - A. Major Ray 1 and Ray 6 Differences 175
  - B. Major Ray 1 and Ray 6 Similarities 177
- VI. General Contrasts Between Ray 1 and Ray 7 178
  - A. Major Ray 1 and Ray 7 Differences 179
  - B. Major Ray 1 and Ray 7 Similarities 181
- VII. General Contrasts Between Ray 2 and Ray 3 182
  - A. Major Ray 2 and Ray 3 Differences 183
  - B. Major Ray 2 and Ray 3 Similarities 184
- VIII. General Contrasts Between Ray 2 and Ray 4 186
  - A. Major Ray 2 and Ray 4 Differences 187
  - B. Major Ray 2 and Ray 4 Similarities 188
- IX. General Contrasts Between Ray 2 and Ray 5 190
  - A. Major Ray 2 and Ray 5 Differences 191
  - B. Major Ray 2 and Ray 5 Similarities 192
- X. General Contrasts Between Ray 2 and Ray 6 193
  - A. Major Ray 2 and Ray 6 Differences 194
  - B. Major Ray 2 and Ray 6 Similarities 195
- XI. General Contrasts Between Ray 2 and Ray 7 197
  - A. Major Ray 2 and Ray 7 Differences 198
  - B. Major Ray 2 and Ray 7 Similarities 199
- XII. General Contrasts Between Ray 3 and Ray 4 201
  - A. Major Ray 3 and Ray 4 Differences 202
  - B. Major Ray 3 and Ray 4 Similarities 203
- XIII. General Contrasts Between Ray 3 and Ray 5 204
  - A. Major Ray 3 and Ray 5 Differences 205
  - B. Major Ray 3 and Ray 5 Similarities 206
- XIV. General Contrasts Between Ray 3 and Ray 6 208
  - A. Major Ray 3 and Ray 6 Differences 209
  - B. Major Ray 3 and Ray 6 Similarities 210
- XV. General Contrasts Between Ray 3 and Ray 7 211
  - A. Major Ray 3 and Ray 7 Differences 212
  - B. Major Ray 3 and Ray 7 Similarities 213
- XVI. General Contrasts Between Ray 4 and Ray 5 215
  - A. Major Ray 4 and Ray 5 Differences 216

   B. Major Ray 4 and Ray 5 Similarities 217
XVII. General Constrasts Between Ray 4 and Ray 6 219
   A. Major Ray 4 and Ray 6 Differences 220
   B. Major Ray 4 and Ray 6 Similarities 222
XVIII. General Contrasts Between Ray 4 and Ray 7 223
   A. Major Ray 4 and Ray 7 Differences 224
   B. Major Ray 4 and Ray 7 Similarities 225
XIX. General Contrasts Between Ray 5 and Ray 6 227
   A. Major Ray 5 and Ray 6 Differences 228
   B. Major Ray 5 and Ray 6 Similarities 229
XX. General Contrasts Between Ray 5 and Ray 7 231
   A. Major Ray 5 and Ray 7 Differences 232
   B. Major Ray 5 and Ray 7 Similarities 233
XXI. General Contrasts Between Ray 6 and Ray 7 234
   A. Major Ray 6 and Ray 7 Differences 235
   B. Major Ray 6 and Ray 7 Similarities 237

SECTION III
UNDERSTANDING HUMAN NATURE
THROUGH AN ANALYSIS OF
THE FIVEFOLD HUMAN ENERGY SYSTEM

I. The Complexity of the Human Being 241
   A. The Fivefold Human Energy System 242
   B. The Five Fields of the Human Energy System 243
   C. The Five Fields and their Order of Presentation 243
II. The Ego as a Faculty within the Egoic (Transpersonal) Field 245
III. Some Key Functions, Operations and Characteristic Dynamics
    of the Ego and its Faculties within the Transpersonal Field 246
IV. The Personality Faculty within the Personality Field 251
V. Some Key Functions, Operations and Characteristic Dynamics
    of the Personality Faculty within the Personality Field 252
   A. Positive Personality Dynamics 252
   B. Negative Personality Dynamics 255
VI. The Concrete Mental Faculty within the Lower Mental Field 258
VII. Some Key Functions, Operations and Characteristic Dynamics
    of the Concrete Mental Faculties within the Lower Mental Field 258
VIII. The Sentient Faculty within the Sentient Field 266
IX. Some Key Functions, Operations and Characteristic Dynamics
    of the Sentient Faculty within the Sentient Field 266

X. The Physico–Dynamic Faculty within the Bio–Field 271
XI. Some Key Functions, Operations and Characteristic Dynamics
of the Physico–Dynamic Faculty within the Bio-field 271
XII. Some Important Differentiations Between Fields 273
   A. Some Distinctions Between the Soul Faculty and Field
      and the Personality Faculty and Field 274
   B. Some Distinctions Between the Personality Faculty and Field
      and the Mental Faculty and Field 275
   C. Some Distinctions Between the Mental Faculty and Field
      and the Etheric–Physical Brain 278
XIII. Important Variable Attributes of the Three Personality Fields 282
   A. Mental Attributes which Vary Most Frequently
      According to the Ray of the Mental Field 282
   B. Emotional Attributes which Vary Most Frequently
      According to the Ray of the Emotional Field 284
   C. Etheric–Physical Attributes which Vary Most Frequently
      According to the Ray of the Etheric–Physical Field 285

SECTION IV
THE DYNAMICS OF THE SEVEN RAYS AS THEY FUNCTION THROUGH THE FIVE FIELDS OF THE HUMAN ENERGY SYSTEM

I. The Soul Ray 290
   A. The Dynamics of the First Ray Soul 291
   B. The Dynamics of the Second Ray Soul 293
   C. The Dynamics of the Third Ray Soul 295
   D. The Dynamics of the Fourth Ray Soul 298
   E. The Dynamics of the Fifth Ray Soul 301
   F. The Dynamics of the Sixth Ray Soul 303
   G. The Dynamics of the Seventh Ray Soul 306
II. The Dynamics of the Seven Types of Personality Rays 309
   A. The Dynamics of the First Ray Personality 311
      1. Positive Ray One Personality Dynamics 311
      2. Negative Ray One Personality Dynamics 311
   B. The Dynamics of the Second Ray Personality 314
      1. Positive Ray Two Personality Dynamics 314
      2. Negative Ray Two Personality Dynamics 314
   C. The Dynamics of the Third Ray Personality 317
      1. Positive Ray Three Personality Dynamics 317
      2. Negative Ray Three Personality Dynamics 318

- D. The Dynamics of the Fourth Ray Personality ... 321
  - 1. Positive Ray Four Personality Dynamics ... 321
  - 2. Negative Ray Four Personality Dynamics ... 322
- E. The Dynamics of the Fifth Ray Personality ... 325
  - 1. Positive Ray Five Personality Dynamics ... 325
  - 2. Negative Ray Five Personality Dynamics ... 326
- F. The Dynamics of the Sixth Ray Personality ... 329
  - 1. Positive Ray Six Personality Dynamics ... 329
  - 2. Negative Ray Six Personality Dynamics ... 330
- G. The Dynamics of the Seventh Ray Personality ... 333
  - 1. Positive Ray Seven Personality Dynamics ... 333
  - 2. Negative Ray Seven Personality Dynamics ... 334

III. The Qualities of the Mental Ray ... 337
- A. List of Qualities for the Ray One Mind ... 339
- B. Commentary on the Dynamics of the Ray One Mind ... 339
- C. List of Qualities for the Ray Two Mind ... 346
- D. Commentary on the Dynamics of the Ray Two Mind ... 346
- E. List of Qualities for the Ray Three Mind ... 352
- F. Commentary on the Dynamics of the Ray Three Mind ... 352
- G. List of Qualities for the Ray Four Mind ... 361
- H. Commentary on the Dynamics of the Ray Four Mind ... 362
- I. List of Qualities for the Ray Five Mind ... 371
- J. Commentary on the Dynamics of the Ray Five Mind ... 371
- K. List of Speculative Qualities for the Ray Six Mind ... 379
- L. Speculative Commentary on the Dynamics of the Ray Six Mind ... 379
- M. List of Speculative Qualities for the Ray Seven Mind ... 382
- N. Speculative Commentary on the Dynamics of the Ray Seven Mind ... 383

IV. An Analysis of Mental Attributes which Vary Most Frequently According to the Ray of the Mental Field ... 389

V. The Qualities of the Emotional Ray and the Ray of the Etheric–Physical Field ... 408

VI. The Ray of the Sentient (Emotional) Field ... 409
- A. List of Qualities for the Ray One Emotional Field ... 413
- B. Commentary on the Dynamics of the First Ray Emotional Field ... 413
- C. List of Qualities for the Ray Two Emotional Field ... 417
- D. Commentary on the Dynamics of the Second Ray Emotional Field ... 417
- E. List of Speculative Qualities for the Ray Three Emotional Field ... 420
- F. Speculative Commentary on the Dynamics of the Third Ray Emotional Field ... 420
- G. List of Speculative Qualities for the Ray Four Emotional Field ... 423

- H. Speculative Commentary on the Dynamics of the Fourth Ray Emotional Field ... 423
- I. List of Speculative Qualities for the Ray Five Emotional Field ... 426
- J. Speculative Commentary on the Dynamics of the Fifth Ray Emotional Field ... 426
- K. List of Qualities for the Ray Six Emotional Field ... 429
- L. Commentary on the Dynamics of the Sixth Ray Emotional Field ... 429
- M. List of Speculative Qualities for the Ray Seven Emotional Field ... 432
- N. Speculative Commentary on the Dynamics of the Seventh Ray Emotional Field ... 432

VII. The Ray of the Etheric–Physical Field (Bio–field) ... 435
- A. List of Qualities for the Ray One Etheric–Physical Body (Field) ... 439
- B. Commentary on the Dynamics of the First Ray Etheric–Physical Body (Field) ... 439
- C. List of Speculative Qualities for the Ray Two Etheric–Physical Body (Field) ... 442
- D. Speculative Commentary on the Dynamics of the Second Ray Etheric–Physical Body (Field) ... 442
- E. List of Qualities for the Ray Three Etheric–Physical Body (Field) ... 445
- F. Commentary on the Dynamics of the Third Ray Etheric–Physical Body (Field) ... 445
- G. List of Speculative Qualities for the Ray Four Etheric–Physical Body (Field) ... 448
- H. Speculative Commentary on the Dynamics of the Fourth Ray Etheric–Physical Body (Field) ... 448
- I. List of Speculative Qualities for the Ray Five Etheric–Physical Body (Field) ... 451
- J. Speculative Commentary on the Dynamics of the Fifth Ray Etheric–Physical Body (Field) ... 451
- K. List of Speculative Qualities for the Ray Six Etheric–Physical Body (Field) ... 453
- L. Speculative Commentary on the Dynamics of the Sixth Ray Etheric–Physical Body (Field) ... 453
- M. List of Qualities for the Ray Seven Etheric–Physical Body (Field) ... 456
- N. Commentary on the Dynamics of the Seventh Ray Etheric–Physical Body (Field) ... 456

VIII. Commentary References ... lxiii

VOLUME TWO
PSYCHOSPIRITUAL TRANSFORMATION AND THE SEVEN RAYS

SECTION V
THE SEVEN RAYS AND THE DYNAMICS OF SOUL/PERSONALITY INTEGRATION

Table of Contents i
How To Use This Book xv
I. The Integration of Soul and Personality 463
   A. Important Realizations 466
   B. The Dynamics of Soul/Personality Integration 469
   C. Phases of Focus in the Process of Integrating Soul and Personality
      Considered with Respect to the Seven Rays 470
   D. Integration Formulae as they Apply to both the Soul Ray
      and the Personality Ray 471
   E. The Relation Between the Seven Techniques
      of Integration and the Seven Integration Formulae 473
   F. Contrasts Between the Strictly Personal and the Spiritual Phases
      of the Integration Process 475
      1. Integration Dynamics for the Energy System
         with a Prominent First Ray 475
      2. Integration Dynamics for the Energy System
         with a Prominent Second Ray 476
      3. Integration Dynamics for the Energy System
         with a Prominent Third Ray 477
      4. Integration Dynamics for the Energy System
         with a Prominent Fourth Ray 478
      5. Integration Dynamics for the Energy System
         with a Prominent Fifth Ray 479
      6. Integration Dynamics for the Energy System
         with a Prominent Sixth Ray 480
      7. Integration Dynamics for the Energy System
         with a Prominent Seventh Ray 482
II. Format for the Presentation of the 49 Soul/Personality Combinations
    in Relation to the Integration Process 484
III. Soul/Personality Combinations with a Ray One Soul 495
   A. Some Contrasts Between the Ray 1 Soul and the Ray 1 Personality 495
   B. Some Contrasts Between the Ray 1 Soul and the Ray 2 Personality 496

- C. The Integration Process for the Individual
  with a Ray 1 Soul and a Ray 2 Personality 497
- D. Some Contrasts Between the Ray 1 Soul and the Ray 3 Personality 502
- E. The Integration Process for the Individual
  with a Ray 1 Soul and a Ray 3 Personality 503
- F. Some Contrasts Between the Ray 1 Soul and the Ray 4 Personality. 508
- G. The Integration Process for the Individual
  with a Ray 1 Soul and a Ray 4 Personality 509
- H. Some Contrasts Between the Ray 1 Soul and the Ray 5 Personality 515
- I. The Integration Process for the Individual
  with a Ray 1 Soul and a Ray 5 Personality 516
- J. Some Contrasts Between the Ray 1 Soul and the Ray 6 Personality 521
- K. The Integration Process for the Individual
  with a Ray 1 Soul and a Ray 6 Personality 521
- L. Some Contrasts Between the Ray 1 Soul and the Ray 7 Personality 527
- M. The Integration Process for the Individual
  with a Ray 1 Soul and Ray 7 Personality 528

IV. Soul/Personality Combinations with a Ray Two Soul 533
- A. Some Contrasts Between the Ray 2 Soul and the Ray 1 Personality 533
- B. The Integration Process for the Individual
  with a Ray 2 Soul and a Ray 1 Personality 533
- C. Some Contrasts Between the Ray 2 Soul and the Ray 2 Personality 538
- D. Some Contrasts Between the Ray 2 Soul and the Ray 3 Personality 540
- E. The Integration Process for the Individual
  with a Ray 2 Soul and a Ray 3 Personality 540
- F. Some Contrasts Between the Ray 2 Soul and the Ray 4 Personality 545
- G. The Integration Process for the Individual
  with a Ray 2 Soul and a Ray 4 Personality 545
- H. Some Contrasts Between the Ray 2 Soul and the Ray 5 Personality 550
- I. The Integration Process for the Individual
  with a Ray 2 Soul and a Ray 5 Personality 550
- J. Some Contrasts Between the Ray 2 Soul and the Ray 6 Personality 556
- K. The Integration Process for the Individual
  with a Ray 2 Soul and a Ray 6 Personality............................. 556
- L. Some Contrasts Between the Ray 2 Soul and the Ray 7 Personality. 561
- M. The Integration Process for the Individual
  with a Ray 2 Soul and a Ray 7 Personality 561

V. Soul/Personality Combinations with a Ray Three Soul 567
- A. Some Contrasts Between the Ray 3 Soul and the Ray 1 Personality 567
- B. The Integration Process for the Individual
  with a Ray 3 Soul and a Ray 1 Personality 568

C. Some Contrasts Between the Ray 3 Soul and the Ray 2 Personality 573
D. The Integration Process for the Individual
   with a Ray 3 Soul and a Ray 2 Personality 573
E. Some Contrasts Between the Ray 3 Soul and the Ray 3 Personality 579
F. Some Contrasts Between the Ray 3 Soul and the Ray 4 Personality 580
G. The Integration Process for the Individual
   with a Ray 3 Soul and a Ray 4 Personality 580
H. Some Contrasts Between the Ray 3 Soul and the Ray 5 Personality 586
I. The Integration Process for the Individual
   with a Ray 3 Soul and a Ray 5 Personality 586
J. Some Contrasts Between the Ray 3 Soul and the Ray 6 Personality 592
K. The Integration Process for the Individual
   with a Ray 3 Soul and a Ray 6 Personality 592
L. Some Contrasts Between the Ray 3 Soul and the Ray 7 Personality 598
M. The Integration Process for the Individual
   with a Ray 3 Soul and a Ray 7 Personality 598

VI. Soul/Personality Combinations with a Ray Four Soul 604
A. Some Contrasts Between the Ray 4 Soul and the Ray 1 Personality 604
B. The Integration Process for the Individual
   with a Ray 4 Soul and a Ray 1 Personality 604
C. Some Contrasts Between the Ray 4 Soul and the Ray 2 Personality 610
D. The Integration Process for the Individual
   with a Ray 4 Soul and a Ray 2 Personality 610
E. Some Contrasts Between the Ray 4 Soul and the Ray 3 Personality 616
F. The Integration Process for the Individual
   with a Ray 4 Soul and a Ray 3 Personality 616
G. Some Contrasts Between the Ray 4 Soul and the Ray 4 Personality 622
H. Some Contrasts Between the Ray 4 Soul and the Ray 5 Personality 624
I. The Integration Process for the Individual
   with a Ray 4 Soul and a Ray 5 Personality 624
J. Some Contrasts Between the Ray 4 Soul and the Ray 6 Personality 630
K. The Integration Process for the Individual
   with a Ray 4 Soul and a Ray 6 Personality 630
L. Some Contrasts Between the Ray 4 Soul and the Ray 7 Personality 636
M. The Integration Process for the Individual
   with a Ray 4 Soul and a Ray 7 Personality 636

VII. Soul/Personality Combinations with a Ray Five Soul 642
A. Some Contrasts Between the Ray 5 Soul and the Ray 1 Personality 642
B. The Integration Process for the Individual
   with a Ray 5 Soul and a Ray 1 Personality 642

  C. Some Contrasts Between the Ray 5 Soul and the Ray 2 Personality 647
  D. The Integration Process for the Individual
    with a Ray 5 Soul and a Ray 2 Personality 647
  E. Some Contrasts Between the Ray 5 Soul and the Ray 3 Personality 653
  F. The Integration Process for the Individual
    with a Ray 5 Soul and a Ray 3 Personality 653
  G. Some Contrasts Between the Ray 5 Soul and the Ray 4 Personality 659
  H. The Integration Process for the Individual
    with a Ray 5 Soul and a Ray 4 Personality 659
  I. Some Contrasts Between the Ray 5 Soul and the Ray 5 Personality 665
  J. Some Contrasts Between the Ray 5 Soul and the Ray 6 Personality 666
  K. The Integration Process for the Individual
    with a Ray 5 Soul and a Ray 6 Personality 666
  L. Some Contrasts Between the Ray 5 Soul and the Ray 7 Personality 672
  M. The Integration Process for the Individual
    with a Ray 5 Soul and a Ray 7 Personality 672
VIII. Soul/Personality Combinations with a Ray Six Soul 678
  A. Some Contrasts Between the Ray 6 Soul and the Ray 1 Personality 678
  B. The Integration Process for the Individual
    with a Ray 6 Soul and a Ray 1 Personality 678
  C. Some Contrasts Between the Ray 6 Soul and the Ray 2 Personality 684
  D. The Integration Process for the Individual
    with a Ray 6 Soul and a Ray 2 Personality 684
  E. Some Contrasts Between the Ray 6 Soul and the Ray 3 Personality 690
  F. The Integration Process for the Individual
    with a Ray 6 Soul and a Ray 3 Personality 690
  G. Some Contrasts Between the Ray 6 Soul and the Ray 4 Personality 696
  H. The Integration Process for the Individual
    with a Ray 6 Soul and a Ray 4 Personality 696
  I. Some Contrasts Between the Ray 6 Soul and the Ray 5 Personality 702
  J. The Integration Process for the Individual
    with a Ray 6 Soul and a Ray 5 Personality 702
  K. Some Contrasts Between the Ray 6 Soul an the Ray 6 Personality 708
  L. Some Contrasts Between the Ray 6 Soul and the Ray 7 Personality 709
  M. The Integration Process for the Individual
    with a Ray 6 Soul and a Ray 7 Personality 709
IX. Soul/Personality Combinations with a Ray Seven Soul 715
  A. Some Contrasts Between the Ray 7 Soul and the Ray 1 Personality 715
  B. The Integration Process for the Individual
    with a Ray 7 Soul and a Ray 1 Personality 715

C. Some Contrasts Between the Ray 7 Soul and the Ray 2 Personality 721
D. The Integration Process for the Individual
   with a Ray 7 Soul and a Ray 2 Personality 721
E. Some Contrasts Between the Ray 7 Soul and the Ray 3 Personality 727
F. The Integration Process for the Individual
   with a Ray 7 Soul and the Ray 3 Personality 727
G. Some Contrasts Between the Ray 7 Soul and the Ray 4 Personality 734
H. The Integration Process for the Individual
   with a Ray 7 Soul and a Ray 4 Personality 734
I. Some Contrasts Between the Ray 7 Soul and the Ray 5 Personality 741
J. The Integration Process for the Individual
   with a Ray 7 Soul and a Ray 5 Personality 741
K. Some Contrasts Between the Ray 7 Soul and the Ray 6 Personality 748
L. The Integration Process for the Individual
   with a Ray 7 Soul and a Ray 6 Personality 748
M. Some Contrasts Between the Ray 7 Soul and the Ray 7 Personality 755

SECTION VI
AN ANALYTICAL APPROACH TO THE FIVEFOLD RAY CHART

I. Ray Exercises in the Abstract 759
   A. Seven Ray Formulae 760
   B. Example 1 761
   C. Example 2 762
   D. Example 3 763
   E. Example 4 765
   F. Example 5 767
   G. Example 6 769
   H. Example 7 771
II. Three Hypothetical Individuals 774
III. Seven Biographical Ray Analyses 790
   A. Annie Besant 790
   B. Albert Schweitzer 800
   C. Albert Einstein 811
   D. Michelangelo Buonarroti 834
   E. Louis Pasteur 847
   F. Joan of Arc 855
   H. Francis Bacon 873
IV. Closing Remarks 897

SECTION VII
APPENDICES AND GLOSSARY

I. Appendix I: Some Ray Tabulations from the Tibetan's Teachings 901
II. Appendix II: A Brief Consideration of the Constellations and Planets from the Perspective of Esoteric Astrology as Presented in the Teachings of the Tibetan Master, Djwhal Khul 909
III. Appendix III: A Brief Discussion of the Meanings of the Planets from the Perspective of Esoteric Astrology 917
IV. Appendix IV: The Personal Identity Profile 923
V. Appendix V: Search for the Soul Ray – a Meditative Technique to assist in the Determination of the Soul Ray 943
VI. Appendix VI: Recommended Reading on the Subject of Esoteric Psychology and the Seven Rays 946
VII. Glossary 951

How To Use This Book

There are a number of reasons why *Tapestry of the Gods* should be studied systematically rather than read casually and selectively. Granted – the idea that there are seven rays conditioning all units of life upon our planet and within our solar system is, essentially, a *simple* idea. It is also true that the essential qualities of the seven rays are not really difficult to understand. Further, on the archetypal level, the seven rays are quite easy to distinguish, and confusion is not a problem. However, in order to produce that complex, multifaceted manifestation called the human being, a number of rays must come together, and it is in their weaving and blending that the archetypal clarity and ease of differentiation begins to disappear.

At first estimation, the task of determining a fivefold ray chart (even a sixfold one) may not seem very formidable. When students are first exposed to the seven ray paradigm, they may expect to discover their ray structures with rapidity. The more they begin to investigate the subject, however, the more subtleties and ambiguities begin to appear. What at first seemed obvious becomes subject to many qualifications and reservations. With increased sophistication a period of uncertainty often supervenes, and it may take the earnest enquirer *years* before a firm and unshakeable intuitive conviction confirming a particular ray structure dawns upon the illumined mind. For this reason, *Tapestry of the Gods* should be *studied as a whole* and not simply used in a piecemeal manner.

A great many people are primarily interested in themselves. There is nothing essentially wrong in such an orientation; self-knowledge is absolutely indispensable, and the Delphic Injunction, "Man Know Thyself" must be fulfilled before the human being can become an illumined server of the Divine Plan. It is, however, quite impossible to *know oneself in a vacuum!* The individual who is also vitally interested in the quality and character of other individuals is the individual who is truly equipped to see himself. This means that the best way for us to understand our own rays is to understand the rays of those with whom our lot is cast; we must understand ourselves *in context*.

The implications are obvious: the science of the seven rays must be studied in a large and general way before the ray structures of particular individuals can be expected to emerge with clarity. *Tapestry of the Gods* is designed with this progression in mind. Volume I offers a fairly comprehensive exploration of the seven rays in relation to human psychology. The rays are treated individually and in relation to each other. Every ray is examined in relation to every vehicle of the human energy system. A close and careful reading of this material is definitely advisable before venturing into Volume II. It is, however, very probable that Volume II will be of greater interest to many students than Volume I, because in Volume II the 42 (more precisely 49) soul/personality ray combinations are carefully explored. Without bothering to read Volume I, some students may be tempted to dive into Volume II in the eager attempt to *"find* themselves." This would be a mistake. The search for their ray structures (and the ray structures of others they seek to understand) will be far more successful if proper attention is given to the explanations and analyses found in the first volume.

At this point, I would like to offer a few simple suggestions to students who hope to gain the maximum benefit from the first two volumes of *Tapestry of the Gods*.

1. Read Volume I first.

2. As you read, think of yourself and others you know well. Begin hypothetically to determine their qualities, but do not jump to conclusions. Reserve judgment. Do not hesitate to write liberally in the margins.

3. When doubts regarding ray structure arise, use the tabulations of contrasts found in Volume I, Section II, and Volume II, Section V. At length your decision will be best if made on the basis of intuition, but in preparation, *check lists* of ray qualities are advisable. If, for instance, when thinking of an individual, you check off 20 qualities which correlate with ray five, and only three or four qualities correlating with ray three, ray five is much more likely to be present than ray five. Of course, it must be remembered, that we all have *all* the rays. It is simply a matter of emphasis in any one life.

4. As you work your way through the book, propose a number of tentative ray charts for yourself (and others). *Using your reasoning faculties* seek to justify or refute the legitimacy of the various charts you propose. You may not have a fifth or a third ray mind, but it is good to subject your possible choices to "sweet reason." In the end, the intuitive apprehension of a first or fourth ray mind may come closer to the mark, but before trusting so-called intuitive realizations too completely, *think the matter through*.

5. When you work with Volume II, seek to *identify* both as a soul and as a personality. When identified as a soul, look at your personality and try to determine what you see. In Section V there are many paragraphs that describe the task of a soul qualified by a particular ray when faced with a particular kind of personality. Does your soul-illumined vision of your personality match any of the descriptive paragraphs? Conversely, seek also to identify as a personality, and try to determine how you experience the voice of the soul. What is its quality? What is your particular manner of accepting or rejecting this voice? In each division of Section V there is a paragraph dealing with this matter. Determine which (if any) seem to pertain to you.

6. When you begin to develop some clearer ideas regarding your soul and personality ray, focus on the paragraphs which describe the *ideal combination* of the two rays. Which such paragraphs appeal to you most? With which do you resonate? Which paragraph (or paragraphs) seem to describe the productive union of your foremost ray qualities (your soul and personality ray)? You can be experimental here: if the section describing the ideal qualities of various soul/personality ray combinations seems incomplete in some respect, use your imagination to invent other ideal combinations. It must be realized that simply knowing your soul and personality ray (however valuable) is not enough. You must know how to *use* those energies in the best possible way. Often, through the use of the creative imagination, optimum methods for expressing your ray qualtiies can be

discovered. Eventually you can combine all five rays in your ray chart (as well as your Sun, Moon and Rising Sign) to create an eightfold 'energy–picture' of your nature. From this eightfold picture you can determine what might be called your 'best composite image' – i.e., the optimum way of fusing and blending *all* your major *ray* and *astrological* energies.

7. Once you feel quite certain of your soul and personality rays, it becomes important to understand how to integrate them more fully. Such an integration continues (according to the Tibetan) even *after* the third initiation. Section V is filled with paragraphs describing the various *integration formulae* for each of the soul/personality ray combinations. Experiment working with these formulae. Apply them to your life situations. Observe your life, and determine where they should be applied. Monitor yourself and determine where you have succeeded in applying them, and where you have failed. Your particular *dual formula* can be used throughout your life, and as you gain practice in its use, your skillful application will grow.

8. When you come to Section VI, which deals specifically with how to approach the analysis of a ray chart, study the examples carefully. After doing so, begin to propose various ray charts *in the abstract* and make a game of interpreting them (perhaps with friends). This will provide you with a needed fluency in the 'language of the rays,' and will enhance your power of combination and your ability to blend ray qualities. It is also an enjoyable and illuminating pastime to make up brief character sketches and attempt to analyze them in terms of the seven rays, as I did in Section VI. Multiple interpretations are, of course, possible, but this only serves to make such exercises more intriguing.

9. One of the most important exercises to sharpen your identification and understanding of the rays is to focus upon well–known contemporary, historical, fictional or mythological figures. I did this throughout Section V and, especially, in the last part of Section VI. After reading the seven biographical ray analyses in Section VI carefully, see if you agree or disagree with the analyses offered. If you disagree, ask yourself why? Can you give good *reasons* for your disagreement? Or perhaps you agree in part and disagree in part. In any case, support your opinions with reasons. After you have worked with and through the seven analyses, and considered the lives of some of the individuals briefly mentioned in relation to every soul/personality combination in Section V, begin to examine the lives of individuals whom you find particularly interesting. Undertake your own extensive ray analyses, and wrestle with the task of creating plausible ray charts for them.

10. Realize that this book is incomplete and is bound to include a number of errors, for human understanding of esoteric psychology and the science of the seven rays is only beginning. It will take the dedicated and intelligent effort of many thinkers to clarify that understanding. Can you suggest ways and means of improving the study of the rays? Can you find errors where they exist and offer suggestions for their correction? Please bring all errors (and all suggestions for improving present methods of studying the rays) to the attention of the University of the Seven Rays Publishing House.

The science of the seven rays is in its infancy. The majority of us cannot yet *see* a ray, nor can we measure a ray objectively; yet the time must soon come when we can do both. It is the task of all serious students to learn what presently can be learned about this fascinating science; to *apply* in service what has been learned; and to discover valid ways of *extending* that learning. This book is a small part of a great effort being undertaken by a number of serious students of esoteric psychology and the seven rays. Hopefully, it will convey some measure of light. I strongly encourage all students of esoteric psychology to dedicate their soul–illumined minds and loving hearts to the elucidation of the science of the seven rays. Struggling and bewildered humanity *needs* this science.

Note: It is strongly recommended that students of *Tapestry of the Gods* take the Personal Identity Profile (found in Appendix IV, page 923, Volume II). The P.I.P. can be an excellent means of indicating ray strengths and inclinations, and can be of real assistance as one seeks to determine one's ray chart.

TAPESTRY OF THE GODS
VOLUME II

Section V

THE SEVEN RAYS
AND THE DYNAMICS OF
SOUL/PERSONALITY INTEGRATION

THE INTEGRATION OF SOUL AND PERSONALITY

One of the major purposes of esoteric psychology is to facilitate the union of soul and personality. This union leads eventually to the transfiguration of the personality. Although the general psychospiritual procedures for bringing about this union are identical for every human being, there are significant individual differences depending upon the condition of an individual's energy system, and the types of rayological and astrological energies which qualify it.

In his *Esoteric Psychology, Vol. II,* the Tibetan has presented a number of "Techniques of Integration" found in the *Old Commentary*. These techniques describe the procedure to be followed by those whose soul or personality is upon one or other of the seven rays as they attempt, first, to integrate their personality and then, coordinate soul and personality.

The techniques or formulas for integration are definitely *ray techniques*. The question may arise as to whether these techniques are to be used according to the ray of the soul or the ray of the personality. There is some ambiguity surrounding this question, and the best answer may be that the techniques or formulas are applicable in relation to *both* the ray of the personality and the ray of the soul.

In the following paragraphs are statements which contribute to the sense of ambiguity:

Statements supporting the idea that it is the ray of the soul to which the aspirant must refer when applying the Techniques of Integration:

> **It is the ray of the ego or soul, slumbering in the early stages within the form, which occultly applies these modes of integration. The soul is essentially the integrative factor, and this shows in the early and unconscious stages as the coherent power of the life principle to hold the forms together in incarnation. In the later and conscious stages, it shows its power by applying these methods of control and unification to the personality. They are not applied, nor can the man avail himself of them, until such time as he is an integrated personality.**
> Esoteric Psychology, Vol. II, p. 346

> *...the integration with which we shall primarily deal as we study the seven Techniques of Integration is that of the personality as it integrates into the whole of which it is a part, through service to the race and to the Plan. Bear in mind that these ray techniques are imposed by the soul upon the personality after it has been somewhat integrated into a functioning unity and is, therefore, becoming slightly responsive to the soul, the directing Intelligence.*
> Ibid., p. 351

Further hints that the Techniques of Integration, indeed, refer to the soul ray can be found in the section of *Esoteric Psychology, Vol. II* dealing with the particular Technique which applies to those upon the first ray. Throughout this three page section (pp. 351–354), there is conveyed a sense of how the first ray individual evolves over the course of a number of lives. Obviously, it is the *true individual*, the individualized Ego, who thus evolves – all the while working under the influence of one particular ray. The personality, though it *may* retain the same ray over the course of several lives, frequently changes rays from life to life, just as it frequently changes astrological influences.

Tapestry of the Gods

The Tibetan, it seems, frequently uses ambiguity as an occult "blind", forcing the reader to think in a fluid, non-rigid manner. Although it is remotely *possible* to interpret the following sentence (referring to a section of the *Old Commentary*) as a description of a technique to be used by a first ray personality, it is difficult to refuse the implication that the Tibetan is referring to a first ray soul when he speaks of "the man upon the first ray":

> **Such is the pattern of thought and the process of the life of the man upon the first ray who is seeking first of all to control his personality and then to dominate his environment.**

Note the feeling of the passage of an extended period of time which permeates the following description of the "man upon the first ray..."

> **At first, his motive is that of selfish, separative achievement, and then comes failure to be satisfied. A higher achievement then takes place as a result of the service of the Plan, until the time eventually comes when the first ray man can be trusted to be God's Destroying Angel - the Angel who brings life through destruction of the form.** *Ibid., p. 352*

The word "eventually" is key. The process of changing from selfish destructiveness to beneficent destructiveness in cooperation with the Divine Plan surely cannot develop over the course of merely one life! Its seems clear that we are dealing with the progress of a first ray *soul* who will be found using, at one time or another, each of the seven possible types of personality ray.

In the sentence immediately following the previous reference to "Destroying Angels," the Tibetan gives us an example of the way he keeps the use of terms fluid in order to provoke thought. He states: "Such integrated personalities are frequently ruthless at first, selfish, ambitious...etc." Why now refer to the "man upon the first ray" as an integrated personality when all that has gone before implies the gradual evolution of a first ray soul? Perhaps it is because the Tibetan often uses terms interchangeably in order to show things *in relationship*. He uses terms like "person" or "individual" to refer to a personality, a soul, or even a Monad. There are also passages in which the terms "egos" and "monadic types" seem to be used interchangeably as on pp. 211–212 of *Esoteric Psychology, Vol. II.*

The reason for this may well lie in the *theory of emanation.* Simply considered, the Monad emanates the ego (spelled sometimes as "*Ego*") or the soul, and the soul emanates the personality. Many intricate technicalities notwithstanding, these three are *all one thing* in different aspects, and the Tibetan does not want us to forget this fact. A personality is really a soul 'in disguise,' so to speak, just as personality and soul are really an extension of the Monad. What we refer to as the personality, is *essentially* the soul, or even more essentially, the Monad. The Tibetan is at pains to remind us (*Ibid.,*p. 358) that *the personality ray is always a subray of the egoic ray,* and thus, essentially, *the personality has no real existence independent from the soul which emanated it.* Thus, it is legitimate to call a personality a soul, just as it is legitimate to call an ego a Monad. The reverse also seems to be true, as when he refers to those with first ray or fifth ray Monads as first ray or fifth ray *people! (Initiation Human and Solar,* p. 187, and *A Treatise on Cosmic Fire,* p. 577–579). The Tibetan's method of writing and "blinding" is an example of the second ray faculty of "Inclusive Reason," which involves, according to the Tibetan, "a very high point of synthetic comprehension,", and which "produces the inherent divine capacity which enables the detail of the sensed Whole to be grasped in meticulous entirety."

In addition to the many statements which present the first ray quality in such a light that it appears to relate to a fundamental (and not a peripheral) aspect of the human being (hence, to the soul and *not* to the personality), there is one commanding piece of evidence which should prove that the seven Techniques of Integration do, indeed, refer to the soul ray, even if not exclusively so. In *Esoteric Psychology, Vol. II*, p. 353, D.K. describes the crisis experienced by the first ray man who "cannot remain satisfied with the gaining of power in the personality sense and in a material world." He seeks to walk with others, to regain feeling and to become inclusive. As the light breaks in upon his situation, "the first thing which is revealed to him is the devastating sight of that which he has destroyed." He is subjected to what is called "the light which shocks," and he seeks to "rebuild that which he has destroyed."

There next follows a most fascinating paragraph which begins with the sentence:

> **It is interesting to note that when this stage is reached (the stage of rebuilding as the first ray man understands it), he will usually pass through four incarnations ....**

The personality ray for the first of these four incarnations is not given, but it is suggested that during the second incarnation the personality ray may be the third or the seventh; that for the third incarnation the personality will be the second; and that during the fourth life "he can function safely *through a first ray personality*[emphasis MDR] without losing his spiritual balance...." There can be no doubt then, that during this entire section on the integration of the personality, it is the *ray of the soul* which is, primarily, being discussed.

Some ambiguity, however, does remain, for there are hints and statements which make it seem that the Techniques of Integration can *also* be applied to the ray of the personality.

Statements or hints supporting the idea that it is the ray of the personality to which the aspirant must refer when considering the Techniques of Integration.

First of all, the Techniques of Integration appear in a section of *Esoteric Psychology, Vol. II* given to a study of "The Ray of Personality." "The Egoic Ray" was treated in the immediately preceding section of some 253 pages. (This fact, however, must not be weighed too heavily because the Technique of Fusion, by means of which soul and personality are fused and blended into one smoothly functioning spiritual organism, and which is obviously keyed to the ray of the soul, is also found just a few pages later within the section on the Ray of Personality).

The most convincing case for believing that the Techniques of Integration refer partially (if not exclusively) to the personality ray appears in the following paragraph which succeeds the presentation of four "formulas" which summarize in a single word the Technique of Integration for each ray:

> As we brood on these words and on the remaining three which are indicated hereafter, we shall bring clearly into our consciousness the keynote for the disciples of the world at this time who are in a position to discover *that their personalities or their souls* [emphasis, MDR] *are on some one or another of these rays*. Ibid., p. 368

By including both the words "personalities" and "souls," the Tibetan seems to be saying that the integration formulas have a *dual* application. Experience in attempting to apply these formulas to the lives of individuals demonstrates that the proposed dual application *does* stand to reason.

The words in the following quotation, suggest that these formulas and techniques can be and are used in relation to the personality ray, though D.K. states the drawbacks of such use in no uncertain terms. When one reads between the lines it again seems clear that these formulas refer *fundamentally* to the soul ray even though they *may* be applied upon the level of the personality. Applying them strictly to the level of personality, however, seems to have its dangers:

> The use of these words by those who are not pledged disciples in connection with their personality rays and personality expression might be definitely undesirable. The third ray personality, emphasising *stillness*, for instance, might find himself descending into the sloughs of lethargy; the first ray personality, seeking to develop *inclusiveness* might go to extremes, deeming himself a centre of inclusiveness. These are Words of Power, when used by a disciple, and must be employed in the light of the soul or may have a striking harmful effect.

In light of the ambiguity, and even though the soul ray must be given the "lion's share" when using these techniques, it would seem wise to learn how these formulae might be effectively applied in relation to *both* the soul and personality (and their respective rays) in order to 1) bring about the integration of the personality, 2) its growing alignment with the soul, 3) the gradual blending of the two, and 4) their eventual fusion.

Important Realizations

Before discussing the problems of integration to be faced by those who have any of the 49 possible combinations of soul and personality rays (seven such combinations being highly unlikely until a very advanced stage of evolution is achieved – if then), it would be well to clarify certain matters. First and foremost: *the soul ray does not manifest only upon the level of the soul or Ego.* Even in the early stages of evolution, long before the individual human being can be called, in any sense, soul–infused, the soul is manifesting through the lower man. The tabulations on p. 39–43 of *Esoteric Psychology, Vol. II*, which apply to both the early and later stages of soul manifestation, demonstrate that rather negative, personality–related manifestations of ray energy do occur as a result of ray energy emanating from the soul. This is not to say that ray energy emanated from the soul can, itself, be considered negative in any way. Rather, the soul's ray is *appropriated* or, rather, mis–appropriated by the individual personality fields and later by the integrated personality field itself.

What this means, in utterly simplistic terms, is that the soul ray energy is not "good" while the energy of the personality ray is "bad.". Those with a soul upon a given ray do, indeed, have personality glamors relating to that ray, because the personality misuses (limits or distorts) the energy of the soul ray and (especially in the pre-spiritual phases of evolution) turns it to personality ends. The soul and its ray energy, however, are *fundamental*, and this means that *the personality will always carry the coloration of the soul ray no matter what may be the temporary ray of that personality in a particular incarnation*. Therefore, certain negative traits, *apparently* associated with the personality, do, indeed, derive from misappropriated soul ray energy and will, therefore, serve as a clue as to which may be the ray of the soul.

Of course, the actual ray of the personality will *also* be the cause of various personality traits and glamors. Actually, the rays of *each* of the personality vehicles will contribute to the quality (and, potentially, to the glamors) of the personality. Interestingly it is possible for an individual (at different times) to demonstrate the positive traits related to the personality ray and negative traits related to the soul ray – and vice versa, which is the more usual expectation.

As the soul seeks to integrate the personality and bring the energy qualities of the personality vehicles into harmony with its own ray quality, the soul has to contend not only with the ray tendencies of the personality and its vehicles, but *with the negative personality reflection of its very own ray qualities*. In fact, the seven one-word formulae, each to be used with one of the seven Techniques of Integration, address the correction of *selfishly misused soul ray energy* even more, perhaps, than they do the correction of the abuses of the personality ray of the current incarnation. We must remember that each personality (no matter what its ray) will demonstrate the qualities and (until a very high stage of evolution is reached) the prominent glamors of its soul ray energy. It is these glamors, especially, which must be rectified if the personality is to become aligned, coordinated and integrated with the soul. A personality may, of course, become powerfully integrated within its own "ring-pass-not" through the selfish use of its own ray and of the appropriated soul-ray energy, but in this type of integration there will be no appreciable blending, fusing or integrating of the personality and its vehicles with the soul. In short, unless the formulae are used, personality integration *in the spiritual sense*, will not occur.

For instance, suppose the soul ray is the second ray and the personality is the first. The personality will demonstrate not only the usual willful first ray glamors, but some of the fear, weakness and over-attachment of the second ray. In order for there to be 1) a true alignment of the personality with the soul, 2) a subsequent coordination and interplay between them, and, finally, 3) an integration of the personality into the life of the soul, the second ray formula of *Centralization* must be used. This is because the personality, though sometimes proud and isolated because of its first ray nature, will be permeated by second ray traits because the personality is, *essentially*, an emanation of a second ray soul. Once there is a detachment from the non-essentials and from the many personality ties (stimulated by the personality's appropriation of the soul's second ray energy of attachment), and also the achievement of a relatively detached centralization, then the soul and personality can be aligned, coordinated, and an increasing integration and fusion will develop between them.

Of course, it would be possible for such a personality to create a selfish, self-centered form of integration (strictly of the personality) without using the Technique of

Integration and its formula *Centralization*. In such a case it would pride itself (first ray) upon its many attachments and ties (second ray), and might live a life of many social and interpersonal satisfactions divorced from a conscious appreciation of the true purpose of the soul. This however, is not the state of personality integration (*in its highest sense*) and, in any case, is only temporary, for the dissatisfactions arising from the misuse of soul energy will usually lead to rectification.

It is important to realize that the term "personality" is defined by the Tibetan in a number of ways, the last of which is very broad and gives the intelligent student much food for thought:

A man can be regarded as a personality in truth when the form aspect and the soul nature are at—one.

This definition seems to suggest that only after the Integration Formula has been used, the personality is aligned with the soul, and soul–personality integration (not just personality integration itself) is proceeding, can a person be thought of as a *truly integrated personality* – or, indeed, even as a *personality* in the fullest sense of the word.

The Dynamics of Soul–Personality Integration

One of the most important themes of esoteric psychology is the union (yoga) of one of the major "pairs of opposites" – soul and personality. The Tibetan has described this process in general (cf., pp. 342–343) and in greater detail for those whose soul is found upon any one of the seven rays.

The possibility of integrating the personality and, then, of expressing the soul through the integrated personality does not even arise until more than half–way through the long cycle of evolution. The ordinary progress of evolution during which the human being has identified his consciousness with one personality vehicle after another (first the physical body, then the emotions and finally the mind) is superseded by a desire for *Self*–awareness. There has been a great reorientation during which the individual "leaves behind the hitherto desirable and aspires to that which has not hitherto been seen."

It is at this point of unfoldment, when the human being is subject to a "process of evolution wherein 'divine attraction' supersedes the attraction of the three worlds," that a knowledge of the rays and their interaction becomes especially valuable. By the time this re–orientation and change of values has taken place, the individual is either an advanced human being or a spiritual aspirant.

This stage of evolution spans a period of development beginning with the uncomfortable realization that there exists a lack of control between the divine and human aspects of the man, and ending with the complete fusion of the soul ray and the personality ray – the consciously achieved blending of soul and personality into one united energy field.

For the purposes of our approach, which is focusing upon certain stages of psychospiritual development which are of importance to aspirants and disciples, we will be considering soul and personality interactions during each of the following phases:

Phases of Focus in the Process of Integrating Soul and Personality Considered with Respect to the Seven Rays

1. The pre–spiritual phase of soul–personality interaction: this is the stage of selfish personality integration during which the personality pursues its own concerns exclusively. While it does not respond to the spiritual motivations and promptings of the soul, the personality does appropriate soul and soul ray energy for its own use. The result is a selfish personality demonstration, qualified by the energy of the personality ray, and reinforced by the misappropriated energy of the soul and its ray.

2. The phase of conflict based on a growing sense of duality: the individual is an advanced human being or an aspirant. A degree of personality integration has occurred. The mind is developed to the point where the individual can function successfully in the world under the direction of the personality ray. There is, however, the aspiration for a different kind of life more in line with the quality of the soul ray. The individual recognizes the presence of the soul ray mostly by the dissatisfaction he feels when engaged in pursuits related only to the personality ray and the rays of the personality vehicles. There ensues a constant warfare between the impulses of the personality ray and that of the 'intruding' soul ray. The conflict at first is unresolved and the situation remains unsettled. This phase marks the beginning of a gradual transference of the center of life interest.

3. The phase of gradual correction, adjustment, accommodation and harmonization: these adjustments are made by the aspirant or disciple who, standing mid–way between soul and personality, has become the detached observer, and seeks to make the personality a fit instrument for cooperation with the energy of the soul and thus, with the Divine Plan. Through the use of the appropriate Integration Formula, alignment and revelation have occurred and the aspirant or disciple comprehends the task ahead.

4. The phase of subordination: the personality is gradually subordinated to the requirements of the Self and begins to work in unison with that Self.

5. The phase of gradual unification and interplay: a gradual integration of the personality into the life of the soul proceeds, and a gradual blending of the soul ray and personality ray into one united energy field. The personality ray is becoming a subray of the soul ray. The Technique of Fusion can be applied.

6. The phase of fusion: the transfiguration of the personality is in process. The personality is soul–infused; the personality is becoming, in the true sense of the word, *the soul in manifestation*.

Throughout this section of the book we will deal with 49 (but more specifically, 42) combinations of soul and personality rays, as these combinations function during the progressive stages of soul–personality integration.

Integration Formulae as They Apply to both the Soul Ray and the Personality Ray

Let us again emphasize that aspirants and disciples are concerned with *two* kinds of personality integration: the first is the integration of the personality per se, and within itself; the second is the integration of the already integrated personality with the soul. This second stage should, perhaps, always be referred to as *soul–personality integration*. However, when D.K. gives formulae for the integration of the personality, *these formuae apply to the second kind of personality integration, soul–personality integration*.

It is important and interesting to realize that strictly personal integration (the first type) is brought about not so much by the use of the Integration Formulae, as by qualities which are, virtually, the *opposite* of these one–word Integration Formulae! It is because a person is already demonstrating *too much* of his ray quality that the Integration Formula (which emphasizes qualities which are an *'antidote'* to that ray quality) must be employed.

The Integration Formulae are not to be applied in the earlier stages of personality integration. It is only after a degree of strictly personal integration has been achieved, that these Formulae can be applied successfully. The earlier phase of strictly personal integration is brought about by the strong and straight–forward emphasis of the individual's ray qualities (overemphasis of which, it is the purpose of the appropriate Integration Formula to moderate or correct). The main point to be remembered here, is that the seven Integration Formulae *do not apply* in the early stages of personality integration – the stages during which the personality is becoming a well–coordinated, efficient, though selfish, organism. They apply only when the time has come to relate the personality directly to the soul.

Before discussing the numerous combinations of soul and personality rays from the point of view of soul–personality integration, it seems a good idea to discuss briefly the seven Formulae derived from the seven Techniques of Integration. *Once a fairly advanced stage of evolution has been reached*, each of these formulae can be effective when applied by the disciple in relation to *either* his soul or personality ray (though the greatest emphasis should almost always be given to applying the appropriate formula in relation to the soul ray). In fact, it would be advisable for each individual engaged in promoting a more complete and harmonious soul–personality interplay, to understand and utilize *two formulae* – one for his personality ray and one for his soul ray.

In any case, it is important to realize, that *the use of the formulae represents a change in the usual direction of evolution and an alteration in technique*. Prior to the time of their application, the integration of the personality was proceeding in a manner thoroughly consistent with the usual 'energy tendencies' of both the soul and personality rays (for *both* the soul ray and personality ray energies are involved in personality integration).

For instance, let us suppose that the first ray of Will or Power is either the soul ray or the personality ray. Prior to the stage of evolution in which conscious soul–personality integration begins, (i.e., prior to the stage in which use of the appropriate Integration Formula is indicated), the individual will probably use will and assertiveness (often selfishly) to gain self-control and to achieve effectiveness in the world. Self-control and effectiveness are strong indicators of what is usually recognized as an integrated personality. This phase occurs before the love aspect of the soul is potently engaged, for the personality, itself, corresponds to the intelligence or activity aspect of divinity (just as the soul corresponds to the love aspect), and the first phases of personality integration necessitate a strong mental polarization. When this first phase of personality integration is complete, we will have a powerful, dominating, self-centered and very integrated and coherent life demonstration, achieved through the *unmodified use of first ray energy*. At this point, a *reversal in procedure* must take place. Certain forms of strenuous, assertive, willful activity (characteristic of the first ray) must be *discontinued*, and a more quiet, receptive attitude (characteristic of the second aspect of divinity) must be developed before the second phase of personality integration (which is really the integration of personality with the soul) can occur. Up to this point, the first ray individual has no doubt utilized the first ray qualities of rebuff and exclusiveness to mobilize and integrate his forces. But – and this is the point – such customary first ray methods are not at all like the first ray Integration Formula which calls for *Inclusion*, (a quality far more characteristic of the second ray than the first). Thus, as a general rule, when personality integration has proceeded as far as it can using the *usual methods* directly expressive of the ray energy of the soul or personality, then the appropriate Integration Formula must be called in. It is this Formula which introduces a balancing aspect of energy which *lifts* the integration process out of the phase of strictly personal integration, into a more spiritual, soul-related phase of activity. The contrast between each Formula and the usual trend of ray expression can be seen in each case. In some cases the contrast is extremely obvious; in one or two, it is more subtle, and requires interpretation. The principle, however, holds good.

The Relation Between the Seven Techniques of Integration and the Seven Integration Formulae

The seven Techniques of Integration are marvellously evocative paragraphs translated by the Tibetan from the *Old Commentary*. They are very comprehensive, and extend from the period of what we are calling *strictly personal integration* to the later phase of *soul–personality integration*. These paragraphs (with the exception of those for ray one) include both the *usual* ray approaches to integration and the *modified* approaches, characterized by the one-word Integration Formulae. The first paragraph of each Technique illustrates what we consider the usual approach to energy expression for the soul or personality upon that particular ray. This usual approach can be positive or negative. When negative, a dis-integrative personality condition will be found to exist. When positive, a strictly personal kind of integration can be developed. This paragraph, in fact, usually depicts a situation needing correction. The ray energy, as it has been used up to that point, can bring the individual no further, and, in fact, in some cases, has caused severe problems.

The paragraphs which follow deal with the extrication from those problems, and the method needed to move beyond strictly personal integration (Personal Psychosynthesis) and bring soul and personality into greater rapport. The one-word Integration Formulae are derived from the final paragraphs in each Integration Technique. Thus, the one-word Integration Formula for any particular ray does *not* embrace the entire Technique of Integration for that particular ray. The Technique is larger, historical, more encompassing, and shows the progress of the individual over time. The Formula is remedial, and offers condensed advice on correcting and balancing the glamors of a particular ray, in order to make the integration of soul and personality possible.

Note: It must always be remembered that, no matter what may be the ray of the personality, it is always a *subray of the soul ray*, just as the personality is always an emanated aspect of its originating source, the soul (as the soul is of the Monad). From this point of view, the personality will always (to a greater or lesser extent) carry some of the same ray qualities as the soul ray, and to these will be added the qualities characteristic of the personality ray of the present incarnation. There is no way to keep these fields of the human energy system completely compartmentalized; always there will be interplay and interdependence, and the 'greater' (in this case the soul) always puts the stamp of its quality upon the 'lesser' (in this case, the personality). Obviously, this model can be continued 'vertically' with respect to the Monad and the soul, but given the stage of evolution of the majority of aspirants and disciples in the world, it is sufficient (because, for the time being, practical) to consider the soul ray (and not the Monadic ray) as the most significant quality in the human energy system.

It must be reemphasized that both the soul ray and personality ray will be involved in the process of strictly personal integration, or "Personal Psychosynthesis," as it is called. However important it may be in the overall development of the individual, Personal Psychosynthesis is characterized by a necessary selfishness, and preceeds the stage of a higher, more selfless integration – "Spiritual Psychosynthesis." During strictly personal integration both the personality ray and the soul ray will be, relatively speaking, *materially focussed*, and the results of the successful completion of this stage will be a relatively strong, independent and efficient personality, able to "find its own place" within the three worlds of human evolution. During Spiritual Psychosynthesis (the integration of soul and personality), the soul ray as well as the personality ray will rise above a rather material focus, and will begin to focus more transpersonally. This is the beginning of the conscious spiritualization of the personality and its ray.

It is difficult to say which ray, soul or personality, may be more influential during the earlier phase of personality integration. In many ways, the influence of the personality ray may be more obvious, but the quality of the soul ray is all-pervasive, for *its influence persists incarnation after incarnation*. There is, it should be realized, a *progressive integration of the personality*, life after life, no matter what the ray of the personality may be; this process of progressive integration taking place over a number of lives (though partially conditioned by the particular personality ray which is temporarily holding sway in any particular incarnation) is *always* conditioned by the quality of the soul ray.

During the stage of Spiritual Psychosynthesis ("the path of the higher integration" when soul and personality are actively blending), the ray of the soul is preeminent, and the Integration Formula, *keyed to the soul ray*, comes into its full usefulness.

Contrasts Between the Strictly Personal and the Spiritual Phases of the Integration Process

(For a refresher upon the methods of strictly personal integration, please refer to Section IV, Vol. I, under the discussion of the positive aspects of the personality ray)

Integration Dynamics for the Energy System with a Prominent First Ray

Method of strictly personal integration: integration through the assertion of the will.

Method of soul–personality integration: application of the first ray Integration Formula – *Inclusion*

Having (through force of will, assertiveness, discipline and control) carried the process of integrating the personality (per se) as far as possible, there arises within the consciousness of the first ray individual a sensed need for *Inclusion*. The soul is, essentially, love. Though the personality may, indeed, have integrated, having successfully used the power of the first ray to do so, too many gaps and cleavages exist between it and its environment. The individual is isolated and insufficiently related in love to his fellow human beings. Additionally, soul consciousness is group consciousness, but due to an overemphasis of ray one qualities, the individual stands alone, isolated from meaningful group participation, and, therefore, less powerful. The soul qualities of love and inclusiveness (Inclusion) must be appropriated and expressed. The theme of Inclusion will, when properly understood and used, relate the individual more intimately and receptively to his soul, and to others. He begins to realize that he "cannot stand and walk alone." Through the use of Inclusion (in many respects a second ray quality) the first ray individual comes into closer rapport with his own love nature (through the accelerating unfoldment of the love petals of the egoic lotus). Thus, a significant barrier to increasing soul–personality coordination and integration is dissolved, for the soul cannot fully infuse a loveless personality.

Note: In every kind of soul–personality relationship, the soul is the creator of balanced fulfillment. The appropriate Integration Formula supplies to the personality a soul quality which had been missing due to the overemphasis within the personality of other qualities. *Without this missing quality supplied by the utilization of the Integration Formula, true rapport between soul and personality could not be achieved and brought to fulfillment.*

Integration Dynamics for the Energy System with a Prominent Second Ray

Method of strictly personal integration: integration through the attractiveness of love.

Method of soul–personality integration: application of the second ray Integration Formula – *Centralization*

Having (through love, magnetic attraction, and a gentle process of fusing and unification) carried the process of integrating the personality (per se) as far as possible, there arises within the consciousness of the second ray individual a sensed need for *Centralization*. The soul is not only essential love, but essential *will* as well; though the soul loves profoundly, it is with a detached and not an attached form of love. Though, shortly before the need for centralization is felt, the personality has probably achieved a good deal of coordination, and may even be rather well–integrated (because the personally centered individual has successfully applied the usual qualities of the second ray to produce physical plane effectiveness), there are still too many personal attachments or adhesions between the personality and its environment. The individual is clinging to many non–essentials from which detachment and release must be achieved if the soul is to exert a greater influence in the life. The life is cluttered with unnecessary ties, and, consequently, the sense of divine identity is often obscured. *Centralization* (in many respects a first ray quality) helps the second ray individual sever unnecessary ties, and detach from irrelevant attachments. *Centralization*, in fact, is an archetypal soul quality (pertaining not just to second ray souls, but to souls on all the rays), for though the soul extends itself into the lower worlds, yet it remains established and *centered* in its own identity. Additionally, when the many personality demands engendered by excessive attachments are reduced, the personality consciousness achieves the freedom to focus more attentively upon the soul, which is the center of love. The consciousness becomes "centered" – centered in love – and thus, soul–personality coordination and integration are facilitated. The increasingly soul–inspired personality can then participate in its daily activities without a consuming involvement in debilitating personal attachments; such attachments throw the consciousness 'off–center', drain energy, and obscure the sense of being a soul. Through the use of the formula *Centralization*, the second ray individual comes into increasing rapport with his own *strength of soul* (note the first ray overtones of this phrase). Thus, significant barriers to soul–personality coordination and integration are thus relinquished, for the soul cannot fully express through a personality which forgets its true origins by clinging too closely to external things of lesser value – including the outer forms of people.

Integration Dynamics for the Energy System with a Prominent Third Ray

Method of strictly personal integration: integration through intelligent adaptability, skillful manipulation and great mobility.

Method of soul–personality integration: application of the third ray Integration Formula – *Stillness*

Having (through intelligent adaptability and mobility, as well as skill in the art of weaving together the energies of thought and act) carried the process of integrating the personality (per se) as far as possible, there arises within the consciousness of the third ray individual a sensed need for *Stillness*. Though the soul seeks action within the three lower worlds (the three lower planes), that action must always be guided by clear vision which depends upon *Stillness*. Though shortly before the need for *Stillness* is felt, the personality has probably achieved a good deal of coordination, and may even be rather well integrated (because the personally centered individual has successfully applied the usual qualities of the third ray to produce physical plane effectiveness), there is still too much poorly–directed or extraneous thought and activity on the level of personality. The individual is too busy with non–essentials, no matter how well (from the worldly point of view) he may seem to perform them. Excessive thought and excessive activity mean that the voice of the soul cannot be heard, that the Plan cannot be clearly envisioned, and that much energy, which should be creating patterns in line with God's Will, is spent creating designs which are merely personal. *Stillness* (in many ways a second ray quality) helps the third ray individual *see* what he is actually doing. The third ray worker, like the worker upon the sixth ray, is very often likely to work blindly, intoxicated by the love of activity, whether mental, physical or both. However, spiritual vision, as the soul sees it, is absolutely crucial if there is to be an increasing coordination and integration between the personality and the soul. Those upon the third ray are in great need of the ancient maxim: "Be *still* and know that I am God." The increasingly soul–inspired personality can then participate in daily activities without being thwarted by misguided activities which render spiritual intentions futile. Through the use of the Integration Formula, *Stillness*, the third ray individual comes into increasing rapport with that aspect of the divine "blueprint" which it is the intention of his soul to manifest. Thus a significant barrier to the increase of soul–personality integration is removed, for the soul cannot fully express through a personality which preoccupies itself with personally motivated motion at the expense of soul–intended action.

Integration Dynamics for the Energy System with a Prominent Fourth Ray

Method of strictly personal integration: integration through shuttle–like mediation which resolves conflict into harmony.

Method of soul–personality integration: application of the fourth ray Integration Formula – *Steadfastness*

Having (through a fluid and flexible adjustment to conflicting demands, and through mediation and harmonization) carried the process of integrating the personality (per se) as far as possible, there arises within the consciousness of the fourth ray individual a sensed need for *Steadfastness*. Though the soul seeks to bridge and harmonize all differences within the lower three worlds, that soul always maintains a point of centered balance, and "steadfast stands." This the personality must also learn to do. Although shortly before the need for *Steadfastness* is felt, the personality has probably achieved a good deal of coordination and may even be rather well integrated (because the personally centered individual has successfully applied the usual qualities of the fourth ray to achieve physical plane effectiveness), there is still too much vacillation between the pairs of opposites, too much pliability, unpredictability and compromise. The fourth ray individual is still the victim of the warring forces – either within his own nature, or within the environment he seeks to harmonize. Excessive identification, with now one side of a struggle, and now the other, renders his position continually unbalanced, unstable and unpredictable. The soul, which seeks for "Two [to] Merge with One," cannot properly function through such a fluctuating medium. *Steadfastness* (in many ways a first ray quality) helps the fourth ray individual hold a balanced center, and refrain from tilting, with disconcerting regularity, towards either side of the struggle which he is seeking to harmonize and pacify. The steadfast, central position will bring what has been called a "Win–Win" resolution to each of the many battles between the pairs of opposites which the fourth ray individual must face. The increasingly soul–inspired personality can then participate in daily activities without falling victim to erratic mood swings or distressing alternations between conflicting perspectives. Through the use of the Integration Formula, *Steadfastness*, the fourth ray individual comes into increasing rapport with the balanced and perfected beauty which the soul intends to manifest. Thus, a significant obstacle to the increase of soul–personality integration is thus neutralized, for the soul cannot fully express through a personality which is constantly divided against itself, and which cannot simultaneously include the opposites which are necessary for the creation of a pattern of divine beauty

Integration Dynamics for the Energy System with a Prominent Fifth Ray

Method of strictly personal integration: integration through observation, analysis, cautious experimentation and the measured application of knowledge.

Method of soul–personality integration: application of the fifth ray Integration Formula – *Detachment*

Having (through a precise analysis of the personality vehicles, and a regulated, measured application of specific knowledge) carried the process of integrating the personality (per se) as far as possible, there arises within the consciousness of the fifth ray individual the sensed need for *Detachment* [from intense preoccupation with the form nature]). Though the soul seeks to *know* all aspects of form, and to shed the light of knowledge within the three worlds of human evolution (wherein form is at its densest), still, the soul maintains the attitude of the detached Knower, never forgetting the distinction between the Knower, the field of knowledge, and the act of knowing which relates them. This basic discrimination must constantly be brought to the attention of the fifth ray individual. Although shortly before the need for *Detachment* is felt, the personality itself has probably already achieved a good deal of coordination and may even be rather well integrated (because the personally centered individual has successfully applied the usual qualities of the fifth ray to achieve physical plane effectiveness), there is still too much preoccupation with knowledge of the form to the exclusion of recognizing the Knower behind the form. Excessive investigation of that which is presented to the senses (whether the sense be subtle or refined) causes the fifth ray individual to lose sight of the subjective synthesis which lies behind the multiplicity of form distinctions. The soul, which ever seeks to project its presence as the Knower into the world of the lower mind and brain consciousness, cannot succeed when the personal consciousness so thoroughly ignores it – forgetting that the soul is the spiritual source of personal consciousness. *Detachment* (in this case, very much a first ray quality) helps the fifth ray individual to terminate his all–absorbing examination of multiplicity, and begin to recognize that completely abstracted, subjective identity which is the true reality behind the near infinitude of objective data. The attitude of the detached "*Self*-remembering" Observer, allows the fifth ray individual to simultaneously entertain in consciousness both the worlds of being and of becoming. The increasingly soul-inspired personality can then participate in daily activities without becoming, literally, so *engrossed* in form that it fails to remember the Knower behind the known. Through the use of the Integration Formula, *Detachment*, the fifth ray individual comes into increasing rapport with the One who forever stands behind and within all multiplicity, and Who intends to manifest His conscious oneness within the field of the personal consciousness. Thus a significant obstacle to the expression of soul–personality integration is dispelled, for the soul cannot express fully through a personality which doubts the soul's very existence, and which is so preoccupied with the complexity of form that it is blind to the simplicity of spirit.

Integration Dynamics for the Energy System with a Prominent Sixth Ray

Method of strictly personal integration: integration by the marshaling of personality forces through ardent desire, militant pursuit and one-pointed focussing.

Method of soul-personality integration: application of the sixth ray Integration Formula – not given.

Note: Although the Tibetan apparently intended to give one word integration formulae for rays six and seven also, He did not do so. Nevertheless, He gave enough within the discussion of the sixth and seventh ray integration processes to offer guidance in the choice of probable integration formulae for these two rays.

Sixth ray Integration Formula: Not given in single-word form, although the Technique of Integration from the *Old Commentary* is fully elaborated, as it is for all other rays.

Proposed phrase to embody the sixth ray Integration Formula: *Peaceful standing still at the center*.

(Perhaps, if a one-word Integration Formula for the sixth ray were to be given, it would be – *Restraint*)

Having (through one-pointed focussing, militant discipline and unswerving pursuit of that which is desired) carried the process of integrating the personality (per se) as far as possible, there arises within the consciousness of the sixth ray individual the sensed need for a *Peaceful standing still at the center*. DESIRE is the great motivating impulse within our solar system (and beyond), and though soul consciousness within the three lower worlds does grow through the pursuit of ever more refined desires leading to lofty aspirations, it is the soul (representing the One SELF) which is, even though often unrealized, the object of all desire (especially during the strictly human phase of evolution). When the individual 'stands' within a state of soul consciousness he realizes that "the Kingdom of God is within." This realization is something which the *personally-focussed* individual, when influenced strongly by the sixth ray, is likely to forget in his almost frantically active and passionate pursuit of the lesser values which lie upon the periphery of reality. Although shortly before the need for a *Peaceful standing still at the center* is felt, the personality, itself, has probably already achieved a good deal of coordination, and may even be rather well-integrated (because the personally-centered individual has successfully applied the usual qualities of the sixth ray to achieve physical plane effectiveness), still, there is far too much rushing forth in pursuit of those things which excite a momentary enthusiasm, but which are not of lasting value or "on target" as far as the vision of the soul is concerned. Investing oneself in a series of misdirected, one-pointed dedications only consumes strength and leads to a sense of futility. Until real alignment with the soul is achieved, nothing the individual may follow leads to lasting satisfaction; once, however, alignment with the soul *is* achieved, it is realized that the only thing worth pursuing is the Pursuer – the soul.

Excessive and blind pursuit, in fact, leads *away* from discovery of the goal – the discovery of the true Self, which is always at the center. The use of either the phrase – *Peaceful standing still at the center* (which conveys the second ray quality of peaceful stillness and the first ray quality of centeredness), or, more emphatically, the use of the one-word Formula, *Restraint*, helps the sixth ray individual see and evaluate truly, and refrain from the intemperate pursuit of, and attachment to, those things which the soul does not desire. The increasingly soul-inspired personality can then participate in daily activities without rushing away from the established center of soul identity – without forgetting the Self. Through the use of the Integration Formula, the sixth ray individual comes into deepening rapport with the soul – the One who always envisions that which is of highest value. Thus inspired, his quests no longer lead to inevitable disappointment. A significant deterrent to the expression of soul-personality integration is rendered unattractive, for the soul cannot express itself fully through a personality which (in hot pursuit of the relatively worthless), mistakes the part for the whole, and the not-Self for the Self.

Integration Dynamics for the Energy System with a Prominent Seventh Ray

Method of strictly personal integration: integration through planned organization, regulation of all personality energies, and a constructively creative approach to all personality activities.

Method of soul–personality integration: application of the seventh ray Integration Formula – not given.

Seventh ray Integration Formula: Not given in single-word form, although the Technique of Integration from the *Old Commentary* **is fully elaborated, as it is for all other rays.**

Proposed phrase to embody the seventh ray Integration Formula: *Stand and suffer within the pentagram, oriented towards the East, attentively awaiting the light which illuminates the Plan.*

(Perhaps, if a one-word Integration Formula for the seventh ray were to be given, it would be *Orientation*).

Having (through the power to efficiently organize, plan, regulate, create and construct) carried the process of integrating the personality (per se) as far as possible, there arises within the consciousness of the seventh ray individual a sensed need which can only be fulfilled by a willingness to *stand and suffer within the pentagram, oriented towards the East, attentively awaiting the light which illuminates the Plan*. Organizing and arranging the life of the physical plane, and creatively constructing designs in the world of matter are, indeed, important soul intentions, but this kind of creative patterning must always be performed *in line with the Plan*. Aligning creativity and organizational power with the Divine Plan is something which the personally-focused individual, when influenced strongly by the seventh ray, is likely to forget to do in his enthusiasm for witnessing the emergence and manifestation of the many forms he loves to create. Although shortly before the need to "stand and suffer, attentively oriented to the Plan" makes itself felt, the personality has, probably, already achieved a good deal of coordination, and may even be rather well-integrated (because the personally-centered individual has successfully applied the usual qualities of the seventh ray to achieve physical plane effectiveness), there is still too much magical or ritualistic manipulation of forces for the sake of purely personal ends and designs. Constructions which are not in line with the Divine Pattern do nothing lasting to decrease the chaos which the seventh ray individual deeply detests. Those upon the seventh ray cannot resist building, but until they build in line with the Plan, their constructions will merely form part of the impedimenta which must be cleared if the Divine Design is to be manifested. Excessive, misguided creation and construction only suffocate the light within dense enclosures of form. The use of the Integration formula – *stand and suffer within the pentagram, oriented towards the East, attentively awaiting the light which illuminates the Plan* (which seems to convey the qualities of the second ray, and a little of the first), helps the seventh ray individual build truly and in conformity to the divine "blueprints". The increasingly soul–inspired personality can then participate in daily activities without manifesting ideas and ideals of lesser worth; he brings into form only that which the soul intends. Through the use of the Integration Formula (shortened as *Orientation*, the seventh ray individual comes into deepening rapport with the soul – the "Master Builder" – the One Who sees in its entirety that part of the Divine Pattern which it is responsible for materializing through the personality. Thus a significant impediment to the expression of soul–personality integration is removed, for the soul cannot express itself fully through a personality which does not care whether the manifestation of its own designs mar or enhance the manifestation of the Greater Design, of which all individually executed designs are intended to be a tiny part.

Concluding Notes

It is interesting to note, when analyzing the ray content of the Integration Formulas, that each carries the quality of the first or second ray, or a combination of the two. The first and second rays, representing as they do the basic duality found in all manifestation, in certain respects, include all the other rays. A great many adjustments necessary for a more healthy psychospiritual functioning (functioning which is in alignment with the soul) can be understood as a need for either more or less first or second ray energy.

It should also be noted that in every case, the Integration Formula calls for a cessation from a certain kind of activity and a subsequent attitude of quiet receptivity. This pattern points to the contrast between the second and third aspects of divinity – the *consciousness aspect* and *activity aspect*, respectively. Alignment, coordination and integration with the consciousness aspect requires a disengagement from blind and blinding activity of the unregulated third aspect of Divinity, correlated with the personality, as the consciousness aspect is with the soul.

FORMAT FOR THE PRESENTATION OF THE 49 SOUL/PERSONALITY COMBINATIONS IN RELATION TO THE INTEGRATION PROCESS

Format for the Introductory Section:
Introductory Tabulations of Differences Between Soul Ray and Personality Ray

In the format we will use in the discussion of each soul and personality ray combination, there will be an introductory tabulation, outlining the significant differences between the spiritual tendencies of the soul when upon a given ray, and the more "personal" tendencies of the personality. In these tabulations, the highest tendencies of the soul ray will be emphasized, and contrasted with the strictly personal, and sometimes obstructive, tendencies of the personality. Although each tabulation will follow this format closely, it should be remembered, as pointed out in the previous section, that the soul ray does not necessarily manifest in an exclusively positive manner. At the current stage of human evolution, the soul ray frequently has a negative (or glamorous) reflection, and this appears when the energy of the soul and its ray are appropriated and distorted by the personality. In such instances, the personality will evidence glamors related to the ray which conditions the soul, and not only glamors related to the personality ray. Conversely, the personality and its ray do not manifest in a purely personal and non-spiritual manner. In discussing the "Technique of Fusion," (by means of which soul and personality are fused into an inseparable unity) Djwhal Khul describes it as "the transmutation of the *higher aspects of the personality ray* [emphasis, MDR] into those of the soul." The personality ray does indeed have its higher aspects, and these, especially when under the guidance of the soul and its ray, manifest as virtues – often difficult to distinguish from the virtues expressed by the soul and its ray.

For instructional purposes, however, and because the integrated personality does so often represent an important obstacle to the expression of the highest qualities of the soul ray, *these tabulations will present the soul in its most positive light and the personality in a strictly personal (and often negative) light*. Thus, personality characteristics described will be those which occur *before* the personality and soul are bound together in the closest cooperation (at which point the personality ray has become a harmonious *subray* of the soul ray).

These tabulations should, therefore, be of special use to those aspirants and disciples who are experiencing the *phase of conflict* between the desires of the rapidly integrating personality and the spiritual intentions of the soul. All this notwithstanding, it will be advisable for students to remember that they are just as likely to suffer opposition to their highest spiritual impulses from the misuse of soul ray energy as they are from personality rebellion colored by the particular quality of their personality ray. In any case, the personality column can also be referenced by those who are seeking a deeper understanding of how their soul ray might express in a limited or distorted manner through the personality. For instance, if one is a second ray *soul*, one might also check the various terms listed under the columns describing the second ray *personality* to discover purely personal and obstructive manifestations of one's second ray soul energy.

The important thing to keep in mind when considering the rays and the fields of the human energy system is the *entirely fluid nature of the interplay between interpenetrating energies and forces*. There occurs a constant fusing and blending, and, given our stage of unfoldment, it it difficult to determine hard and fast boundaries between the energies which condition specific fields. Not only will energies from a 'superior' field influence an 'inferior' field (as the personality ray will influence the mind, and the soul ray will influence, not only the personality, but the mind as well, etc.) but an inferior field will somewhat influence those superior to it, as the emotional vehicle and its ray will influence the coherency and stability of the thought process. For those with very analytical rather than intuitive minds, the attempt to understand this condition of mutual interdependence (i.e., 'overlays' and 'sub-colorations') can be exasperating, but, in consolation, it should be realized that the intuition can function as a mental 'organ' of incredible precision; given sufficient experience, based upon much careful and analytical thought, the qualities of the rays of the various vehicles can be intuitively discerned with a fair degree of reliability. Reasoning, however, should precede any wholesale attempt at intuitive determination.

The student is also asked to bear in mind that all that is subsequently said of the relationships between the soul ray and the personality ray is necessarily subject to a great number of qualifications. The rays of the mind, the emotions and the etheric-physical nature cannot (due to the tremendous number of variables such consideration would introduce) be considered in the following 49 comparisons, and they, along with numerous astrological factors exert a very important qualifying influence on any combination of soul and personality rays.

Ultimately each individual will have to be considered on his or her own individual merits. It cannot be stressed too often that every individual is *unique* – a product of a unique combination of energies (though every individual has each of the constituent energies in greater or lesser measure) and of a unique evolutionary history.

Included among these introductory tabulations will be seven which *will be virtually irrelevant* for almost every student – namely, seven tabulations which deal with the relationship between a soul and personality upon the same ray. To the knowledge of the author, in all of D.K.'s writings, such a state of affairs is discussed only once – on p. 354 of *Esoteric Psychology, Vol. II*. In this reference there is a brief but intriguing mention of the possibility of combining a first ray soul with a first ray personality. It should be noted that this combination occurs quite *late* in the evolutionary process, after a considerable amount of soul–personality integration and fusion has been achieved.

> **...in the fourth life he [the first ray individual] can function safely through a first ray personality without losing his spiritual balance, if we might use such a phrase. Through this type of personality, his first ray soul can demonstrate, because the disciple has 'recovered feeling, gained divine emotion, and filled his waiting heart with love.' In such cases as this, the astral body is usually upon on the second ray, the mental body upon the fourth ray, and the physical body upon the sixth ray. This naturally tends to balance or offset the intensity of the first ray vibrations of personality and soul.**

Tapestry of the Gods

In all fairness, a quotation from *Esoteric Astrology*, p. 91 must be mentioned. It will give heart to those who want to believe that identical soul and personality rays are frequently found. A closer examination of what the Tibetan writes, however, leaves many questions unanswered:

> **Strictly speaking, what I have to say now concerns the pure first ray type because** *Aries is the zodiacal sign through which the first Ray of Will or Power reaches our planetary life*. **Such pure types are rare indeed and at this period of evolution well nigh unknown. Most people are governed by their personality ray and** *as the present first ray types are expressing themselves through personalities on all the rays* **[emphasis, MDR], I would simply ask you to consider what I have to say from the angle of character effects, of problems presented and of quality unfolded.**

From a casual reading of this paragraph it would appear that first ray souls express themselves through personality vehicles upon all the rays, including the first. This *may*, indeed, be possible, and there does seem to be some basis for the assumption, because the only 'double-ray' emphasis mentioned or discussed in all of D.K.'s writings relates to a situation in which the soul and personality are both upon the first ray. But those rare cases in which both the soul and personality are found upon the first ray may very well occur because there are (at this time) no first ray souls which are really *pure first ray souls*, or pure types.

Just what does D.K. mean by "pure types?" He says they are "well nigh unknown" at this period of evolution, but such, we know, is obviously *not* the case for first ray souls – *in general*. Even within his own group of disciples–in–training, there were quite a few people to whom D.K. assigned a first ray soul (twelve, to be exact), and these were people very much like ourselves, of no great degree of accomplishment. Obviously, these twelve individuals could not have been *pure types*, even though they were known as first ray souls. It would seem that a pure type, would be an individual who had not only a first ray soul, but, also, an *atmic triadal polarization* (cf. *A Treatise on Cosmic Fire*, p. 177). Further, a really pure type might have, not only a first ray soul with an atmic triadal polaization (i.e., an emphasis upon the atmic or *first ray* aspect of the spiritual Triad, but a *first ray Monad*, as well. Now *that* would be an utterly *pure* first ray type! The Tibetan may, in fact, be inferring that only the individual with a *first ray Monad* can be called a "pure first ray type," for the Monadic ray, is, after all, the "primary ray". It is important to note that there are relatively few first ray Monads in manifestation, and even fewer in incarnation (cf. *A Treatise on Cosmic Fire*, p. 579).

Interestingly, Aries has much to do with Shamballa and with the power of the Monad. Aries also is the primary distributor of ray one energy to our planet. Aries, via its hierarchical ruler Uranus, is deeply related to "fire electric" which is the quality of the Monad.

The implication in all this, is that "present first ray types" who *do* express themselves through personalities which may be on all the rays (including the first), are not really what D.K. would call real first ray egos:

> "As to the first ray egos, there are no pure first ray types on the planet. All so-called first ray egos are on the first subray of the second ray, which is in incarnation. There is not sufficient intelligence and love in the world to balance the dynamic will of an ego on the ray of the destroyer". *Esoteric Psychology, Vol. I, p. 26–27*

This, perhaps, explains why so-called first ray souls (or Egos) are sometimes (late in evolution) found with first ray personalities. The great occultist, Helena P. Blavatsky may have been one.

From all this, some students may be eager to infer that soul and personality combinations upon the same ray might be possible for individuals whose souls are upon the other six rays as well. This possibility must remain an inference, however, because none of the almost fifty disciples instructed by Djwhal Khul had identical soul and personality rays. These were people, who by all trustworthy accounts, were very much like students of esotericism and spirituality in the present day. With only one exception, they had "passed" the first initiation. A number of them were working on, or had completed, the second initiation and a few (as can be inferred from certain passages in their instructions) were preparing for the third initiation. Here were people of a fairly advanced spiritual status, *none of whom* had identical soul and personality rays. Even among those who may be presumed to have taken the third initiation, such as, for instance, Alice Bailey, *never* are instances of identical soul and personality rays mentioned. (Alice Bailey is said to have had a second ray soul and a first ray personality). Even in the cases of Hercules, the Buddha and the Christ – great Indiviudals who had reached such a high stage of unfoldment that it might be presumed that the personality would be *purely the reflector of soul quality* (and thus, *virtually identical* in quality to the soul) – the soul and personality rays *always differed*. In *The Destiny of the Nations* we learn that Hercules has a first ray soul and a second ray personality; the Buddha (in his last incarnation as the Prince Siddhartha) a second ray soul and a first ray personality; and the Christ (at the time of his manifestation through the vehicles of the initiate Jesus), a second ray soul and a sixth ray personality. Further, in all the hypothetical or sample ray tabulations offered by the Tibetan, there is not one which shows soul and personality to be qualified by the same ray.

In light of the apparent rarity of identical soul and personality rays, it would seem wise to regard such an instance as a special case, and not assign identical rays in a 'wholesale' manner, as some ray analysts seem inclined to do. The inference of frequent identicality would be risky at best, and, perhaps, even reckless. A greater understanding of the successive stages of soul unfoldment will help us pinpoint those stages and special instances in which there is a higher probability of the two rays being the same. It must also be remembered that since the personality ray is always a subray of the soul ray, the quality of the soul ray will, at a fairly advanced stage of evolution, be quite manifest through the personality, and the *mistaken perception of identicality* may arise as a result.

The seven tabulations and explanations presenting identical soul and personality rays are, therefore, offered more for the sake of completeness than for their broad applicability. They do have a certain utility, however, for people whose souls are to be found on all the rays (no matter what the ray of the personality might be), for whatever may be the ray of the soul, certain negative reflections or distortions of that ray will (until a very high stage of evolution is reached) *always manifest through the personality.*

Note: The 49 tabulations will not usually differentiate ray characteristics according to ray type. The (A), (B) and occasional (C) types have been noted rather fully in the tabulations to be found in Section II, Volume I. At this point, students should understand how to differentiate subsidiary types, and can analyze the tabulations for themselves, should they so desire. Differentiations and combinations according to type will, however, be utilized in various sections of the commentary which follows each tabulation. For instance, in Section 1 of each discussion of the *usual* 42 soul and personality ray combinations, various abuses or glamors of the combination will be proposed. Sometimes, however, the proposed glamor will refer only to certain individuals possessing a particular combination of rays, and sometimes to all. When a glamor refers more or less equally to all individuals found with a particular ray combination, there will be no notation of (A), (B) or (C). When the glamor refers to only certain individuals with that ray combination, an explanatory parenthesis will follow the glamor. If, for example, a glamor is followed by the notation (3B + 1), it means that this glamor is found in those whose soul is predominantly upon the (B) type of the third ray, and whose personality can be on *either* the (A) *or* (B) type of the first ray; if the notation reads (3B + 1A), the indication is virtually the same, *except* that it means the glamor would apply (again) to those whose soul is upon the (B) type of the third ray, but whose personality is found only upon the (A) type of the first ray. There are a number of possibilities: (3B + 1), (3B + 1A), (3B + 1B), (3A + 1), (3A + 1A), (3A + 1B), (3 + 1A), (3 + 1B). The principle is always the same. Please bear in mind that, in this matter of discriminating one type from another, there are no hard and fast lines of demarcation. Even though a person upon a particular ray may incline more towards one type than another, the fundamental ray quality *includes both types.* The *type notation* is intended to bring added clarity to the task of trying to understand the inclination or the emphasis, but the (A), (B) and (C) categories *cannot be considered absolute.*

The list of glamors is not complete; there will not be a glamor for every one of the possible combinations, but the student is encouraged to think of a particular glamor (or of a particular strength) which would correlate with any of the many combinations of types.

Format for Section 1

This section will offer a discussion on the pre-spiritual phase of evolution for each soul and personality ray combination, with the exception of seven in which soul and personality ray are identical (since identical soul and personality rays could not occur in a pre-spiritual phase). In the pre-spiritual phase the soul ray is appropriated by the personality, and reinforces the personality demonstration. This is a selfish phase, and the two ray energies are combined to produce largely negative and selfish results. In this section, the individual's *primary* desire or motive is correlated with the soul ray, and his *secondary* desire or motive (indicated by the word "also") is correlated with the personality ray. What is primary or secondary will, of course, depend to a certain extent upon the *degree to which the soul or personality ray has emerged* – an emergence which varies widely from individual to individual. There are many human beings in whom *neither* the soul or personality rays has emerged (though, even at an early stage of evolution, such rays [especially the soul ray] may be capable of detection). For the purposes of this study, it is assumed that the personality ray is in full expression, and that the soul ray energy has emerged as a force to be reckoned with, but is *not manifesting spiritually*, being, instead, misappropriated by the personality. That such a 'negative' emergence of the soul ray does, indeed, occur well before the individual can be considered *spiritual* (i.e., an advanced human being, an aspirant or a disciple) is definitely established on pp. 39-43 of *Esoteric Psychology, Vol. II*.

Format for Section 2

This section will offer a brief description of the essence of the conflict between the particular soul ray and personality ray under discussion.

Format for Section 3

This section will offer a discussion on how the soul/personality conflict is perceived when the consciousness of the aspirant or disciple is identified primarily with the soul. From this perspective, the personality will then be seen as an obstacle.

It must be remembered that what is normally called the *individual*, is really (from the esoteric perspective) the "soul-in-incarnation" – an emanation of the soul, projected into form. The individual is actually a unit of consciousness (an "I") immersed in the matter of the three lower worlds of human evolution. To be even more accurate, this unit of consciousness is *essentially* a projection of the Monad. For practical purposes, however, the individual or unit of consciousness should be considered as *neither* the soul upon its own plane, or the personality – and certainly not as an emanation of the Monad; that will come later.

For practical purposes, the individual unit of consciousness occupies a fluctuating position which might be described as *between* the soul and personality. Sometimes this unit of consciousness is identified with the soul on its own plane. At such times, it virtually *becomes* the soul (for such is the nature of consciousness, that it *becomes* that with which it identifies). When thus identified, the individual can then be called the *inner man*. At other times, the individual or unit of consciousness is identified with the personality, at which point (from the perspective of consciousness) it virtually *becomes* the personality. The individual can then be called the *outer man*. Thus, at different moments in the life, the individual (i.e., the disciple, the unit of consciousness, the soul–in–incarnation, etc.) may be identified *primarily* with either the soul on its own plane or the personality (and, later in evolution, with higher centers within the total human energy system). The individual's perspective and *sense of self* will vary greatly depending upon his level of identification.

The level of identification can change instantaneously, with the individual focusing now as the soul, now as the personality – depending upon the situation, and his intention. It is interesting that the greater includes the lesser, but the lesser does not include the greater. When the individual identifies with personality or focuses, principally, as a personality, he cannot simultaneously identify with the soul or focus as the soul. But sometimes (when he is experienced and practiced), he can focus, primarily, as soul while holding the realization that he is *also* the personality. This is a tiny reflection of God's capacity to be both transcendent and immanent. Of course, there may be rare moments when the individual focuses as the soul, and forgets completely that he has a personality. Given the practical demands of living upon the earth, however, such a situation cannot, and should not, occur with great frequency, otherwise the individual would become completely abstracted from physical plane living. Though this might be very satisfying spiritual enjoyment, it would negate the usefulness of the incarnation.

Section 3 in the Format discusses the individual's perspective when in a high or exalted state of consciousness – identified not only *with* the soul but *as* the soul. Section 4 discusses the individual's perspective at a much lower and more normal state of consciousness when identified not only *with* the personality, but as a personality. At such moments of lower identification the soul on its own plane may seem almost like a foreign or intruding entity. Of course, there is also the possibility that the individual may hold a position of identification mid–way between soul and personality, identifying fully with neither. This is a position frequently assumed by the struggling aspirant or disciple. He is "neither fish nor fowl." At different times, he seems to look in two opposite directions, and, sometimes, in two opposite directions simultaneously like the Roman god Janus. But really, for the usual aspirant or disciple, no 'position in consciousness' is utterly stable. He is 'riding' up and down upon what might be called 'an elevator in consciousness'; his sense of identity alters with every change in his 'level of identification.'

It is difficult to choose suitable terminology to discuss these subtleties. No words really suffice. We are in a realm of paradox, for we are saying that the individual can *be* more than one thing. This is true. He can be many things, depending upon his moment–to–moment level of identification. Actually, he is *all* aspects of himself – Monad, soul and personality – *simultaneously*. Only, however, when he is consciously the Monad, can he identify with all levels of his being *simultaneously*. When we understand more about the *dynamics of identification*, some of these mysteries will be clarified.

Format for Section 4

This section will offer a discussion on how the soul/personality conflict is perceived when the consciousness of the aspirant or disciple is identified primarily with the personality. From this perspective, the soul will then be seen as an intruding and disruptive energy.

Format for Section 5

This section will offer a discussion on how the soul ray and personality ray can be combined for maximum positive effect. Examples of their ideal combined expression will be put forward. This section, obviously pertains to the period of soul/personality integration and subsequent fusion.

Format for Section 6

This is an important section discussing the actual dynamics of soul/personality integration, which can be brought about through the use of the Integration Formulae – one of which is keyed to the soul ray and the other to the personality ray.

Format for Section 7

This is a more practical and concrete section discussing special vocational aptitudes and abilities relating to the combination in question. In a general way it will be useful in vocational guidance. The vocations presented, however, are by no means *exclusive* to any particular ray. In fact, it is probable that all professions include individuals whose soul or personality is found upon all the rays. Certain vocations, however, may more frequently be followed by those upon a particular ray or rays, and such tendencies were taken into consideration in the tabulating of vocational aptitudes and orientations. It is anticipated that students, once they grasp the basic principles, will be able to think of many additional vocational aptitudes and orientations keyed to the 42 major soul and personality ray combinations.

Format for Section 8

This is the final section. It will attempt to offer lists of well-known individuals (historical, contemporary, fictional or mythological) whose soul ray can reasonably be assumed to be the soul ray being discussed in the combination, and for whom a strong subsidiary ray (probably the personality ray or the mental ray) is the other ray of the combination under discussion. Some of these lists are longer than others. Certain lists might have only one or two entries, which, themselves, may be quite hypothetical. There are certain types of soul/personality ray combinations which tend to emerge into prominence, and others which are far less conspicuous. Naturally, advanced individuals with a first ray soul are not that difficult to find; they come forward and rise "to the top," as the Tibetan says. Even though some of these lists may be quite short, they can be supplemented by careful research, which students are encouraged to undertake. The attempt to think in these rayological terms about well-known figures (whether real or fictional) is an excellent exercise in the new psychology.

Note: When seeking to use Section V of *Tapestry*, it is of the utmost importance for all students to remember that *every human being is utterly unique*. No description of the interaction of soul and personality rays, no matter how astute, can convincingly capture individual uniqueness. As previously stated, astrological factors, evolutionary status, and karmic liabilities (to mention only a few of the most pertinent considerations) must be investigated in each case if there is to be a more thorough understanding of the individual. The various tabulations and explanations, however, should give careful and intuitive readers some significant understanding of their identity and soul/personality dynamics. If as as result of what follows, students can achieve a better grasp of their soul and personality rays (and, eventually, of their fivefold ray chart), and the manner in which the soul and personality can best be integrated, then Section V will have served its purpose.

List of Tabulations Contrasting the Qualities of 49 Combinations of Soul and Personality Rays

I. Ray One Soul:

1/1, 1/2, 1/3, 1/4, 1/5, 1/6, 1/7

II. Ray Two Soul:

2/1, 2/2, 2/3, 2/4, 2/5, 2/6, 2/7

III. Ray Three Soul:

3/1, 3/2, 3/3, 3/4, 3/5, 3/6, 3/7

IV. Ray Four Soul:

4/1, 4/2, 4/3, 4/4, 4/5, 4/6, 4/7

V. Ray Five Soul:

5/1, 5/2, 5/3, 5/4, 5/5, 5/6, 5/7

VI. Ray Six Soul:

6/1, 6/2, 6/3, 6/4, 6/5, 6/6, 6/7

VII. Ray Seven Soul:

7/1, 7/2, 7/3, 7/4, 7/5, 7/6, 7/7

Note: It must be remembered in connection with each of the seven tabulations representing identical soul and personality rays (1/1, 2/2, 3/3, 4/4, 5/5, 6/6, 7/7), that, in all probability, the soul would only choose a personality ray identical to its own *at quite an advanced stage in the process of evolutionary unfoldment*; at such a stage, the worst excesses or weaknesses of personality would probably no longer be obstacles to soul expression, and may even have ceased altogether. In fact, the personality manifestation would be very much a reflection of positive soul qualities though, of course, constrained by the inherent limitations of the personality field, itself, which can *never* reflect the full breadth and power of the soul field.

In most cases of identical soul and personality rays, tables of *contrasting* qualities would, consequently, have little meaning, because *only positive qualities would manifest* (since the stage of evolution would be very advanced) and sharp contrasts would rarely exist. The sharply contrasting qualities, as here presented, would have their main practical usefulness in those instances in which a very advanced individual were having something of a relapse, or a brief struggle with a recrudescence of negative qualities long ago subdued. It is also recognized that very advanced individuals experience certain "temptations" as did the Master Jesus during the forty days in the desert following the baptism initiation. If such an individual were conditioned by the same soul and personality ray, it is likely that some of the temptations would reflect the negative qualities of that particular ray. If this were the case, then the lower manifestations of the ray, as listed in the tabulations, would be useful as an indication of the nature of the struggle. It is the opinion of the author, however, that the seven tabulations featuring the contrasts between identical soul and personality rays should be used to identify soul/personality dynamics *only as a last resort*, when no other more plausible combination of rays seems possible.

Soul/Personality Combinations with a Ray One Soul

Some Contrasts Between the Ray 1 Soul and the Ray 1 Personality

Ray 1 Soul		Ray 1 Personality
* selfless spiritual will	vs.	* the expression of selfish personal will
* isolated unity	vs.	* personal coldness and aloofness; isolated disunity
* the use of power for the Plan	vs.	* the selfish appropriation of power for personal ends
* destructiveness to clear a path for the manifestation of the Plan	vs.	* inconsiderate, egotistically motivated destructiveness to satisfy personal desire
* spiritual impersonality and divine indifference	vs.	* unfeeling impersonality and callous indifference
* centralization within the identity of the Divine Self	vs.	* centralization within the limited, personal identity
* assertion of Divine Law	vs.	* assertiveness of the personal ego
* imposition of the Divine Fiat	vs.	* personality domination
* the primacy of the ONE	vs.	* the primacy of the little ego
* deep spiritual humility from sensing the vastness and grandeur of the ONE	vs.	* pride and a sense of personal superiority due to a limited, self-centered perspective
* determination to persist and survive as a spiritual being	vs.	* determination to persist and survive as an isolated personality

Abbreviated Commentary

1. As the author infers (on the basis of statements by the Tibetan) that the appearance of identical soul and personality rays is a rarity occurring only in the very late stages of the path of discipleship, and probably upon the path of initiation, it is not really meaningful to enlarge upon the dynamics of the possible interaction between a ray one soul and a ray one personality in the pre-spiritual phases of evolution. If a student is utterly convinced that this combination represents his soul and personality ray, enough is given throughout the book, for him to work out the implications.

2. Such conflicts as might occur would be based upon the counterpulls of the higher and lower qualities. Essentially the contrast would be between the selfless, synthetic spiritual will and the selfish, exclusive personal will.

3. As regards the ideal expression of the combination of the ray one soul and the ray one personality, it is clear that this combination would present a remarkable opportunity for an unusually pure expression through the human energy system of the Will of God – the energy which emanates from Shamballa.

Some Contrasts between the Ray 1 Soul and the Ray 2 Personality

Ray 1 Soul		Ray 2 Personality
* spiritual will	vs.	* personal love
* dynamic expression of spiritual power	vs.	* personal passivity and weakness
* spiritual assertiveness	vs.	* placid reliance upon personal magnetism
* willingness to initiate drastic action for the sake of preserving spiritual values	vs.	* disinclination to engage in any kind of drastic action
* firmness based upon spiritual certainty and strength	vs.	* yielding and infirmity based upon the sense of personal powerlessness
* insistence upon the upholding of spiritual principle	vs.	* sacrifice of spiritual principle to personal ease and comfort
* ease achieving spiritual detachment	vs.	* binding personal attachments
* soul–inspired fearlessness	vs.	* personal fear based upon undue sensitivity
* austere spiritual solemnity	vs.	* meaningless joviality, levity
* spiritually motivated exclusiveness	vs.	* unwise inclusiveness for the sake of personality satisfaction
* ease expelling what is spiritually worthless	vs.	* retention of much that is spiritually worthless
* strong rejection of the spiritual non–essentials	vs.	* emphasis upon many non–essentials cherished and held by the personality
* keen sense of spiritual priorities	vs.	* disinclination to take the drastic measures necessary to determine priorities
* brief and trenchant emphasis upon spiritual essentials	vs.	* elaboration upon the details of personal, daily living
* destruction of that which inhibits spiritual expression	vs.	* preservation of that which comforts personality, though it inhibits spiritual expression
* eagerness to take independent action for the sake of a spiritual principle	vs.	* unwillingness to stand alone for the sake of a spiritual principle
* "isolated unity" discovered in individual isolation	vs.	* the love of personally satisfying companionship
* stern, spiritually motivated strictness and discipline	vs.	* leniency and permissiveness for the sake of preserving personal satisfaction
* powerful attitude of spiritual centralization	vs.	* loss of center, based upon an excessive number of ties
* strong sense of identification with the spiritual Self	vs.	* weak sense of identity from too much identification with other personal selves
* fast, decisive soul–inspired action	vs.	* hesitation, tentativeness and inaction based upon personal fear
* impatience based on a sense of spiritual urgency	vs.	* an unworthy patience arising from personal inertia
* soul–inspired indignation	vs.	* excessive patience and tolerance contributing to the preservation of non–spiritual values
* the dominance of the spiritual Self	vs.	* compliant subservience to the dominion of the lesser self

* the imposition of spiritual law	vs.	* over–protectiveness which shelters from the impact of spiritual law
* power to stand by as others learn difficult spiritual lessons on their own	vs.	* excessive guarding of others, which prevents them from learning their difficult spiritual lessons on their own
* healthy spiritual Self–respect	vs.	* tendency to lack self–respect
* realization of the superiority of the spiritual Self	vs.	* an unseemly sense of personal inferiority
* reliance upon the immortality of the spirit	vs.	* preoccupation with a sense of personal vulnerability
* lofty, spiritually–inspired indifference to criticism and unkind comment	vs.	* extreme personal susceptibility to criticism or unkind comment
* frank enunciation of spiritual truth, even when it may offend	vs.	* fear of speaking the painful truth even when it is necessary
* easily achieved spiritual impersonality	vs.	* tendency to be too close and too personal

The Integration Process for the Individual with a Ray 1 Soul and a Ray 2 Personality

1. The pre–spiritual phase; soul energy appropriated by a selfish personality: At this pre–spiritual phase of unfoldment, the individual's motives (based upon the personality distortion of first ray soul energy and the self–centered use of second ray personality force), are to achieve great personal power arising from the unrestrained imposition of his personal will, *as well as* the complete fulfillment of personal love (or the complete satisfaction of studious enquiry [2B]). The person wants primarily to dominate and control others, and wield authority unopposed, but he *also* wants to be constantly loved, consistently popular, warmly admired, well–cared–for, and to live a soft, comfortable, well–protected, well–insulated life – closely attached to those people, places and things he loves and finds personally satisfying.

Negatively and glamorously, these two ray influences can combine to produce: the despot who is convinced of his own benevolence (1A + 2A); the dictator who believes himself to be benign (1A + 2A); the ruler who fancies himself the wisest of all (1A + 2B); the insecure ruler who aggrandizes himself by appropriating "men of learning" and their knowledge (1 + 2B); the vain leader who loves adulation and flattery (1 + 2A); the power–hungry autocrat with a deceptively pleasant mask; domination through allurement (1 + 2A); the insatiable ego who aggrandizes himself through personal love (1 + 2A); the use of personal magnetism and charm to achieve power over others (1A + 2A); the typical negative example of the "iron fist in the velvet glove"; etc.

2. The phase of conflict; pure soul energy conflicts with personality force: The essential conflict between the ray one soul and the ray two personality is the struggle between spiritual detachment and personal attachment.

3. The soul/personality integration process from the perspective of the consciousness identified primarily with the ray one soul: It will be the task of the soul to impose its well–developed impersonality and detachment upon a personality which, because of sensitivity, tends to remain attached to others. The soul seeks to liberate the personality from the many non-essentials with which it has surrounded itself, and which it has accumulated through a personal use of the Law of Attraction. The will of the first ray soul seeks to destroy the bondage of strictly personal love, personal popularity, personal magnetism and attraction and, instead, dynamically direct the personality towards a soul-inspired goal despite the inevitable illusion of personal pain. The soul must force the personality to "act now," rather than wait until studious enquiry is completely satisfied. Faced with the necessary task of increasing personal tempo through the application of pressure, and reducing personal fear through desensitization, the soul seeks to propel the personality forward regardless of its tendency to attach, accumulate and cling. The soul must, in short, destroy what the personality (for its own selfish sake) seeks to preserve.

4. The soul/personality integration process from the perspective of the consciousness identified primarily with the ray two personality: For the personality, the integration process will be one of severity, relinquishment and renunciation. At first, the second ray personality may find it personally painful to obey a will which demands the disruption of its own life and the lives of those who are "near and dear." Such personalities are particularly solicitous of the care, comfort and sensitivites of those for whom they have, wisely or unwisely, assumed responsibility. They may shrink in fear from fulfilling the impersonality and demonstrating the (apparent) insensitivity (really, divine indifference) demanded by the first ray soul. In the past, principle may often have been sacrificed to ease and kindness, but if integration is to be a success, this will no longer be possible. The second ray personality discovers that it can no longer preserve *all* its cherished comforts and relationships; some of them have to go, and only those can be retained which conform to Divine Purpose. The good opinion of others, so dear in the past, must be sacrificed. The pain of wrenching detachment must be endured. An agreeable but spiritually useless personal softness and sensitivity can no longer remain unchallenged; a new kind of spiritual 'hardness' must enter the life so that the dynamic will of the soul can be accomplished.

5. The ideal combination of first ray soul energy and second ray personality force: Dynamic spiritual will is expressed lovingly and with wise understanding. Unalterable Divine Purpose is patiently and tactfully implemented. The tendency towards detachment masters the tendency towards attachment, and yet, attachment is skillfully employed to ameliorate the impact of "that which must be." The law always prevails but is compassionately applied. Here is an individual who understands what it means to "temper justice with mercy." Truth is never compromised but is expressed with tact. An individual with this combination of rays is capable of a deep, essential impersonality, but he expresses it with a winning "personal touch"; thus, he masters the art of being *impersonally personal*. When destruction must come, it is executed as benevolently and compassionately as possible. Such an individual is capable of grasping and implementing sweeping syntheses, but they are always performed with consideration for their effect upon those least able to withstand the repercussions. The guiding theme for the highest ideals of those with this combination might well be the following words spoken by Abraham Lincoln, at his second inaugural address:

> With malice toward none; with charity for all; with firmness in the right, as God gives us to see the right, let us strive to finish the work we are in; to bind up the nation's wounds; to care for him who shall have borne the battle, and for his widow, and his orphan – to do all which may achieve and cherish a just and lasting peace among ourselves, and with all nations.

Lincoln, who was a disciple upon the first ray (i.e., he had a first ray soul) very probably had a second ray personality.

6. The combined effect of the two integration formulae: The primary integration formula is *Inclusion*, keyed to the first ray soul. The secondary integration formula is *Centralization*, keyed to the second ray personality. The first formula corrects the exclusive and isolative tendencies induced by the first ray, and the second formula corrects the second ray tendencies towards diffusion and over-expansion, and an energy-draining attachment to life's peripheral attractions. Used together, these two formulae provide the individual striving for soul/personality integration with the composite quality of 'centralized inclusion,'(i.e., the "centered" attitude of the "outer man" which complements the attitude of inclusiveness which it is the will of the "inner man" to cultivate). The proper use of the formulae makes it possible for the individual to stand detached, yet lovingly centered within his personality consciousness, while within those moments of exalted consciousness pervaded by soul quality, he learns to gather to his heart those whom he previously rejected. These formulae provide a remarkable balance of inclusive strength and, loving, self-collected detachment; they have an unusual effectiveness together because the first ray formula, *Inclusion*, is based upon a second ray quality and the second ray formula, *Centralization*, is based upon a first ray quality.

In the earlier stages of evolution, before successfully applying these formulae, an individual with this ray combination often finds himself rebuffing everyone except those few upon whom he wished to lavish his protective love and patronage. Even his love and attachment for them serves the purpose of self-aggrandizement, and he rejects them, too, unless they flatter him and feed his need to be loved.

The intelligent use of the combined formulae ends the period in which a normally self-centered, first ray individual, strays further from his spiritual center, and deepens his alienation and isolation from the true Self by indulging in selfish love. Despite illusions to the contrary, selfish love cannot bring the cycle of isolation to an end. Through the application of the two formulae, the individual learns, primarily, to lovingly touch and include the *essence* of those he formerly rejected or cast aside, and his growing secondary ability to regain his personal center by detaching himself from all selfish personality loves (while yet remaining lovingly related to the all), contributes to his primary, soul-inspired objective of inclusiveness.

7. Some examples of vocational aptitudes and orientations relating to the combination of the first ray soul and the second ray personality:

* the head of state who has the true welfare of the people at heart
* the leader who evokes love
* the director who seeks to direct with wisdom and thorough comprehension

* the ruler who rules with compassion and understanding
* the fearless commander known for his tranquility
* the manager who manages by consensus
* the governor who governs with genuine respect for the consent of the governed
* the authority who attracts and persuades rather than imposes
* the law–maker who always remembers the impact of the law upon those least able to protect themselves
* the executive who never forgets the "human equation" in all his decisions
* the presiding officer with the "personal touch"
* the "good–natured," "good-humored" disciplinarian

In general: vocations and professions which require great will power, strength and stamina, the ability to stand firmly on principle, and (when necessary) the power to destroy obstacles, *as well as* a wise and loving attitude, great empathy and understanding, studiousness, and the ability to teach or compassionately heal.

8. A proposed list of well–known individuals (historical, contemporary, fictional or mythological) whose soul ray can reasonably be considered the first, with a strong subsidiary second ray influence (whether or not the second ray is, strictly speaking, the personality ray):

Akbar the Great: the greatest of the Mughal emperors of India. He has been called the "unifier of India." The fourth ray was also prominent.

Amelia Earhart: aviatrix. Earhart was the first woman pilot to fly solo across the Atlantic ocean. A strong ray five was also in evidence.

Mohandas Gandhi: the most prominent leader in the movement for Indian independence, and the foremost prophet of nonviolence in the 20th century. A strong sixth ray was also in evidence.

Michail Gorbachev: statesman, reformer, General Secretary of the Soviet Union. The seventh ray (Uranian impulse) also appears to be prominent – in alignment with the soul ray of Russia.

Hercules: an ancient disciple and teacher whose struggles to achieve soul consciousness and livingness have been immortalized as the "Labors of Hercules"

John F. Kennedy: 35th president of the United States. Rays four and six were also important aspects of his ray chart.

Abraham Lincoln: 16th president of the United States. Lincoln preserved the Union during the Civil War and brought about the emancipation of the slaves. The fourth ray was also strongly in evidence.

Robert E. Lee: chief commanding officer of the Confederate armies during the United States Civil War. The seventh ray was also strongly in evidence.

Madame Helena Roerich: author, educator and spiritual warrior – amanuensis for the Agni Yoga Teaching. A strong sixth ray influence may also be detected.

Franklin D. Roosevelt: 32nd president of the United States.

King Solomon the Wise: traditionally remembered as the greatest king of Israel. His reputed power as a magician is attributable to a strong seventh ray.

Walt Whitman: American poet – defender and prophet of democracy. A strong ray four influence was also present.

Some Contrasts between the Ray 1 Soul and the Ray 3 Personality

Ray 1 Soul		Ray 3 Personality
* spiritual will	vs.	* personal intelligence
* spiritual "being"	vs.	* personal "doing"
* realization of the oneness of spirit	vs.	* preoccupation with the 'manyness' of form
* direct perception through "straight knowledge"	vs.	* entrapment in the convoluted, reasoning mind
* straight spiritual purpose	vs.	* involvement in a proliferation of personal aims and objectives
* fearless expression of spiritual truth	vs.	* self-protective untruthfulness
* fearless, direct action based on spiritual purpose	vs.	* deviousness or "crookedness" in order to preserve personal advantage
* bold and clear enunciation of the facts as perceived	vs.	* frequent equivocation and resort to ambiguity or unclarity
* brave confrontation to preserve spiritual values	vs.	* circuitous avoidance of obstacles which should be met and responsibilities which should be shouldered
* spontaneous, exuberant selfless action	vs.	* calculated, premeditated action for personal profit
* impersonal self-sacrifice	vs.	* clever (often self-deceiving) evasion of self-sacrifice
* spiritual staunchness and firm spiritual commitment	vs.	* self-serving fluidity and indulgence in a selfish non-committal attitude
* emphasis upon fundamental spiritual values	vs.	* emphasis upon a diversity of extraneous personal activities
* vigorous emphasis upon spiritual essentials	vs.	* distraction with many tangential preoccupations
* assertion of spiritual priorities	vs.	* distaste for putting "first things first"
* power to focus with dynamic intensity	vs.	* difficulty achieving focus due to distracted diversification
* power to stand steadfastly upon spiritual principle	vs.	* tendency to yield to selfishly motivated expediency
* clear-sighted capacity for immediate and undeferred action	vs.	* paralysis of action rooted in the tangled consideration of too many variables
* undeviating fulfillment of divine law, purpose and intention	vs.	* sidetracking and deviation leading to the non-fulfillment of same
* disciplined concentration upon immediate evolutionary necessities	vs.	* preoccupation with personally interesting (though evolutionarily unnecessary) possibilities and eventualities
* destruction of "maya" through clear-cut, spiritually necessary action; destroying the web	vs.	* the creation of "maya" through confused overactivity; 'weaving the ensnaring web'
* decisiveness based upon the clarity of perception arising from the steadfast adherence to the Spiritual Will	vs.	* muddled decision-making based upon uncertain perception caused by a tendency to deviate from the Spiritual Will

• clear groundedness in fact and actuality	vs.	• lost and meandering in theory and hypothesis
• uncompromising presence of mind through identification with the Presence	vs.	• absentmindedness and obliviousness to the environment
• powerful spiritual effectiveness upon the physical plane	vs.	• ineffectivness upon the physical plane due to excessive ideation and impracticality
• utter spiritual simplicity	vs.	• debilitating complexity; the paralysis of too many perspectives
• great capacity for spiritual abstraction	vs.	• excessive preoccupation with matter; materialism
• intense spiritual fixity and centralization	vs.	• personal instability and chaotic activity, manifested as rushing from point to point
• the power to stand alone and unmoved	vs.	• the inclination towards perpetual motion
• spiritually purposeful stillness at the center	vs.	• purposeless rambling around the periphery
• power to organize and execute according to the intention of the soul	vs.	• frequent displays of chaos and disorganization
• habitual spiritual daring	vs.	• self-protective, tactical maneuvering
• spiritual synthesis centered in the heart	vs.	• complex mental analysis; an overly mental approach to life
• brevity due to an understanding of the spiritual essentials	vs.	• prolixity, due to an overstimulation of the throat center; the tendency to speak and write superfluously
• the promotion of spontaneity and authenticity	vs.	• manipulativeness which stifles spontaneity and authenticity – one's own and that of others
• great generosity of spirit	vs.	• personal parsimony

The Integration Process for the Individual with a Ray 1 Soul and a Ray 3 Personality

1. The pre-spiritual phase; soul energy appropriated by a selfish personality: At this pre-spiritual phase of unfoldment, the individual's motives (based upon the personality distortion of first ray soul energy, and the self-centered use of third ray personality force), are to achieve great personal power arising from the unrestrained imposition of his personal will, *as well as* a cleverly intelligent, self-serving mastery of circumstances and the environment. The person wants, primarily, to dominate and control others, and wield authority unopposed, but he also wants to demonstrate his superior intelligence at every opportunity, manipulate money and other people for his own material and intellectual satisfaction, keep incessantly busy in the pursuit of his own self-centered interests, and evade responsibilty through selfish, strategic planning.

Negatively and glamorously, these two ray influences can combine to produce: the all-powerful executive who trusts only himself to run every single phase of an operation (1 + 3B); a egotistical person who prides himself on his outstanding efficiency; the relentlessly ambitious person who seeks power deviously and unscrupulously; (1 + 3B); the power-hungry individual who "reaches the top" through trickery; the individual who can deceptively disguise his intention to control others; the leader who habitually deceives those he leads; the autocrat whose 'god' is money – i.e., the plutocrat (1 + 3B); the authority who is convinced of his own genius (1 + 3A); the ruler who seeks to impose his elaborate philosophy or system of thought (1 + 3A); the one who sows destruction through treachery (1B + 3B); the established ruler who relies heavily upon intelligence reports to maintain his iron grip (1A + 3); the one who dominates others through manipulation; etc.

2. The phase of conflict; pure soul energy conflicts with personality force: The essential conflict between the ray one soul and the ray three personality is the struggle between the intention to uphold the highest principles and values through the use of the firm spiritual will, and the materialistic and intellectual distortion of those principles and values through the manipulative misuse of human intelligence.

3. The soul/personality integration process from the perspective of the consciousness identified primarily with the ray one soul: It will be the task of the first ray soul to "straighten out" the devious, complicated maneuverings common to the third ray personality. The soul seeks to impose its firm spiritual intention on a very mobile personal mechanism which has many plans and pursuits of its own. Guiding such a personality in a straight line, preventing sidetracking, unnecessary diversification, ramification and proliferation will be the soul's formidable concern. It must force the personality to plan strictly in accordance with spiritual will, to recognize the singleness of soul purpose, and to avoid the scattering of its energies. The soul must pressure the wandering, speculative, theoretical personality into an immediate reckoning with *real need*, rather than a preoccupation with the abstract, the tangential, the distant, and the non-essential. The soul must impose deliberate sacrifice and grounded commitment upon a personality highly adept at evading such requirements.

4. The soul/personality integration process from the perspective of the consciousness identified primarily with the ray three personality: For the third ray personality, the pressure towards integration will be felt as constraint and a severe limitation upon its proclivity for diversity and mobility. This type of personality feels most comfortable approaching things obliquely, circuitously, cautiously; it senses the soul trying to force it into a straight and fearless execution of spiritual intention, and consequently feels as if its "hands are tied," its customary, intelligent resourcefulness curtailed. The personality feels pinned down, as if it can't *move*. For integration to be successful, the personality must learn to give up *its* plans, *its* schemes, *its* many lines of interest and activity, and align itself with what it is likely to consider a too-simple, monolithic, all-exacting, one-dimensional purpose. Under the impress of the soul, the personality learns that it has a natural tendency to step out-of-bounds, and that its customary busy, peripheral excursions must be severely curtailed. Skillfully intelligent self-seeking must be eliminated and numerous personally advantageous options relinquished. Trickiness and deviousness can no longer remain unchallenged. A new clarity, straightness and simplicity must enter the life.

5. The ideal combination of first ray soul energy and third ray personality force: Dynamic spiritual will is expressed with creative intelligence and adaptability. Irresistible, invincible spiritual intentions are implemented with constant, tireless activity. All means necessary for victory or achievement are manipulated with brilliant dexterity. Here is an individual who, ideally, knows exactly what he wants and has the power and flexible intelligence to get it. Spiritual objectives are carried forward firmly and with an intelligent readiness for many possible contingencies. As an integrated soul/personality, such an individual has a firm and purposeful attitude which overcomes any tendency towards dispersion, busyness and diffusion, and yet his natural versatility eliminates any danger of falling into crystallization. He is able to implement his spiritual purposes all the more effectively through the creation of many possible channels of expression. He executes his powerful plans adroitly, with strategic skill. There is an inherent ability to retain power which is enhanced through intelligent speculation and foresight. Adaptability and intelligent response contribute to his prodigious capacity to survive and achieve victory. The state of soul–inspired "being" is perfectly complemented by ingenious "doing." There is a profound identification with the Oneness of the Divine Identity, and yet the remarkable ability to play an active role within the 'Divine Diversity.' Divine laws and principles are supported and explained with flawless, eloquent reasoning. Truth is expressed fearlessly, and yet the "right word" (the 'politic' word) can always be found and skillfully enunciated. Great abstract principles upon which universal laws are based are thoroughly comprehended, and yet a way to work such principles into the immediate fabric of current reality is never wanting. Individuals with this combination of rays have more than enough will to confront obstacles fearlessly, and yet they have a constant ability to maneuver wherever necessary so that precious energy can be economized. They have an uncommon understanding of the Purpose of Deity, and the skill to set in motion the wide–ranging plans which are necessary for the manifestation of that Purpose. In the task of executing their interpretation of the Divine Will, they draw upon the great web of interrelated energies; they utilize the astrological science and the science of cycles to intelligently impose the purposes of the inner spiritual government of the planet, as they understand them. Those with this combination are well placed in government; they can ensure that government operates intelligently!

6. The combined effect of the two integration formulae: The primary integration formula is *Inclusion*, keyed to the first ray soul. The secondary integration formula is *Stillness*, keyed to the third ray personality. The first formula corrects the exclusive and isolative tendencies induced by the first ray, and the second formula corrects third ray tendencies towards a busy scattering of attention, wasted thought, and physical overactivity (with their resultant disturbances and obscurations of consciousness). Used together, these two formulae provide the individual striving for soul/personality integration with the composite quality of 'still inclusion,' (i.e., the stillness which fosters the inclusive attitude), making it possible for him to achieve a quietude within his personal consciousness which is supportive of those rare moments of exalted consciousness when, pervaded by the presence of the soul, he begins to gather to his heart those entities whom he previously rejected.

In the earlier stages of evolution, before successfully applying these formulae, an individual with this ray combination often finds himself ceaselessly and restlessly searching for highly intelligent ways of grasping whatever and whomever he wants, and rejecting everything and everyone else. He misuses his power and his mind. He is ruthless and manipulative. His life is one of ceaseless activity in the pursuit of his ambitions. Through grasping and strategem, he acquires what he wants, but, in the process, he destroys his relationship to others. Thus, he brings upon himself a deepening state of isolation.

The intelligent use of the formulae, however, transmutes the abuses of the past. The individual learns, primarily, to stand together with others (protecting and embracing them where he once destroyed them or cast them aside) and his growing secondary ability (acquired in the stillness) to act with true, clear intelligence, contributes to his primary, soul-inspired objective – inclusive relationship. In the stillness, the spiritual essences which are to be embraced and included are realized. This ray combination is usually highly extroverted, and focussed on objective living and achievement; the two integration formulae counteract this tendency; they give the individual a greatly heightened sensitivity to the subtler, intangible, "attractive" aspects of life. The soul, no matter what its ray, is, essentially, *love* and is always group conscious; *Inclusion* and *Stillness* contribute to the growth of group–conscious love.

7. Some examples of vocational aptitudes and orientations relating to the combination of the first ray soul and the third ray personality:

* the head of state who has a profound understanding of economics
* the leader with an astute sense of timing
* the director who understands the effectiveness of indirect direction
* the ruler who takes pains to enhance the intellectual power of those he rules
* the fearless commander capable of subtle strategems
* the manager who can skillfully manipulate interpersonal situations for the benefit of all
* the governor who governs adaptably through the utilization of many options
* the authority who never becomes rigid because he has so many ways to wield his authority
* the lawmaker with excellent powers of reasoning
* the executive who can coordinate a diversity of far–flung enterprises
* the presiding officer who can work behind the scenes to ensure that all goes smoothly
* the disciplinarian who administers disciplines which serve an intelligent purpose
* the supervisor whose success is enhanced through creative thinking
* the field of governmental planning
* the field of political strategy

In general: vocations and professions which require great will power, strength and stamina, the ability to stand firmly on principle, and (when necessary) the power to destroy obstacles, *as well as* acute intelligence (whether active or abstract), great adaptability and resourcefulness, abundant creative and communicative abilities, and (frequently) strong business aptitudes.

8. **A proposed list of well-known individuals (historical, contemporary, fictional or mythological) whose soul ray can reasonably be considered the first, with a strong subsidiary third ray influence (whether or not the third ray is, strictly speaking, the personality ray):**

Yasir Arafat: wily, elusive leader of the Palestine Liberation Organization

Julius Caesar: probably the most celebrated personage of ancient Rome, and one of the greatest generals in the history of the West

Cleopatra: Queen of Egypt, who captivated both Julius Caesar and Mark Antony. Even today she stands as the prototype of the *femme fatale*

Benjamin Disraeli: British statesman and novelist – twice prime minister

Indira Gandhi: former prime minister of India

Iago (fictional): manipulative villain in Shakespeare's *Othello*

Lyndon Baines Johnson: 36th president of the United States – architect of the "Great Society"

Richard M. Nixon: 37th president of the United States. Nixon was the architect of a new policy towards Communist China. Interestingly, China has a first ray soul and a third ray personality.

Odysseus (fictional): hero of Homer's epic poem, the *Odyssey*. Odysseus was known for his courage, endurance, skill and resourcefulness.

Cardinal de Richilieu: astute French statesman and prince of the Catholic Church

Theodora: Byzantine empress, wife of the emperor Justinian I. An individual of surpassing intelligence and political sagacity, Theodora was probably the most powerful woman in Byzantine history. She was influential in devising laws which protected the rights of women.

Some Contrasts between the Ray 1 Soul and the Ray 4 Personality

Ray 1 Soul		Ray 4 Personality
* spiritual unity	vs.	* personal duality
* emphasis upon spiritual Will	vs.	* emphasis upon personal charm and appeal
* spiritual synthesis through subservience to Divine Will	vs.	* warring with the polarities: perpetual struggle between the "pairs of opposites"
* singleness of spiritual purpose	vs.	* personal ambivalence and self–contradiction
* firm decisiveness and unwavering spiritual intent	vs.	* constant indecisiveness and debilitating vacillation
* strong spiritual detachment and self–control	vs.	* excessive personality responsiveness and loss of self–control
* facility for establishing spiritual priorities	vs.	* easily "torn" in the attempt to establish priorities
* self–confidence based upon a firm sense of identity	vs.	* lack of personal self–confidence based upon constantly shifting psychological attitudes
* strong sense of spiritual assuredness or certainty	vs.	* constant uncertainty and unstable psychological balance
* strong sense of spiritual Self–centralization	vs.	* tendency to shuttle to and fro as a link or go–between rather than hold the center; "mercurial"
* undeviating spiritual orientation	vs.	* vacillating orientation; "rajas" and "tamas" (activity and inertia) vie for supremacy
* soul–inspired domination of emotional fluctuation	vs.	* subject to widely contrasting emotions and mood swings
* spiritually stalwart and steadfast; the "rock"; the "tower of strength"	vs.	* personally pliable; the tendency to give way under pressure
* ability to stand in "isolated unity," glorying in spiritual detachment	vs.	* personal need for much rapport, interaction and interplay with others
* great capacity for the exertion of unremitting spiritual pressure upon the self and others	vs.	* personal indolence and laziness followed by the spasmodic expenditure of energy
* spiritually positive to the environment; mastery over circumstances	vs.	* too negative to the environment; easily affected or thrown off balance
* facility for holding a point of tension regardless of stress and strain (whether within the individuality or within the environment)	vs.	* tendency to abandon the necessary point of tension due to the inability to tolerate unresolved stress and strain, even when such stress and strain indicate the rightful resistance to negativity
* implacable resistance to that which opposes spiritual principles	vs.	* unbecoming compromise with the adversary; inclination towards 'unrighteous' compromise
* unassailable spiritual integrity	vs.	* the 'dis–integrated' state of being "one's own worst enemy"
* loyal adherence to spiritual laws and principles	vs.	* betrayal of laws and principles through self–division and divided loyalties

* power to "take sides" for the preservation of spiritual values	vs.	* unprincipled refusal to "take sides" thus avoiding spiritual commitment
* spiritual courage under tremendous adversity	vs.	* "moral cowardice"
* wages spiritual warfare only to uphold high impersonal principles and purposes	vs.	* instinctually combative nature which is easily triggered; fights for the establishment of personal harmony and comfort
* uses full spiritual will to prevail in battle	vs.	* fights for temporary accommodation rather than to prevail
* power to perform with true spiritual impersonality necessary tasks which may be painful to self or to others	vs.	* tendency to suffer remorse, regret or self-recrimination for the inflicting of pain or the violation of harmony, even when such action is morally or spiritually necessary or justified
* strength to disregard pain, whether mental, emotional, or physical	vs.	* hypersensitivity to (and absorption in) pain
* speaking spiritual truth at at all costs	vs.	* tendency to lie to avoid uncomfortable feelings
* power to state the "plain, unvarnished truth" with brevity and simplicity	vs.	* colorful exaggeration and inaccuracy
* prompt, unhesitating action based upon inner spiritual conviction	vs.	* procrastination based upon ambivalence and inner divisions
* calmness based upon fearless identification with the immortal Self	vs.	* personal turmoil and agitation based upon excessive sensitivity and a dread of pain; overresponsiveness to the not-Self
* complete freedom from worry	vs.	* tendency to worry, fret and chafe
* high reliability based upon a strong will and singleness of purpose	vs.	* low reliability, based upon a vacillating will and division of purpose; irresolute and erratic
* ability, when necessary to remain detached and abstracted from form – no matter how attractive the form	vs.	* overattraction and susceptibility to beauty of form; difficulty resisting allurement
* strong sense of organization and a tendency to assign people to well-defined spheres of activity	vs.	* tendency to mix and blend, thus blurring lines of distinction; encourages and participates in indiscriminate mixing – hence, the tendency towards promiscuity
* willing subordination to Divine Law	vs.	* perverse contrariness, inclining to insubordination; instinctively rebels against the principle of hierarchical organization and the imposition of spiritual authority
* great seriousness of spirit; solemnity	vs.	* frivolity, silliness, foolishness: "lightmindedness"

The Integration Process for the Individual with a Ray 1 Soul and a Ray 4 Personality

1. The pre-spiritual phase; soul energy appropriated by a selfish personality: At this pre-spiritual phase of unfoldment, the individual's motives (based upon the personality distortion of first ray soul energy, and the self-centered use of fourth ray personality force), are to achieve great personal power arising from the unrestrained imposition of his personal will, *as well as* an agreeable feeling of personal peace and harmony through the tension–releasing expression of conflicting bio–psychic impulses. The person wants primarily to dominate and control others, and wield authority unopposed, but he *also* wants to be constantly surrounded by what he considers beautiful or attractive, to be spontaneously self–expressive without discipline or control, self–indulgently dramatic or moody (as he pleases), and greatly appreciated for his colorful, unpredictable temperament.

Negatively and glamorously, these two ray influences can combine to produce: a despot who imposes his iron will through the process of war and conflict (1 + 4B); the capacity to attain and hold power by "playing enemies off" against each other; the fulfillment of destructive intentions by mollifying or placating victims – allowing them to think that all is agreeable and harmonious while intending their ruin (1B + 4A); the ascent to authority through the betrayal of allies, through double–dealing; grasping control by feigning harmonious cooperation (1 + 4A); precipitating conflict under the false pretense of establishing peace; the glorification of war and struggle (1 + 4B); inciting rebellion with the purpose of seizing power (1 + 4B); an individual who will make a self–serving, unprincipled peace ("make peace with the devil") to boost his authority and prestige (1A + 4A); egotistic self–valuation as the world's greatest arbiter or "man of peace" (1 + 4A); the ruler who must be surrounded by beauty and magnificence in order to sustain his grandiose self–image (1 + 4A); the tyrant with a perilous psychological balance (1 + 4B); the despot with a split personality (1 + 4B); the indecisive leader; megalomania with manic–depressive tendencies (1 + 4B); imperious theatrics; bombastic temperamentalism (1B + 4B); etc.

2. The phase of conflict; pure soul energy conflicts with personality force: The essential conflict between the ray one soul and the ray four personality is the struggle between the soul–inspired refusal to compromise on spiritual principle, and the over–eagerness for compromise characteristic of a weak and vacillating nature that cannot sustain the tension required to hold to principles in the face of strenuous opposition.

3. The soul/personality integration process from the perspective of the consciousness identified primarily with the ray one soul: It will be the task of the ray one soul to desensitize the over–responsive, environmentally–sensitive, reactive fourth ray personality. The soul seeks to impose its "peaceful, silent will" upon a personality habitually embroiled in stress, strain, strife and turmoil. The soul is endowed with firm resolution and must stem the personality's tendency to irresolute vacillation between alternatives. The driving, directedness of the soul must be imposed upon a personal mechanism which often makes but little progress as a result of inconclusiveness. Because very little will be accomplished otherwise, the first ray soul must "step in" and settle what are often self–destructive, self–defeating personality conflicts, and direct the personal capacitites toward the steadfast achievement of firmly intended soul objectives. A never–ending series of fourth ray personality crises must be made to count for something *purposeful*; combat and turmoil for their own sake are hardly positive and evolutionary; they are, in fact, a meaningless waste of energy. Concentrated first ray power can force a more rapid reliquishment of useless interpersonal and intrapersonal battles, by acting as a demanding spiritual energy which guarantees spiritual victory in the midst of incessant personality struggles. The first ray soul can and must bring *stability* to this most unstable of personality types.

If the personality is the type which is too ready to "make peace," the first ray soul must '*break* the peace!' A personally satisfying peace has nothing to do with the austere, spiritual Will of the soul. Thus, in relation to the fourth ray personality, the soul has two opposing tasks. When the fourth ray personality is purposelessly conflicted, the first ray soul must restore balance and peace; when, on the other hand, the personality accommodates itself too readily to circumstances, forgetting laws and principles, the soul must instigate disruption, destroying personality equilibrium. The soul cannot tolerate a pleasing tranquility which serves no evolutionary purpose – i.e., a useless or (worse) "unjust peace."

4. The soul/personality integration process from the perspective of the consciousness identified primarily with the ray four personality: The first ray pressure towards integration will be felt as a harsh curb upon the personality's flexible accommdation and compromise with circumstances and with people. The fourth ray personality may, under the lash of the soul, feel itself driven suddenly and rapidly forward when it does not feel inclined to move, for this type of personality often seeks refuge in inertia, indolence or lethargy – energy states which are not tolerated under the impatient, will–directed first ray thrust. On the other hand, when the fourth ray personality is in the "rajasic" or hyperactive state (an often–conflicted state), it may wish to race forward recklessly and impetuously; under such a stimulus, the first ray soul would be experienced as a retarding and stabilizing force, insisting upon purposeful rather that wild action. The personality may resist first ray pressure by accentuating its ill–regulated fourth ray traits, but eventually it begins to experience the futility of reactive rebellion. The uselessness of both purposeless accomodation, and of aimless, energy–depleting combat begins slowly to dawn within the personal consciousness. Unreliability, inconstancy, uncontolled moodswings, "half–wayness" – all these are eventually experienced as sources of frustration, militating against the expression of deeper purpose. As it comes more and more under the impress of the first ray soul, the fourth ray personality with its tendency toward the easy forming of relationships, and towards a spontaneous "give–and–take" with others, will itself feel driven into isolation and a state of regimented nonresponsiveness. The ease with which it previously achieved harmonization and agreeable interplay with others will seem imperiled. In short, the fourth ray personality will be forced to take a stand, and not always a pleasant one. The urge toward compromise for its own sake, and for the pleasant feeling such compromise brings, will be overruled by the will of the soul, and this will cause the discomfort of having to endure friction and dissonance for the sake of the preservation of principle. This personality is used to "sitting on the fence" and the charge of irresolute "half–wayness" is frequently more than justified – but the first ray soul insists that the personality go "all the way." Forced off the fence, the personality learns that "right is right" even if personal feelings get hurt.

5. The ideal combination of first ray soul energy and fourth ray personality force: Dynamic will is expressed harmoniously. An unwavering insistence upon upholding and executing spiritual principles arouses a crisis in which conflicts are resolved in accordance with those spiritual principles. A firm attitude masters the tendency to compromise for the sake of comfort, and yet the capacity for principled compromise (i.e., "righteous compromise") is always present. With such individuals, their capacity for purposeful self-discipline always controls any tendency they might have to waste energy in purposeless combat, but they know when and how to fight if they have to, and they can *always* be counted on to put up a good fight. Here is an individual who achieves his unwavering intentions, not only through the exertion of his powerful will, but through his facility for establishing rapport with others, and his understanding of the value of "give and take." Nonetheless, he will never sacrifice his deepest purposes, and he refuses to see his *principles* compromised or weakened (however much he may compromise on nonessential matters). This combination also expresses the union of power and aesthetic sensibility. There is a realization that Divine Law is essentially beautiful, and that the Divine Might must be expressed in ways which are expressive and dramatic. An individual with this combination understands the role of government as the foremost patron of the arts, for the arts are understood as a means of impressing great principles upon the mind of the people. There may also be a tendency to believe, as Napoleon did (Napoleon being a first ray soul with a fourth ray personality), that *imagination* is the greatest power in the world; thus, imagination and arresting drama are seen as tools of leadership. Above all, there is the power to "make peace." Divine Law is recognized and preserved, but there exists that broad tolerance and understanding of contrasting peoples and values which allows for astute negotiation, and reconciliation. The desire for synthesis is one of the strongest motives: *synthesis through identification* (R1) and *synthesis through harmonization* (R4). Identification with divinity is approached through a love of the beautiful.

6. The combined effect of the two integration formulae: The primary integration formula is *Inclusion*, keyed to the first ray soul. The secondary integration formula is *Steadfastness* keyed to the fourth ray personality. The first formula corrects the exclusive and isolative tendencies induced by the first ray; the second formula corrects tendencies towards vacillation, irresoluteness, instability, indecisiveness and moral cowardice characteristic of the fourth ray personality. Used together, these two formulae provide the individual striving for soul/personality integration with the composite quality of 'steadfast inclusion,'(i.e., the steadfastness of the personal consciousness which fosters spiritual inclusiveness). The proper use of these two formulae make it possible for the individual to stand with steadfastness in the center of his normal personality consciousness (choosing neither one side nor the other of the warring opposites within his personality vehicles or within the environment). This personal steadfastness, in turn, enhances those rare moments of exalted consciousness when, pervaded by the presence of the soul, he gathers to his heart all those whom he has previously rejected.

In the earlier stages of evolution, before successfully applying these formulae, an individual with this ray combination is often found throwing himself into the great battle of the opposites, rejecting now one side and now the other – never making a lasting peace, never maintaining allies, always attempting to enforce his dominating but unpredictable will upon the battlefield of life. Rays one and four together can stimulate war – a state of extreme conflict in which rejection and repudiation are the inevitable results. Such an individual becomes, naturally enough, the one who stands alone and isolated, hemmed in on all sides by enemies of his own making.

The intelligent use of the formulae, however, transmutes the abuses of the past. Accomplished in the arts of war, the individual now chooses to fight (if he must) only for peace. Through the formulae, he learns, primarily, to stand in loving being with others (protecting and embracing them, where once he destroyed them or cast them aside), and his growing secondary ability to stand steadfastly and peacefully between the warring polarities (thus refraining from exclusive identification with either one) assists him with his primary objective of achieving a strong, loving and inclusive attitude. He achieves peace and harmony without – love and union within. Above all, he becomes the strong and steadfast "messenger of peace."

7. Some examples of vocational aptitudes and orientations relating to the combination of the first ray soul and the fourth ray personality:

* the head of state who champions the arts
* the leader who understands how to dramatize his ideas
* the director with a gift for spontaneity
* the ruler who is adept in the art of peacemaking
* the fearless commander – born for combat
* the manager who excells in conflict resolution
* the governor who is able to placate constituencies which have contrasting values
* the authority who lightens his impact with humor
* the lawmaker whose success rests upon his ability to compromise
* the executive who succeeds through unpredictability
* the presiding officer who understands how to enliven proceedings
* the disciplinarian who knows how to build bridges to those he must discipline

In general: vocations and professions which require great willpower, strength and stamina, the ability to stand firmly on principle, and (when necessary) the power to destroy obstacles, *as well as* a strong creative imagination, spontaneity, expressivity, aesthetic sensitivity, and the ability to bring harmony out of conflict, beauty out of ugliness, and at–one–ment out of divisiveness.

8. A proposed list of well–known individuals (historical, contemporary, fictional or mythological) whose soul ray can reasonably be considered the first, with a strong subsidiary fourth ray influence (whether or not the fourth ray is, strictly speaking, the personality ray):

Alexander the Great (Alexander III): king of Macedonia. A great conqueror, he overthrew the Persian Empire, and laid the foundations for the Hellenistic world of territorial kingdoms.

Otto von Bismark: 19th century Prussian statesman who founded the German Empire and became its first chancellor

Napoleon Bonaparte: French general and later, emperor of France

Winston Churchill: author, orator, statesman and artist. Churchill was twice prime minister of Great Britain.

David, King of Israel: a courageous yet self-divided individual. David was known as a great musician.

George Gurdjieff: occultist, who emphasized struggle, conflict, and the expression of spirituality through the sacred dance. A strong third ray influence was also present.

Alexander Haig: United States general, politician and statesman

Hamlet (fictional): Prince of Denmark in the play *Hamlet*, by William Shakespeare

Henry VIII: king of England

Adolf Hitler: German dictator, leader of the Third Reich. Some have felt that Hitler had both a ray one soul and a ray one personality.

Lorenzo di Medici ("the Magnificent": Florentine ruler and a great patron of the arts

Benito Mussolini: the first of Europe's Fascist dictators and authoritarian head of the Italian state for more than 20 years

Theodore Roosevelt: 26th president of the United States, author, explorer, and amateur soldier. A strong ray six quality was also present, and (surprisingly) ray five.

Some Contrasts between the Ray 1 Soul and the Ray 5 Personality

Ray 1 Soul		Ray 5 Personality
* spiritual synthesis	vs.	* preoccupation with concrete analysis; little capacity for perceiving or understanding wholeness
* vision in vast spiritual wholes	vs.	* focus upon disconnected parts
* realization of the broad, sweeping panorama, as seen from the summits of spirit	vs.	* the limitations of specialization and particularization
* breadth of spirit	vs.	* personal narrowness
* the overcoming of all divisions	vs.	* unable to see beyond a multitude of illusory separations and cleavages
* focus within the world of Being	vs.	* intellectual thralldom to the world of form
* all–encompassing spiritual intuitions	vs.	* disbelief based upon the restrictions of concrete–mindedness
* emphasis upon the great spiritual essentials	vs.	* engrossed in the details and minutiae of the world of matter
* brevity based upon emphasis of that which is spiritually vital	vs.	* longwindedness based upon absorption in the multitude of fragmentary perceptions registered by the concrete mind
* expansive action from the heart – the seat of the "Life principle"; great–heartedness	vs.	* action constricted by the pettiness of concrete intellect
* absolute "Identification" with the One Life	vs.	* slavery to a strictly objective attitude; the systematic cultivation of the separation between subject and object resulting in an intellectual "split" between the observer and the observed
* the apotheosis of spiritual "fire"	vs.	* a presentation of self devoid of "fire"
* the power and charisma generated by identification with the One Life	vs.	* a nonmagnetic persona
* great depth of feeling arising from profound identification with the source of spirit	vs.	* disconnection from feelings and vitality, conveying the impression of a disembodied intellect
* power to initate great spiritual projects	vs.	* small capacity to initiate; confinement to study and analysis
* involvement of the entire being in spiritual enterprises	vs.	* an attitude of skeptical reservation which may invest the mind, but not the other aspects of self
* immense spiritual courage	vs.	* the restrictiveness of common sense
* irresistable spiritual dynamism	vs.	* plodding, linear activity
* great breadth of spiritual vision	vs.	* unimaginative, pedestrian and literal
* total conviction and commitment	vs.	* excessive skepticism interferes with conviction and commitment

The Integration Process for the Individual with a Ray 1 Soul and a Ray 5 Personality

1. The pre-spiritual phase; soul energy appropriated by a selfish personality: At this pre-spiritual phase of evolutionary unfoldment, the individual's motives, (based upon the personality distortion of first ray soul energy, and the self-centered use of fifth ray personality force) are to achieve great personal power arising from the unrestrained imposition of his personal will, *as well as* narrow, materialistic, intellectual certainty. The person wants, primarily, to dominate and control others and wield authority unopposed, but he *also* wants to take everything apart (either analytically or actually) reduce all life experience to nothing but rationalistic formulae, control matter mechanically for selfish ends, and reject any kind of knowledge that is not materialistic or derived strictly from the five physical senses.

Negatively and glamorously, these two ray influences can combine to produce: the quest for personal power understood in purely materialistic terms; willful destructiveness through the abuse of scientific knowledge (1B + 5); the arms race, and those who advocate achieving domination through the use of lethal technology (1B + 5B); the "military-industrial complex"; the tyranny of technocracy; the domination of men by machines (1 + 5B); government basing its principles of rulership upon narrow, materialistic scientific orthodoxy; the "Prussian" mentality; repressive power supported by scientific research and discovery (1 + 5A); amoral, "social Darwinism" – i.e., official policies which espouse the idea that it is natural for only the most powerful and intelligent to survive; pride of race based upon presumed, 'scientific' differences in intellectual capacity (1A + 5A); the leader who promotes disunity and cleavage based upon the distinctions and classifications of the concrete mind; laws which separate people by emphasizing their differences – i.e., institutionalized racism, and other forms of legalized "pigeonholing"; the willingness to disrupt and dismember Nature purely for the sake of power – i.e., power *over* Nature rather than cooperation *with* Nature; extreme egotism based upon an impelling sense of difference; the "hanging judge" – adamant and merciless; the energy of the "black lodge" (cf., tabulation, p. 89, *The Externalization of the Hierarchy*); etc.

2. The phase of conflict; pure soul energy conflicts with personality force: The essential conflict between the ray one soul and the ray five personality is the struggle between the vision of synthesis based upon "Identification" with the One Life, and the determination to 'divide' the great synthesis through an entirely mental process of objective analysis, in which subject and object remain forever separate and distinct.

3. The soul/personality integration process from the perspective of the consciousness identified primarily with the ray one soul: It will be the task of the ray one soul to broaden the ray five personality, and bring it to the point where it can see things "en large" to a greater extent. The soul wishes to press forward according to its keen sense of purpose, but the personality is liable to be caught up in the examination of its narrow, particularized field of study. Wishing to achieve dramatic results, the soul exerts its will dynamically, but the personality prefers a rather unspectacular approach – slow, cautious and non-assertive. The soul demands that the personality realize that it is not knowledge alone that counts, but the responsible, purposeful application of that knowledge in line with the Divine Purpose. The soul mobilizes to prevent the personality from becoming overly-fascinated with what is interesting in itself, but irrelevant to soul intention. Mere curiosity often leads away from the actualization of soul purpose. Spirit is primary and form, secondary; this, the soul knows, and, thus, urges the personality forward, forcing a disengagement from a too time-consuming preoccupation with the examination of form.

4. The soul/personality integration process from the perspective of consciousness identified primarily with the ray five personality: The first ray pressure towards integration will be felt by the fifth ray personality as an urge to committed action rather than prolonged investigation. The personality does not like to trouble itself with assuming a position of leadership because such activities take precious time away from its own specialized enquiries and discoveries. The task of supervising and regulating others seems tedious and mentally uninteresting. The responsibility of inspiring and empowering others appears foreign and frightening, because the fifth ray personality senses (correctly) that it does not have the emotional equipment to arouse others to enthusiasm and success. Under the impress of the first ray soul, the personality begins to realize that a broader, more dynamic, more inspired, more magnetic assertiveness is spiritually necessary, and that a strictly mental, dispassionate, experimental approach will have to be modified and expanded if the inner demand is to be met, and integration with the Higher Self is to succeed. This type of personality will have to learn to actually *embody* that which its mind *knows*.

5. The ideal combination of first ray soul energy and fifth ray personality force: Dynamic will is expressed through a mastery of concrete fact and a practical command of material energies. Spiritual purpose is intelligently implemented through a completely accurate and intimate knowledge of energies and forces inherent in matter. Those with this combination can scientifically arouse the kundalini power with potent results. Advanced individuals of this type can, when necessary, unleash divine destructiveness through their command of precise formulas which hold the key to Nature's powers. Through the utilization of these energies, Divine Law can be imposed upon form through a mastery of appropriate technologies. On a very lofty turn of the spiral one can imagine the scientific use of natural law in the Department of the Manu. Here, also, we find an individual whose innate capacity to rule and govern is augmented by a wealth of technical knowledge, enabling him to make the very well-informed decisions. When this combination applies to the field of government, governmental policies are based upon enlightened, scientific understanding. Knowledge is wedded to power. The ability to see the "big picture" prevails over the tendency to specialize and get bogged down in the details of form, but such an individual will see even vast panoramas clearly and in detail. An individual endowed with this combination of rays will approach the process of Identifcation with divinity through a mentally-reverent realization of matter as the "garment of God." The capacity to achieve the broad and synthetic vision characteristic of those upon the first ray is enhanced by a brilliant illumination of the mind. The first ray is the "conqueror of death," and for those with a first ray soul and fifth ray personality, death is conquered through knowledge, and the "Kingdom of Heaven" is not only "taken by storm," but 'taken by science.'

6. The combined effect of the two integration formulae: The primary integration formula is *Inclusion*, keyed to the first ray soul. The secondary integration formula is *Detachment*, keyed to the fifth ray personality. The first formula corrects the exclusive and isolative tendencies induced by the first ray, and the second formula corrects the fifth ray tendencies towards mental attachment to matter, and an obsessive preoccupation with investigating or manipulating concrete form while ignoring the reality of that which is "formless." Used together, these formulae provide the individual striving for soul/personality integration with the composite quality of 'detached inclusion,'(i.e., the detachment of the "outer man" from a spiritually-blind, all-engrossing interest in material form, and detachment which contributes to the development of spiritual inclusiveness within the consciousness of the "inner man"). When identified with the soul, the individual is, at last, learning to warmly embrace the essential reality of others, but if his personality is fixated only upon the form, and is blind to anything but the material aspect of those whom he is learning to approach, the soul-inspired attempt to be lovingly inclusive will fail. The proper use of these integration formulae, however, will enable the individual to detach his personal consciousness from its excessive fascination with the fluctuating conditions of matter, and this detachment, in turn, will enhance those rare moments of exalted consciousness when, pervaded by the presence of the soul, he succeeds in gathering to his heart those whom he has previously rejected.

In the earlier stages of evolution, before successfully applying these formulae, an individual with this ray combination often finds himself preoccupied with acquiring a detailed knowledge of matter and form, which, because selfishly and separatively used to augment his personal power, only increases his sense of isolation and alienation. Using knowledge as a means to dominate not only his environment but all those he contacts, he banishes himself to the outer circle of his life. He becomes unapproachable, untouchable, animated by an "impelling sense of separation." This can be a very negative combination which, if badly abused, may attune an individual to the vibration of the "Black Lodge."

The intelligent and successful use of the formulae, however, transmutes the abuses of the past. The individual learns, primarily, to stand together with others (protecting and embracing them, where he once destroyed them or cast them aside), and his growing secondary ability to understand the God 'within' and 'behind' the material form contributes to his primary soul-inspired objective of loving inclusion. Although this is usually a very material combination, through the use of the formulae the individual increases his *subjective sensitivity* greatly; he comes into deep subjective rapport with the essential, formless Life from which the form has emanated. His emphasis changes from a previous preoccupation with power and knowledge, to a sensitive, loving inclusion of others and an appreciation of subtle realities unavailable to the testimony of the senses. Again we see how these Integration Formulae, *balance or correct the usual tendencies of the rays*. The soul, itself, is the balancing or "midway point" between Monad and personality, just as the heart chakra is, from one important perspective, the middle chakra. A balanced condition is required for those who wish to enter into the consciousness of the soul.

7. Some examples of vocational aptitudes and orientations relating to the combination of the first ray soul and fifth ray personality:

* the head of state who does all he can to promote scientific discovery and application
* the leader with true common sense
* the director of a large, technical enterprise, such as the Atomic Energy Commission
* the ruler with a profound respect for exact knowledge
* the fearless commander intimately familiar with the technology of weaponry
* the bold explorer who must rely upon technical expertise for the success of his expedition
* the manager who demands accuracy from his subordinates
* the autocrat who is utterly sure of his facts
* the lawmaker who, through research, is familiar with the many technicalities of the law
* the executive who insists upon automation
* the disciplinarian who demands a strict accounting of the truth
* the field of military technology; the "military–industrial complex"
* the head of a munitions company
* a magnate in heavy industry
* the modern general in a technological army
* the director of governmental investigations

In general: vocations and professions which require great will power, strength and stamina, the ability to stand firmly on principle, and (when necessary) the power to destroy obstacles, *as well as* solid common sense, keen analytical abilities, the capacity for research, and scientific and/or technical expertise.

8. A proposed list of well–known individuals (historical, contemporary, fictional or mythological) whose soul ray can reasonably be considered the first, with a strong, subsidiary fifth ray influence (whether or not the fifth ray is, strictly speaking, the personality ray):

Henry Ford: automobile manufacturer who revolutionized United States industry with his assembly line method of production. Ray seven is probably strong as well.

J. Edgar Hoover: former head of the Federal Bureau of Investigation

Alfred Krupp: industrialist in the field of armaments

Gordon Liddy: author, government agent, exponent of *will*

Alfred Nobel: manufacturer of explosives and philanthropist. He left the bulk of his fortune in trust to establish the Nobel prizes.

Harry S. Truman: 33rd president of the United States. The decision to use the first atomic bomb fell to him.

Some Contrasts Between the Ray 1 Soul and the Ray 6 Personality

Ray 1 Soul		Ray 6 Personality
* spiritual will	vs.	* personal desire
* uncompromising spiritual detachment	vs.	* desperate attachment
* emotional control through the application of spiritual will	vs.	* ill–controlled emotionalism and frequent lack of restraint
* identification with the One Self within the individual self	vs.	* personal worship, devotion and adoration of a self or selves external to the individual self
* spiritual centralization: the one who stands unmoved at the spiritual center of his life	vs.	* flight from center: the one who rushes away from his own spiritual center towards a center outside himself
* spiritual strength and Self–reliance	vs.	* personal dependency; overleaning on others
* spiritual impersonality	vs.	* excessively personal emphasis
* divine indifference	vs.	* anxiety and overconcern based upon personal fears and attachments
* wide, synthetic breadth of vision	vs.	* a passionately narrow vision
* impartiality based upon an identification with spiritual law, and an unshakable realization of the One Identity	vs.	* bias based upon partiality and personal favoritism
* commitment to the "greatest good of the greatest number"	vs.	* ignoring the "greatest good of the greatest number" in the fanatical pursuit of "special interests"
* the soul–inspired leader	vs.	* the personally excited follower
* spiritual severity based upon the acceptance of essential values	vs.	* personal sentimentality based upon an emotional clinging to lesser values
* uncompromising spiritual realism	vs.	* unrealistic attitudes and escapism

The Integration Process for the Individual with a Ray 1 Soul and a Ray 6 Personality

1. The pre–spiritual phase; soul energy appropriated by a selfish personality: At this pre–spiritual phase of evolutionary unfoldment, the individual's motives (based upon the personality distortion of first ray soul energy, and the self–centered use of sixth ray personality force), are to achieve great personal power arising from the unrestrained imposition of his personal will, *as well as* the uncompromising satisfaction of the ideals and goals to which the personality is passionately devoted. The person wants, primarily, to dominate and control others and wield authority unopposed, but he *also* wants to ignore everything except the object or path of his devotion, spurn even reasonable, mundane responsibilities if they do not relate specifically to his quest, fanatically follow his ideal regardless of destructive consequences, and cling desperately to that which he believes he loves.

Negatively and glamorously, these two ray influences can combine to produce: willful destructiveness aggravated by unbalanced, emotional extremism (1B + 6B); repressive theocratic rule – an unholy alliance of church and state (1A + 6); governmental 'inquisitions'; the wedding of tyranny and fanaticism (1 + 6B); the lust for power, self-righteously pursued; a leader who demands total, unquestioning loyalty (1 + 6A); the relentless purging and liquidating of those who deviate from narrow, orthodox ideology (1B + 6B); the obliteration of the 'unfaithful' (1B + 6B); governing power basing its principles of rulership upon religious intolerance (1A + 6); a morbid devotion to power (1 + 6A); a ruler who believes himself to be a 'god' and who cultivates the 'worship' of his personality (1 + 6A); unabashed nepotism and favoritism towards those to whom one is devoted (1A + 6A); the arousal of destructive mass emotion or hysteria for cynical political ends (1B + 6B); lofty idealism used as an excuse for the ruthless acquisition of personal power; etc.

2. The phase of conflict; pure soul energy conflicts with personality force: The essential conflict between the ray one soul and the ray six personality is the struggle between the firm, unemotional spiritual will to uphold Divine Law, and the passionately emotional pursuit of fanatical personal desire.

3. The soul/personality integration process from the perspective of the consciousness identified primarily with the first ray soul: It will be the task of the ray one soul to strengthen the sense of centralization in the ray six personality. The soul upon the first ray knows that victory is in its own hands, whereas the sixth ray personality usually depends upon some source of sustenance outside itself. The first ray soul knows *itself* as the source of unfailing strength, whereas the personality almost invariably relies upon others (human or divine) for its strength. The problem centers upon the contrast between being "inner-directed" (R1), or "outer-directed" (R6) – being "Self-directed" (R1), or "other-directed" (R6). The soul must discipline the emotional excesses of the personality and widen its point of view. The soul imposes a severe form of Self-control, teaching the personality that it must function according to impartial law rather than emotional preference. A vision of the "big picture" and the true, enduring, spiritual values is imposed by the soul. This is meant to overcome the narrow, fanatical adherance to spiritually limited devotions and idealisms.

4. The soul/personality integration process from the perspective of the consciousness identified primarily with the ray six personality: As the pressure of the ray one soul exerts itself, the personality is initially likely to feel as if a cold, impersonal force is suppressing its enthusiasms and excitements. A greater *Will* is perceived as interfering with the fulfillment of the personality's very definite, focused desires. The ray six personality wants to direct all its energy towards a revered person or object of devotion, but begins to sense a devaluation of that person or object as a broader and clearer vision of the Whole is *forced* into its consciousness by the soul. The personality's objects of devotion begin to pale in significance. As the limitations of personality attachments are mercilessly revealed, the personality is likely to feel that fate or destiny is depriving it of everything loveable – everything worth living for. Under the harsh light and uncompromising vision of reality emanating from the first ray soul, the personality is forced into a state of bewildering disillusionment. Thus does the sixth ray personality come to realize that narrow personal love and attachment act as a chain limiting the freedom of consciousness. Vague longings arise to abandon the role of the "frenzied follower" and, instead, play the role of the self-confident leader. Eventually the personality realizes that, all along, it has been laying emphasis upon little things and that, somehow, in its impassioned searching and one-pointed devotion to limited causes and limited people, it has missed the "main point," – the "big picture." The larger issues and larger responsibilities, as understood by the first ray soul, begin to dawn.

And so, the unit of consciousness, still aware of itself as a sixth ray personality, but more and more identified with the first ray soul, seeks to detach from limited loves and limited pursuits. It seeks to look to *itself* as a source of power and energy, and not only to others upon whom it has mistakenly projected the essence of its own strength. It seeks to dedicate itself only to that which is truly important for the welfare of the whole and for the execution of the Divine Will, and not to that which is merely personally appealing or exciting. The sixth ray personality, beginning now to fuse with the first ray soul, *devotes itself* to the "greatest good of the greatest number."

5. The ideal combination of first ray soul energy and sixth ray personality force: Dynamic will is expressed with one-pointed ardor and fervent devotion. Divine destructiveness, when necessary, is zealously and unhesitatingly enacted. Complete sacrifice of the form life is executed with total self-abnegation. The individual's small part in the fulfillment of God's Purpose is fearlessly carried forward to the point of self-immolation; he expresses utter loyalty to Divine Law. Firmness, coolness and absolute self-control master the tendency towards emotionalism and irrational excesses. The highest purpose is upheld with no thought of compromise. High-minded conviction is sustained with unshakeable faith, and the goal is achieved at all costs. This is an individual who can rarely be thwarted. He consecrates his life to the fulfillment of a greater purpose – often of a political nature. In the lives of advanced individuals with this combination of rays, impersonality triumphs over personalism. They understand the value of fulfilling their duty impersonally and yet ardently. Their centralization within the One Self overcomes any tendency they might have to rush away from the center of identity, and yet the capacity for well-directed, enthusiastic pursuit is ever "at the ready." Ideally, individuals of this type have the ability to stand as strong and inspiring embodiments of divinity. Through the blending of the first and sixth rays, their innate capacity for Identification with the One Life is borne on the wings of mystical abstraction. They rise above all identification with form.

6. The combined effect of the two integration formulae: The primary integration formula is *Inclusion*, keyed to the first ray soul. The secondary integration formula is proposed as *Peaceful Standing Still at the Center*, or, simply, *Restraint*, keyed to the sixth ray personality. The first formula corrects the exclusive and isolative tendencies induced by the first ray, and the second formula corrects the unrestrained, passionate pursuit of the 'partial' and 'peripheral' so common to the emotionally undisciplined sixth ray personality. Used together, these formulae provide the individual striving for soul/personality integration with the composite quality of 'restrained inclusion,' (i.e., the personal restraint which fosters spiritual inclusiveness). The reoriented individual with a first ray soul is pledged to love where once he hated. He seeks to attract where once he repelled. He must employ a gentler approach than heretofore, in order to become a loving and inclusive center of strength. To accomplish this, he requires a personality which is under control, and will not rush forward and *seize* those who should, instead, be naturally attracted. The sixth ray personality needs patience and tempering if it is to be a useful instrument to its powerful soul – a soul which due to the integration process is newly intent upon treading the Way of Love. The proper use of the formulae enables the individual to restrain his personal consciousness from violent attachments to people, places and things, and this restraint, in turn, enhances those rare moments of exalted consciousness when, pervaded by the presence of the soul, he gathers to his heart those he has previously rejected.

In the earlier stages of evolution, before successfully applying these formulae, an individual with this ray combination often finds himself willfully pursuing his narrow desires, demanding their satisfaction, racing towards their gratification. His unrestrained, relentless determination to grasp only what he wants (regardless of consequences) drives others away from him, landing him in a state of utter isolation. There is too much of the straight line in this combination. When the indivdual is enlightened, the straight–line approach leads undeviatingly towards accomplishment. When in a benighted state, however, this individual will rush straight to the outer rim of his life, trampling anyone who dares to oppose him. In the impassioned pursuit of domination he crushes all opposition, and thereby, temporarily, destroys the "Path of Return" to his spiritual center.

The intelligent use of the formulae, however, transmutes the abuses of the past. The individual learns, primarily, to stand together with others (protecting and embracing them, where once he destroyed them or cast them aside), and his growing secondary ability to release himself from the fury of his desires, allows him to drop the lesser things which he once held in his impassioned grip, and open his arms, inclusively, to those he is learning to love. Thus, he begins to experience increasingly centered, loving and inclusive relationships with others. His usual tendency to dominate, over–do and drive others away through excessive, fiery intensity is balanced by a more restrained, and open-armed approach. Integration with the soul grows as he refrains from pursuing that which can result merely in increased personal power and personality satisfaction; instead, he pursues (with illumined devotion) that which will bind him to others in the bonds of spiritual intimacy.

7. Some examples of vocational aptitudes and orientations relating to the combination of the first ray soul and the sixth ray personality:

* the statesman who is a true patriot
* the leader who sets an example by living up to the ideals he enunciates
* the director with great power to motivate
* the ruler who inspires self–sacrifice
* the fearless commander who arouses great loyalty in those he commands
* the manager who "coaches" others towards their best performance

* the authority who easily mobilizes enthusiastic cooperation with his plans
* the lawmaker or politician animated by high, uncompromising idealism
* the executive who uplifts his employees with a glowing vision of possible accomplishment
* the pioneer who will sacrifice everything to break new ground
* the true "spartan"

In general: vocations and professions which require great will power, strength and stamina, the ability to stand firmly on principle, and (when necessary) the power to destroy obstacles, *as well as* high idealism, undeviating devotion, great enthusiasm and persistent emotional intensity.

8. A proposed list of well-known individuals (historical, contemporary, fictional or mythological) whose soul ray can reasonably be considered the first, with a strong subsidiary sixth ray influence (whether or not the sixth ray is, strictly speaking, the personality ray).

Susan B. Anthony: pioneer crusader for the woman suffrage movement in the united states

Annie Besant: militant idealist, orator, social crusader, president of the Theosophical Society, and president of India's National Congress

Fidel Castro: revolutionary, head of the Cuban Government since 1959

Giuseppe Garibaldi: Italian revolutionary and one of the most skillful guerilla generals of all time. He was the most distinguised soldier of the Risorgimento, the movement that united Italy. It is reputed that Helena Blavatsky (disguised as a man) fought in his regiments.

Emma Goldman: political activist, called the "Mother of Anarchy"

Judith: legendary biblical heroine who cut off the head of the tyrant Holofernes, thus liberating her people from oppression

Nicholai Lenin: idealistic revolutionary, considered the father of the Russian Revolution

Martin Luther: founder and leader of the 16th century Protestant Reformation

Moses: Hebrew prophet and lawgiver

Othello (fictional): the protagonist in Shakespeare's *Othello*

Vanessa Redgrave: actress, political activist

George Sand: the pen name of Amandine-Aurore Dupin, prolific 19th century romantic novelist. Sand, a social rebel who asserted her independence by frequently dressing in men's clothing, protested passionately against social conventions which bound a woman to her husband against her will.

Harriet Tubman: a leading abolitionist before the U.S. Civil War. She organized the "underground railroad," which guided slaves to freedom in the North. She became known as the "Moses of her people."

Mao Zedong: founder of the Chinese Communist State

Some Contrasts Between the Ray 1 Soul and the Ray 7 Personality

Ray 1 Soul		Ray 7 Personality
* unimpeachable spiritual authenticity	vs.	* loss of Self through slavery to social conditioning
* the moment–to–moment rebirth of the essential Self	vs.	* stifling the rebirth of the essential Self through adherence to meaningless rituals, routines and procedures
* destruction and radicalism for the sake of spiritual freedom	vs.	* building purely for material security; unconsciously refortifying the socially acceptable forms which confine consciousness
* soul–inspired liberation from form	vs.	* imprisonment within form; locked into deadening formalities
* unconstrained action of the spiritually motivated free will	vs.	* compulsiveness and conditioned response
* dynamic spiritual initiatives	vs.	* overly cautious reliance upon precedents
* the soul–inspired willingness to dare on behalf of spiritual progress	vs.	* insistence upon absolute physical plane safety and material security
* bold and fearless declaration of spiritual truth	vs.	* unnecessary secrecy; also, the concealment of truth through artificial and superficial forms of social interaction
* the power to take unilateral action for the sake of spiritual values	vs.	* avoiding personal initiatives by excessive reliance upon group action
* ultimate spiritual abstraction	vs.	* densest material concretion and crystallization
* commitment to spiritual essentials	vs.	* self–limiting concern for externals and outer appearances
* spontaneous originality and unconventionality as reflections of unconditional spiritual freedom	vs.	* restrictive conventionalism which inhibits originality [at least for one type of personality upon this ray – (7A)]
* spiritual dynamism to break the mould	vs.	* subservience to habit and tradition
* a broad sweep of synthetic spiritual vision	vs.	* limitation of vision due to overconcern for detail
* immediate mobilization: ability to arise to spiritual emergencies	vs.	* difficulty altering unvarying procedures and sequences of action, even in emergencies
* death and abstraction as spiritual acts; freedom from the prison of the physical body	vs.	* identification or preoccupation with the physical body
* shattering the prison of the spirit	vs.	* carefully building the prison of the spirit

The Integration Process for the Individual with a Ray 1 Soul and a Ray 7 Personality

1. The pre–spiritual phase; soul energy appropriated by a selfish personality: At this pre–spiritual phase of evolutionary unfoldment, the individual's motives (based upon the personality distortion of first ray soul energy, and the self–centered use of seventh ray personality force), are to achieve great personal power arising from the unrestrained imposition of his personal will, *as well as* a rigidly ritualized, tightly ordered physical plane safety, security and 'perfected' materialistic living. The person wants primarily to dominate and control others, and to wield authority unopposed, but he *also* wants a highly predictable (hence, relatively risk–free) life, to avoid having to think for himself or act upon his own initiative, and to have the solid assurance that all physical plane appetites and imagined material needs will be satisfied on schedule.

Negatively and glamorously these two ray influences can combine to produce: the ruler who imposes absolutely rigid laws upon his people; the tyranny of Procrustus (1 + 7A); the paranoid leader who refuses to tolerate any kind of innovation (1 + 7A); the preservation of state power through the severe suppression of all individual expression (1 + 7A); a governmental policy which forces conformity and standardization in order to forstall the threat of change (1 + 7A); the decision to overthrow all valuable, well–established laws, and impose those of one's own invention (1B + 7B); the ever–dissatisfied revolutionary (1B + 7B); the attempt to gratify unlawful ambition through the improper use of magic (1 + 7C); the attempt to destroy individuality through compulsory ritual (1B + 7C); potentates who indulge their egomania by building imposing monuments to honor themselves; the determination to dominate and control the forces of nature for purely self–exalting purposes; great destructiveness through the invocation of daemonic forces (1B + 7C) etc.

2. The phase of conflict; pure soul energy conflicts with personality force: The essential conflict between the ray one soul and the ray seven personality is the struggle between the inherent freedom of the spirit and the subservience of the spirit to form.

3. The soul/personality integration process from the perspective of the consciousness identified primarily with the first ray soul: It will be the task of the first ray soul to shatter the many forms and patterns which hold the seventh ray personality prisoner. The soul seeks to impose a sweeping sense of divine freedom and unfettered individual will upon a personality which is habitually over–regulated, over–scheduled, over–particular, and over–attentive to the "thousand–and–one" petty details which distract it from the realization that form is essentially illusory. The soul wishes to extricate the personal consciousness from preoccupation with externals and to have it realize the essential reality of *formless* spirit. The soul, animated by the will–to–sacrifice, whispers of the beauty of death, which is really spiritual life; but the seventh ray personality prefers its own version of 'life,' which means, enwrapping the spirit in illusory 'safety' through the process of psychosocial mummification.

Rapid, direct action is a predominant quality of the first ray soul, but it is frustrated by the difficulty of breaking the well–established, self–protective rhythms of the seventh ray personality. The soul dares to renounce form and thus be free; the personality preserves its routines thus saving itself from the terror of pure spontaneity – the horror of a totally unconditioned act of will.

4. The soul/personality integration process from the perspective of the consciousness identified primarily with the seventh ray personality: The first ray pressure towards integration will be sensed by the seventh ray personality as an intruding, abstracting force, disrupting comfortable, well–established rhythms, and destroying well–accustomed patterns of behavior. The personality prefers a predictable context, in which the rules are well–known, and expectations are well–defined. The death–dealing, sacrifice–demanding first ray energy destroys all that, and leaves 'no–*thing*' in its place. The personality feels as if it is being driven from one shattered refuge to another. When none remain, the desperate personality will immediately seek another consciousness–numbing form to shelter itself from the fear of naked abstraction, but no sooner is a spiritually purposeless form created (or inhabited), than it is again shattered by soul impulse. The personality discovers there is nowhere to hide, no covering it can build around itself, no edifice it can erect to flee the pure abstraction of spirit. At length the seventh ray personality (as it becomes a subray of the first ray soul) learns that there is no safety in form, and that its creations and constructs are meant to house or embody formless principles. A well–ordered world designed strictly for personal safety and comfort, gives way to a well–ordered world designed to reflect, symbolize and contain Divine Purpose.

5. The ideal expression of the combination of the ray one soul and the ray seven personality: Dynamic spiritual will is expressed rhythmically and with exquisite timing, as well as with complete regard for the best laws, rules and social conventions. Ideally, individuals with this combination are committed to uphold the highest values of society, as those values are embodied in law. This is a combination conferring great strength, and is characteristic of those who both make the law and enforce the law. Such individuals stand as steadfast '*pillars*' within any organization of which they are a part; the structure and stability of all social systems depend upon them. They especially value ethical action as a reflection of Divine Law and Divine Will. These are people of prodigious will, but they are never crude in their application of power; they execute their intentions with finesse and practical effectiveness. Spiritual laws and principles are always implemented with consummate skill–in–action; governmental programs are superbly structured to meet (in a most responsible manner) the needs of those governed. People of this type put forth dynamic initiatives based upon the newly emerging divine ideas, and always find ways to embody such ideas in the best possible form; thus, they work to promote the smooth evolution of civilization rather than chaos and disruption, because their initiatives are so skillfully *presented* upon the material plane. Their freedom and spontaneity of spirit masters any tendency they might have towards formalism and the habitual following of precedent, and yet they invariably maintain a deep respect for *appropriate action.*. This can be a revolutionary combination, but sweeping changes are always skillfully administered. Pioneering programs are resourcefully and excellently organized. Great reforms can be initiated by these individuals because their power to forcefully present the totally new is complemented by their great skill in restructuring that which already exists. This is the combination of the unrelenting yet skillfully pragmatic social revolutionary – one who has the forcefulness and inventiveness to institute great changes for the better.

6. The combined effect of the two integration formulae: The primary integration formula is *Inclusion*, keyed to the first ray soul. The proposed secondary integration formula, keyed to the seventh ray personality is: *'Stand and suffer within the pentagram, and, oriented towards the East, await the Light which illuminates the Plan* – or, far more simply, *Orientation*. The first formula corrects the exclusive and isolative tendencies induced by the energy of the first ray. The second formula corrects the tendencies towards selfish building and organizing according to short-sighted, materially-minded personal plans, but without an attentive orientation to the Divine Design as revealed by the soul. Used together, these formulae provide the individual striving for soul/personality integration with the composite quality of 'oriented inclusion,' (i.e., the attentive spiritual orientation which fosters an understanding of the part which everyone is to play within the Divine Plan, as well as the loving, synthetic will to embrace or include the 'players'). The formula makes it possible for the individual to orient his personal consciousness towards the practical specifics of manifesting the Plan. This orientation, in turn, enhances those rare moments of exalted consciousness when, pervaded by the presence of the soul, he gathers to his heart, as co-workers in the Divine Manifestation, those whom he had previously rejected.

In the earlier stages of evolution, before successfully applying these formulae, an individual with this ray combination often finds himself preoccupied with building many forms designed to meet only his personal need and desire, and to enhance his power upon the physical plane. These tightly organized forms either act as barriers to his fellow human beings (shutting them out), or imprison them (shutting them in). Craving complete control, he consolidates his power over others, organizing them into patterns of servitude. He creates a perfectly organized, 'totalitarian' structure. Far from the center of his being he works, his back to the light, forcing others to conform *exactly* to the dictates of his powerful will. Filled with the energy of rejection and working in the dark, his isolation and spiritual alienation increase.

The intelligent use of the formulae, however, transmutes the abuses of the past. The individual learns, primarily, to stand together with others (protecting and embracing them, where once he destroyed them or cast them out). In inclusive love, he now appreciates who they are and their place in the Divine Pattern, and his growing secondary ability to orient himself to the East, and sense the practical things which must be done to fulfill the Plan, contributes to his primary, soul-inspired objective. He begins building lovingly for all. Instead of building a "power-base" upon the physical plane for himself alone, he builds-up a power-base for all. Under the influence of a spiritually-oriented inclusiveness, the constructive work he undertakes (in strict conformity with the Plan) is for the many whom he embraces with a breadth of understanding inspired by the capaciousness of his first ray soul.

7. Some examples of vocational aptitudes and orientations relating to the combination of the first ray soul and the seventh ray personality:

* the statesman with a superb sense of timing
* the leader who is a brilliant organizer
* the director who understands the best way of executing the many details of a project
* the ruler, fastidiously aware of the rank and privileges of his subjects
* the fearless commander whose campaigns are designed down to the last detail
* the manager who is invariably courteous and polite
* the governor who always observes proper protocol
* the authority whose task it is to enforce the law
* the lawmaker who understands all the ethical implications of the legislation he proposes
* the executive who always insists upon the proper performance of business practices
* the presiding officer who requires the strict following of parliamentary procedure
* the politician with a masterful sense of ceremony
* the disciplinarian
* the drill sergeant!

In general: vocations and professions which require great will power, strength and stamina, the ability to stand firmly on principle, and (when necessary) the power to destroy obstacles, *as well as* the power to organize or reorganize, the ability to build, a facility for creating or maintaining standards, and the capacity to skillfully manifest ideas through form.

8. A proposed list of well-known individuals (historical, contemporary, fictional or mythological) whose soul ray can reasonably be considered the first, with a strong subsidiary seventh ray influence (whether or not the seventh ray is, strictly speaking, the personality ray):

Francisco Franco: Spanish general and virtual dictator of Spain from 1939–1975

Thomas Jefferson: third president of the United States and principal author of the Declaration of Independence. There is a strong fifth ray influence in Jefferson's energy system. (Note: A convincing argument might be made for a seventh ray soul and a first ray personality.)

General Horatio Kitchener: British general in the Boer War, and World War I. Kitchener had extraordinary powers of organization. The Tibetan assigns him a first and seventh ray.

George D. Marshall: Chief of Staff of the U.S. Army during World War II. He was, according to Churchill, "the organizer of victory."

Bernard Montgomery: field marshall and one of the outstanding Allied commanders in World War II

Solon: Athenian statesman and poet who embodied the cardinal Greek virtue of moderation. He provided his fellow countrymen with a balanced constitution and a humane code of laws. Because he was an excellent mediator, the fourth ray was undoubtedly influential.

Josef Stalin: dictator of the Soviet Union (a strong ray three influence [3B], can also be detected – probably on the level of the concrete mind)

Margaret Thatcher: Prime Minister of Great Britain

George Washington: Commander of the Continental Army during the Revolutionary War, and first president of the United States. Washington was also an active Mason.

Soul/Personality Combinations with a Ray Two Soul

Some Contrasts Between the Ray 2 Soul and the Ray 1 Personality

Ray 2 Soul		Ray 1 Personality
* spiritual love and wisdom	vs.	* personal wilfulness and aggression
* the will to preserve and save	vs.	* inconsiderate destructiveness in order to achieve personal advantage
* joy and spiritual positivity	vs.	* wrath and anger
* spiritual inclusiveness; accepting others despite their imperfections	vs.	* personal exclusiveness; rejecting others because of their imperfections
* spiritual attachment to the heart and soul of others	vs.	* cold detachment; rebuffing others
* spiritual achievement through the power of magnetic attraction	vs.	* accomplishment through grasping assertiveness and, even aggressiveness
* loving impersonality	vs.	* callous impersonality
* spiritual intimacy	vs.	* isolative aloofness
* extreme spiritual sensitivity and intuition	vs.	* hardness, insensitivity, imperviousness
* deep, empathic understanding	vs.	* inability (or lack of desire) to get close enough to others to really understand them
* kindness and long–suffering patience	vs.	* personal demands and impatience
* gentle tact based upon spiritual love	vs.	* harsh, blunt expression of opinion despite the wounds it may cause
* group love and cooperation	vs.	* personal egotism and lack of cooperation; unilateral undertakings unrelated to the group
* humble, spiritual decentralization	vs.	* selfish personal centralization and self–aggrandizement
* well–considered action based on profound thought	vs.	* rash, unconsidered action
* the "wise use of slow action"	vs.	* violence
* spiritually evocative; non–coercive	vs.	* dominating, coercive and controlling

The Integration Process for the Individual with a Ray 2 Soul and a Ray 1 Personality

1. The pre–spiritual phase; soul energy appropriated by a selfish personality: At this pre–spiritual phase of evolutionary unfoldment, the individual's motives (based upon the personality distortion of second ray soul energy and the self-centered use of first ray personality force), are to achieve the complete fulfillment of personal love, (or the complete satisfaction of studious enquiry [2B]), *as well as* great personal power arising from the unrestrained imposition of the personal will. The person wants, primarily, to be constantly loved, consistently popular, warmly admired, well–cared–for, and to live a soft, comfortable, well–protected, well–insulated life – closely attached to those people, places and things which he loves and finds personally satisfying, but he *also* want to dominate and control others, and wield authority unopposed. (The inherent contradiction of this combination is extremely evident, just as there was an inherent contradiction associated with the combination of the first ray soul and the second ray personality).

Negatively and glamorously, these two ray influences can combine to produce: the essentially weak but willful person; the spoiled individual who believes that he has a right to self–indulgence; the socialite who always wants to be noticed and appreciated (2A + 1A); the fearful, "motherly" type, who forces his overprotectiveness on those for whom he imagines he is totally responsible (2A + 1); the 'helper' whose ego is invested in keeping those he helps dependent upon him; the intimate advisor who loves to tell others what to do (2B + 1); the overly–responsible person who destroys the character of others because he does too much for them (2A + 1B); the savior who, in glorifying his role as savior, robs others of their strength (2A + 1); the religiously inclined individual who believes that he personally has the power to "save the world" (2A + 1); the person with a deep inferiority complex who compensates by acting superior – superior as a source of love (2A + 1), or superior as a source of wisdom (2B + 1); the person who becomes so thoroughly absorbed in study that he remains selfishly aloof from others (2B + 1); the person who wants to say "Yes" but always finds himself saying "No"; the self–consciously humble person who forces others to be humble too; the one who 'hates' those who do not 'love'(2A + 1); the comfort–loving person who will use the full force of his personal will to preserve his personal comforts; the 'wise' individual who is destructively critical of all forms of wisdom except his own (2B + 1B); the 'sage' who prides himself on the supremacy of his world view and the scope of his understanding (2B + 1), etc.

2. The phase of conflict; pure soul energy conflicts with personality force: The essential conflict between the ray two soul and the ray one personality is the struggle between the need to express unconditional soul love and wisdom and the urge to express personal will regardless of destructive consequences.

3. The soul/personality integration process from the perspective of the consciousness identified primarily with the second ray soul: It will be the task of the second ray soul to pervade with spiritual love and wisdom a personality that is instinctively self–centered, self–willed and resistant to altruism. The soul seeks to impose a broader, and more inclusive perspective, but the personality is innately exclusive, overly–assertive and infused with the quality of rebuff, contributing to its repudiation of and by others – hence its isolation and alienation. The soul works to dissolve the many barriers the personality has built around itself; through the steady and consistent infusion of light, the soul reveals to the personality the unhappy consequences of egotism and lovelessness. By a process of constant 'softening,' the soul trains the personality to cease rupturing interpersonal links. Softening, smoothing, restraining, amerliorating, cushioning, enfolding, illuminating, quieting – these are the methods by which the second ray soul brings love and wisdom into the consciousness of a personality which would rather force its way through the world – alone.

4. The soul/personality integration process from the perspective of the consciousness identified primarily with the first ray personality: The second ray pressure towards integration will be felt by the first ray personality as a subtle and frustrating, weakening experience. The personality will feel robbed of its strength, its edges dulled, its impacts lessened, and its sharp lines of personal distinction blurred. The first ray personality prides itself on its strength; it is not used to blending, merging, and deferring. It does not immediately see why it should "hold back," and stop itself from grasping that which it desires, because, after all, it is perfectly capable of getting what it wants! And yet every straight line of assertive action is subtly and gently changed into a curved line of more mutual, considerate action. From deep within itself (which is another way of describing soul action) the personality feels itself being *rounded*, and rendered more magnetic. The real meaning of love and relationship begins to dawn upon the personal consciousness, which realizes the truth of the age–old saying: "it's easier to catch flies with honey than with vinegar." Gradually, and subtly, under the steady, persistent impress of the soul, the personality mellows, realizing that real strength need not hurt others, and that, after all, "life is with people."

5. The ideal expression of the combination of the ray two soul and the ray one personality: Loving understanding is expressed with power and firmness. The union of love and will is solidly achieved, with love preponderating. The tendency towards attachment masters the personality tendency towards detachment, and yet the balance is preserved. Love is poured forth, but always with detachment; thus a state of "detached attachment" comes to fruition. The individual masters the lesson of becoming "impersonally personal." The "Will to Unify" is powerfully implemented. Wise and gentle understanding is conveyed with strength. Comprehensive studies are relentlessly pursued. This combination can create an unusually effective educator: one who will accumulate a wealth of knowledge, but who will strenuously insist that knowledge be applied directly and forcefully in service. The most benevolent motives are powerfully carried into life experience. Here is an individual who understands the meaning of humility and decentralization, but who is sufficiently "centered" to be a vigorous, effective and practical world server. Deep love is expressed without a trace of sentimentality. The heart–felt yearning to save and salvage is firmly buttressed by first ray fortitude. Redemption becomes the theme of the life, but those who are helped are never weakened or made dependent; they are encouraged to stand on their own feet and rely upon themselves. The "heart of gold" is found beneath what may sometimes seem a rather distant or, even, forbidding exterior. With this combination, we find experts in the art of "tough love."

6. The combined effect of the two integration formulae: The primary integration formula is *Centralization*, keyed to the second ray soul. The secondary integration formula is *Inclusion*, keyed to the first ray personality. The first formula corrects second ray tendencies towards diffusion, overexpansion, and an energy–draining attachment to life's peripheral attractions, whereas the first formula corrects the exclusive and isolative tendencies characteristic of the first ray personality. Used together, these two formulae provide the individual striving for soul/personality integration with the composite quality of 'inclusive centralization,' (i.e., the tolerant and inclusive personal attitude which fosters the discovery of one's spiritual center). The proper use of the formulae make it possible for the individual to cultivate a more loving and accepting personal consciousness, supportive of those rare moments of exalted consciousness when, pervaded by the presence of the soul, and detached from all lesser attractions, he takes his stand firmly and, immovably within the "center of all love."

In the earlier stages of evolution, before successfully applying these formulae, an individual with this ray combination often finds himself unable to relate to others in a loving and intimate way no matter how hard he tries to do so. Although he is attracted (almost indiscriminately) to many people, there is always something within himself which quickly repels them, causing him constant frustration over his inability to express and receive love. Using his first ray qualities he might even try to force others to love him. He does not yet understand real love, spiritual love. Never, at any time, is he really centered in his essence, which is the "center of all love." His love is still personal and selfish, and while it remains so, he will remain off balance, driving away from himself that which he most desires.

Through the intelligent use of these formulae, the individual learns, primarily, to stand within the center of the love and wisdom of his second ray soul, loving others purely, wisely and with detachment; his growing secondary ability to include others where he once rebuffed them, attracts to him many with whom he can now share his newer, purer and more centered form of love – spiritual love.

These two formulae (as in the case of the identical [though reversed] formulae for the first ray soul and second ray personality) provide a perfectly balanced energy configuration. The second ray soul must learn Centralization, and it is aided in this task by its first ray personality. The first ray personality (though it is essentially a subray of the second ray soul) still must learn to be inclusive; this is naturally aided by the very inclusive tendencies of its 'sponsoring' soul. The combined formula, 'inclusive centralization,' can be aptly portrayed by the point within the circle – a powerful occult symbol, conveying the ideas of unity and identity.

7. Some examples of vocational aptitudes and orientations relating to the combination of the second ray soul and the first ray personality:

* the server who teaches those he serves to become self–reliant

* the teacher who insists that students embody and become an example of the best that they learn

* the therapist who refuses to allow his clients to act like weaklings

* the humanist who loves all of humanity, but believes that people must earn the respect they receive

* the unifier who requires that everyone live up to his reponsibility in the unification process

* the illuminator who teaches that the greatest understanding comes from the "hard knocks" of first hand experience

* the 'guru' who thinks it best to hold the mirror up to his chela's weaknesses without delay

* the scholar who will risk danger and hardship to acquire the knowledge he seeks
* the healer who teaches his patients to draw upon their own unsuspected reserves of healing power
* the counselor who reminds counselees of their own strength
* the social worker who does not allow fit people to become dependent
* the meditator who disciplines his personality vehicles with ease

In general: vocations and professions which require a wise and loving attitude, great empathy, studiousness, and the ability to teach or compassionately heal, *as well as* great will power, strength and stamina, the ability to stand firmly on principle, and (when necessary) the power to destroy obstacles.

8. A proposed list of well–known individuals (historical, contemporary, fictional or mythological) whose soul ray can reasonably be considered the second, with a strong subsidiary first ray influence (whether or not the first ray is, strictly speaking, the personality ray):

Alice A. Bailey: amanuensis for the Tibetan, author, lecturer, founder of the Arcane School

Robert Browning: one of the great poets of the Victorian Age. His poetic genius is most evident in his mastery of the dramatic monologue as a technique for powerful poetic narrative and rich psychological portraiture. Browning is said to be a high initiate, and, according to Dr. Douglas Baker, a Master of the Wisdom.

The Buddha (Siddhartha Gautama): founder of Buddhism. In the esoteric tradition, the Buddha is known as the "Lord of Light," and the "Lord of Wisdom." In many respects, both He and the Christ are the World Saviors.

Sigmund Freud: founder of psychoanalysis. Freud was also strongly influenced by the fifth ray, and the seventh to no small degree.

Pythagoras: a great sage, founder of the school of wisdom at Crotona. Presumably, a strong fourth ray influence was also in evidence. He Who was once Pythagoras is now said to be the Chohan Koot Hoomi – the Tibetan's Master.

Albert Schweitzer: author, theologian, philosopher, musician and physician. Schweitzer established what became a world–renowned missionary hospital at Lambaréné in French Equatorial Africa.

Mother Theresa: regarded by many as a living saint, and an embodiment of the energy of love. There is also a strong sixth ray present in her energy system, and it is possible that she has transferred onto the second ray from the sixth.

Some Contrasts Between the Ray 2 Soul and the Ray 2 Personality

Ray 2 Soul		Ray 2 Personality
* expression of spiritual magnetism and attraction	vs.	* reliance upon personal magnetism and attraction
* loving spiritual impersonality	vs.	* close personal attachments
* soul–inspired patience	vs.	* personal inertia; self–indulgent slowness to act
* the love of love	vs.	* the love of being loved
* sensitivity to the heart and soul of others	vs.	* debilitating personal sensitivity; fearfulness
* compassion for the weak and vulnerable	vs.	* personal weakness and vulnerability
* pity based upon a loving heart	vs.	* self–pity
* wide tolerance based upon loving understanding	vs.	* unwisely permissive
* inclusive attitude towards knowledge and understanding	vs.	* includes too many personally related non–essentials
* attachment to the spiritual consolations of the divine heart of love	vs.	* attachment to personal comfort
* radiation of spiritual joy	vs.	* insistence upon "being happy"

Commentary

1. As it is assumed that identical soul and personality rays are a rare occurrence, appearing only in the very last stages of evolution, it is not really meaningful to discuss the dynamics of soul/personality interaction in a pre–spiritual phase of evolutionary unfoldment.

2. If it is true that the combination of a second ray soul with a second ray personality would not appear until the second ray qualities had been balanced over many lives by the acquisition of a great deal of strength and independence (first ray qualities), the spiritual maturity of the individual would negate the possibility of a pronounced or prolonged stage of soul/personality conflict – as frequently occurs during a somewhat earlier stage of evolution, when the soul is just beginning to impose itself upon established personality rhythms. It is important to remember that, no matter what rays may condition the personality fields during a particular incarnation, the experiences of past lives (colored by many different combinations of rays) have been *built into the character of the individual* (being stored as spiritual qualities within the causal body, and as "skandas" or "tendencies" within the permanent atoms). Such ray–qualified qualities and tendencies *do*, in fact, exert their influence on an individual's *present* character.

Such rare conflicts as there might be, would be based upon the higher and lower possibilities of the second ray. Essentially: the contrast would be between a radiant, inclusive, impersonal, all–encompassing love, and an attached, personal, overly–sensitive and fearful holding of others to the self. It can be assumed that for such an individual, the use of second ray energy in a strictly personal sense would be quite rare. In general, however, it would always be necessary to guard against an overaccentuation of second ray energy, with the result of too much attachment and too much loving understanding (if the latter can be imagined). The presence of a highly developed quality becomes an overaccentuation when the compensatory qualities of other rays are severely diminished or missing. For instance, second ray virtues become vices unless they are balanced by rays along the 1–3–5–7 line of energy.

As regards this particular combination, it must be remembered that the two greatest exponents of second ray energy, the Buddha and the Christ, *both* worked through personalities which were *not* upon the second ray – the Buddha through a first ray personality and the Christ through a personality upon the sixth ray. Certainly, these great Individuals were expressions of the *purest* kind of second ray energy available to humanity, and those who associated with them directly must have experienced an overwhelming flow of second ray quality. It therefore stands to reason that the combination of a second ray soul and second ray personality is *not* absolutely necessary for the manifestation of an unusually pure expression of second ray energy, and, in those cases in which the presence of the second ray seems unusually pure and powerful, it must not too hastily be assumed that this necessarily entails the presence of *both* a second ray soul and second ray personality.

3. As regards the ideal expression of the combination of the ray two soul and the ray two personality, it is clear that the personality would serve as a pure channel for the unimpeded flow of the soul's love–wisdom.

Contrast Between the Ray 2 Soul and the Ray 3 Personality

Ray 2 Soul		Ray 3 Personality
* spiritual love	vs.	* personally motivated intellectuality
* deep feeling of the heart	vs.	* unfeeling thought of the selfish, self–interested mind
* inclusive spiritual synthesis and fusion	vs.	* discriminating separativeness
* deep intuitive comprehension	vs.	* confusions and uncertainties of the unenlightened reasoning process
* profound subjectivity	vs.	* blindness to spiritual subtleties caused by an excessively objective and intellectual attitude
* silent, non–verbal understanding	vs.	* overly verbal or wordy
* tolerance born of love and wisdom	vs.	* criticism, copiously produced by the intellectually proud mind
* clear perception arising from stillness	vs.	* clouded perception arising from an over–active mind and body
* great luminosity of soul	vs.	* the veiling of light through the creation of an over–abundance of forms, whether mental or physical
* instinctive spiritual truthfulness	vs.	* facile deviation from truthfulness
* wholesome spiritual simplicity	vs.	* entanglement in unnecessary complexities
* sensitive stillness contributing to effectiveness in the art and science of meditation	vs.	* busyness militating against effective meditation
* slow but sure spiritual constructiveness	vs.	* wasted energy through excessive activity
* sensitive, magnetic evocation of the identity of others	vs.	* manipulation of others for personal ends
* spiritual loyalty and faithfulness to the end	vs.	* elusive, non–committal attitude
* a wise understanding of the very next spiritual step ahead	vs.	* preoccupation with impractical or excessively abstract eventualities lying far ahead
* facility for the accumulation and handling of detail (especially in the realm of scholarly studies)	vs.	* sloppiness and inaccuracy; small concern for detail, (especially mundane detail)
* loving cooperation	vs.	* competitive maneuvering for advantage
* expansion of consciousness	vs.	* increase of information
* trust and joyful openness	vs.	* wariness and suspicion

The Integration Process for the Individual with a Ray 2 Soul and a Ray 3 Personality

1. The pre–spiritual phase; soul energy appropriated by a selfish personality: At this pre–spiritual phase of evolutionary unfoldment, the individual's motives (based upon the personality distortion of second ray soul energy and the self-centered use of third ray personality force), are to achieve the complete fulfillment of personal love, (or the complete satisfaction of studious enquiry [2B]), *as well as* a cleverly intelligent, self-serving mastery of circumstances and the environment. The person wants, primarily, to be constantly loved, consistently popular, warmly admired, well-cared-for, and to live a soft, comfortable, well-protected, well-insulated life – closely attached to those people, places and things which he loves and finds personally satisfying, but, he *also* wants to demonstrate his superior intelligence at every opportunity, manipulate money and other people for his own material and intellectual satisfaction, keep incessantly busy in the pursuit of his own self-centered interests, and evade responsibilties through selfish, strategic planning.

Negatively and glamorously these two ray influences can combine to produce: the overly soft-hearted individual who "arranges" the lives of others, so they do not have to do so themselves (2A + 3B); the person, who feeling weak and inadequate, compensates by pretending to be more intelligent than others (2B + 3A); the studious individual who is contemptuous of the mental limitations of others and filled with detailed, verbal criticism of those limitations (2B + 3A); the person who does not know when to stop taking-on responsibility, and then becomes hyper-active in the frantic attempt to do everything he promised to do (2A + 3B); similarly, one who tries to make up for a deep-seated feeling of inferiority by undertaking far too many activities (2A + 3B); a life lived with entirely too much 'scatter' and 'spread'; the person who attempts to offer too comprehensive a picture in too complex a manner, and finishes by confusing those he intended to enlighten (2B + 3A); one who sees and talks about an extraordinary number of possibilities, but carries out very few; one who is content with amassing and thinking about knowledge he never uses (2B + 3A); one who is always protecting his sensitive psyche through evasive maneuvers (2A + 3); one who uses constant financial manipulations to cushion and enwrap his life with many material comforts (2A + 3B); one who, desperately wanting to be popular and well-liked, uses his financial skill to "buy" the love and appreciation of others; etc.

2. The phase of conflict; pure soul energy conflicts with personality force: The essential conflict between the ray two soul and the ray three personality is the struggle between a deeply subjective attitude characterized by wisdom and loving understanding, and a far more objective, materialistic attitude based upon a determination to face life chiefly through intellectual acuity, resourcefulness and adaptability.

3. The soul/personality integration process from the perspective of the consciousness identified primarily with the second ray soul: It will be the task of the second ray soul to quiet and sensitize the third ray personality. The soul is faced with a personality which is over-active, over-talkative and frequently so busy that it "crowds out" the impressions that might be received from others. The soul senses a complicated maze of words and actions interfering with the straight and simple nurturing love it seeks to express. Breathing forth calm, silence and stillness, the soul seeks to reveal to the personality the 'noise' which that personality so constantly generates and in which it so constantly lives. Further, the soul impresses upon the personality the thought that "less is more" – that it is not always necessary to meddle, interfere, or "have a [manipulative] hand in" the affairs of others. It is the soul's intention to teach the personality how to *allow*, and how to *trust in love*. Inherent in others is the possibility of their success, and that they do not have to be manipulated into doing, but will act (at the right time) of their own accord. This, the third ray personality very much needs to learn. In essence, the soul is imposing a more subjective, internal attitude upon a personal mechanism which has, heretofore, been firmly convinced of the efficacy of the active, external approach to "getting things done."

4. The soul/personality integration process from the perspective of the consciousness identified primarily with the third ray personality: The pressure towards integration exerted by the the second ray soul will be felt by the third ray personality as a subtle changing of the "rules of the game." The personality likes to have the "strings" in its own hands so that it can "pull" them. When the soul requires a trustful "letting–go," the personality feels an indefinable malaise. The individual with this type of personality does not like to admit that, "It's out of my hands"; he feels most comfortable when he is able to "*do* something." A disturbing feeling of helplessness, and lost control develops until the personality begins to see that 'doing' is a "two–way street," a reciprocal activity; that one need not do everything oneself, and that things work out well when others are allowed to initiate actions, on their own, without interference (however subtle).

Then, there is the matter of openness and honesty. In order to accomplish its ends, the third ray personality understands how to disguise, complicate, evade, mislead others and, generally, "cover its tracks"; the second ray soul, however, inclines towards honest, self–disclosure. The maxim, "Truth is good for the soul," bears the signature of the second ray. But the third ray personality realizes that if it embraces truth, simply and without complication, it loses one more "maneuvering advantage," and it is no longer possible to "move behind the scenes" to bring things about. However, the uncompromising illumination thrown by the second ray soul upon the actual results of the unending stream of third ray plans and activities, reveals their futility, and soon convinces the personality that it is useless to weave and maneuver "in the dark," i.e., whether that darkness is caused by a distrust of others' motives, a distrust of the value of truth, or a distrust of that which the light of intuition reveals.

5. The ideal expression of the combination of the ray two soul and the ray three personality: Love and understanding are actively expressed with great intellectual resourcefulness. Intangible, subjective realizations are verbalized with outstanding interpretive finesse. A multitude of ways are devised to express a deeply–felt humanitarianism. This is an individual capable of originating ingenious strategies to unite in cooperative enterprise those who work for the expansion of consciousness. Philanthropic motives are supported by excellent business skills. Intuitive insights are creatively communicated, and a diversity of methods is generated to convey wisdom and illumination. A profound and inclusive understanding of reality is eloquently articulated. Those with this combination of rays can argue tirelessly for the value of a broad, humanistic education as necessary for the optimum development of the human soul and intellect. They can weave together, with unusual skill and intelligence, the many details of a vast and comprehensive knowledge. The wise use of slow action masters the tendency towards excessive activity and wasted motion, but such people remain flexible and mobile, ready and able to go anywhere and do anything to further love, wisdom and understanding. The heart fuses with the ever-active mind. Benevolence and loving kindness are expressed with intellectually sophisticated "savoir-faire."

6. The combined effect of the two integration formulae: The primary integration formula is *Centralization*, keyed to the second ray soul. The secondary integration formula is *Stillness*, keyed to the third ray personality. The first formula corrects the second ray tendencies towards diffusion, overexpansion, and an energy-draining attachment to life's peripheral attractions, whereas the second formula corrects third ray tendencies towards a busy scattering of attention, wasted thought and physical over-activity (with their resultant disturbances and obscurations of consciousness). Used together, these two formulae provide the individual striving for soul/personality integration with the composite quality of 'still centralization,' (i.e., the personality stillness which fosters the ability to find one's spiritual center). The formulae make it possible for the individual (by detaching his loving attention from the periphery of life) to gather his consciousness to the center of his being and (aided by the newfound stillness of his personality), become sensitive to that which is *central* to his expression as a soul.

In the earlier stages of evolution, before successfully applying these formulae, an individual with this ray combination often finds himself desperately overextended, attached to far too many things, and wildly active in the pursuit of those things. Restless activity, and a too-inclusive, expansive, undiscriminating attitude towards love and attachment keeps him constantly "un-centered" and off balance. He is too involved and too busy to seek the center of his being.

The intelligent use of these formulae, however, transmutes the abuses of the past. The individual learns, primarily, to stand within the center of the love and wisdom of his second ray soul, loving others purely, wisely and with detachment, and his growing secondary ability to find clarity and right-action through stillness helps him remain spiritually "centered".

7. Some examples of vocational aptitudes and orientations relating to the combination of the second ray soul and the third ray personality:

* the server who thinks of every possible contingency which may arise during the course of his service
* the teacher who persistently encourages intelligent, verbal self-expression among her students
* the therapist with outstanding interpretive skill
* the humanist who realizes the importance of historical perspective in the development of humanity
* the unifier with a skill for pulling a great diversity of 'threads' together
* the compassionate helper who will "go anywhere and do anything" to render his help effective
* the illuminator who is broadly eclectic in her methods

* the light–bearer who spreads knowledge far and wide
* the sage who uses every means at her disposal to communicate her ideas
* the guru who is adept at sharpening the intellect of his chelas
* the scholar with a strong penchant for philosophical thought
* the healer who combines psychological understanding with herbal medicines
* the counselor with a multitude of constructive alternatives for her clients
* the social worker who is keenly aware of the financial dimensions of social welfare
* the astrologer who focuses extensively upon the timing of events in relation to the expression of subjective soul potentials
* the meditator with unusual facility for the creative development of seed thoughts

In general: vocations and professions which require a wise and loving attitude, great empathy and understanding, studiousness, and the ability to teach or compassionately heal, *as well as*, acute intelligence (whether active or abstract), great adaptability and resourcefulness, abundant creative and communicative abilities, and (frequently) strong business aptitudes.

8. A proposed list of well–known individuals (historical, contemporary, fictional or mythological) whose soul ray can reasonably be considered the second, with a strong subsidiary third ray influence (whether or not the third ray is, strictly speaking, the personality ray):

Martin Buber: Jewish religious philosopher, biblical translator and interpreter. Buber is best known for his development of the ethical concept of "I and Thou".

Meister Eckehart: the greatest German speculative mystic. Although mysticism flourishes, primarily, under the sixth ray, Eckehart's mysticism was broad characterized by the lucidity of the second ray. The Tibetan refers to him as an occultist.

Marilyn Ferguson: new–age educator, author of *The Aquarian Conspiracy*, and editor of "The Brain–Mind Bulletin"

Hypatia: Alexandrian Neo–Platonist philosopher, mathematician and educator. Hypatia was considered the most learned woman of the ancient world.

Henry James: American novelist. A strong ray four was also in evidence.

Origen: the most influential and seminal theologian and biblical scholar of the early Greek Church

Plato: Greek philosopher, who with Socrates and Aristotle laid the philosophical foundations of western culture. The first ray appears to have been a strong influence.

Socrates: Greek philosopher, and teacher of Plato. The first ray was definitely an important influence.

Some Contrasts Between the Ray 2 Soul and the Ray 4 Personality

Ray 2 Soul		Ray 4 Personality
* spiritual love and wisdom	vs.	* personal expressiveness
* serenity based upon deep faith in and understanding of Divine Love	vs.	* persistent personal crises and conflicts – mental, emotional, and even physical
* tranquility based upon clear spiritual vision	vs.	* moodiness based upon blind reaction to the fluctuations of the form life
* undimmed spiritual positivity	vs.	* unstable alternation between "highs" and "lows"; unpredictable personality reactions
* scholarly inclinations in the pursuit of Divine Wisdom	vs.	* rejection of the scholarly path in the pursuit of "experiential" living
* a profoundly spiritual/religious attitude and world-view	vs.	* 'artistic' temperamentalism
* soul-inspired restraint of the passions; wise dispassion	vs.	* surrender to the emotional fluctuations of the passions
* slow, steady and stable spiritual progress	vs.	* a personal life filled with constant self-inflicted reversals
* quiet faithfulness and spiritual loyalty	vs.	* fickleness due to self-contradiction and divided loyalties
* the wise avoidance of extremes	vs.	* constant alternation between the extremes
* capacity to "stand" within "the center of all love"	vs.	* difficulty achieving a centered position due to constant vacillations
* upholding of spiritual values through the application of detached spiritual love	vs.	* relinquishing of spiritual values because of the felt need for tension-reduction, resulting in unwise compromise and "peace at any price"
* selfless concern for others	vs.	* selfish concern with one's never-ending problems and turmoils
* gentleness and loving-kindness	vs.	* contrariness and combativeness
* humility and "occult obedience"	vs.	* temperamental rebelliousness; the refusal to be quiet and disciplined
* quiet joy	vs.	* frequent bouts with depression

The Integration Process for the Individual with a Ray 2 Soul and a Ray 4 Personality

1. The pre-spiritual phase; soul energy appropriated by a selfish personality: At this pre-spiritual phase of evolutionary unfoldment, the individual's motives (based upon the personality distortion of second ray soul energy and the self-centered use of fourth ray personality force) are to achieve the complete fulfillment of personal love (or the complete satisfaction of studious enquiry [2B]), *as well as* an agreeable feeling of personal peace and harmony through a tension-releasing expression of conflicting bio-psychic impulses. The person wants primarily to be constantly loved, consistently popular, warmly admired, well–cared–for, and to live a soft, comfortable, well–protected, well–insulated life – closely attached to those people, places, and things which he loves and finds personally satisfying, but, he *also* wants to be constantly surrounded by what he considers beautiful or attractive, to be spontaneously self–expressive without discipline or control, self–indulgently dramatic or moody (as he pleases), and greatly appreciated for his colorful, unpredictable temperament.

Negatively and glamorously, these two ray influences can combine to produce: a fearful, self–tortured person (2 + 4B); one who over–dramatizes himself, or becomes the 'entertainer' in the effort to be loved and appreciated; one who is filled with self–pity because of the constant turmoils and personal crises in which he finds himself (2A + 4B); one with a deep–seated inferiority complex, aggravated by psychological instability; an over–sensitive, vulnerable person who is always giving in, and compromising so that he doesn't have to be assertive (2A + 4A); one who is too permissive, realizes it, tries to combat the tendency, and continually reverses himself in the process (2A + 4B); an individual who is too protective and is always worrying about someone or something (2A + 4); one who is constantly in a state of apprehension and usually falls victim to pessimism or negativity; one who always has to be "in love" or "in a relationship" (2A + 4A); one who becomes promiscuous in the desire to be loved by (and in harmony with) everyone (2A + 4A); one who values unity and loving relations so much that he desires peace and harmony at any price (2A + 4A); the person who, convinced of his own wisdom, believes he can reconcile all differences and solve all conflicts (2B + 4A); a person so determined to be inclusive that he can never decide upon what (or whom) to relinquish (2 + 4A); one who always has difficulty deciding upon whom to love – faithfully (2A + 4A); one who moves at an excruciatingly slow pace, largely because of inner and outer conflict (2 + 4B); an individual who is too 'soft,' being unable to function unless those around him are in a state of love and harmony (2A + 4A); one who "enables" another's weaknesses because of "moral cowardice" and the inability to abide unpleasantness (2A + 4A); etc.

2. The phase of conflict; pure soul energy conflicts with personality force: The essential conflict between the ray two soul and the ray four personality is the struggle between the serene expression of spiritual love–wisdom, and the dramatic expression of widely fluctuating states of personal feeling and emotion.

3. The soul/personality integration process from the perspective of the consciousness identified primarily with the second ray soul: It will be the task of the second ray soul to bring serenity to the many turmoils and crises of the fourth ray personality. The soul, endowed with a steady, loving radiance, impervious to the fluctuations of form, seeks to share this radiance with a personality that is constantly reactive and fluctuating. Abiding, as it does, in the "center of all love," the second ray soul naturally seeks to bring the vacillating personality to a "centered" position, from the vantage point of which, clear perceptions will no longer be obscured by the smoke and din of battle. With undimmed positivity the soul pours its warming, encouraging influence into a personality which suffers from frequent bouts of negativity and lost confidence. With an all–embracing sense of inclusiveness, the second ray soul pervades the personal psyche, for the love and wisdom of the second ray soul already *contain* the many opposites between which the fourth ray personality oscillates. The soul seeks to demonstate that *both sides* of a conflict must be brought together in unity, for both sides are different aspects of the same thing. Gradually, after demonstrating the waste and futility of conflict, the soul brings the personality to a condition of greater peacefulness. It is the broad, impersonal, complete view of the whole (greater than all strictly personal sensitivities – however deeply–felt) that the second ray soul seeks to convey. The soul seeks to guide this most *human* ("all too human" of personality types to a wise understanding of its true place within the larger whole.

4. The soul/personality integration process from the perspective of a consciousness identified primarily with the fourth ray personality: The second ray pressure towards integration will be felt by the fourth ray personality (initially, at least) as a diminution of its expressive power, and the quieting and neutralizing of its dramatic flair. The vibrant fourth ray personality has no great love of serenity – at least not for any length of time. It loves the feeling of poignant contrasts, sudden emotional changes of pace; it loves to be moved by the muse and inspired by spontaneous urges. The calm of the second ray soul – no matter how spiritual, no matter how radiant – appears unappealing, even insipid – altogether lacking in what the personality recognizes as "life" and "vitality." Living a colorful, exciting life, filled with surprises and "aesthetic moments" is the joy of the fourth ray personality, and this proves difficult to relinquish. Gradually, however, it begins to dawn upon the fourth ray person that the steady outpouring of loving radiance is a greater thing than personal expressivity (no matter how engaging), and that fluctuating personality extremes only inhibit the flow of this all–pervading, all–inclusive love. After agony and ecstasy have run their course, something greater appears. After the pain of being strictly human, comes the joy of realizing that "the soul of things is sweet." The fourth ray personality begins to relinquish its central place on the stage to the rising of a greater 'star' – the soul. Beyond the delights of personal self–expression lies the beauty of love and wisdom.

5. The ideal expression of the combination of the ray two soul and the ray four personality: Loving understanding is expressed harmoniously and beautifully, with complete skill–in–action. Radiant serenity and confidence master inner and outer conflict, fret, turmoil and the agony of dissonance, but an intimate understanding of the causes of inharmony strengthens the personality as an agent of harmony, serving the wise and loving soul. Many conflicting personal and environmental energies are wisely and gently fused into a whole; psychological and environal synthesis is created. Love is served, and love is expressed through the ability to end conflicts constructively, bringing peace and equilibrium to the inner and outer environment. There is a deep understanding of the joy and pain of the human condition, accompanied by the harmonizing skill to alleviate the pain, and the inspirational sensitivity to express the joy. Because of a broad, heart–felt understanding of diverse and contrasting human qualities, there is an unusual capacity to reconcile differences between many types of people. Many are drawn together and unified through a pronounced facility for building bridges of rapport. There is a willingness (even an eagerness) to fight and struggle, if necessary, to express wisdom and understanding through beautiful or imaginative forms. The teacher teaches through his aesthetic sensibilities. The educator makes his subject "come alive" through a vibrant, engaging, entertaining presentational style. A wise understanding of human nature is expressed through drama or through dramatic action. The one who seeks to save and salvage finds success through his deep understanding of, and identification with, the "human predicament."

6. The combined effect of the two integration formulae: The primary integration formula is *Centralization*, keyed to the second ray soul. The second ray integration formula is *Steadfastness*, keyed to the fourth ray personality. The first formula corrects the second ray tendencies towards diffusion, overexpansion, and an energy–draining attachment to life's peripheral attractions, whereas the second formula corrects the tendencies towards vacillation, irresoluteness, instability, indecisiveness and moral cowardice characteristic of the fourth ray personality. Used together, these two formulae provide the individual striving for soul/personality integration with the composite quality of 'steadfast centralization' (the steadfastness of personality consciousness which fosters the ability to find and maintain one's spiritual center). The formulae make it possible for the individual to cultivate a more serene and stable personal consciousness, supportive of those rare moments of exalted consciousness when (pervaded by the presence of the soul) he takes his stand firmly and immovably "in the center of all love." Thus, as a soul he stands centered in spiritual love, detached from all outer bonds; as a personality he stands, steadfastly, midway between the warring opposites, yet embracing and valuing them both.

In the earlier stages of evolution, before successfully applying these formulae, the individual often finds himself excessively attached to many personalities and to many extraneous things, torn between competing commitments, irresolutely swinging from one peripheral attachment to another. The constant turmoils and fluctations of his life and the excessive number of his attachments lead him far from his spiritual center.

The intelligent use of these two formulae, however, transmutes the abuses of the past. The individual learns, primarily, to stand within the center of the love and wisdom of his second ray soul, loving others purely, wisely and with detachment, and his growing secondary ability to achieve a poised, steadfast and balanced personality consciousness helps him maintain his spiritual "centeredness."

7. Some examples of vocational aptitudes and orientations relating to the combination of the second ray soul and the fourth ray personality:

* the server who establishes excellent rapport with those he serves
* the teacher who dramatizes his subject, teaching through the arts, through entertainment and the evocation of the imagination
* the therapist who utilizes the arts extensively in his therapeutic practices
* the humanist animated by a "renaissance spirit"
* the unifier capable of working–through the difficulties of reconciling many differences
* the illuminator who draws constantly upon the revealing power of the intuition
* the "light–bearer" who fights and struggles to express the light through art

* the guru who teaches his chelas that "beauty is truth"
* the scholar who makes his learning "come alive" through the use of many lively stories and anecdotal illustrations
* the healer who works particularly through color and sound
* the counselor who encourages his clients to struggle with their internal conflicts rather than simply smooth them over
* the social worker who is willing to fight to see that his clients get fair treatment

In general: vocations and professions which require a wise and loving attitude, great empathy and understanding, studiousness, and the ability to teach and heal, *as well as* a strong creative imagination, spontaneity, expressivity, aesthetic sensitivity and the ability to bring harmony out of conflict, beauty out of ugliness and at–one–ment out of divisiveness.

8. A proposed list of well–known individuals (historical, contemporary, fictional or mythological) whose soul ray can reasonably be considered the second, with a strong subsidiary fourth ray (whether or not the fourth ray is, strictly speaking, the personality ray):

Roberto Assagioli: Italian psychiatrist and founder of Psychosynthesis

Nadia Boulanger: teacher of musical composition whose students have included many of the leading composers of the 20th century

Charles Dickens: generally regarded as the greatest English novelist. His thorough understanding of human nature and his dramatic gifts, imparted the quality of universality to his work.

Fyodor Dostoyevsky: perhaps the greatest Russian novelist, renowned for the depth of his psychological penetration, and the intensity of his characterization. The sixth ray is also strongly in evidence. Dostoyevsky may be an example of an individual undergoing the transformation from a sixth to a second ray soul.

Dane Rudhyar: sage, philosopher, astrologer, artist and composer. Rudhyar was also strongly influenced by the third ray.

Carl Jüng: Swiss psychiatrist and scholarly author. Jüng named his psychological orientation Analytic Psychology. His prodigious scholarship suggests the presence of the fifth ray, as well.

Carl Rogers: American psychologist who originated the nondirective, or client–centered approach to psychotherapy. His version of unconditional love is called "unconditional, positive regard."

Jean–Jacques Rousseau: French philosopher, composer, and educator of the Enlightenment

Sapppho: one of the greatest lyric poets of Western Civilization. She was also a renowned teacher of the arts of poetry, music and dancing. It would seem that a strong seventh ray was also in evidence.

Some Contrasts Between the Ray 2 Soul and the Ray 5 Personality

Ray 2 Soul		Ray 5 Personality
* soul–inspired love and wisdom	vs.	* preoccupation with limited concrete knowledge and analytical thought
* irrefutable recognition of the reality of soul life, love and light	vs.	* materialistic skepticism
* great intuitive sensitivity; the revelations of the "soft heart"	vs.	* the limitations of "common sense"; the limitations of the "hard head"
* the magnetism of the loving heart	vs.	* non–magnetic personality radiation due to an interfering mind
* the wise, inclusive, "rounded–out" point of view	vs.	* the narrow, restricted view of the strict specialist
* direct experience of the eternal verities proclaimed by the world's great religions	vs.	* sense–blinded rejection of the eternal verities proclaimed by the world's great religions
* love of pure, subjective truth	vs.	* acceptance of only that which can be immediately verified and practically applied
* deep identification with others through empathic love	vs.	* separation from others due to a detached, overly–objective attitude
* great warmth of soul	vs.	* cool, unfeeling personality reactions
* a broad and wise tolerance	vs.	* the harsh criticism of a keen, overly–discriminating mind
* deep appreciation for meaning based upon a broad synthesis of accumulated detail	vs.	* blinded to meaning by the accumulation of unsynthesized facts
* fluidity of thought leading to a well–developed faculty for synthesis	vs.	* stubborn fixity of thought based upon the assurance of correctness and accuracy
* reverence and deep humility	vs.	* irreverence and mental arrogance, based upon a condescending attitude towards subtle ideas which are difficult to prove by conventional means
* profound spiritual morality based on a deep feeling of fellowship with all humanity	vs.	* the amorality of the overly–fascinated mind

The Integration Process for the Individual with a Ray 2 Soul and a Ray 5 Personality

1. The pre–spiritual phase; soul energy appropriated by a selfish personality: At this pre–spiritual phase of evolutionary unfoldment, the individual's motives (based upon the personality distortion of second ray soul energy and the self–centered use of fifth ray personality force) are to achieve the complete fulfillment of personal love (or the complete satisfaction of studious enquiry [2B]), *as well as* a narrow, materialistic intellectual certainty. The person wants, primarily, to be constantly loved, consistently popular, warmly admired, well-cared-for, and to live a soft comfortable, well-protected, well-insulated life – closely attached to those people, places, and things which he loves and finds personally satisfying, but, he *also* wants to take everything apart (either analytically or actually), reduce all life experience to nothing but rationalistic formulae, control matter mechanically for selfish ends, and reject any kind of knowledge that is not materialistic and derived strictly from the five physical senses. As can be seen, these are very contradictory orientations.

Negatively and glamorously, these two ray influences can combine to produce: one who seeks to amass detailed knowledge for himself alone (2B + 5A); one who, seeking comfort and material well-being, enlists all his mechanical aptitudes to that end (2 + 5B); one who becomes utterly and coldly preoccupied with study, especially the selfish accumulation of unutilized facts (2B + 5A); the individual who detachedly studies and analyzes everyone and everything, without actually participating in life experientially (2B + 5A); one who has great contempt for the mental limitations of others, demanding, with harsh criticism, that they verify or substantiate everything they say or write (2B + 5A); one who senses the Whole and yet remains apart, analyzing everything and everyone as if from a distance (2B + 5A); one who is very cold and non-magnetic (2B + 5); an individual who tries to compensate for inferiority feelings through the presumption of mental certainty (2A + 5); one who is afraid of bold initiatives and uses the rationality of a narrow and rigid mind to justify this fear – "it can't be done and there is no use trying"; the diffident person who observes but does not take action; the overly-protective person who finds a "thousand-and-one" 'scientific' reasons to justify his fears for his loved ones (2A + 5A); the overly attached person who expresses his 'love' (really, fearful concern) through an attitude of constant criticism of that which he loves (2A + 5A); the one whose progress is extremely slow (and whose writing and conversation are extremely tedious) due to preoccupation with a vast amount of detailed knowledge (2B + 5A); the unwarranted presumption of great wisdom based upon the limited certainties of the concrete mind (2B + 5); etc.

2. The phase of conflict; pure soul energy conflicts with personality force: The essential conflict between the ray two soul and the ray five personality is the struggle between the deep, intuitive love of the heart and the strictly analytical and rational approach to knowledge, which rejects all that does not appeal to "common sense."

3. The soul/personality integration process from the perspective of the consciousness identified primarily with the second ray soul: It will be the task of the second ray soul to broaden the understanding of the fifth ray personality, dissolving the barriers (erected by concrete thought) which prevent an acceptance of the subtler realities. The soul consciousness, rich in intuitions and exquisitely attuned to the value of spiritual intangibles, is faced with a personality which functions in a linear, analytical fashion, utilizing only the head, and repudiating (as unreliable) the testimony of the heart. The soul, ever sensitive to the wisdom beyond and within knowledge, seeks so to illumine the personal mind, that the personality can begin to see its preoccupation with narrowly-defined, concrete areas of specialization as a serious limitation. Consciousness, under the inspiration of a second ray soul, is filled with a faith arising from breadth of vision and an awakened intuition; the general nature of truth is realized even if the many details and "matters of fact" are not yet externally verified. The second ray soul has a remarkable ability to verify truth "inwardly," and it is a reliance upon this capacity that it tries to convey to the skeptical, doubting, concretely–intellectual fifth ray personality. The second ray soul (of all the soul types) is the great representative of the powers of the *heart* (in all the many ways the term "heart" can be interpreted). Life lacking heart is woefully incomplete, even though the fifth ray personality is likely to feel very satisfied with the surety of that which it knows – mentally. The soul, in subtle ways, demonstrates to this mentally self–sufficient personality the many areas in which "the way of the head" is simply inadequate. Thus gradually, the "mental fixation" of the personality is dissolved; the 'knot' of concrete consciousness is loosened, and the broader ways of "heart understanding" begin to overcome the restrictions of a too commonsensical, too "hardheaded" outlook.

4. The soul/personality integration process from the perspective of the consciousness identified primarily with the fifth ray personality: The second ray pressure towards integration will be felt by the fifth ray personality as a subtle but persistent devaluation of the technical interests which have, hitherto, been all–consuming. The personality has been engrossed in its specialized fascinations and enthusiasms, learning "more and more about less and less." These narrowly focussed interests have been quite satisfying, no matter how unrelated they have been (at least in the consciousness of the personality) to the larger picture. The world of the fifth ray personality has been very small but very secure.

Now, from deep within the consciousness, arises a sense of the inadequacy of all that had been the focus of personality preoccupation. The heart begins to stir, and longings for things that cannot be measured, quantified or definitely *fixed in mind* begin to arise. The personality feels as if its mental security is being dissolved in an ocean of uncertainties. Its "rock–solid" discriminations no longer seem to hold. Instead of differences, distinctions and 'perfect' mental clarity, it becomes hard to separate one thing from another, or one person from another. The perception of the meaning and scope of truth begins to undergo a profound change. The sense of the inescapable interrelatedness of all things intrudes upon the personal consciousness. The sensed urge towards unification takes the joy out of being a specialist. "Standing back," and observing the world from a protected point of mental objectivity, begins to seem arid. Participation of the whole self is demanded as the personality realizes that it is intimately involved in the *Wholeness*. The urge towards inclusiveness, and comprehension of the Whole overcomes the mental passion for narrow certainty; everything has changed.

5. The ideal expression of the combination of the ray two soul and the ray five personality: The loving understanding of the heart is expressed through the application of scientific knowledge and with solid common sense. Those who seek to serve and save through compassion utilize the latest, scientifically developed procedures which translate benevolent impulses into effective, working techniques; the persistent urge to ameliorate human conditions takes form through the development of new technologies which improve the condition of those in need. Individuals qualified by this combination of rays so value the pure truth, that they work diligently to discover concrete examples substantiating that truth, and develop practical/technical means for implementing the truth. The capacity for scholarship is greatly advanced through meticulous experiment and research. The gift for amassing encyclopedic knowledge is fortified by easy mental access to a great number of pertinent references. The validity and reasonableness of a broadly inclusive and synthetic world–view is supported by the citation of many specific instances of confirmation which point to the reality of wholeness. Those in the "helping professions" improve their abilities to serve through solid analysis and sensibility. Preoccupation with essential quality and subjective reality masters preoccupation with form and matter, but a strong commonsensical, realistic attitude provides a balance against excessive subjectivity. The ability to see the whole pattern and the multitude of interrelationships masters the tendency to see just the detail or the part, but, even though the scope of enquiry be great, the details are never ignored. Compassion and mercy master the tendency to "sit in judgment," yet such individuals are "hard headed" enough to avoid becoming unrealistic "bleeding hearts." The heart masters the concrete intellect, yet uses that intellect to serve more effectively in the material world. The way of wisdom and divine understanding is shown to be based upon solid evidence. These are individuals who have an extraordinary ability to demonstrate that humanity's religious and spiritual impulses are rooted in scientific fact and natural law. They are able to demonstrate the factual nature of the "Law of Love." Love is proven to 'work,' *and* to be an energy as real as light or heat.

6. The combined effect of the two integration formulae: The primary integration formula is *Centralization*, keyed to the second ray soul. The secondary integration formula is *Detachment*, keyed to the fifth ray personality. The first formula corrects the second ray tendencies towards diffusion, overexpansion, and an energy–draining attachment to life's peripheral attractions, whereas the second formula corrects fifth ray tendencies towards a mental attachment to matter, and an obsessive preoccupation with investigating or manipulating concrete form while ignoring the reality of that which is "formless."

Used together these two formulae provide the individual striving for soul/personality integration with the composite quality of 'detached centralization' (i.e., the kind of mental detachment which fosters the ability to find and maintain one's spiritual center). The formulae make it possible for the individual to cultivate a personal consciousness which can detach itself from a preoccupation with matter. A personal consciousness free of the glamor of materiality serves as a complement to those rare moments of exalted consciousness when (pervaded by the presence of the soul), the individual takes his stand firmly and immovably "in the center of all love." His vision becomes that of one who is thoroughly abstracted from matter, and profoundly cognizant of God (a Being Whose nature is Love) standing behind the "garment" of matter and form which He 'wears' during the period of manifestation. Thus, as a soul, the individual stands centered in spiritual love and wisdom, detached from all outer bonds; as a personality, he stands interested in (yet not captivated by) matter – his eyes trained upon the divinity which lies within and behind appearances.

In the earlier stages of evolution, before applying these formulae, the individual often finds himself excessively attached to form and matter, and to their utilization for personal comfort and security. His fascination for 'things,' and how they can be made to serve his "creature comforts," leads him far from his spiritual center.

The intelligent use of these two formulae, however, transmutes the abuses of the past, allowing the individual to see how the illusory 'spell' of matter prevented him from recognizing the subtle presence of the God of Love within the material form. He learns, primarily, to stand within the center of the love and wisdom of his second ray soul, loving others purely, wisely and with detachment, and he utilizes his growing secondary ability (the ability to disengage his personality consciousness from excessive fascination for the 'movements of matter') as a means of maintaining and sustaining his *centered*, soul–inspired identification with the God of Love.

7. Some examples of vocational aptitudes and orientations relating to the combination of the second ray soul and the fifth ray personality:

* the compassionate server who is filled with the spirit of common sense
* the teacher who excels in the impartation of illuminating facts
* the educator with an unusual ability to evoke lucidity of mind
* the therapist whose therapeutic methods rely upon instrumentation
* the psychologist with keen analytical abilities
* the humanist who enthusiastically values the contributions of technology to modern civilization
* the unifier who emphasizes the use of communications technology to draw people together
* the guru who insists that his chelas experiment with their theoretical knowledge
* the consummate "light–bearer"
* the scholar who verifies every detail of his research
* the healer who employs the most modern, scientific techniques
* the counselor who depends upon "down–to–earth" techniques which have been proven to work
* the nurturer who utilizes precise, factual information to improve the quality of nurture offered

In general: vocations and professions which require a wise and loving attitude, great empathy and understanding, studiousness, and an ability to teach or compassionately heal, *as well as* keen analytical abilities, the capacity to conduct research, and scientific and/or technical expertise.

8. **A proposed list of well-known individuals (historical, contemporary, fictional or mythological) whose soul ray can reasonably be considered the second, with a strong subsidiary fifth ray influence (whether or not the fifth ray is, strictly speaking, the personality ray):**

Bhagavan Das: Indian sage and educator, author of *The Science of the Emotions*

Fritjof Capra: educator in the field of science, and author of *The Tao of Physics*. Capra's work relates the "new physics" to the transformation of consciousness.

Christopher Hills: author of *Nuclear Evolution*. Hills approaches the expansion of consciousness from a scientific perspective.

Hippocrates: the "Father of Medicine"

Patanjali: the great sage of India who was the foremost exponent of the system of esoteric training known as Raja Yoga. He was the author of the Yoga Sutras which formed the basis of Alice Bailey's book, *The Light of the Soul*.

Peter Russell: author of *The Global Brain*

Some Contrasts Between the Ray 2 Soul and the Ray 6 Personality

Ray 2 Soul		Ray 6 Personality
* all–inclusive spiritual love	vs.	* narrow personal devotion
* deep, yet detached, loving understanding	vs.	* intense, even violent, personal emotion
* the attractiveness of the loving soul	vs.	* a passionate personality which follows goals without intelligent discrimination, often achieving those goals through intrusion
* the wisdom to love non–possessively	vs.	* extreme possessiveness and jealousy
* "unconditional positive regard"; love for the 'sinner' regardless of his 'sins'	vs.	* love given only to those who completely and continuously live up to one's expectations
* spontaneous forgiveness	vs.	* persecution of those who do not stand for one's ideal
* experiencing the center of love divine within one's *Self*	vs.	* unremitting longing for someone or something other than one's *Self*
* a very broad and synthetic world view	vs.	* unreasoning fanaticism
* the embodiment of pure reason	vs.	* blind faith and foolish single–mindedness
* wide tolerance based upon love and wisdom	vs.	* extreme intolerance based upon the conviction of personal rectitude
* gentle soul love	vs.	* unregulated personal intensity
* the patience of understanding love	vs.	* impatience driven by furious desire; inordinate haste
* assiduous cultivation of the discipline of meditation	vs.	* over–reliance upon fervent personal prayer
* teaching through wise and loving evocation	vs.	* insistence that others follow one's preaching
* the loving wisdom to appraise others realistically	vs.	* greatly exaggerated estimation or deprecation
* spontaneous joyfulness and happiness	vs.	* overly earnest and humorless

The Integration Process for the Individual with a Ray 2 Soul and a Ray 6 Personality

1. The pre–spiritual phase; soul energy appropriated by a selfish personality: At this pre–spiritual phase of evolutionary unfoldment, the individual's motives (based upon the personality distortion of second ray soul energy, and the self–centered use of sixth ray personality force), are to achieve the complete fulfillment of personal love (or the complete satisfaction of studious enquiry [2B]), *as well as* the uncompromising satisfaction of the ideals and goals to which the personality is passionately devoted. The person wants primarily to be constantly loved, consistently popular, warmly admired, well–cared–for, and to live a soft, comfortable, well–protected, well–insulated life – closely attached to those people, places and things which he loves and finds personally satisfying, but he *also* wants to ignore everything except the object or path of his devotion, spurn tedious mundane responsibilities which do not relate specifically to his quest, fanatically follow his ideal regardless of destructive consequences, and cling desperately to that which he believes he loves. There are some similarities between these two sets of desires, but they vary in intensity.

Negatively and glamorously, these two ray influences can combine to produce: the fearful and overly-attached person who clings tenaciously to those he loves (2A + 6A); the person who feels helpless and vulnerable and leans upon others in the hope that they will take care of him (2A + 6A); the masochistic person who prefers to remain in a servile position relative to his 'superiors'(2A + 6A); the person filled with such a strong sense of protectiveness and responsibility for another that he allows that person no freedom from his obsessive concern; the person with such low self-esteem that devotion to another person becomes his whole "reason for living" (2A + 6A); an individual who wants so much to be loved by a particular person that he will remain utterly loyal and devoted to that person despite constant mistreatment and abuse (2A + 6A); the lover who is filled with such insecurity that he is frequently swept by waves of intense jealousy (2A + 6B); the person who, selfishly, seeks wisdom for himself alone, and devotes himself fanatically to its pursuit (2B + 6B); the scholar so intent upon pursuing "omniscience" that he studies with passionate one-pointedness, leaving no time for balanced living (2B + 6B); the person who has such a desire to be popular and appreciated that he will go to unrealistic lengths to secure the recognition of others (2A + 6B); the overly-meek, religiously inclined person who believes that he must wait for God to guide him in all matters (2A + 6A); the person who is so intent on achieving completeness that he never knows when enough is enough (2B + 6B); the extremely conscientious server who, because of his over-pitiful heart, believes he has a responsibility to 'save' all those who ask for help, and even those who don't (2A + 6); the devoted lover who knows he cannot live if he is separated from the one he loves (2A + 6); the "motherly" type of individual who is totally unrealistic about the true nature of the one for whom he devotedly cares (2A + 6A); the individual with an irresistable "Messiah complex" (2A + 6B); etc.

2. The phase of conflict; pure soul energy conflicts with personality force: The essential conflict between the ray two soul and the ray six personality is the struggle between the need to express a broad, unconditional soul-love, and the passionate desire to focus a narrow, devoted, personal 'love' upon an idealized "other."

3. The soul/personality integration process from the perspective of the consciousness identified primarily with the second ray soul: It will be the task of the second ray soul to moderate the extremism of the sixth ray personality. The soul seeks to present a broad, inclusive, widely tolerant perspective to a personality which is fanatically driven to propel itself towards limited objectives and limited loves. The soul knows that limited objects of devotion will ever fail to satisfy, and seeks to expand the consciousness of the personality so that a truer sense of values and of proportion can be established. The soul has the constant problem of "reining in" (ever so gently) a personality which is always rushing off after an idealised vision. Armed with the brilliant light of revelation, the soul consistently demonstrates to the impassioned personality the relative worthlessness and insignificance of all it held dear. Gradually, the soul weakens and dissolves the personality's furious grip upon the inconsequential. Imperceptibly, the soul teaches the personality (after numerous disillusionments) to remove the "blinders" which prevented a vision of the beauty of the Whole – not just the idealised beauty of one or two things within the Whole. For the loving soul, there is nowhere to "run" because the "center of all love" (which is the most desirable object of devotion) is *everywhere to be found.* The second ray soul teaches the sixth ray personality to idealize the divine center within itself (the spiritual essence) and to focus its devotion there.

4. The soul/personality integration process from the perspective of the consciousness identified primarily with the sixth ray personality: The second ray pressure towards integration will be felt by the sixth ray personality as an unwelcome and disquieting reduction of personal intensity. The personality is convinced that "broad is the way, that leadeth to destruction" and "narrow is the way, which leadeth unto life." The sixth ray personality is narrow and intense. The pleasure of intensity is self-validating; something done intensely feels significant and important. However, as the soul influence begins to pervade the personal consciousness, the personality senses itself weakening, spreading, and *relaxing* (a dreadful word for the sixth ray zealot!). An uncomfortable feeling of futility begins to arise; the goals which inspired so much dedication and impassioned questing no longer seem so worthwhile. When this perception is registered, there may be a rebellious redoubling of previous efforts, but at length it becomes difficult for the personality to summon the motivation to chase after former 'idols.' *Many* things and *many* ways now begin to reveal their desirability; intolerance is no longer so easy, and rejection of the 'worthless' no longer such a simple and obvious task. The personality begins to learn that the fury of its former pursuit blinded it to the larger reality. The many who aspire along different paths are now noticed, and the value of their paths acknowledged. The personality begins to sense its relative unimportance, for it sees itself as only one of innumerable others – *all* following their vision, *all* devoted to their ideals. Life seems less secure, the future less certain, the path to be trodden less direct, but the world – *larger!*

5. The ideal expression of the combination of the ray two soul and the ray six personality: Loving understanding is expressed with complete devotion and self-sacrifice. Broad, inclusive love masters narrow, emotional loyalties and attachments, but *spiritual* loyalty and attachment are never relinquished. The love of the heart masters the emotion of the solar plexus, but an intense feeling-sensitivity remains. Impersonal love prevails, but a warm, "personal touch" is still preserved. The expression of *love for all* becomes a cherished ideal. The pursuit of wisdom, and of the detailed patterns of pure truth is furthered by unflagging zeal. For individuals with this ray combination, the profound spiritual realizations, foundational to the world's great religions, become living *facts* within their consciousness, and there arises the commitment and idealism to *live* those realizations and share them tirelessly with others. Deep humility is supported by a willing, self-abnegation, a devotion to the "heart of all love." There is total emotional commitment to a life of salvage and redemption. The will to sacrifice one's own spiritual progress in order to bring love, illumination, healing and release to others becomes the all-consuming passion of the life.

6. The combined effect of the two integration formulae: The primary integration formula is *Centralization*, keyed to the second ray soul. The secondary integration formula is proposed as *Restraint*, keyed to the sixth ray personality. The first formula corrects the second ray tendencies towards diffusion, overexpansion, and an energy–draining attachment to life's peripheral attractions, whereas the second formula corrects the unrestrained, passionate pursuit of the 'partial' and 'peripheral,' so common to the emotionally undisciplined sixth ray personality. Used together, these formulae provide the individual striving for soul/personality integration with the composite quality of 'restrained centralization,' (i.e., the emotional and personality restraint which fosters the ability to find and maintain one's spiritual center). The formulae make it possible for the individual to cultivate a more moderate, dispassionate personality consciousness, supportive of those rare moments of exalted consciousness when, pervaded by the presence of the soul, he takes his stand firmly and immovably "in the center of all love." Because he learns to restrain his personal consciousness from violent attachments to people, places and things, he finds that deeper *center* within his nature from which he can relate to all beings with love and wisdom, and yet remain detached from their form aspect.

In the earlier stages of evolution, before successfully applying these formulae, an individual with this ray combination often finds himself throwing himself into one attachment after another, clinging so tightly that it is extremely difficult to pry him loose. For all their intensity, these attachments occur without proper discrimination, and chain the individual to the periphery of his life, where he becomes so thoroughly 'fastened' that he cannot find his way back to his spiritual center.

The intelligent use of these two formulae, however, transmutes the abuses of the past. The individual learns, primarily, to stand within the center of the love and wisdom of his second ray soul, loving others purely, wisely and with detachment, and his growing secondary ability to restrain the fury of his desires, and pursue only that which is truly of spiritual value, assists him in maintaining his spiritual "centeredness." No more will he rush from the center to the periphery, and from a state of centered spiritual detachment into a passionate attachment to particular peripheral forms. His desires are now directed towards spiritual realities, the most important of which is to be found in the central core of his own being.

7. Some examples of vocational aptitudes and orientations relating to the combination of the second ray soul and the sixth ray personality:

* the compassionate server who dedicates everything he is and has to his service
* the teacher who always inspires great enthusiasm in his students
* the educator who is remarkably idealistic
* the therapist with unusual ability to motivate his patients
* the humanist who offers a glowing vision of human possibilities
* the unifier who arouses in others the aspiration to come together
* the illuminator who inspires people to follow the light

* the guru who emphasizes devotion among his chelas
* the scholar who counts all as lost if he does not complete his enquiry
* the healer intensely animated primarily by faith
* the counselor who is *always* "there" for his clients
* the social-worker who sees his work as a cause
* the nurturer who nurtures with unflagging persistence and loyalty
* the priest, minister or rabbi who excels in arousing religious commitment

In general, vocations or professions which require a wise and loving attitude, great empathy and understanding, studiousness, and the ability to teach or compassionately heal, *as well as* high idealism, undeviating devotion, great enthusiasm and persistent emotional intensity.

8. A proposed list of well-known individuals (historical, contemporary, fictional or mythological) whose soul ray can reasonably be considered the second, with a strong subsidiary sixth ray (whether or not the sixth ray is, strictly speaking, the personality ray):

Elizabeth Barrett Browning: English poet, wife of Robert Browning. She wrote love poems that are gentle, yet passionately sincere.

Ralph Waldo Emerson: essayist, poet, and Unitarian minister. Emerson was the leading light of the American Transcendentalist movement.

Judith Hollister: ecumenist, founder of the Temple of Understanding

Pope John XXIII: the pope renowned for his efforts to achieve Christian unity. His influence was responsible for the modern ecumenical movement in the Catholic Church. The mediating influence of the fourth ray was also in evidence.

Helen Keller: author and educator who was blind and deaf. Given the nature of her handicaps, her accomplishments were extraordinary. She devoted her life to publicly aiding the deaf and blind.

Charles W. Leadbeater: prominent member of the Theosophical Society, psychic, occult investigator, author of many books on the Ageless Wisdom. The fifth ray was also prominent.

Abraham Maslow: psychologist, founder of the Psychology of Self-Actualization

Dr. Benjamin Spock: the "Father of modern pediatrics." A strong fifth and seventh ray are also evident.

Paramahansa Yogananda: Indian sage, teacher of Kriya Yoga, and founder of the Self-realization Fellowship

Some Contrasts Between the Ray 2 Soul and the Ray 7 Personality

Ray 2 Soul		Ray 7 Personality
* deep spiritual subjectivity	vs.	* preoccupation with pragmatism
* spiritual orientation towards the expansion of consciousness	vs.	* excessive concern with matters of form
* natural realization of the loving soul as the essence of individual reality	vs.	* over–absorption with the form and processes of the physical body
* the joy of accumulating and bearing the light of the soul	vs.	* encapsulating the light of the soul in tight, repressive forms
* intuitive focus upon the essential quality of the human being	vs.	* a limiting focus upon external appearances
* loving interpersonal rapport; the spontaneous release of warm feelings	vs.	* insistent subjection of interpersonal relations to artifical social rituals
* the wise and loving evocation of individual identity; giving people permission to be who they are	vs.	* the inclination to standardize others
* the love of setting people at ease; spiritual informality	vs.	* rigid and formal attitudes which arouse discomfort in others
* moment–to–moment trust in the adequacy of the wise and loving soul	vs.	* personal insecurity if without a form, formula, pattern or outline to follow
* a broad and loving ecumenical spirit	vs.	* superficial sectarianism
* spontaneous mercy and humanitarianism	vs.	* the pettiness which imposes the "letter of the law"
* the realization of essential spiritual democracy	vs.	* class–conscious superciliousness and condescension
* allowing spiritual intuition to guide interpersonal interactions	vs.	* fixation upon structuring all interpersonal interactions
* wise and loving group consciousness	vs.	* stifling the group by forcing it to become a rigid organization
* the radiant light of the soul	vs.	* the instinctual life of the form
* the radiant love of the soul; ability to fuse the opposites through love	vs.	* immersion in sexuality (the physical symbol of the fusion of the opposites)

The Integration Process for the Individual with a Ray 2 Soul and a Ray 7 Personality

1. The pre–spiritual phase; soul energy appropriated by a selfish personality: At this pre–spiritual phase of evolutionary unfoldment, the individual's motives (based upon the personality distortion of the second ray soul energy, and the self–centered use of the seventh ray personality force), are to achieve the complete fulfillment of personal love, (or the complete satisfaction of studious enquiry [2B]), *as well as* a rigidly ritualized, tightly ordered life conducive to physical plane safety, security and 'perfected' materialistic living. The person wants, primarily, to be constantly loved, consistently popular, warmly admired, well–cared–for, and to live a soft, comfortable, well–protected, well–insulated life – closely attached to those people, places and things which he loves and finds personally satisfying, but he *also* wants a highly predictable (hence, relatively risk–free) life, to avoid having to think for himself or act upon his own initiative, and to have the solid assurance that all instinctual appetites and imagined material needs will be satisifed on schedule.

Negatively and glamorously, these two ray influences can combine to produce: a timid person who protects himself from the risks of initiatives by relying upon established precedents (2A + 7A); a fearful person who depends upon personal routines and rituals to allay anxieties (2A + 7C); an overly–sensitive person who is always concerned with security and stability (2A + 7A); a person who is afraid of not being comfortable and in "good–looking" surroundings; one who becomes a complete conformist out of the desire to be well–liked and popular (2A + 7A); one who feels he can only function when he is with other people and "playing by the rules"; an overly–conscientious student, unwilling to risk originality – a "grind" (2B + 7A); a person, who attempting to be too inclusive or complete, becomes absolutely mired in details (2B + 7); one who is a victim of inertia and habitual–bound behavior, resulting in a very slow pace (2 + 7A, 7C); a person with low self–esteem and plagued by compulsions (2A + 7A, 7C); a socially insecure person who plays the role of "outrageous non–conformist" in order to gain attention (2B + 7B); a religiously oriented person who feels warm and comfortable with certain established rituals, and wants to make sure they never vary (2A + 7C); a person with a strong inferiority complex who resorts to social affectation as a compensation; a teacher who rigidly insists upon repetitive and stultifying class procedures (2B + 7A); etc.

2. The phase of conflict; pure soul energy conflicts with personality force: The essential conflict between the ray two soul and the ray seven personality is the struggle between the love of internal quality and preoccupation with manifested actuality.

3. The soul/personality integration process from the perspective of the consciousness identified primarily with the second ray soul: It will be the task of the second ray soul to impress upon the personality the value of subjectivity. The soul understands the essential *quality* of which all form is an emanation; the seventh ray personality, however, is usually all too attentive to the form. The second ray soul is ever sensitive to the "heart." It seeks to pervade the personal consciousness with a deep, impersonal love, to ameliorate the personality's tendency to judge by appearances or according to artificial, socially contrived standards. The radiant soul seeks to express itself with a loving spontaneity which understands all and forgives all, but it encounters, in the personality, an orientation towards rigidity and conventionality. Sowing love and wisdom in all experiences, the second ray soul looks for a harvest of right human relations and illumination; the personality is wedded to other values, and they are far more material, far more sensuously (and even sensually) based. The soul's task is to influence the personality to release its grip upon the material plane. Too often the seventh ray personality, like Martha in the New Testament, has no time for the "Christ" – the Christ aspect being the soul. Gradually, the soul teaches the personality how to love, and how to await the response of love without dictating what that response *should* be, or judging its appropriateness according to conventional standards. The seventh ray personality does not like surprises, but the soul, trusting in the inherent goodness of life, understands that all surprises arising from openness to the spirit will be beneficent ones.

4. The soul/personality integration process from the perspective of the consciousness identified primarily with the seventh ray personality: The second ray pressure towards integration will be felt by the seventh ray personality as a loosening, amorphous influence. The personality has certain forms and practices which it treats as, virtually, "sacred observances." Endless repetition of these forms and practices, however, tends to numb the consciousness into a sense of false security – a feeling that "all is in order" and that "all's right with the world." The broadening, inclusive influence of the soul begins to dissolve that security, and to include within the purview of consciousness that which the personality would rather not consider, things which make the world seem as chaotic as it *really is* (on this plane and at this stage of global evolution). The personality does not want to abandon the customary; sometimes, it does not even want to *understand* the customary; it simply wants to *perform* it. The soul however brings understanding, and with it the shallowness, meaninglessness and repressive, limiting nature of numerous habits, customs, and formalities are revealed. The personality is made to question *why* it does the things it does; strict, unquestioning adherence to the comfortable routine is no longer satsifying under the illuminating 'eye' of the brilliant second ray soul. The personality seeks to hide within form, but the soul challenges the personal consciousness to risk adventuring into a state of relative formlessness where anything can happen – especially in the area of human interaction. All real spiritual progress, at length, calls for the relinquishing of previous conditioning and the exposure to new experiences. The seventh ray personality, of all personality types, has the greatest difficulty relinquishing the many forms of conditioning to which it has been subjected (hence, its sometimes violent attempts to throw off old conditioning only to become the slave of a new, 'unconventional' kind of conditioning); the gradually dawning trust and positivity inspired by the loving second ray soul gradually makes this relinquishment an inevitability. The personality lets go of the security of established form and is compensated by receiving the surety of spiritual love and wisdom.

5. The ideal expression of the combination of the ray two soul and the ray seven personality: A deep feeling for human unity is expressed in group "movements," through well-structured programs, and with real attention to (and an understanding of) the importance of organization. Individuals with this combination have abundant loving understanding, and an innate respect for *right practice* which contributes greatly to its successful expression. There is a strong commitment to humanism which manifests through the creation of new and innovative patterns of social interaction – patterns which facilitate the expression of "right human relations." The urge to unify people takes the form of practical and appropriate *action* upon the physical plane; people are drawn together for cooperative and loving purposes in ways that are unusually well-organized and coordinated. Here we find those who have a great talent for skillfully designing and creating material forms which embody or symbolize the light of wisdom streaming forth from a deeply intuitive consciousness; their craftsmanship is guided by the power of love. With individuals of this type, the wisdom of the heart masters the presumed rightness of personality method and outer technique, but efficient means and methods for expressing subtle realizations are never wanting. The inner work, however, is always seen to be more important than its outer expression – at least, it is understood that the heart must be in all acts before these acts can truly be called an expression of spirituality, no matter how rightly or perfectly they may be performed. Essential love triumphs over (and yet expresses itself through) perfected forms. Great empathy for humanity provides the patience for a slow, sequential and painstaking reconstruction of the "shrine of human living." The loving wisdom which heals is applied with consummate skill upon the etheric–physical plane.

6. The combined effect of the two integration formulae: The primary integration formula is *Centralization*, keyed to the second ray soul. The secondary integration formula is proposed as *Orientation*, keyed to the seventh ray personality. The first formula corrects the second ray tendencies towards diffusion, overexpansion, and an energy-draining attachment to life's peripheral attractions, whereas the second formula corrects seventh ray tendencies towards selfish building and organizing according to short-sighted, materially-minded personal plans, but without an attentive orientation to the Divine Design as revealed by the soul. Used together, these formulae provide the individual striving for soul/personality integration with the composite quality of 'oriented centralization,' (i.e., the attentive spiritual orientation of the personality which helps the individual detach from peripheral attachments, and find and maintain his spiritual center). The formulae make it possible for the individual to cultivate a spiritually-oriented and attentive personality consciousness, supportive of those rare moments of exalted consciousness when, pervaded by the presence of the soul, he takes his stand firmly and immovably "in the center of all love."

In the earlier stages of evolution, before successfully applying these formulae, an individual with this ray combination often finds himself closely attached to many people and things and working diligently to create outer forms which only increase the extent of his attachment to externals. The many forms he creates under selfish impulse confine him to the worlds of form, and separate him further from the central point of his spirituality – the soul. At length, so 'successful' is his unenlightened constructiveness, that the light of the soul is totally obscured, hidden within the many forms and patterns he has built. He is 'safe,' 'secure,' utterly attached, and exiled from his essence.

The intelligent use of these two formulae, however, transmutes the abuses of the past. The individual learns primarily, to stand within the center of the love and wisdom of his second ray soul, loving others purely, wisely and with detachment, and his growing secondary ability to orient himself to the divine Plan (while ceasing from entombing the spirit in nonessential constructs) makes it possible for him to create forms which will always be expressive of his spiritual "center." Thus, during all excursions into form (whether psychological or actual), he will remain centered in the consciousness of his soul.

7. Some examples of vocational aptitudes and orientations relating to the combination of the second ray soul and the seventh ray personality:

* the server whose preferred method of service is "karma yoga"

* the teacher whose lesson plans are consistently well-organized

* the educator whose philosophy of education emphasizes the inculcation of ethical principles
* the therapist who emphasizes the importance of "body work"
* the humanistic pyschologist who sees the value of behavioristic therapy
* the humanist who believes that society can best be improved through the creation of new patterns of behavior, the keynote of which is decent human relations
* the unifier who excels through his ability to organize cooperative networks
* the illuminator who focuses upon the interpretation of symbols
* the guru who teaches strict rules and practices of spiritual development
* the scholar who researches the history of fraternal orders and their laws, customs and rituals
* the healer with an excellent understanding of how to work with the etheric body
* the counselor who stresses involvement in well-structured programs of action as the best means of client improvement
* the social worker who stresses the importance of improvment in administrative methods
* the nurturer endowed with remarkable tact and timing
* the priest, minister or rabbi who values, preserves and interprets the religious rituals associated with his faith
* the "light bearer" who creates the rituals of the New Age

In general: vocations or professions which require a wise and loving attitude, great empathy and understanding, studiousness, and the ability to teach or compassionately heal, *as well as* the power to organize or reorganize, the ability to build, a facility for creating or maintaining standards, and the capacity to skillfully manifest ideas through form.

8. A proposed list of well-known individuals (historical, contemporary, fictional or mythological) whose soul ray can reasonably be considered the second, with a strong subsidiary seventh ray (whether or not the seventh ray is, strictly speaking, the personality ray):

Clara Barton: humanitarian and founder of the American Red Cross, known as the "angel of the battlefield." A strong ray six influence is also evident.

Confucius: Chinese teacher, philosopher and political theorist, whose ideas have deeply influenced the civilization of all eastern Asia.

The Dalai Lama: leader of the exiled Tibetan Buddhist community, and a unifier of East and West. The mediating power of the fourth ray is strongly in evidence.

Manly Palmer Hall: philosopher, sage, scholar. Dr. Hall is the founder and president of the Philosophical Research Society. A strong ray three influence is also in evidence.

Maria Montessori: Italian physician and educational reformer – originator of the educational system which bears her name (the Montessori Method)

Sir Thomas More: English saint and humanist, martyred for refusing to accept the Act of Supremacy, establishing the king as supreme head of the Church of England. A strong sixth ray is also present.

Florence Nightingale: pioneer in the development of military and civilian nursing and of hospital care. A strong first ray and sixth ray are also apparent.

Emmanuel Swedenborg: Swedish scientist, mystic, philosopher and theologian. Swedenborg was strongly influenced by the fifth ray.

Soul/Personality Combinations with a Ray Three Soul

Some Contrasts betweeen the Ray 3 Soul and the Ray 1 Personality

Ray 3 Soul		Ray 1 Personality
* incisive spiritual intelligence	vs.	* personality action motivated by self–will and the love of personal power, rather than intelligence
* appreciation of the divine "many"	vs.	* exaltation of the personal ego above all the "many"
* understanding and appreciation of the theory behind the "divine blueprint"	vs.	* constant repudiation of theoretical 'nonsense' in favor of direct, "no–nonsense" action
* great sophistication of abstract, academic thought	vs.	* conviction of the uselessness of abstract, academic thought
* a soul–inspired vision of the spiritual advantages of variety and multiplicity	vs.	* a personality bull–headedly determined to follow a simple, direct way, instead of giving any consideration to the many possible ways
* creative thought and action keyed to manifesting the Divine Plan	vs.	* thought and action which exalt and empower the personality with no regard for more important plans and purposes
* great flexibility and adaptability in the execution of spiritually motivated projects	vs.	* stubborn, willful resistance to the spiritual demand for flexibility and adaptability
* the mastery of intelligent change as the primary modality for facilitating spiritual accomplishment	vs.	* the head–strong refusal to change
* a careful weaving of the web of interrelated spiritual energies	vs.	* careless destructiveness, which fails to consider consequences upon already woven textures of interrelated energies; the determination to do exactly as one pleases
* intelligent understanding and skillful application of the many ways, options and circuitous means to achieve spiritual effectiveness	vs.	* blundering straight forward without due consideration of alternative possibilities; almost no ability to handle indirect approaches skillfully
* soul–inspired communicativeness	vs.	* unresponsiveness and taciturnity
* well–developed capacity to "network," and thus establish many channels of communication and interaction	vs.	* personal isolation and unrelatedness
* spiritually tactful and tactical	vs.	* bluntness
* cautious subtlety in spiritual efforts	vs.	* crude imposition of the personal will despite disruptive effects

The Integration Process for the Individual with a Ray 3 Soul and a Ray 1 Personality

1. The pre–spiritual phase; soul energy appropriated by a selfish personality: At this pre–spiritual phase of evolutionary unfoldment, the individual's motives (based upon the personality distortion of third ray soul energy and the self–centered use of first ray personality force) are to achieve a cleverly intelligent, self–serving mastery of circumstances and the environment, *as well as* great personal power arising from the unrestrained imposition of his personal will. The person wants, primarily, to demonstrate his 'superior' intelligence at every opportunity, manipulate money and other people for his own material and intellectual satisfaction, keep incessantly busy in the pursuit of his own self–centered interests, and evade responsibilities through selfish, strategic planning, but he *also* wants to dominate and control others, and wield authority unopposed.

Negatively and glamorously, these two ray influences can combine to produce: the calculating opportunist who will stop at nothing until he gets what he wants; one who dedicates his full intelligence to achieving personal power; the manipulative, isolated person who coldly treats people as if they were 'things'; one who plots and plans to remove anyone in his way (3B + 1B); one who dwells so consistently in his thought life that he totally removes himself from contact with others (3A + 1); one who is so enamored of his own elaborately–contrived philosophy, that he forces others to think according to his sytem (3A + 1); the recklessly hyperactive individual who "knocks people over" as he rushes from place to place (3B + 1); one who, filled with intellectual pride, demands to be noticed and admired for his intelligence (3A + 1); the intensely materialistic person who does whatever is necessary to gratify his desires (3B + 1); the extremely critical individual who is blunt in the delivery of his criticism; one to whom everything is a game – to be won at all costs; one who callously and consistently abandons principle for expediency; the individual whose morality is for sale as long as his personal power is increased; one who uses subtle devious means to increase his personal authority; the person who "knows it all" and therefore feels self–important (3A + 1); one who is extremely resourceful at finding reasons and justifications for the many willful things he does (3A + 1); one who lays traps for others so that he can "come out on top"; one whose head is always filled with big, impractical plans and schemes in which he tries to force others to participate; etc.

2. The phase of conflict; pure soul energy conflicts with personality force: The essential conflict between the ray three soul and the ray one personality is the struggle between the need to achieve a wide comprehension of (and intelligent mastery over) contextual variables, and the impatient desire to cut right through complex considerations (no matter how necessary they may be) in the interests of expeditious action.

3. The soul/personality integration process from the perspective of the consciousness identified primarily with the third ray soul: It will be the task of the third ray soul to render the first ray personality more cautious and circumspect. The soul–identified consciousness sees widely, and all around any subject under consideration, whereas the personal consciousness upon the first ray has no time for such 'useless,' 'academic' perspectives. The third ray soul understands the broad consequences and ramifications of action to be taken, as well as the many related contingencies. It seeks to teach the personality to respect such possibilities and eventualities as worthy of consideration. Sensing the possibility of ill–considered, disruptive action on the part of the personality, the soul seeks to impress upon the personal consciousness the value of the tactical approach. The soul realizes that the shortest distance between two points is not always the straight line, but the personality distrusts indirectness or obliqueness. The soul realizes the extent to which *many* variables have to be taken into simultaneous consideration in order for plans to materialize as intended, whereas the personality craves only the simplicity of direct action. It will be the consistent aim of the soul to demonstrate to the personality that every line of action has many potential 'branches,' and that those branches have branches of their own. Seeing and knowing that this is a world of immense variety, the soul seeks to impress its vision of divine multiplicity upon a personality which unadaptably and monolithically seeks to preserve the simplicity of egotism.

4. The soul/personality integration process from the perspective of the consciousness identified primarily with the first ray personality: The third ray pressure towards integration will be felt by the first ray personality as an 'unnecessarily' confusing experience. The personality, which is used to seeing exactly what it wants and moving rapidly to possess it, becomes frustrated by the great number of options and alternatives offered by the 'multi–viewed' perspective of the third ray soul. Everything that was clear is no longer so; definiteness changes to indefiniteness, certainty to uncertainty, assurance to tentativeness. Under soul pressure the world suddenly becomes irritatingly complex – from the personality point of view. Instead of *one*, there are now *many*. The personality feels its strength weakening from repeated exposure to diversity. A "unified front" is no longer so easy to achieve. Monolithic certainty is fragmented by the growing need to reckon with a host of variables. Gradually, it begins to dawn upon the personality that the enjoyment it derives from a feeling of consolidated strength must give way to an appreciation of the value of relativity. Under the pervading influence of the third ray soul, self-assured personal power begin to seem a very small thing compared to the opportunity to appreciate the wonders of the Divine Mind. Self–will, once so eagerly enforced, begins to be seen as an obstacle to the intelligent, adaptable mastery of circumstances. The personality senses that it has been standing in the way of its own deeper desires for more intelligent living.

5. The ideal expression of the combination of the ray three soul and the ray one personality: Intelligent comprehension is expressed with dynamic power. Creative plans and large projects are executed with unfaltering one–pointedness. Broad abstract understanding is anchored into practicality by a powerful will. There is a highly developed ability to communicate, aided by an impressive presentation of self. Individuals with this combination possess excellent strategic skills, complemented by the stamina to turn strategy into actuality. Their great mental fertility is matched by abundant charisma and vitality. Mobility masters immobility; adaptability overcomes inflexibility; nevertheless, such individuals are firm, well–centered and self–possessed.

Their mastery of intelligent manipulation supercedes any tendencies they might have towards unintelligent willfulness, but they do have a strong will, and it supports them in their many activities. They are eminently capable of executing a number of complex tasks successfully, with simplicity and certainty, and their undoubted strength enables them to endure. Their energy is great, as is their intelligence. There is also the ability to be (simultaneously) both eminently *reasonable* and *forceful*. They have a facility for travelling and making many contacts but, if they have a good reason, they know how to remain (albeit temporarily) fixed and immovable at the center. People of this kind have a great love of creative thinking and doing, which are, in the long run, more important to them than their very real personal power. With this combination, power supports intelligence, but is secondary to it. This is an excellent combination for an executive who must oversee and direct many aspects of a complex project.

6. The combined effect of the two integration formulae: The primary integration formula is *Stillness*, keyed to the third ray soul. The secondary integration formula is *Inclusion*, keyed to the first ray personality. The first formula corrects third ray tendencies towards a busy scattering of attention, wasted thought, and physical overactivity (with their resultant disturbances and obscurations of conciousness), whereas the second formula corrects the exclusive and isolative tendencies induced by the first ray. Used together, these two formulae provide the individual striving for soul/personality integration with the composite quality of 'inclusive stillness,'(i.e., an inclusive attitude towards others, which quiets the conscience, and renders the personal consciousness receptive (in the stillness) to the divinely intelligent ways of serving others which the soul reveals. Through the wise use of these formulae, the individual withdraws quietly to the center of his being, senses the outlines of the Divine Plan (heretofore obscured by the 'noise' of his overactive life), and then embraces all those, who with himself, are meant to carry forward with intelligence their tiny portion of the Divine Plan. Thus, the formulae make it possible for the individual to cultivate a more open and inviting personal consciousness, supportive of those moments of exalted consciousness when, pervaded by the presence of the soul, he stands silent and still, intent upon hearing, and then executing with all his creative intelligence, a Plan greater in every way than his own tiny plans.

In the earlier stages of evolution, before successfully applying these formulae, an individual with this ray combination often finds himself utterly preoccupied with his own, excessive, spiritually–unaligned thought and activity, and rejecting the heart–felt intimacy which would lead to a quieter, more trusting, less manipulative attitude. He rebuffs others, refuses to listen to the soul, and has no rest.

The intelligent use of these two formulae, however, transmutes the abuses of the past. The individual ends his busy entrapment in externals, and his insistence on keeping other people at a distance (and hence, *external* to himself). He learns, primarily, to act and think only in accordance with the divinely intelligent Plan, and his growing secondary ability to embrace others, rather than cast them aside, ensures that whatever he *thinks* and *does* (under the impress of his highly *intelligent* soul), will benefit the many with whom he has chosen to cooperate.

7. Some examples of vocational aptitudes and orientations relating to the combination of the third ray soul and the first ray personality:

* the intelligent executive with the daring to take bold initiatives and the rugged endurance to see them through
* the resourceful business person with strong leadership abilities
* the intellectual who is also a brave "man of action"; the intellectual activist
* the historian with a particular interest in political history
* the mathematician with the will and tenacity for long hours of abstract thought
* the philosopher for whom power is a predominating theme of thought
* the planner of staightforward, "do–able" plans
* the strategist who also understands what it is like "in the field" or "under the gun"
* the creative thinker with the fortitude to stand up for his thoughts
* the magician who has the stamina for the prolonged and successful manipulation of energy
* the communicator who tells the truth as he sees it
* the writer who has the courage of his convictions
* the philanthropist who is courageous is the selection of his beneficiaries
* the financial analyst who does not mince words
* the broker with the "guts" to stick with his decisions
* the satirist
* the critic who is biting in his commentary

In general: vocations and professions which require acute intelligence (whether active or abstract), great adaptability and resourcefulness, abundant creative and communicative abilities, and (frequently) strong business aptitudes, *as well as* great will power, strength and stamina, the ability to stand firmly on principle, and (when necessary) the power to destroy obstacles.

8. A proposed list of well–known individuals (historical, contemporary, fictional or mythological) whose primary ray can be assumed to be the third, with a strong, subsidiary first ray influence (whether or not the first ray is, strictly speaking, the personality ray):

Karl Marx: revolutionist, sociologist and economist, author of Das Kapital, and *The Communist Manifesto*. The energy of the sixth ray was also pronounced.

H.L. Mencken: American editor and critic, known as "the Voltaire of his time"

J.P. Morgan: U.S. financier, industrial organizer, and art collector. The fourth ray was also influential.

John D. Rockefeller: U.S. industrialist and philanthropist, founder of the Standard Oil Company

Bertrand Russell: philosopher, mathematician, logician, social critic – one of the greatest intellects of the 20th century. Both rays five and six are strongly accented, as well.

Shylock (fictional): the implaccable moneylender in *The Merchant of Venice* by William Shakespeare

Gertrude Stein: avant–garde writer, eccentric and self–styled genius, whose Paris home was a salon for the leading artists and writers of her day. The fourth ray was also influential.

Voltaire (François–Marie Arouet): one of the greatest French authors, and a courageous crusader against tyranny, bigotry and cruelty. A strong fourth ray influence was also present.

Some Contrasts Between the Ray 3 Soul and the Ray 2 Personality

Ray 3 Soul		Ray 2 Personality
* spiritual intelligence	vs.	* personal love
* the "wise head"	vs.	* the "foolish heart"
* spiritual detachment arising from a wide and abstract mental horizon	vs.	* personal attachment based upon the desire for personal intimacy
* good judgment based upon keen mental discrimination	vs.	* quality of judgment adversely influenced by the desire to maintain warm, friendly interpersonal relations
* a thorough comprehension of the laws of reasoning	vs.	* a gentle ignoring of careful thinking and conceptual accuracy in conducting the affairs of daily living
* the pursuit of great thought	vs.	* the pursuit of a soft and comfortable life
* the cultivation of thought which rises boldly above mundane considerations	vs.	* fear of the consequences of living according to great thought
* time insistently spent in the generation and discussion of lofty ideas and theoretical concepts, expressed with acuity	vs.	* small talk for the sake of pleasant sociability; declining to express one's thought with acuity, in order to be loved or, at least, liked
* great energy and activity ready for expenditure in the divine creative process	vs.	* personal inertia and reticence to act
* the power to "make things happen"	vs.	* the disinclination to bestir oneself
* soul-inspired manipulation of energies	vs.	* passivity; the one to whom things "happen"
* commercial resourcefulness as an aid to the manifestation of spiritual ideas	vs.	* often too soft for the demanding adaptability and 'busyness' of the business world
* a flexible and intelligent handling of the important general ideas	vs.	* over-attentiveness to a mass of detail retards rapidity of action
* deep and serious thinking	vs.	* frivolity and superficial gaiety

The Integration Process for the Individual with a Ray 3 Soul and a Ray 2 Personality

1. The pre-spiritual phase; soul energy appropriated by a selfish personality: At this pre-spiritual phase of evolutionary unfoldment, the individual's motives (based upon the personality distortion of third ray soul energy, and the self-centered use of second ray personality force) are to achieve a cleverly intelligent, self-serving mastery of circumstances and the environment *as well as* the complete fulfillment of personal love (or the complete satisfaction of studious enquiry [2B]).

The person wants, primarily, to demonstrate his 'superior' intelligence at every opportunity, manipulate money and other people for his own material and intellectual satisfaction, keep incessantly busy in the pursuit of his own self-centered interests, and evade responsibilities through selfish, strategic planning, but he *also* wants to be constantly loved, consistently popular, warmly admired, well–cared–for, and to live a soft, comfortable, well–protected, well–insulated life – closely attached to those people, places and things which he loves and finds personally satisfying.

Negatively and glamorously, these two ray influences can combine to produce: the caculating manipulator who deceives through a pleasant manner; the "wheeler–dealer" with a trustworthy face (3B + 2); the opportunist who uses 'love' and personal magnetism to get what he wants (3 + 2A); the vague, absent–minded thinker who is too weak and ineffectual to accomplish anything (3A + 2); the impractical theorist afflicted with inertia (3A + 2); one who constantly loses himself in abstract thought, compounding his difficulty with supplient passivity upon the physical plane (3A + 2A); the selfish materialist who is strongly motivated by the desire for a soft life (3B + 2A); one who utilizes his considerable intelligence purely for the purpose of protecting himself from the impacts of normal living (3B + 2A); one who is filled with intellectual pride because of his learnedness (3A + 2B); a cleverly elusive individual who is well–practiced in escaping from disagreeable encounters (3B + 2A); a person who has considerable difficulty making himself clear and is too timid to really try (3A + 2A); one who is not only chronically disorganized but acts quite helpless as well (3 + 2A); one who seeks to demonstrate his intellectual prowess in order to be loved or socially accepted (3A + 2A); the "chameleon" who adaptively 'becomes' the person others want him to be or think he should be (3 + 2A); etc;

2. The phase of conflict; pure soul energy conflicts with personality force: The essential conflict between the ray three soul and the ray two personality is the struggle between the need to express acute, spiritual intelligence and the desire for a life in which the complete satisfaction of personal love is paramount.

3. The soul/personality integration process from the perspective of the consciousness identified primarily with the third ray soul: It will be the task of the soul to activate and 'intellectualize' the personality consciousness. The highly intelligent soul seeks to acquaint the personal consciousness with "the acute energy of divine mental perception." Given the potential clarity and lucidity of the second ray personality, this need not be a difficult task, except for the impediment of close, personal ties. The mentally–oriented soul (and frequently the orientation is very abstract) faces a real difficulty in bringing the personality to the point where it is willing to relinquish (for the sake of greater mental acuity and dexterity) its deep and sensitive attachments to those it loves (and the places and things it loves, as well). The soul seeks to induce greater mental and physical activity in a personality which is focused (subtly and non–cognitively) upon the quality of its close personal relationships. Endeavoring to induce a state of mental abstraction, in which all the experiences of life can be examined from the point of view of a detached, 'distant,' mental analysis, the third ray soul has difficulty 'convincing' the personal consciousness to 'leave' the familiar, the "near and dear," and depart for those 'colder' realms of lofty thought where everything is seen rationally, philosophically and divorced from personal feeling. (These remarks are, of course, particularly true when the soul is influenced by the energy of type (3A), and is focused more within the higher mind than upon the physical plane).

From another point of view, the soul encounters a sometimes sluggish, inert personality whose mobility is severely curtailed, again, by the personal ties it has formed. The soul seeks to have the personality detach sufficiently to begin manipulating its material environment more effectively and in line with the Plan. The potential activity of the third ray soul is great, but the second ray personality (still, calm and closely attached) is resistant to the required degree of activation.

4. The soul/personality integration process from the perspective of the consciousness identified primarily with the second ray personality: The third ray pressure towards integration will be felt by the second ray personality as both an 'impersonalizing' and agitating process. The personality feels most comfortable loving, relating and being close to others. The soul influence forces it to begin to question and doubt the value of such intimacy. The personality is forced to *think reasonably* about the most cherished and comfortable things in its life, and it has no wish to do so. The light of an expanded historical, sociological, biological (in short, *academic*) perspective is felt as an intrusion upon the personality's enjoyment of the loving, comfortable, happy and satisfying attachments which had always been taken for granted as supremely valuable. Under the impress of soul quality, the personality begins to suspect that it has been *unintelligent* about the way it has been living its life – content, but unintelligent. This is an uncomfortable feeling. Mental discipline and increased mental activity are, at length, seen as a necessity by a personality which has been loathe to discipline its mind or think in an active, intellectual manner. Further, the personality begins to glimpse the *many things that can be done*, given sufficient intelligence and activity. The fascinating variety of possible activities begins to dawn upon it, as well as the realization that very little of that variety has been sampled due to personal slowness, inertia and attachment. The feeling of being prodded to "get moving," arises constantly within the personal consciousness; otherwise (so the personality realizes) the possibility of participating in a significant number of all those interesting activities will be sacrificed. The personality is forced to learn that only those attachments and relationships which serve the goal of sharpening and expanding the intelligence can be sustained without frustrating the will of the soul.

5. The ideal expression of the combination of the ray three soul and the ray two personality: The profound thoughts of a highly intelligent mind, and the fascinating concepts engendered by brilliant, mental creativity are expressed lovingly, sensitively and with heart. An intelligent comprehension which is detached and objective, prevails over an approach to living which is too soft and easy-going to be effective, and yet the quality of loving-kindness is present in all the many intelligent activities which such an individual characteristically initiates. The benefits of far-seeing, strategic planning are increased by a willingness to wait patiently until the plans materialize. A good business head masters a well-meaning but often misguided heart, and yet a humanitarian attitude of care and consideration is preserved in all business transactions. Astute executive abilities become all the more effective because of a loving and magnetic presentation of self. Speedy execution of responsibilities wins out (when necessary) over slow movement and the love of comfort, and yet this individual is always inclined to utilize his considerable intelligence to protect others and ameliorate their life circumstances. Here is one who may easily accumulate a great deal of money through the exercise of formidable financial skills, and then share that money, generously and whole-heartedly, with others. Serenity and contemplativeness create a personal attitude conducive to sustained, deeply intellectual thinking. Philosophical reasoning and speculation are supported by a calm, unemotional temperament well-suited to prolonged, patient enquiry. An abstract perspective is rendered more accessible and comprehensible by one who has a sensitive "personal touch" and a great love of teaching. Others might justly say of such an individual: "He makes difficult subjects easier to follow because he's so kind and approachable." This is an individual with great creativity and mental resourcefulness, who has the patience and interpersonal skills to make his innovations clearly understandable. Individuals of this type also have excellent linguistic or communicative abilities which are enhanced by a talent for achieving a warm and comfortable rapport with many different people.

6. The combined effect of the two integration formulae: The primary integration formula is *Stillness*, keyed to the third ray soul. The secondary integration formula is *Centralization* keyed to the second ray personality. The first formula corrects third ray tendencies towards a busy scattering of attention, wasted thought, and physical overactivity (with their resultant disturbances and obscurations of consciousness), whereas, the second formula corrects second ray tendencies towards diffusion, over-expansion, and an energy-draining attachment to life's peripheral attractions. Used together, these two formulae provide the individual striving for soul/personality integration with the composite quality of 'centralized stillness,' (i.e., the personal centralization which contributes so much to creating the stillness in which right spiritual thought and action can be perceived). The individual who uses these formulae releases himself from all attachments which keep him bound to the periphery of his life, and quiets all agitations of consciousness which prevent him from seeing and cooperating with the Plan as it *is*. Thus, the formulae make it possible for the individual to cultivate a more detached and centered personal consciousness, supportive of those moments of exalted consciousness when, pervaded by the presence of the soul, he stands silent and still, intent upon hearing, and then executing with all his creative intelligence, a Plan greater in every way than his own tiny plans.

In the earlier stages of evolution, before successfully applying these formulae, such an individual often finds himself unproductively active, and persistently generating new peripheral attachments, virtually guaranteeing futile, uncentered activity. He finds himself overattached and overextended – interested in everything and involved in everything, restless and uncentered, "spread too thin" to find his center.

The intelligent use of these two formulae, however, transmutes the abuses of the past. He restores economy of motion and a stable, centered self-possession. The individual learns, primarily, to act and think only in accordance with the divinely intelligent Plan, and his growing secondary ability to stand detached, centered and 'unafraid of being out of love' (so to speak), will free his hands for the active and intelligent (though wise and loving) execution of his tiny part in the Plan.

7. Some examples of vocational aptitudes and orientations relating to the combination of the third ray soul and the second ray personality:

* the intelligent executive with an attractive "personal touch"
* the resourceful business person who easily promotes unity and good–feeling among his employees and customers
* the intellectual with broad and inclusive interests
* the theorist who, always balancing his head with his heart, never abandons his close contact with people
* the academician who always makes his subjects personally relevant and inviting to his students
* the historian with a particular interest in democracy and the impact of historical trends upon the "common man"
* the philosopher with well–developed humanistic orientation
* the teacher of philosophy
* the speculative thinker with a comprehensive point of view
* the "far–out" professor who is an excellent teacher
* the planner who is ever mindful of human impact studies
* the strategist endowed with calm and great patience
* the creative 'think–tanker' who always remembers the concerns of ordinary people
* the magician who effectively employs the magnetism of love
* the articulate communicator with the "common touch"
* the clever writer whose works are filled with fun and good humor
* the compassionate critic, who really understands human foibles
* the philanthropist with great compassion for the suffering of the individual
* the financial analyst who never forgets the "human equation"
* the broker with a talent for "hand–holding"

In general: vocations or professions which require acute intelligence (whether active or abstract), great adaptability and resourcefulness, abundant creative and communicative abilities, and (frequently) strong business aptitudes, *as well as* a wise and loving attitude, great empathy and understanding, studiousness, and the ability to teach or compassionately heal.

8. A proposed list of well-known individuals (historical, contemporary, fictional or mythological) whose soul ray can reasonably be considered the third, with a strong subsidiary second ray influence (whether or not the second ray is, strictly speaking, the personality ray):

Mortimer Adler: contemporary philosopher and educator, who has been instrumental in making philosophy accessible to the average, intelligent individual.

St. Thomas Aquinas: the foremost philosopher and theologian of the Catholic Church. An Aristotelian thinker, he provided the classical systematization of Latin theology.

Lewis Carol: mathematician and logician who created *Alice in Wonderland*. The fourth ray was also very influential.

Nicolaus Copernicus: Polish astronomer whose findings confirmed the heliocentric view of the solar system. The fifth ray was also a strong influence.

Albert Einstein: theoretical physicist, philosopher, humanitarian, who revolutionized humanity's understanding of the physical universe. Clearly, the fifth ray was also of outstanding importance. (See the ray analysis of Albert Einstein in Section VI, Vol. II)

Edward Gibbon: the greatest English historian of the 18th century. Gibbon was the author of *The History of the Decline and Fall of the Roman Empire*. The fifth ray was very strongly represented in his energy system; the Tibetan's commentary in which he states that "the third and fifth rays make the perfectly balanced historian who grasps his subject in a large way and verifies every detail with patient accuracy" is an excellent description of Gibbon.

Benedict de Spinoza: a 17th century Rationalist who was author of one of the most consummate systems of metaphysics in the history of philosophy.

Alfred North Whitehead: mathematician, author, educator and metaphysician

Norbert Wiener: mathematician who established the science of cybernetics. Ray five was also extremely influential.

Some Contrasts Between the Ray 3 Soul and the Ray 3 Personality

Ray 3 Soul		Ray 3 Personality
* the bending of all thought towards the understanding and manifestation of the Divine Plan	vs.	* active and devious scheming towards the creation and manifestation of selfish, purely personal plans
* the power to grasp the essence of truths	vs.	* the self–serving manipulation, distortion and disguising of truths
* "acute energy of divine mental perception"	vs.	* the prostitution of intelligence to purely personal and material ends
* sharp–mindedness and great interpretive capacity	vs.	* sharp–mindedness used to deceive or mislead others
* facility for the comprehension of spiritual abstractions	vs.	* vague, impractical thought and absentmindedness
* communication as the means of revealing and sharing lofty thought	vs.	* over–talkativeness and carelessness in the use of words
* cultivation of financial resourcefulness to aid in the manifestation of the Plan	vs.	* the selfish acquiring and misuse of money and other material resources
* the capacity to handle many threads of energy in the interests of divinely inspired creativity	vs.	* chaos, scatter and disorganization; living a 'tangled' life "at loose ends"

Commentary

1. As it can reasonably be inferred (on the basis of statements by the Tibetan) that the appearance of identical soul and personality rays is a rarity occuring only in the very late stages of the path of discipleship, and probably upon the path of initiation, it is not really meaningful to discuss the dynamics of the possible interaction between a ray three soul and a ray three personality in the pre–spiritual phase of evolution.

2. Such contrasts as there might be would be based upon the counterpulls of the higher and lower qualities of the third ray. Essentially, the contrast would be between the selfless use of the "acute energy of divine mental perception" to manipulate the many energies relevant to the manifesting of the Divine Plan, and the selfish abuse of high intelligence for the manipulation of energies and forces for purely personal ends.

3. As regards the ideal expression of the combination of the ray three soul and the ray three personality, it is clear that this combination would present a remarkable opportunity for an unusually pure expression of Divine Intelligence (the Mind of God) through the human energy system.

Note: For additional commentary on issues relating to identical soul and personality rays, please refer to the sections on ray combinations 1/1 and 2/2.

Some Contrasts Between the Ray 3 Soul and the Ray 4 Personality

Ray 3 Soul		Ray 4 Personality
* profound intelligence	vs.	* submersion in personal dramatics
* the power to think deeply until the truth is reached	vs.	* discontinuity and lack of self-discipline which interfere with the thoughtful approach to truth; rebellion against the disciplined life of the mind
* striking capacity for exactitude of thought (especially thought unrelated to concrete objects)	vs.	* loose analogical, free-associative thinking; inaccurate and unexacting
* uncompromising intellectual integrity	vs.	* beliefs and opinions compromised for the sake of a peaceful, tension-free personal life
* powerful abstract thought which rises far above personal vicissitudes	vs.	* personal moodiness and temperamentalism
* the power of lofty concepts to generate a thought life free from the distortions and negativities of the strictly personal perspective	vs.	* pessimism, worry and lack of confidence
* abundant energy to act continuously in the execution of spiritual enterprises	vs.	* spasmodic activity under the alternating influences of "rajas" (activity) and "tamas" (inertia)
* emphasis upon the essential pattern of thought behind appearance	vs.	* preoccupation with personal beauty and appeal
* capacity to create long-range plans and strategems for the materialization of spiritual values	vs.	* aversion to planning; disruption of carefully created plans through thoughtless spontaneity and improvisatory, inspirational, "in-the-moment" living
* soul-inspired caution and economy	vs.	* personal improvidence and prodigality
* the mastery of calculated, indirect action to accomplish spiritual objectives	vs.	* disruptively confrontational and pugnacious
* natural facility in business and commerce	vs.	* a frequently self-indulgent, "artistic temperament" unsuited to the demands of business and commerce

The Integration Process for the Individual with a Ray 3 Soul and a Ray 4 Personality

1. The pre-spiritual phase; soul energy appropriated by a selfish personality: At this pre-spiritual phase of evolutionary unfoldment, the individual's motives (based upon the personality distortion of third ray soul energy and the self-centered use of fourth ray personality force) are to achieve a cleverly intelligent, self-serving mastery of circumstances and the environment, *as well as* an agreeable feeling of personal peace and harmony through a tension-releasing expression of conflicting bio-psychic impulses. The person wants, primarily, to demonstrate his 'superior' intelligence at every opportunity, manipulate money and other people for his own material and intellectual satisfaction, keep incessantly busy in the pursuit of his own self-centered interests, and evade responsibilities through selfish, strategic planning, but he *also* wants to be constantly surrounded by what he considers beautiful or attractive, to be spontaneously self-expressive without discipline or control, self-indulgently dramatic or moody (as he pleases), and greatly appreciated for his colorful, unpredictable temperament.

Negatively and glamorously, these two ray influences can combine to produce: the dishonest person with divided loyalties; the devious individual who uses his fertile imagination to invent new fictions as his need requires; the manipulative person who understands how to sow discord as he plays one party against another for his own advantage (3 + 4B); one who seeks to subtly control the behavior of others by pretending to be in harmony with them (3 + 4A); one who is filled with an abundance of impractical ideas and is too emotionally unstable and inconsistent to actualize any of them (3A + 4B); an abstracted, overly-intellectual person, whose temperamentalism makes him unsuited for practical living (3A + 4B); a person whose great intellectual pride persistently provokes arguments and fractious interpersonal relationships (3A + 4B); an evasive, overly-expedient person who lacks moral courage (3B + 4A); an amoral schemer who is forever compromising away the few principles he may have (3 + 4A); one who sees issues from so many perspectives, and is so indecisive that clear decision and action is a great rarity; one whose activity is so great and continuity so small that he seldom accomplishes anything of significance (3B + 4B); a highly critical person with intellectual pretensions as an arbiter of aesthetic taste (3A + 4A); one who believes that beautiful things and "beautiful people" can simply be bought and sold (3B + 4A); one who purposely misleads others with many "tall tales"; one who combines a confused, overly-complex thinking with intense psychological conflict – the result being personality fragmentation and, even, disintegration (3A + 4B); one who seeks to arrange the lives and circumstances about him so that conflict and crisis (no matter how healthy) are avoided at any cost (3 + 4A); a person for whom accuracy of detail is almost meaningless; hyperactive and manic-depressive tendencies rolled into one (3B + 4B); an overly-adaptable person who constantly changes his position in order to harmonize with those around him (3B + 4A); etc.

2. The phase of conflict; pure soul energy conflicts with personality force: The essential conflict between the ray three soul and the ray four personality is the struggle between acute, spiritually-inspired, intellectual comprehension and manipulation of energy, and a mind-obscuring, personal captivity to fluctuating and conflicted psychological and physical states.

3. The soul/personality integration process from the perspective of the consciousness identified primarily with the third ray soul: It will be the task of the third ray soul to render the fluctuating fourth ray personality more reasonable and intelligent. The third ray soul gazes at all life-phenomena as from a "philosophical distance"; the constant vicissitudes of the personality are not a matter of any significant interest. And yet the soul is frustrated in its attempts to master the world of thought and manipulate various environments (physical as well as non-physical) by the *undependability* of its fourth ray personality. The soul wishes to think with a pure form of intellectuality, undisturbed by changes of mood – the unpredictable alternation of excessively positive or negative attitudes. It must teach the personality to conform to the dictates of reason despite ambivalent feelings. It must teach the value of logical consistency to a personality which almost prides itself on a temperamental disposition to illogic. A more cautious, provident, far-seeing way of living is what is required, and towards this end, the intelligent soul must guide its rebellious, rather unmanageable personality.

4. The soul/personality integration process from the perspective of the consciousness identified primarily with the personality: The third ray pressure towards integration will be experienced by the fourth ray personality as a demanding intellectual energy, intruding unwelcomely upon a life of spontaneity and expressivity – for it is commonly believed (especially by the individual with a fourth ray personality) that intellectual thought interferes with natural, self–expression. Thus, the personal consciousness of such an individual has no desire to engage in pure intellectualism, or in theoretical abstractions – both of which, initially, seem excruciatingly boring. An emotionally responsive life filled with contrasts is the life that appeals – a life of vivacious immediacy. The personality is frustrated merely by the thought of having to *think* about everything – which is precisely what the third ray soul would have it do. Instead, the personality seeks to be inspired; it has virtually no desire for mental consistency.

Yet, despite its protests and rebellions, the personality slowly begins to find its preoccupation with self–expression dissatisfying. The adventures possible to the versatile intellect begin to beckon, and the personality begins to sense that, despite the emotional and aesthetic satisfactions of a spontaneous and expressive life style, it has lived in a manner quite uninformed and rather unintelligent. New learnings arise: that moods interfere with mental functioning; that the power to think abstractly broadens the understanding; that consistency and continuity (both of thought and action) lead to increased effectiveness and mastery over the environment. Needless vacillation ends; the personal consciousness "stands back" and begins to take the long–range view. World understanding, as seen from a lofty, capacious, intellectual perspective begins to dawn upon the consciousness of a personality which is beginning to value the mind over the transient pleasures of its own, irresponsible reactivity.

5. The ideal combination of third ray soul energy and fourth ray personality force: Intelligent comprehension and creative activity are expressed in the spirit of interplay and compromise. Difficult theoretical considerations are imaginatively illustrated in picturesque symbols and colorful analogies. There is a lively talent for dramatizing academic issues. Philosophical abstractions are presented in a delightful and engaging manner. Here is an individual who can implement his elaborately thought–out plans all the more effectively because of his natural ability for "give–and–take." A masterful manipulation of the environment is enhanced by an exquisite sensitivity to potential harmonies and discords; an unusual talent for adaptability becomes even more successful because of the ability to establish a sensitive and flexible rapport with many kinds of people and situations. Individuals of this type can convey their sharply-honed communication skills via many 'bridges.' They often have the power to express themselves brilliantly in a number of languages, and this creates many channels of rapport. This combination is characteristic of the tactician who masters many personal and environal vicissitudes; his strategies succeed because (even in adversity) he has learned how to remain in harmony with others, with his environment, and with himself. He is mentally astute, but colorful and entertaining, as well. He possesses both mental and emotional creativity, and his facility for unusually intelligent verbal expression is presented in an aesthetically pleasing manner. This is a very imaginative combination of rays, producing considerable literary skill, especially in the area of fiction. The power to sustain activity (or concentration upon higher abstract studies) masters the tendency towards vacillation and spasmodic, irregular thought and action. Such individuals are very capable of utilizing beauty and charm when motivating others to cooperate with their extensive plans and arrangements. This combination of rays also inclines towards an excellent blending of business and artistic aptitudes. It is frequently found in the entertainment industry – especially among producers, agents, and all those who have a gift for intelligently managing the talent of others.

6. The combined effect of the two integration formulae: The primary integration formula is *Stillness*, keyed to the third ray soul. The secondary integration formula is *Steadfastness*, keyed to the fourth ray personality. The first formula corrects third ray tendencies towards a busy scattering of attention, wasted thought, and physical overactivity (with their resultant disturbances and obscurations of consciousness), whereas the second formula corrects the tendencies towards vacillation, irresoluteness, instability, indecisiveness and moral cowardice characteristic of the fourth ray personality. Used together, these two formulae provide the individual striving for soul/personality integration with the composite quality of 'steadfast stillness' (i.e., the personal steadfastness which contributes to a quieting and attuning of all aspects of the energy system, and a subsequent alignment with Divine Intelligence as apprehended by the soul). Upon the level of personality, the individual steadfastly refuses to engage in an unbalanced warfare between any of the many pairs of opposites, and his outer serenity eventually helps him achieve that quiet at the center of his being which reveals the Divine Plan. Thus, the formulae make it possible for the individual to cultivate a more equilibrized and stable personal consciousness, supportive of those rare moments of exalted consciousness when, pervaded by the presence of the soul, he stands silent and still, intent upon hearing, and then executing with all his creative intelligence, a Plan greater in every way than his own tiny plans.

In the earlier stages of evolution, before successfully applying these formulae, such an individual often finds himself preoccupied with numerous scattered activities and lines of thought, all peripheral to the center of his spiritual consciousness; further he is constantly being torn between them, trying to relate and harmonize widely disparate qualities of energy. He is restless, unproductive, struggling on the periphery of his life, and embroiled in numerous conflicts which have little or nothing to do with his soul purpose. Purposeless activity (both mental and physical) and persistent stress and strain obscure the Path of Return to the center of his being.

The intelligent use of these two formulae, however, transmutes the abuses of the past. The individual brings an end to the disintegrating effect of constant struggle between the polarities, and his inner consciousness becomes clear, quiet and aligned with his inner and highly intelligent purpose. He learns, primarily, to act and think only in accordance with the divinely intelligent Plan, and his growing secondary ability to make peace upon the plane of personality, guarantees that he will have the skill to implement harmoniously (as well as intelligently) that tiny aspect of the great Plan for which he is spiritually responsible.

7. Some examples of vocational aptitudes and orientations relating to the combination of the third ray soul and the fourth ray personality:

* the intelligent executive who is well versed in conflict resolution
* the resourceful business person who is responsive to the need for beauty in the business environment
* the intellectual who has keen aesthetic sensibilities
* the theorist whose theories are created largely to resolve cognitive dissonance
* the academician who enthusiastically builds bridges between various academic disciplines
* the historian who focuses especially upon the history of art
* the literary critic
* the philosopher who knows many stories and anecdotes to illustrate his ideas
* the "far-out" professor who is also a lively entertainer in class
* the planner who is always ready for inevitable, necessary compromises
* the strategist who is ever cognizant of the conflicts which his strategy may generate and the possible means of resolving those conflicts
* the creative thinker who excels in analogical thought
* the magician who is masterful in the manipulation of sound and color
* the articulate communicator who delights his audience through the use of picturesque language
* the philanthropist who is especially interested in endowing the arts
* the financial analyst who always strives for a balanced interpretation of his figures
* the broker who continually "hedges his bet"

In general: vocations and professions which require acute intelligence (whether active or abstract), great adaptability and resourcefulness, abundant creative and communicative abilities, and (frequently) strong business aptitudes, *as well as* a strong creative imagination, spontaneity, expressivity, aesthetic sensitivity and the ability to bring harmony out of conflict, beauty out of ugliness, and at-one-ment out of divisiveness.

8. A proposed list of well-known individuals (historical, contemporary, fictional or mythological) whose soul ray can reasonably be considered the third, with a strong subsidiary fourth ray influence (whether or not the fourth ray is, strictly speaking, the personality ray):

Steve Allen: comedian, author, versatile entertainer, producer of "The Meeting of Minds"

Woody Allen: film–maker, actor, comedian

James Joyce: Irish novelist, best known for his difficult, intricate, but incredibly interesting novels *Ulysses* and *Finnegans Wake* (which is still imperfectly understood)

Molière (Jean–Baptiste Poquelin): French comic playwright

Francis Parkman: often called America's greatest historian. Parkman is best known for his seven–volume history of the Anglo–French struggle for North America, in which he displayed a rare talent for dramatic exposition combined with the strict historical accuracy of the scholar. A strong ray five influence is to be noted.

Jean Paul Sartre: French Existentialist philosopher, novelist, and playwright. The influence of the first ray is also noticeable.

Steven Spielberg: film–maker. The influence of the second ray is present as well.

Mark Twain: American humorist and satirist. There was also a pronounced ray one influence, quite possibly at the level of the mind, and an idealistic ray six may have been the true reason for his cynicism and interest in religious/moral issues.

Jules Verne: French author whose writings laid much of the foundation of modern science fiction. A strong fifth ray influence is also evident (whether qualifying a vehicle of the personality, or coming through his Sun sign, Aquarius).

Some Contrasts Between the Ray 3 Soul and the Ray 5 Personality

Ray 3 Soul		Ray 5 Personality
* abstract spiritual thought	vs.	* literal, concrete thought
* broad abstract comprehension	vs.	* narrow materialistic focus
* astute metaphysical insight	vs.	* a "matter–of–fact," 'unsoaring' persona
* a powerful philosophical mentality	vs.	* a pedestrian, "nuts–and–bolts" mentality
* great spiritual/intellectual creativity	vs.	* a non–creative, descriptive/objective approach to thinking
* fertile capacity for inspired brainstorming; resourceful, divergent thinking	vs.	* too much fixity of thought for facile brainstorming
* capacity to discover meaning and implication within any system of relationships	vs.	* preoccupation with collections of facts and often unconcerned about their meaning, in the larger sense
* facility for devising speculative theories which penetrate into new realms of truth	vs.	* a personal focus conservatively confined to currently verified knowledge
* considerable imaginative capacity; intellectual 'dreaming'	vs.	* unimaginative and unintuitive; "commonsense" restricting the comprehension of more subtle and elusive forms of truth
* great capacity to handle intangible complexities	vs.	* incapable of coping with intangibles
* fluidly adaptable thought and action applied to the manifestation of the Plan	vs.	* fixed, concrete thinking, leading to rigid, unadaptable activity
* capacity to weave together many diverse lines of thought	vs.	* the limitations of linearity and particularity (i.e., fascination with the apparent separateness of things)
* pronounced capacity for interdisciplinary thought	vs.	* the ignorance arising from specialization
* powerful communicative skills	vs.	* limited communicativeness – restricted to specialty areas

The Integration Process for the Individual with a Ray 3 Soul and a Ray 5 Personality

1. The pre–spiritual phase; soul energy appropriated by a selfish personality: At this pre–spiritual phase of evolutionary unfoldment, the individual's motives (based upon the personality distortion of third ray soul energy, and the self–centered use of fifth ray personality force), are to achieve a cleverly intelligent, self–serving mastery of circumstances and the environment, *as well as* a narrow, materialistic intellectual certainty. The person wants primarily to demonstrate his 'superior' intelligence at every opportunity, manipulate money and other people for his own material and intellectual satisfaction, keep incessantly busy in the pursuit of his own self–centered interests, and evade responsibilities through selfish, strategic planning, but he *also* wants to take everything apart (either analytically or actually), reduce all life experience to nothing but rationalistic formulae, control matter mechanically for selfish ends, and reject any kind of knowledge that is not materialistic or derived strictly from the five physical senses.

Negatively and glamorously, these two ray influences can combine to produce: a flagrant form of intellectual pride reinforced by a narrow intellectual assurance; an extreme prejudice in favor of rationality, negating the validity of any psychological process which is not "rational" in the narrowest sense of the term (3A + 5A); a world view based solely upon the testimony of materialistic reasoning and worldly science (3B + 5); persistent agnosticism and skepticism; one who repudiates intuition and faith; one who seeks to manipulate others through the application of technology (3B + 5B); one who is inclined to prostitute all knowledge to selfish, materialistic ends; one whose severe criticism of others is based upon the presumption of his own mental superiority and of their ignorance (3A + 5A); a person utterly preoccupied with analysing *everything*, whether abstract or concrete; one who is completely distrustful of the value of feelings and emotions; one who, being incapable of empathy, holds everyone and everything at a mental distance; one who seeks selfishly to manipulate his environment through the misuse of scientific knowledge (3B + 5); one who is so absorbed in "left–brain" mental processes that "holistic" thinking becomes a virtual impossibility (3B + 5); an utterly calculating and premeditative individual who will not allow himself to be spontaneous; one so fascinated by the acquisition and manipulation of knowledge that moral considerations regarding the use of that knowledge are ignored (3A + 5); one who furthers his selfish manipulation of money through the use of mathematical and statistical processes (3B + 5A); one who, for the sake of efficiency and the improvement of his finances, would gladly replace any man with a machine (3B + 5B); an impractical, theoretical person who spends a great deal of time gathering data on speculative considerations which have no possible relevance to human need and no conceivable means of being applied (3A + 5A); an individual with an intensely overactive, discriminating mind – quite divorced from his heart (3A + 5A); etc.

2. The phase of conflict; pure soul energy conflicts with personality force: The essential conflict between the ray three soul and the ray five personality is the struggle between the spiritual need to comprehend abstract thoughts related to the divine Plan, and the personal tendency to confine the mind to narrow, materialistic, concrete thinking.

3. The soul/personality integration process from the perspective of the consciousness identified primarily with the third ray soul: It will be the task of the third ray soul to expand the theoretical horizon of the fifth ray personality. The soul seeks the broadest possible abstract comprehension of a wide variety of interrelated variables; the personality prefers to focus strictly and concretely on that which lies before it. The soul seeks to induce in the personal consciousness a sense of implication and relationship. Being well–aware of the abstract *category* to which every concrete 'thing' belongs, the soul hopes to lift the focus of the personality from the specific to the general. However, the third ray soul is faced with a personality which insists upon a close and concrete approach to particular objects of interest; the soul, conversely, focuses upon the broad and distant perspectives which reveal the general context in which things are placed. The soul, therefore, must instill in the personality the capacity for broad and intelligent generalization. It must teach the personality to think in terms of the *abstract meaning* of the knowledge acquired or discovered. On the highest levels of mind, something akin to the essential truth *can* be discovered. The soul knows this; the concrete–thinking, fifth ray personality does not.

4. The soul/personality integration process from the perspective of the consciousness identified with the fifth ray personality: The fifth ray personality will quite possibly experience the third ray pressure towards integration as a blurring of its sharply focussed vision. The personality wishes to see every particular thing with utmost clarity, allowing no detail to escape examination. As soul consciousness begins to pervade the personal consciousness, however, the eyes of the personality are drawn further and further away from those few, small, isolated objects of interest upon which it had been focusing. As the vantage point of vision recedes, more and more objects of potential interest are revealed by the rapidly enlarging horizon. The exact details of these objects are not distinct, however, their mutual relationships as co–variables within a single context *are.* This soul–inspired process of *abstraction* is (initially, at least) not comfortable for the personality, which strains forward to recapture the closer view; it does not yet care to view the larger "web of relationships." And yet, gradually, it begins to dawn upon the personal consciousness, that specialized knowledge, isolated from the larger context of variables is a significant limitation. The fifth ray personality has, it seems, always wanted to know more and more about less and less; now, from deep within its consciousness, arises the contrary urge which can be expressed as wanting to know less and less about more and more. At any rate, a broadening of the field of knowledge is in order. The personality discovers that the mind which thinks about relationships between *many things* instead of *few*, can be just as active as before – even more so – but a new flexibility and scope are required. At length, the personal consciousness, abandons its insistence upon exhaustive knowledge, and begins to take delight in the relativistic universe. It abandons its dread of the large and the general; it accepts a new fluidity, and no longer insists upon absolutely fixed and definite mental outlines.

5. The ideal expression of the combination of the ray three soul and the ray five personality: Intelligent comprehension and creative activity are expressed with complete respect for accuracy. Theory is well supported by fact. Broad conceptions are reinforced by a mastery of detailed particulars. The individual is equally at home with thoughts which are vast in scope or focused for "pinpoint accuracy." The highest flights of abstract thinking can with facility be translated into suitable technical applications. Talent for higher mathematics is supported by excellent skills in applied mathematics. Those endowed with this combination of rays have a wide comprehension of abstract realities accompanied by the capacity to discover the reflections of such realities in concrete form. This is perhaps the most mentally astute of all the combinations; the power to analyze is nowhere stronger. They have the further ability to speculate intelligently about the future, and to support their speculations by reliable, factual data. Here, also, we may find considerable facility for interdisciplinary comprehension, the quality of which is enhanced by a knowledge of many specifics from each of the various disciplines. The ability to see the abstract blueprints and significant trends of any issues is complemented by highly–developed empirical and observational powers. Ideas for ingenious utilitarian inventions can, under the combined influence of these energies, be made into technically workable actualities. Outstanding business abilities are reinforced by solid commonsense and technical "know–how." Business is wedded to science. The manifold thoughts of an unusually fertile mind become both specific and immediately applicable. This combination can create the extremely versatile and flexible thinker who knows *exactly* what he is talking about.

6. The combined effect of the two integration formulae: The primary integration formula is *Stillness*, keyed to the third ray soul. The secondary integration formula is *Detachment*, keyed to the fifth ray personality. The first formula corrects third ray tendencies towards a busy scattering of attention, wasted thought, and physical overactivity (with their resultant disturbances and obscurations of consciousness), whereas the second formula corrects the fifth ray tendencies towards mental attachment to matter, and an obsessive preoccupation with investigating or manipulating concrete form while ignoring the reality of that which is "formless." Used together, these two formulae provide the individual striving for soul/personality integration with the combined quality of 'detached stillness' (i.e., the detachment [from excessive interest in the modifications of material substance] which leads to that inner quietude in which the intelligent Plan of the soul can be intelligently registered). The individual, released from purposeless activity and from a mental focus upon the outer material form, achieves a concentrated mental sensitivity to the soul. The proper use of the formulae make it possible for him to cultivate a less crystallized, more spiritually–penetrating personal consciousness, supportive of those rare moments of exalted consciousness when, pervaded by the presence of the soul, he stands silent and still, intent upon hearing, and then executing with all his creative intelligence, a Plan greater in every way than his own tiny plans.

In the earlier stages of evolution, before successfully applying these formulae, such an individual often finds himself actively engrossed in materialism and utterly focused upon the *appearance* of matter to the exclusion of its animating principle – its *life*. He is endlessly restless, and intellectually preoccupied with the external evidence of something subtle and subjective which he does not sense, and which he would not even wish to understand if he did. Activity and mentality obscure his reality. He is convinced of his intelligence, and of the foolishness of those who believe in the reality of intangibles. He thinks and does too much; he feels and knows too little. And thus he cannot find his way back to the center of his being where Divine Intelligence stands revealed.

The intelligent use of these two formulae, however, transmutes the abuses of the past. The individual learns, primarily, to act and think only in accordance with the divinely intelligent Plan, and his growing secondary ability to discriminate between matter and *That* which is the living cause of all things material, enables him to manipulate matter purely for the expression of spirit. He becomes a quieted, refocused individual, sensitive to the divine intelligence of his soul, and forever free from the illusion that matter is, itself, reality. This highly active and mental individual becomes transformed into the intelligent servant of "things not seen."

7. **Some examples of vocational aptitudes and orientations relating to the combination of the third ray soul and the fifth ray personality:**
   * the intelligent executive who avails himself of the latest scientific developments in his field
   * the resourceful business person who always "has a handle" on the numbers generated in all aspects of his business
   * the intellectual with formidable powers of definition
   * the theorist who insists upon research and experimentation in order to confirm his theories
   * the "far–out" professor with a knack for helping his students distinguish truth from error
   * the academician who thinks with great precision
   * the historian who "verifies every detail with patient accuracy" (*Esoteric Psychology, Vol. I*, p. 205)
   * the philosopher who tends towards logical positivism
   * the planner who avails himself of the latest technology whenever possible
   * the mathematician "who soars into heights of abstract thought and calculation, and who can also bring his results down to practical scientific use" (*Esoteric Psychology, Vol. I*, p. 205)
   * the strategist who invariably takes all pertinent facts and figures into his calculations
   * the creative thinker with a flair for mechanical invention
   * the magician whose approach to his art is utterly scientific
   * the articulate communicator who expresses himself with utter lucidity
   * the philanthropist who values and endows scientific research
   * the financial analyst whose analyses are extremely trustworthy
   * the broker who bases advice to his clients upon a careful analysis of highly accurate data
   * the writer who is a master of the pen
   * the critic who can substantiate the reason for his every criticism

   In general: vocations and professions which require acute intelligence (whether active or abstract), great adaptability and resourcefulness, abundant creative and communicative abilities, and (frequently) strong business aptitudes, *as well as* keen analytical abilities, the capacity for research, and scientific and/or technical expertise.

8. A proposed list of well-known individuals (historical, contemporary, fictional or mythological) whose soul ray can reasonably be considered the third, with a strong, subsidiary fifth ray influence (whether or not the fifth ray is, strictly speaking, the personality ray):

Archimedes: Greek mathematician, scientist and inventor. He is considered the founder of theoretical mechanics, and pioneered the deducing of mathematical laws from experimental observations.

Aristotle: Greek philosopher, logician and scientist. Aristotle is considered the most eminent representative of the Realist school of philosophy in the history of Western thought.

Isaac Asimov: author of an extraordinary variety of books on both science and science fiction, founder of Mensa (a society limited to those of extremely high intelligence). Ray four energy also seems to be significantly present.

David Boehm: theoretical physicist, author of *Wholeness and the Implicate Order*

Rudolf Carnap: original and leading exponent of Logical Positivism

Isaac Newton: English physicist and mathematician who was the culminating figure in the scientific revolution of the 17th century. A strong seventh ray influence is evident, as is the influence of the first ray.

John von Neuman: mathematician, inventor of the modern computer

Some Contrasts Between the Ray 3 Soul and the Ray 6 Personality

Ray 3 Soul		Ray 6 Personality
* spiritual intelligence	vs.	* all-consuming personal desire
* preservation of intellectual values	vs.	* recourse to emotionalism
* great capacity for abstract reasoning	vs.	* a tendency to emphasize blind, unreasoning faith
* the wisdom of a relativistic world view	vs.	* unbending absolutism
* tentative philosophical perspectives	vs	* unwisely-assumed certainty
* breadth of intellectual comprehension	vs.	* passionate narrowness
* original, creative thought	vs.	* over-eagerness to be guided
* soul-inspired, individualistic thinking	vs.	* an easy relinquishment of personal authority
* detachment based upon broad vision and an intelligently critical world view	vs.	* intense, uncritical attachment to both people and ideals
* the cautious handling of the consequences of action	vs.	* often oblivious to the consequences of action
* the reservation of judgement until all pertinent variables have been considered	vs.	* hasty leaping to conclusions under emotional impulse
* wise handling of economic contingencies	vs.	* impractical idealism in the handling of financial affairs
* adaptability, expediency and efficiency	vs.	* rigidly unadaptable in the pursuit of chosen goals
* astute in the assessment of implications	vs.	* gullible and blind to implications
* understanding the value of multiple options	vs.	* restricted (for better or worse) to one, undeviating way
* fertile, creative mentality	vs.	* imitates the object of devotion
* sagacious in the calculation of the future	vs.	* rushes into the future without reasoned forethought
* wise in the ways of the world	vs.	* foolishly 'otherworldly'

The Integration Process for Individuals with a Ray 3 Soul and a Ray 6 Personality

1. The pre-spiritual phase; soul energy appropriated by a selfish personality:

At this pre-spiritual phase of evolutionary unfoldment, the individual's motives (based upon the personality distortion of third ray soul energy, and the self-centered use of sixth ray personality force), are to achieve a cleverly intelligent, self-serving mastery of circumstances and the environment *as well as* the uncompromising satisfaction of the ideals and goals to which the personality is passionately devoted. The person wants, primarily, to demonstrate his 'superior' intelligence at every opportunity, manipulate money and other people for his own material and intellectual satisfaction, keep incessantly busy in the pursuit of his own self-centered interests, and evade responsibilities through selfish, strategic planning, but he *also* wants to ignore everything except the object or path of his devotion, spurn even reasonable, mundane responsibilities if they do not relate specifically to his quest, fanatically follow his ideal regardless of destructive consequences, and cling desperately to that which he believes he loves.

Negatively and glamorously these two ray influences can combine to produce: the manipulative person who will "pull any strings" to fulfill his ideals; the devious opportunist for whom a 'noble end' or a high ideal justifies any means (3B + 6); the amoral schemer who pretends to high ideals and noble aims in order to accomplish his ends; the materialistic person who seeks to arouse enthusiasm and intense desire in others purely for his own commercial advantage (3B + 6B); the "con-artist" who knows how to play upon people's dreams and emotions (3B + 6); one who is utterly devoted to making money (3B + 6); the impractical thinker animated by unrealistic ideals (3A + 6); one whose vague and abstracted thought process is matched by his emotion-impelled obliviousness to the normal requirements of physical plane living (3A + 6); one whose confused thinking is further weakened by bewildered idealism (3A + 6); the philosopher who idealistically refuses to deal with money or assume any kind of financial responsibility (3A + 6A); the metaphysician who is totally devoted to the unattainable (3A + 6); one who, having reached certain conclusions through fallacious reasoning, seeks passionately to impose those conclusions upon others (3 + 6B); one who is not only extremely critical but extremely biased; the intellectual who becomes unreasonably devoted to his own thought (3A + 6); the theorist who passionately spreads his ideals far and wide without stopping to consider whether they are really true (3A + 6B); one who is torn in the struggle between faith and reason (3A + 6); the hyperactive, 'busy-all-the-time' person who drives himself (and others) incessantly (3B + 6B); one who is always scattered and "spread too thin," but who refuses to give up any of his activities, forcing himself to do them all (3B + 6B); one who wearies others psychologically and physically because he never stops (3 + 6B); one who is a virtual 'expert' in futile adventures and wasted energy (3 + 6B); etc.

2. The phase of conflict; pure soul energy conflicts with personality force: The essential conflict between the ray three soul and the ray six personality is the struggle between the spiritual need to apply abstract reasoning to the understanding and manifestation of the Divine Plan, and irrational, personal devotion to desires, ideals and enthusiasms which prevent intelligent cooperation with the divine Plan.

3. The soul/personality integration process from the perspective of the consciousness identified primarily with the third ray soul: It will be the task of the third ray soul to make the sixth ray personality more thoughtful and more reasonable. The soul with its great capacity for highly intelligent, abstract thinking is faced with a personality which often chooses not to think; it would prefer to remain blinded and bewildered by intense emotion, devotion and idealism. The soul seeks to instill a sense of perspective within the personal consciousness, but perspective requires a de-intensification of the unbalanced, over-emphatic focus with which the sixth ray personality habitually faces its few, all-absorbing interests. The third ray soul envisions the *many* – the wide variety of interrelated energies and forces which are woven together to create divine manifestation; the personality sees only the *one* – its obsessive enthusiasm of the moment. The soul seeks to stimulate the personal consciousness with a vision of the many possibilities, the many relationships, the many variables, no one of which is all–important, and every one of which must, at length, be *comprehended* by the acute, abstract mind. It is the soul's difficult task to teach the personality to release its tenacious grip (physical or psychological) upon its one particular object of all–consuming devotion, and take *at least several things* in its 'hands'; then, perhaps, the soul can instruct the personality to use these several things together. Anything to bring some respect for variety into the monochromatic personality life! How can the soul become the "divine manipulator" if the personality will not release its tenacious grip upon one thing. The soul needs a "free hand" to fulfill its destiny.

4. The soul/personality integration process form the perspective of the consciousness identified primarily with the sixth ray personality: As the third ray soul exerts its pressure towards integration, the personality will feel itself somewhat distracted from its all–consuming interests. The personality desires only to have more and more of that which it loves: it wants to dwell only upon its ideals, or draw ever–closer to its object of devotion. It has no time for *other* things, especially *many* things. It has no wish to widen its interests; its loyalties are absolutely determined, "once and for all" (until, that is, the loyalties change suddenly, becoming, then, the *'real* loyalties' – absolutely determined, of course, "once and for all.)" The personality becomes distressed as, from deep within its consciousness, there arises a vision of numerous possible interests and activities. It may strenuously attempt to reinforce its former limited focus, but, slowly, there grows the suspicion that there is more to the world than the few things, ideals or people it loved so well; in short, there grows an uncomfortable feeling that something has been missing all along. The personality senses that it has grown rigid through one–pointedness, and further, that it has become *unthinking* because it had believed that all important issues were decided. New learnings arise: mobility, lightness of touch, a willingness to reserve judgment until all the variables have been considered, and a recognition of the need to see the broader picture instead of rushing off to idealize one small part of that picture. The personality sees that it must restrain its zeal and begin to *compare* the many possible ways and means.

5. The ideal combination of the third ray soul and the sixth ray personality: Intelligent conceptions and creative ideas are expressed enthusiastically and zealously. The individual is an unending source of unsuspected alternatives and options which he easily "sells" because of his enthusiasm and reasonableness. A life filled with resourceful activity is lived with intense optimism. Creative business practices are pursued with continuous drive; the individual is a master of intelligent adaptation and he persists until he succeeds. Intelligence and forethought master ardent devotion and the unthinking pursuit of "causes," and yet the mind uses emotional energy productively. There is a gift for speculation and the faith to follow it. The rational masters the irrational, and yet emotional ardor remains to stimulate rational pursuits. Great value is placed upon the capacities of the higher mind, with the personality fueling the aspiration to engage in the higher kind of thinking. Theories and systems are advanced with excitement and conviction; the individual believes completely in his ideas. Theological thinking is supported by great faith. Wide, complex and sophisticated views are presented with persuasive emotional appeal. Much extroversion is possible in this combination, as the individual seeks to motivate others by impressing them with the content of his best thinking. There is a pronounced ability to project and adapt many ideas in the most persuasive and convincing manner.

6. The combined effect of the two integration formulae: The primary integration formula is *Stillness*, keyed to the third ray soul. The secondary integration formula is proposed as *Restraint*, keyed to the sixth ray personality. The first formula corrects third ray tendencies towards a busy scattering of attention, wasted thought, and physical over-activity (with their resultant disturbances and obscurations of consciousness), whereas the second formula corrects the unrestrained, passionate pursuit of the 'partial' and 'peripheral,' so common to the emotionally undisciplined sixth ray personality. Used together, these two formulae provide the individual striving for soul/personality integration with the composite quality of 'restrained stillness' (i.e., the personal and emotional restraint which quiets the personality field and allows an intent and *still* focussing upon the abstract realities of the Divine Plan as comprehended by the acutely intelligent soul). These formulae subdue commotion within all fields of the energy system, restraining the urge to rush 'noisily' from the center to the periphery. Thus, correct application of the formulae make it possible for the individual to cultivate a more moderate, tempered and emotionally-disciplined personal consciousness, supportive of those rare moments of exalted consciousness when, pervaded by the presence of the soul, he stands silent and still, intent upon hearing, and then executing with all his creative intelligence, a Plan greater in every way than his own tiny plans.

In the earlier stages of evolution, before successfully applying these formulae, an individual with this combination of rays often finds himself utterly preoccupied with far too many non-essential activities, rushing in a frenzy from activity to activity. He is restless, unrestrained, and utterly unwilling to disengage from the impassioned commotion which he so consistently generates. No one wastes more energy on more false hopes than he. No one runs about so ceaselessly, so far from "home."

The intelligent use of these two formulae, however, transmutes the abuses of the past. The "Word" of the soul breaks upon the ear of one who is usually far too busy and overheated to hear it. The individual learns, primarily, to act and think only in accordance with the Divine Plan, and his growing secondary ability to restrain his passionate desires, and redirect his aspirations away from the non-essential and towards that which is spiritually essential, ensures the intelligent soul of a faithful and utterly focused instrument for the manifestation of that aspect of the Plan for which it is responsible.

7. Some examples of vocational aptitudes and orientations relating to the combination of the third ray soul and the sixth ray personality:

* the intelligent executive animated by high idealism

* the resourceful business person who excells at promoting his business

* the economist who passionately espouses a particular economic theory

* the business executive who his devoted to his firm
* the intellectual who has the conviction to live up to his highest and best thinking
* the theorist who will not deviate from his theoretical conclusions
* the futurist as visionary
* the academician who feels humble before the greatness of the human intellect
* the historian whose major focus is the history of religion
* the philosopher with a particular interest in mysticism or metaphysics
* the planner of idealistic (or utopian) enterprises
* the "far–out" professor whose enthusiasm serves as a tremendous motivation for his students
* the strategist who works to advance certain "special interests" in which he thoroughly believes
* the creative thinker with a talent for propagating his ideas
* the magician whose attitude in conducting the magical process is one of faith, receptivity and openness to guidance
* the articulate communicator with great rhetorical abilities
* the critic who criticizes with fervor and ideological conviction
* the ardent polemicist
* the passionate apologist
* the "brains" behind the "cause"
* the financial analyst who believes his figures always support a particular financial philosophy
* the broker who vigorously encourages his clients to have faith in his advice

In general: vocations and professions which require acute intelligence (whether active or abstract), great adaptability and resourcefulness, abundant creative and communicative abilities, and (frequently) strong business aptitudes, *as well as* high idealism, undeviating devotion, great enthusiasm and persistent emotional intensity.

8. A proposed list of well–known individuals (historical, contemporary, fictional or mythological) whose soul ray can reasonably be considered the third, with a strong subsidiary sixth ray (whether or not the sixth ray is strictly speaking, the personality ray):

Giordano Bruno: 16th century philosopher, astronomer and mathematician, burned at the stake by the Inquisition for his 'heretical' views

Andrew Carnegie: steel industrialist and philanthropist, author of "The Gospel of Wealth"

Joseph Goebbels: journalist, orator, leading propagandist of the Nazi Party and minister of propaganda of Adolf Hitler's Third Reich

Nicolò Machiavelli: 16th century Italian author, political theorist, statesman and patriot. It appears that the fourth and first rays were also influential.

Blaise Pascal: French religious philosopher, mathematician, scientist. His mental ray was almost certainly the fifth. His life presents a fascinating study of the battle between reason and devotion.

Leon Trotsky: the most intellectually brilliant leader of the Russian Communist revolution. Trotsky was also strongly conditioned by the first ray.

Some Contrasts Between the Ray 3 Soul and the Ray 7 Personality

Ray 3 Soul		Ray 7 Personality
* focusing consciousness within the higher dimensions of the mind	vs.	* preoccupation with the body and its instinctual nature
* realization of the many ways	vs.	* acceptance of only the socially approved and sanctioned way
* acute spiritual intelligence	vs.	* conventional, personal rituals and routines
* great capacity for abstract or metaphysical thinking	vs.	* strictly objective thought and action focused on external patterns
* deep and searching thought which reserves judgment pending the consideration of multiple variables	vs.	* superficial judgmentalism
* great adaptability, flexibility and versatility	vs.	* imprisoned by rigid conditioning and repetitive practices
* creative, independent thinking	vs.	* a too–ready acceptance of established forms
* emphasis upon the intellectual essence behind the form	vs.	* over–valuation of form to content; captivated by appearances
* a soul–inspired vision of many possible intellectual orientations	vs.	* sectarianism
* the capacity for diversified simultaneous activities	vs.	* the limitation of rigidly following one strictly procedural activity at a time
* remarkable cleverness and inventiveness	vs.	* locked into tradition and precedent; often dull and predictable
* understanding how to dispense with details when developing broad conceptions	vs.	* hampered by excessive attention to very small details
* capacity to create highly flexible plans which evolve as need requires	vs.	* inflexibility in the creation and changing of plans
* realization of the value of a multi–optioned approach to accomplishment	vs.	* feeling constrained to do everything "by the book"

The Integration Process for the Individual with a Ray 3 Soul and a Ray 7 Personality

1. The pre–spiritual phase; soul energy appropriated by a selfish personality: At this pre–spiritual phase of evolutionary unfoldment, the individual's motives (based upon the personality distortion of third ray soul energy, and the self–centered use of seventh ray personality force) are to achieve a cleverly intelligent, self-serving mastery of circumstances and the environment, *as well as* a rigidly ritualized, tightly ordered life conducive to physical plane safety, security and 'perfected' materialistic living. The person wants, primarily, to demonstrate his 'superior' intelligence at every opportunity, manipulate money and other people for his own material and intellectual satisfaction, keep incessantly busy in the pursuit of his own material and self-centered interests, and evade responsibilities through selfish, strategic planning, but he *also* wants a highly predictable (hence, relatively risk-free) life, to avoid having to think for himself or act upon his own initiative, and to have the solid assurance that all his instinctual appetites and imagined material needs will be satisfied on schedule.

Negatively and glamorously, these two ray influences can combine to produce: one who manipulates the physical environment solely to provide for his own selfish safety and security (3B + 7); the magician who wields ritualistic control over material forces purely for his own benefit (3B + 7C); one who levels excessive intellectual criticism at those who depart from conventional modes of thinking (3A + 7A); the judicial thinker whose reasoning always lends support to a strictly literal interpretation of the law (3A + 7A); the clever opportunist who misuses his intelligence to achieve greater social status and position (3 + 7A); the selfish materialist for whom everything of value must be tangible or visible (3B + 7A); one who seeks to acquire vast monetary wealth so that it can be transformed into the *appearance* of wealthiness, thereby elevating his reputation (3B + 7); one who wishes to acquire large sums so that he may erect monuments to himself (3B + 7); one who believes that everyone and everything can be bought and sold – the economic determinist (3B + 7); the impractical thinker who specializes in untenable schemes to transform the social order (3A + 7B); the individual with an overly fertile mind and imagination who foolishly and constantly attempts to materialize the most improbable schemes (3 + 7B); the unethical individual who advances his self-interest by "playing the bureaucratic game" (3B + 7A); an individual adept at "pulling strings" within "the establishment" of which he is solidly a part (3B + 7A); the calculating materialist who joins fraternal orders strictly to advance his business success (3B + 7C); one who is ever seeking to "revise the system" so that it works to his own advantage (3B + 7B); etc.

2. The phase of conflict; pure soul energy conflicts with personality force: The essential conflict between the ray three soul and the ray seven personality is the struggle between the spiritual need to understand and lay plans to manifest the abstract "blueprints" within the Mind of God, and the personal desire to build or manifest concrete forms purely for one's own safety, security and what might be called one's 'stability within the realm of matter.'

3. The soul/personality integration process from the perspective of the consciousness identified primarily with the third ray soul: It will be the task of the third ray soul to invest with meaning and flexibility the many forms created by the seventh ray personality. The soul must teach the personality to think of the implications of what it does rather than simply *perform* long-established routines and rituals. The consciousness of the third ray soul is broad, and within it, many things are seen in comparison; relative values emerge in perspective. The soul with its breadth of vision is faced with a personality which is content to repeat, without really understanding that which it repeats. Repetition brings the illusion of safety and security, which the seventh ray personality is intent upon achieving. The thoughtful and thought-provoking soul must lift the personality from its numbing "cultural trance," thus ending the cycle of mindless repetition – the cycle of not really *knowing* what one is *doing*. The soul with its great love of change and variety is frustrated by the dull, personal customs of its ritualistic personality. If there must be rituals, let the rituals be designed for intelligent ends! If there must be repeated personal observances, let such be filled with meaning. The soul sees its personality "locked into" predictable forms of response. And yet, evolution and development call for adaptability and flexible responsiveness. The soul, therefore, attempts to teach the personality how to awaken to the many changes occurring around it, and how to meet those changes with forms of thought and action which result in *progress* – not simply the repetition of past patterns. The flexible third ray soul wants the personality to *change its habits*.

4. The soul/personality integration process from the perspective of the consciousness identified primarily with the seventh ray personality: The third ray pressure towards integration will be felt by the seventh ray personality as a destabilization. The personality feels most comfortable when it is allowed to continue doing what it has always done – rhythmically, ritualistically, repeatedly. The personality feels threatened and shakey, as the soul calls for intelligent *change*. The personality believes that many forms of action require no further thought, and certainly not deep and probing thought. If the performance is solid and dependable, why interfere with tortuous questions, doubts, comparisons, and 'time-wasting' analyses? And yet, from deep within the personal consciousness (that area of consciousness which is the province of the soul) there arises the disturbing thought that all the many personal patterns (comfortable and reassuring though they be) may, after all, be quite *meaningless*, or antiquated, or 'mal-adaptable.' The challenged personality may counter by attempting to be even stricter in its ritualized observances, but gradually, its will to repeat the old is undermined. It begins to realize that all over the world are peoples, groups and individuals with their own customary ways of doing things, and that *no one way* is the absolutely right way. The personality begins to learn the need for thoughtful comparison. Under soul impulse it begins to examine the many patterns *relative* to each other, and the realization of the indisputable actuality and validity of the *many* patterns begins to replace its earlier fixation upon "my pattern," "our pattern," or the "perfect pattern." Even when the personality is bent upon the radical work of restructuring and reorganizing (type 7B), the soul forces it to *think* about the relative significance of the new patterns it is creating. The personality, of course, feels frustrated that it can no longer 'hide' behind and within formality, but at length it realizes that there are divine patterns and designs which a new flexibility of mind can begin to reveal. Above all, the personality learns that deep *thinking* must correct superficial *doing* in order to transform it into *intelligent doing*.

5. The ideal expression of the combination of the ray three soul and the ray seven personality: Intelligent conceptions and creative ideas are expressed in a precise and highly-organized manner. This is the combination of an ingenious, yet utterly practical individual – adept in the art of intelligent materialization. Virtually anything he conceives, he can manifest, however, the creative conception always takes precedence over the chosen means of manifestation. He never allows himself to be limited by rigid, sequential proceduralism; of course, he understands the value of right procedure, but he always remains a flexible, creative thinker – *using* form, and not used by it. This individual would make an excellent planner. He would be equipped with far-seeing vision, wide-mindedness and an intelligent grasp of all the many trends and variables to be considered; but he would also understand the immediate situation, and the practical demands of daily operations. This is also a superb financial combination. Both the third and seventh rays are related to the matter aspect – both in its etheric and dense material forms. Money is simply a materialization of etheric energy – crystallized prana. Just as the individual with this combination has a talent for manipulating the fluid ethers, he also understands the fluidity of money and makes it serve the process of manifestation. The magical potential of this combination is very great: ray three is often called the "magician" and ray seven the "ritualist." Magic is essentially the art and science of manifestation; it is a process of precipitating ideas into form. The individual with this combination understands the many ideas, and also the ritualistic methods of clothing those ideas with a physical sheath. This combination, more than any other, is adapted to intelligent living upon the physical plane. At an advanced stage of evolution, it produces the supremely intelligent executive in the *business* of manifesting the Divine Plan.

6. The combined effect of the two integration formulae: The primary integration formula is *Stillness*, keyed to the third ray soul. The secondary integration formula is proposed as *Orientation*, keyed to the seventh ray personality. The first formula corrects third ray tendencies towards a busy scattering of attention, wasted thought and physical over–activity (with their resultant disturbances and obscurations of consciousness), whereas the second formula corrects seventh ray tendencies towards selfish building and organizing according to short–sighted, materially–minded personal plans, but without an attentive orientation to the Divine Design as revealed by the soul. Used together, these formulae provide the individual striving for soul/personality integration with the composite quality of 'oriented stillness' (i.e., the attentive spiritual orientation of the personality which promotes an intent and *still* focusing upon the abstract realities of the Divine Plan as comprehended by the soul). These formulae bring the "light of the East" to the personality consciousness, and with this light comes the assurance that all building of forms will be guided by the intelligent intention of the soul. This intention, once so difficult to apprehend (because of the 'noise,' commotion and restlessness resulting from the negative reflection of third ray energy within the personality field) can now be truly divined in the clarifying stillness. The attentive, spiritually–oriented personality is given the intuitive realization of the exact design which must be built. The process of materialization can then safely begin, supervised by the intelligent soul, whose influence filters through the transparent stillness into the consciousness of the personality. Thus, these formulae make it possible for the individual to cultivate a more aligned and spiritually–oriented *personal consciousness,* supportive of those rare moments of *exalted consciousness* when, pervaded by the presence of the soul, he stands still and silent, intent upon hearing, and then executing with all his creative intelligence, a Plan greater by far than his own tiny plans.

In the earlier stages of evolution, before successfully applying these formulae, an individual with this ray combination often finds himself engaged in intense physical and mental activity upon the periphery of his being – arranging, manipulating, building and manifesting that which has no true relation either to his soul purpose or the divine Plan. Far from his true spiritual center, he builds to suit himself and according his own varied and spiritually–irrelevant plans. His materializations are not attuned to the Divine Mind.

The intelligent use of the two formulae, however, transmutes the abuses of the past, guaranteeing that all thought created, and all action taken, will be in line with the intelligent will of the soul, and, consequently, in line with as much of the Will of the Great Architect of the Universe as that soul can understand. The individual employing these formulae thus learns, primarily, to act and think only in accordance with the Divine Plan, and his growing secondary ability to rightly orient himself towards the eternal Light (so that when he builds, the Light shines upon and through his work) ensures that the great intelligence of his soul will be expressed through appropriately constructed forms.

7. Some examples of vocational aptitudes and orientations relating to the combination of the third ray soul and the seventh ray personality:

* the intelligent executive who is a superb organizer
* the resourceful business-person with the ability to create smoothly functioning groups and organizations
* the intellectual with a "hands on" approach
* the theorist who seeks to create tangible structures and patterns for the implementation of his ideas
* the academician who loves the rituals of academia
* the "far-out" professor who always comes up with unconventional ideas which are essentially useful, practical and "down-to-earth"
* the futurist with a vision of many innovative patterns of human relationship and interaction
* the historian with a special interest in social mores and customs
* the philosopher who focuses upon law and ethics
* the planner who charts and diagrams every aspect of a plan
* the strategist whose schemes respect the prevailing rules and regulations, and never overstep the bounds of decency
* the creative thinker with an impressive ability to manifest his thoughts
* the magician with a comprehensive yet practical understanding of "times and cycles"
* the articulate communicator who chooses his words meticulously and polishes every phrase
* the informative writer who focuses upon the meaning of human behavior
* the critic of social customs and mores
* the financial analyst with a good record for prediction and reliability
* the broker who cautiously follows well-accepted procedures

In general: vocations and professions which require acute intelligence (whether active or abstract), great adaptability and resourcefulness, abundant creative and communicative abilities, and (frequently) strong business aptitudes, *as well as* the power to organize or reorganize, the ability to build, a facility for creating or maintaining standards, and a capacity to skillfully manifest ideas through form.

8. A list of well-known individuals (historical, contemporary, fictional or mythological) whose soul ray can reasonably be considered the third, with a strong subsidiary seventh ray influence (whether or not the seventh ray is, strictly speaking, the personality ray):

Euclid of Alexandria: the most prominent mathematician of antiquity. His treatise on Geometry, the *Elements* has exerted a continuous and major influence on human affairs.

James A. Baker III: political strategist, White House Chief of Staff, Secretary of the Treasury under Ronald Reagan. Baker has been something of a "magician" in the deft and skillful manifestation of his intentions. A ray one influence is also noticeable.

Henry George: economist and land reformer

Marc Edmund Jones: astrologer and occult philosopher

Immanuel Kant: the foremost thinker of the Enlightenment, and one of the great philosophers of all time. A pronounced fifth ray emphasis is also present.

Johannes Kepler: Renaissance astronomer and astrologer who discovered the three principles of planetary motion, through which he clarified the spatial organization of the solar system. The fifth ray was also prominent in his ray chart.

Andrew Mellon: financier and philanthropist

Julius Rosenwald: merchant and philanthropist who paid for the contruction of over 5,000 schools for Negroes in 15 southern states. He also established Chicago's Museum of Science and Industry.

Soul/Personality Combinations with a Ray Four Soul

Some Contrasts Between the Ray 4 Soul and the Ray 1 Personality

Ray 4 Soul		Ray 1 Personality
* spiritual beauty	vs.	* personal power
* the capacity for promoting reconciliation	vs.	* the creation of interpersonal enmity through inconsiderate self–assertiveness
* one who is characterized by the great spiritual gift of intra–psychic conflict leading to harmony within and without	vs.	* the insistence upon being strong, refusing to allow intra–psychic conflict because it is seen as a sign of personal weakness
* facility for maintaining the midway point between the pairs of opposites (soul and personality)	vs.	* immovable consolidation of consciousness within the lower, personal self
* exquisite sensitivity to color	vs.	* ignoring of subtle differences in color and quality
* cultivation of imagination as a spiritual faculty expressive of divinity	vs.	* tough personal realism
* openness to artistic inspiration	vs.	* hardness and insensitivity
* great facility as a bridging agent producing divine harmony and unification	vs.	* a refusal to extend oneself to others; reaffirming one's own position and refusing to consider positions taken by others
* the exaltation of aesthetic creativity	vs.	* focus upon survival and self–promotion
* pronounced capacity for attunement and rapport with others	vs.	* personal isolation and separation from others
* talent for the artistic dramatization of soul qualities	vs.	* the unadorned expression of personal will
* the soul–inspired ability to so identify with others that a facility for impersonating them is easily achieved; the natural actor	vs.	* the identity of the lower self is so emphasized that the individual is inflexibly trapped within it; one who can only identify with himself or herself; the isolation of egoism

The Integration Process for the Individual with a Ray 4 Soul and a Ray 1 Personality

1. The pre–spiritual phase; soul energy appropriated by a selfish personality: At this pre–spiritual phase of evolutionary unfoldment, the individual's motives (based upon the personality distortion of fourth ray soul energy, and the self–centered use of first ray personality force) are to achieve an agreeable feeling of personal peace and harmony through tension–releasing expression of conflicting bio–psychic impulses, *as well as* great personal power, arising from the unrestrained imposition of the personal will. The person wants, primarily, to be constantly surrounded by what he considers beautiful or attractive, to be spontaneously self–expressive without discipline or control, self–indulgently dramatic or moody (as he pleases), and greatly appreciated by others for his colorful, unpredictable temperament, but he *also* wants to dominate and control others and wield authority unopposed.

Negatively and glamorously, these two ray energies can combine to produce: an moody, unstable person who "takes his moods out on others" through violence or cruelty (4B + 1); a capricious, temperamental individual who feels sufficiently self-important to inflict his temperamentalism on others (4B + 1); one who feels he must be stimulated by beauty at all times, believes that he has a natural 'right' to such privilege, and demands that others provide it; one who, convinced that he is a great artist, expects others to be equally convinced, and pay him tribute accordingly; the narcissistic artist who believes that it is his prerogative to say, do or create anything he pleases; the frustrated artist who believes that people do not recognize his true greatness; one who, loving the stimulation of battle, irrationally plunges into conflict and strife with very destructive consequences for himself and others (4B + 1B); one who enjoys promoting crisis because of the scope it gives him for the exercise of his will (4B + 1); one whose desire for peace is so strong that he forces others to desist from any kind of conflict, even when such conflict is productive and clarifying (4A + 1A); one who, feeling unconfident and unstable, overcompensates by assuming a bombastic, dictatorial manner (4B + 1B); one who is consumed with his own suffering, and perversely isolates himself from others to prolong that suffering (4B + 1); a manic-depressive temperament that leads to extreme aggression or morbid self-destructiveness (4B + 1B); unbridled spontaneity, egotistically expressed; exaggerated personal dramatics expressed with vehemence (4B + 1B); etc.

2. The phase of conflict; pure soul energy conflicts with personality force: The essential conflict between the ray four soul and the ray one personality is the struggle between spiritual need to create and express beauty and harmony, and the personal desire to achieve power and preeminence even if it means destroying inter-personal harmony, or harmony between the self and the environment.

3. The soul/personality integration process from the perspective of the consciousness identified primarily with the fourth ray soul: It will be the task of the fourth ray soul to refine and sensitize the first ray personality. The 'cultured' soul is faced with a personality that often hardens itself to fine perceptions, nuances, subtle contrasts – for when survival is at stake, and power is the issue, the love of the beautiful weakens the resolve (at least the first ray personality thinks so). The soul seeks to correct this misperception; it seeks to lift the focused personal consciousness towards a realization of the motivating *power* that lies in beauty and harmony. The personality believes it is most powerful when least sensitive, and so it refuses to dwell upon that which delights, enraptures, captivates. The soul, however, slowly begins to pervade the personal consciousness with intimations of the beautiful, "moving" and inspiring the personality in spite of itself. By subjecting the personality to constant constrasts, the soul breaks down crystallized insensitivity. Gradually the soul wears away the preoccupied focus upon the separated self, and provides currents of beauty that are so irresistable, that the personality is lured away from its stubborn refusal to experience aesthetic loveliness.

From another perspective, the soul must teach the personality that compromise is not capitulation. The soul understands the value of both sides of the warring "pairs of opposites"; the soul triumphs when both sides win. The personality, however, is interested in one-sided victory. It seeks undisputed triumph over an enemy, and accommodation and compromise are seen as unworthy. As soul-inspired sensitization proceeds, however, the personality begins to "feel for" its opponent. Personality isolation is gradually overcome, and bridging become possible. The soul succeeds in showing the personality that each enemy is but an aspect of its very self, and that at length (for the sake of wholeness), the enemy, too, must share in the victory.

4. The soul/personality integration process from the perspective of a consciousness identified primarily with the first ray personality: The fourth ray pressure towards integration is experienced by the first ray personality as weakening and self-division. The personality feels most comfortable when willfully carrying out its own purposes, its consciousness uncomplicated by doubts, misgivings, and reservations. It does what it *will* – undeflected and unrestrained. Its power (or, so it feels) comes from within itself; the personality stands unmoved. But from deep within its consciousenss, there begins to arise the desire to notice that which is beautiful and appealing. Pausing in the midst of powerful acts, the person finds himself fascinated and attracted by contrasting colors, by harmonious strains of music, by beautifully shaped forms. He stands there *powerless*, immobile, under the spell of loveliness. When he reawakens to his former, limited state of mind, he realizes that he has not succeeded in executing his will, and perhaps, for a time, he tries to do so even more vehemently. But the soul's enchantment continues to draw him away from his preoccupation with the exercise of crude will. The personality begins to realize that the beautiful is the desirable, and that it has been wasting its strength upon ugliness. A further realization dawns – that the beautiful provides a new and different kind of power – a power which is *moving*, animating and inspiring. Through beauty, the strength of love and harmony pervade the personal consciousness – a strength arising from perfectly adjusted (i.e. harmonious) relationship. The personality sees that personal isolation and self-accentuation bestowed only the illusion of power, but that, in a larger sense, there was only powerlessness. The personality proceeds to dedicate its strength to the expression of beauty and harmony in all relationships.

5. The ideal expression of the combination of the ray four soul and the ray one personality: The urge to create harmony and beauty is expressed dynamically. The individual may be a proponent of the finest and highest aesthetic culture, with sufficient personal power to make a striking impact upon the world. Strength and steadfastness serve the task of revealing beauty and creating loveliness. There may be a noteworthy ability to be a "peace maker," a strong "agent of reconciliation," – nor will such an individual give up until peace and reconciliation are achieved. Here is one who can demonstrate that peace is not weakness, but rather, that it is only for the strong. But if it is necessary to fight, he can be a powerful combatant – as long as the battle is in the name of peace. The individual is ideally suited to mediate, and achieve "righteous compromise," because he is known as one who has the fortitude to live by, and uphold, high, selfless principles. This combination holds a great capacity for synthesis, unifying others through harmonization, and preserving that harmony through the enforcement of essential laws. Tremendous dramatic power is a potential here; histrionic gifts become charismatic because of a commanding personal presence. This ray combination suggests one who may have great artistic abilities, and the personal determination to express them at all costs, and despite all obstacles. Here also, is the naturally great intuitive, who has the stamina to anchor his intuitions and see that they stay anchored. There is also an ability to "stand up for" the testimony of the intuition, and to put oneself "on the line" in defense of all types of sensitive receptivity, aesthetic or otherwise. This is a strong individual, able to endure and persist in his soul–appointed task of creating harmonious linkages between diverse individuals. The linkages may be within the psyche as well, and much personal strength will also be required if the task is to be completed.

6. The combined effect of the two integration formulae: The primary integration formula is *Steadfastness*, keyed to the fourth ray soul. The secondary integration formula is *Inclusion*, keyed to the first ray personality. The first formula corrects the fourth ray tendencies towards vacillation, irresoluteness, instability, indecisiveness and moral cowardice, whereas the second formula corrects the first ray tendencies towards isolated exclusivity. Used together, these two formulae provide the individual striving for soul/personality integration with the composite quality of 'inclusive steadfastness,' (i.e., the inclusive personality attitude which promotes peace on the outer planes, and a steadfast and harmoniously balanced spiritual orientation upon the inner). The formulae make it possible for the individual to cultivate a more attractive and loving personal consciousness, supportive of those rare moments of exalted consciousness when, pervaded by the presence of the soul, he stands steadfastly poised and centered between the many warring pairs of opposites – at peace with them all. From the spiritual center of his being, he goes forth as "peacemaker"; intuitively, he understands the eternal war and its eternal solution; upon the outer plane of daily living, he stands with his arms opened to an inclusive and strong embrace of the many people and situations needing the gifts of reconciliation and peace.

In the earlier stages of evolution, before successfully applying these formulae, an individual with this ray combination often finds himself embroiled in constant warfare. He rejects others, fighting with them and with himself. He becomes an isolated antagonist. He craves harmony, but causes nothing but conflict and rebuff. If he should, unexpectedly, conclude a peace, it will be nothing but partial and temporary, and soon disrupted by his own unpredictable, alienating behavior.

The intelligent use of the two formulae, however, transmutes the abuses of the past. No longer is the individual selfishly submerged in personal and environal battles; he makes himself available as a steadfast and inclusive peace–maker, resolved to mediate and assist in the harmonization of the many conflicts raging about him. By using the formulae, the individual learns, primarily, to stand so steadfastly and peacefully in the center of his being, that he brings peace and synthesis to all the warring forces, within and without, and his growing secondary ability to embrace others rather than reject them, ensures the peacemaking soul of a strong and loving personality to serve as its agent of peace in the three worlds.

7. Some examples of vocational aptitudes and orientations relating to the combination of the fourth ray soul and the first ray personality:

* the peacemaker who stands staunchly for the highest human values and principles
* the mediator who is strict and firm with both disputing parties

* the negotiator who will only negotiate from strength
* the arbitrator who will not bend the law
* the intermediary who is tireless in his bridging work
* the translator who is brief and direct
* the harmonizer who refuses to mince words
* the warrior who is an implaccable combatant
* the 'martial artist' possessed of complete self-control
* the creative artist who expresses himself fearlessly
* the beautifier who creates an effect of striking simplicity
* the painter who is daring in his use of form and color
* the composer with a taste for grandeur
* the musician who performs with power and solemnity
* the actor who excels in portrayals of strength
* the dramatist with a penchant for dramatic shock
* the architect who designs bold structures with simple lines
* the city planner with a feeling for the special requirements of governmental facilities

In general: vocations and professions which require a strong creative imagination, spontaneity, expressivity, aesthetic sensitivity, and a marked ability to bring harmony out of conflict, beauty out of ugliness, and at–one–ment out of divisiveness, *as well as* great will power, strength and stamina, the ability to stand firmly on principle, and (when necessary) the power to destroy obstacles.

8. A proposed list of well–known individuals (historical, contemporary, fictional or mythological) whose soul ray can reasonably be considered the fourth, with a strong subsidiary first ray influence (whether or not the first ray is, strictly speaking, the personality ray):

Ludwig van Beethoven: a outstanding musical genius, regarded by many as the greatest composer who ever lived. (Some have suggested that Beethoven's soul ray was the first. The first ray, however, [in addition to being the personality ray] may lie at an even deeper [perhaps Monadic] level.)

Benvenuto Cellini: artist of the Italian Renaissance – goldsmith, adventurer, autobiographer

Isadora Duncan: acknowledged prophetess of interpretive dance

Johann Wolfgang von Goethe: a German writer universally acknowledged to be one of the giants of world literature. He had the many–sidedness of the great Renaissance personalities as poet, dramatist, novelist, scientist, philosopher, critic, journalist, painter, theatre manager, statesman, educationalist, and natural philosopher. In Goethe's life, the influence of *all* the rays can be detected, but the fifth is quite present (which is, perhaps, surprising in the life of a great poet).

Pablo Piccaso: one of the most prolific and versatile artists of the 20th century. He expressed through a variety of mediums – painting, drawing, engraving, collage, sculpture, constructions, pottery, etc. The complexity and versatility of his work suggests the additional influence of the third ray.

Richard Wagner: the leading German composer of the late 19th century, creator of the operatic form called the "music drama". There is reason to believe that the fourth ray was in process of transformation into the second.

Some Contrasts Between the Ray 4 Soul and the Ray 2 Personality

Ray 4 Soul		Ray 2 Personality
* spiritual beauty	vs.	* personal love
* uncompromising preservation of beauty	vs.	* too willing to sacrifice beauty to the preservation of personal affection
* life as art and art as life	vs.	* fearful avoidance of the extremes which artistic perception and artistic living demand
* a deep compulsion to embrace the pain of beauty	vs.	* shrinking from the inseparability of beauty and pain
* insistence upon the necessary and essential spirituality of both the light and the dark	vs.	* rejecting all darkness in the attempt to create a shallow personal positivity and superficial happiness
* following the creative urge to the point of extremity	vs.	* disinclination to disrupt personal comfort by allowing creative arousal
* the spirituality of artistic passion	vs.	* a calm, too tranquil, too unexcitable disposition
* "beauty is truth and truth is beauty"	vs.	* the sense of values is too closely tied to the preservation of pleasant interpersonal warmth of feeling
* quickness of the highly imaginative, free–associative psyche	vs.	* a tendency towards quiet inertia
* strenuous mediative efforts for the sake of promoting reconciliation	vs.	* ineffectual good–naturedness
* the animated expression of the dramatic contrasts found at deep levels of individual reality	vs.	* a preference for undramatic, un–exciting living
* considerable courage to confront opposition in the cause of peace, harmony and unity; an accomplished warrior in the war that leads to peace	vs.	* personal timidity and fear of confrontation
* an irresistable urge to unify the heights and depths of human nature; reconciling the "four quarters" to complete the mandala of human identity	vs.	* reticence to deal with the unpleasant, undesirable aspects of human nature

The Integration Process for the Individual with a Ray 4 Soul and a Ray 2 Personality

1. The pre–spiritual phase; soul energy appropriated by a selfish personality: At this pre–spiritual phase of evolutionary unfoldment, the individual's motives (based upon the personality distortion of fourth ray soul energy, and the self–centered use of second ray personality force), are to achieve an agreeable feeling of personal peace and harmony through tension–releasing expression of conflicting bio–psychic impulses, *as well as* the complete fulfillment of personal love (or the complete satisfaction of studious enquiry [2B]). The person wants primarily to be constantly surrounded by what he considers beautiful or attractive, to be spontaneously self-expressive without discipline or control, self-indulgently dramatic or moody (as he pleases), and greatly appreciated by others for his colorful, unpredictable temperament, but he *also* wants to be constantly loved, consistently popular, warmly admired, well-cared-for, and to live a soft, comfortable and well-protected, well-insulated life – closely attached to those people, places and things which he loves and finds personally satisfying.

Negatively and glamorously, these two ray influences can combine to produce: an unreliable, irresponsible person who is quite helpless and ineffectual (4 + 2A); one who is not only caught up in constant suffering and crisis, but who feels an overwhelming pity for himself as well (4B + 2A); the "artistically temperamental" individual who craves popularity and constant personal support (4B + 2A); one whose "moral cowardice" is exacerbated by an insatiable "love of being loved" (4A + 2A); one who becomes petulant unless he is surrounded by 'beauty' in pleasant and comfortable surroundings (4A + 2A); one who is always compromising away principles, being too weak to take a stand (4A + 2); one who must have "peace at any price," being too soft-hearted to face any kind of unpleasantness (4A + 2A); one whose sole preoccupation is to ensure that his personal life is harmonious as well as safe and well-cushioned (4A + 2); a person who has a terrible time saying "No!" (4A + 2); one who is simply too inclusive; one who has a very difficult time moving forward, due to constant indecision and inertia (4A + 2); one who consistently relies upon being charming and attractive because he has no real capacity for initiative (4A + 2A); a person who is constantly embroiled in 'romantic' relationships and always becoming attached (4 + 2A); one who habitually finds himself "torn" between alternatives and incapable of letting go of either (4B + 2); one who thinks himself the 'world's best' liason between people because he understands them so well – the glamor of the 'all-wise' intermediary (4A + 2B); one who in mediating, softens differences unduly, being too sensitive to tolerate the tension of differences (4A + 2A); one whose intense, internal psychological conflicts and struggles are made more desperate by his belief that he must remain absolutely calm on the surface (4B + 2B); etc.

2. The phase of conflict; pure soul energy conflicts with personality force: The essential conflict between the ray four soul and the ray two personality is the struggle between the spiritual need to express the vibrancy of divine beauty (with its great and contrasting "opposites"), and the desire to avoid any kind of disturbance in the hope of sustaining a pleasant and personally comforting calm, no matter how dull or uneventful.

3. The soul/personality integration process from the perspective of the consciousness identified primarily with the fourth ray soul: It will be the task of the fourth ray soul to enliven the second ray personality, rendering it more vibrant and exciting. The soul is thrilled by the great color and contrast of the divine spectacle, and animated by a love for expressing the omni-present beauty it perceives. When identified with the soul consciousness, the individual with this ray combination seeks to find ways for releasing the aesthetic rapture and excitement he feels. The interior life of the soul-conscious individual is filled with the tensions of contrasting polarities, and he must resolve these tensions through self-expression. The personality, however, is often deliberately unresponsive; it does not wish to respond to the soul's call for an interior struggle which leads to the expression of beauty. The personality does not wish to bear the pain of revelation. It becomes necessary, then, for the soul to find ways to disrupt the often stultifying serenity in which the personality customarily cloaks itself. Beauty is something far more than pleasantness; it includes terror as well as loveliness. The soul seeks to guide the personality into a state of willing vulnerability to life's dynamic polarities, so that the joy and pain of the 'drama of spirit–in–form' can be expressed.

4. The soul/personality integration process from the perspective of the consciousness identified primarily with the second ray personality: The fourth ray pressure towards integration will be sensed by the second ray soul as a disquieting and troublesome experience. The personality is usually content and easy to please. The last thing it desires is to be subject to dramatic fluctuations and contrasts, and yet this is precisely what begins to occur as soul energy pervades the personal consciousness. The fourth ray soul understands "crucifixion" intimately; it is torn and rent by the opposites and, yet, determined to bring them together in the synthesis of beauty and harmony. The personality, however, wants no part of the necessary agony, preliminary to "at–one–ment." And yet, try as it may to avoid the struggle, from deep within the personal consciousness there begins to arise a sense of the the pain and distress of unreconciled opposites; this perception destroys the personality's self–satisfied calm, the gentle, peaceful, 'happy,' tranquility it so much prizes. The personality would like to ignore its growing awareness of unresolved dissonances, and it may, for a time do so. In cannot, for long however, resort to its former quietue – devoid of the *thrill* of beauty. The issue arises: shall life be calm and comfortable, or a thrilling, yet agonizing, experience of bringing painful dissonance into harmony? Increasingly, the calm and easy–going way is seen as the shallow way. The unity of an unruffled calm gives way to the promise of a new unity of harmonized polarities – a unity filled with beauty.

5. The ideal expression of the combination of the ray four soul and the ray two personality: The urge to create harmony and beauty is expressed serenely and lovingly. The individual may be a representative of the highest aestheticism, whose personal warmth and magnetisim contribute greatly to his determination to bring refinement and beauty to the world. There exists an unusual ability to establish bridges of rapport with widely contrasting types of people, and this gift is enhanced by an unoffending manner which relaxes people and puts them at ease. This is the combination of the gracious artist who endears himself to many. There is also a remarkable ability to bring peace and harmony to distressed situations. The many interpersonal adjustments necessary to the tasks of harmonization and reconciliation are easily accomplished with the aid of an attractive, pleasing, charming and eminently *approachable* personality. The ability to unify and "make whole" is highly developed. The positive and negative poles of all fundamental polarities are deeply respected, and no one and nothing of value is excluded. There is often a profound knowledge of sound and color which can be successfully applied to bring comfort and healing. There may also be considerable psychological skill, as the reconciling of conflicts within the psyche is one of the major purposes of psychotherapy; a loving and evocative personal manner is an additional benefit, complementing the therapeutic value of skillful conflict resolution. The ability to triumph over the ravages of conflict, and radiantly impart the fruits of victory to others is another gift of this blend of rays. There is also an extremely responsive imagination and remarkable intuitive receptivity; unusual sensitivity to visual imagery and to light increases the individual's "bridging" connection to the higher worlds. The willingness to engage in struggle, stress and strain incident to the process of reconciling the various pairs of opposites makes this individual an effective teacher – one who can effectively share the harvest of the many lessons learned from his struggles. This is the combination of one who has a unique capacity for radiating the joys of beauty.

6. The combined effect of the two integration formulae: The primary integration formula is *Steadfastness*, keyed to the fourth ray soul. The secondary integration formula is *Centralization*, keyed to the second ray personality. The first formula corrects the fourth ray tendencies towards vacillation, irresoluteness, instability, indecisiveness and moral cowardice, whereas the second formula corrects second ray tendencies towards diffusion, over-expansion, and an energy-draining attachment to life's peripheral attractions. Used together, these two formulae provide the individual striving for soul/personality integration with the composite quality of 'centralized steadfastness' (i.e., the centered personality attitude which helps the "inner man" achieve a steadfast, harmoniously balanced sprital orientation). The individual who uses these formulae releases himself from many lesser loves, the many attachments which kept him bound to the periphery of his life. His personal centeredness strengthens his steadfast, soul-inspired refusal to enter the war between the opposites *on one side or the other*. Inestead, he enters the war *on both sides*. From this balanced and centered position in consciousness, he becomes impressed with the solution to the perpetual dilemma of bi-polar conflict. With firm resolution he stands, at peace, observing (and yet participating) in the battle – bringing the *warring two* together for a mutual victory. Out of this victory, beauty is born. Thus, the formulae facilitate the cultivation of a more detached and centered personal consciousness, supportive of those rare moments of exalted consciousness when (pervaded by the presence of the soul) the individual stands steadfastly poised between the many warring pairs of opposites, holding them in a state of dynamic equilibrium (a state of dynamic peace), and drawing them towards mutual victory.

It should not be thought that his peace is without suffering. He becomes a center of reconciliation for warring energies, and as they play through him, he suffers. He steadfastly refuses to "choose sides" and, thus, cannot escape the rending agony caused by contending polarities. He will not move from the center where he "steadfast stands," and out of his suffering arises his immense capacity to express beauty.

In the earlier stages of evolution, before successfully applying these formulae, the individual with this ray combination often finds himself torn by many interpersonal and circumstantial dilemmas and far too personally attached to extricate himself. He cannot stop fighting and he cannot let go. He in uncentered and unbalanced. He struggles on one side or the other, and cannot find the centralized position from which he can find release from turmoil.

The intelligent use of the two formulae, however, transmutes the abuses of the past. No longer is he the helpless plaything of the warring pairs of opposites. With firm deliberation he takes his stand within the center of his consciousness. Through the use of the formulae, the individual learns, primarily, to stand so steadfastly and so peacefully in the center of his being, that he brings peace, beauty and synthesis to the warring forces within and without, and his growing secondary ability to stand detached, centered and unafraid will give the peacemaking soul a personal instrument which cannot be lured into the fray, but which will always act as a calm center of peace, love and wisdom.

7. Some examples of vocational aptitudes and orientations relating to the combination of the fourth ray soul and the second ray personality:

* the peacemaker who radiates loving concern for people
* the mediator whose skill rests largely upon his innate wisdom and intuitive abilities
* the negotiator with seemingly endless patience
* the arbitrator who conceives his work as that of a humanitarian
* the intermediary who easily draws separated parties together
* the translator/interpreter with a special gift for tact, and a special sensitivity to the psychology of those for whom he translates or interprets
* the harmonizer whose success is largely attributable to his intimate understanding of character
* the warrior whose battles are silently waged, and lead inevitably to peace
* the creative artist whose work is consistently educational or instructive
* the beautifier for whom beautification is an act of love
* the painter whose works are filled with light
* the composer whose themes are sweet, attractive and unifying
* the musician whose tone emanates loveliness
* the actor who exudes personal warmth
* the dramatist who creates very sympathetic characters
* the bard as teacher
* the architect who designs for comfort and intimacy
* the city planner who gives special attention to health care and other therapeutic facilities
* the psychologist whose service is to bring peaceful fusion to the psyches of those he treats
* the compassionate humanist
* the exponent of culture whose work flourishes because of his sincere love for people

In general: vocations and professions which require a strong creative imagination, spontaneity, expressivity, aesthetic sensitivity, and a marked ability to bring harmony out of conflict, beauty out of ugliness, and at–one–ment out of divisiveness, *as well as* a wise and loving attitude, great empathy and understanding, studiousness, and the ability to teach or compassionately heal.

8. A proposed list of well–known individuals (historical, contemporary, fictional or mythological) whose soul ray can be reasonably considered the fourth, with a strong subsidiary second ray (whether or not the second ray is, strictly speaking, the personality ray):

Robert Burns: celebrated as the national poet of Scotland, Burns was also a great writer and collector of songs.

Gaetano Donizetti: one of the most prolific of 19th century Italian opera composers

Wolfgang Amadeus Mozart: Austrian composer regarded as one of the greatest musical geniuses of all time. He is ranked as one of the world's three or four leading composers of opera. The third ray also seems prominent in the ray chart of his personality, and there are seventh ray reverberations as well – perhaps via Aquarius.

Franz Schubert: one of the principal Austrian composers of the early 19th century. Schubert's music bridged the Classical and Romantic periods. A lyric composer, he is particularly noted for the extraordinary melodic and harmonic gifts displayed in his many songs (over 600) and chamber works.

George Frederic Watts: English painter and sculptor whose work was infused with grandiose allegorical themes. Watts believed that art should reveal a universal message. (On p. 206 of *Esoteric Psychology, Vol. I*, the Tibetan informs us that "Watts was fourth and second rays." Further, on p. 203, when speaking of the second ray, he states, "The artist on this ray would always seek to teach through his art, and his pictures would have a meaning."

Some Contrasts Between the Ray 4 Soul and the Ray 3 Personality

Ray 4 Soul		Ray 3 Personality
* spiritual beauty	vs.	* personality–centered intellectualism
* profound aesthetic expressivity	vs.	* intelligence used too exclusively as a tool of trivial expediency
* a gift for synthesizing a great diversity of people or qualities of energy	vs.	* constant, busy–minded analysis
* great capacity to identify with and respond to human predicaments	vs.	* strangulation of spontaneous human feeling in excessive thought
* vibrant 'life–in–the–moment'; deep trust in spontaneity	vs.	* mind–induced abstraction from spontaneous living; manipulatively controlling outcomes because of basic distrust
* colorful living as an expression of spirituality	vs.	* calculated, self–serving guardedness which neutralizes the color and contrasts of life
* celebrating life as a great drama	vs.	* cloaking the drama of life with over–intellectualization
* deeply in touch with the subjective dynamics of the psyche	vs.	* entangled in materialistic objectivity; loud extroversion
* an embodiment of aesthetic elegance and refinement	vs.	* crude commercialism
* a deep understanding of and commitment to true mediation and a benefit to both conflicted parties	vs.	* patching up differences through expedient manipulation rather than through genuine conflict resolution
* depth of intuitive insight bridging apparently separated dimensions of consciousness	vs.	* entrapment in the benighted convolutions of concrete mind
* great finesse in the harmonizing of people and their potentials	vs.	* "pulling strings" to pull people together, often unsuccessfully, because of small understanding of the principles of interpersonal harmony
* willingness to confront obstacles in the pursuit of harmonization and reconciliation	vs.	* the craftiness to "get around" obstacles rather than confront them
* great skill–in–action; mastery of the "art of living"	vs.	* futile overactivity

The Integration Process for the Individual with a Ray 4 Soul and a Ray 3 Personality

1. The pre–spiritual phase; soul energy appropriated by a selfish personality: At this pre–spiritual phase of evolutionary unfoldment, the individual's motives (based upon the personality distortion of fourth ray soul energy and the self–centered use of third ray personality force) are to achieve an agreeable feeling of personality peace and harmony through tension–releasing expression of conflicting bio–psychic impulses, *as well as* a cleverly intelligent, self-serving mastery of circumstances and the environment. The person wants, primarily, to be constantly surrounded by what he considers beautiful and attractive, to be spontaneously self-expressive without discipline or control, self-indulgently dramatic or moody (as he pleases), and greatly appreciated for his colorful, unpredictable temperament, but he *also* wants to demonstrate his 'superior' intelligence at every opportunity, manipulate money and other people for his own material and intellectual satisfaction, keep incessantly busy in the pursuit of his own self-centered interests, and evade responsibilities through selfish, strategic planning.

Negatively and glamorously, these two ray influences can combine to produce: the artist, so hungry for recognition, that he involves himself in crass, self-promotional commercialism (4 + 3B); one who is so eager for "peace at any price," that he will countenance any kind of deviousness and deceit to bring it about (4A + 3); one who adds futile over-activity to a life already torn with constant conflict and crisis (4B + 3B); a "moral coward" who persistently finds a way to evade or circumvent the necessity of taking a stand (4A + 3); an undisciplined, dissolute person, adept at finding a rationalization for everything he does (4B + 3); a perversely combative individual whose attacks are usually indirect or underhanded (4B + 3); one who adds confused and overly-complicated thinking to his constant psychological conflicts (4B + 3A); one who affects lofty aesthetic tastes and surpassing intellectualism (4A + 3A); the individual whose activity patterns are either erratic or chaotic (4B + 3B); one who seeks the gratification of his unregulated passions through calculation and cunning; an inconsistent and unreliable person with far too many impractical ideas to ever get anything done (4B + 3A); an exaggerative, highly inventive 'story teller' who thinks nothing of bending the truth and twisting the facts; a compulsive worrier whose mind can always think of innumerable ways something can go wrong; an improvident spendthift who wastes his money on far flung schemes that have no chance of materializing (4 + 3A); the ambivalent and indecisive person who sees things from so many different perspectives that he can never really make up his mind; etc.

2. The phase of conflict; pure soul energy conflicts with personality force: The essential conflict between the ray four soul and the ray three personality is the struggle between the spiritual need to remain open to intuitive inspiration in order to express divine beauty and harmony imaginatively and spontaneously, and the cynical, untrusting determination to calculate all possible 'moves' intellectually, leaving no room for higher inspiration – all in order to ensure the gratification of one's material and selfish interests.

3. The soul/personality integration process from the perspective of the consciousness identified primarily with the fourth ray soul: It will be the task of the fourth ray soul to render the third ray personality sensitive to beauty and to intuition conveyed through imagery. The soul knows the limitations of intellect; this type of personality does not, and tends to rely overmuch upon it. The soul, which ever seeks to remain open to "artistic inspiration," (to the possibility of embodying some great truth or concept in pictorial or auditory image, or in some other form of beauty) is faced with a personality which can easily desensitize itself to beauty through excessive thought and overactivity; the 'noise' level and distractedness of the personality frequently render it impervious to aesthetic impression. The soul consciousness, ever intent upon cultivating refinement and expressivity, seeks to redirect an intellect which rarely, if ever, pauses to appreciate any form of loveliness. The soul is on intimate terms with beauty; the personality manipulates the mental, emotional and physical 'contents' of life as if from a distance – moving them here, moving them there according to self-interested plan, but not really pausing to contemplate the beauty or essential quality of that which it consistently rearranges. In colloquial terms, the soul is saying to the busy third ray personality (as it might justifiably say to the sixth ray personality as well) "stop, and smell the roses." Only in moments of attentive stillness can it be realized that "a thing of beauty is a joy forever." The soul tries to teach its restless personality to take those moments.

4. The soul/personality integration process from the perspective of the consciousness identified primarily with the third ray personality: The fourth ray pressure towards integration will be felt by the third ray personality as a call to non-rationality, irrelevant pleasure and non-accomplishment. Clearly the personality feels most comfortable when it is *busy*, whether or not the constant activity has any significant value in itself. The personality wants to "get on with" the many seemingly 'important' things it proposes to do. To the glamored consciousness of the third ray personality, there is no *time* to simply stop and *appreciate*, and of all activities, the apparent non-activity of aesthetic contemplation seems the greatest waste of time. The personality is, therefore, *annoyed* at the increasing calls which arise from deep within its consciousness, to appreciate (and express) the beautiful. But as the soul continues to pour its influence into the personal consciousness, the personality will find its former actitivies more and more hollow, less and less attractive and alive. They lose their appeal, and the attention is increasingly drawn to the beautiful, the harmonious, the innately lovely and the dramatic. Personal activities are, gradually, evaluated and refined, and the intellect is rendered up as the servant of the urge to beautification and harmonization. The personal consciousness turns inward, and when aesthetic impressions are received, they are rendered intelligently vocal or translated into a variety of expressions. The new life is one of greater risks, and fewer guarantees – of greater spontaneity and fewer manipulative controls, but it is a *vibrant* life, engaging *all* human faculties in a vitally expressive outpouring, rather than the power of thought and physical activity alone.

5. The ideal expression of the combination of the ray four soul and the ray three personality: The urge to create harmony and beauty is expressed with active intelligence and adaptability. This combination yields the artist who can express himself through a great diversity of channels. It may further indicate a proponent of the highest aesthetic culture, whose many skills and contacts in the financial community bring substantial material assistance to the fulfillment of his aims. Peace-making, in all its many forms, is a special gift of those upon the fourth ray, and, when in combination with the third ray, resourcefulness, inventiveness and adaptability greatly enhance the prospects for reconciliation. Skill in conflict resolution is heightened by the ability to devise many effective strategems for success. Righteous compromise is always possible. If peace cannot be had by one means, then there are always new avenues of approach; the road to peace is never blocked because the imagination generates so many options. Individuals upon the fourth ray have powerful imaginations which can tap the "image-bank" of the human race – the "collective unconscious." With the assistance of the third ray, these images can be articulately expressed through speech and writing. The apparently separate dimensions of human consciousness (subjective and objective) are successfully bridged, and brought into the light through reasoned discourse. The great drama hidden within humanity's collective psyche is skillfully communicated or portrayed in words. The living power of symbols is grasped by the penetrating intuition, and the power of acute intelligence is ready to interpret and explain, enriching and sensitizing many minds. This combination brings a gift for fusing and blending. The fourth ray reconciles dissonant elements within any whole, and the third ray weaves those elements closely together. The planet Mercury is intimately involved in the process. The task of relating and linking the many elements can be achieved innovatively, and in a remarkable variety of ways. The revelation of divine beauty is facilitated through the combined power of visual image and the spoken or written word.

6. The combined effect of the two integration formulae: The primary integration formula is *Steadfastness,* keyed to the fourth ray soul. The secondary integration formula is *Stillness*, keyed to the third ray personality. The first formula corrects the fourth ray tendencies toward vacillation, irresoluteness, instability, indecisiveness and moral cowardice, whereas the second formula corrects the third ray tendencies towards a busy scattering of attention, wasted thought, and physical overactivity (with their resultant disturbances and obscurations of consciousness). Used together, these two formulae provide the individual striving for soul/personality integration with the composite quality of 'still steadfastness,' (i.e., the stillness of the personal consciousness which contributes to a centering of the inner consciousness steadfastly between the warring "pairs of opposites"). If there is peace and quiet without, there can be steadiness and harmonious balance within. Thus, these formulae facilitate the cultivation of a more quiet and restful personal consciousness, supportive of those rare moments of exalted consciousness when (pervaded by the presence of the soul) the individual stands steadfastly poised between the many pairs of "opposing forces," holding them in a state of dynamic equilibrium (a state of dynamic peace), and drawing them together towards mutual victory.

In the earlier stages of evolution, before successfully applying these formulae, an individual with this ray combination often finds himself chaotically and futilely scattering his energies – the unstable victim of the fluctuating dualities. Restless without, and tortured within, he has no peace and no stability. He wastes his life in commotion and conflict, refusing to rest, struggling incessantly. The "dust of the road" and the "smoke of the battle" never have a chance to settle. He is lost. The intelligent use of the two formulae, however, transmutes the abuses of the past. The period of restless fluctuation gives way to a period in which the versatile intelligence becomes the instrument of peace. The individual learns, primarily, to stand so steadfastly and so peacefully in the center of his being, that he brings peace, beauty and synthesis to the opposing forces within and without, and his growing secondary ability, to remain still and quiet until he knows exactly what he should do, ensures that the peacemaking soul will have at its disposal a personal instrument which can act intelligently and efficiently as its agent.

7. Some examples of vocational aptitudes and orientations relating to the combination of the fourth ray soul and the third ray personality:

* the peacemaker armed with an understanding of the world's best thought
* the mediator whose excellent reasoning abilities enhance his success
* the negotiator who is also a shrewd bargainer
* the arbitrator with a keen mind for the implications and ramifications of his decisions
* the intermediary who travels rapidly "to and fro"
* the translater/interpreter with an exceptional facility for languages
* the harmonizer capable of generating innumerable ways of reducing tensions
* the warrior whose best strategies are indirect
* the creative artist with a keen business sense
* the beautifier who weaves together many unusual elements
* the painter whose themes are full of interesting thought
* the composer whose music is characterized by a complex, multi–layered texture
* the musician who brings unusual intelligence to the interpretation of his art
* the actor capable of portraying many different kinds of characters
* the dramatist whose plot–construction is superb
* the eclectic architect who successfully harmonizes a diversity of styles
* the acutely intelligent humanist
* the city planner whose designs give special attention to the needs of the business community
* the psychologist whose special service is providing insight into many ways in which psychological conflicts may be reconciled and psychological synthesis achieved
* the exponent of culture who articulates his views brilliantly

In general: vocations and professions which require a strong creative imagination, spontaneity, expressivity, aesthetic sensitivity, and a marked ability to bring harmony out of conflict, beauty out of ugliness, and at–one–ment out of divisiveness, *as well as*, acute intelligence (whether active or abstract), great adaptability and resourcefulness, abundant creative and communicative abilities, and (frequently) strong business aptitudes.

8. A proposed list of well-known individuals (historical, contemporary, fictional or mythological) whose soul ray can reasonably be considered the fourth, with a strong subsidiary third ray influence (whether or not the third ray is, strictly speaking, the personality ray):

Hector Berlioz: French composer, critic and conductor, Berlioz was a many-sided genius. The outstanding characteristics of his music were its dramatic expressiveness and its variety.

Claude Debussy: French composer of the late 19th and early 20th century. Debussy developed a highly original system of harmony and musical structure that expressed the ideals to which the Impressionist and Symbolist painters and writers of his time aspired. A pronounced seventh ray influence is also apparent.

Mercutio (fictional): the brilliant, half-mad friend and companion of Romeo in Shakespeare's *Romeo and Juliet*

Giacomo Rossini: the leading composer of Italian opera during the early part of the 19th century. The almost frenetic 'activity level' of many of Rossini's compositions is striking. Elements of the second ray are also apparent.

Some Contrasts Between the Ray 4 Soul and the Ray 4 Personality

Ray 4 Soul		Ray 4 Personality
* spiritual expressiveness	vs.	* personal expressiveness
* the power to bridge and relate the personal and spiritual aspects of human nature, and later, the spiritual and the divine asepcts	vs.	* bridging only within the confines of the lower personal self
* conflict waged with the purpose of harmonizing soul and personality	vs.	* the struggle to achieve selfish personal harmony
* power to express the synthesis of true beauty	vs.	* preoccupation with the lower forms of beauty, which are only ugliness when seen from the divine perspective
* the artistry to express high spiritual principles	vs.	* the use of art purely for expression of personal thought and emotion
* the power to express divine archetypes in image; imagination as an instrument of expression for the collective mind of humanity and even for the Divine Mind	vs.	* imagination reflecting purely personal experience
* conflict resolution which does not abandon or compromise the highest spiritual values and principles	vs.	* conflict resolution which frequently abandons or compromises the highest spiritual values and principles for the sake of temporary, personal peace
* intuitive spontaneity contributing to creative living and skill–in–action	vs.	* unregulated spontaneity leading to erratic, unpredictable behavior
* the "mathematical exactitude" of the exquisitely cultivated intuition	vs.	* the inaccuracy of an untrained mind relying upon psychic hunches instead of real intuition
* the finesse to reconcile the heights and depths (the flowers and the roots) of human living	vs.	* a victim of the many pairs of opposites; unaccountably subject to mood swings

Commentary

All that has been said in the sections dealing with ray combinations 1/1, 2/2, and 3/3, concerning the presumable rarity of identical soul and personality rays applies here, but even more so. When dealing with the "rays of attribute" (rays four, five, six and seven), special consideration must be given to the science of ray dynamics as the disciple approaches and passes beyond *the period of the transfiguration of the personality.* At that stage in the evolutionary cycle, if the soul ray is one of the four rays of attribute, it may very well be in the process of being transferred or shifted onto one of the three "rays of aspect," i.e., rays one, two or three (cf. *Discipleship in the New Age, Vol. I*, pp. 572–573). From a number of indications give by the Tibetan, by the time an individual has become an initiate of the third degree, his soul is often found upon one of the first three rays or, at least, is in the process of blending into, or shifting onto, one of the first three rays – though the quality built–in during past experience upon the rays of attribute does not simply vanish (cf. *Discipleship in the New Age, Vol. I*, p. 216). It stands to reason (though it cannot easily be confirmed) that the stage of evolution close to the time of the third initiation (and, more probably, somewhat *after* the third initiation) is that stage at which there would have been sufficient spiritual development within the personality to enable the soul to choose a subray (i.e., a personality ray) *identical with its own* – without dangerous results. The long progress of evolution would have created enough experience upon the various contrasting rays so that *balance* would not be destroyed by identical soul and personality rays. However, it can easily be seen that if souls upon a ray of attribute are often in process of transferring to a ray of aspect as the Transfiguration approaches (or soon afterwards), and if identical soul and personality rays are not likely to be found until the period immediately preceding the Transfiguration (and, more likely, [if at all] *even later*), then, *there is not a great deal of likelihood of finding identical soul and personality rays upon the rays of attribute*!

There does, however, exist the interesting possibility that a soul upon a ray of attribute, and intending to transfer to a particular ray of aspect, might, in that incarnation (or in the several during which such a transference is occurring), choose for a personality ray that particular ray of aspect *to which it is attempting to transfer*. For instance: a soul upon the fourth ray, intending to transfer to the second ray, would then choose for its subray or personality ray, the second ray, thereby facilitating the transference. This interesting possibility would not, however, provide a situation in which there were identical rays of *attribute* – only the possibility of identical rays of *aspect*. In the particular case cited, there would be (once the transference were completed) an identity between the newly established second ray soul, and the second ray personality. Just how long such an identity would prevail is, given our present point of understanding, impossible to estimate. It must be remembered that the soul can change its subray for purposes of service (cf., p. 107, *Discipleship in the New Age, Vol. II*), and that the personality ray *is* a subray of the soul (cf. *Esoteric Psychology, Vol. II*, p. 358), though not necessarily the *only* subray of the soul. Therefore, it is conceivable that once the transference from the fourth ray soul to the second ray soul were complete, the soul could, for the sake of balance, change its subray (in this case, its personality ray) from the fourth ray to some other ray.

What is here being speculatively discussed is an extremely subtle matter dealing with unrevealed intricacies of the science of the seven rays and the science of initiation. Real understanding will have to await either further revelation or experimentation. It should, however, provide a caution to those ray analysts who wish to assign identical rays of attribute to soul and personality, *regardless of the point in evolution of the individual concerned*.

At any rate, it does not seem really profitable to discuss potential interactions between identical soul and personality rays when the rays concerned are *rays of attribute*, because the likelihood of the existence of such combinations (at least, given the author's present premises and line of reasoning) is rather negligible. For those readers who believe that such combinations do, in fact, exist, sufficient is given in the tabulations, and in the format for handling the many other combinations, for them to work out the implications for themselves.

Some Contrasts Between the Ray 4 Soul and the Ray 5 Personality

Ray 4 Soul		Ray 5 Personality
* spiritual beauty	vs.	* concrete knowledge
* divine incentive to harmonize and synthesize	vs.	* tendency to create cleavages through over–analysis
* vibrant, aesthetic expressivity	vs.	* a lack–luster, pedestrian, excessively–commonsensical attitude
* vivid realization and expression of the divinity of play	vs.	* harsh criticism of everything that seems foolish or nonsensical
* ultra–sensitivity and responsiveness to subtle psychological nuances and changes	vs.	* non–responsiveness to most psychological nuances and changes
* great magnetic charm	vs.	* flat, non–magnetic personality radiation
* brilliant creative imagination expressed as a divine faculty	vs.	* over–mentalization severely limits imaginative freedom and power
* highly refined intuitive apprehension	vs.	* skepticism and disbelief limits the functioning of the intuition
* an immediate intuitive attunement and identification with many types of people	vs.	* an overly objective, mentally–filtered assessment of people which fails to appreciate the true nature of their other–than–mental dimensions
* harmonious adjustability which confers the skill–in–action to live creatively	vs.	* brittle unresponsiveness through excessive fixity of thought
* can easily access the psycho–spiritual riches which emerge through improvisation	vs.	* caught in the psycho–spiritual impoverishment of strictly logical, 'correct' thinking
* easily moved by divine inspiration	vs.	* deflects inspiration through excessive rationalism
* unpredictable, non–linear living, which surprises, delights and evokes joy	vs.	* predictable linearity which robs life of the joy of unexpectedness

The Integration Process for the Individual with a Ray 4 Soul and a Ray 5 Personality

1. The pre–spiritual phase; soul energy appropriated by a selfish personality: At this pre–spiritual phase of evolutionary unfoldment, the individual's motives (based upon the personality distortion of fourth ray soul energy, and the self–centered use of fifth ray personality force), are to achieve an agreeable feeling of personal peace and harmony through a tension–releasing expression of conflicting bio–psychic impulses, *as well as* a narrow, materialistic, intellectual certainty. The person wants primarily to be surrounded by what he considers beautiful or attractive, to be spontaneously self–expressive without discipline or control, self–indulgently dramatic or moody (as he pleases), and greatly appreciated for his colorful, unpredictable temperament, but he *also* wants to take everything apart (either analytically or actually), reduce all life experience to nothing but rationalistic formulae, control matter mechanically for selfish ends, and reject any kind of knowledge that is not materialistic or derived strictly from the five physical senses. (The contrast between these two ray types is striking and they are difficult to blend. Since these rays are, respectively, the soul and personality ray of humanity, the difficulty of the task of synthesis set before the human kingdom can be more easily understood).

Negatively and glamorously, these two ray influences can combine to produce: one whose personality schisms and cleavages are aggravated by an overly-analytical, separative mind (4B + 5); one whose natural indecisiveness is exacerbated by a thought process which is too meticulous and focused upon minutia (4 + 5A); one whose habitual conflict with others is considerably worsened by his harsh criticism and his tendency to see only differences between people – i.e., one who sustains conflict and prevents peace by over-emphasis upon petty distinctions (4B + 5); unregulated hedonism justified by an attitude which can see no reality beyond the five senses; one who irresponsibly and capriciously gives into impulses, later justifying his actions by saying he has an exact understanding of their causes; a split or dissociated personality – divided into many "complexes" or "sub-personalities" (4B + 5); one who, though his various behaviors are strikingly self-contradictory, acts in a strangely objective, detached, dissociated manner (4B + 5); one who excuses his moral cowardice and refusal to take definitive, principled action by saying that he is merely "standing back" and studying the situation (4A + 5A); one who prolongs conflicts unnecessarily through the misuse of technology (4B + 5B); one whose concepts of beauty are arid and mechanical (4 + 5B); the artist whose expressive powers are curtailed by his preoccupation with correctness of technique; etc.

2. The phase of conflict; pure soul energy conflicts with personality force: The essential conflict between the ray four soul and the ray five personality is the struggle between the spiritual intuition which reveals the mystery and synthesis of beauty, and the separative, commonsensical intellect which focuses upon the fragmentary and the ordinary.

3. The soul/personality integration process from the perspective of the consciousness identified primarily with the ray four soul: It will be the task of the ray four soul to animate the fifth ray personality by loosening its rational-analytical 'cramp.' The flexible and harmonizing soul is faced with a personality in the grip of an inflexible, concrete-minded thought process. The soul seeks to teach the personality the art of "at-one-ing," through bridging, fusing and unifying, but this is difficult, because the personality's aim is to determine the distinctness of things, and to keep that distinctness clearly in mind. Intuition is the psychospiritual 'organ' which erradicates the notion of essential difference, but the rational/analytical personality discounts intuition as imprecise and unreliable. The fourth ray soul is frustrated by the fragmented consciousness of the fifth ray personality, and seeks to lead it to an appreciation of subtly beautiful apprehensions which cannot be defined in words or measured with instrument and apparatus. The soul, thus, begins to radiate an influence which gradually alerts the personal consciousness to the 'feel' of life's polarities; this radiation starts to change an often colorless and monotonous quality of consciousness into something far more vibrant. Intuition beings to master intellect. The sense of drama gradually overcomes flat, unresponsive affect. The realization and expression of beauty enlivens the ordinariness of the personality's prosaic, "matter-of-fact" approach to life.

4. The soul/personality integration process from the perspective of the consciousness identified primarily with the fifth ray personality: The fourth ray pressure towards integration will be felt by the fifth ray personality as an invasion of the intellect by irrational or irrelevant fantasy. The personality feels most comfortable thinking clearly, solving problems rationally, and separating itself mentally from the 'irrational' currents of energy found in other aspects of the energy system – namely, the emotional field and the soul field. When currents which the artist might call "the muse" or "inspiration" begin to enter the personal consciousness, the personality feels that its mental integrity is being compromised. It wants no part of the unreal, the fanciful, the imaginary – in short, the non-factual. And yet, beneath its protests, the personality realizes the drabness, the colorlessness of its life – a life that is severely limited. A full life does not always "make sense," and though the personality may redouble its concentration in order to throw off these subtle, internal invitations to 'foolishness,' the way of the "divine fool" becomes ever more attractive. The personality begins to realize that a man is not merely a mind, and that a mind is not merely an intellect. A new and essential learning arises – that man is meant to *experience fully*, and not merely to *know intellectually*, and that only in this way can life be suffused with beauty. As the personality relaxes its mental grip, and allows itself to be surprised by loveliness, the poverty of its narrow, erstwhile perspective is seen for what it is. The personality, now increasingly soul-infused, begins to know, or rather intuit and *express*, the beauty which is transcendently inaccessible to strictly rational processes.

5. The ideal combination of the fourth ray soul energy and the fifth ray personality force: The urge to create harmony and beauty is expressed with extensive technical "know-how." Precise knowledge of the technical means of expression serves to enhance the quality of that which is expressed. Technology serves art. Art and machine are united; art and artifact are wedded. The urge to end dissonance and promote harmony is furthered by an intensely concentrated mind which understands, scientifically and mathematically, the true nature of dissonance and harmony. A profound understanding of human character is sharpened still further by penetrating analytical powers. The ability to express dramatic nuance rides on a technique which is faultlessly correct. A full and colorful imagination is enriched through the addition of concrete detail. Eloquence and colorful speech are supported by a precise knowledge of the meaning of words. A great talent for expression in color and sound is perfected through a detailed, analytical and factual understanding of both. Peace and cooperative, mutual interplay are enhanced by the fruits of scientific enquiry and technical innovation. The individual becomes an expert in the bridging process because he knows exactly how to build the bridge; he becomes the *scientific bridge-builder*. A clear-minded knowledge of factual reality serves as the basis for creating interpersonal and intra-personal resolution of conflict. One whose purpose is to unify the psyche, has a full and detailed comprehension of the natural laws of the psyche. Intuitive, buddhic consciousness is supported by "hard-headed," rational-mindedness. The art of intuitively linking the various dimensions of reality becomes a specialized and technical science – the science of the Antahkarana.

6. The combined effect of the two integration formulae: The primary integration formula is *Steadfastness*, keyed to the fourth ray soul. The secondary integration formula is *Detachment*, keyed to the fifth ray personality. The first formula corrects the fourth ray tendencies towards vacillation, irresoluteness, instability, indecisiveness and moral–cowardice, whereas the second formula corrects the fifth ray tendencies towards mental attachment to matter, and the obsessive preoccupation with investigating or manipulating concrete form, while ignoring the reality of that which is "formless." Used together, these two formulae provide the individual striving for soul/personality integration with the composite quality of 'detached steadfastness,' (i.e., that detachment from a preoccupation with the modifications of matter which helps bring peace, steadiness, balance and harmony to a tumultuous psyche). With the help of the formulae, the personality begins to see *behind* the many material forms to the formless reality of the One Life, and the inner consciousness, too, takes its poised and steadfast stand upon a point of observation from which the *wholeness* of the One Subjective Life – with all its many apparently–conflicting polarities – can be intuited. Thus, these formulae facilitate the cultivation of a less materially–obsessed, more spiritually–penetrating personal consciousness, supportive of those rare moments of exalted consciousness when (pervaded by the presence of the soul) the individual stands steadfastly poised between the many pairs of "warring forces", holding them in a state of dynamic equilibrium (a state of dynamic peace), and drawing them together towards mutual victory.

In the earlier stages of evolution, before successfully applying these formulae, an individual with this ray combination often finds himself fragmented – preoccupied with the many material divisions of matter, and torn in many directions by internal and external warring forces he cannot control. His psyche is in 'pieces'; his perception of the outer world is also in pieces; and he cannot bring the many pieces together. So great is the battle between the many conflicting aspects of himself, and so engrossing his preoccupation with concrete matter, that he cannot *see–through* to the unifying, subjective essence which lies behind all multiplicity, and which would bring peace and wholeness to his war–torn nature.

The intelligent use of the two formulae, however, transmutes the abuses of the past. It brings an end to unbalanced, 'matter–blinded' living, followed by the discovery of a reliable vantage point from which the two halves of every whole can be unified, and the reality behind the distressed form known. The individual learns, primarily, to stand so steadfastly and so peacefully in the center of his being, that he brings peace, beauty and synthesis to the opposing forces within and without, and his growing secondary ability to see a unifing God within multifarious forms ensures the peacemaking soul that it will have at its disposal a personal instrument which will help *knowledgeably and scientifically* unite the many to each other, and to the One Who contains all things, thus negating the reality of all division and conflict.

7. Some examples of vocational aptitudes and orientations relating to the combination of the fourth ray soul and the fifth ray personality:

* the peacemaker who focuses upon how to apply scientific research and discovery in the cause of peace

* the negotiator whose mind is so clear, and whose facts are so 'straight,' that an equitable solution is easier to find
* the arbitrator with a precise knowledge of all the pertinent facts and details of the issue which must be decided
* the intermediary who makes full use of communications technology
* the translator/interpreter whose use of language is precise and technically correct
* the harmonizer who has a technical understanding of the laws of vibration
* the warrior who avails himself of technology in order to triumph
* the creative artist who can analyze and explain with complete lucidity the methodology of the creative process
* the designer with a special interest in the relationship between aesthetics and technology
* the painter with extensive knowledge of the chemical and material properties of the various media he employs
* the composer who clearly understands the mathematical dimensions of music
* the musician with a solid understanding of the science of acoustics
* the actor with real expertise in the area of technical theatre
* the dramatist whose plays are examples of the most uncompromising realism
* the storyteller whose stories are enriched with a wealth of descriptive detail
* the imaginative writer with a flair for science fiction
* the architect with well–developed engineering abilities
* the city planner who is inclined to give special attention to the needs of the scientific community
* the psychodramatist endowed with penetrating powers of analysis
* the exponent of culture who values the sciences, and attempts to unite them to the arts

In general: vocations and professions which require a strong creative imagination, spontaneity, expressivity, aesthetic sensitivity, and a marked ability to bring harmony out of conflict, beauty out of ugliness, and at–one–ment out of divisiveness, *as well as* keen analytical abilities, the capacity for research, and scientific and/or technical expertise.

8. A proposed list of well-known individuals (historical, contemporary, fictional or mythological) whose soul ray can reasonably be considered the fourth with a strong subsidiary fifth ray influence (whether or not the fifth ray is, strictly speaking, the personality ray):

Johann Wolfgang von Goethe: although described more fully under the 4/1 section, Goethe must be mentioned here. He was unquestionably an initiate in whose consciousness art and science were magnificently synthesized.

Edgard Varèse: Whether or not Varèse was, strictly speaking, a fourth ray soul, there can be no doubt that his approach to music unified the fourth and the fifth rays. Such compositions as *Hyperprism*, *Ionisation*, and *Density* reveal his scientific leanings. He was one of the pioneers of electronic music.

Leonardo da Vinci: Renaissance painter, sculptor, architect and engineer. Leonardo was the quintessential artist–scientist. The seventh ray, also, was powerfully present.

Rudolph Steiner: scientist, artist, editor and founder of Anthroposophy. It seems clear that Steiner was either a fourth or fifth ray soul. He was strongly attracted to the works of Goethe, editing the poet's scientific works, and also working upon the standard edition of Goethe's complete works. As in the case of Goethe, the quality of Steiner's life was a strong representation of the union of the fourth and fifth rays.

Note: When considering the significance of the contribution of both Goethe and Steiner, it is well to remember that the soul ray of humanity is the fourth, while its personality is the fifth. Interestingly, Steiner was born in Austria – a country with a fourth ray soul and fifth ray personality.

Some Contrasts Between the Ray 4 Soul and the Ray 6 Personality

Ray 4 Soul		Ray 6 Personality
* the expression of spiritual beauty	vs.	* fanaticism; the ugliness of excess
* alive to all forms of beauty	vs.	* frequently so preoccupied with the pursuit of personal goals that obliviousness to beauty is the result
* mastery of the art of righteous compromise	vs.	* ardent, emotionally–motivated refusal to compromise
* the gifted mediator between one human being and another, regardless of their idealistic persuasions	vs.	* the unbending partisan upholding only one point of view
* the achievement of spiritual balance	vs.	* passionate, unbalanced overemphasis
* wide spiritual tolerance based upon an appreciation for the absolute necessity of all the many "pairs of opposites"	vs.	* narrow intolerance based upon strictly personal preferences and attachments
* wise recognition that man is human as well as divine	vs.	* idealistic denunciation (or even persecution) of man's strictly human, fallible nature
* the flexibility and pliability leading to harmonization and unity	vs.	* the rigid idealism which leads to separation and cleavage
* soul–inspired appreciation of divine proportion	vs.	* lack of proportion on every hand
* the joyful expression of the humor and playfulness of the "Divine Child"	vs.	* overly–earnest inability to laugh at oneself and to play
* the capacity to empathize with, or dramatically portray, a wide variety of human beings	vs.	* rigid incapacity to identify with anyone except those who embody one's ideals
* the soul–inspired capacity to act as the coordinating general, presiding over the spiritual battle in which there is no victor unless both sides win	vs.	* demands an uncompromising victory over (or conversion of) those who do not believe 'correctly'
* a mastery of spiritual "give–and–take"; the "light touch"; alternating strokes leading to accomplishment	vs.	* counterproductive personal intensity; excessive pressure which destroys good results
* perfected "creative living" through skill–in–action	vs.	* too one–pointedly focused to live even normally, let alone beautifully and creatively

The Integration Process for the Individual with a Ray 4 Soul and a Ray 6 Personality

1. The pre–spiritual phase; soul energy appropriated by a selfish personality: At this pre–spiritual phase of evolutionary unfoldment, the individual's motives (based upon the personality distortion of fourth ray soul energy, and the self–centered use of sixth ray personality force) are to achieve an agreeable feeling of personal peace and harmony through tension–releasing expression of conflicting bio–psychic impulses, *as well as* the uncompromising satisfaction of the ideals and goals to which the personality is passionately devoted. The person wants, primarily, to be surrounded by what he considers beautiful or attractive, to be spontaneously self-expressive without discipline or control, self-indulgently dramatic or moody (as he pleases), and greatly appreciated for his colorful, unpredictable temperament, but he *also* wants to ignore everything except the object or path of his devotion, spurn even reasonable mundane responsibilities if they do not relate specifically to his quest, fanatically follow his ideal regardless of destructive consequences, and cling desperately to that which he believes he loves.

Negatively and glamorously, these two ray influences can combine to produce: the tortured and self-torturing individual whose pain is aggravated by emotional extremism (4B + 6); the combative person who fights furiously (and "at the drop of a hat") due to emotional blindness and fanaticism (4B + 6B); one who worries excessively, but is too passive and dependent upon others to take those steps which would make worry unnecessary (4 + 6A); a moody, unstable individual given to emotional outbursts and violence (4B + 6B); one whose emotional nature is so intense, that his love of dramatic expression too easily becomes melodrama (4B + 6); one whose unregulated passions are aggravated by obsessive drives (4B + 6); the hedonist utterly addicted to his pleasures; the manic-depressive who uses drugs to 'rocket' him out of the depressive cycle (4B + 6); one whose inconsistency and changability are worsened by lack of self-restraint; one who cannot resist involving himself in relationships, and cannot let go once he is in them (4 + 6A); the aesthete whose ideals are so lofty that he cannot live in the 'real' world (4A + 6); one with a maladaptive "artistic temperament" which he refuses to compromise; one whose love of the arts becomes an all-consuming passion to the detriment of other activities necessary for balanced living; the romanticist who is extraordinarily naive (4A + 6A); one who is so idealistically devoted to peace ("at any price") that he fails to see the values which are sacrificed because of his pacifism (4A + 6A); etc.

2. The phase of conflict; pure soul energy conflicts with personality force: The essential conflict between the ray four soul and the ray six personality is the struggle between the spiritual need for the realization and expression of divine proportion and balanced beauty, and a fanatical, desire-driven overemphasis which destroys all balance and proportion.

3. The soul/personality integration process from the perspective of the consciousness identified primarily with the ray four soul: It will be the task of the ray four soul to bring moderation, balance and beauty to the ray six personality. The soul seeks to demonstrate to the personality that there are two sides to every issue in this world of contrasting polarities, but, of course, the sixth ray personality sees only one, and that one is pursued with undue emphasis. The soul seeks to have the personality abate its furious pace, or variegate the transfixity of its gaze so that the many beauties of the world can be seen, but the personality sees only one thing at a time, and rejects other things as valueless or uninteresting. The soul must teach the personality *alternation* – a periodic relaxation of its focused intensity, so that a reciprocal "give-and-take" relationship with life can be established. Every stick has two ends, every "up" a "down," every "north" a "south," every "high" and "low." The sixth ray personality, however, ignores polarities, especially the 'lower' pole (which is often repudiated), and this unbalances the psyche. The fourth ray seeks to transform a soaring, vertical line into a four-quartered mandala, thus bringing the various "opposites" into a "holistic" relationship with each other. The sixth ray personality, however, must be convinced of the beauty of contrast before this rounding out can be achieved.

4. The soul/personality integration process from the perspective of the consciousness identified primarily with the sixth ray personality: The fourth ray pressure towards integration is sensed by the sixth ray personality as a splitting of the stream of aspiration, or as an induction of ambivalence. The personality is most comfortable when it can simply continue to pursue, without distraction, that which it desires or aspires to pursue. The contrast, or opposing point of view, which the soul consistently offers, is not something the personality wishes to see. To the personal consciousness upon the sixth ray, value has nothing to do with balanced polarities, or a dynamic equilibrium between the opposites; value is the possession of the one thing prized above all, and anything opposed to that thing (or even different from it) is to be rejected as perilous or worthless. This type of personality forgets that beautiful flowers have roots; of course, it is irrational to claim love for the flower and hatred for the roots. Man is an "animal *plus* a living god" – *both* – not simply a living god. The soul has its personality, and God has His "devil." The personality, however, does not like to be reminded of what might be called 'the rejected polarity.' The wise, fourth ray soul knows that there is no light without dark, no happiness without sadness, and that all qualities, in this bi-polar world, are defined by their opposites. The personal consciousness qualified by the sixth ray, however, desires unrelieved light, unending happiness, etc., and while these are theoretically possible in the absolute sense, they lead to tedium and boredom in the bi-polar world of "becoming." The personality may reject the soul's intimation of the value of both poles, and redouble its unbalanced pursuit, but at length it wearies and grows tired. A world without the inspiration of beauty is tiresome and boring, and there can be no beauty without recognizing and honoring the interplay of the opposites. Though the personality is irritated by what it perceives to be the 'devaluation of the beloved,' it must gradually awaken to the loveliness which appears from the synthesis of all the many apparently conflicting energies and forces. At length the personality looks around and notices (everywhere) the *presence* of a beauty after which it need not strain. It relaxes its tension and simply *appreciates* the present loveliness. The personality broadens through the devotion to *omnipresent beauty*.

5. The ideal combination of the fourth ray soul and the sixth ray personality: The urge to create harmony and beauty is expressed fervently and zealously. The expression of beauty becomes one's greatest ideal, and loveliness is, virtually, worhipped. Aesthetic pursuits become a passion; divine beauty is impressed upon the consciousness, and the entire life is given, one-pointedly, to the revelation of that beauty. The artistic urge expresses itself, particularly, through religious or devotional themes. The spirit of accommodation for the sake of harmony masters one-pointed, conflict-producing narrowness, and yet utter dedication is preserved. Ability to compromise and see the other's point of view supercedes separative emotional loyalties, but unflinching loyalty to fairness, balance and equality remains. Support for bi-partisan ventures prevails over partisan devotions, but devotion to those who speak for cooperative, bi-partisan interplay is easily aroused. The individual with this combination can become an excellent mediator or negotiator, always animated by the highest idealism, capable of persisting with tenacious dedication until the ideals of "righteous compromise" and harmony are achieved. This is also the combination of the ardent humanist – one who believes passionately in the divinity of humanity. Histrionic abilities are pronounced; great actors with impressive emotional intensity are found here, as well as eloquent speakers with a wonderful flair for oratory. Everything is given or sacrificed to serve one's art, or one's conception of beauty. This combination can well indicate the devoted person who becomes a martyr for his art, or a martyr in the cause of peace.

6. The combined effect of the two integration formulae: The primary integration formula is *Steadfastness*, keyed to the fourth ray soul. The secondary integration formula is proposed as *Restraint*, keyed to the sixth ray personality. The first formula corrects fourth ray tendencies towards vacillation, irresoluteness, instability, indecisiveness and moral cowardice, whereas the second formula corrects the unrestrained, passionate pursuit of the 'partial' and 'peripheral,' so common to the emotionally undisciplined sixth ray personality. Used together, these two formulae provide the individual striving for soul/personality integration with the combined qualities of 'restrained steadfastnesss,' (i.e., the restraint of personal desire and aspiration which promotes a harmoniously balanced and steadfast orientation within the inner psyche). Restraint without; steadfastness within. The individual subdues his over-eager personality, and prevents it from destroying his soul-inspired ability to "make peace." As he applies the formulae, he steadily restrains himself from participating in the fluctuations of the "pairs of opposites." Standing balanced and steadfast at the center of his being, and refusing to follow the lure of the attractive but utterly limited visions which beckon from the periphery, he becomes sensitive to the impression of divine beauty and harmony, and dedicates himself to their expression. Thus, these formulae facilitate the cultivation of a less impetuous, less frenzied, more moderate and controlled personal consciousness, supportive of those rare moments of exalted consciousness when (pervaded by the presence of the soul) the individual stands steadfastly poised between the many pairs of "warring forces," holding them in a state of dynamic equilibrium (a state of dynamic peace) and drawing them together towards mutual victory.

In the earlier stages of evolution, before successfully applying these formulae, an individual with this combination of rays often finds himself too passionately and intensely consumed by the battle between the warring, bi-polar energies and forces, both within his own nature and the environment. He experiences nothing but conflict on every hand, and he fights passionately. He is the play-thing of passion. He knows no restraint, and finds no stability. He fights upon the periphery of his life, and, submerged by his rampant and conflicting desires, loses complete touch with his spiritual center.

The intelligent use of the two formulae, however, transmutes the abuses of the past. He concludes the period of what might be called 'vehement fluctuation,' and travels a straight path towards the revelation of divine beauty and bi-polar peace. Thus, the individual learns, primarily, to stand so steadfastly and so peacefully in the center of his being, that he brings peace, beauty and synthesis to the warring forces within and without, and his growing secondary ability to restrain a desire for lesser things, and pursue only that which is of great spiritual value, ensures his peacemaking soul that it will have at its disposal a personal instrument which will be utterly devoted to the task of bringing peace and beauty to the world.

7. Some examples of vocational aptitudes and orientations relating to the combination of the fourth ray soul and the sixth ray personality:

* the peacemaker who sacrifices himself as a martyr in the cause of peace
* the mediator animated by the highest idealism
* the negotiator who (understanding the nature and value of idealism) excels when working with partisans and special interest groups
* the arbitrator who, in all settlements, upholds his vision of what is fair
* the intermediary who cannot be deflected from his mission
* the harmonizer who will not settle for anything less than perfect harmony
* the warrior who fights with a fury born of intense belief
* the creative artist who sacrifices everything for his art
* the passionate humanist
* the beautifier whose work inspires the urge for "uplift"
* the painter whose canvases glow with passion
* the composer of religious or devotional music
* the musician capable of great emotional expressivity
* the actor as activist
* the dramatist whose plays espouse a "cause"
* the storyteller whose stories always have a "moral"
* the romantically idealistic poet
* the architect whose structures reflect the thrust of aspiration
* the city planner who gives special attention to the needs of the religious community
* the psychodramatist who easily inspires others to express themselves emotionally
* the exponent of culture capable of arousing and motivating many to support the arts

In general, vocations and professions which require a strong creative imagination, spontaneity, expressivity, aesthetic sensitivity, and a marked ability to bring harmony out of conflict, beauty out of ugliness, and at–one–ment out of divisiveness, *as well as* high idealism, undeviating devotion, great enthusiasm and persistent emotional intensity.

8. A proposed list of well-known individuals (historical, contemporary, fictional or mythological) whose soul ray can reasonably be considered the fourth, with a strong subsidiary sixth ray influence (whether or not the sixth ray is, strictly speaking, the personality ray):

Michelangelo Buonaroti: artistic genius, leading sculptor, painter, architect of the Italian Renaissance. (See ray analysis in Section VI, Volume II.)

Lord Byron: 19th century English poet and satirist, whose poetry and personality captured the imagination of Europe. His attitude of ironic despair and his aspirations for political liberty made him the universal symbol of the Romantic poet.

Vincent Van Gogh: painter, generally considered the greatest Dutch painter after Rembrandt.

El Greco: a true Renaissance Humanist who achieved greatness as a religious painter and portaitist.

Edgar Allen Poe: poet, critic, writer of short stories often of a myterious or macabre nature. Poe was the creator of the American Gothic tale and of the whole detective fiction genre. His analytical powers suggest the presence of ray five, as well. Astrological factors account for his fascination with the bizzare and perverse.

Percy Bysshe Shelley: poet, philosopher, reformer, novelist and essayist. Shelley was one of the greatest and most controversial of the English Romantic thinkers. The third ray may also be present.

Some Contrasts Between the Ray 4 Soul and the Ray 7 Personality

Ray 4 Soul		Ray 7 Personality
* spiritual beauty	vs.	* strict personal order
* soul–inspired spontaneity	vs.	* personal rigidity; fear of spontaneity
* skillfully improvisatory	vs.	* wedded to customary, crystallized, procedures
* seeks novel artistic forms to express divine understanding	vs.	* controlled and limited by worn and ordinary modes of expression
* facile access to deeply–subjective psychological depths	vs.	* concern with outer behavior and surface matters
* highly imaginative	vs.	* imagination limited by established forms and conditioned responses
* delights in free–form expression of ideas through art	vs.	* tightly, inelastically formal
* playfully, delightfully unpredictable	vs.	* stultifyingly–predictable routinization of life
* easily accessing intuitive inspiration	vs.	* following convention rather than trusting any "inner" source of guidance; proceeding "by the book" and according to precedent
* identifies easily with a wide diversity of people	vs.	* often displays an exclusive, haughty or snobbish attitude
* broadly tolerant of contrast and difference	vs.	* intolerantly sectarian
* joyfully acknowledges individuality	vs.	* rejects individual ideosyncrasies as abnormal (except [7B])
* imaginatively open to new possibilities	vs.	* "knee–jerk" conservatism which 'freezes the flow of time'
* keenly receptive and sensitive to subjective nuances within the psyche	vs.	* limited by a strictly objective and physically practical point of view
* freely interactive with others	vs.	* controls and standardizes his own behavior and the behavior of others
* rejoices in the expressive freedom of the human spirit; an example of the "Renaissance–mentality"	vs.	* slavery to tradition despite the adverse repercussions of such an attitude upon the freedom of the human spirit

The Integration Process for the Individual with a Ray 4 Soul and a Ray 7 Personality

1. The pre–spiritual phase; soul energy appropriated by a selfish personality: At this pre–spiritual phase of evolutionary unfoldment, the individual's motives (based upon the personality distortion of fourth ray soul energy, and the self–centered use of the seventh ray personality force) are to achieve an agreeable feeling of personal peace and harmony through tension–releasing expression of conflicting bio–psychic impulses, *as well as* a rigidly ritualized, tightly ordered life conducive to physical plane safety, security and 'perfected' materialistic living. The person wants, primarily, to be constantly surrounded by what he considers beautiful or attractive, to be spontaneously self-expressive without discipline or control, self-indulgently dramatic or moody (as he pleases), and greatly appreciated for his colorful, unpredictable temperament, but he *also* wants to live a highly predictable (hence, relatively risk-free) life, to avoid having to think for himself or act upon his own initiative, and to have the solid assurance that all his instinctual appetites and imagined material needs will be satisfied on schedule.

Negatively and glamorously, these two ray influences can combine to produce: a precious person with pretensions of status (4A + 7); one who poses and pretends, conveying the impression of artificiality and stilted mannerism (4A + 7A, 7C); an ultrarefined aesthete who looks down upon any form of imperfection (4A + 7A); one who is satisfied with superficial beauty of appearance, rather than beauty of character (4A + 7A, 7C); one whose concepts of beauty are entirely conventional (4A + 7A); one who seeks to delight and entertain in order to be socially esteemed; an unstable, unconfident person who seeks personal reinforcement through social position (4 + 7A, 7C); one who must 'decorate' himself in the latest colors and styles in order to feel worthwhile (4A + 7A, 7C); one who compensates for his constant instabilities and vacillations by recourse to compulsiveness (4B + 7A); one whose only relief from internal conflict and crisis is a rigid adherence to personal rituals (4B + 7C); one who, because of his contrary and undisciplined temperament, seeks to turn the established order "upside-down" so he does not have to conform (4B + 7B); one who compounds the ineffectualness of his overly-compromising, overly-conciliatory nature by refusing to be 'impolite' under any circumstances (4A + 7A); one for whom maintaining personal harmony is absolutely dependent upon the upholding of tradition and custom (4A + 7A, 7C); one who tightly organizes everyone and everything in his environment to satisfy his deep desire for undisturbed harmony (4A + 7A); one so in love with the drama of spectacle that he is easily "carried away" by empty show; a morally undisciplined person, deeply captivated by the "glamor of the physical body" (4 + 7B); a difficult and combative person, who fights for a perfection of form which can never be achieved (4B + 7); a thoroughly indecisive person who persistently defaults to doing things as they have been done before (4 + 7A); the individual whose deep inner agonies center upon never being able to express himself perfectly in form; etc.

2. The phase of conflict; pure soul energy conflicts with personality force: The essential conflict between the ray four soul and the ray seven personality is the struggle between, on the one hand, the spiritual need for improvisation and spontaneity in order to receive and express new ways of creating beauty by harmonizing dissonance, and, on the other, the personal desire to think and behave in established ways which lead predictably to material and psychological security.

3. The soul/personality integration process from the perspective of the consciousness identified primarily with the fourth ray soul: It will be the task of the fourth ray soul to create in the seventh ray personality a willingness to experiment with new experiences. When consciousness is identified with the fourth ray soul, it never knows what is going to happen next, or where a new perception of beauty, or a potential for inspired expression will arise. Such a soul remains open to the muse, does not systematically plan, and awaits the descent of intuitive gifts which present new ways of revealing divinity. The fourth ray soul, however, is faced with a personality which (whether conservative or revolutionary) attempts to leave nothing to chance. The soul lives open to revelation; the personality creates a "closed system" in which everything is *under control*. The soul, knowing that divine gifts often arrive as a surprise, is frustrated by the personality's refusal to remain 'creatively unorganized.' After all, if everything is superbly organized, there is no room for that unexpected 'something,' coming from 'somewhere,' which can transform a situation from competent–but–commonplace to captivating. Slowly the soul infiltrates the personal consciousness with contrasting currents of thought which demand an unexpected response, a change of pace. The soul seeks to challenge the often deadening regularity of the seventh ray personality with elements of unpredictability. The stress and strain which consciousness experiences as it tries to cope with life's contrasting, bi–polar energies will disrupt the self–protective 'sameness' of seventh ray routine. From the soul's perspective, if the personality continues to experience "business as usual," it is not spiritually alive, and is no fit vehicle to receive startling impressions of divine beauty.

Even the more experimental seventh ray personality [type (7B)] needs to relax its structure. This type of personality may be subject to sudden and startling developments, but after the flash of revelation which stimulates a revolution or great reordering, the new order is institutionalized, and preserved with the same kind of rigidity one might expect from the more tightly controlled (7A) personality type. Any type of seventh ray personality has much to learn when attempting to blend and fuse with a spontaneous, improvisatory fourth ray soul.

4. The soul/personality integration process from the perspective of the consciousness identified primarily with the seventh ray personality: The fourth ray pressure towards integration will be felt by the seventh ray personality as an invitation to unnecessary risk and ineffectiveness. The personality is most comfortable when it knows exactly what it has to do, and then proceeds to do it, step by step, with no hesitation, no delay and no "wild cards." For a personality accustomed to having everything proceed "like clockwork," it is decidedly unsettling to wait to be "moved" by something as vague and unpredictable as an inspiration. The intuition, with which the fourth ray has such resonance, is from the perspective of the seventh ray personality, notoriously unreliable in terms of *time*; it comes when it will, and there is no compelling it. The personality is, therefore, threatened when it is asked to disrupt its perfectly–ordered schedule to await something intangible and untimed. It has no time for such impractical, non–productive activities. But slowly, within the depths of the personal consciousness, there arises a longing for the beauty and harmony which cannot be contained by a predictable, well–ordered life – a beauty and harmony which cannot be commanded by the will, nor made to appear in a timely fashion. The personality may wish to reject such intimations and longings as vagaries, but it will find itself increasingly dissatisfied with a life that, superficially at least, works too well. Learning that if it is to be stimulated and enlivened by the beautiful, it must give up its insistence upon iron–clad guarantees, the personality gradually discovers that things may work out just as well, even better, if they are not exactly and rigidly arranged in advance. Experiencing the dread of not knowing how things will work out is the price to be paid by the seventh ray personality as it seeks to approach the mystery of divine beauty.

5. The ideal expression of the combination of the ray four soul and the ray seven personality: The urge to create harmony and beauty is expressed through an exquisite sense of form. The love of color exceeds the love of structure, and yet the two are marvelously well-integrated. Aesthetic expression conforms to the highest standards; every creative effort is refined and polished to the point of consummation. Beauty is expressed in perfect form – art "in excelsis." The creative imagination is highly developed; images are full, colorful and structurally complete – vivid models of that which is to be manifested. This combination bestows the capacity to create distinguished portrayals of character, which are both refined and meticulously executed; character-appearance and outer behavioral patterns are presented in a manner exceptionally true-to-life. The individual may well possess the gift of eloquence, and the written or spoken word will be presented with careful attention to style. There will be a special talent for expression in color and/or sound, and the form of expression will be splendidly organized in a manner reminiscent of ritual and magic. The process of peacemaking will be pursued with consummate skill-in-action, diplomacy and perfect timing, facilitating the task of tension-reduction. When peace is achieved, it is perfectly instituted and administered in accordance with lawful procedures, both of which contribute to the preservation and stability of the peace. This combination brings about perfected interplay between the pairs of opposites, rhythmically and harmoniously manifested. The "bridge" (or antahkarana) linking the various dimensions of subjective and objective reality is solidly built and well-maintained through regular use. Buddhic intuitions which present themselves as beautiful imaginary forms are anchored upon the physical plane. The understanding of beauty-in-relationship is expressed in concrete symbols. This is a combination which, more than any other, is designed to bring beauty into the world.

6. The combined effect of the two integration formulae: The primary integration formula is *Steadfastness*, keyed to the fourth ray soul. The secondary integration formula is proposed as *Orientation*, keyed to the seventh ray personality. The first formula corrects fourth ray tendencies towards vacillation, irresoluteness, instability, indecisiveness and moral cowardice, whereas the second formula corrects seventh ray tendencies towards selfish building and organizing according to short-sighted, materially-minded personal plans, but without an attentive orientation to the Divine Design as revealed by the soul. Used together, these two formulae provide the individual striving for soul/personality integration with the composite quality of 'oriented steadfastness' (i.e., the attentive, spiritual orientation of the personality which reinforces the steadfast and harmoniously balanced perspective of the "inner man"). If the personality upon the outer planes is oriented towards the light which shines in the East (i.e., the "light of the soul,") and the soul-infused consciousness of the disciple (the inner man) is perfectly balanced between the "pairs of opposites," there is created a potent alignment for the manifestation of beauty, peace and harmony upon the physical plane. Thus, these formulae facilitate the cultivation of a more attentive, impressionable, 'light-permeable' personal consciousness, supportive of those rare moments of exalted consciousness when (pervaded by the presence of the soul) the individual stands poised between the many pairs of warring forces, holding them in a state of dynamic equilibrium (a state of dynamic peace), and drawing them together towards mutual victory.

In the earlier stages of evolution, before successfully applying these formulae, an individual with this ray combination often finds himself embroiled in conflict, and manifesting many tangible forms conceived by an unstable and conflicted consciousness – forms reflective of his troubled personal condition, having little or nothing to do with the manifestation of soul intention. The beglamored individual thinks he has produced beauty, when, in fact, he has only contributed more clutter to the pile of irrelevant, light–suffocating forms. To the clear–seeing eye, his cherished forms serve only to reveal the state of his agonized, imbalanced psyche. But learning must proceed in this manner. Under the broadening influence of the soul, his 'beauty' stands revealed to him as ugliness, and his cherished forms as obstructions to the Plan. He realizes that he is in a "distant land," exiled and confined to crystallized constructs of his own design, far – very far – from the 'land of beauty' (his soul–center).

The intelligent use of the two formulae, however, transmutes the abuses of the past. He terminates the period of soul–blind creativity and discovers in himself (slowly at first) the proper orientation and steadfast spiritual poise to creatively manifest spiritual beauty and harmony as they are known to the soul. Thus, using these formulae of integration, he learns, primarily, to stand so steadfastly and so peacefully in the center of his being, that he brings peace, beauty and synthesis to the warring forces, within and without, and his growing secondary ability to orient his personal vision to the inner design of beauty illuminated by his soul, ensures that soul that it will have at its disposal a personal intrument which will build only those habitations which will be true embodiments of beauty and vessels to contain the energy of peace.

7. Some examples of vocational aptitudes and orientations relating to the combination of the fourth ray soul and the seventh ray personality:

* the peacemaker who is adept at devising and administrating new patterns of behavior which promote the maintenance of peaceful relations

* the mediator well–versed in the customs of those to be reconciled

* the negotiator whose etiquette is impeccable

* the arbitrator who adheres strictly to legal procedures

* the intermediary who always sustains a constructive rhythm of interaction between the two parties

* the translator/interpreter who is utterly dependable and responsible in the performance of his function

* the harmonizer who has a talent for saying just the right word at the right time

* the warrior who performs, with consummate grace, the movements required by the martial arts

* the creative artist with an exceptional ability to manifest his ideas as perfectly as he conceives them

* the beautifier with a keen eye for spatial composition
* the painter endowed with an exquisite sense of form
* the composer who creates innovative forms
* the musician who is scrupulously faithful to the style in which compositions were intended to be performed
* the actor whose portrayals are suave and sophisticated
* the dramatist whose plays are elegantly constructed
* the storyteller with a masterful sense of timing
* the dancer whose disciplined body faithfully reflects her every intention
* the architect for whom beauty of form precedes function
* the city planner whose designs have great organic integrity
* the psychodramatist who polishes 'scenes' until all psychological revelations have been extracted
* the exponent of culture who stands as a pillar of society

In general: vocations and professions which require a strong creative imagination, spontaneity, expressivity, aesthetic sensitivity, and a marked ability to bring harmony out of conflict, beauty out of ugliness, and at–one–ment from divisiveness, *as well as* the power to organize or reorganize, the ability to build, a facility for creating or maintaining standards, and the capacity to skillfully manifest ideas through form.

8. A proposed list of well-known individuals (historical, contemporary, fictional or mythological) whose soul ray can reasonably be considered the fourth, with a strong subsidiary seventh ray (whether or not the seventh ray is, strictly speaking, the personality ray):

Alban Berg: one of the principal figures responsible for bringing maturity to the atonal style of 20th–century music. Berg was called the "classicist of modern music." The second ray, as well, seems to have played an important part in his energy system.

Felix Mendelssohn: Romantic composer whose music is known for its lyricism and vivacity. He observed classical models and practices, while initiating key aspects of Romanticism.

Anna Pavlova: perhaps the most renowned ballerina in the tradition of classical ballet

Raphael: painter and architect of the early 16th century. He is considered by many the consummating artist of the High Renaissance, giving incomparable expression to the spirit of Humanism.

Soul/Personality Combinations with a Ray Five Soul

Some Contrasts Between the Ray 5 Soul and the Ray 1 Personality

Ray 5 Soul		Ray 1 Personality
* search for exact knowledge	vs.	* love of personal power
* dedication to science and pure research	vs.	* dedication to assertive self–advancement
* emphasis upon the intellect as an instrument of enquiry, investigation and discovery	vs.	* emphasis upon the will as a means of promoting personal authority
* rationality as the justification of action	vs.	* powerful personal ambition as the justification for action
* great capacity for living the pure life of the mind	vs.	* rejection of the pure life of the mind as insufficiently vital or practical
* modesty in the face of the endlessness of knowledge	vs.	* arrogance based upon excessive self–emphasis
* great analytical ability	vs.	* brushing exact analysis aside
* laborious patience in the pursuit of truth	vs.	* impatience in the satisfaction of personal demands
* meticulous attention to knowledge in detail	vs.	* careless dismissal of the highly detailed approach because it retards rapid action
* thorough understanding of cause–and–effect relationships	vs.	* rash oversimplification
* knowledge before action	vs.	* action before knowledge
* precision of action based upon exact knowledge	vs.	* impetuous, often destructive action based simply on the will–to–act, and the will to make a strong impact
* insistence upon scientific verification	vs.	* assertion of personal opinion as 'truth,' without recourse to scientific verification
* scientifically detached objectivity concerning one's self	vs.	* intense self-centeredness which makes it difficult to regard the self objectively

The Integration Process for the Individual with a Ray 5 Soul and a Ray 1 Personality

1. The pre–spiritual phase; soul energy appropriated by a selfish personality: At this pre–spiritual phase of evolutionary unfoldment, the individual's motives (based upon the personality distortion of fifth ray soul energy, and the self–centered use of first ray personality force) are to achieve narrow, materialistic, intellectual certainty, *as well as* great personal power, arising from the unrestrained imposition of the personal will. The person wants primarily to take everything apart (either analytically or actually), reduce all life experience to nothing but rationalistic formulae, control matter mechanically for selfish ends, and reject any kind of knowledge that is not materialistic or derived from the five senses, but he *also wants* to dominate and control others, and wield authority unopposed.

Negatively and glamorously, these two ray influences can combine to produce: the stubborn, self-assured, materialistic thinker, who instinctively discounts any evidence which challenges his authority (5A + 1); the harsh critic who does not care if his criticism hurts or destroys others (5 + 1B); one who examines all people and circumstances with an attitude of cold detachment, and from a position of proud isolation; the investigator who will use any means, however inhumane, to get the information he is seeking – for instance, the sadistic scientist (5A + 1B); the amoral scientist who feels more powerful because his discoveries are utilized for purposes of war and destruction (5 + 1B); the arid, non-magnetic individual who deliberately cuts himself off from his fellow human beings; the inveterate skeptic who severely derides those who have faith as gullible fools; one who, suffering from an idée fixe, forcefully "hammers home" his opinions at every occasion; one who, believing his mental prejudices to be proven facts, rudely resists all attempts to point out his errors; one who loves technology but rejects people (5B + 1B); one for whom great knowledge serves only as an incentive to pride and separativeness (5A + 1); one whose "hard-headedness" easily turns to "hard-heartedness"; etc.

2. The phase of conflict; pure soul energy conflicts with personality force: The essential conflict between the ray five soul and the ray one personality is the struggle between the spiritually-pure need to know, and the selfish desire for personal power.

3. The soul/personality integration process from the perspective of the consciousness identified primarily with the fifth ray soul: It will be the task of the fifth ray soul to convey to the first ray personality a love of knowledge for its own sake, and not for the power and advancement it can bring. The consciousness identified with the fifth ray soul is truly fascinated with the world, and takes great delight in understanding how things *are*, and how things *work*, whether or not the personality benefits materially from such knowledge. The soul, characterized thus by the quality of *pure interest*, is faced with a personality which is often engulfed in egotism – feeling that all people and all things are to be used for its own aggrandizement. The soul is naturally frustrated because the personal consciousness refuses to see things as they are, to observe with pure disinterestedness, and to keep *self* from distorting the understanding of what is seen. It will be the soul's difficult responsibility to guide the personality towards a truly detached attitude – not the detachment which is unaffected by ties to others (for this, the first ray personality already has), but the detachment which creates a new perspective in consciousness leading to illumined knowledge of the "garment of God." For the fifth ray soul, light is paramount, and the lust for personal power, which obscures the light, a definite hindrance.

4. The soul/personality integration process from the perspective of the consciousness identified with the first ray personality: The fifth ray pressure towards integration will be felt by the first ray personality as something of an irrelevance – almost an impertinence. The personality feels most comfortable when doing precisely what it pleases; people and things either further its purposes or, they are are in the way. Certainly, there is little inclination to stop and *make a study* of situations, purely for the pleasure of learning. Those with a strong first ray frequently refer, with some scorn, to certain lines of thought as "merely academic," – i.e., *useless* in terms of accomplishment. This sense of being asked to engage in the useless acquisition of knowledge is precisely what the first ray personality may experience as the fifth ray becomes more influential. The personality has no time, so it thinks, for patient, detached observation and analysis prior to acting. Should the personality 'waste its time' in doing so, it would have to slacken its pace, and might risk sacrificing that which it intends to grasp for itself. The personality, therefore, resists the call to *know with purity* as something unnecessary in the life of a "mover and a shaker." Gradually, however, under the impress of the soul, there begins to arise within the personal consciousness an unsettling perception of its own ignorance. Gradually, it is realized that power without knowledge is, itself, useless. The vision of an endlessly fascinating world awaiting discovery enters the consciousness, along with the realization of the counterproductivity of impetuous, benighted blundering. A new and important learning begins to grow – that knowledge is a good in its own right, and that eventually, "knowledge is power." The personality temporarily holds its will-to-power in abeyance and takes the time to understand, with real clarity, at least a few of the many particulars before its eyes.

5. The ideal combination of the fifth ray soul and the first ray personality: The pursuit and application of concrete knowledge are expressed with power and endurance. Patient research is supported by relentless personal strength. An individual with this ray combination is likely to have a penetrating power of analysis, with the will to stay focused upon the object of attention for long periods of time. Fortitude and one-pointed persistence serve the spirit of selfless, scientific enquiry and discovery. Once discovery is made, this individual would have the bravery to present the discovery unequivocally, no matter how upsetting or revolutionary its implications. The urge towards specific, focused research masters the attitude of focused self-importance, and yet, self-confidence is abidingly present to sustain the search for knowledge. Here is an individual who, understanding the necessity for experimentation, has the courage to undertake experiments which are particularly demanding and even dangerous. There is a tremendous capacity for sheer common sense, and for "no-nonsense" action which gets the job done. The fifth ray individual is unusually objective about his own feelings and emotions, and when the fifth ray is complemented by the first, emotions are strictly controlled, and never allowed to interfere with the functioning of the will. Technical and mechanical ability will be outstanding, accompanied by a real understanding for how to use such ability to leverage personal power. All discoveries are utilized to help humanity triumph over its adversaries. Here, one might find a scientist who realizes that knowledge is a matter of life and death; in fact, his research may focus upon "life-and-death" issues. The keen particularity of the fifth ray supercedes the first ray desire to see only "the big picture," but an understanding of the value of simplicity assists in transforming knowledge of particular facts into essential, immediately-useful action. With this combination, analysis is primary, but synthesis, with its concern for the essential, is also present.

6. The combined effect of the two integration formulae: The primary integration formula is *Detachment*, keyed to the fifth ray soul. The secondary integration formula is *Inclusion*, keyed to the first ray soul. The first formula corrects the fifth ray tendencies towards mental attachment to matter, and the obsessive preoccupation with investigating or manipulating concrete form while ignoring the reality of that which is "formless," whereas the second formula corrects the exclusive and isolative tendencies characteristic of the first ray personality. Used together, these two formulae provide the individual striving for soul/personality integration with the composite quality of 'inclusive detachment,'(i.e., the magnetic, inclusive and accepting attitude within the personal consciousness which facilitates, within the inner psyche, a detachment from matter, and an attachment to the subjective reality which unifies all things). Aided by these formulae, the individual detaches his inner consciousness from the perspective of fragmentation (induced by the discriminating fifth ray), and begins to experience a stronger and more loving relationship to the many who are subjectively related (despite appearances to the contrary caused by what might be called 'the illusion of fragmentation,' which life in the three worlds imposes upon the human consciousness). Thus, these formulae make it possible for the individual to cultivate a more inviting and embracing personal consciousness, supportive of those rare moments of exalted consciousness, when (pervaded by the presence of the soul) he *knows,* past all doubting and seeming, the indisputable *reality* of that great subjective Entity –the planetary God– whose "garment" of matter has long been the object of his fascination and enquiry.

In the earlier stages of evolution, before successfully applying these formulae, an individual with this ray combination often finds himself engrossed in matter and utterly isolated from his fellow human beings. Knowledge of the outer form is his one, great, all-consuming interest and he rebuffs others so that he may occupy himself ever more exclusively with that interest. As his enquiries proceed, he becomes more and more unapproachable – an isolated *mind* at work. His life is filled with barriers: between himself and other people, and between his materialistic mind and the perception of the unifying reality lying behind and within all matter. He is "caught in concrete" and repels those who might help him break free.

The intelligent use of these formulae, however, transmutes the abuses of the past. The individual terminates his slavery to the misperception that form is reality. He realizes, too, that he does not stand alone, and he begins to embrace those he previously rejected. By using the formulae, the individual learns, primarily, to detach himself from the illusion of multiplicity, and to know the One God who is the Unity behind all material diversity, and his growing secondary ability to embrace others within that Unity, rather than reject them as heretofore, ensures the soul of a strong and loving instrument with which to investigate diversity and prove its relationship to a seamless, subjective Unity.

7. Some examples of vocational aptitudes and orientations relating to the combination of the fifth ray soul and the first ray personality:

* the scientist whose major focus of interest is researching the means for releasing vast amounts of power

* the researcher for whom no research project is too arduous

* the investigator who is ready and willing to face danger fearlessly in order to carry out his investigations

* the enquirer who asks his questions with uncompromising detachment and impersonality

* the experimenter capable of controlled, yet relentless, persistence in conducting a difficult and prolonged program of experimentation
* the analyst who has a knack for grasping the essential point
* the specialist with a keen sense of priorities, knowing, in no uncertain terms, the relative importance of his field of expertise
* the objective observer whose accuracy and efficiency are enhanced by great discipline and self-control
* the inventor who rises to the challenge of harsh necessity
* the engineer who enjoys his work most when there are tremendous obstacles to be overcome
* the technician who can be trusted to let nothing stand in the way of the execution of his responsibilities
* the mechanic who is a totally independent and self-reliant "troubleshooter"
* the repair-person who is completely confident that he can fix anything

In general: vocations and professions which require keen analytical abilities, the capacity for research, and scientific and/or technical expertise, *as well as* great will power, strength and stamina, the ability to stand firmly on principle, and (when necessary) the power to destroy obstacles.

8. A proposed list of well-known individuals (historical, contemporary, fictional or mythological) whose soul ray can reasonably be considered the fifth, with a strong subsidiary first ray influence (whether or not the first ray is, strictly speaking, the personality ray):

Thomas Alva Edison: one of the outstanding geniuses in the history of technology. Edison held 1,093 patents which included the incandescent electric lamp, the phonograph, the carbon telephone transmitter, and the motion picture projector. He also created the first industrial-research laboratory.

Thomas Henry Huxley: 19th century English physician, biologist, and "bull dog" for Charles Darwin in the advancement of the Theory of Evolution

Louis Pasteur: French chemist, microbiologist, whose contributions to humanity's welfare were among the most valuable and varied in the history of science and industry. (See ray analysis in Section VI, Volume II)

Igor Sikorsky: outstanding pioneer of aircraft design, and developer of the helicopter. He always insisted upon being the test pilot for any airplane or helicopter he designed.

Some Contrasts Between the Ray 5 Soul and the Ray 2 Personality

Ray 5 Soul		Ray 2 Personality
* the scientific pursuit of pure truth	vs.	* preoccupation with the demands of personal love and affection
* relentless, painstaking investigation	vs.	* aversion to extreme efforts which disrupt ease and comfort
* uncompromising tough–mindedness	vs.	* undiscriminating soft–heartedness
* hard–headed recognition of straight fact, unswayed by affection or sentiment	vs.	* unwisely allowing personal love and affection to influence the hard–won, rational conclusions of the mind
* well–suited to understand matter and handle concrete, physical plane reality	vs.	* often too 'soft' and vulnerable to cope practically and effectively with concrete physical plane reality
* scientifically applied spiritual detachment serving the clear perception of reality	vs.	* personal attachment blurs the perception of reality
* standing back for improved vision	vs.	* great difficulty standing back; prefers closeness and intimacy
* insistence on preserving the totally objective point of view	vs.	* allowing personal magnetism and attraction to interfere with objectivity
* uncompromisingly impersonal approach to truth	vs.	* the "personal equation" looms overly large
* presentation of the exact scientific facts even when they are socially upsetting or unpopular	vs.	* softening facts in order to preserve personal popularity
* independent self–verification of the accuracy of thoughts	vs.	* too likely to be swayed by the opinions of those who are closely related
* a vision of truth based upon the *separative* modalities of thought – analysis and discrimination	vs.	* loathe to implement any kind of separative act, hence an avoidance of analysis and discrimination
* spiritual skepticism as an instrument of truth and an antidote for gullibility in spiritual matters	vs.	* often too open and willing to accept on trust
* putting all ideas to the test by means of strict rationality	vs.	* a distrust of rationality which may be a disguise for mental laziness
* willingness to make great sacrifices in the pursuit of knowledge	vs.	* too much love of fun and enjoyment

The Integration Process for the Individual with a Ray 5 Soul and a Ray 2 Personality

1. The pre–spiritual phase; soul energy appropriated by a selfish personality: At this pre–spiritual phase of evolutionary unfoldment, the individual's motives (based upon the personality distortion of fifth ray soul energy, and the self–centered use of second ray personality force) are to achieve narrow, materialistic, intellectual certainty, *as well as* the complete fulfillment of personal love (or the complete satisfaction of studious enquiry [2B]). The person wants primarily to take everything apart (either analytically or actually), reduce all life experience to nothing but rationalistic formulae, control matter mechanically for selfish ends, and reject any kind of knowledge that is not materialistic or derived from the five senses, but he *also* wants to be constantly loved, consistently popular, warmly admired, well-cared-for, and to live a soft, comfortable, well-protected and well-insulated life, closely attached to those people, places and things which he loves and finds personally satisfying.

Negatively and glamorously, these two ray influences can combine to produce: one with an exclusively mental focus, complacently over-absorbed in his studies (5A + 2B); one who, focusing upon his area of interest, attempts to achieve encyclopedic knowledge of a virtual infinitude of particulars, thus becoming overwhelmed by inapplicable minutiae (5A + 2B); one who has only harsh criticism and self-satisfied contempt for the mental limitations of others (5A + 2B); one who is filled with doubt, but is too timid to discover whether his doubt is really warranted (5 + 2A); one who confines his enquiries strictly to the world of the senses (or their instrumental extensions), and becomes threatened or, even, frightened at the thought that subjective or spiritual things may be real (5 + 2A); one who has become comfortably satisfied with the commonsense view of the world, and is too lazy to disturb himself by looking beyond it; the convinced materialist who, having justified his materialism rationally, thinks it only sensible to live a "soft life" of comfort and easy gratification; one who becomes so aware of the infinitude of knowledge, and is so filled with the sense of his own personal limitations, that he easily falls into self-pity and a sense of inferiority (5A + 2B); one who hesitates to present the facts as he knows them, because he desires to remain popular and well-liked (5 + 2A); one who, having assured himself of the unchanging veracity of his factual knowledge, is smugly indulgent with those who are foolish enough to question him (5 + 2B); one whose relaxed, unassuming personality entirely disguises his mental commitment to develop technologies which threaten the welfare of human beings (5B + 2); in general, one who is inclined to employ his very capable mind for destructive purposes, but gets away with it because he appears harmless; etc.

2. The phase of conflict; pure soul energy conflicts with personality force: The essential conflict between the ray five soul and the ray two personality is the struggle between the spiritual need to discover and apply true knowledge at all costs, and the personal desire to *do* nothing and to *know* nothing that would disrupt cherished relationships and comfortable circumstances.

3. The soul/personality integration process from the perspective of the consciousness identified primarily with the fifth ray soul: It will be the task of the fifth ray soul to infuse the second ray personality with the *urge to know,* no matter how much the "truth" may hurt. The consciousness identified with the fifth ray soul is forever asking questions, searching, enquiring, investigating, seeking to discover the true nature of matter and form. Faced with a personality which is often disinclined to use the mind in a strictly rational manner (being, in general, far more interested in feelings and sentient sensitivities), the soul must find a way to awaken it to a genuine and purely mental "interest in things," beyond the kind of interest which such a personality naturally has in those things (and people) to which it is closely *attached.* Such attachment inhibits pure knowledge, for the personality does not really understand (nor does it wish to understand), with any kind of objectivity, the various objects of its attachment – whether people, places or things. Objective understanding might, so the personality thinks, disturb the quality of its relationships, and it is right – only it little suspects that the disturbance will be for the better, and will be a disturbance of sentiment but not of real quality. The soul is frustrated that the personality will not truly observe, but tends to overestimate whatever it loves, and, especially, the people it loves. The second ray personality draws "too close" for the exercise of truly objective understanding. The soul, therefore, seeks to have the personality "stand back," and look on with unbiased disinteresteness, no matter what the heart and feelings may say to the contrary. Only in this way will the truth be revealed (in all its purity and lucidity), and well–meaning (or, self–comforting) distortions of the truth be relinquished.

4. The soul/personality integration process from the perspective of the consciousness identified primarily with the second ray personality: The fifth ray pressure towards integration will be felt by the second ray personality as a growing (and very unwelcome) inclination towards cold, and even clinical, detachment. The consciousness when identified with the second ray personality feels most comfortable when it can enjoy *contact*, close and reassuring relations, the warmth of accumulation – whatever and whomever may be magnetically accumulated. There are some things the personality simply does not wish to question. The thought of treating the "near and dear" people and things with scientific detachment, and without familiarity, is most uncomfortable. And yet, deep within the consciousness of the second ray personality the call for truth in all things, for exact evaluation, slowly begins to arise. It is a difficult thing for an individual with this ray combination (especially at the intermediary stage of development here being discussed) to suspend the action of what is normally called the "heart" in order to allow the head to convey its mode of light and revelation. Here, as is the case with all the ray combinations, one of the individual's early tendencies may be to compartmentalize, allowing (in this particular instance), the second ray personality, at times, to have its way entirely, and at other times, completely forgetting the inclinations of the personality and abiding entirely with those of the soul. But, in terms of the integration process, compartmentalization is counterproductive, and does not lead towards soul/personality fusion. The personality must at length accede to the 'unpleasant' task of objectivity, or it will begin to have intimations that the closeness it so much cherishes is warm but unenlightened. The personality learns, at length, that it cannot tolerate a state of comfortable darkness, no matter how unflattering and disconcerting the truth may be. The glare of the harsh light of pure knowledge is better than the blindness of a comfortable mole.

5. The ideal expression of the combination of the ray five soul and the ray two personality: The pursuit and application of concrete knowledge are expressed lovingly, responsibly, and with great attention to human impact. This combination is one of those in which mind and heart are united; the mind of God is scanned with focused intensity so that some new, practical understanding of natural law may be won for the edification (and the comforting) of humanity. The love of pure research grows stronger than the love of an "easygoing" life, and yet the sense that the fruits of research must ameliorate the lives of the human family is never lost. Here we may find an individual who must *know* the truth, no matter how he may *feel* about it – personally, and yet the personal touch never fails to soften the glare of plain truth. One can imagine an accomplished surgeon – a master with the scalpel, but kind of heart. Ideally, there will be a perfect blend of scientific detachment and loving attachment. A kind and loving, humanitarian outlook is an excellent support for one who seeks to promote the application of specialized, technical knowledge for the advancement of the race. A "high-powered" scientific mind dwells within a gracious person. Here may also be found the student of any one of the multitudinous aspects of reality – one who *loves* his field, approaching its study with innocence, fascination, wonderment, and infinite respect. Such an individual will realize that the mysteries of Nature (in all their mind-baffling intricacy) are mysteries created by Love. This is also the ray combination of an expert who has spent years mastering all the many particulars of his field, but has the tact and loving patience to do an admirable job of teaching what he knows.

6. The combined effect of the two integration formulae: The primary integration formula is *Detachment*, keyed to the fifth ray soul. The secondary integration formula is *Centralization*, keyed to the second ray personality. The first formula corrects the fifth ray tendencies towards mental attachment to matter, and the obsessive preoccupation with investigating or manipulating concrete form (while ignoring the reality of that which is "formless"), whereas the second formula corrects the second ray tendencies towards diffusion, overexpansion, and an energy-draining attachment to life's peripheral attractions. Used together, these two formulae provide the individual striving for soul/personality integration with the composite quality of 'centralized detachment,' (i.e., the attainment of a centered personality consciousness [loving, yet detached] which complements the will of the "inner man" to detach from what might be called 'the mystification of matter' [the illusion of the ultimate reality of material form]). The "inner man" is enabled to detach his spiritual-mind from a preoccupation with the modalities of matter and form; the "outer man" detaches his heart from peripheral attractions, however pleasant. Thus, these formulae make it possible for the individual to cultivate a firmer, more centered, more detached personal consciousness, supportive of those rare moments of exalted consciousness, when (pervaded by the presence of the soul) he *knows,* past all doubting and seeming, the indisputable *reality* of that great subjective Entity (the planetary God), whose "garment" of matter has long been the object of his fascination and enquiry.

In the earlier stages of evolution, before successfully applying these formulae, an individual with this ray combination often finds himself engrossed in the endless questions concerning form and matter, and all-too-comfortably attached to that which he seeks to understand. He is too attached to material appearances to really understand what lies behind them, nor does he really want to. There is more than enough diversity to occupy his mind totally, and more than enough attractions to keep his personality "enthralled," (i.e., *imprisoned*). He goes no further than a superficial materialistic enquiry leading to results which enhance his comfort and personal satisfaction. He is blind to the Presence. His eyes are focused too closely on the immediate foreground. He is warm, "cozy," interested, satisfied, and as divorced from the center of his life as he is from subjective understanding.

The intelligent use of the two formulae, however, transmutes the abuses of the past. He seeks intangible reality, and releases the grip with which both his mind and heart have fastened upon the fragments and nonessentials of life. He learns, primarily, to recognize the One Identity behind all material forms, and his growing secondary ability to stand detached from all lesser loves, introduces him to that *central Place* where divine Love is wedded to divine Knowledge. It is a domain of his consciousness which might be called 'the Temple of Intelligent–Love,' and there, his fifth ray soul holds sway.

7. Some examples of vocational aptitudes and orientations relating to the combination of the fifth ray soul and the second ray personality:

* the scientist as humanitarian

* the researcher with a calm demeanor and tireless patience

* the investigator who is frequently guided by subjective sensitivity and intuition

* the enquirer who always exercises tact and consideration

* the experimenter who is humane in both his objectives and procedures

* the analyst who always uses his heart as well as his head

* the specialist with an inclusive awareness of other specialties

* the objective observer whose undisturbed tranquility renders his observations even more accurate

* the inventor whose inventions are particularly designed to comfort, ameliorate or salvage the lives of others

* the engineer who consistently seeks to understand the human impact of his work

* the technician for whom cooperation with others comes very naturally

* the mechanic who always seems to have a positive, "can do" attitude

* the repair–person who serenely and cheerfully goes about his task

In general: vocations and professions which require keen analytical abilities, the capacity for research, and scientific and/or technical expertise, *as well as* a wise and loving attitude, great empathy and understanding, studiousness, and the ability to teach or compassionately heal.

8. **A proposed list of well-known individuals (historical, contemporary, or mythological) whose soul ray can reasonably be considered the fifth, with a strong subsidiary second ray influence (whether or not the second ray is, strictly speaking, the personality ray):**

Luther Burbank: plant breeder whose successful production of many useful varieties of fruits, flowers, vegetables, grains and grasses encouraged the development of plant breeding into a modern science

George Washington Carver: agricultural chemist, experimenter and educator. Carver was a great benefactor of the American South and a black hero.

Charles Darwin: English naturalist who demonstrated the principle of organic evolution through natural selection. The third ray energy may have been represented as well.

Edward Jenner: physician and surgeon who discovered the process of vaccination. Jenner did more than any other person to reduce the menace of smallpox.

Jonas Salk: scientist, physician, discoverer of the vaccine for polio myelitis

Some Contrasts Between the Ray 5 Soul and the Ray 3 Personality

Ray 5 Soul		Ray 3 Personality
* spiritual science	vs.	* personal business
* conscientious experimentation and verification	vs.	* loose speculation and theorization
* spiritual pragmatism and common sense	vs.	* impractical "big ideas"
* directed, purposeful activity in the pursuit of truth	vs.	* often purposeless overactivity
* highly developed power to define	vs.	* tendency towards fluid indefiniteness
* highly accurate descriptive abilities	vs.	* inaccurate registration of sensation due to submergence in thought and activity, and, hence, inaccurate descriptions
* patience to determine concrete specifics	vs.	* dealing in "glittering generalities"
* great emphasis upon the importance of factual detail	vs.	* irresponsible and even "slippery" ignoring of pertinent detail
* enunciation of exact truth	vs.	* 'creative' disregard for exact truth and accuracy
* dedication to pure research	vs.	* absorption in commercialism
* the spiritual wonderment arising from pure and 'innocent' observation	vs.	* jaded cynicism: the attitude of, "I've seen it all."
* laser–like focus on soul–inspired investigations; deep concentration upon the *One*	vs.	* scattering of personal energies; preoccupation with the *Many*.
* serious, economical, purposeful use of words	vs.	* oververbalization
* excellent methodical procedures	vs.	* unmethodical, often–random approaches
* revelation arising from convergent thinking	vs.	* obscuration arising from undisciplined, divergent thinking
* keen observational ability and undeflectable presence of mind	vs.	* vagueness, distraction and absentmindedness
* uprightness and personal rectitude	vs.	* amoral expediency
* highly practical use of the mind	vs.	* empty intellectualism

The Integration Process for the Individual with a Ray 5 Soul and a Ray 3 Personality

1. The pre–spiritual phase; soul energy appropriated by a selfish personality: At this pre–spiritual phase of evolutionary unfoldment, the individual's motives (based upon the personality distortion of fifth ray soul energy, and the self–centered use of third ray personality force is to achieve narrow, materialistic, intellectual certainty, *as well as* cleverly intelligent, self-serving mastery of circumstances and the environment. The person wants, primarily, to take everything apart (either analytically or actually), reduce all life experiences to nothing but rationalistic formulae, control matter mechanically for selfish ends, and reject any kind of knowledge that is not materialistic or derived from the five senses, but he *also* wants to demonstrate his 'superior' intelligence at every opportunity, manipulate money and other people for his own material and intellectual satisfaction, keep incessantly busy in the pursuit of his own self-centered interests, and evade responsibilities through selfish, strategic planning.

Negatively and glamorously these two ray influences can combine to produce: the ultimate skeptic and critic; one whose approach to people and life situations is entirely mental, lacking all heart and feeling; an irreverent person who is disdainful of all thinking rooted in subtle sensitivity, intuition or other transcendent impulses (5 + 3B); one whose orientation is so analytical, that he becomes lost in distinctions, and is unable to put things back together (5A + 3); one who knows a tremendous amount and thinks incessantly about what he knows, but is too lacking in will and practicality to use or apply it (5A + 3A); one who is not only harshly critical of the 'inadequate' thinking of others, but is swelled with mental pride (5A + 3A); one whose motive for research is purely mercenary (5 + 3B); one who coldly manipulates others in order to study what they will do; the dishonest scientist who manipulates the results of his experiments (5A + 3); a narrow-minded investigator who cares only for his own speciality, and will "pull any strings" to make sure that it receives preferential treatment; one who will work strenuously on destructive or morally-questionable projects purely because he finds them mentally interesting (5 + 3A); one who is so mentally detached and absorbed that he lacks any warmth or personal magnetism; an inquisitor who is devious in his methods of enquiry (5A + 3); one who is thoroughly committed to finding economical ways to have machines replace as many human beings as possible (5B + 3B); the confirmed materialist whose concrete thinking and reasoning rejects as unreal anything abstract or subtle (5B + 3B); one with such a thoroughly mechanistic and deterministic view of reality that he sees the universe as a great mechanism (5B + 3); one who is overly enamored of definition, mistaking words for the substance of experience (5A + 3A); one whose incessant intellectuality prevents the development of normal, natural relationships based on personal closeness or intimacy; etc.

2. The phase of conflict; pure soul energy conflicts with personality force: The essential conflict between the ray five soul and the ray three personality is the struggle between the spiritual need to know and verify the truth, and the personal desire to manipulate knowledge, people and circumstances for one's own selfish benefit – almost always at the expense of the truth.

3. The soul/personality integration process from the perspective of the consciousness identified primarily with the fifth ray soul: It will be the task of the fifth ray soul to gather and focus the scattered, ill-directed forces of the third ray personality. The soul seeks precise knowledge and its concrete application, whereas the personality prefers to dabble with many thoughts and many activities, a tendency often leading to confusion and ineffectuality. Consciousness, when identified with the fifth ray soul, pursues a highly focused line of enquiry which yields definite revelation. The soul, bending every mental quality to the solution of one important, specific problem at a time, seeks to prevent the personality from diffusing energy, for the personality frequently refuses to settle down to the task at hand. Thus, faced with a personality which is easily deflected from singleness of purpose, which easily takes flight into inaccurate generalization, and for which diversification easily produces futility, the soul seeks to induce prolonged concentration upon concrete issues. The soul must guide the personality from the "many" to the "one"; from the indefinite to the definite; from divergency to convergency; from copious talk to concrete action. The personality scans the distant horizon for a glimpse of exciting, though remote, possibilities; the soul brings everything remote into the foreground where it can be closely examined. The "far–away look" of the third ray personality is transformed into the sharp, observant, fifth ray gaze, alert to every detail.

4. The soul/personality integration process from the perspective of the consciousness identified primarily with the third ray personality: The fifth ray pressure towards integration will initially be felt by the third ray personality as a loss of numerous interests and potentials. The personality feels most comfortable when it is incessantly active, in mind or body, and engaged in a wide variety of mental or physical interactions. The soul, however, has other intentions, and begins to exert a counteractive influence. Thus, every time the personality begins reaching for a new contact, or tries to extend itself into a new field of activity, it feels itself pulled back to a central focus, and forced to engage in a narrowly restricted, highly disciplined enquiry. The third ray personality usually becomes bored if forced to focus for long upon a small range of mental data or physical activity, but it soon discovers, arising within its consciousness, a surprisingly insistent demand for certainty, for precise and definite knowledge requiring keen observation (undisrupted by commotion), and for careful experimentation rather than undisciplined speculation. The personality will, in revolt, temporarily attempt to seek refuge in variety, but gradually it capitulates to the soul–demand for a more scientific and truthful approach to living. Gradually, there dawns the realization that hyperactivity (whether mental or physical) leads *away* from knowledge and truth, and that things *as they actually are,* are far more interesting than things as one would have them be.

5. The ideal expression of the ray five soul and the ray three personality: The pursuit of concrete knowledge is accompanied by an innovative understanding of a diversity of possible applications for such knowledge. "One–hundred–and–one" uses are found for the products of pure research. Here we find the researcher whose fertile and resourceful imagination devises many ways to adapt his discoveries to present conditions. In general, pure research is valued more than commercial enterprise, but business skills are effectively used to spread and implement the benefits of the research process. The love of facts is well–served by respect for the principle of economy. This is another combination in which the impulse to theorize and the impulse to verify are well blended, there being, in this case, a decided preference for verification. There will also be great facility for applied mathematics; figures will be easily manipulated and adapted to a diversity of contexts. This is, perhaps (with the possible exception of the ray three soul and the ray five personality) the most analytically gifted combination; the powers of discrimination are very highly developed. There is the capacity to shed much light upon specific fields of enquiry, accompanied by the ability to articulate and interpret that light in words. The individual will have great expertise in his field, but he will also have the flexibility of mind to understand how his field and many other fields are tied together through many 'threads' of relationship. Thus he becomes an expert with interdisciplinary understanding. While discovery is valued more highly than utility, the utilitarian attitude is never abandoned. As a matter of fact, business prowess provides the means of financing research and investigation. Under this combination, science and industry are united. When certain "types" (or, more accurately, "subtypes") within each ray are accented, there is ingenious technological inventiveness. The inventions will be eminently *useful* and will be skillfully marketed and adapted to prevailing commercial trends. There will also be a special aptitude for conducting research in (or inventing new means of) travel, locomotion and conveyance.

6. The combined effect of the two integration formulae: The primary integration formula is *Detachment*, keyed to the fifth ray soul. The secondary integration formula is *Stillness*, keyed to the third ray personality. The first formula corrects the fifth ray tendencies towards mental attachment to matter, and the obsessive preoccupation with investigating or manipulating concrete form, while ignoring the reality of that which is "formless," whereas the second formula corrects the third ray tendencies towards a busy scattering of attention, wasted thought, and physical overactivity (with their resultant disturbances and obscurations of consciousness). Used together, these two formulae provide the individual striving for soul/personality integration with the composite quality of 'still detachment,' (i.e., a still and quiet disposition of the "outer man," which complements the intention of the "inner man" to achieve detachment from a mental preoccupation with matter and form). Stillness without; detachment within. For ages the evolving individual has been captivated by the illusory reality of material forms. At the stage of evolution when the integration of soul and personality become a possibility, he must release himself from this very plausible "seeming," and understand that which matter and form both veil and reveal. In any one incarnation the individual works upon both the outer (personal) and inner or deeper (i.e., soul–inspired) layers of his psyche, availing himself of the potency of the integration formulae. In this case, the two formulae make it possible for him to cultivate a more quiet, collected, and *purposefully active* personal consciousness, supportive of those rare moments of exalted consciousness when (pervaded by the presence of the soul), he *knows,* past all doubting and seeming, the indisputable *reality* of that great subjective Entity – the planetary God – whose "garment" of matter has long been the object of his fascination and enquiry.

In the earlier stages of evolution, before successfully applying these formulae, an individual with this ray combination often finds himself attentively engrossed by the modifications of matter – his inner light veiled in hectic material thought and activity. Restless, the victim of excessive activity of mind and body, he is utterly preoccupied with the movements and events within the veils of matter. His eyes are blinded by a fascination with multiplicity, and with the many possible interrelationships of that which he sees. His motion is too great and his vision too narrowly focused to glimpse the *life* behind the multiplicity of fragmentary forms. He fails to sense the origin of things, or of himself.

The intelligent use of the two formulae, however, transmutes the abuses of the past. He concludes that period of his evolutionary journey in which he is the victim of an overactive attachment to illusory externals. Aided by concentration upon the formulae, the individual learns, primarily, to recognize the One Identity behind all form (the Unity behind all material diversity), and his growing secondary ability to quiet himself, and act only when acting serves the purposes of his ever-enquiring soul, loosens the hold which "maya" has upon him, thus ensuring the soul of an intelligent and versatile instrument with which to investigate the amazing diversity and *prove* it to be an emanation of the one invisible, all-containing, subjective Life.

7. Some examples of vocational aptitudes and orientations relating to the combination of the fifth ray soul and the second ray personality:

* the scientist endowed with strong business aptitudes

* the researcher who is extremely versatile in the development of research strategies

* the investigator, willing and inclined to travel extensively in pursuit of information

* the enquirer with an unusual ability to propose intelligent, thought-provoking questions

* the experimenter who utilizes a wide range of eclectic approaches, realizing that if one thing doesn't work, something else will

* the analyst with a gift for giving well-reasoned interpretations and explanations of the implications of his analyses

* the specialist who understands how a broad network of variables relates to his specialty

* the objective observer with a talent for building extensive theories based upon his observations

* the inventor of machines and instruments which promote travel and, in general, the ability to "move through space"

* the engineer who brings notable fertility of thought and resourcefulness to the solution of engineering problems

* the technician who handles his instruments with a manual dexterity amounting, almost, to virtuosity

* the mechanic who consistently knows how to get the job done in the most economical manner

* the repair-person who is adept at finding ingenious ways to make something work again

In general: vocations and professions which require keen analytical abilities, the capacity for research, and scientific and/or technical expertise, *as well as* acute intelligence (whether active or abstract), great adaptability and resourcefulness, abundant creative and communicative abilities, and (frequently) strong business aptitudes:

8. A proposed list of well-known individuals (historical, contemporary, fictional or mythological) whose soul ray can reasonably be considered the fifth, with a strong subsidiary third ray (whether or not the third ray is, strictly speaking, the personality ray):

Alexander Graham Bell: inventor of the telephone

Guglielmo Marconi: a distinguished Italian physicist who was the inventor of a successful system of radio telegraphy and exploited the commercial possibilities of wireless communication to an unlimited number of receivers at the same time.

Some Contrasts Between the Ray 5 Soul and the Ray 4 Personality

Ray 5 Soul		Ray 4 Personality
* unrelenting examination of the "garment of God" to find the 'Wearer' of the "garment"	vs.	* pursuit of knowledge is sacrificed to the preservation of personal taste and aesthetics
* the scientific pursuit of pure knowledge	vs.	* pursuit of personal expressivity
* unobscured lucidity of thought, and keen critical thinking	vs.	* volatile feelings interfere with mental clarity and critical discrimination
* steadfast concentration and undivided mental focus	vs.	* capriciousness and inconsistency; ingrained self–division and ambivalence
* stability and reliability growing out of a fixed mental orientation	vs.	* personal instability due to fluctuating emotions and moods
* insistence upon accuracy and precision	vs.	* exaggeration for dramatic effect; conspicuous disregard for accuracy
* innate common sense	vs.	* abandonment of common sense in favor of play, fantasy and frequent foolishness
* ultrarealism and factuality; 'non–fictionalism'	vs.	* rejection of pure 'factuality'; overemphasis upon 'fictional' thought and imaginative (i.e., unrealistic) living
* uncompromising rationality and logic as methods of enhancing spirituality	vs.	* frequent recourse to irrationality (creative or otherwise) as a method for alleviating personal tensions
* keen ability to analyze the quantitative basis of reality	vs.	* repudiation of analysis and quantification as dull and uninteresting
* constant recourse to "cause–and–effect" thinking	vs.	* a pronounced distaste for (and inability for) linear, sequential thinking based upon the tracing of causes and effects
* the zenith of objectivity	vs.	* unstable, mood–influenced subjectivism
* an innate ability to recognize and respect the distinct lines of demarcation and the separative boundaries necessary for intelligent spiritual living	vs.	* inappropriate mixing and blending; promiscuity on all levels
* great technical/mechanical skill and inventiveness	vs.	* often an aesthetic aversion to machines and the handling of "nuts–and–bolts" matters

The Integration Process for the Individual with a Ray 5 Soul and a Ray 4 Personality

1. The pre–spiritual phase; soul energy appropriated by a selfish personality: At this pre–spiritual phase of evolutionary unfoldment, the individual's motives (based upon the personality distortion of fifth ray soul energy, and the self–centered use of fourth ray personality force) are to achieve narrow, materialistic, intellectual certainty, *as well as* an agreeable feeling of personal peace and harmony through the tension–releasing expression of conflicting bio–psychic impulses. The person wants, primarily, to take everything apart (either analytically or actually), reduce all life experience to nothing but rationalistic formulae, control matter mechanically for selfish ends, and reject any kind of knowledge that is not materialistic or derived from the five physical senses, but he *also* wants to be consistently surrounded by what he considers beautiful or attractive, to be spontaneously self-expressive without discipline or control, self-indulgently dramatic or moody (as he pleases), and greatly appreciated for his colorful, unpredictable temperament.

Negatively and glamorously these two ray influences can combine to produce: one who deeply wishes to give his life to science, study and research, but has insufficient personal stability to do so successfully (5A + 4B); a harshly critical thinker who is consistently getting into fights because of his combative attitude (5 + 4B); one who causes cleavages between himself and others through an overly discriminating attitude and excessive moodiness (5A + 4B); one who is torn between the urges to be both rational and irrational; one who compounds his problem of debilitating social awkwardness with a notable lack of self-confidence; one for whom decisions present a constant dilemma, because he persistently overanalyzes everything; one whose gnawing sense of life's aridity is compounded by his inability to rid himself of interpersonal and intra-personal dissonances (5 + 4B); one who, knowing a great deal, disguises or compromises his knowledge for the sake of personal peace and emotional comfort (5 + 4A); an individual afflicted mentally by doubt and skepticism, and emotionally by pessimism and negativity; one whose materialistic rationality justifies living a hedonistic and morally unbalanced personal life (5 + 4B); one who focuses destructive analysis and deadening rationality upon the arts, robbing them of their mysterious power to inspire (5B + 4); one who focuses so exclusively upon a narrow, restricted area of enquiry that he loses his mental and emotional balance and begins to "go to pieces" – the "mad scientist" (5 + 4B); etc.

2. The phase of conflict; pure soul energy conflicts with personality force: The essential conflict between the ray five soul and the ray four personality is the struggle between the spiritual need to acquire exact knowledge at all costs, and the personal desire to reduce tension and preserve harmony, even if it means compromising the search for knowledge.

3. The soul/personality integration process from the perspective of the consciousness identified primarily with the ray five soul: It will be the task of the ray five soul to bring keen observation and detached, mental stability to an emotionally impressionable, fluctuating personality. The soul values factual knowledge above things, whereas the personal consciousness is invested in its own expressivity, often to the detriment of mental concentration. The soul seeks to evoke a passion for exactitude from a personality which has little use for particulars. Faced with a personality which interprets most things in terms of their "feeling-tone," the soul seeks (temporarily, at least) to dampen the volatile reactivity of the feelings, so that pure, lucid vision may eventuate – vision uncontaminated by any mood, emotion or bias. The soul must guide the personal consciousness to seek a steadfast, centralized position, where it is unlikely to be pulled off balance. It is the soul's intent to persevere in its focused enquiry until the light of knowledge dawns. When the individual is identified with the consciousness of the soul, he experiences frustration at the disruptive instabilities thrown up by the vacillating personality. The soul must stabilize the personality before it can possibly persist throughout the lengthy time–spans required to complete all significant research efforts.

4. The soul/personality integration process from the perspective of the consciousness identified primarily with the fourth ray personality: The fifth ray pressure towards integration will initially be experienced by the fourth ray personality as an attack of aridity. The personality is most comfortable when it can continue to be its vibrant, responsive, spontaneous self. It changes when it feels like changing; when it can readily express contrasting moods and emotions when and as it will, the personality feels that all is well. It has no wish to become strictly "mental"; when under the impress of the fifth ray soul, it feels threatened with the neutralization of its colorful nature. The fourth ray personality dislikes the thought that its very sensitive aesthetic responsiveness no longer counts as a primary function. And yet, as the soul continues to work its intelligent will, from deep within the personal consciousness there arises a growing inclination towards unbiased observation and impartial examination – in short, towards the *exact comprehension of things*, whether or not they are beautiful or ugly, harmonious or dissonant. In the serious study of these things, personality preferences have to be set aside; they simply do not count. This growing emphasis upon the intellect will, initially, cause rebellion, and the personality will, with desperate vigor, seek to re–indulge its temperamental tastes. Increasingly, however, it will be beset by the gnawing feeling that it is missing something important, that its responses and reactions are somehow obscuring the face of reality. If it does not quiet down, become serene, and see things *exactly as they are,* the personality will begin to feel stupid – somehow lacking in commonsense and realism. Gradually, new learnings arise, and are accepted and integrated within the personality consciousness: especially the learning that *knowledge of reality is beautiful,* and that factual understanding, at length, contributes to the significance of the expressivity and creativity which the personality so much values.

5. The ideal combination of the fifth ray soul energy and the fourth ray personality force: The pursuit and application of concrete knowledge is accompanied by a colorful and entertaining manner. When working ideally, this is a fortunate blend of energies, each tempering the other. The presentation of knowledge will never be dry, and expressivity will never be empty and unrelated to the world of facts and common sense. Here, one might expect to find the ability to present factual, natural things with excitement and drama. With this combination of rays might also be found the artist who begins to investigate his medium so thoroughly and carefully, that learning all about the technical means of expression becomes almost more important than that which is to be expressed. All the arts have their technical side, which this type of individual easily masters, providing the artistic community with invaluable technical support. One has only to think of photography to realize the importance of technical knowledge in the creation of that which has aesthetic appeal. In general, with this combination, science proves itself the master of art, and yet scientific findings are beautifully, colorfully and appealingly expressed. Here is one who can present the beauty of scientific fact, who can dramatize the story of science, picturesquely portraying the romance of the quest for knowledge. Scientific research is also furthered by the ability to establish harmonious rapport with diverse individuals. One can imagine the reconciliation of disagreements within the scientific community being facilitated with the help of a scientifically–inclined individual equipped with a strong fourth ray. There is an unusual ability to blend analysis with synthesis, as well as fact with imagination. In the quest for knowledge, analysis may reveal numerous discrepancies and apparent contradictions, but when soul consciousness upon the fifth ray is equipped with the fourth subray of "Harmony through Conflict," the reconciliation of discrepancies and contradictions is much facilitated. The logical procedures of the concrete mind are also complemented by fourth ray intuitive and analogical thinking. The most advanced scientific enquiry of the present is heavily dependent upon the utilization of revelatory metaphor, for the creation of which the fourth ray is ideally suited. The fifth ray, it must be remembered, is the primary energy by means of which thoughtforms are created; with the help of the imaginative fourth ray, the thoughtforms will usually be colorful and interesting. In general, this is an outstanding combination for presenting concrete knowledge in an attractive, fascinating manner.

6. The combined effect of the two integration formulae: The primary integration formula is *Detachment*, keyed to the fifth ray soul. The secondary integration formula is *Steadfastness,* keyed to the fourth ray personality. The first formula corrects the fifth ray tendencies towards mental attachment to matter, and the obsessive preoccupation with investigating or manipulating concrete form, while ignoring the reality of that which is "formless," whereas the second formula corrects the tendencies towards vacillation, irresoluteness, instability, indecisiveness and moral cowardice characteristic of the fourth ray personality. Used together, these two formulae provide the individual striving for soul/personality integration with the composite quality of 'steadfast detachment,' (i.e., the development of a steadfast and stable personality attitude which complements and fortifies the determination of the "inner man" to detach from his obsession with the material aspect of reality). Upon the outer plane he stands midway between the warring forces of his nature and of the environment. And upon the inner planes he learns to detach himself from the illusion that the testimony of the senses (gross or subtle) is reality itself. Thus, assisted by the right use of these two formulae, the individual is enabled to cultivate a more serene, balanced and peaceful personal consciousness, supportive of those rare moments of exalted consciousness when (pervaded by the presence of the soul), he *knows* past all doubt and seeming, the indisputable *reality* of that great subjective Entity – the planetary God – whose "garment" of matter has long been the object of his fascination and enquiry.

In the earlier stages of evolution, before successfully applying these formulae, an individual with this ray combination often finds himself himself utterly enthralled by the innumerable modifications of matter, and captivated by the fluctuating pairs of opposites. Opposing energies turn him this way and that – he has no stability. He is minutely interested in everything that occurs upon the battlefield of life; his analysis of vicissitudes is even too complete, but his vision is still obscured. Blinded by conflict, he fails to see the One Who does not fight. Blinded by too close an examination of obvious things, he fails to see the One Who is not obvious, and who dwells behind all things. A distressed and materially–minded individual, he is still far from his spiritual center.

The intelligent use of the two formulae, however, transmutes the abuses of the past. Aided by the potency of these formulae, he brings to a conclusion the period of personal inconstancy, and of attachment to the durable illusion of "objective reality." The individual learns, primarily, to recognize the One Identity behind all form (the great Unity behind all material diversity), and his growing secondary ability to steadfastly reconcile the warring pairs of opposites (within his nature and within the environment) clears the personality consciousness of the smoke and din of battle, thus ensuring the ever–enquiring fifth ray soul of a sensitive, stable, balanced and *intuitive* personal instrument, useful in the task of scientifically unveiling the great subjective Reality which is the intangible matrix from which all material forms emanate.

7. Some examples of vocational aptitudes and orientations relating to the combination of the fifth ray soul and the fourth ray personality:

* the scientist who is always alive to the beauty of scientific knowledge
* the researcher with a gift for dramatizing the significance of his discoveries
* the investigator whose delightful, entertaining manner lightens his labors with humor
* the enquirer who poses questions to himself and others in a non–linear, unpredictable, "right–brained" manner
* the experimenter whose strong improvisatory streak helps him formulate creative experimental procedures
* the analyst with an intuitive gift based upon a powerful imagination
* the specialist who builds bridges of relationship between his own and other specialties
* the objective observer with sufficient sensitivity to feel the subjectivity of that which he is observing objectively
* the inventor for whom the law of analogy is the source of some of his best ideas
* the engineer who specializes in the building of bridges and other means of connection
* the technician who focuses upon the technical means for enhancing the expression of beauty
* the mechanic with a real imaginative "feel" for adjusting all parts of a mechanism so they function harmoniously
* the repair–person who attempts to restore whatever he repairs to a condition of beauty (repair being for him as much an art as a technology): for instance, a specialist in auto–body restoration and painting
* the plastic surgeon

In general: vocations and professions which require keen analytical abilities, the capacity for research, and scientific and/or technical expertise, *as well as* a strong creative imagination, spontaneity, expressivity, aesthetic sensitivity, and a marked ability to bring harmony out of conflict, beauty out of ugliness, and at–one–ment out of divisiveness.

8. **A proposed list of well-known individuals (historical, contemporary, fictional or mythological) whose soul ray can reasonably be considered the fifth, with a strong subsidiary fourth ray influence (whether or not this fourth ray is, strictly speaking, the personality ray):**

Tycho Brahe: Danish astronomer, artist and craftsman. Brahe gave the majority of his life to making accurate astronomical measurements. The accuracy of his many measurements was extraordinary considering that they were made without the benefit of the telescope. He was also a man of refined artistic and aesthetic tastes.

Robert Fulton: developer of the first successful steamboat, Fulton was also an accomplished artist. In addition, ray two was a significant influence.

Rudolf Steiner (see discussion under the fourth ray soul and fifth ray personality): Rudolf Steiner was both an occult scientist and artist. It is possible that he is a fifth ray soul working under the Master Hilarion upon the development of the psychic sciences. In this case, the fourth ray would form a prominent part of the personality equipment.

Some Contrasts Between the Ray 5 Soul and the Ray 5 Personality

Ray 5 Soul		Ray 5 Personality
* pursuit of spiritual science	vs.	* pursuit of orthodox, form-limited materialistic science
* scientific investigation of dimensions of nature undetectable by the five senses	vs.	* thought imprisoned within spheres of knowledge circumscribed by the five senses
* close cooperation with and validation of the great spiritual truths of religion and philosophy	vs.	* harsh repudiation of religion and philosophy as superstitious and unscientific
* unbiased, fair-mindedness	vs.	* mentally confined to the prejudices of the orthodox scientific community
* the spiritual power to unite "three minds": the lower (concrete) mind, the "Son of mind" or soul, and the higher (abstract) mind – pure manas	vs.	* restriction to the sphere of influence of the concrete mind
* mind as an instrument of spiritual love and union	vs.	* mind as the "slayer of the real" – an instrument producing separation and cleavage
* mind as the revealer of the true nature of human identity as soul; mind, the servant of Raja Yoga	vs.	* mind used to obscure the true nature of of human identity as soul
* mind leading to the Higher Self	vs.	* mind precipitating man into the "eighth sphere" – severed from soul
* detailed analysis within the context of synthesis; realization of the broader spiritual implications of scientific discoveries	vs.	* minute analysis within a narrow field, isolated (through ignorance) from the larger context: knowledge within a vacuum
* scientific inventiveness aiding the manifestation of the Divine Plan	vs.	* inventiveness turned to trivial or even destructive ends

Commentary

Please refer to the commentary following the tabulation of contrasts between the fourth ray soul and the fourth ray personality for a complete discussion of the reasons why no commentary will be offered for any combinations of identical soul and personality rays when the ray in question is one of the rays of attribute.

Some Contrasts Between the Ray 5 Soul and the Ray 6 Personality

Ray 5 Soul		Ray 6 Personality
* spiritual science	vs.	* inflexible personal belief
* the earnest pursuit of irrefutably accurate knowledge	vs.	* passionate adherence to cherished convictions, whether or not they can be substantiated
* the cultivation of the soul–inspired intellect as an excellent means of understanding God and His Creation	vs.	* innate distrust of the intellect
* unbiased consideration of all tenable hypotheses	vs.	* the refusal, because of strong biases, to consider all hypotheses fairly and openly
* extremely accurate appraisement of facts	vs.	* extreme exaggeration, proportional to the degree of devotion, or the intensity of attachment to a particular point of view
* luminous knowledge	vs.	* the obscurations of emotionality
* surpassing mental objectivity and detachment	vs.	* mental distortions induced by sentimentality and intense personal attachments
* unwavering mental discipline	vs.	* heated passions overcome rational thought
* profound respect for and adherence to the experimental method	vs.	* tenacious reliance upon faith as the only path to truth and understanding
* a spiritual common sense which fully understands the nature, place and rightful requirements of matter in the process of living the spiritual life upon the physical plane	vs.	* impractical escapism; obliviousness to the commonsense requirements of physical plane living; sacrificing a "level head" to wish–fulfillment
* accurate 'this–worldly' knowledge – *on all planes*; hence, presence of mind, and attunment with immediate reality	vs.	* flight into impractical "other–worldliness" – hence, taking refuge in 'absence' from immediate reality
* healthy, soul–inspired skepticism	vs.	* foolish credulity
* noteworthy independence of thought and action	vs.	* debilitating personal dependency

The Integration Process for the Individual with a Ray 5 Soul and a Ray 6 Personality

1. The pre–spiritual phase; soul energy appropriated by a selfish personality: At this pre–spiritual phase of evolutionary unfoldment, the individual's motives (based upon the personality distortion of fifth ray soul energy, and the self–centered use of sixth ray personality force) are to achieve narrow, materialistic, intellectual certainty, *as well as* the uncompromising satisfaction of the ideals and goals to which the personality is passionately devoted. The person wants, primarily, to take everything apart (either analytically or actually), reduce all life experience to nothing but rationalistic formulae, control matter mechanically for selfish ends, and reject any kind of knowledge that is not materialistic or derived from the five physical senses, but he *also* wants to ignore everything except the object or path of his devotion, spurn even reasonable, mundane responsibilities if they do not relate specifically to his quest, fanatically follow his ideal regardless of destructive consequences, and cling desperately to that which he believes he loves.

Negatively and glamorously, these two ray influences can combine to produce: the harshly critical person who inflicts criticism with fury (5 + 6B); the narrow-minded materialist who passionately refuses to deviate from his limited point of view (5 + 6B); the confirmed skeptic devoted to his skepticism; the one who, thinking he knows, and assured that his views make perfect sense, will persecute anyone who does not think as he thinks (5A + 6B); one who can easily fall victim to idée-fixe; the crystallized thinker with utterly rigid emotional attitudes; one whose interests are totally focused, severely restricted in scope, and fanatically pursued; the mentally prejudiced, emotionally biased individual; an unbalanced person, exclusively devoted to the exercise of the mind (5A + 6); one whose need to know is so intense, that he justifies any means to reach the knowledge he desires; one whose desire for knowledge (and lack of original thinking) inclines him to become passively dependent upon those who supposedly have the knowledge he requires (5 + 6A); one whose excessive discrimination leads to a separative attitude which he seeks to maintain at all costs (5A + 6); an individual whose love of analytical classification inclines him first to "pigeon-hole" others, and then to zealously defend the 'correctness' of his classification (5 + 6B); one who is so convinced of the value of certain theories or explanations that he becomes a tireless and tiresome proselytizer for them (5A + 6B); etc.

2. The phase of conflict; pure soul energy conflicts with personality force: The essential conflict between the ray five soul and the ray six personality is the struggle between the spiritual need for exact knowledge, and the personal desire for an intense devotional attachment to some person, cause or ideal, despite the fact that such attachment may inhibit or distort progress towards knowledge.

3. The soul/personality integration process from the perspective of the consciousness identified with the fifth ray soul: It will be the task of the fifth ray soul, initially, to inspire the sixth ray personality with an appreciation for rationality. The soul is faced with a personality given to emotionality and, frequently, to irrationality. No matter what the ray of the soul, its demand of the personality is "more light and less heat," (for the personality is, generically, motivated by the "heat" of desire), but this is especially the case when a fifth ray soul is accompanied by a sixth ray personality. The mental and the emotional fields are two of the great "pairs of opposites," and with this particular ray combination, these opposites are very much at odds – even more so than when the soul is upon the third ray and the personality upon the sixth, for rays three and six are closely related. The soul, therefore, seeks to impose the regime of the mind upon a personality whose emotional or aspirational intensity is often extremely difficult to restrain. Patient, unbiased observation and experimentation are required, but the personality is naturally impatient, strongly biased, blind with passion, and well-assured that its conclusions need not be submitted to experimentation. The soul, therefore, is frustrated by a personality which, initially at least, rejects mental values and prefers to submerge itself in sentiency and sentimentality. For the soul, of course, belief is not enough; the soul seeks to have the personality learn the value of *proof*. Gradually the soul must find a way to dry the waters of feeling, and subdue and direct the fires of emotional aspiration if there is to eventuate sufficient lucidity of consciousness to lead to exact knowledge. The soul must lead the personality to the point where it can envision the pursuit and application of knowledge as an ideal end worthy of its devotion.

4. The soul/personality integration process from the perspective of the consciousness identified primarily with the sixth ray personality: The fifth ray pressure towards integration will be felt by the sixth ray personality as a sharply critical voice demanding rational self-restraint. The personality feels most comfortable when it can simply (to use a colloquial phrase) "go for it." Why should the personality (so it thinks) stop to question the desirability of the goals and objectives it passionately desires to achieve? Their value seems self-evident! The personality enjoys the intensity of pursuit, the uncontaminated purity of its adherence to the desirable; the questioning mind seems an unwelcome annoyance – even a threat. But as the influence of the fifth ray soul grows within the personal consciousness, the urge to question everything (and worse! – *prove* everything) is precisely what arises. Doubt and skepticism – those great *apparent* enemies of faith– begin to corrode the unquestioning devotion and idealism of the discomfited personality. Fear arises. The emotional certainty, so much prized by a personality for which belief was formerly all sufficient, is now under seige by the enquiring mind. The personality is both irritated and frightened by these constant internal calls for analysis, close examination and verification; it wants to feel; it does not want to look, nor does it wish to stop to think about what makes sense. What is truth, after all? To the personality, it is a matter of faith and conviction; to the soul, only that qualifies as truth which has been rigorously confirmed by the scientific method – or, at least by common sense. Under this relentless pressure to know, to "find out," the personality will, most likely, rebel, experience a beligerent 'revival' of its faith, and self-righteously shut the door on all further enquiry, but, increasingly, it will find itself wondering about the *true nature* of that to which it so tenaciously clings. Perforce, the personality must begin to open its eyes; the erosion of its *blind* faith has already begun, and if faith is to be reacquired, it will have to be a faith based upon sound knowledge – soul knowledge. The personality eventually learns that it is gratifyingly possible to become just as intensely devoted to the pursuit of the ideal of scientific knowledge, as it was to lesser objects of devotion unrelated to mental values.

5. The ideal expression of the combination of the fifth ray soul and the sixth ray personality: The pursuit and application of concrete knowledge are fueled by ardent, one-pointed devotion. This is the ray combination of an individual who *believes* in science, and in the undisputable value of exact knowledge. Science and concrete knowledge are so loved, that they are pursued to the exclusion of all else. Narrow lines of technical enquiry, which to most people would be dry or tedious, are investigated with unabating enthusiasm. The chances for successful investigation are greatly increased by a capacity for iron discipline. The need to know precisely, masters the need to believe, and yet passionate belief hastens the acquisition of knowledge. There is an unusual capacity to understand that science and religion are both saying the same thing. The individual realizes that research into unseen dimensions, can, in fact, be conducted just as effectively, as research into the realms of sensory knowledge. While realism masters *blind* faith and idealism, this individual's ideal becomes the discovery of the *real*, and faith (being the "evidence of things not seen") leads the probing consciousness ever closer to the unveiling of hidden reality. In this case, faith functions as an aspect of the intuition, which adds its revelatory power to the use of the scientific method. In this combination we find the ability to unite science and religion, with the scientific approach always predominating. Here, too, is an individual who will sacrifice all to achieve discovery. Once discovery has been achieved, the power of the sixth ray will help such an individual awaken others to its value, and motivate them to find a means of application. Ideally, this combination produces one who has abiding faith in the value of scientific knowledge, and who will promote and defend its worth tirelessly, and without thought of himself. The capacity to arouse and enthuse others in the cause of science, and in the technical mastery of energies and forces, is pronounced. Here we may find the martyr in the cause of scientific revelation. Science has become his god, because science, rightly understood, leads to God.

6. The combined effect of the two integration formulae: The primary integration formula is *Detachment,* keyed to the fifth ray soul. The secondary integration formula is proposed as *Restraint,* keyed to the sixth ray personality. The first formula corrects the fifth ray tendencies towards mental attachment to matter, and an obsessive preoccupation with investigating or manipulating concrete form, while ignoring the reality of that which is "formless," whereas the second formula corrects the unrestrained, passionate pursuit of the 'partial' and 'peripheral,' so common to the emotionally undisciplined sixth ray personality. Used together, these two formulae provide the individual striving for soul/personality integration with the composite quality of 'restrained detachment,'(i.e., the restraint of the "outer man" (the personality) which complements the inner man's intent to detach his consciousness from a preoccupation and false identification with the many forms of matter). The formulae enable the individual to restrain the outgoing rush of desire within his personal consciousness while he (within the depths of his consciousness – that 'place' where he 'becomes' the "inner man" – the true disciple) learns to detach himself from the illusion that the testimony of the senses (gross or subtle) is reality itself. Thus the individual cultivates a less impassioned, less intense, more controlled personal consciousness, supportive of those rare moments of exalted consciousness when (pervaded by the presence of the soul), he *knows,* past all doubt and seeming, the indisputable *reality* of that great subjective Entity – the planetary God – whose "garment" of matter has long been the object of his fascination and enquiry.

In the earlier stages of evolution, before successfully applying these formulae, an individual with this ray combination often finds himself *enthralled* (literally, imprisoned) by the innumerable modifications of matter, and tenaciously and devotedly adhering now to one, now to another of those modifications – all of them on the periphery of subjective reality. His very intensity leads him away from that which he most desires, and his preoccupation with multiplicity blinds him to the essential Unity which he must, one day, discover as the true object of his spiritual quest.

The intelligent use of the two formulae, however, transmutes past abuses, and ends the period of 'unrestrained attachment' to the illusion of "objective reality." The individual learns, primarily, to recognize the One Identity behind all material form (i.e., the great subjective Unity behind all material diversity), and his growing secondary ability to restrain his passionate pursuit of the worthless and non-essential, (while learning the nature of real values by attending to spiritual guidance from the deeper and profoundly knowledgeable levels of his consciousness [the levels of soul]), erases the former futility of his outer life, and helps him adhere to a vision of the true Life veiled by the form. At last he sees the One, and he steadies his gaze upon it. Thus the 'great Investigator,' the fifth ray soul, is assured of a personal instrument which will be properly directed, controlled, focused and utterly dedicated to the task of demonstrating the reality of the invisible Oneness, which is the true quest of every spiritual scientist.

7. Some examples of vocational aptitudes and orientations relating to the combination of the fifth ray soul and the sixth ray personality:

* the scientist consistently animated by the highest idealism

* the "hard-headed" realist who attempts to prove the essential reality and tangibility of those apparently unreal and intangible dimensions of life which are usually approached only through faith, belief and religious practices

* the researcher who counts all as lost unless he achieves his research objectives

* the investigator who never doubts that he will find what he is looking for

* the enquirer who is ever-optimistic that his questions will be answered

* the experimenter whose persistence is proverbial

* the analyst who zealously propagates his conclusions

* the specialist who "lives, eats and breathes" his specialty – exclusively

* the objective observer who gazes with focused intensity

* the inventor filled with faith in the value of his inventions

* the engineer intent upon assisting a specific cause or "special interest" (political, environmental, social, religious, etc.) with his expertise

* the technician who devotes his life to improving the quality of work done within his field

* the mechanic filled with infectious enthusiasm for his work

* the repair-person who is almost incapable of letting go of a project until it is completed

In general: vocations and professions which require keen analytical abilities, the capacity for research, and scientific and/or technical expertise, *as well as* high idealism, undeviating devotion, great enthusiasm and persistent emotional intensity.

8. A proposed list of well-known individuals (historical, contemporary, fictional or mythological) whose soul ray can reasonably be considered the fifth, with a strong subsidiary sixth ray influence (whether or not the sixth ray is, strictly speaking, the personality ray):

Ernst Haeckel: zoologist and an enthusiastic proponent of Darwin's theory of evolution. He was, reputedly, "more Darwinist than Darwin himself."

Joseph Lister: celebrated British surgeon and medical scientist. Lister was the pioneer of antisepsis – the use of chemicals to prevent surgical infections. He was also a deeply religious man.

Gregor Mendel: the Austrian monk whose discoveries of the first laws of heredity laid the foundation of the science of genetics. Given the nature of his experiments with *varieties* of garden peas, the presence of the third ray is also a possibility.

Charles Proteus Steinmetz: one of the world's foremost electrical engineers. Steinmetz developed fundamental ideas concerning alternating current systems and devised caculating methods that enabled engineers to design more efficient electrical machinery. He exemplified the engineer with a social consciousness. The third ray was also pronounced.

Some Contrasts Between the Ray 5 Soul and the Ray 7 Personality

Ray 5 Soul		Ray 7 Personality
* independent research into the nature of reality	vs.	* conformity; dependency upon patterns of social conditioning
* healthy reliance upon verification	vs.	* habitual acceptance of that which is usual, customary or normal
* dedication to pure knowledge	vs.	* dedication to maintaining appearances
* innate truthfulness	vs.	* the politic or polite disguising of the truth
* embracing of confirmed knowledge despite its social consequences	vs.	* disregard or suppression of knowledge if it threatens traditions and established social conventions, or even new social arrangements
* revelation of "embarassing facts"	vs.	* discomfited by "embarassing facts" which are promptly "swept under the rug"; ignoring of 'inconvenient' truths
* the constant search for scientific improvements in methods and procedures	vs.	* the constant attempt to preserve and fortify comfortable routines
* pursuit of iconoclastic discoveries – the knowledge that destroys "sacred cows"	vs.	* preservation of meaningless rituals and the protection of unproductive but time–honored "sacred cows"
* a spirit of free–minded enquiry	vs.	* enquiry limited by adherence to established precedent
* strong belief in the free dissemination of facts to benefit many	vs.	* instinctive reliance upon secrecy to prevent disturbance to the smooth functioning of the established organizational structure
* intellectual detachment from biological rhythms and compulsions	vs.	* susceptibility to biological compulsions – especially sexual compulsions
* cultivation of the mind as the preferred instrument of spiritual release	vs.	* excessive attention to the body and its processes
* research and development of the true science of spirituality	vs.	* easily deceived by superstitious magical practices rather than scientific magical practices

The Integration Process for the Individual with a Ray 5 Soul and a Ray 7 Personality

1. The pre–spiritual phase; soul energy appropriated by a selfish personality: At this pre–spiritual phase of evolutionary unfoldment, the individual's motives (based upon the personality distortion of fifth ray soul energy, and the self–centered use of seventh ray personality force) are to achieve narrow, materialistic, intellectual certainty, *as well as* a rigidly ritualized, tightly ordered life conducive to physical plane safety, security and 'perfected,' materialistic living. The person wants, primarily, to take everything apart (whether analytically or actually), reduce all life experience to nothing but rationalistic formulae, control matter mechanically for selfish ends, and reject any kind of knowledge that is not materialistic or derived strictly from the five physical senses, but he *also* wants a highly predictable (hence, relatively risk–free) life, to avoid having to think for himself or act upon his own initiative, and to have the solid assurance that all his instinctual appetites and imagined material needs will be satisfied on schedule.

Negatively and glamorously, these two ray influences can combine to produce: the harsh critic of all that does not exactly conform to his standards of sensible thought and action; the exponent of strict, scientific orthodoxy (5 + 7A); the materialistic thinker, interested exclusively in appearances and externals (5 + 7A); one whose mind is so entirely focused upon form and physical process, that he denies any reality to feeling and subjectivity (5 + 7A); the excessively analytical individual whose thought procedures are rigidly routinized (5 + 7A); one so fascinated by technology that he organizes human beings and their interactions inhumanly – as if people were machines and their human responses mere mechanistic functions (5B + 7A, 7B); one who classifies and organizes all things into separate and distinct categories (5A + 7A); the individual with a fetish for exactitude of definition (5A + 7A); the detached and socially awkward individual who is incapable of interpersonal spontaneity, and can only relate to others by means of unimaginative formalities (5 + 7A); the utterly arid and non–magnetic person whose individuality has been swallowed up in the rigid observance of rules and regulations (5 + 7A, 7C); one whose pride of mind leads to "scientific sectarianism," analogous to religious sectarianism (5A + 7A); one so assured of the correctness of his thought and his rationality, that his 'informed' opinions become a comfortable, self–consistent collection of views – rigid, unadaptable and rapidly obsolete (5 + 7A, 7C); an uncompromisingly irreverent thinker who has no use for any traditional values or patterns (5 + 7B); the mechanistic thinker who, espousing that the concept of free–will is meaningless, believes that all human behavior is programmed, and all human responses are conditioned (5B + 7A, 7B); etc.

2. The phase of conflict; pure soul energy conflicts with personality force: The essential conflict between the ray five soul and the ray seven personality is the struggle between the spiritual need to enquire until exact knowledge is achieved, and the personal desire to conform to some pattern (new or old), even if conformity inhibits the progress of meaningful enquiry.

3. The soul/personality integration process from the perspective of the consciousness identified primarily with the fifth ray soul: It will be the task of the fifth ray soul to lead the seventh ray personality towards a love of knowledge and away from an excessive love of form. The soul does not care if time–honored traditions and customs are shown to be useless or worse, or if new plans for restructuring and reorganizing are shown to be foolish; it seeks to see things exactly as they are – to know the truth no matter how disillusioning. The soul, however, is faced with a personality which seeks to be comforted by rhythms, a personality which allays its anxieties through the creation of order and routine. These patterns of action become solidly ingrained habits which numb the enquiring mind. Some patterns become so ingrained and so comfortable that they are considered beyond questioning. This proves frustrating to the soul, which wishes to examine all things impartially. The soul must lead the personality to the point where it begins to understand exactly what it is really *doing*. Stability, security and the feeling of reassurance evoked by sameness, formality and frictionless routine must not be allowed to interfere with the endless quest for knowledge.

4. The soul/personality integration process from the perspective of the consciousness identified primarily with the seventh ray personality: The fifth ray pressure towards integration will initially be felt by the seventh ray personality as an unwelcome voice questioning the validity of personality patterns that have become so well established that they are "second nature." The personality feels most comfortable creating order and form as a hedge against the unexpected and chaotic. Within its ordered world, it lives a life of satisfaction, free from the intrusion of elements which do not "fit," and cannot be predicted and regulated. It has no wish to begin scrutinizing its highly organized life, disrupting well-nurtured 'automaticisms' with questions. But from deep within its consciousness arises the voice of the 'spiritual investigator' asking such questions as: What am I really doing?; Why am I doing it?; What is it really accomplishing?; Are my habit patterns blinding me to reality?; etc. The personality wishes to continue its well-programmed activity, but the soul forces it to "stand back" mentally, and learn. The personality may reassert itself, and insist upon continuing its unexamined, patterned activity, but slowly there will arise within the personal consciousness the sense of being an ignorant automaton. The personality will, eventually, find unknowledgable action (no matter how well-performed) distasteful, and its days of an unquestioning conformity to long-programmed patterns and styles, (religious, national, ethnic, civic, bureaucratic, modish, etc.) will end. The personality comes to learn that exact knowledge makes possible the creation of patterns which are truly magical, rational and, hence, spiritually effective.

5. The ideal expression of the combination of the ray five soul and the ray seven personality: Scientific and technical knowledge are pursued systematically, methodically and with great organizational skill. Right procedure and exactitude of method and measurement strengthen the effectiveness of research. The discovery and revelation of *what actually is* overcomes unquestioning adherence to established patterns, and yet such patterns are enriched by the infusion of new knowledge. The love of facts and truth – "no matter what" – masters the attempt to "keep up appearances," and yet the "appearance" of manifested ideas (i.e., the quality of their presentation in form) is, in the long run, enhanced by increased knowledge. Here we find the capacity to discover a wealth of knowledge and then organize it brilliantly. There may be a particular interest in understanding the processes of manifestation scientifically; such an individual may possess the skill to prove that magic is a scientific process. This is, potentially, an exceedingly occult combination, conferring the capacity to determine exact formulae for the laws of Nature, and then to wield those laws effectively upon the physical plane. The blend of these two rays adds an exquisite sense of timing to investigative abilities; the investigation of all cyclic phenomena in Nature would be a natural focus. More conventionally, this is the ray combination of the researcher who is capable of designing and administering programs of action which implement the results of his research in the most organized and most effective manner. It is a combination which gives the capacity for the perfect material application of scientific discovery. Consummate engineering skill can be anticipated. Here would be found the brilliant inventor with an unusual capacity to materialize his ideas so that they become practical inventions. With the fifth ray soul and the seventh ray personality, knowledge is easily transformed into concrete actuality.

6. The combined effect of the two integration formulae: The primary integration formula is *Detachment,* keyed to the fifth ray soul. The secondary integration formula is proposed as *Orientation,* keyed to the seventh ray personality. The first formula corrects the fifth ray tendencies towards mental attachment to matter, and an obsessive preoccupation with investigating or manipulating concrete form, while ignoring the reality of that which is "formless," whereas the second formula corrects the seventh ray tendencies towards selfish building and organizing according to short-sighted, materially-minded personal plans, but without an attentive orientation to the Divine Design as revealed by the soul. Used together, these two formulae provide the individual striving for soul/personality integration with the composite quality of 'oriented detachment,' (i.e., the "outer man's" orientation towards the inner Light which complements the "inner man's" will to detach from the light-concealing, illusory reality of the many forms of matter). These formulae enable the individual to stand within the center of his personal consciousness, his attention oriented towards the center of his spiritual life, and attentively await the appearance of a 'subjective template,' a soul-inspired design, to guide his personal actions within the three lower worlds. When identified with the inner 'heights' of his consciousness (nearest to the soul on its own plane), he learns the even more difficult task of detaching himself from the illusion that the testimony of the senses (gross or subtle) is reality itself. Thus, by using these formulae, the individual cultivates a more aligned, more spiritually-oriented personal consciousness, supportive of those rare moments of exalted consciousness when (pervaded by the presence of the soul) he *knows,* past all doubt or seeming, the indisputable *reality* of that great subjective Entity – the planetary God – whose "garment" of matter has long been the object of his fascination and enquiry.

In the earlier stages of evolution, before successfully applying these formulae, the individual with this ray combination often finds himself thoroughly engrossed in the investigation and organization of matter and form – actively involved upon the periphery of subjective life. What he knows, he knows exactly. What he organizes, he organizes exactly. But he does not know the Truth, and he does not organize in alignment with the Plan. He is an eager student within what might be called the 'prison of crystallized form.' He investigates everything but the 'One Thing' which would dissolve the many-celled prison to which he has confined himself; he does not investigate the One Life, nor does he even suspect it exists. Only at the center of his being can he find access to the "One behind the Many," and, at this stage of his development, he prefers the dark and densified conditions at the periphery.

The intelligent use of the two formulae, however, transmutes the abuses of the past. Aided by the potency of these formulae, he terminates the period of personal disorientation and inattentiveness to subjective, spiritual design, and of ignorant attachment to the illusion that objective form is real. The individual learns, primarily, to recognize the reality of the One Identity behind all form (the great subjective Unity behind all material diversity), and his growing secondary ability to register a more subjective "blueprint" to guide him in the reorganization and reconstruction of both his life and his environment, ensures his soul of an utterly reliable, rightly oriented personal instrument which can build forms exactly suited to embody and reveal divine knowledge upon the outer plane of manifestation.

7. Some examples of vocational aptitudes and orientations relating to the combination of the fifth ray soul and the seventh ray personality:

* the scientist as reformer and renovator
* the researcher whose research methods are impeccable
* the investigator whose success depends upon his timing and his knowledge of cycles
* the enquirer whose questions are unfailingly polite and courteous
* the experimenter who ensures that his experiments conform to the highest scientific standards
* the analyst with a superb ability for classification
* the surgeon with consummate surgical technique
* the reliable specialist with an exact understanding of his function within the corporate whole
* the objective observer with highly developed spatial perception, useful in such professions as surveying or map–making
* the inventor with the skill–in–action to manifest his ideas successfully
* the engineer with a talent for building and construction
* the technician who is unusually well–organized
* the mechanic with a remarkable ability to fine–tune mechanisms until they function like a perfect organism
* the repair–person with an excellent knack for understanding exactly how things fit together
* the expert in robotics

In general: vocations and professions which require keen analytical abilities, the capacity for research, and scientific and/or technical expertise, *as well as* the power to organize or reorganize, the ability to build, a facility for creating or maintaining standards, and the capacity to skillfully manifest ideas through form

8. **A proposed list of well-known individuals (historical, contemporary, fictional or mythological) whose soul ray can reasonably be considered the fifth, with a strong subsidiary seventh ray influence (whether or not the seventh ray is, strictly speaking, the personality ray):**

Oswold Avery: microbiologist who identified DNA as the chemical substance of which genes are composed

Galileo Galilei: Italian astronomer, mathematician and physicist. He was the first man to use the telescope to study the skies, and amassed evidence that proved the Earth revolves around the Sun.

Dimitry Mendeleyev: chemist who established a periodic classification of the elements

Max Plank: German physicist, originator of the Quantum Theory

Ivan Petrovich Pavlov: Russian physician and physiologist, chiefly known for his development of the concept of the conditioned reflex. Pavlov was strongly endowed with first ray energy as well.

Nikola Tesla: prophetic inventor, who discovered the rotating magnetic field. The fourth ray was also strongly represented in his make-up, augmenting and enhancing his intuitive abilities and his incredible powers of visualization. (Due to his almost magical control of electrical energies, some might wish to argue for a seventh ray soul.)

Soul/Personality Combinations with a Ray Six Soul

Some Contrasts Between the Ray 6 Soul and the Ray 1 Personality

Ray 6 Soul		Ray 1 Personality
* spiritual idealism	vs.	* the love of personal power
* the mystical approach to reality	vs.	* adamant egotism
* divine dualism	vs.	* selfish, personal monism (the attitude that one is "the only one in the world")
* devotion to a cause which far transcends the interests of the little personal self	vs.	* strong emphasis upon the little personal self as the major center of interest
* passionate yearning for the divine and the "beyond"	vs.	* proud, self-satisfaction
* the exaltation of fervent emotion into spiritual rapture	vs.	* the harsh suppression of emotion
* release through spiritual surrender	vs.	* stubborn, self-willed refusal to relinquish personal authority
* exquisite sensitivity to transcendent ideals and subtleties	vs.	* callous, earthbound realism
* divinely inspired enthusiasm	vs.	* repressive self-containment
* fervent self-immolation for the sake of an ideal	vs.	* personal survival as the first priority; the rejection of self-sacrifice
* consummate tenderness towards the object of devotion	vs.	* impenetrable hardness and frequent cruelty
* intense, unseverable attachment to the beloved ideal or individual	vs.	* a cold detached attitude based upon a preference for selfish isolation
* the inspiration to follow a chosen leader	vs.	* the determination to follow none but oneself
* unusual receptivity to divine guidance	vs.	* proud rejection of any form of guidance as the attempted imposition of an alien will
* unalterable loyalty	vs.	* the arrogant expectation of loyalty from others
* irrepressible high-minded idealism; "eyes upon the stars"	vs.	* repudiation of idealism as unreality; eyes undeviatingly upon the little self

The Integration Process for the Individual with a Ray 6 Soul and a Ray 1 Personality

1. The pre-spiritual phase; soul energy appropriated by a selfish personality: At this pre-spiritual phase of evolutionary unfoldment, the individual's motives (based upon the personality distortion of sixth ray soul energy, and the self-centered use of first ray personality force) are to achieve the uncompromising satisfaction of the ideals and goals to which the individual is passionately devoted, *as well as* great personal power, arising from the unrestrained imposition of the personal will. The person wants, primarily, to ignore everything except the object or path of his devotion, spurn even reasonable mundane responsibilities if they do not relate specifically to his quest, fanatically follow his ideal regardless of destructive consequences, and cling desperately to that which he believes he loves, but he *also* wants to dominate and control others and wield authority unopposed.

Negatively and glamorously, these two ray influences can combine to produce: the religious fanatic who will mercilessly crush anyone who opposes him (6B + 1B); the dogmatist who imposes his dogma on others; the sadistic individual who is convinced that his excesses are justified by the overwhelming importance of his cause (6B + 1B); the uncompromising idealist who tries to force everyone to conform to his ideal; the self-righteously separative person who ploughs a deep furrow between the church (whatever the religion) and everything 'secular'; one who is so narrow and utterly one-pointed that he rejects everything that is not upon the straight line he pursues; a rash and foolhardy person, rushing forward and blinded to real danger by the feeling of invincibility (6B + 1); one who, in exalting the object of his devotion, is really exalting himself; the idealist who egotistically presents himself as the foremost representative of the ideal; the selfish devotee who demands to be his teacher's favorite – the "second in command" (6A + 1); one who justifies his own authoritarianism by the 'guidance' he receives (6A +1); one who clings to an object of devotion because of the personal power it brings him (6A + 1); one who is so utterly extreme in his views that he leaves no room for any accommodation or compromise; one who, filled with a sense of his own unworthiness, humbles and humiliate others (6A + 1); one who, longing to be the "mouthpiece" of higher beings, deludes himself into thinking that the illusory 'messages' he receives are a confirmation that he is the one and only chosen messenger of those higher beings (6A + 1); one so crystallized in his false idealism that he will steadfastly persist in his "wrong-headedness" long after his actions have been shown to be useless, futile or counterproductive (6 + 1A); one who easily blazes with anger, wrath and fury (6B + 1B); rash militancy leading inevitably to destructiveness (6B + 1B); one who exalts the virtue of loyalty, especially, loyalty from others towards himself (6A + 1); a "pied piper" with the will and charisma to lead others into futility and danger; one who yearns so passionately for the other world that he brings on his own death (6 + 1B); fanatical asceticism uncompromisingly carried to the point of self-destruction (6 + 1B); etc.

2. The phase of conflict; pure soul energy conflicts with personality force: The essential conflict between the ray six soul and the ray one personality is the struggle between the spiritual need to sacrifice oneself, totally, devotedly and without reservation, for one's highest ideals, and the personal inclination to view oneself as the world's "most important person," who must survive and have his own way at any cost – including the sacrifice of his highest ideals.

3. The soul/personality integration process from the perspective of the consciousness identified with the sixth ray soul: It will be the task of the sixth ray soul to induce humility and self-sacrifice in the consciousness of the first ray personality. The soul has a truer sense of perspective; it understands the nature of greatness, the vastness of the plan and the tininess of the role it is intended to play; the personality, however, sees things egotistically. The soul is faced with a personality intent upon preserving its "sovereign prerogatives." Realizing that each entity, figuratively, 'revolves around' a still greater Entity, the sixth ray soul attempts to inspire the first ray personality to lift its gaze towards that higher center and away from itself; but the personality remains stubbornly centered in itself, i.e. "self–centered." The soul must induce in the personal consciousness a vision of the Path of spiritual development, its extraordinary length (by ordinary human measures), and the great distance that yet remains to be travelled before the self–important personality can achieve the goal. By presenting a vision of that great and distant goal, the soul hopes to awaken the personality from its proud and stultifying self–satisfaction. The only way towards the distant goal must include aspiration – a sincere and fiery reaching beyond the egotism of the lower, personal self. The soul seeks to teach the personality to relinquish its inflated opinion of itself, and in all humility, to aspire to (and, even, surrender to) something greater.

4. The soul/personality integration process from the perspective of the consciousness identified primarily with the first ray personality: The sixth ray pressure towards integration will initially be felt by the first ray personality as a call to self–abasement – to humility, humiliation and loss of self. The personality feels most comfortable when it feels most important. Confident, centered and able to force the world to comply with its desires, the first ray personality has no wish to feel "meek and lowly." Turning its gaze upward is not something it does easily, whether the higher position is occupied by another individual, God, the state or the flag. The first ray personality often sees itself as a fortress, sufficient unto itself. And yet, under the impress of the sixth ray soul, there arises within the depths of the personal consciousness a yearning for something else, something greater. The personality begins to experience the uncomfortable feeling that although it is a "sovereign lord," it is, so to speak, 'lord over a little land.' As the soul pours its vision into the personal consciousness, the personality grasps the significance of its impoverished 'kingdom,' and, within the confines of its own awareness, is *humiliated*. Such an individual may try to eradicate the vision through renewed ego–inflation, but the exercise is futile. One cannot artificially transform the part into the whole. At length, the personality learns the meaning of humility, and that the greatness it so much craved, can only be achieved when its lowly but authentic place in a transcendent Greatness is recognized.

5. The ideal combination of the sixth ray soul and the first ray personality: Idealism and one–pointed devotion are expressed with great strength and endurance – fearlessly. Personal fortitude contributes powerfully to the achievement of passionately held convictions and ideals. This is an exceedingly potent combination, embodying a devotion and idealism which are unrelenting. Anything that must be done to achieve an ideal *will* be done. These rays have much in common, but will struggle mightily over the primacy of the little self. When the struggle subsides, with the sixth ray soul as victor, these energies complement each other impressively. Self–surrender and self–sacrifice master the tendency to self–aggrandizement, but the dignity of the personal self is always preserved. Humility masters personal pride, but genuine self–respect remains. Complete devotion to a cause triumphs over self–importance, and yet it is realized that a strong personality makes a better servant. Devoted attachment is seen to be more important than aloofness and detachment, but it is firmly understood that attachment must never become weakness. This blend of rays is characteristic of an individual whose loyalty (firm and unwavering) cannot be questioned. It is, above all, the combination of the martyr who, with full and fearless possession of his faculties, wills to sacrifice his life for the highest cause he can conceive.

6. The combined effect of the two integration formulae: The primary integration formula is proposed as *Restraint,* keyed to the sixth ray soul. The secondary integration formula is *Inclusion,* keyed to the first ray personality. The first formula corrects sixth ray tendencies towards the unrestrained, passionate pursuit of the 'partial' and 'peripheral,' whereas the second formula corrects the exclusive and isolative tendencies characteristic of the first ray personality. Used together, these two formulae provide the individual striving for soul/personality integration with the composite quality of 'inclusive restraint' (i.e., the loving and inclusive attitude of the "outer man" which complements the will of the "inner man" to restrain himself from all errant quests, and, instead, quest only after the essence – that which is of supreme value, *Divine Love*). As he applies these formulae, he learns, within his personal consciousness, to feel the magnetism of love, and begins to draw others to him where once he cast them aside. At the still deeper level of spiritual motive, he scans the many possible lines of idealistic approach, but now refuses to rush off along any one of them, because, at last, he begins to sense their limitations – that they lead only towards the periphery of his life, and away from that which he most desires. He, therefore, restrains himself because he is intent upon achieving only that which is of the very highest value. Thus, through the use of these formulae over time, the individual cultivates a warmer, more embracing personal consciousness, supportive of those rare moments of exalted consciousness when (pervaded by the presence of the soul), he widens his vision, restrains his passionate aspiration, and achieves the realization of his ideal: union with "the Beloved," Who embodies the essence of *Divine Love* – omnipresent and inescapable. Upon fulfilling the formulae, he discovers that his search is over, for that which he sought in one direction only, is *everywhere* to be found.

In the earlier stages of evolution, before successfully applying these formulae, an individual with this ray combination often finds himself devotedly rushing off after his limited vision of the ideal, and cruelly excluding (and usually harming) those who appear to obstruct or threaten the fulfillment of that vision. Nothing can stop the relentless progress of his quest. Whoever stands between him and the attainment of his ideal, is trampelled, crushed or cast aside. He imagines that he will find his heart's desire, but in alienating so many, he becomes alienated from his inner Self – which is the source of the spiritual treasure he seeks – in fact, the very treasure itself.

The intelligent use of the formulae, however, transmutes the abuses of the past. The individual learns, primarily, to restrain his urgent impulse to pursue a narrow vision of divinity or the ideal, and to refrain from grasping only that which the narrow vision reveals; consequently, he learns to identify with all true visions, and to love the whole and not just a part. Further, his growing secondary ability to warmly and magnetically include the many he had heretofore rejected, ensures the dedicated soul of a strong yet kind personal instrument to serve upon the outer plane in the task of inspiring others with inclusive spiritual idealism and inclusive spiritual love.

7. Some examples of vocational aptitudes and orientations relating to the combination of the sixth ray soul and the first ray personality:

* the idealist with the will to forge his ideals into actualities
* the devotee, unhesitatingly ready to sacrifice himself for the object of his devotion
* the missionary who is willing to face any danger
* the proselytizer who persuades through his commanding presence
* the minister who stands as a pillar of strength to his congregation
* the orator whose orations crackle with 'electricity'
* the prophet who fearlessly denounces the abuses of his contemporaries
* the visionary with the strength and charisma to impress his vision upon others
* the motivator with a "never–say–die" attitude
* the martyr who approaches his chosen fate fearlessly
* the crusader who is virtually unstoppable
* the loyalist, firm and unflinching in his loyalty
* the activist who is uncompromising in what he seeks to see accomplished
* the moralist with the discipline to live by his highest principles
* the mystic with the will to persist until union with the divine is achieved

In general: vocations and professions which require high idealism, undeviating devotion, great enthusiasm and persistent emotional intensity, *as well as* great will power, strength and stamina, the ability to stand firmly on principle, and (when necessary) the power to destroy obstacles.

8. A proposed list of well–known individuals (historical, contemporary, fictional or mythological) whose soul ray can reasonably be considered the sixth, with a strong subsidiary first ray influence (whether or not the first ray is, strictly speaking, the personality ray):

John Brown: militant abolitionist whose raid on the Federal arsenal at Harpers Ferry, Virginia, in 1859 made him a martyr to the anti–slavery cause

The Master Jesus: the fiery sixth ray initiate, overshadowed by the World Teacher – the Christ

Saint Joan of Arc: mystical visionary and military captain. St. Joan became the heroine of the French nation during the final phases of the Hundred Years War with England.

John the Baptist: the prophet heralding the coming of the Messiah

Kent (fictional): the loyal servant to King Lear, in Shakespeare's play, *King Lear*

Ayatollah Khoumeini: spiritual and temporal leader of Iranian Revolution

Martin Luther King: an eloquent black Baptist minister who for nearly twenty years led the first mass civil rights movement in the United States, regarding himself as a "drum major" for justice, peace and righteousness. The seventh ray was probably also a significant influence in King's energy system.

Mahommet: a great disciple of the Master Jesus, and founder of Islam. Mahommet, according to the Tibetan, was "overshadowed" by the Master Jesus, just as the Master Jesus was overshadowed by the Christ.

Carry A. Nation: militant crusader against alcohol, alcoholism and numerous other 'sinful' abuses. Nation, leader of the W.C.T.U. (Women's Christian Temperance Union) personally carried out "saloon–smashing" expeditions.

Thomas Paine: political journalist, patriot and champion of the rights of the common man

Some Contrasts Between the Ray 6 Soul and the Ray 2 Personality

Ray 6 Soul		Ray 2 Personality
* spiritual ardor	vs.	* personal ease and comfort
* the pursuit of martyrdom	vs.	* fear of pain
* easily inspired by the highest ideal, no matter how demanding	vs.	* attracted by the promise of effortlessness
* unrelenting haste towards the goal	vs.	* inertia; difficulty rousing oneself
* intensity of love	vs.	* broad, pleasant, superficial affection
* rising towards the "highest light"	vs.	* hampered by multiple personal and environal attachments
* passionate intensity leading to accomplishment	vs.	* easy–going unexcitability leading to non–accomplishment
* ardent spiritual discipline	vs.	* seeks to avoid all strenuous applications of force
* the benefits of fiery zeal	vs.	* experiencing fieriness as disturbing; frequent bouts with laziness
* uncompromising adherence to the ideal	vs.	* readiness to abandon the ideal because of personal weakness
* the power to detach violently whenever spiritually necessary	vs.	* difficulty with all detachments, especially violent ones
* constant readiness to tread the "high road"	vs.	* too easily succumbing to the 'drag' of the personality
* one–pointedness as the guarantor of idealistic achievement	vs.	* non–dynamic 'spread' of energies which disperses the strength needed for achievement
* the power to destroy that which prevents the realization of the ideal	vs.	* virtually no destructive power even when it is absolutely necessary
* instant mobilization for necessary action	vs.	* often overly absorbed in study, and loathe to take action
* irrepressible faith	vs.	* self–pity and defeatism
* ready response to the call to rise above human frailty	vs.	* calm resignation to the naturalness of human frailty
* intense spiritual earnestness	vs.	* ineffectual personal pleasantness

The Integration Process for the Individual with a Ray 6 Soul and a Ray 2 Personality

1. The pre–spiritual phase: soul energy appropriated by a selfish personality: At this pre–spiritual phase of personality unfoldment, the individual's motives (based upon the personality distortion of sixth ray soul energy, and the self–centered use of second ray personality force) are to achieve the uncompromising satisfaction of the ideals and goals to which the individual is passionately devoted, *as well as* the complete fulfillment of personal love (or the complete satisfaction of studious enquiry [2B]). The person wants, primarily, to ignore everything except the object or path of his devotion, spurn even reasonable mundane responsibilities if they do not relate specifically to his quest, fanatically follow his ideal regardless of destructive consequences, and cling desperately to that which he believes he loves, but, he *also* wants to be constantly loved, consistently popular, warmly admired, well–cared for, and to live a soft, superficially pleasant, comfortable, well–protected and well-insulated life, closely attached to those people, places and things which he loves and find personally satisfying.

Negatively and glamorously these two ray influences can combine to produce: a persistently self–abnegating person with a strong streak of masochism (6A + 2A); one submerged in a profound sense of unworthiness and self–pity (6A + 2A); one who is usually found leaning upon others and unable to let go (6A + 2A); one whose attitude is so servile that he has no conception of what it means to stand up for himself (6A + 2A); one who is always attached to someone or something; an extremely passive person who believes that God will provide all if one only waits (6A + 2); one who believes that God or a "higher power" is guiding and supervising his every move (6A + 2); one who compounds the problem of his excessive otherworldliness with a weak and ineffectual presentation of self (6A + 2); one whose estimation of others is unrealistically positive; one who is extremely indulgent and permissive with those to whom he is devoted (6A + 2A); an extremely naive person who believes that those he loves are "all sweetness and light" and can do no wrong (6A + 2); one who sees the world "through rose colored glasses" (6A + 2); an overly emotional sentimental person, moved to tears at the slightest provocation (6A + 2A); one who will do anything to be loved by the person to whom he is devoted (6 + 2A); one so passionately devoted to a certain teaching that he reads and studies nothing else (6 + 2B); the militant idealist who supports and strengthens his idealism with excessive study (6B + 2B); the overzealous teacher who forces his students to learn *everything* he has learned (6B + 2B); one who believes the world would be perfect if everyone were taught in one certain way (6 + 2B); the well meaning person who, with tedious kindness, shares the same moral lessons over and over again (6 + 2B); the incurable romantic in search of perfect love (6 + 2A); the classic "bleeding heart" (6A + 2A); one with a pronounced "savior complex," eagerly out to 'save' everyone, especially the downtrodden or those who have not "seen the light"; etc.

2. The phase of conflict; pure soul energy conflicts with personality force: The essential conflict between the ray six soul and the ray two personality is the struggle between the spiritual need to be devoted to high ideals at any cost, and the personal desire for the warm comforts of love and learning, often achieved at the expense of high and demanding ideals.

3. The soul/personality integration process from the perspective of the consciousness identified primarily with the sixth ray soul: It will be the task of the sixth ray soul to arouse the second ray personality to more strenuous effort in the cause of attainment. The sixth ray soul is motivated by spiritual extremism, whereas the second ray personality dislikes putting itself under stress. The urgent (and 'urging') soul is faced with a personality which would rather "take it easy," proceeding gradually, comfortably and, above all, without disrupting its warm and close attachments to certain people and things. The soul must persuade the personality that a seductive combination of lethargy and overattachment are preventing it from realizing and attaining *higher things*. Slowly, the soul infuses the personal consciousness with a glorious vision of a Path leading to heights which can only be attained if the personality bestirs itself and releases its grip upon the "near and dear." The soul well knows that the many accumulations with which the personality has surrounded itself only stand in the way, that they act as a weight preventing aspiration and ascent. The soul must present a vision so attractive and inspiring that, at length, the personality will dare to leave the *many* attachments behind, and, instead, follow *one* Path to a lofty goal.

4. The soul/personality integration process from the perspective of the consciousness identified primarily with the second ray personality: The sixth ray pressure towards integration will initially be felt by the second ray personality as a yearning for something which its present attachments fail to satisfy. The second ray personality, perhaps influenced by the quality of the second ray planet Jupiter, desires complete satisfaction. With its considerable magnetism and charm, it attracts both people and things which contribute to that satisfaction, and it holds them close, creating, at length, a completely satisfying environment – warm, pleasant, agreeable, lovely. This type of personality has no wish to relinquish these many satisfying ties to pursue a vague "something higher," and yet, deep within the personal consciousness, as the soul pours forth its influence, there arise intimations of heights far more dazzling and attractive than the many little loves which hold the personality in womb–like comfort. A yearning for something unknown; an aspiration towards something more perfect – these are the unsettling effects of the influence of the sixth ray soul, making lesser attachments seem pale and unworthy. Especially under the inspiration of the sixth ray soul, does the personality experience soul influence as a "call." At the beginning of the Piscean Age (with its powerful sixth ray influence) Christ/Jesus sounded a call strongly qualified by the sixth ray – that a man must leave his home, his wife, and all things familiar, to follow Him – the embodiment of the highest ideal. This call to follow the highest ideal is most uncomfortable to the second ray personality, which may attempt, temporarily, to ignore the call and hold the "near ones" even nearer. But at length, there is no choice but to forsake lesser things for greater; the alternative – suffocation in one's own personal satisfactions. And thus, as the influence of the soul prevails, one love, a love more ideal, a love more transcendent, now replaces the lesser loves. To that *one love* the individual becomes devoted.

5. The ideal expression of the combination of the ray six soul and the ray two personality: Idealism and one–pointed devotion are expressed slowly, considerately and in a sweet, kindly manner. Intensity of belief and conviction prevail over both the desire to be loved and the desire for personal comfort, but sensitivity to others mellows the sometimes harsh effects of intensity. Personal kindness and serenity, and the considerate "go slow" approach facilitate the fulfillment of cherished ideals. Passion for the "right" replaces a well–meaning but ill–advised and indiscriminate tolerance, but there is always sufficient "heart understanding" to prevent righteousness from becoming fanaticism. When this ray combination is functioning positively, there will be a great gift for humility. The greatness of God or the ideal is understood, and the little ego never interferes. Further, there is an intense desire to serve and save; such an individual will be unweariyingly tenacious in his determination to serve the ideal by serving and saving others. Although a passion for the ideal comes first, there is a real "feeling for people," and a wish to avoid having them suffer, even though the fulfillment of the ideal may require suffering. We might call the attitude of such an individual 'humanistic idealism' – an attitude in which compassion for humanity is always considered in the process of fulfilling ideals. Here, too, we may find the preacher/teacher – one who has discovered a particular moral, religious or idealistic teaching of great value, and who dedicates his life to presenting that point of view to whomever will listen. In addition there is great trust, faith and receptivity; an attitude of uplifted openness, patiently awaiting "guidance from above." Few combinations will be more loyal; high-minded devotion and loving attachment blend to create an individual who will never abandon the care of those he loves, no matter how great the self-sacrifice or lengthy the time required. The capacity to cherish will be intense.

6. The combined effect of the two integration formulae: The primary integration formula is proposed as *Restraint,* keyed to the sixth ray soul. The secondary integration formula is *Centralization,* keyed to the second ray personality. The first formula corrects the sixth ray tendencies towards the unrestrained, passionate pursuit of the 'partial' and 'peripheral,' whereas the second formula corrects the second ray tendencies towards diffusion, overexpansion, and an energy-draining attachment to life's peripheral attractions. Used together, these two formulae provide the individual striving for soul/personality integration with the composite quality of 'centralized restraint,' (i.e., the quiet and peaceful centralization of the personal consciousness which complements the determination of the "inner man" to restrain himself from pursuing anything but that which is of the highest spiritual value). These formulae enable him to detach from the effects of many personal ties so that he can "center" his personal consciousness, while within the inner recesses of consciousness (the realm of consciousness pertaining to the soul) he learns the attitude of restraint, which allows him to see divinity or the ideal on every hand, rather than only in one specific direction. By using these formulae over time, the individual succeeds in cultivating a more detached and independent personality consciousness, supportive of those rare moments of exalted consciousness when, (pervaded by the presence of the soul) he expands his vision, restrains his passionate aspiration, and eventually achieves the realization of his very highest ideal: union with "the Beloved," Who embodies the essence of *Divine Love* – omnipresent and inescapable.

In the earlier stages of evolution, before successfully applying these formulae, an individual with this ray combination often finds himself rushing off after his vision of the ideal, and becoming so attached to what he grasps, that he is powerless to regain his center. Upon the periphery of his life, he clings to a narrow form of fulfillment. He will not let go, nor admit the possibility of deeper values and wider loves. When he tires of that to which he has attached himself (as he inevitably must) he will "latch on" to another tiny aspect of the whole, and cling to it with equal tenacity and earnestness. So narrow is his vision, and so poorly developed his power to release, that he cannot find his way back to the center of his being.

The intelligent use of the combined formulae, however, transmutes the abuses of the past. The individual learns, primarily, to restrain the urgent impulse to pursue a narrow vision of divinity or the ideal, and to refrain from grasping only that which his narrow vision reveals; consequently, he learns to identify with all true visions, and because of his restraint, he comes to love the whole and not just the part. Further, his growing secondary ability to detach himself from many lesser personal loves, and stand firmly within the center of personal consciousness, promotes the primary (soul) process, since from a detached and "centered" position the individual with a second ray personality can begin to access the "heart of love," and hence, participate more easily in the divinity of *all* people and *all* things. Thus the soul is assured of a personal instrument endowed with love, and well able to help the soul achieve the goal of loving the *many,* wisely and dispassionately.

7. **Some examples of vocational aptitudes and inclinations relating to the combination of the sixth ray soul and the second ray personality:**

* the idealist who is capable of waiting with "long–suffering patience" for the fulfillment of his ideals

* the devotee totally in love with the one to whom he is devoted

* the missionary who arrives with not only a doctrine, but with compassionate, humanitarian concern

* the church educator

* the proselytizer who understands the value of 'conversion by inclusion,' whereby the most cherished thoughts and practices of the ones to be converted are somehow included within the presentation of the new faith

* the minister who seeks to elevate his congregation through education

* the orator more inclined toward gentle persuasion than declamation

* the prophet with a tolerant understanding of human foibles and the inevitable slowness of constructive change

* the visionary who sees all the more clearly because of his tranquility

* the motivator who understands how to magnetize (through warmth and kindness) those he wishes to motivate

* the martyr who accepts all abuse with gentle resignation

* the quiet crusader motivated by compassion

* the loyalist who remains quietly and calmly attached to the very end

* the activist whose friendliness and cooperativeness enlist many in the cause

* the moralist whose personality is so positive and appealing that people find it agreeable to adopt his point of view

* the mystical quietist

In general: vocations and professions which require high idealism, undeviating devotion, great enthusiasm and persistent emotional intensity, *as well as* a wise and loving attitude, great empathy and understanding, studiousness, and the ability to teach or compassionately heal.

8. A proposed list of well-known individuals (historical, contemporary, fictional or mythological) whose soul ray can reasonably be considered the sixth, with a strong subsidiary second ray influence (whether or not the second ray is, strictly speaking, the personality ray):

George Fox: founder of the Society of Friends known as the Quakers

Ronald Reagan: 40th president of the United States: an idealist with an unusually warm, friendly and pleasing persona

Some Contrasts Between the Ray 6 Soul and the Ray 3 Personality

Ray 6 Soul		Ray 3 Personality
* spiritual earnestness	vs.	* calculation, premeditation and frequent insincerity
* spiritual dedication to the *One*	vs.	* personal preoccupation with the *many*
* the faith which touches reality	vs.	* intellectual reasoning within the "veils of maya"
* profound mysticism; sensitive receptivity to the higher worlds	vs.	* materialism; astute adaptability confined to the lower three worlds
* yearning for that which transcends the little personal self	vs.	* preoccupied self–interest
* zealous fulfillment of spiritual destiny	vs.	* clever self–protective evasion of responsibility
* uncompromising idealism	vs.	* unidealistic expediency
* clear–sighted spiritual vision	vs.	* obscuration of the vision through overly–complex, relativistic thinking
* penetrating spiritual intuition	vs.	* prideful intellectuality which repulses intuition
* high–minded honesty	vs.	* devious manipulation for personal advantage
* realization of the essential simplicity of the highest moral and spiritual values	vs.	* inability to see or think with simplicity
* the transmutation of emotion into the exaltation of divine love	vs.	* emotional sensitivity stifled and devitalized by an overly–busy thought life, and excessive physical activity
* one–pointed focus leading to spiritual accomplishment	vs.	* scattered thoughts and activities dissipating energy and preventing true accomplishment
* clarity of motive through clarity of vision	vs.	* mixed motives and confused vision
* firm and loyal commitment to one's highest ideals or spiritual values	vs.	* an elusive, non–committal attitude based upon constant maneuvering for a more advantageous position

The Integration Process for the Individual with a Ray 6 Soul and a Ray 3 Personality

1. The pre–spiritual phase; soul energy appropriated by a selfish personality: At this pre–spiritual phase of evolutionary unfoldment, the individual's motives (based upon the personality distortion of sixth ray soul energy, and the self–centered use of third ray personality force), are to achieve the uncompromising satisfaction of the ideals and goals to which the individual is passionately devoted, *as well as* a cleverly intelligent, self–serving mastery of circumstances and the environment. The person wants, primarily, to ignore everything except the object or path of his devotion, spurn even reasonable mundane responsibilities if they do not relate specifically to his quest, fanatically follow his ideal regardless of destructive consequences, and cling desperately to that which he believes he loves, but, he *also* wants to demonstrate his 'superior' intelligence at every opportunity, manipulate money and other people for his own material and intellectual satisfaction, keep incessantly busy in the pursuit of his own self-centered interests, and evade responsibilities through selfish, strategic planning.

Negatively and glamorously, these two ray influences can combine to produce: the unscrupulous idealogue who uses devious means to ensure that his ideals prevail; the sly proselytizer who seeks to convert others through sophistry (6 + 3A); the unrealistic, "otherworldly" individual who is, more often than not, entangled in vague and overly-involved thought (6A + 3A); the utopian visionary who delights in dreaming up grandiose schemes which can never possibly materialize (6 + 3A); the "head-in-the-clouds" individual with an almost total lack of common sense (6 + 3A); the injudicious person who rushes furiously towards one ill-conceived goal after another, squandering his energy in futile hyperactivity (6B + 3B); one who drives himself to such a degree that he is 'busy' all the time (6B + 3B); the fanatic who insists that everyone must learn to reason as he does; one who is motivated by unintelligent, "blind" faith, but will go to great lengths employing his reasoning to justify whatever he believes (6 + 3A); the dogmatic theologian who is convinced of the infallibility of his own reasoning (6 + 3A); one who believes that God has entitled him to be rich, by fair means or foul (6 + 3B); an unhappy blending of the religious and commercial instincts (6 + 3B); one who is intensely devoted to obtaining great material wealth (6B + 3B); one so passionately determined to reach his goal that he will use dishonest means to get there (6B + 3B); one who compounds his problem with addiction by the fertility with which his mind invents rationalizations (6A + 3); one who wants only one thing and irresponsibly evades the normal duties of life if they do not pertain to just that one thing (6 + 3A); etc.

2. The phase of conflict; pure soul energy conflicts with personality force: The essential conflict between the ray six soul and the ray three personality is the struggle between the spiritual need for a transcendent union with divinity achieved through faith and ardent aspiration, and the personal desire to manipulate the three worlds of human evolution through the power of intellectual reasoning, almost invariably at the expense of the mystical life.

3. The soul/personality integration process from the perspective of the consciousness identified primarily with the sixth ray soul: It will be the task of the sixth ray soul to demonstrate to the third ray personality the limitations of the reasoning process. When consciousness is identified with the sixth ray soul, it is possessed by an unquenchable aspiration for the ecstasy of mystical transcendence. Even when sixth ray idealism is expressed in a manner which is not outwardly religious or spiritual, the pursuit of ecstasy, rapture, glorification and union is, nevertheless, implicit. With this combination of rays, however, the sixth ray soul finds itself faced with a personality which is usually preoccupied with mental processes, or with the application of intensely active thought to an unusually active physical plane life. As long as the personality is absorbed in hyperactive thinking and doing, it will not be able to participate in mystical exaltation – a state of union which can only be achieved through prayer, aspiration and meditation.

The soul seeks to impress the personal consciousness with the need to cease from its incessant activities long enough to catch a glimpse of the transcendent *vision*. The soul realizes that the personality reasons and acts so incessantly, simply because it does not yet *see*. If the "higher light" were to come into view, the lower activity would be temporarily suspended, and later, would take its proper place. The soul must teach the personality that there are certain higher opportunities it cannot make for itself, and that, through an attitude of stillness and upward-gazing receptivity, certain highly desirable "gifts of the spirit" (which cannot possibly be reached through reason) can be bestowed. Although frequently frustrated by complicated, chaotic or pointless motion within its personality, the soul gradually infuses the personal consciousness with a numinous vision. The resulting sense of awe subdues personality activity. The soul thus succeeds in revealing a lofty realm inaccessible to the reasoning intellect; the quieted personality, attracted to the intangible as never before, begins to listen and gaze enraptured towards the summit where shines the "Highest Light."

4. The soul/personality integration process from the perspective of the consciousness identified primarily with the third ray personality: The sixth ray pressure towards integration is initially felt by the third ray personality as a hopelessly idealistic interference with the continuation of its important business. The personality has everything well in hand, weaving and manipulating thoughts, people, circumstances and the environment for its own good and sufficient reasons. The last thing it wishes to do is to "cease from its doing" and follow an ever-receding, patently unattainable vision. The personality does not choose to exchange its role of efficient thinker and actor for the role of humble follower of a higher light – a light which, more often than not, cannot be understood, reached or captured by the mind. Under the impress of the soul, the proud-minded personality feels itself beginning to lose control; it begins to realize that its well-developed and capable intelligence will not bring it to the "promised land" presented as a glorious vision by the soul. Deep within the personal consciousness there arises an emotional yearning, an aspiration for that which, hitherto, it would have called "unreasonable." Such urges are distressing to a personality which has prided itself on cleverness of mind and reasoning abilities. The personality naturally feels frustrated by this intrusion of ostensibly irrational idealism, and at first, rejects it as unfounded. Gradually, however, the lure of the transcendent heights begins to lift the personality out of its intellectual convolutions. It begins to sense, that for all its many activities, it is really getting nowhere, and is, in fact, missing a goal far higher and far more desirable. While it is extremely difficult for the third ray personality to simplify its life, it does so. Instead of running in many directions in pursuit of many objectives, it begins to "walk the straight and narrow," in pursuit of *one* objective – the transcendent vision as presented by the soul.

5. The ideal expression of the combination of the ray six soul and the ray three personality: Idealism and one-pointed devotion are expressed intelligently, resourcefully and cleverly. Here there is no question of "blind faith" or "bewildered idealism"; an advanced individual with this ray combination has thought through *why* he *believes,* and can articulate his conclusions. One would expect to find the usual sixth ray sense of righteousness, moral purity and sincerity of motive, and these would prevail over expediency and moral flexibility, yet there is sufficient intelligence and adaptability to prevent crystallization into rigid attitudes. Sincerity and simplicity master the tendency towards indirectness and complexity, but the individual always remains astute. The love of religion is felt to be more important than business activity, but business skills are turned to good account in the support of religious activities. Here, for instance, we might find the successful business person who lays much of his profit upon the altar of his church. Here also, is one who can find numerous excellent *reasons* to justify his faith, but reason, per se, is ever the servant of faith. This combination offers a blend of *abstract* idealism and *abstract* intelligence – the result being an ability to clothe mystical perceptions in appropriate philosophical concepts. On a somewhat less remote level, it is a ray–blend which can produce an extremely resourceful and versatile proselytizer. The third ray personality, when functioning intelligently bestows a pronounced ability to plan, and to actively execute plans; this ability is used to help bring the ideal into manifestation.

6. The combined effect of the two integration formulae: The primary integration formula is proposed as *Restraint*, keyed to the sixth ray soul. The secondary integration formula is *Stillness,* keyed to the third ray personality. The first formula corrects sixth ray tendencies towards the unrestrained, passionate pursuit of the 'partial' and 'peripheral,' whereas the second formula corrects third ray tendencies towards a busy scattering of attention, wasted thought, and physical overactivity (with their resultant disturbances and obscurations of consciousness). Used together, these two formulae provide the individual striving for soul/personality integration with the composite quality of 'still restraint,' (the stillness of the "outer man" which complements the determination of the "inner man" to restrain himself from pursuing anything but that which is of the highest spiritual value). Stillness brings greater clarity to the consciousness and reduces the psycho–mental confusion which ever results in a confusion of values (i.e., those things which are *worth* desiring and pursuing). Seeing more clearly, the individual can restrain himself from worthless pursuits more effectively. These formulae thus make it possible for him to quiet his personal consciousness and personality vehicles, while within the soul–pervaded "higher reaches" of his consciousness, he learns that attitude of restraint, which allows him to see divinity or the ideal on every hand rather than only in one specific direction. Thus, eventually, he expands his inner vision and achieves the realization of his very highest ideal: union with "the Beloved," Who embodies the essence of *Divine Love* – omnipresent and inescapable.

In the earlier stages of evolution, before successfully applying these formulae, an individual with this ray combination often finds himself devotedly rushing off after his vision of the ideal, and thrown into a state of ceaseless overactivity of mind and body in the attempt to make that ideal an actuality. This can be an incredibly restless combination, unusually subject to glamor and maya. There is a breathless, hurried quality to all he does. The solar plexus and throat centers are hyperactive. He runs around the periphery of his life, chasing one desirable objective after another, anxious to commit, but too restless to stay committed for long. His passions are too aroused and his mind too active to see with clarity. His life demonstration is utterly *centrifugal.* The uncontrolled force racing through him 'spins him out' farther and farther from the center of his being.

The intelligent use of the combined formulae, however, transmutes the abuses of the past. The individual learns, primarily, to restrain his urgent impulse to pursue a narrow vision of divinity or the ideal, and to refrain from grasping only that which his narrow vision reveals; consequently, he learns to identify with all true visions, and because of his restraint, he learns to love the whole and not just the part. Further, his growing secondary ability to stand *still* at the center of his personal consciousness with quieted mind, emotions and body, produces a personality control which furthers the process of restraint engineered by the soul. This controlled personality quietude removes a significant obstacle from the soul's primary intention of ensuring that inclusive spiritual vision and inclusive spiritual love become the distinguishing features of the individual's consciousness.

7. Some examples of vocational aptitudes and orientations relating to the combination of the sixth ray soul and the third ray personality:

* the idealist who justifies his ideas with philosophical astuteness
* the devotee who serves his cause without pausing to rest
* the missionary whose financial resourcefulness helps those he seeks to serve meet their material financial needs, just as his fiery faith and commitment help them fulfill their spiritual needs
* the proselytizer, highly adaptable in his methods of persuasion
* the minister with a talent for fund raising
* the orator with remarkable abilities to articulate difficult concepts
* the enthusiastic sportscaster
* the ubiquitous prophet, travelling constantly to impart his message
* the visionary who lays elaborate, far–reaching plans for his visions to become actualities
* the motivator with a great repertoire of motivational approaches
* the martyr with the shrewdness to time his sacrifice for greatest effect
* the crusader known for his impassioned reasoning
* the loyalist whose flexibility and mobility prevent him from falling into traps
* the activist whose success is reinforced by excellent strategic thinking
* the moralist whose positions on various issues are thought–through from every conceivable angle
* the mystic whose mind is as active as his aspirational longings are intense

In general: vocations and professions which require high idealism, undeviating devotion, great enthusiasm, and persistent emotional intensity, *as well as* acute intelligence (whether active or abstract), great adaptability and resourcefulness, abundant creative and communicative abilities, and (frequently) strong business aptitudes.

8. A proposed list of well–known individuals (historical, contemporary, fictional or mythological) whose soul ray can reasonably be considered the sixth, with a strong subsidiary third ray influence (whether or not the third ray is, strictly speaking, the personality ray):

St. Augustine: bishop of Hippo in Roman Africa from 396 to 430. Augustine is generally recognized as having been the greatest thinker of Christian antiquity. His theology is the source of the religious philosophy of predestination.

William Jennings Bryan: Democratic and Populist leader who ran unsuccessfully three times for the presidency of the United States. Bryan was a fiery and magnetic orator, regarded by his supporters as a life–long champion of liberal causes, such as Labor, Prohibition and women's suffrage. He was also closely identified with monetary reform. A strong ray one influence is to be noted, as well.

Bob Dylan: song–writer, poet, idealistic protester. Dylan has experienced more than one religious conversion.

Richard Vigurie: ideologically militant direct–mail specialist for conservative causes

Zig Ziglar: "born again" business executive with a great flair for the promotion of positive thinking

Some Contrasts Between the Ray 6 Soul and the Ray 4 Personality

Ray 6 Soul		Ray 4 Personality
* unrelenting spiritual aspirations	vs.	* constant personality fluctuations
* uncompromising spiritual idealism	vs.	* easy acquiescence to cyclic negativity
* rising above the limitations of the form nature	vs.	* swinging helplessly between the "pairs of opposites"
* soul–inspired loyalty to lofty causes	vs.	* divided loyalties and inconstancy
* passionate, high–minded certainty	vs.	* ambivalence and infirmity
* unwavering spiritual commitment	vs.	* compromise for the sake of personal peace and harmony
* unrelenting spiritual effort	vs.	* frequent inability to sustain effort
* constant envisioning of the ideal	vs.	* quality of vision subject to mood swings
* the serenity of assured faith	vs.	* constant personal turmoil and crises
* great joy and optimism fostered by clear and true spiritual vision	vs.	* frequent pessimism, dejection and deflation
* maintenance of the highest moral standards	vs.	* moral cowardice; wavering on moral principles
* immediate pursuit of the spiritually desirable	vs.	* delay through procrastination
* utter reliability and predictability	vs.	* the unreliability of a self–conflicted person
* serious battle only for the sake of worthy ideals	vs.	* confused combat to no worthy end
* deep earnestness	vs.	* frequent bouts of foolishness and frivolity
* holding steadfast despite disapproval	vs.	* need to be entertaining and pleasing
* single–minded, one–pointed fulfillment of duty	vs.	* 'two–mindedness', capriciousness and irresponsibility

The Integration Process for the Individual with a Ray 6 Soul and a Ray 4 Personality

1. The pre–spiritual phase; soul energy appropriated by a selfish personality: At this pre–spiritual phase of evolutionary unfoldment, the individual's motives (based upon the personality distortion of sixth ray soul energy, and the self–centered use of fourth ray personality force), are to achieve the uncompromising satisfaction of the ideals and goals to which the individual is passionately devoted, *as well as* an agreeable feeling of personal peace and harmony through a tension–releasing expression of conflicting bio–psychic impulses. The person wants, primarily, to ignore everything except the object or path of his devotion, spurn even reasonable mundane responsibilities if they do not relate specifically to his quest, fanatically follow his ideal regardless of destructive consequences, and cling desperately to that which he believes he loves, but he *also* wants to be constantly surrounded by what he considers beautiful or attractive, to be spontaneously self-expressive without discipline or control, self-indulgently dramatic or moody (as he pleases), and greatly appreciated for his colorful, unpredictable temperament.

Negatively and glamorously these two ray influences can combine to produce: the melodramatic person, all too often in the throes of fluctuating emotionalism (6 + 4B); one who, sensing the polarities of life as irrevocably separated, fluctuates wildly and violently between them (6B + 4B); and an excessively dependent person who has very little self-confidence (6A + 4); an individual who feels very defensive about his beliefs and is instantly ready to fight if they are challenged – the combative idealist (6B + 4B); one who blends unrestrained religious fervor with lack of moral discipline; a person easily addicted, indulging in one excess after another; the unstable, hysterical individual – especially prone to religious hysteria (6 + 4B); the self-abasing, self-flagellating person (6 + 4B); one who, living at an uncomfortably high pitch of emotional intensity, is always in a state of crisis (6B + 4B); an utterly unrealistic person who lets his fantasies run away with him; one who compounds the problems caused by his otherworldliness with an attitude of foolish improvidence; an idealistic perfectionist for whom nothing on earth is ever beautiful enough (6 + 4A); the naive idealist who will settle for nothing less than perfect peace and harmony in all situations, even if it means "making peace with the devil" – pacifistic appeasement (6A + 4A); the fanatical aggressor who perpetually incites conflict (6B + 4B); in general, one for whom emotional control presents an almost insuperable obstacle; etc.

2. The phase of conflict; pure soul energy conflicts with personality force: The essential conflict between the ray six soul and the ray four personality is the struggle between the spiritual need to follow one's highest ideal with unswerving devotion, and the personal desire to achieve peace and harmony at all costs, even if one's ideals must be compromised.

3. The soul/personality integration process from the perspective of the consciousness identified primarily with the sixth ray soul: It will be the task of the sixth ray soul to assist the fourth ray personality to end its perpetual internal and external ambivalences, and focus its aspiration upon a single, magnetic point. For the soul, there is always one thing – a person, a cause, an ideal or a great being – which is seen as the 'object' of greatest worth; the fourth ray personality, however, can rarely decide to pursue an objective single-mindedly, and if it does seem to decide, it shortly reverses itself with a contradictory decision. The soul's frustration arises from its desire to hasten towards the goal which it has selected, with all personality forces fully mobilized; yet, it is faced with a personality which is often too embroiled in crisis and conflict to move forward with any degree of rapidity. Further, the personality has considerable difficulty holding to a commitment; vacillation always undoes its resolution. The soul must pervade the personal consciousness with a vision so numinous, so exalting, that the contrariness of the personality is resolved, and a single direction pursued. The sixth ray soul's greatest 'weapon' is its capacity to inspire enthusiasm; as it does so, the personal consciousness becomes so enamored of new and lofty possibilities, that it stops wasting its energy in fruitless conflicts, and seeks to collect and harmonize its energies so that it can move forward, sincerely, earnestly, and with keen aspiration, towards that single, maximally desirable objective which has been placed in its line of vision by the soul.

4. The soul/personality integration process from the perspective of the consciousness identified primarily with the fourth ray personality: The sixth ray pressure towards integration will be felt by the fourth ray personality as a call to abandon its vibrant humanity for the sake of remote, transcendent objectives. The personality feels most comfortable when it is most 'human' – reacting, interacting, experiencing and harmonizing the many contrasts which are part and parcel of being a normal human being. This is all part of what might be called 'the drama of being human' with its delights, surprises, reversals, defeats and victories. For the highly developed fourth ray personality, it is thrilling to be in the midst of life's many contrasts, living vibrantly and colorfully, identifying alternately with the many pairs of opposites. Compared to such an exciting life, the call of the soul seems monochromatic; instead of variety, color, and contrast – a single, unvarying objective! Consistency instead of fluctuation; sameness instead of surprise; and, of course, self–denial (detested by the average fourth ray type) – which means the impossibility of experiencing and enjoying those things in human living which pertain to the 'lower pole,' the more material aspect of the nature. This is not an appealing prospect for a personality which wishes to be, according to its estimation, fully human instead of idealistically out of touch with the engaging vicissitudes of the human condition. The soul, however, gradually demonstrates to the personality that the human condition, as it now exists, is not really all that desirable, and that a devotion to transcendent things will, at length, make human living all the more vibrant and interesting. At first the personality is not easily convinced, because it does not like the discipline of a steady, unrelieved orientation towards a single objective, no matter how high the objective. Eventually, however, there arises within the personal consciousness, a realization of the futility of human living (no matter how vibrant, exciting and colorful) when it is disconnected from a sense of that which a human being can and must become. The image of the *ideal* human, with transcendent, god–like qualities, living in an *ideal* environment (whether earthly or supermundane) becomes stronger, as does the realization that it is impossible to become such a being without aspiring to the heights, and without recognizing (with reverence) Those who are already '*up there*' and ready to assist. In short, the value of idealism and devotion becomes patent to the personal consciousness, which, with ardor and aspiration, begins to transcend the futility of preoccupation with the strictly human state.

5. The ideal expression of the combination of the ray six soul and the ray four personality: Idealism and one–pointed devotion are expressed beautifully and harmoniously. Here is an individual capable of the loftiest spiritual aspiration, and his intuitive sensitivity to beauty leads him ever closer to his goal. Not only does he idealize the beautiful, but the fourth ray in his equipment enables him to *create* beauty as well. Idealism and aesthetic refinement are blended, and the result is a strongly perfectionistic streak. When it comes to representing the ideal to others, the use of color and contrast, and, in general, the arts and all things beautiful, play a prominent role. There may be an unusual talent for expressing emotion or religious aspiration through music. This is an individual gifted with passion, intensity and fervor which he loves to use dramatically. He will have a gift for dramatic oratory, and his language will be picturesque and colorful. In the contest between the soul ray and its subray (the personality ray), unyielding devotion and commitment to an ideal master vacillation and pliability, and yet there remains the capacity to reconcile one's ideal to the ideals of others. Sincerity and one–pointed loyalty master ambivalence and divided loyalties, neverthless the "other point of view" can always be recognized and appreciated. When the sixth ray subdues and utilizes the fourth, faith and optimism prevail over personal ambivalences, moods and negativities, but there remains the sensitivity to sense such fluctuations in others and to help lift their sights when cyclic bouts with negativity threaten to dim their vision. Perceptive steadiness overcomes numerous personal instabilities, for the goal is never lost to sight. Those characterized by this ray combination are noted for their readiness to fight for, or defend their ideals. This is an idealistic individual who seeks to have his highest dreams come true; once the conflict and combat of his personality have been harmonized, he becomes capable of achieving interpersonal harmony, and the cooperation this engenders assists in the actualization of his dreams. Here is an individual who is capable of manifesting his highest ideals and yearnings through creative living and artistic expression, but the ideals are paramount, and art is the form of expression. (This combination stands in contrast to the fourth ray soul and sixth ray personality, in which the individual idealizes his art – art always being primary, and constituting the individual's highest personal ideal.)

6. The combined effect of the two integration formulae: The primary integration formula is proposed as *Restraint*, keyed to the sixth ray soul. The secondary integration formula is *Steadfastness*, keyed to the fourth ray personality. The first formula corrects sixth ray tendencies towards the unrestrained, passionate pursuit of the 'partial' and 'peripheral,' whereas the second formula corrects the tendencies towards vacillation, irresoluteness, instability, indecisiveness and moral cowardice characteristic of the fourth ray personality. Used together, these two formulae provide the individual striving for soul/personality integration with the composite quality of 'steadfast restraint,' (i.e., the steadfast attitude of the "outer man" which complements the determination of the "inner man" to restrain himself from pursuing anything but that which is of the highest spiritual value). Steadfastness brings equililibrium to the consciousness and reduces the psycho–mental turmoil which ever results in ambivalence and uncertainty with regard to values. Being more balanced in his personal life, and less likely to be drawn into any of the numerous possible conflicts between the various "pairs of opposites," the individual can more effectively restrain himself from the narrow pursuit of lesser values. These formulae, therefore, make it possible for him to stand with steadfastness in the center of his personality consciousness (choosing neither one side nor the other of the warring opposites within his personality vehicles), while within the soul–pervaded "higher reaches" of his consciousness, he learns that attitude of restraint from impetuous pursuit which allows him to see divinity on every hand, rather than only in one specific direction. Thus, eventually, he expands his inner vision and achieves the realization of his very highest ideal: union with "the Beloved," Who embodies the essence of *Divine Love* – omnipresent and inescapable.

In the earlier stages of evolution, before applying these formulae, an individual with this ray combination, often finds himself devotedly rushing off after his limited vision of the ideal, and torn by constant inner and outer conflict as he tries to live up to that ideal.

This is a combination given to tremendous struggle. The individual wars with others (and even more so with himself) as he attempts to preserve his idealistic orientation. But his ideals are narrow and unsatisfying, and his personality inconstant and undependable – incapable of holding the tension of a steady orientation. There is too much passion and too much vacillation for a clear vision of reality. The result is melodramatic living, far from the spiritual center of his being.

The intelligent use of the combined forumlae, however, transmutes the abuses of the past. The individual learns primarily to restrain his urgent impulse to pursue a narrow vision of divinity or the ideal, and to refrain from grasping only that which his narrow vision reveals; consequently, he learns to identify with all true visions, and because of his restraint, he learn to love the whole and not just the part. Further, his growing secondary ability to stand steadfastly between the warring polarities (thus refraining from exclusive identification with either one) assists him with his primary effort to achieve restraint. The personality holds a balanced position which includes and synthesizes both polarities, just as the soul is seeking to influence the consciousness towards a more inclusive and loving vision which recognizes the omnipresence of divinity.

7. Some examples of vocational aptitudes and orientations relating to the combination of the sixth ray soul and the fourth ray personality:

* the idealist possessed of refined aesthetic sensibilities

* the devotee with a fighting spirit

* the missionary with a gift for compromise

* the proselytizer with the ability to arrest attention through improvization and change of pace

* the minister whose hamonizing skill–in–action brings peace to the factions within his congregation

* the orator with a great dramatic flair

* the prophet who guides his people towards at–one–ment

* the visionary whose visions are filled with beauty

* the motivator who paints inspiring 'pictures' with his vivid imagination

* the martyr who sacrifices himself so that warring parties may be reconciled

* the crusader who seeks eventual union with the "infidel"

* the loyalist who is sufficiently tolerant to act as a mediating link to those who have other loyalties

* the activist who succeeds because he is able to harmonize the differences between those he seeks to arouse

* the moralist who always considers opposing points of view

* the mystic enraptured by the beauty of higher realms

In general: vocations and professions which require high idealism, undeviating devotion, great enthusiasm and persistent emotional intensity, *as well as* a strong creative imagination, spontaneity, expressivity, aesthetic sensitivity, and a marked ability to bring harmony out of conflict, beauty out of ugliness, and at–one–ment out of divisiveness.

8. A proposed list of well–known individuals (historical, contemporary, fictional or mythological) whose soul ray can reasonably be considered the sixth, with a strong subsidiary fourth ray influence (whether or not the fourth ray is, strictly speaking, the personality ray):

John Bunyan: English Puritan minister and preacher. He was an author of religious allegories, the most famous of which is *The Pilgrim's Progress*.

Johnny Cash: singer and composer whose work sparked a revival of interest in American country–and–western music. Some ray one energy is also present.

Aaron Copland: one of the most significant composers of the 20th century. Copland thoroughly integrated the American folksong into his highly expressive personal style, capturing in a unique manner the idealism which animates the American psyche. The presence of the third ray must also be considered.

Harriet Beecher Stowe: woman of letters, philanthropist, moralist, author of *Uncle Tom's Cabin*

Arthur Sullivan: English composer who, with W.S. Gilbert, established the distinctive English form of the operetta. Sullivan's more serious and ambitious compositions were based upon religious or chivalric themes.

Leo Tolstoy: one of the greatest Russian novelists, reformer, moral thinker and religious puritan. A strong ray one influence is also present.

Charles Wesley: English evangelist, and (with his brother, John) founder of the Methodist movement. Charles was an eloquent preacher and wrote many hymns which are still loved, and in constant use in Protestant churches today.

Some Contrasts Between the Ray 6 Soul and the Ray 5 Personality

Ray 6 Soul		Ray 5 Personality
* earnest spiritual aspiration	vs.	* pursuit of worldly knowledge
* deep, unshakeable faith	vs.	* skeptical disbelief
* profoundly reverent attitude	vs.	* critical irreverence
* firmly convinced religiosity	vs.	* disdain for the religious spirit
* abiding faith in non–material realities	vs.	* contempt for the 'irrational' concept of non–material realities
* lofty spiritual emotion	vs.	* emotional impoverishment
* the highest abstract idealism	vs.	* the limitations of commonsensical pragmatism
* penetrating intuitive apprehension based upon faith	vs.	* non–intuitive, analytical linear–mindedness
* unusually open to higher guidance	vs.	* the repulsion of guidance through excessive rationalism
* high–minded morality	vs.	* the amorality of the inquisitive, obsessively interested mind
* the quest for mystical union and at–one–ment	vs.	* harsh criticism of the mystical attitude
* the faith which transforms	vs.	* the belittlement which prevents progress
* great receptivity to abstract ideals and values	vs.	* rejection of all ideas and things which are not definite and delimited
* passionate adherence to the ideal or to the object of devotion	vs.	* clinical detachment which negates warmth of feeling
* unbounded spiritual enthusiasm	vs.	* a cool, mental attitude which negates enthusiasm
* intensely magnetic	vs.	* non–magnetic personality radiation
* born along on waves of aspiration and inspiration	vs.	* a plodding, pedestrian, step–by–step approach to living

The Integration Process for the Individual with a Ray 6 Soul and a Ray 5 Personality

1. The pre–spiritual phase; soul energy appropriated by a selfish personality: At this pre–spiritual phase of evolutionary unfoldment, the individual's motives (based upon the personality distortion of sixth ray soul energy, and the self–centered use of fifth ray personality force) are to achieve the uncompromising satisfaction of the ideals and goals to which the individual is passionately devoted, *as well as* a narrow, materialistic intellectual certainty. The person wants, primarily, to ignore everything except the object or path of his devotion, spurn even reasonable mundane responsibilities if they do not relate specifically to his quest, fanatically follow his ideal regardless of destructive consequences, and cling desperately to that which he believes he loves, but, he *also* wants to take everything apart (either analytically or actually), reduce all life experience to nothing but rationalistic formulae, control matter mechanically for selfish ends, and reject any kind of knowledge that is not materialistic or derived strictly from the five senses.

Negatively and glamorously these two ray influences can combine to produce: one whose emotional and mental rigidity inclines towards idée fixe; the religious inquisitor who persecutes those whose ideas and beliefs are not 'correct'(6 + 5A); the narrow-minded, dogmatic theologian or idealogue, who presumptuously judges the truth or falsity of others' beliefs (6 + 5A); the "true believer" who "picks apart" (i.e., subjects to rigorous, destructive analysis) the beliefs of all those who do not think or believe as he does (6 + 5A); one who is constantly trying to prove or justify his extremely narrow views; the superstitious person who manages to find a pseudoscientific explanation for his unfounded beliefs (6 + 5A); one who, indiscriminately accepting so called "higher-guidance," believes unquestioningly in the scientific accuracy of the guidance (6A + 5); the escapist or addict who misuses his technical knowledge (for instance, a knowledge of chemistry) to facilitate his flights from reality (6A + 5B); one who concretizes his estimation of the "other world," envisioning and longing for a technological heaven (6A + 5B); one who, searching for 'truth' believes that the truth can always be 'correctly' embodied in definite, concrete words; also, one who easily becomes devoted to the inconstestable 'correctness' of such definite, concrete words; therefore, the absolute literalist who believes in the so-called "inerrancy" of scriptural revelation; the virulently intolerant person who looks with a cold, clinical eye upon the misfortunes of those who fall outside the scope of his sympathies, his interest being confined to analyzing such people in order to prove that their difficulties arose from their false beliefs or ideals (6B + 5A); etc.

2. The phase of conflict; pure soul energy conflicts with personality force: The essential conflict between the ray six soul and the ray five personality is the struggle between the spiritual need to rise towards mystical union through prayer, aspiration and faith, and the personal desire to achieve knowledge exclusively by means of the sense-conditioned concrete mind – a skeptical and doubting attitude which challenges the very existence of those spiritual realities the soul-inspired consciousness pursues.

3. The soul-personality integration process from the perspective of the consciousness identified primarily with the sixth ray soul: It will be the task of the sixth ray soul to inspire the fifth ray personality with respect for the intangible – for that which faith reveals. When the consciousness is identified with the soul, it aspires to the heights, and to achieve a quality of vision and inspiration inaccessible to the mind bent upon the understanding and manipulation of concrete things. The soul is faced with a personality which doubts and even rejects the possibility of abstract, intangible or mystical states. To the personality such states are illusions. The soul-inspired consciousness desires (or, rather, aspires) to *soar*, but the consciousness identified with the conditioning energy of the personality will not take flight. The soul seeks to have the personal consciousness take a "leap of faith," but the commonsensical personality views such a leap as the ultimate foolishness – at least initially. It will be difficult, but the soul must persuade the mentally self-assured personality that it doesn't know as much as it thinks it knows, and further, that there is more to life than the mind. This the soul can accomplish by presenting to the personal consciousness ideals that are so magnetic, numinous, arousing and inspiring that the personality will come to view its little bit of learning as so many "dry bones." Soul success in the 'conversion' process is not unusual, for one very frequently sees those of a scientific or technical persuasion turning towards the comforts of religion in later life.

4. The soul/personality integration process from the perspective of the consciousness identified primarily with the fifth ray personality: The sixth ray pressure towards integration will initially be felt by the fifth ray personality as a mindless call to abandon good sense and, instead, surrender to the vain wishes, impossible dreams and foolish hopes of the emotional nature. Those with a fifth ray personality are often uncomfortable with the "excesses" of the emotions which, they believe, should be kept strictly under mental control. This type of personality wishes to pursue the life of the mind, very frequently to the exclusion of other personality potentials. It certainly does not want to have to deal with the interference of strong emotional and aspirational drives which, to put it mildly, "disrupt the train of thought." But due to the insistent impress of the soul, there gradually arises, from deep within its consciousness, a vision of sublime and transcendent possibilities (whether spiritual, religious or secularly idealistic) which cannot be reached through the linear, analytical mental processes. And with the vision come longings which, distressingly, resist rational explanation, for there is no "good and sensible reason" (so thinks the consciousness when conditioned by the fifth ray personality) that such longings should arise. The personality, determined to hold on to its rationality, may, for a time, resist the 'nonsense' it feels welling up within it, but at length it will develop a strong distaste for the unrelieved study and application of dry facts. The vision proves too alluring, and the ordinary life of the personality, too insipid. The powers of feeling, emotion and aspiration assert themselves and overwhelm the independence of the concrete mind. The man becomes motivated to ascend towards the ideal, and the mind becomes the servant of his idealism.

5. The ideal expression of the combination of the ray six soul and the ray five personality: Idealism and one-pointed devotion are expressed through scientific and technological pursuits. Here is an individual who is able to facilitate the fulfillment of his highest dreams and wishes by means of his technical expertise. An individual with this ray combination may often be a utopian who believes that the ideal or utopian condition will be achieved through advancements in science, industry and technology. For this person, however, the exalted vision always remains more important than the means of implementing the vision. He never gets so "caught up" in mechanism and gadgetry that he forgets the *dream*. Faith becomes the master of skepticism, and belief the master of doubt, but there is always a healthy common sense to keep a rampant wish-life in check. This combination offers the opportunity to blend science and religion, or faith and reason. For an advanced individual of this type, there is no essential conflict between religion and science; his heart is filled with faith, and his mind is filled with evidence which justifies his faith. Such an individual may well *believe* before he knows with exactitude. He will put his fine mind and scientific abilities to the task of *proving* that which he already accepts on faith, and he will not rest until exact knowledge is his. This, of course, would be an excellent combination for verifying the famous words of St. Paul: "faith is the substance of things hoped for, the evidence of things not seen." This is also of course, would be an excellent combination for verifying the famous words of St. Paul: "faith is the substance of things hoped for, the evidence of things not seen." This is also one of the ray combinations in which intellect and intuition may be constructively related. In addition, the individual with a sixth ray soul and a fifth ray personality may have theological abilities. While, negatively, there are many ways to abuse theology, positively, theology can serve as a means for human intelligence to understand the relationship between the mind and heart of God. In general, it might be said, that the mind will find good and sufficient reasons, based upon reliable evidence, for any ideal pursued. Here, devotion and idealism remain the principle motivations, but their direction and expression are always balanced by a keen intellect with recourse to abundant factual knowledge.

6. The combined expression of the two integration formulae: The primary integration formula is proposed as *Restraint*, keyed to the sixth ray soul. The secondary integration formula is *Detachment*, keyed to the fifth ray personality. The first formula corrects sixth ray tendencies towards the unrestrained, passionate pursuit of the 'partial' and 'peripheral,' whereas the second formula corrects fifth ray tendencies towards mental attachment to matter, and the obsessive preoccupation with investigating and manipulating concrete form, while ignoring the reality of that which is "formless." Used together, these two formulae provide the individual striving for soul/personality integration with the composite quality of 'detached restraint,' (i.e., the detachment of the "outer man" from his exclusive concern with superficial, material phenomena – a detachment which complements the determination of the "inner man" to restrain himself from pursuing anything but that which is of the highest spiritual value. Obviously, matter is not! And so the ability of the outer man to see beyond and through an obsessive interest in matter, renders the consciousness more subtle, and more able to appreciate those intangible realities which the soul on its own plane values so highly, and is attempting to teach the individual to value. Thus, within his normal, personality consciousness, the individual learns no longer to regard matter as something wholly objective, while, within the soul-pervaded, "higher reaches" of his consciousness, he learns the attitude of restraint, which allows him to see divinity on every hand, rather than only in one specific direction. Through the use of these formulae over time, the individual cultivates a less engrossed, more detached, spiritually-sensitive, subtly-discerning personal consciousness, supportive of those rare moments of exalted consciousness when (pervaded by the presence of the soul), he widens his vision and achieves the realization of his very highest ideal: union with "the Beloved," Who embodies the essence of *Divine Love* – omnipresent and inescapable.

In the earlier stages of evolution, before successfully applying these formulae, an individual with this ray combination often finds himself devotedly rushing off after his vision of the ideal, and thoroughly engrossed in attempting to understand the strictly material, objective, external and superficial aspects of the vision to which he has attached himself. He is utterly absorbed in the particular, and passionately devoted to miniscule, material considerations. This combination can be extremely narrow in scope. Fifth ray specialization compounds the problem of sixth ray one-pointedness. He cares a great deal about things of small import. His attention is 'riveted' upon outer,

The intelligent use of the combined formulae, however, transmutes the abuses of the past. The individual learns, primarily, to restrain his impulse to pursue a narrow vision of divinity or the ideal, and to refrain from grasping only that which his narrow vision reveals; consequently, he learns to identify with all true visions, and because of his restraint, he learns to love the whole and not just the part. Further, his growing secondary ability to detach his personal consciousness from the constant examination of the obvious, and look for something less tangible and more spiritually real behind that which is objective, contributes added depth of perception to the primary process which the soul is seeking to see accomplished. Both the sixth and the fifth rays, in their own very different ways, tend to become mesmerized by external form. It is the goal of the sixth ray soul to see "the Beloved" everywhere, within all the many possible partial ideals and perspectives. The fifth ray personality, when inspired by the soul, seeks the immaterial "One" behind the material "many." It is easily seen how these two efforts can complement one another, and how, at length, the individual using the formula 'detached restraint' can discover what might be called the " *Beloved One – everywhere.*"

7. Some examples of vocational aptitudes and inclinations relating to the combination of the sixth ray soul and the fifth ray personality:

* the realistic idealist

* the well–balanced devotee animated by a healthy dose of "every–day understanding"

* the missionary who uses his mechanical inventiveness and ingenuity to ameliorate the lives of those he seeks to serve

* the proselytizer who convinces through common sense as well as zeal

* the minister who believes that the testimony of science can only strengthen and justify faith

* the orator who backs up his rhetoric with documented facts

* the prophet who speaks in specific, concrete detail of things to come

* the visionary who envisions a technological utopia

* the motivator who has made a detailed, well–researched study of motivational technique

* the martyr who continues to present indisputable facts with lucidity despite danger to his person

* the crusader who employs the latest technology to win his crusade

* the loyalist who justifies his position through exhaustive analysis

* the activist who can attribute much of his success to being so very well informed

* the moral–revivalist who inspires people to see moral abuses in an unbiased manner, exactly as they are

* the mystic with a strong capacity to think and act scientifically

In general: vocations and professions which require high idealism, undeviating devotion, great enthusiasm, and persistent emotional intensity, *as well as* keen analytical abilities, the capacity for research, and scientific and/or technical expertise.

8. A proposed list of well-known individuals (historical, contemporary, fictional or mythological) whose soul ray can reasonably be considered the sixth, with a strong subsidiary fifth ray influence (whether or not the fifth ray is, strictly speaking, the personality ray):

Mary Baker Eddy: discoverer and founder of the religious faith known as Christian Science

Jimmy Carter: 39th president of the United States. Carter was a Navy engineer by profession, but the idealistic vision of his soul compelled him to become a peacemaker. The seventh ray is also influential, as is the sign of peace, Libra.

Thomas De Torquemada: Grand Inquisitor of Spain during the latter part of the fifteenth century. A pronounced ray one emphasis is also to be seen.

Some Contrasts Between The Ray 6 Soul and the Ray 6 Personality

Ray 6 Soul		Ray 6 Personality
* high spiritual aspiration	vs.	* low personal desire
* mystical union and at–one–ment	vs.	* escapism, delusion and unreality
* practical and humble service upon the plains of earth	vs.	* selfish attempt to leave practical service (and even practical living) far behind
* broad tolerance of many paths to reality or God	vs.	* narrow intolerance of all but one path
* universal encouragement of all worthy ideals	vs.	* bigoted persecution
* serenity arising from spiritually sublimated emotion	vs.	* unrestrained emotionalism
* faith which has become lost in vision	vs.	* blind faith
* purposeful self–immolation which spiritual sacrifice requires	vs.	* reckless, immoderate expenditure of personal energy resulting in "burn out"
* loyal adherence to the highest ideals or spiritual values	vs.	* frenzied clinging to lesser things
* the straight beam of accurate intuition	vs.	* bewildered psychism
* spiritual discernment	vs.	* foolish gullibility

Commentary

Please refer to the commentary following the tabulation of contrasts between the fourth ray soul and the fourth ray personality for a full discussion of the reasons why no commentary will be offered for any combination of identical soul and personality rays when the ray in question is one of the rays of attribute.

Some Contrasts Between the Ray 6 Soul and the Ray 7 Personality

Ray 6 Soul		Ray 7 Personality
* ardent spiritual aspiration	-vs.	* over–attentiveness to the 'normal,' mundane sphere of activity
* an upward, idealistic orientation	vs.	* preoccupation with conventional expectations
* open and receptive to divine inspiration	vs.	* routinization dulls receptivity
* deep sentient appreciation for the formless, abstract aspects of reality	vs.	* form–bound consciousness
* spontaneous, enthusiastic response to spiritual impression	vs.	* personal rigidity; fear of spontaneity
* ability to rise far above the concerns of the physical body	vs.	* excessive body–consciousness as a form of materialism
* the sublimation of the sexual instinct	vs.	* over–indulgence in sexuality
* the unfettered expression of deep feeling	vs.	* feeling regulated (and even crushed) by conventional forms of expression; decorum to be preserved at all costs
* one–pointedly passionate pursuit of ideals and objectives	vs.	* uninspired, lukewarm moderation; disinclined to break established rhythms for an all–out push
* the inspired power to motivate	vs.	* the capacity to train but not enfire
* the power to relinquish all forms which prevent the realization of the abstract nature of divinity	vs.	* entrapped by the demand for form
* direct and uncomplicated fulfillment of spiritual desires and aspirations	vs.	* over–reliance upon formulae and patterns of action; too close a following of established patterns and "proper channels"
* ability to reject all but the highest values	vs.	* encumbered by unnecessary social observances; the burden of enculturation
* utter earnestness and sincerity	vs.	* the insincerity of hiding one's identity behind pre–programmed forms of social interaction
* easily moved by spiritual ardor	vs.	* overscheduling, and the ritualization of life activities inhibit vital excitations
* devotion to long–cherished ideals of proven value	vs.	* superficial rejection of anything old (7B)

The Integration Process for the Individual with a Ray 6 Soul and a Ray 7 Personality

1. The pre–spiritual phase; soul energy appropriated by a selfish personality: At this pre–spiritual phase of evolutionary unfoldment, the individual's motives (based upon the personality distortion of sixth ray soul energy, and the self–centered use of the seventh ray personality force), are to achieve the uncompromising satisfaction of the ideals and goals to which the individual is passionately committed, *as well as* a rigidly ritualized, tightly ordered life, conducive to physical plane safety, security and 'perfected,' materialistic living. The person wants, primarily, to ignore everything except the object or path of his devotion, spurn even reasonable mundane responsibilities if they do not relate specifically to his quest, fanatically follow his ideal regardless of destructive consequences, and cling desperately to that which he believes he loves, but he *also* wants a highly predictable (hence, relatively risk–free) life, to avoid having to think for himself or act upon his own initiative, and to have the solid assurance that all physical plane appetites and imagined material needs will be satisfied on schedule.

Negatively and glamorously, these two ray influences can combine to produce: the religionist who becomes fanatically devoted to a specific form of church ritual (6 + 7A, 7C); a dogmatist who insists that people conform to the letter of the law (6 + 7A, 7C); any form of rigid, emotional adherence to an unchanging form or a routinized pattern of action; a habitual follower, who always wants to do exactly what was done before (6A + 7A); one who is utterly dependent upon another to meet all his needs for stability and security (6A + 7A); an extremely narrow, intolerant individual, bigoted and sectarian (6 + 7A); a gullible and superstitious person; one who easily becomes addicted, and cannot break the habit (6 + 7A, 7C); a very crystallized person, resistant to all change (6 + 7A); one who very easily gets into a rut and is too rigid to break out of it (6 + 7A, 7C); one who is afraid to act without seeking permission from an authority (6 + 7A, 7C); a fanatical zealot who tries to force others to conform to certain patterns of behavior (6B + 7A); a reactionary "law and order" type (6 + 7A); one who believes that the only way to reach "heaven" is through the fulfillment of certain rituals (6 + 7C); one who feels he must pray and always in exactly the same way (6 + 7A, 7C); one who, being emotionally overwrought, manages to maintain emotional control only through compulsive or ritualistic behavior (6 + 7A, 7C); one who is indiscriminate, ardent, enthusiastic over everything new (6B + 7B); a wildly utopian individual who wants to overthrow everything about the established order (6B + 7B); one who easily falls prey to obsessive behaviour, especially in the area of sexuality; one who develops blind faith in procedures, routines and rituals he does not at all understand (6 + 7A, 7C); enflamed militarism aggravated by rigid discipline (6B + 7A); one who drives others mercilessly, leaving no room for the demands of their individuality (6B + 7A); the nostalgic individual who longs for the stability and security of the "good old days" (6A + 7A); an intense clinging to matter, form and physical plane life; etc.

2. The phase of conflict; pure soul energy conflicts with personality force: The essential conflict between the ray six soul and the ray seven personality is the struggle between the spiritual need to escape from the confines of form, and the personal love of form, formalism and formality.

3. The soul/personality integration process from the perspective of the consciousness identified with the sixth ray soul: It will be the task of the sixth ray soul to teach the seventh ray personality to value the possibilities of abstraction. The soul seeks to see the personal consciousness detach from its anchorage in physical form, and ascend into the realm of the formless (though, technically speaking, there is no state of vibration upon the cosmic physical plane which is really free of form – cosmically considered). When consciousness is identified with the soul, it soars to the heights, and seeks to attach itself to states of awareness in which there are no demonstrable 'outlines' such as appear in the "three worlds of human evolution" – the physical, emotional and mental planes. The soul, however, is faced with a personality which *loves* form – the more tangible, the better. This is a personality given to *patterned* behavior, and the consciousness becomes preoccupied with maintaining such patterns – rituals, routines, etc. The soul demands freedom from these patterns, but it can only hope to prevail over the habit patterns of the regimented or self-regimenting personality by demonstrating to the personal consciousness that such patterns are *prisons*. When consciousness is influenced by the sixth ray soul it is easily moved, inspired and motivated, and the response in consciousness is to 'fly' towards the source of influence. Naturally, if consciousness is confined by unvarying patterns of action, and by the compulsive fixation upon what must be done next, there will be no possibility of a free and full response of the aspirational nature. The soul must convince the personality that its stability, its predictability, its "groundedness" (while valuable in a secondary sense) are all holding it *pinned* to earth, and thus separated from sublime, mystical experiences within higher dimensions of consciousness.

4. The soul/personality integration process from the perspective of the consciousness identified primarily with the seventh ray personality: The sixth ray pressure towards integration will initially be felt by the seventh ray personality as a loss of rootedness and security. The seventh ray personality feels most comfortable when its 'feet' are planted firmly and squarely on the ground; this is not a personality with its "head in the clouds." It feels however, with some justification, that a powerful influence is pulling it away from earth – from all that is definite, predictable, reliable and grounded. The seventh ray personality is not one to proceed by faith rather than plan. Organization brings security and protection from life's innumerable uncertainties; of all the personality types, the seventh ray (though at times [when distributed by Uranus] it may appear unpredictable) dislikes uncertainty most of all. And yet the voice of the soul, arising from the innermost depths of personal consciousness calls for *release* from the elaborate 'security system' created and maintained by a materially vigilant personality. The personality feels insecure as the soul calls it "up and away" from customary rhythms and self-stabilizing procedures. Further, the goal to which the soul calls is rather nebulous, indefinite, intangible – hardly appealing to a personality which wants to know "where its next meal is coming from." So, naturally, the personality will rebel against the seeming uncertainty of the faith-inspired way of life required by the soul, and may, for a time, become even more compulsive in the attempt to make life safer, more predictable and materially secure. But personal security is bought at the cost of repetitive action, and repetition, at length (and in contrast with the possibility of mystical ecstasy and rapture), reveals itself as a prison. The personal consciousness will, therefore, reach a point of surrender, as the attraction towards a transcendent or mystical vision becomes irresistible. It realizes that comfortable forms and procedures can in no way substitute for the ideal. Then, with aspirational longing, it will reach away from its earthly anchorage towards the higher, formless, abstract dimensions of consciousness.

5. The ideal combination of the sixth ray soul and the seventh ray personality: Idealism and one-pointed devotion are expressed practically, through organizational work and in institutional or bureaucratic settings. This combination bestows upon an individual the desire, and often the ability, to achieve a perfected manifestation of the lofty ideals to which he aspires. While the love of the abstract ideal in itself is valued more highly than the perfected expression of that ideal, the ability to embody the ideal in form is considerable. Thus idealism prevails over materialism, yet a wise and effective orientation towards matter remains. This combination of rays confers the ability to achieve mystical union through the observation of right spiritual practices and various forms of ritual. The soaring aspiration of the religious impulse is expressed through the power to build beautiful forms. The great cathedrals of the Middle Ages are an expression of irrepressible sixth ray aspiration and consummate seventh ray constructiveness. When these rays are ideally combined, form is sanctified and consecrated to the service of a transcendent ideal. Here too we find a devotion to ideal values and the ability to codify these values in perfectly balanced systems of laws and rules. With this combination, all values receive their consummated expression. An individual influenced by these two rays is utterly committed to a certain vision, and determined to see that vision expressed perfectly in form and pattern. On a more mundane level, administrative and managerial abilities contribute to the complete actualization of the "causes" or "special interests" to which the individual is passionately devoted. A fine sense of form, organization and a knowledge of the laws of manifestation precipitate and ground ideals which might otherwise remain abstract.

6. The combined use of the two integration formulae: The primary integration formula is proposed as *Restraint*, keyed to the sixth ray soul. The secondary integration formula is proposed as *Orientation,* keyed to the seventh ray personality. The first formula corrects sixth ray tendencies towards the unrestrained, passionate pursuit of the 'partial' and 'peripheral,' whereas the second formula corrects seventh ray tendencies towards selfish building and organizing according to short–sighted, materially–minded personal plans which are not in accordance with the Divine Plan. Used together, these two formulae provide the individual striving for soul/personality integration with the proposed composite quality of 'oriented restraint,' (i.e., the "outer man's" orientation to the inner Light which complements the determination of the "inner man" to restrain himself from pursuing anything but that which is of the highest spiritual value). If the seventh ray personality averts its eyes from the inner Light, it creates what might be called 'darkened structures.' The individual begins to idealize these structures and becomes devoted to maintaining them. This is a form of imprisonment and prevents the integration of soul and personality. Through the right use of the integration formulae, the individual, when identified with the personality, learns to orient himself towards the divinely inspired spiritual "blueprint" or 'working pattern' to be found within the inner recesses of his nature, and, when identified with the soul, he learns the attitude of restraint, which allows him to see divinity on every hand rather than only in one specific direction. Thus, through the use of these formulae over time, the individual cultivates a more aligned, spiritually attentive, inwardly oriented personal consciousness, supportive of those rare moments of exalted consciousness when (pervaded by the presence of the soul), he widens his vision and achieves the realization of his very highest ideal: union with "the Beloved," Who embodies the essence of *Divine Love* – omnipresent and inescapable.

In the earlier stages of evolution, before applying these formulae, an individual with this ray combination often finds himself devotedly rushing off after his limited vision of the ideal, and rapidly building crystallized and self–limiting forms as monuments to that ideal. He seizes upon an ideal, and seeks to institute it in form. He quests in the dark, and builds in the dark, and what he creates separates him from the light to be found at the center of his own being.

The intelligent use of the combined formulae, however, transmutes the abuses of the past. The individual learns, primarily, to restrain his urgent impulse to pursue a narrow vision of divinity or the ideal, and to refrain from grasping only that which his narrow vision reveals; consequently, he learns to identify with all true visions, aided by his developing restraint, he learns to love the whole and not just the part. Further, his growing secondary ability to sensitize his normal personality consciousness to impressions of a higher design (which can serve as the pattern to which his constructive building and organizational efforts can conform), promotes the primary integrative intent of the soul, for the personality is no longer so eager to build limited ideals into form and thereby add to the imprisonment of the consciousness. Inclusive spiritual vision and inclusive spiritual love, therefore, become the distinguishing features of the individual's consciousness, and the forms subsequently built (through the agency of the personality's seventh ray energy) embody this inclusive perspective. Thus the combined efforts of the integrated soul and personality are aligned with the Plan.

7. Some examples of vocational aptitudes and orientations relating to the combination of the sixth ray soul and the seventh ray personality:

* the idealist as organizer
* the devotee who expresses himself through ritualized forms of devotion
* the missionary who understands and respects the customs and mores of the people to whom he ministers
* the proselytizer who enhances his powers of persuasion with an attitude of unfailing politeness
* the zealot who, for all his impassioned idealism, minds his manners
* the minister who stands as a pillar in his community
* the orator whose orations are always exquisitely polished
* the prophet whose enunciations focus upon laws and ethical conduct
* the visionary with the power to envision the pattern of the "new order"
* the motivator who is also an excellent trainer
* the martyr who times his sacrifice for maximum benefit to those he serves
* the crusader whose respect for rhythmic activity prevents him from "burning out"
* the loyalist as conservative, adhering faithfully to the established order
* the passionate activist with a keen sense of how things must be reorganized if the ideal is to be achieved
* the moral–revivalist who translates his fervor into offering practical guidance on how a morally responsible person must behave in various social contexts

* the mystic with the conviction that he must bring his revelations into manifestation

In general: vocations and professions which require high idealism, undeviating devotion, great enthusiasm and persistent emotional intensity, *as well as*, the power to organize or reorganize, the ability to build, a facility for creating or maintaining standards, and the capacity to skillfully manifest ideas through form.

8. A proposed list of well-known individuals (historical, contemporary, fictional or mythological) whose soul ray can reasonably be considered the sixth, with a strong subsidiary seventh ray influence (whether or not the seventh ray is, strictly speaking, the personality ray):

Thomas Becket: Chancellor of England under Henry II, and subsequently Archbishop of Canterbury

William Booth: founder and first general of the Salvation Army

John Calvin: French theologian and ecclesiastical statesman who was one of the most important leaders of the Protestant Reformation in the 16th century. A strong, rationalistic ray five influence was also present.

Saint Francis of Assisi: known as the "seraphic saint." St. Francis was the founder of the Franciscan orders of men and women, and is regarded as the principal patron saint of Italy. There is no doubt that the second ray was also highly influential. The soul may have been refocusing upon the second ray, or the Monadic ray may have been the second.

St. Ignatius Loyola: founder of the Society of Jesus (the Jesuits), and one of the most influential figures of the Catholic Reformation of the 16th century. The third ray was also active in his nature.

Colonel Oliver North: impeccably well-mannered zealot, allegedly responsible for much of what has become known as the "Iran-Contra Affair"

Philip II: King of Spain from 1556–1598, and champion of the Roman Catholic Counter-Reformation. The fourth ray was also influential.

Don Quixote (fictional): the idealistic protagonist in Miguel de Cervantes novel by the same name.

Thomas à Kempis: author of the *Imitation of Christ*, a devotional book that, with the exception of the Bible, has been considered the most influential work in Christian literature

Woodrow Wilson: 28th president of the United States. A high-minded idealist, Wilson was largely responsible for the establishment of the League of Nations, the modern world's first permanent organization for international cooperation. For students who may be interested, the Tibetan gives an account of the founding of the League of Nations from an esoteric perspective (in *Telepathy and the Etheric Vehicle*). Woodrow Wilson was the final recipient (in a long line of intermediaries) of an idea which originated within the Hierarchy.

Soul/Personality Combinations with a Ray Seven Soul

Some Contrasts Between the Ray 7 Soul and the Ray 1 Personality

Ray 7 Soul		Ray 1 Personality
* the builder, building in line with the Plan	vs.	* destructiveness which serves no spiritual purpose
* meticulous attention to detail in the manifestation of spiritually intended patterns	vs.	* habitual disregard of fine detail
* great patience in execution	vs.	* blatantly impatient
* exquisite timing	vs.	* rashly inappropriate timing
* great respect for and observance of spiritual and societal laws and rules	vs.	* willful insistence upon doing what one wants to do when one wants to do it; "riding roughshod" over the law
* well–regulated spiritual living	vs.	* spontaneous rejection of any regulations which restrain egoism
* the innate understanding of how to keep oneself "within due bounds" with all one's fellow human beings	vs.	* the aggressive crossing of personal boundaries; violation of the "space" and integrity of others
* innate understanding of the spirituality of real group process	vs.	* considerable difficulty working in group formation because of assertive individualism
* promotion of the team–spirit	vs.	* the person who has to be "number one"
* skill in the fostering of enlightened consensus	vs.	* a dictatorial, dominating nature
* considerateness and consistent decency	vs.	* rudeness
* consummate polish and refinement	vs.	* bluntness
* mastery of the art of diplomacy	vs.	* the proverbial "bull in the china shop"
* the power and patience to achieve perfected consummation	vs.	* bold beginnings lacking finesse
* a gift for the creation of organizational harmony	vs.	* the disruption of organizational harmony by refusing to "fall in line," and humbly "play one's part"
* the preservation of rhythm as a key to spiritual accomplishment	vs.	* the disruption of rhythm through headstrong, unilateral action

The Integration Process for the Individual with a Ray 7 Soul and a Ray 1 Personality

1. The pre–spiritual phase; soul energy appropriated by a selfish personality: At this pre–spiritual phase of evolutionary unfoldment, the individual's motives (based upon the personality distortion of seventh ray soul energy, and the self–centered use of first ray personality force) are to achieve (often through the selfish use of some consciously or unconsciously applied magical process) a rigidly ritualized, tightly ordered life conducive to physical plane safety, security, and 'perfected' materialistic living *as well as* great personal power, arising from the unrestrained imposition of the personal will. The person wants, primarily, to lead a highly predictable (hence, relatively risk-free) life, to avoid having to think for himself or act upon his own initiative, and to have the solid assurance that all physical plane appetites and imagined material needs will be satisfied on schedule, but, he *also* wants to dominate and control others and wield authority unopposed.

Negatively and glamorously these two ray influences can combine to produce: the rigid conformist who forces others to conform as well (7A + 1); the bureaucrat whose life is governed by numberless petty rules and restrictions, and who insists that the lives of others be similarly governed (7A + 1A); the haughty, supercilious person who "lords it over" others; the condescending individual who is convinced he is supremely important; the ultrafastidious person who enforces his pettiness; one who insists upon formality at all times because it inflates his regal sense of self (7A, 7C + 1); one who regiments others drastically (7A + 1); one who uses black magic to destroy those who oppose him (7C + 1B); one who practices sex-magic to gain power over others (7C + 1); the superficial socialite who seeks social prominence; one who organizes others forcibly and cruelly; one who uses draconian measures to standardize others, allowing them absolutely no room to express their individuality (7A + 1); one who rejects absolutely everything about the old order (even the good) and will stop at nothing to overthrow it (7B + 1B); one known for his routinized rigidity as well as his stubborn refusal to change (7A + 1A); an extremely sectarian individual who has no hesitation rejecting and excluding others; one who makes the law the servant of his egotism; one who builds or erects monuments to exalt his ego (7 + 1A); the body-conscious person, preoccupied with gratifying his physical instincts and demonstrating his physical strength (7 + 1A); one who utilizes ritual in order to increase his personal power (7C + 1); etc.

2. The phase of conflict; pure soul energy conflicts with personality force: The essential conflict between the ray seven soul and the ray one personality is the struggle between the spiritual need to build, and the personal desire to destroy: the creation of form to perfectly express the archetypal 'soul design,' and the shattering of form so that the lower self can be free of irksome restraints upon its personal prerogatives.

3. The soul/personality integration process from the perspective of the consciousness identified primarily with the seventh ray soul: It will be the task of the seventh ray soul to teach its first ray personality to learn the value of proceeding patiently through lawful *little steps*. When consciousness is identified with the seventh ray soul, it seeks to be engaged in constructive action in accordance with the Divine Plan; with measured self-restraint, it subordinates itself to higher rules and observes them in detail. However, the personality has no such patience; it proceeds as *it* will. The soul, therefore, seeks to impose a regimen of spiritual "law and order" upon a personality which all too easily becomes a "law unto itself." Gradually, the soul seeks to impress upon the personality that willful license is only destructive in the long run, and ultimately self-defeating. By presenting the personal consciousness with a detailed vision of the manifested Plan (or at least that part of it which the individual can be instrumental in manifesting), the soul hopes to show the personality how it can *fit* within that Plan – constructively. The ultimate fate of every renegade from spiritual law is isolation and impotence. While the first ray personality does not fear isolation, and may, in fact, enjoy it, impotence is another matter. The soul begins to demonstrate to the personality that real power lies in organized relationship and not in rebellious separativeness.

4. The soul/personality integration process from the perspective of the consciousness identified primarily with the first ray personality: The seventh ray pressure towards integration will initially be felt by the first ray personality as a binding and 'stricturing' of its will. The personality feels most comfortable when it can do precisely as it intends. It resents what it perceives as "red tape," and as the tying of its hands by numerous precedents and petty conventions. This is the personality which is inclined to "kick over the traces"; it has no wish to sacrifice its personal 'sovereignty' by conforming to a maze of regulations *made by others*. But persistently, from the inner depths of the personal consciousness, there arises the soul–inspired vision of a great structure of orderly, synthesized, hierarchical relationships. The realization begins to dawn that all of creation is organized and coordinated through lawful action, and that those who abide by the law, and assume their proper place and function, benefit from the beneficence of the law. The price, however, is conformity to the Divine Pattern through the restraining of personal will. At first this may seem too great a cost for the ruggedly independent first ray personality. It may rebelliously return to its former isolated independence, but, before long, the personality cannot fail to realize that its illusion of personal power is simply an illusion. Its strength is the strength of one, whereas the *lawfully related* individual is supported by the organized strength of the whole. Gradually, the personality will feel impelled to commit its will to the fulfillment of a larger design, becoming, in cooperation with its seventh ray soul, a constructive agent in the manifestation of the Divine Plan. Thus, with proper alignment, its purposeless destructiveness ends.

5. The ideal combination of the seventh ray soul and the first ray personality: The urge to order and reorder (to structure and restructure) is expressed with steadfast, personal fortitude. Right procedure in line with the Plan prevails over the assertion of concentrated, self–centered force, and yet personal strength enhances the individual's effectiveness in manifesting the Plan. Those endowed with this combination of rays are among the world's best organizers; they know, in detail, what it takes to bring a mass of people or an array of actions into a truly organic relationship, and they have the will power to see that the structure they have created is maintained as intended. On a more material level, such people are the world's great builders, and, such is their relation to the mineral kingdom (which is both the first and seventh Kingdom of Nature), that what they build, stands. The seventh ray seeks to shape matter to an intended design, and with the assistance of the first ray, the forceful impact upon matter is very great. Those influenced by this combination of rays are in a position to assertively uphold the laws, community standards and social propriety. As lawmakers, they have the capacity to create beneficent laws which reflect the Divine Plan, and to legislate in accordance with human need; further, they have the power to see that such laws are enforced. Their strength and endurance are also invaluable in the arduous task of perfectly linking spirit and matter. Ideally, this is the combination of the white magician endowed with the strength of will and endurance to ensure that his magical operations come to fruition. In those instances in which a necessary exactitude of pattern and arrangement must be imposed, this is the combination which can successfully do so. This combination is also endowed with the power of destruction, the better to make way for the establishment of a truly perfected form. Especially in the New Age, the seventh ray will be the *re–former*; those with this combination can easily become renovators – those who institute the new; because of the first ray, they will firmly and forcefully *insist* upon the new. Such people will bring in the New Age, and will not compromise until transformation has been achieved.

6. The combined effect of the two integration formulae: The primary integration formula is proposed as *Orientation*, keyed to the seventh ray soul. The secondary integration formula is *Inclusion* keyed to the first ray personality. The first formula corrects seventh ray tendencies towards selfish building and organizing according to short–sighted, materially–minded personal plans, but not in accordance with the Divine Plan, whereas the second formula corrects the exclusive and isolative tendencies characteristic of the first ray personality. Used together, these two formulae provide the individual striving for soul/personality integration with the composite quality of 'inclusive orientation,'(i.e., the loving and inclusive attitude of the "outer man" which complements the will of the "inner man" to orient himself towards the spiritual 'design' which his soul intends to actualize). The design is intended to manifest as an ordered expression of soul love, but its expression upon the outer plane is thwarted as long as the personality relates to others in a repellent and unloving manner. The proper use of the formulae make it possible for the individual to stand within the center of his personality consciousness and, figuratively, extend his arms to include in loving cooperation the many he previously rejected, while, within the inner, soul–inspired 'heights' of his consciousness, he learns to orient himself with exquisitely refined attentiveness, towards the Divine Light which, streaming from the "East," begins to reveal a tiny portion of the great "Tracing Board" upon which the 'blueprints' of the Divine Plan are inscribed. Oriented thus, he stands, waits and suffers in expectant uncertainty until, at last, he is impressed by the perfected vision of that fragment of the divinely intended design which it is his responsibility and privilege to manifest (in strength, and yet with love and inclusiveness); then and only then is he ready to *work* in full cooperation with the Plan.

In the earlier stages of evolution, before applying these formulae, an individual with this ray combination often finds himself preoccupied with building and organizing structures which imprison (rather than embody) the light, and, (in the process), excluding from his constructive efforts all who offer their cooperation. He works alone and in the dark. He builds for himself, by himself, and cares not whether his constructions will have to be cleared away at a later date because they were untrue to the intended design. He works under the spell of maya, forcing his purposeless forms upon the world.

The intelligent use of the combined formulae, however, transmutes the abuses of the past. The individual learns, primarily, to manifest with consummate skill his small part in the *true Plans* of the Great Architect of the Universe, and his growing secondary ability to include and love those who are drawn to him, contributes to his primary purpose of divine manifestation – for it is the many working in perfect cooperation who, *together*, must build on earth the reflection of that great "temple not made with hands, eternal in the heavens."

7. Some examples of vocational aptitudes and orientations relating to the combination of the seventh ray soul and the first ray personality:

* the fearless magician with nerves of steel
* the spiritualist who *commands* apparitions to make themselves known
* the ceremonialist/ritualist with absolute control over his every act
* the manifester who can virtually will his ideas into manifestation
* the alchemist who submits his energy system to drastic transformations
* the organizer – rapid, decisive and sure
* the administrator who is always guided by first principles and essential values
* the regulator who strictly enforces regulations
* the manager who expects and demands individual initiative of those he supervises
* the trainer who drills his trainees relentlessly
* the legislator whose laws are stern
* the judge who refuses to bend the law
* the architect who designs massive, powerful structures
* the builder whose constructions are always strong and solid
* the artist who attacks his medium aggressively
* the craftsman whose works are strong and durable enough to take considerable abuse
* the designer with a gift for uncompromising simplicity of line
* the diplomat, always polite and always firm
* the revolutionary who will stop at nothing short of "overthrow"

In general: vocations and professions which require the power to organize or reorganize, the ability to build, a facility for creating or maintaining standards, and the capacity to skillfully manifest ideas through form, *as well as* great will power, strength and stamina, the ability to stand firmly on principle and (when necessary) the power to destroy obstacles.

8. A proposed list of well-known individuals (historical, contemporary, fictional or mythological) whose soul ray can reasonably be considered the seventh, with a strong subsidiary first ray influence (whether or not the first ray is, strictly speaking, the personality ray):

Aleister Crowley: magician, author, poet. Crowley's reputation is clouded by his egotism, and his often bizzare and extravagant behavior. He is, nevertheless, the 20th century's most widely read 'authority' on ceremonial magic.

Merlin: (the name, at least, is fictional): legendary, archetypal magician, adviser to King Arthur

John Marshall: fourth chief justice of the United States Supreme Court. Marshall was the principal founder of the American system of constitutional law, including the doctrine of judicial review.

S. L. MacGregor-Mathers: author, scholar, founder of the magical Order of the Golden Dawn

Albert Pike: Civil War general, scholar, ritualist. Pike organized and established the present form of Scottish Rite Freemasonry.

Emily Post: authority on social behavior and author of *Etiquette: The Blue Book of Social Usage*

Frank Lloyd Wright: regarded as the most abundantly creative genius of American architecture. His works were dominated by a profound sense of principle. The fourth ray was also influential.

Paracelsus: physician, surgeon, alchemist and chemist, the "Medical Luther." The fifth ray was also strongly in evidence.

Some Contrasts Between the Ray 7 Soul and the Ray 2 Personality

Ray 7 Soul		Ray 2 Personality
* bringing the soul into perfected manifestation upon the physical plane	vs.	* preoccupation with personality love and affection
* excellent organizational, managerial and administrative abilities	vs.	* lacks speed in organization and is disinclined to manage or administrate
* pronounced capacity to function easily within the usual, large organizational setting	vs.	* often requires too much personal kindness and reassurance to function well within the impersonal setting of the usual large organization
* strong spiritual inclination to act in a way that respects a hierarchical chain of command	vs.	* exudes an overly–warm, personal, democratic touch, which has a leveling effect upon hierarchical functioning, and is inappropriate where a stratified chain of command must be maintained; overfamiliarity
* conformity to the strict and lawful discipline necessary for spiritual or professional effectiveness	vs.	* excessive desire for ease and comfort makes strict discipline uncongenial
* a highly conscientious following of prescribed rules for spiritual conduct and accomplishment	vs.	* one who, because of an overly–relaxed, casual attitude, fails to perform a number of necessary actions
* a soul–inspired understanding of the reasons why the law must apply to all, impersonally and without exception	vs.	* an overly permissive attitude with respect to the law; the unwise attempt (because of tender personal feeling) to shield those close to one from the full impact and consequences of the law
* courage in the execution of dangerous magical process	vs.	* timidity and fear of danger
* the inclination to function as a "pillar" of society or of any organization of which one may be a part	vs.	* a sense of being too weak or sensitive to uphold onerous burdens
* mastery of the etiquette necessary to fulfill official public, political or social responsibilities	vs.	* personal attachments interfere with disciplined social interaction; difficulty maintaining an image of strength and dignity
* the spiritual demand for concrete, manifested results	vs.	* "softness," and the human equation interfere with "running a tight ship" in which results have to come first regardless of personal consequences

The Integration Process for the Individual with a Ray 7 Soul and a Ray 2 Personality

1. The pre–spiritual phase: soul energy appropriated by a selfish personality: At this pre–spiritual phase of personality unfoldment, the individual's motives, based upon the personality distortion of seventh ray soul energy, and the self–centered use of second ray personality force), are to achieve (often through the selfish use of some consciously or unconsciously applied magical process) a rigidly ritualized, tightly ordered life conducive to physical plane safety, security, and 'perfected' materialistic living, *as well as* the complete fulfillment of personal love (or the complete satisfaction of studious enquiry [2B]). The person wants, primarily, to lead a highly predictable (hence, relatively risk–free) life, to avoid having to think for himself or act upon his own initiative, and to have the solid assurance that all physical plane appetites and imagined material needs will be satisfied on schedule, but, he *also* wants to be constantly loved, consistently popular, warmly admired, well–cared–for, and to live a soft, comfortable, superficially pleasant, well–protected and well–insulated life, closely attached to those people, places and things which he loves and finds personally satisfying.

Negatively and glamorously, these two ray influences can combine to produce: the timid conformist (7A + 2); one who overburdens himself with the consideration of details (7 + 2B); one who, refusing to vary the many little steps of his routine, further compounds his problem by insufficient rapidity of action; one whose well–trained politeness and dread of self–assertion result in an inability to stand up for himself or make his will felt (7A, 7C + 2); a fragile and rather rigid person whose sensitivity is so great that he is easily overwhelmed; one who becomes so comfortable with and attached to the ease of certain procedures or rituals that he is extremely loathe to change (7A, 7C + 2A); one whose personal stability and sense of belonging are entirely invested in maintaining long–cherished customs and traditions (7A, 7C + 2A); one who always follows precedent, being too hesitant or fearful to do what has not been done (7A, 7C + 2); one who is the victim of both an insatiable desire to circulate with the right social "set," and a persistent "love of being loved" – such a person will easily sacrifice his individuality and originality in order to be well–liked and accepted; the superficial individual who constantly wastes time in the pursuit of pleasant sociability; one who perverts the magical process in order to achieve the satisfaction of personal love and comfort – i.e., the use of "sex–magic" to attract others (7C + 2A); one whose need to work within an organizational setting, or to be attached to others is so great that he can hardly tolerate being alone (7 + 2A); the obsessive/compulsive person with a low self–image; one who builds purely for the sake of sheltering himself physically and emotionally (7A, 7B +2); one whose consciousness is caught up in material externals, such as excessive attention to the physical body in order to be physically attractive (7 + 2A); etc.

2. The phase of conflict; pure soul energy conflicts with personality force: The essential conflict between the ray seven soul and the ray two personality is the struggle between the spiritual need to express the Divine Design perfectly through form, and the personal need to remain comfortably attached to certain people and things, even if such attachments make one loathe to undertake the rigorous discipline and effort demanded by the work of spiritual manifestation.

3. The soul/personality integration process from the perspective of the consciousness identified primarily with the seventh ray soul: It will be the task of the seventh ray soul to impress the second ray personality with the need for organization, so that the magical work of manifestation can go forward uninhibited by inertia or unrelinquished attachments. The magical process is exacting; it involves strict discipline and an attentive following of tried and tested formulae. Anyone who participates in such a process must have himself well in hand; mistakes can be lethal and excuses are useless. In this instance, however, the seventh ray soul is faced with a personality which has very little inclination to submit itself to the rigorous demands of the magical process, with its specific formulae and *well-timed* actions. Second ray laziness is a problem; so is fear, for the magical work of manifestation (whether in the magician's study or the corporate board room) requires firm and fearless self-control, as well as the masterful control of many potentially dangerous forces which threaten to overwhelm the one who does not subdue them. So frequently, when an individual is conditioned by the second ray, he wants nothing to do with asserting control over others, or over those unruly parts of himself which cause trouble – at least, he does not enjoy asserting control in a firm and decisive manner. The soul then, must guide the personality towards adopting a more rigorous, athletic "tone," so that the individual will be able to successfully perform the sequence of arduous steps demanded by the process of manifestation. Both rays are rays of relationship, but the seventh ray promotes the kind of relationship possible to those who perfectly play their part in an exactly organized whole, whereas the second ray promotes relationships built around an unstructured personal intimacy. In order to bring the personality to the point where it is willing to "gird its loins" and sacrifice its personal loves and comforts (or, at least, put them in right perspective) it is clear that the soul must succeed in impressing upon the personality the beauty of *corporate life* (in the same sense that Hierarchy is an example of corporate life), and the value of well-structured cooperation which can arise within the perfectly organized group doing its share to manifest the Divine Plan.

4. The soul/personality integration process from the perspective of the consciousness identified primarily with the second ray personality: The seventh ray pressure towards integration will be felt by the consciousness identified with the second ray personality as an annoying imposition of tightly scheduled requirements and demands. The second ray personality has a strong tendency towards self-indulgence; it enjoys the pleasant life. Under the influence of the soul, however, it begins to experience something akin to spiritual "performance quotas." That easy-going dilation of time is no longer possible; it becomes more and more difficult for the personality to linger in self-satisfying situations, indefinitely prolonging the pleasure of contact. There is too much *work* to be done, and too many tangible results to be manifested. The personality feels the discomfort of being held to account; it is not used to "functioning like clockwork," or putting all things aside until the required assignment is completed. This pressure to be a responsible spiritual functionary may well be sensed as mechanical and almost inhuman. The personality may seek to return to its cozier, less materially productive ways, but its conscience (the intruding voice of the soul) will steadily remind it of the cost of self-indulgence, and the refusal to set time boundaries. As the Plan moves forward into manifestation, and as, within the larger environment, one divine idea after another precipitates into tangible form, the personality will begin to feel as if it is not "keeping pace." It is overcome by that uneasy feeling that the "train has already left the station." The personality's only legitimate recourse is to begin to *act,* responsibly, efficiently and *"on time."* It realizes that it must "fall into line," "shape-up," and make that extra, comfort–disrupting effort so that it may play its designated part in the Divine Plan *appropriately*.

5. The ideal expression of the combination of the ray seven soul and the ray two personality: The urge to order and reorder (to structure and restructure) is expressed with tact and consideration – with love and wisdom. The Plan is seen and understood in clarity and detail, but for best effect, it is implemented gently and slowly, with every attempt to cushion any adverse or unsettling impacts. Realization and execution of the intended design (in all exactitude) prevails over the attachments, fears, timidities and personal vulnerabilities which would prevent that design from being perfectly manifested, and yet, during the manifestation process, harmlessness and sensitivity always smooth the way. This is the combination of the excellent executive or manager whose sunny disposition and personal magnetism promotes loving cooperation and group spirit throughout his organization. The urge to work correctly overcomes the predilection for personal comfort, and yet any tendencies towards compulsive perfectionism are softened by a warm and relaxed attitude. There is a great appreciation for impersonal principles of law, and for proper codes of right action, especially as these are applied for humanitarian purposes. Such an individual will have a deep concern when he discovers that people's practical needs for living are not being met; animated by compassion and protectiveness, he will do all he can, in practical ways, to ameliorate such conditions. This is the combination of the magician who works not only through formulae but through love; his personal radiance magnetically attracts many subtle cooperators, whose joy it is to assist him in his work. When this combination characterizes the lawmaker or legislator, it indicates one who never forgets his humanity, and the humanity of those for whose welfare laws are being made. The seventh ray has a great appreciation for the value of traditions and customs; in this case there is a realization of the protective and bonding value of a society's cyclic observances. This is one of the great healing combinations – the seventh ray providing the ability to manipulate etheric energy currents, and the second ray conferring that loving understanding which warms the heart and places the healer deeply en rapport with the one to be healed. Above all, we find one who is ready and willing to work upon the "plains of earth" as a dedicated "karma yogi" for the salvation and redemption of his fellow human beings.

6. The combined effect of the two integration formulae: The primary integration formula is proposed as *Orientation*, keyed to the seventh ray soul. The secondary integration forumla is *Centralization*, keyed to the second ray personality. The first formula corrects seventh ray tendencies towards selfish building and organizing according to short–sighted, materially–minded personal plans, but not in accordance with the Divine Plan, whereas the second formula corrects second ray tendencies towards diffusion, overexpansion, and an energy–draining attachment to life's peripheral attractions. Used together, these two formulae provide the individual striving for soul/personality integration with the composite quality of 'centralized attentiveness,' (i.e., the detached and centered attitude of the "outer man" which complements the will of the "inner man" to orient himself towards the spiritual 'design' which his soul intends to actualize). That manifestation requires hard *work* in exact *conformity* with soul intent, and the personality must have its "hands free," and its forces gathered to the center, in order so to work. The proper use of the formulae makes it possible for the individual to stand detached yet lovingly centered within his normal personality consciousness, while, within the inner, soul–inspired 'heights' of his consciousness (that realm of consciousness where the presence of the soul can be definitely encountered), he learns to orient himself with exquisitely refined attentiveness, towards the Divine Light, which, streaming from the "East", begins to reveal a tiny portion of the great "Tracing Board170 upon which the "blueprints" of the Divine Plan are inscribed. Oriented thus, he stands, waits and suffers in expectant uncertainty until, at last, he is impressed by the perfected vision of that fragment of the divinely intended design which it is responsibility and privilege to manifest (in love, and yet in strength and integrity); then and only then is he ready to *work* in full cooperation with the Plan.

In the earlier stages of evolution, before applying these formulae, an individual with this ray combination often finds himself preoccupied with building and organizing structures which imprisoned (rather than embody) the light, and (to compound his difficulty) deeply attached to, and encumbered by, that which he has built. He is really too weak to work, and he works far too slowly and without the benefit of light. He builds for comfort and for the preservation of that which is pleasant to him. His constructions smother the divine life in a well–planned 'coziness' which is heart–warming to the form–engulfed consciousness and hateful to the soul.

The intelligent use of the combined formulae, however, transmutes the abuses of the past. The individual learns, primarily, to manifest with consummate skill his small part in the true Plans of the Great Architect of the Universe, and his growing secondary ability to detach himself from all binding and encumbering attachments (while yet remaining lovingly related to all), contributes to his primary purpose of manifesting the divine, for the second ray functioning through the personality brings clarity of perception, great patience and much light – just what the seventh ray soul needs if it is to orient itself "Eastward," await the dawning of the true design, and then build patiently, in conformity with that design, the divinely intended forms translucent to the Divine Light.

7. Some examples of vocational aptitudes and orientations relating to the combination of the seventh ray soul and the second ray personality:

* the beneficent magician for whom magic is a work of compassion
* the spiritualist who sincerely and in tenderness seeks to reunite those parted by death
* the ceremonialist/ritualist filled with brotherly love and spirit of group cooperation
* the manifester who understands the value of the "wise use of slow action"
* the alchemist who excels at dissolving (through the gentle warmth of the fire of love) all blockages to the transformational process
* the organizer who patiently assembles and coordinates that which must be organized
* the administrator who "catches more flies with honey than with vinegar"

* the planner who is content to proceed patiently
* the regulator who is always willing to listen
* the manager whose warm and friendly manner easily elicits cooperation
* the trainer who achieves his best results through the use of encouragement
* the legislator who regularly sponsors humanitarian legislation
* the judge who always tempers justice with mercy
* the architect who emphasizes the humanity of his structures by creating designs with many curves
* the builder who works slowly, patiently and with great clarity of consciousness
* the artist whose creations seem to radiate light
* the craftsman who imbues his creations with love
* the designer whose creations always have an inviting, attractive quality
* the diplomat who is gifted with extraordinary tact
* the revolutionary, content with a quiet and gradual 'humanitarian revolution'

In general: vocations and professions which require the power to organize or reorganize, the ability to build, a facility for creating or maintaining standards, and the capacity to skillfully manifest ideas through form, *as well as* a wise and loving attitude, great empathy and understanding, studiousness, and the ability to teach or compassionately heal.

8. A proposed list of well-known individuals (historical, contemporary, fictional or mythological) whose soul ray can reasonably be considered the seventh, with a strong subsidiary second ray influence (whether or not the second ray is, strictly speaking, the personality ray):

Alvar Aalto: Finnish architect whose work exemplifies the best of 20th-century Scandinavian architecture. The presence of ray four is also to be noted.

John James Audubon: American naturalist and artist best known for his colorful and realistic water colors and paintings of birds. A strong ray four was also in evidence.

Walt Disney: American motion-picture and television producer who pioneered the art of animated cartoon films. A strong ray four is also likely.

Oliver Wendell Holmes: distinguished historian and philosopher of the law, and for 30 years a justice of the United States Supreme Court

Some Contrasts Between the Ray 7 Soul and the Ray 3 Personality

Ray 7 Soul		Ray 3 Personality
* conformity to divine order	vs.	* personal disorderliness
* adherence to the cyclic regularities of the spiritual order	vs.	* constantly involved in "irregularities"
* right spiritual practice	vs.	* mentally proud disregard for established rules and precedents
* one who reliably sticks to the established rules (whether established by others or himself)	vs.	* changing the rules (or making them up) as one goes along
* well–grounded spirituality	vs.	* futile intellectualism; overly theoretical, vague and impractical
* skillful manifestation; talent for the actualization of soul–intended design	vs.	* entertaining too many options and possibilities inhibit the precipitation of clear–cut results
* strict conformity to the divine pattern of the Plan	vs.	* a too fluid adaptability leads to modifications which are untrue to original intent
* fastidious in the performance of detailed duties and responsibilities	vs.	* cares little for exacting performance
* refinement of execution	vs.	* unrefined technique
* thoroughly planned and systematic construction	vs.	* an often hasty or sloppy throwing together of the elements of construction
* uprightness and rectitude; spiritually "upstanding"	vs.	* shifty, devious and tricky: constantly maneuvering for personal advantage
* strict conformity to spiritual and social law	vs.	* dexterous evasion of the law for the sake of self–interest
* exemplary behavior and propriety as reflections of an elevated, trustworthy character	vs.	* careless of convention and of propriety
* well–regulated action leading to successful manifestation	vs.	* hectic overactivity; unnecessary 'busy–ness'
* sequential activity leading to solid results	vs.	* the constant attempt to do too many things at the same time
* extremely clear lines of thought and activity	vs.	* confused, jumbled lines of thought and activity; "wires" often "crossed"
* an embodiment of the best and highest standards	vs.	* abandoning standards whenever it seems expedient or convenient to do so

The Integration Process for the Individual with a Ray 7 Soul and a Ray 3 Personality

1. The pre–spiritual phase; soul energy appropriated by a selfish personality: At this pre–spiritual phase of evolutionary unfoldment, the individual's motives, (based upon the personality distortion of seventh ray soul energy, and the self–centered use of the third ray personality force), are to achieve (often through the selfish use of some consciously or unconsciously applied magical process) a rigidly ritualized, tightly ordered life conducive to physical plane safety, security, and 'perfected' materialistic living, *as well as* a cleverly intelligent, self-serving mastery of circumstances and the environment. The person wants, primarily, to lead a highly predictable (hence relatively risk-free) life, to avoid having to think for himself or act upon his own initiative, to have the solid assurance that all physical plane appetites and imagined material needs will be satisfied on schedule, but he *also* wants to demonstrate his 'superior' intelligence at every opportunity, manipulate money and other people for his own material and intellectual satisfaction, keep incessantly busy in the pursuit of his own self-centered interests, and evade responsibilities through selfish, strategic planning.

Negatively and glamorously, these two ray influences can combine to produce: the earthbound person entirely concerned with financial manipulations (7A, 7B + 3B); one for whom material results are the only measure of efficacy (7 + 3B); one who serves "maya" – effortlessly wrapping himself within the veils of matter (7 + 3B); the bureaucrat whose life within his organization consists of a continuous series of devious maneuvers (7A + 3B); the haughty individual whose condescending manner is made more insufferable by his mental pride (7 + 3A); the stilted individual whose chief affectation is a pretense to mental superiority (7 + 3A); one who, because of his excessive concern for personal security, engages in numerous deceptions to mislead those who seek to know what he is thinking or doing; the abuse of magical powers chiefly for the sake of obtaining great wealth – i.e., the magician whose intent is purely material (7C + 3B); one who exploits the "system" (legal or other) to serve his own selfish ends, and then argues brilliantly to justify his maneuver; one who cleverly seeks to create laws and rules which simply serve his own self-interest (7A, 7B + 3); one who to all appearances is an upstanding citizen, a pillar of the community, but really is involved with numerous "shady deals" (7 + 3B); one who utilizes sex-magic to bring others under his manipulative control (7C + 3); the spiritualist who makes a practice of bewildering clients; one abnormally sensitive to "omens," but whose confused interpretations distort the truth (7C + 3A); one who is adept in the misuse of magical words to veil and hide the light (7C + 3); one who intends, by subtle, surreptitious means, to standardize the lives of others, depriving them of their individuality (7A + 3); etc.

2. The phase of conflict; pure soul energy conflicts with personality force: The essential conflict between the ray seven soul and the ray three personality is the struggle between the spiritual need to understand and adhere to the Divine Order and the personal desire to 'creatively' arrange (and disorder!) life's energies and forces in any manner, provided that they serve personal self-interest.

3. The soul/personality integration process from the perspective of the consciousness identified primarily with the seventh ray soul: It will be the task of the seventh ray soul to influence the third ray personality towards right procedure and towards a strict regulation of its chaotic activity so that such activity conforms to the divinely intended pattern. The seventh ray soul knows what lines it must not cross; under its influence a human being learns to keep himself "within due bounds" with all his fellow men. But the soul is faced with an imaginative and intellectual personality for whom no such bounds exist. If the personal mind can conceive how something personally advantageous (though illegal, unethical or inappropriate) can be intelligently accomplished, there are often insufficient scruples to prevent the attempt. Fertile, third ray creativity accepts few if any restraints, and the seventh ray soul, which ever influences towards principled, ethical, *well–regulated* behavior, clearly has cause for frustration. The soul must impress upon the personality that just because something is "do-able," it is not necessarily permissible. The Divine Pattern (even to the small extent that an individual human being can conceive it) is a very definite and specific thing; its outlines are clear. The third ray personality, with its hyperactivity of mind and/or body, frequently distorts this clarity, and does not *perform true to form*. Further, the seventh ray soul is oriented towards the achievement of concrete results. With at least one type of third ray orientation (3A), ideas are abundant but accomplishment is wanting. There is too little of what might be called the 'will–to–bring–through,' and too little continuity of effort. Therefore the soul is faced with the task of restricting the numerous options for action generated by the personality, so that its continuous "side–tracking" will no longer frustrate the expression of soul intent. In general, the soul seeks to teach the personality to rid itself of spiritually obstructive "irregularities" – those thoughts and acts which *deviate* from divine intent. It is the difficult task of the seventh ray soul to bring the third ray personality to the point where its abundant energy is consecrated to the manifestation of that which is *meant to be*, and not merely to the manifestation of that which is arbitrarily and irresponsibly conceived.

4. The soul/personality integration process from the perspective of the consciousness identified primarily with the third ray personality: The seventh ray pressure towards integration is felt by the third ray personality as a blatant restriction of creativity. The third ray personality is most comfortable when it can freely conceive, and intelligently enact that which it has conceived. It dislikes walls made of rules and regulations; these it tries to circumvent – colloquially speaking, it tries to "*get around* them." The personality likes variety of mind and activity, and yet the influence of the soul inclines towards the rhythmic repetition of a few emphases – those things which, spiritually, are important. To those influenced by the third ray, sameness is a great bore, and the repetitive pattern which the personality feels encroaching upon its fluid and versatile consciousness is a source of no small frustration. It has no wish to limit its 'behavioral repertoire' to what it perceives as certain rigid routines, no matter how spiritually important.

And yet, from deep within the personal consciousness, there arises the disturbing intimation of futility. A voice seems to say that the patterns of thought and action created by the personality are essentially ill–conceived and ultimately ugly and useless. Behind the scenes, the soul is at work, presenting the design of the Plan *as it is*, and demonstrating to the personal consciousness that its hyperactivity brings only illusory accomplishment, for that which is created *untrue* to form will have to be redone. The personality in its pride of mind will at first reject such a dismal assessment; it will console itself by exercising its undisputed intellectual power and creative fertility, but at length, the saying of Christ, "by their fruits ye shall know them" brings the truth home. In a moment of truth, the personality sees that nothing true and lasting has been created, for all its incessant effort and activity. Slowly it resolves to curb the excessive and deviant modifications of its mental substance, inevitably attended, as they are, by excessive and deviant modifications of behavior. *Fewer* and *truer* thoughts and actions indicate the way of integration; the personality consecrates itself to the manifestation of the *true design*. In short, it decides to work correctly, and "get something done."

5. The ideal expression of the combination of the ray seven soul and the ray three personality: The urge to order and reorder (to structure and restructure) is expressed with adaptability, resourcefulness and versatile intelligence. The capacity to create order prevails over disorderly ways; right procedure masters randomness or haphazardness, and yet, although behavior is characterized by greater formality, it never loses its fluidity and adjustability. For an individual with this combination of rays, exact conformity to the design of the Plan supercedes individually focused creativeness and manipulativeness, and yet a talent for creative manipulation remains, the better to serve the Plan. This is one of the ray combinations which suggests outstanding financial ability; the individual has the astute, creative intelligence to precipitate, concretize or manifest whatever he intends. He has, in short, exemplary executive ability which he can use to fulfill his extremely practical intentions. If the law happens to be his field of interest, there is abundant intelligence brought to bear on all legal issues; legal decisions are elegantly reasoned through. Here is an individual who has a keen sense of his proper place and function within the whole, and his resourceful intelligence allows him to perform this function regardless of the many vicissitudes to which he may be subjected. As might be expected, the consummate magician is found with this combination, for no two rays are more suited to the magical arts – the arts of manifestation. The ability to manipulate energies and forces in order to precipitate thought is distinctive. Here, especially, the capacity to use sound or words to magically actualize ideas reaches its culmination; the same is only slightly less true with the converse of this combination – the ray three soul and the ray seven personality. The seventh ray is, perhaps, the most stabilizing of the seven; this combination marks an individual who can be called upon to lend his stabilizing influence to the vitalizing and maintenance of any enterprise, and his resourceful intelligence will be sure to find a method of stabilization which works. The seventh ray individual has a great need to express an idea perfectly in concrete form; in this instance, the capacity to do so prevails over the tendency to rest content with simply "knowing about" or discussing the idea; words turn into deeds, which, in essence, is one important way of describing the magical process.

6. The combined use of the two integration formulae: The primary integration formula is proposed as *Orientation* keyed to the seventh ray soul. The secondary integration formula is *Stillness*, keyed to the third ray personality. The first formula corrects seventh ray tendencies towards selfish building and organizing according to short–sighted, materially–minded personal plans which are not in accordance with the Divine Plan, whereas the second formula corrects third ray tendencies towards a busy scattering of attention, wasted thought and physical overactivity (with their resultant disturbances and obscurations of consciousness). Used together, these two formulae provide the individual striving for soul/personality integration with the composite quality of 'still orientation,' (i.e., the stillness of the personal consciousness which enhances the orientation of the inner consciousness towards that Divine Design which it is the will of the soul to actualize). The manifestation of this design requires great clarity of consciousness, and will be thwarted by a personality which habitually abides in a state of confusion. Stillness reduces confusion, enhances focus and clarity and complements that exacting spiritual orientation of the inner psyche without which truly spiritual manifestation cannot occur. Thus, the proper use of these formulae make it possible for the individual to quiet his personal consciousness and restless personality vehicles, while within the inner soul-inspired 'heights' of his consciousness (that realm of consciousness where the presence of the soul can be definitely encountered), he learns to orient himself (with exquisitely refined attentiveness) towards the Divine Light, which, streaming from the "East," begins to reveal a tiny portion of the great "Tracing Board" upon which the "blueprints" of the Divine Plan are inscribed. Oriented thus, he stands, waits and suffers in expectant uncertainty until, at last, he is impressed by the perfected vision of that fragment of the divinely intended pattern which it is his responsibility and privilege to manifest (with great intelligence, and yet with a clarity of outline made possible by stillness and a disciplining of wild activity); then and only then is he ready to *work* in full cooperation with the Plan.

In the earlier stages of evolution, before successfully applying these formulae, an individual with this ray combination often finds himself preoccupied with building and organizing structures which imprison (rather than transmit) the light, as well as hyperactively engaged in manipulating all aspects of his personal environment in ways which further distort the expression of his soul's intent. His personal methods are tangled and even chaotic. He builds and weaves with no true understanding of any plan or pattern upon which to model his activity. His creations are nothing but obstructions, and encumber the Path to the center of his being, from which perspective soul/personality integration can be achieved and the Divine Design be known.

The intelligent use of the combined formulae, however, transmutes the abuses of the past. The individual learns, primarily, to manifest with consummate skill his small part in the *true Plans* of the Great Architect of the Universe, and his growing secondary ability to refrain from the futile expenditure of personal energy contributes to his primary, soul-inspired objective of clearly intuiting his piece of craftsmanship within humanity's execution of the Divine Design. Eventually true vision and true economy are merged; he sees exactly what he has to do, and wastes no energy in creating the nonessential.

7. Some examples of vocational aptitudes and orientations relating to the combination of the seventh ray soul and the third ray personality:

* the magician with unusual ability to manipulate the numerous energies and forces necessary to the successful performance of the magical process

* the ceremonialist/ritualist who excels in the utilization of mantra

* the spiritualist who understands the best means of promoting communication between the physical and the subtle worlds

* the manifester who has a highly intelligent grasp of all the many variables involved in the process of manifestation he has undertaken

* the alchemist who assists the process of psychospiritual transformation with an intelligently selected variety of herbs and minerals

* the organizer whose success is attributable in great measure to his high level of intelligent activity
* the administrator who is able to keep his finger on the pulse of the many activities under his supervision
* the regulator who persistently exercises a well-informed caution
* the manager whose style is to encourage frequent verbalization of a wide range of ideas
* the planner who excels at forseeing numerous contingencies
* the trainer who finds numerous innovative methods to promote mental creativity in his trainees
* the legislator who understands the many ramifications of the laws he participates in creating
* the judge whose reasoning abilities are unusually astute
* the architect who has the versatility to come at a difficult design problem from a number of angles
* the builder who seems to be able to work on many different aspects of construction at virtually the same time
* the facile artist whose creations are always full of thought and interest
* the craftsman with unusual manual dexterity
* the designer who eclectically weaves various styles together
* the diplomat who is always able to suggest a "way around" an apparent difficulty
* the revolutionary as strategist
* the reformer gifted with acute intelligence

In general: vocations and professions which require the power to organize and reorganize, the ability to build, a facility for creating or maintaining standards, and the capacity to skillfully manifest ideas through form, *as well as* acute intelligence (whether active or abstract), great adaptability and resourcefulness, abundant creative and communicative abilities, and (frequently) strong business aptitudes.

8. A proposed list of well-known individuals (historical, contemporary, fictional or mythological) whose soul ray can reasonably be considered the seventh, with a strong subsidiary third ray influence (whether or not the third ray is, strictly speaking, the personality ray):

Sir Francis Bacon: lawyer, courtier, statesman, utopian philosopher and master of the English tongue. (See ray analysis in Section VI, Volume II.)

John Dee: alchemist, mathematician, and astrologer to Queen Elizabeth I of England.

Benjamin Franklin: statesman, diplomat, printer, inventor, scientific investigator. Franklin was remarkable for both his versatility and accomplishment. The power of the fifth ray is also pronounced.

Buckminster Fuller: innovator, architect, engineer, cartographer, inventor, philosopher and poet. Fuller's creative genius was principally focused upon redesigning man's relation to his environment. He attempted to develop, on a global basis, comprehensive, long-range plans designed "to make man a success in Universe [sic]." The influence of the fifth ray is also present.

Some Contrasts Between the Ray 7 Soul and the Ray 4 Personality

Ray 7 Soul		Ray 4 Personality
* a "pillar of strength" in the "Father's House"	vs.	* personal fluctuation and temperamental instability
* extremely well–regulated approach to spiritual living	vs.	* the victim of unpredictability and inconsistency
* a creator of organizations or one who functions optimumly within them	vs.	* ill–suited for the regularities of organizational living
* spirituality enhanced by solidly grounded pragmatism	vs.	* frequent recourse to the fictional, the fanciful and the entertainingly unreal
* commands respect and serious consideration	vs.	* foolishness and erratic action make it difficult to be respected or taken seriously
* the stability and solidity to bear a great weight of spiritual responsibility; "Atlas" standing four–square	vs.	* unsteady, and hence easily overwhelmed by pressure
* characteristically able to support soul intent with a solid financial base	vs.	* prodigal, improvident and financially unreliable
* courage in the conscientious exactment of laws and principles	vs.	* insufficiently steadfast to take an unwavering stand on laws and principles
* great skill as an executive, manager or administrator	vs.	* not well–equipped for the steady exertion of the will in positions of control
* polite, smooth and frictionless execution of soul intentions	vs.	* interpersonal conflict and combat, easily triggered by changeable moods
* the power to bring spirit and matter together	vs.	* torn between the demands of spirit and matter
* steady, rhythmic movement contribute to success	vs.	* given to "fits and starts"
* noteworthy confidence in carrying plans towards materialization	vs.	* worry, fret and distinct lack of self–confidence; constant personal crises
* pronounced self–control and self–discipline	vs.	* pronounced lack of self–control and self–discipline
* the spiritual steadiness to conform to the Plan	vs.	* the pliability which cannot hold steady

The Integration Process for the Individual with a Ray 7 Soul and a Ray 4 Personality

1. The pre–spiritual phase; soul energy appropriated by a selfish personality: At this pre–spiritual phase of evolutionary unfoldment, the individual's motives (based upon the personality distortion of seventh ray soul energy, and the self–centered use of fourth ray personality force) are to achieve (often through the selfish use of some consciously or unconsciously applied magical process) a rigidly ritualized, tightly ordered life, conducive to physical plane safety, security and instinctual gratification, *as well as* an agreeable feeling of personal peace and harmony through a tension–releasing expression of conflicting bio–psychic impulses. The individual wants, primarily, to lead a highly predictable (hence relatively risk–free) life, to avoid having to think for himself or act upon his own initiative, and to have the solid assurance that all physical plane appetites and imagined material needs will be satisfied on schedule, but he *also* wants to be constantly surrounded by what he considers beautiful or attractive, to be spontaneously self–expressive without discipline or control, self–indulgently dramatic or moody (as he pleases), and greatly appreciated for his colorful, unpredictable temperament.

Negatively and glamorously, these two ray influences can combine to produce: the overly–cultured individual who will not tolerate that which does not live up to his aesthetic standards (7 + 4A); the rigidly conservative individual, who dismisses the value of new forms of artistic expression (7A + 4); the wildly iconoclastic individual who rejects all old forms of artistic expression (7B + 4B); the superficial individual who is completely captivated by external beauty of appearance; one for whom the preservation of a rigidly ordered, tastefully arranged environment is more important than the people who are found within that environment (7 + 4A); one who very easily loses his balance if an aesthetically exact arrangement of his environment is disturbed in any way (7 + 4A); one whose consciousness is sensually engrossed with a fascination for the physical body and the undisciplined gratification of its appetites (7 + 4B); one who creates or participates in hedonistic rituals (7C + 4); one who organizes too tightly, and refuses to tolerate the slightest friction or inharmony in the performance of that which he has organized (7 + 4A); one who very easily falls into a mannered, stilted, affected attitude of the poseur (7 + 4A); one who finds it very difficult to be natural and spontaneous unless "playing a role" (7 + 4B); the overly–polite individual who will do anything to preserve harmony (7A + 4A); one who, seeking the overthrow of all old and established forms, will fight wildly, confusedly, and ungovernably to that end (7B + 4B); the conformist who compounds his fear of individual initiative by profound self–doubt and lack of confidence (7A + 4); the individual whose excessive respect for precedent and continuous vacillation renders spontaneous decision–making very difficult (7A + 4); etc.

2. The phase of conflict; pure soul energy conflicts with personality force: The essential conflict between the ray seven soul and the ray four personality is the struggle between the spiritual need to manifest the Divine Design (steadfastly maintaining its expression in form), and the personal desire to indulge in various forms of tension–relieving behavior, which render the person insufficiently stable or responsible to manifest and maintain properly.

3. The soul/personality integration process from the perspective of the consciousness identified primarily with the seventh ray soul: It will be the task of the seventh ray soul to stabilize the fourth ray personality, submitting it to the disciplines of divine law. The soul seeks to impose a number of necessary controls upon this most unstable of personality types. When individual consciousness is identified with the soul, it functions in a well–regulated manner, moving systematically from idea, through method to manifestation. When identified with the fourth ray personality, consciousness becomes the plaything of moods and fluctuating bio–psychic states, rendering tangible accomplishment very uncertain. The soul must guide its personal mechanism towards a respect for regularity and steadiness of rhythm. Faced with a personality which revels in its capricious reactivity, the soul attempts to persuade the personal consciousness to place a higher value upon well-planned, predictable methods in which very little, if anything, is left to chance. Within the consciousness of the soul resides a vision of a materialized spiritual synthesis – a smoothly functioning, organically perfected whole upon the physical plane. It is this vision of *right relationship through exact arrangement* that the soul must present to the personal consciousness, so that the futility of uncontrolled stress, strain and friction can be seen. The futility of *partial* harmonization can also be demonstrated when compared to a vision in which *all* parts within any whole function organically. Through the continuous presentation of such visions, the soul will succeed in subduing the personality instabilities which prevent proper manifestation in line with the Plan. The soul is the "white magician," and it needs a stable, steadfast instrument to cooperate in the "Great Work." It is not easy for a fourth ray personality to become such an instrument, but, if the point of personal *balance* can be found, then that which is manifested by the seventh ray soul through the fourth ray personality can be remarkable for its beauty.

4. The soul/personality integration process from the perspective of the consciousness identified primarily with the fourth ray personality: The seventh ray pressure towards integration will initially be felt by the fourth ray personality as a curtailment of spontaneity and imagination. The personality feels most comfortable when it can respond, fully, naturally and without any inhibition. But the voice of the seventh ray soul is the voice of propriety – highly serious, even solemn. This voice, which under soul impression, arises (eventually) within the inner depths of the personal consciousness, is also the voice of spiritual law, presenting duties which cannot be treated irresponsibly. In colloquial terms, the fourth ray personality may begin to feel compelled to "clean up its act." The voice of the soul demands maturity; adolescent behavior (a favorite of the fourth ray personality) cannot last forever, and, at length one must "get serious," and "do what is expected" – if not by society as a whole, at least, what is expected by one's conscience. Needless to say, the personality is likely to view such responsible sobriety as an impoverishment, a joyless exercise in unimaginative regularity. The life of a "square" is very unappealing to such a colorful person, and a revolt into the former life of cyclically fluctuating extremes is, at first, likely. (How often has one heard from certain artistic or temperamental individuals that they are not the "corporate type?!") But adults have certain privileges which adolescents do not, and an adolescent way of life, continued into adulthood, is depleting and exhausting. At length, there comes the realization that a life lived *in control* of oneself, is far better than undisciplined reactivity, with its inevitable wear and tear upon the organism. The personality must and will come to the point where it gives up its fight against assuming a responsible role within some group, association or organization. It soon discovers that the harmony it seeks is much more easily found within an organization whose members courteously abide by the laws and rules of right human relations.

5. The ideal expression of the combination of the ray seven soul and the ray four personality: The urge to order and reorder (to structure and restructure) is expressed with an understanding of how to maintain beauty and harmony in the intended final arrangement. This is one of the outstandingly artistic combinations. The capacity to create perfection of form is enhanced by the ability to endow those forms with beauty of color. When music is the art, the composer's "architecture" is sublime, but his gift for melody cannot be denied. This is the combination of the great architect whose designs fulfill the highest structural and aesthetic standards; both the functional and poetic aspects of the architectural art are *in excelsis*. As the seventh ray is related to "groundedness," it provides stability wherever it appears. Here we might also find a stable, reliable community servant whose ability to bring harmony out of conflict reduces tensions and promotes interpersonal effectiveness in community organizations. In all organizational work, such an individual can become a valued peace-maker. In this combination, stability and right procedure prevail over temperamental instabilities, and yet pliability and the spirit of accommodation remain, preventing rigidity. Steadfast conformity to the divine Plan masters the urge to appease for the sake of personal peace and comfort, and yet the spirit of righteous compromise endures – compromise in matters concerning application, but never concerning matters of principle. This ability to compromise and seek equitable solutions aids the precipitation and implementation of the envisioned order. One can see that when both these rays are functioning optimally, there may be a very high degree of "skill-in-action." When the process of "white magic" is the focus, the magician is animated by a keen sense of beauty. The magical properties of sound and color are thoroughly understood, and that which the magician manifests, under law, brings harmony and beauty to the world. Here is an individual who may seek to renovate and transform the world (or, more modestly, his own life) and beauty and harmony will be key goals of the transformation process. Both are rays of synthesis, and both can combine to produce a great at-one-ment upon the outer or physical plane. In general, of this ray combination it might be said that *order is adorned with beauty*.

6. The combined use of the two integration formulae: The primary integration formula is proposed as *Orientation*, keyed to the seventh ray soul. The secondary integration formula is *Steadfastness*, keyed to the fourth ray personality. The first formula corrects seventh ray tendencies towards selfish building and organizing according to short-sighted, materially-minded personal plans which are not in accordance with the Divine Plan, whereas the second formula corrects fourth ray tendencies towards vacillation, irresoluteness, instability, indecisiveness and moral cowardice. Used together these two formulae provide the individual striving for soul/personality integration with the composite quality of 'steadfast orientation,' (i.e., the steadfastness of the personal consciousness which enhances the orientation of the inner consciousness towards the Divine Design which it is the will of the soul to actualize). An unstable personality mechanism will thwart the attempts of the soul to see the pattern and make it an actuality. The dust and confusion of personality conflict can obscure the vision and skew the orientation of the inner man, and unbalanced personality reactions can destabilize the often delicate and sequential stages of the manifestation process. The proper use of the formulae make it possible for the individual to stand steadfastly within the center of his normal personality consciousness, *unswayed* by the attractions and repulsions of the many pairs of opposites within his nature or his environment, while within the soul-inspired 'heights' of his consciousness (that realm of consciousness where the presence of the soul can be definitely encountered), he learns to orient himself (with exquisitely refined attentiveness) towards the Divine Light, which, streaming from the "East," begins to reveal a tiny portion of the great "Tracing Board" upon which the 'blueprints' of the Divine Plan are inscribed. Oriented thus, he stands, waits and suffers in expectant uncertainty until, at last, he is impressed by the perfected vision of that fragment of the divinely intended pattern which it is his responsibility and privilege to manifest (with beauty and harmonizing sensitivity, and yet with stability and centered steadfastness); then and only then is he ready to *work* in full cooperation with the Plan.

In the earlier stages of evolution, before successfully applying these formulae, an individual with this ray combination often finds himself preoccupied with building and organizing structures which imprison (rather than embody and transmit) the light, and also struggling with himself and fighting with others in the unbalanced effort to adorn and render "enchanting" the spiritually obstructive organizations and edifices he creates. The many patterns and forms which flow from him into manifestation are (due to fourth ray emphasis) beautiful and alluring, but they lead the consciousness further into form and away from his spiritual center where the true pattern and real beauty can be apprehended. A well-built and beautiful prison is still a prison.

The intelligent use of the combined formulae, however, transmutes the abuses of the past. The individual learns, primarily, to manifest with consummate skill his small part in the *true Plans* of the Great Architect of the Universe, and his growing secondary ability to refrain from unnecessarily stressful, unbalanced creative agonies contributes to his primary, soul-inspired objective of clearly intuiting that aspect of the divine construction upon which he has the responsibility to labor. It is clear that if the personality perspective is balanced and steadfastly centered between the pairs of opposites, personality gifts can be properly placed at the disposal of the soul, the better to truly beautify that aspect of the Divine Design which it is the duty of the soul to manifest. Agonies mispent on spiritually worthless manifestations are then at an end.

7. Some examples of vocational aptitudes and orientations relating to the combination of the seventh ray soul and the fourth ray personality:

* the magician who has mastered the utilization of sound and color

* the ceremonialist/ritualist whose "floor work" is a fine example of elegance and beauty

* the choreographer with a great theatrical flair

* the spiritualist as a reliable "bridge" between two dimensions of consciousness

* the manifester who, in bringing a new idea forward, carefully adjusts new ideas to established values

* the planner who aesthetically balances all phases of his scheme

* the organizer with exceptional skill for reducing tension among those he organizes

* the administrator whose success is largely the result of his ability to compromise while still upholding the structure of established policy

* the regulator who never forgets his own fallible humanity and the humanity of others

* the manager who is always ready to "work–through" difficulties in order to maintain harmonious relations with those he supervises
* the trainer who freshens–up the training process with his delightful humor and entertaining manner
* the legislator who succeeds in passing many laws because he realizes that "a half loaf is better than no loaf at all"
* the judge who sees his role as an opportunity to bring people into harmony with the law and society's most important standards
* the architect whose designs are characterized by a rare aestheticism
* the builder whose constructions are well balanced and finely proportioned
* the artist who has mastered both form and color
* the craftsman whose pieces show great refinement
* the designer whose style is most characterized by the dramatic interplay of contrasting colors
* the diplomat with a gift for immediately sensing obstructive tension and its antidote
* the revolutionary who fights for a righteous accommodation with the old order
* the reformer who proceeds creatively and with a well–developed skill–in–action

In general: vocations and professions which require the power to organize and reorganize, the ability to build, a facility for creating or maintaining standards, and the capacity to skillfully manifest ideas through form, *as well as* a strong creative imagination, spontaneity, expressivity, aesthetic sensitivity, and a marked ability to bring harmony out of conflict, beauty out of ugliness, and at–one–ment out of divisiveness.

8. A proposed list of well-known individuals (historical, contemporary, fictional or mythological) whose soul ray can reasonably be considered the seventh, with a strong subsidiary fourth ray influence (whether or not the fourth ray is, strictly speaking, the personality ray):

Charles Baudelaire: French symbolist poet of the 19th century

Aubrey Beardsley: the leading English illustrator of the 1890's and one of the outstanding figures in the Aesthetic movement of the period

"Beau" Brummel: English dandy and undisputed connoisseur of fashion in the early 19th century

Bob Geldoff: rock musician, actor and principal organizer of the international famine relief effort – Live Aid

Samuel F.B. Morse: American artist and inventor of the electric telegraph. A strong fifth ray influence is to be noted.

Antonio Stradivari: the most renowned of all violin makers. Stradivari raised the craft of violin making to its highest pitch of perfection.

August Strindberg: regarded as the greatest Swedish playwright, Strindberg exerted a profound influence on European and American drama.

J.R.R. Tolkein: scholar and philologist – author of epic trilogy, *The Lord of the Rings*, and, also, *The Hobbit*. The fifth and second rays were, it would seem, also present.

Oscar Wilde: Irish writer and wit who was a major spokesman for the Aesthetic movement of the 19th century

William Butler Yeats: Irish poet, dramatist, and occultist with a strong interest in magic and ritual

Some Contrasts Between the Ray 7 Soul and the Ray 5 Personality

Ray 7 Soul		Ray 5 Personality
* pronounced social grace and finesse	vs.	* socially naive and frequently non–magnetic; often lacking in social graces
* reliance upon ritual as the preferred means of manifesting the divine Plan	vs.	* irreverently and harshly critical of ritual
* innate skill in achieving the union of mind, emotions and body	vs.	* excessive reliance upon the mind to the exclusion of the other personal faculties
* great capacity for orchestrating practical synthesis	vs.	* over–reliance upon analysis and narrow specialization; difficulty synthesizing
* relating all; linking all	vs.	* the mind which divides
* practical occultism in action	vs.	* too often stopping short at simply knowing or discovering the facts
* invocation of the transformative powers of Nature which 'sleep in the depths'	vs.	* cut off from the surge of transformative power because of an overly mentalized focus
* deep respect for and guarding of Nature's occult secrets	vs.	* a mentality which brings all to light, whether appropriately or inappropriately; nothing is held sacred
* elevation to positions of executive, managerial or administrative control	vs.	* ill–suited because of narrow, technical interests, for the more interpersonal task of regulating or controlling the behavior of others
* masterful coordination of a diversity of people through an understanding of how to create an organization which is really a vital organism	vs.	* too specialized and technical to successfully relate and coordinate a diversity of people
* responsibility accepted for preserving the structure of laws and ethics within society	vs.	* overly interested in knowledge for its own sake rather than in its socially responsible application
* one who seeks to achieve the perfection of form	vs.	* the pursuit of knowledge becomes so overwhelmingly important that beauty or perfection of form passes largely unnoticed
* the spiritualization of matter	vs.	* preoccupation with matter itself; frequent blindness to the spirit within
* frequently animated by a strong artistic or expressive impulse	vs.	* usually devoid of the artistic or expressive impulse

The Integration Process for the Individual with a Ray 7 Soul and a Ray 5 Personality

1. The pre–spiritual phase; soul energy appropriated by a selfish personality: At this pre–spiritual phase of evolutionary unfoldment, the individual's motives (based upon the personality distortion of seventh ray soul energy, and the self-centered use of fifth ray personality force is to achieve (often through the selfish use of some consciously or

Tapestry of the Gods

unconsciously applied magical process) a rigidly ritualized, tightly ordered life, conducive to physical plane safety and security, *as well as* a narrow, materialistic, intellectual certainty. The individual wants, primarily, to lead a highly predictable (hence relatively risk-free) life, to avoid having to think for himself or act upon his own initiative, and to have the solid assurance that all instinctual appetites and imagined material needs will be satisfied on schedule, but he *also* wants to take everything apart (either analytically or actually), reduce all life experience to nothing but rationalistic formulae, control matter mechanically for selfish ends, and reject any kind of knowledge that is not materialistic or derived strictly from the five senses.

Negatively and glamorously, these two ray influences can combine to produce: the utterly materialistic person whose mental scope is strictly limited by the prejudices of the scientific community (7A + 5); one whose interests, being exclusively confined to that which is revealed by the senses, has a materialistically rational, 'sensible' explanation for everything (7A + 5); one who limits himself by rigid scheduling and an overly-meticulous attitude; an individual almost incapable of spontaneous action – his over-reliance upon precedent and his need to analyze before acting will prevent it (7A + 5); an individual excessively preoccupied with detail, trivia and minutiae; the rigid grammarian who insists upon the absolutely 'correct' use of language at the expense of the ideas being expressed (7A + 5A); the unimaginative literalist – totally disinterested and almost incapable of abstract thought or interpretation; one who deliberately seeks to condition or standardize the behavior of others through scientific or mechanistic techniques (7A, 7B + 5B); hence, one who expects the members of an organization to function more like machines than human beings (7A, 7B + 5B); an individual whose mind is completely preoccupied with form, matter and objectivity; the stiff, formal person with a noticeable lack of personal magnetism; one who, in executing his regulatory functions, harshly and condescendingly criticizes the errors committed by those he supervises; one who judges and disciplines others in a petty manner – according to the "dead letter" of the law, and with reference to insignificant legal "technicalities" (7A + 5); hence, one who has great difficulty understanding the "spirit" of the law, and not just the form in which it is written (7A + 5); the magician who utilizes scientific knowledge for his own selfish purposes (7C + 5); the ritualist who performs with precision but without understanding or magnetic appeal (7C + 5A); the routinized person who functions in a dull, linear and thoroughly predictable manner (7A, 7C + 5); the unimaginative functionary; one who seeks to radically restructure the pattern of human living strictly along technological lines – without any understanding of human sensitivity (7B + 5B); the technological utopian (7B + 5B); the inflexible person prone to fixity of thought; the person whose life becomes stagnant because of compulsiveness and overanalysis (7A + 5A); etc.

2. The phase of conflict; pure soul energy conflicts with personality force: The essential conflict between the ray seven soul and the ray five personality is the struggle between the spiritual need to create a practical synthesis of idea and expression upon the physical plane, and the personal desire to focus intellectually, exclusively and *separatively* upon one or two small fragments within the whole, with no thought of how the many fragments can be synthesized.

3. The soul/personality integration process from the perspective of the consciousness identified primarily with the seventh ray soul: It will be the task of the seventh ray soul to bring the specialized fifth ray personality to an understanding of (and practical interaction with) the many *other* areas of specialization within the synthesis the soul is attempting to create. The seventh ray soul has an outstanding ability to coordinate in a rhythmic and organic manner the many parts within any whole; however, in this instance, the soul is faced with a personality which prefers to go ever more deeply into the particularized understanding of some limited area of specialization. In doing so, the personal consciousness becomes cut–off from other areas of enquiry. The soul is frustrated because it tries to create links between the many parts and pieces, but the personality is quite satisfied to remain insulated and focused upon what, from the larger, spiritual perspective, must appear as unimportant technicalities or, worse, irrelevant minutiae. The soul must find a way to induce the personality to enter willingly into a larger and more effective cooperation. One way for the soul to accomplish this task is to pose to the personal consciousness the questions: What is knowledge for? What good does it really do? How can knowledge change things for the better? What part does a particular kind of knowledge play within the larger pattern? The soul seeks to inspire in the personality a determination to apply what it knows in a way which conforms to the Divine Design, which means in *cooperation* with many others whose specialized knowledge is *equally needed* if that which God intends is to be manifested. The love of knowledge for its own sake, the love of pure research is all to the good but, eventually, what is discovered must be used to serve the greater good in a practical manner, thus contributing to the *integrity* of the whole. The seventh ray soul is building a New World Order; the personality can participate as it should when it develops a sense of proportion, learning where its special interests really *fit* within that emerging Order.

4. The soul/personality integration process from the perspective of the consciousness identified primarily with the fifth ray personality: The seventh ray pressure towards integration will initially be felt by the fifth ray personality as the voice of social responsibility interfering with the pusuit of its all–consuming interests. This type of personality feels most comfortable when it can "stick to what it knows." Other considerations are an unwelcome interference. "What *is* it?" tends to outweigh the significance of "What *good* is it?" A selfish engrossment of the mind is at work here, and there is very little attempt to understand the impact of an avid mental interest upon the condition of the social order. Throughout this century there has been much discussion about the interference of the state or society with the pursuits of the individual. Should socio–political values intrude themselves upon the practice of the arts or the sciences? This question has been of particular relevence within the Soviet Union, a nation whose soul ray is the seventh. This is also an important question for the fifth ray personality when associated with a seventh ray soul. The personality feels that the keenness of its pursuit of pure truth, of knowledge for its own sake, is being limited or dulled by social and ethical questions. It does not want to relinquish its purely mental approach, nor waste time on questions pertaining to the socially responsible implementation of knowledge. It does not wish to trouble itself with thoughts of laws and limitations. As the pressure to do so slowly arises within its consciousness (due to the steady impress of the soul), rejection of social responsibility, and an even more avid pursuit of special interests are temporarily likely. But slowly the personality realizes that the very energy (time and money) which enables it to continue pursuing its speciality is a gift of society (be it the society called a nation, or the smaller society called a corporation, or any one of the smaller groups in which an individual may be a member). In any normal and reasonably healthy human society, the social structure supports each individual in many ways, and the individual, consequently, has an obligation to support society by behaving as a social being. It begins to dawn upon the personal consciousness that without social integrity, the efforts of all members of a society eventually fail. Such thoughts, nourished by the seventh ray soul, bring the personal consciousness to the point where it is willing to think in terms of how to contribute what it knows to improve the social structure of which it is a part. In short, narrow personality interests expand to include the larger pattern.

5. The ideal expression of the combination of the ray seven soul and the ray five personality: The urge to order and reorder (to structure and restructure) is expressed with expert knowledge of all technical details involved in the expression. Technology contributes to the implementation of the Divine Order and the manifestation of the Plan. A deep respect for custom, law, social convention and the social order prevails over purely mental interests, and yet there always remains, as a contribution to group integrity, a keen mind bent on factual truth. Positively, the welfare of the social order is seen to rest upon the edifice of scientific enquiry. All seventh ray combinations convey a potential for one or another way of working with the law; in this case, there may be a pronounced capacity for legal research. Here is also an individual who may take a great interest in various types of institutions (historical and contemporary) and will be inclined to learn everything about their functioning in meticulous detail. There are few combinations which have a greater ability to handle details (especially a great number of tiny details). This ability ensures that when an idea is manifested, it is worked into matter and form with precision. The ability to understand and manipulate matter is highly advanced, and it can be imagined that this combination of rays would be most important in industry, or in large organizations whose purposes are technological. This is the combination of the white magician who understands that the magical art has a strictly scientific basis; he will pursue an exact, cause–and–effect understanding of why his magical operations work, and will make unwearied efforts to bring magic and science into closer cooperation. Another way of saying this, is that this combination is one of those most likely to produce the *practical occultist*. The seventh ray is deeply involved in alchemy, which is a process of initiatory transformation. This combination is unusually alchemical, and is unusually well–suited to bring about a deep understanding of matter so that it can be knowledgeably transmuted into spirit. As with the opposite of this combination (the fifth ray soul and seventh ray personality), there may be a strong ability for technological invention; here, however, the vision of a technologically transformed civilization will predominate, and specific inventions will be seen as a means to that larger end. Exact knowledge is understood to contribute its important share to the optimal structuring and restructuring of civilization. The renovation of the forms and patterns of human living is carried forward with the help of scientific understanding and solid common sense.

6. The combined effect of the two integration formulae: The primary integration formula is proposed as *Orientation*, keyed to the seventh ray soul. The secondary integration formula is *Detachment*, keyed to the fifth ray personality. The first formula corrects seventh ray tendencies towards selfish building and organizing according to short-sighted, materially-minded personal plans which are not in accordance with the Divine Plan, whereas the second formula corrects fifth ray tendencies towards mental attachment to matter, and the obsessive preoccupation with investigating or manipulating concrete form while ignoring the reality of that which is "formless." Used together, these two formulae provide the individual striving for soul/personality integration with the composite quality of 'detached orientation,'(i.e., the detachment of the "outer man" from his exclusive concern with superficial, material phenomena – a detachment which enhances the orientation of the "inner man" towards the Divine Design which it is the will of the soul to actualize). When the attention of the personal consciousness is obsessively fixed upon matter, the inner consciousness cannot achieve a proper 'sighting' of the Divine Pattern which determines the manner in which matter is to be organized. The soul-infused individual must see that pattern and express it; a concrete-minded personality, totally insensitive to subtle spiritual *arrangements,* will thwart the desired expression. It will be unable to appreciate the synthesis of the manifesting pattern. The proper use of the formulae makes it possible for the individual to stand poised within the center of his normal personality consciousness and detach himself from the lower mind's blinding fascination with the diversity of material forms, while, within the soul-inspired 'heights' of his consciousness (that realm of consciousness where the presence of the soul can be definitely encountered), he learns to orient himself (with exquisitely refined attentiveness) towards the Divine Light, which, streaming from the "East," begins to reveal a tiny portion of the great "Tracing Board" upon which the 'blueprints' of the Divine Plan are inscribed. Oriented thus, he stands, waits and suffers in expectant uncertainty until, at last, he is impressed by the perfected vision of that fragment of the divinely intended pattern which it is his responsibility and privilege to manifest (with fifth ray accuracy and precision, but with sufficient detachment from the outer aspect of matter to be cognizant of [and to work in cooperation with] the spiritual essence which substands it); then and only then is he ready to *work* in full cooperation with the Plan.

In the earlier stages of evolution, before successfully applying these formulae, an individual with this ray combination often finds himself preoccupied with building and organizing structures which imprison (rather than embody and transmit) the light, and, also, so mentally engrossed in the technical requirements of building and organizing his creations that not even a glimpse of the subjective, substanding reality is possible. His consciousness is 'form-bound' and he sees only what is immediately before his eyes. He builds with precision and with meticulous attention to detail, but his solid structures, and perfected patterns of activity only succeed in entrapping him far from the center of his being. His skill and technological expertise are wasted because they are employed in the manifestation of nonessential patterns.

The intelligent use of the combined formulae, however, transmutes the abuses of the past. The individual learns, primarily, to manifest with consummate skill his small part in the *true Plans* of the Great Architect of the Universe, and his growing secondary ability to detach from the mental illusion of material multiplicity and fragmentation contributes to his primary, soul-inspired objective of clearly intuiting that aspect of the Divine

Construction for which he has responsibility. It is clear that if the Divine Design is to be apprehended, the consciousness must not be under the spell of maya. Not matter, but that which molds matter must be the focus of the attention. Not just *any work* which gratifies the urge to create form, but only the *specific work* which it is the duty of the individual to manifest.

7. Some examples of vocational aptitudes and orientations relating to the combination of the seventh ray soul and the fifth ray personality:

* the magician as scientist

* the ceremonialist/ritualist who seeks to acquire a precise understanding of the subtle and material effects of his every word and gesture

* the spiritualist who eagerly participates in research concerning the relationship between the subtle and objective dimensions

* the alchemist for whom psychospiritual transformation is a bold scientific experiment, in which he is both the experimenter and the experiment

* the organizer whose success depends upon his keen ability to analyze organizational dynamics

* the administrator who relies heavily upon statistical data in the formulation of policy

* the planner whose plans proceed with strict logic and rationality

* the regulator who checks and double-checks the accuracy of his facts and figures before making a decision

* the manager known for the unusual clarity of his explanations

* the trainer who consults landmark "studies" to establish training techniques of proven value

* the legislator who consistently supports the allocation of funds for pure research

* the judge who takes the trouble to make himself aware of the numerous technicalities of the law

* the architect who is aware of the latest technological improvements in the field of construction

* the builder who understands "nuts and bolts" – exactly how everything is supposed to fit together

* the artist who excels in working with metals and minerals: for instance, metal sculpture would be a field well suited to an individual with this ray combination

* the craftsman who employs innovative technologies in the creation of his pieces

* the designer who excels in industrial design

* the diplomat who is invariably truthful, lucid and "matter-of-fact"

* the revolutionary who realizes the importance of scientific discovery and innovation in the task of achieving the new order

* the reformer who enlists the aid of scientific knowledge in his undertakings

In general: vocations and professions which require the power to organize or reorganize, the ability to build, a facility for creating and maintaining standards, and the capacity to skillfully manifest ideas through form, *as well as* keen analytical abilities, the capacity for research, and scientific knowledge and/or technical expertise.

8. A proposed list of well-known individuals (historical, contemporary, fictional or mythological) whose soul ray can reasonably be considered the seventh, with a strong subsidiary fifth ray influence (whether or not the fifth ray is, strictly speaking, the personality ray):

Roger Bacon: Franciscan philosopher and alchemist who was one of the earliest and strongest advocates of experimental science

Rachel Carson: biologist and author of *The Silent Spring*. She planted the seeds of the environmental movement, and introduced the general public to the importance of ecology.

William Cecil (Lord Burghley): master of Renaissance statecraft and secretary to Elizabeth I of England

Marie Curie: physicist who, with her husband Pierre, received the Nobel Prize for Physics for their investigation of radioactivity. Later Mme. Curie received a second Nobel Prize for her discovery of radium and polonium. (Mme. Curie was designated by the Tibetan as a ray seven soul.)

William James: eminent American psychologist and philosopher. James was the leader of the philosophical movement known as Pragmatism.

Alfred Kinsey: sociologist, researcher of sexual mores

Franz Mesmer: 18th century physician whose system of therapeutics became known as "mesmerism," the forerunner of the modern practice of hypnotism. He postulated that a person may act to transmit universal forces in the form of "animal magnetism."

B.F. Skinner: psychologist and one of the most influential exponents of Behaviorism. Skinner was an advocate of social engineering and programmed learning. Some ray two influence is also likely.

Andreas Vesalius: Renaissance physician who revolutionized the study of biology and the practice of medicine by his careful description of the anatomy of the human body. The fourth ray may have been influential as well.

Christopher Wren: English astronomer and geometrician of great distinction, but remembered chiefly as the architect of St. Paul's cathedral in London, and for designing the buildings for three reigns

Some Contrasts Between the Ray 7 Soul and the Ray 6 Personality

Ray 7 Soul		Ray 6 Personality
* spiritual magic	vs.	* prayer to fulfill personal desires
* balanced spiritual practices; progress through moderation	vs.	* personal extremism, fanaticism and unnecessary asceticism
* the spiritualization of matter; uniting that which is "high" and that which is "low"	vs.	* escapist flight from involvement with the physical plane
* attending to the etheric–physical vehicle as a vital aspect of the transformational process	vs.	* unintelligent (and often abusive) treatment of the etheric–physical vehicle
* a soul–inspired mission to unite the real and the ideal	vs.	* unrealistically and exclusively focused upon the ideal
* the dream becomes reality	vs.	* the dream remains the "impossible dream"
* grounded spiritual idealism	vs.	* ungrounded wishful thinking
* creation of the concrete forms which embody spirit	vs.	* emotional gravitation towards that which is formless, abstract and frequently useless in the practical sense
* well–regulated spiritual living in accord with important individual and planetary cycles	vs.	* unregulated, passionate intensity which fails to account for the importance of the time factor
* strict control of emotion via the skillful spiritual will	vs.	* rampant emotionalism
* a paragon of worldly and spiritual discretion	vs.	* in constant danger of excess and indiscretion
* spiritual progress based upon the exercise of strict control according to well–established rules	vs.	* passive openness to arousal from without; suspension of the will while waiting to be "moved"
* powerful organizational abilities	vs.	* disruption of organizational harmony through an overly–reactive emotional nature
* the capacity to create a practical synthesis upon the physical plane	vs.	* caring too much about only one or two things to create a synthesis of many things
* noted integrity, self–reliance and the confident strength to 'build oneself' spiritually	vs.	* "over–leaning on others"

The Integration Process for the Individual with a Ray 7 Soul and a Ray 6 Personality

1. The pre–spiritual phase; soul energy appropriated by a selfish personality: At this pre–spiritual phase of evolutionary unfoldment, the human being's motives (based upon the personality distortion of seventh ray soul energy, and the self–centered use of sixth ray personality force) are to achieve (often through the selfish use of some consciously or unconsciously applied magical process) a rigidly ritualized, tightly ordered life conducive to physical plane safety and security *as well as* the uncompromising satisfaction of the ideals and goals to which the personality is passionately devoted. The individual wants, primarily, to lead a highly predictable (hence, relatively risk–free) life, to avoid having to think for himself or act upon his own initiative, and to have the solid assurance that all physical plane appetites and imagined material needs will be satisfied on schedule, but he *also* wants to ignore everything except the object or path of his devotion, spurn even reasonable mundane responsibilities if they do not relate specifically to his quest, fanatically follow his ideal regardless of destructive consequences, and cling desperately to that which he believes he loves.

Negatively and glamorously, these two ray influences can combine to produce: the routinized person, irrevocably attached to a certain form of procedure (7A, 7C + 6); the ritualist, so totally devoted to a specific ritual, that he will not tolerate even the thought of change (7C + 6); a rigidly conditioned person, who becomes filled with a sense of guilt and shame if he does not conform to his conditioning (7A + 6); one who, blindly, and with passionate insistence, demands a totally new order, ignoring many excellent values from the past (7B + 6B); the fanatical revolutionary (7B + 6B); the utopian whose visions of future innovations are so idealistic as to be impossible of achievment (7B + 6); one who easily develops crystallized attitudes and actions (7A, 7C + 6); the rigid conservative or reactionary (7A, 7C + 6); the militant defender of "law and order" (7A + 6B); one whose one–pointed cause is to preserve forms which have outlived their usefulness – for instance, the die–hard preservationist, or one who is utterly dedicated to the preservation of obstructive "blue laws" (7A + 6); an extremely superstitious person who stands in awe of signs and omens (7C + 6); a sectarian, bigoted person, who is so convinced of the superior value of his organization's system (be it church, corporation, club, etc.) that he disapproves of anyone who is not totally committed to doing just as he and his organization do; the rigidly bureaucratic person who demands unquestioning loyalty to the organization, whether that organization is as large as the "state" or as small as a club (7A + 6); the unimaginative conformist who relinquishes all initiative, and with full devotion, passively does exactly what is expected of him, in every particular (7A, 7C + 6A); the person who severely limits the scope of his consciousness through repetitive behavior and a very narrow outlook (7A, 7C + 6); one whose life freezes into unvarying predictability (7A, 7C + 6); one who, in seeking spiritual union through sexual union, easily becomes addicted to such practices – for instance, a devotee of tantric rituals (7C + 6); one who suffers from a combination of compulsive behavior and hysterical emotionalism; one for whom the practice of magical ritual becomes dangerous because of an uncontrolled emotional body (7C + 6); the fastidious perfectionist whose unrealistically lofty idealism makes any form of contentment impossible; etc.

2. The phase of conflict; pure soul energy conflicts with personality force: The essential conflict between the ray seven soul and the ray six personality is the struggle between the spiritual need to manifest and maintain (upon the physical plane) the new forms which embody the Divine Plan, and the personal desire to find one of many possible methods of escape from one's Self, into realms of oblivion or of the abstracted ideal. In either case, the escape results in the *illusion* of freedom from form, even if, on many occasions the person remains a prisoner of the worlds of form – as with drug addiction.

3. The soul/personality integration process from the perspective of the consciousness identified primarily with the seventh ray soul: In the simplest terms, it will be the task of the seventh ray soul to "ground" the sixth ray personality. The seventh ray soul has a great respect for the physical plane on its own terms; the sixth ray personality rarely sees the physical plane as it really is, and often has a strong distaste for concentrating, for any length of time, upon strictly physical plane issues. Even in those rare instances when the personal consciousness is concentrating upon an object in the world of the senses, that concentration is suffused with the conditioning influences of idealism, devotion or strong emotional attitudes, all of which easily distort perception. The soul, then, is faced with a personal consciousness far more at home on the astral (emotional) plane than in the world of tangible actuality. The soul seeks to find ways for the personality to reduce its emotional intensity, so that a realistic appraisement can be made of the requirements demanded for effective manifestation. The emotional "rush," the impassioned or exalted emotional states which the sixth ray personality so much enjoys, are ill-suited for realistic understanding of (or actions upon) the physical plane. Such emotional excitations disturb the rhythm, timing and sequence of execution and, hence, disrupt the process of manifestation. When consciousness is identified with the ray seven soul, moderation and balance are shown in all things, and constructive action upon the physical plane results; moderation and balance are the very qualities which the soul must somehow impress upon an often immoderate, unbalanced, over-emphatic personal consciousness, which, because of a distorted assessment of physical plane actualities, initiates ill-regulated actions with unintentionally destructive or blundering results. The soul is intent upon creating a *New World Order*; the sixth ray personality, however, is often still busy clinging to fragments of the old world, or seeking to escape from the world altogether. The seventh ray concepts of the "sacredness of Earth," and of "heaven on earth" are much needed by the sixth ray personality. The soul must induce the personality to refocus (at least, on occasion) its upward gazing consciousness *downward towards divinity* thus making possible a true appreciation of the spiritual value of our physical planet, and in general, of the plane of concrete manifestation. The personality, then, idealistically devotes itself to the holy task of uniting "Father Heaven and Mother Earth."

4. The soul/personality integration process from the perspective of the consciousness identified primarily with the sixth ray personality: The seventh ray pressure towards integration will initially be felt by the sixth ray personality as an unwelcome restraining, moderating and grounding influence. The personality feels most comfortable when it can think continuously of that which it adores – when it can continuously direct its activity towards the object of its idealistic love. The seventh ray soul, however, breaks this fanatical continuity, knowing that "for everything there is a season." Not one thing at all times, but a number of things at appropriate times – such is one of the key messages of the seventh ray soul to its sixth ray personality. The pressure to be less emphatic is perceived by the personality as a sapping of strength and intensity, for the personality loves "building up a head of steam," rolling forward without interruption, and sustaining the momentum generated. It dislikes having to "co-measure" its actions with physical plane requirements; when under the spell of "mad desire" or wild aspiration, the physical plane becomes almost an irrelevancy. Yet slowly, as the soul applies its moderating influence, there arise, within the inner recesses of the personal consciousness, glimpses of a radiant planet and a transformed humanity; the "dusty plains of earth" are seen as they could be, once transfigured through Divine Intention. A Divine Design promising a beautiful, rhythmic interdependency between all things begins to flash into awareness, and with it, the call to *divine materialism* and *practical mysticism* – both of which will be required to make this vision a reality. The personality, sensing the incredible patience and practical responsibility required to manifest even a small part of this vision, feels beset by a great weight. It wants heaven now! It wants its unrestrained desires and aspirations gratified immediately. It does not want to have to deal with the myriad physical plane details which are part of the laborious task of constructing heaven on earth. Impatiently and rebelliously, it redoubles its efforts to reach its former, narrow, goal – looking neither to the right nor the left, oblivious to the mundane obstructions presented by concrete matter. But the soul has worked its magic upon the personality; abstract goals seem ever to recede, and the more concrete objects of devotion, once grasped, fail to satisfy. The personality is beset by futility. It begins to realize that its goals are as nothing compared to the Grand Design which God is in the process of materializing. It realizes that all its "furious followings" are an escape from cooperating intelligently with the manifestation of the Divine Plan. Bowing in humility to the limitations of time, and to the unavoidable constraints of *things as they are*, the personality more patiently begins to devote itself to the arduous task of becoming a builder of the Great Temple.

5. The ideal expression of the combination of the seventh ray soul and the sixth ray personality: The urge to order and reorder (to structure and restructure) is expressed as a one-pointed ideal. Forms and patterns, which it is the intention of the soul to express, are carried forth into manifestation avidly, zealously and devotedly. This is an individual who *works* with one-pointed ardor to transform the many details of the Divine Plan into actualities. If such an individual becomes devoted to the process of manifestation, he will sacrifice everything (even himself) to ensure that the ideal is properly materialized. The discipline and organizational skill required to create perfect procedures, at length regulate blind, emotional impulsiveness, nevertheless, an abundant supply of spontaneous enthusiasm remains. The sense of perfect timing masters emotional disregard for proper rhythm, but the individual remains open to inspiration *all* the time. This is the combination of an individual who, because of his strong faith in a particular organization, devotes himself to supporting and sustaining it – seeing that its rules, policies and protocols are upheld. On a more spiritual level, there may be found an almost mystical belief in the "Divine Order," but it is the Divine Order *in manifestation,* not simply in its idealized state. The *mastery* of life-in-matter overcomes the *evasion* of life-in-matter, and yet it is never forgotten that the function of form is to embody the ideal. On the occult side, this is the combination of the magician who is filled with fiery faith in the value of his art, and fiery zeal in its practice; as a ritualist, such an individual will proceed with reverence and solemnity, and his work will be all the more effective because of his single-minded devotion. In the field of law we find a lofty social idealism, a sincere determination to uphold honored ethical precepts. In general, this is the ray combination of an individual who is devoted to the task of upholding an idealized way of life; he will be the loyal defender and preserver of traditional customs, and other valued patterns of social interaction. Whatever the process of manifestation or of building, this individual will throw himself into it without reservation; one can well-imagine finding here those who are willing to martyr themselves in order to bring in the "New World Order." They are consecrated, without reservation, to the redesign of human civilization.

6. The combination of the two integration formulae: The primary integration formula is proposed as *Orientation*, keyed to the seventh ray soul. The secondary integration formula is proposed as *Restraint*, keyed to the sixth ray personality. The first formula corrects seventh ray tendencies towards selfish building and organizing according to short-sighted, materially-minded personal plans which are not in accordance with the Divine Plan, whereas the second formula corrects the unrestrained, passionate pursuit of the 'partial,' and 'peripheral,' so common to the emotionally undisciplined sixth ray personality. Used together, these two formulae provide the individual striving for soul/personality integration with the composite quality of 'restrained orientation,'(i.e., the restraint of the "outer man" which enhances the spiritual orientation of the "inner man" towards the Divine Design which it is the will of his soul to manifest). The soul-oriented individual sees the Divine Pattern and is intent upon its manifestation. But if the personality is both 'super-heated' and misguided, rushing madly to grasp one non-essential form after another, the inner consciousness will become clouded, and the process of manifestation will be severely disrupted. The proper use of the formulae make it possible for the individual to stand within the center of his personality consciousness, restraining the impetuousity of personal desire as it seeks to race towards an engagement with peripheral things, while, within the soul-inspired 'heights' of his consciousness (that realm of consciousness where the presence of the soul can be definitely encountered), he learns to orient himself (with exquisitely refined attentiveness) towards the Divine Light, which, streaming from the "East," begins to reveal a tiny portion of the great "Tracing Board" upon which the 'blueprints' of the Divine Plan are inscribed. Oriented thus, he stands, waits and suffers in expectant uncertainty until, at last, he is impressed by the perfected vision of that fragment of the divinely intended pattern which it is his responsibility and privilege to manifest (with sixth ray commitment and enthusiasm, and yet with the poise and restraint which prevent the useless expenditure of energy on errant quests); then, and only then, is he ready to *work* in full cooperation with the Plan.

In the earlier stages of evolution, before successfully applying these formulae, an individual with this ray combination often finds himself preoccupied with building and organizing structures which imprison (rather than embody and transmit) the light, and, moreover, so unrestrainedly devoted to such building and organizing, that his consciousness fails to register anything else as important. With unrelenting dedication he builds the prison-house of his soul. His working tools are always in his hands, but his back is to the light. With passion he works, and rapid is the emergence of spiritually irrelevant forms. He becomes obsessively devoted to the perpetuation of the non-essential structures he has created, and will not release his grip upon them even though it holds him fast to the periphery of his life. With misguided fervor, he remains deeply committed to living in 'darkened mansions' of his own making, thereby repudiating his spiritual center.

The intelligent use of the combined formulae, however, transmutes the abuses of the past. The individual learns, primarily (through right spiritual orientation), to manifest with consummate skill his small part in the *true Plans* of the Great Architect of the Universe, and his growing secondary ability to restrain his impulse to pursue aspirations leading to the periphery rather than the center of his life, contributes to his primary, spiritually constructive objective. It can be seen that when the personality restrains itself from following well-meaning but misguided aspirations, its aspirational energy is then free to contribute to the true spiritual constructiveness which the soul intends. Wild enthusiasm for manifesting what are really nothing more than "obstructions in space" is transformed into a disciplined, idealistic devotion to manifesting the Plan.

7. Some examples of vocational aptitudes and orientations relating to the combination of the seventh ray soul and the sixth ray personality:

* the white magician whose faith, ardor and devotion to Hierarchy are his shield during dangerous encounters with the lower forces of Nature or with the "dark forces"
* the ceremonialist/ritualist imbued with the quality of reverence
* the spiritualist with a special facility for accessing the astral plane
* the alchemist whose fiery aspiration contributes greatly to the transformational process
* the zealous organizer
* the administrator who carries forward even his mundane functions with infectious enthusiasm
* the regulator who administers moral and ethical admonitions
* the loyal manager who possesses the power to inspire loyalty
* the trainer with a superior talent for motivating his trainees
* the legislator who attempts to legislate his idealism into law
* the judge with a strong conservative value system
* the architect whose works express a great "up-sweep" symbolizing aspirational longing
* the builder who pursues construction with unflagging persistence
* the artist who produces meticulously organized creations on religious themes
* the craftsman, so absorbed in his work that nothing can deflect him
* the choreographer whose dances express a fervent, emotional intensity
* the designer whose designs consistently make an idealistic statement

* the utopian afire with a burning vision of an ideal future order
* the revolutionary eager to sacrifice himself for his cause
* the ardent reformer

In general: vocations and professions which require the power to organize or reorganize, the ability to build, the facility for creating and maintaining standards, and the capacity to skillfully manifest ideas through form, *as well as* high idealism, undeviating devotion, great enthusiasm, and persistent emotional intensity.

8. A proposed list of well–known individuals (historical, contemporary, fictional or mythological) whose soul ray can reasonably be considered the seventh, with a strong subsidiary sixth ray influence (whether or not the sixth ray is, strictly speaking, the personality ray):

Eliphas Levi: ceremonial magician, whose writings were largely responsible for the revival of an interest in magic during the 19th century. A strong fourth ray was undoubtedly present.

Charles A. Lindbergh: aviator, experimenter, environmentalist. There was also a strong ray five influence in Lindbergh's energy system.

Israel Regardie: author, magician, secretary to and biographer of Aleister Crowley

Queen Victoria: Queen of the United Kingdom of Great Britain and Ireland from 1837 to 1901. Her long reign made the monarchy respectable, thereby guaranteeing its continuance – not so much as a political power, but as a political institution.

Thomas Watson, Sr.: corporate reformer, visionary, founder of IBM

Some Contrasts Between the Ray 7 Soul and the Ray 7 Personality

Ray 7 Soul		Ray 7 Personality
* divine magic; white magic	vs.	* magical procedures for the fulfillment of personality desires; 'grey' magic, or worse
* mastery of rituals needed to hasten the externalization of spiritual plans	vs.	* numbing repetition of meaningless personal and social rituals
* intelligent creation of tangible forms to embody spiritual ideas	vs.	* building of forms for strictly personal ends
* executive work within the context of the Divine Plan	vs.	* planning for the manifestation of purely personal designs
* highly developed capacity to spiritualize matter	vs.	* engrossment in materialism; subject to crystallization
* skill in uniting that which is subjective with that which is objective	vs.	* superficiality; a thoroughly extroverted consciousness which judges solely by appearances
* the patience to achieve spiritual consummation	vs.	* looking for completion in small, external, inconsequential things; preoccupation with precipitations and not their causes
* the union of the great pairs of opposites – spirit and matter	vs.	* deluded by sex–magic; mistaking the *symbol* of union for the reality
* behavior performed artfully, in conformity with the highest ethical standards	vs.	* cultured artificiality; mannerism
* the infusion of spirit into the interpretation of the law	vs.	* petty conformity to the "letter of the law"
* the power to create in conformity to the newly intended pattern	vs.	* conformity to the old mould

Commentary

Please refer to the commentary following the tabulation of contrasts between the fourth ray soul and fourth ray personality for a full discussion of the reasons why no commentary will be offered for any combination of identical soul and personality rays when the ray in question is one of the rays of attribute.

TAPESTRY OF THE GODS
VOLUME II

Section VI

AN ANALYTICAL APPROACH TO THE FIVE-FOLD RAY CHART

RAY EXERCISES IN THE ABSTRACT

We have reached the point in the development of our subject at which it would be profitable to examine seven complete ray formulae out of all the many possible. The seven formulae offer a variety of ray combinations, and will test the imaginative power of the interpreter. The Tibetan, Himself, utilizes this approach to understanding on pp. 295–298, and 442–445 of *Esoteric Psychology, Vol. II*.

It is suggested that the student examine each formula before reading the subsequent interpretation of its potentials. The student should attempt to grasp the general quality and character of the kind of individual which the formula might represent, including possible vocations. Individuals at widely varying stages of evolution may have the same ray formulae, and consequently, each of these formulae could be interpreted very differently, according to the state of evolution of the individual to whom it pertains. It is most important, however, to focus upon how each of the formulae should be interpreted during the stages of *aspiration* or *discipleship*. Each aspirant or disciple has certain issues to solve and problems to overcome; some of the most important of these are indicated by the ray chart. The composite liabilities of each formula should be estimated (worst case scenario), as well as the composite potentials (best case scenario). The student should also form an impression of the "next step ahead" (i.e., the next evolutionary step forward) – assuming, of course, that the chart belongs to the typical aspirant or disciple.

The entire exercise is purely conjectural and speculative; there is no strictly *"right way"* to interpret any of the ray combinations, but there are *reasonable ways*. As students grow more proficient in the interpretation process, they can return to these combinations in order to elaborate them, or, better still, generate for themselves others with which to practice. It must be remembered that no ray formula can give a full picture of individual character and potentials: astrological information, karmic and environmental issues, as well as the individual and group history of the entity in question would all have to be considered if there is to be a reasonably complete assessment.

Some of the formulae chosen for interpretation are fairly unusual, while some (judging from the composition of the Tibetan's groups of disciples–in–training) are more commonly found. Even if two individuals had the *same* formula, the process of interpretation would have to be different for each, so many are the additional variables.

Seven Ray Formulae

The format used to describe a ray chart is the customary one:

			4
1.	I	6	6
			3

			3
2.	II	5	2
			7

			5
3.	III	7	6
			6

			1
4.	IV	1	6
			7

			7
5.	V	4	2
			1

			2
6.	VI	3	1
			3

			4
7.	VII	2	2
			7

Note: In the discussions which follow, "Best Case" and "Worst Case" scenarios are examined. In the cases numbered 2., 3, 5 and 6, the "Worst Case Scenario" cannot be considered to apply in full force, for, since the ray combination is not one of the usual ones, the individual would have to be an "awakening disciple" (i.e., an individual who is quite advanced upon the Path of Evolution). This means that the negative descriptions should only be considered as relating to those inevitable moments (inevitable even in the lives of awakening disciples) when glamor and illusion hold sway.

Example 1

```
        4
    1   6   6
        3
```

General Character

Here is an subject with great drive (R1 + R6), capable of excessive personal and emotional intensity (R6). The chart shows the potential of a strong will (R1), idealistically applied (R6). Moderation might be difficult to achieve (R1 + R6), but the fourth ray mental quality could be enlisted in the attempt to do so. There would clearly be battles between will (R1) and desire (R6), and the struggle could lead to mental crises (R4). In any case, the balancing potential of the ray four mind would be needed to mediate between emotional impulsiveness (R6), and the imposition of the will (R1). There is little humor and little perspective on the self indicated here, but the ray four mind could supply some. The subject would be given to considerable physical activity [(R3) driven by (R6) and (R1)]. Restraint would be a great need.

Possible Vocation

This could be the chart of an inspiring leader (R1 + R6), capable of arousing and motivating many (R6), as well as of accomplishing a great deal upon the physical plane (R3 + R1). There would be a strong gravitation towards political idealism (R1 + R6), with unrelenting devotion to great and impersonal (R1) causes. A gift for oratory (R6) and colorful expression (R4) are also probable. Here is someone who would never give up (R1 + R6). He would carry out his will no matter what the cost.

Worst Case Scenario

At its worst, this is the chart of a destructive fanatic (R1 + R6), mentally at war with himself and others (R4). There is too much intensity because of the combination of the first ray and two sixth rays. The blast of willful, devotional energy would not be restrained, and would tend to induce scattered physical activity. The subject would continually "overdo." The fourth ray mind would bring mental instability, and the turmoil of incessant inner and outer conflict. This could be the chart of an individual *unwilling* to regulate himself.

Best Case Scenario

This is also the chart of a selfless leader (R1) who through the keenest idealism (R6), is ready to sacrifice everything he has (even his life) for his cause (R6). Balanced judgment (R4) and an ability to resolve conflict (R4) and good humor (R4) help him moderate the intensity of his eneriges, preventing them from having too harsh an impact upon others and the environment. Here we find a tireless worker, who will drive himself until the task is completed (R1 + R6), and who has the physical stamina to do so (R3 + R1). All within his range of influence would be inspired by his enthusiasm (R6) and his determination to overcome all opposition (R1).

The Problem of the Disciple

The disciple or aspirant with this chart would need to learn the difference between will (R1) and desire (R6). This would be an emotional individual learning the lessons of self control. The "peaceful, silent will" of the soul aspect (R1) seeks to quell emotionalism (R6), and moderate excessive drive and enthusiasm (R6). Through sensitive, intuitive thinking (R4), and an attempt to balance warring forces, dynamic energies would be turned to constructive use, and the individual would no longer disrupt or destroy his own best efforts.

Example 2

```
        3
   ll 5 2
        7
```

General Character

The subject is a calm (R2) and loving person (R2), unusually practical and competent (R5 + R7), and gifted with an extremely versatile, intelligent mind (R3). This is a person capable of expansive learning and understanding (R2 + R3), and yet who has more than enough common sense (R5) to make her voluminous learning immediately useful in everyday situations (R5 + R7).

Possible Vocation

This could be the chart of an scholar or teacher (R2), who would appreciate both the theoretical approach to her subject (R3) and its technical applications (R5 + R7).

Worst Case Scenario

At its worst, this chart describes one who suffers from extreme mental pride (R5 + R3) and a cold contempt for the mental limitations of others (R2B, reinforced by R5 and R3). The subject would be totally and selfishly involved in the acquisition of knowledge for herself alone (R2 + R5). As a teacher she would speak over the heads of her students (R3) and be harshly critical of even tiny flaws in their thinking (R3 + R5) or methodology (R5 + R7). She would be given to pedantry (R2 + R5), filled with self–satisfaction (R2), and determined to shine as an individual of great learning (R2 + R5 + R3).

Best Case Scenario

Ideally, this chart describes the energy system of an unusually accomplished scholar (R2 + R5 + R3), whose humility (R2) is as great as her learning (R2 + R5). Her mind would be exceptionally versatile (R3), and she would succeed as both a specialist (R5) in one or more scientific/academic disciplines (R5 + R3), and a generalist (R2 + R3) with a comprehensive theoretical grasp of vast expanses of knowledge. She would possess excellent teaching abilities (R2): clarity (R2 + R5), human understanding (R2) and abundant patience (R2). Everything she did would presented in a well–organized manner (R7 + R5); at no time, however, would she become dull or pedantic. Although her grasp of her subject would be inclusive and meticulous (R2 + R5), she would have the mental flexibility and versatility (R3) to adapt her presentation to the needs of her students (R3 + R2). Under her guidance, even demanding academic efforts (R5 + R3) would become a joy (R2). She would love to learn (R2 + R5 + R3) and, by her quiet example (R2) inspire others to do the same.

The Problem of the Disciple

The disciple with this ray chart is faced with the necessity of distinguishing between wisdom (R2) and knowledge (R5 + R3). On the personality level she might be something of a "bookworm," constantly into her researches (R5) and innovative experimentations (R3 + R5). She would appear to others as an extremely mental type (R5 + R3), consumed with a love of knowledge – living (it would seem) only to study (R2B + R5). Without the influence of the love aspect of the soul (R2), the life might tend to become arid (R5 + R3). The love of humanity (R2) must blend with the love of "things mental" (R5 + R3). Love (R2) must transform knowledge (R5 + R3) into wisdom. Breadth of understanding (R2 + R3) must take the place of preoccupation with specialized pursuits (R5 + R3). This disciple is faced with the need for using her considerable scientific and academic skills to promote human unity (R2) and loving, intuitive understanding (R2).

Example 3

```
         5
    III  7  6
         6
```

General Character

This is the chart of a highly intelligent, analytical (R3 + R5), practical (R7 + R5) "man of the world," animated by considerable idealism (R6). Business and financial skills would be pronounced (R3 + R7), and there might be unusual mathematical facility (R3 + R5). Against all this practical efficiency and competency (R3 + R7 + R5), would be an impulsive bio–pyschic nature (R6) prompted by insistent emotional and physical needs (R6). There is a cleavage here between the sophisticated (R7 + R3) intellectual (R3 + R5), and the emotional 'child' who is at odds with the controlled (R7 + R5) and intellectual (R3 + R5) aspects of himself.

Possible Vocation

This individual could easily succeed in the financial or business community (R3 + R7 – the two rays most associated with money). Business ventures (R3 + R7) would very likely involve technical "know–how" (R5). A business involving computers, for instance, or other kinds of electronic equipment (R5), would provide an excellent outlet for his particular combination of soul, personality and the mental rays. Mathematics and academic philosophy (R3 + R5) also would be strong possibilities. The field of communications (R3), especially its technical aspects (R5), would be congenial to him. He might be attracted to a variety of academic pursuits, especially history (R3 + R5). There is even the possibility of working in relation to the theoretical aspects (R3) of law (R7).

Worst Case Scenario

At its worst, this is the chart of an individual suffering from a great cleavage between mind (R3 + R5) and feelings (R6 conditioning the physical and emotional natures) – i.e., between the rational aspects (R3 + R5) and irrational aspects (R6) of himself. He could, for instance, be a scheming (R3), self–serving bureaucrat (R7) with narrow, intolerant views (R5 + R6 and R7). His uncontollable desires (R6) for material wealth (R3 + R7) would drive him into shrewd, even unethical (R3), financial manipulations (R3 + R7), but he would usually be cautious (R3) and sophisticated enough (R7) to avoid detection. The victim of obsessive emotions (R6) and physical desires (R6), he would manipulate others (R3) to gratify those desires, all the while "keeping up appearances" (R7). He would be by turns excessively emotional (R6) and coldly clinical (R5 + R3). He would use others (R3), always analyzing them (R3 + R5) and keeping them at a distance – except when he needed them to satisfy his emotional and physical dependencies (R6). He would be virtually incapable of expressing any genuine warmth or true love (lack of R2).

Best Case Scenario

At its best, this is the chart of a brilliant (R3 + R5) and practical thinker (R7 + R3 + R5) animated by strong feelings of devotion (R6) to those less fortunate than himself. He emotional sensitivity (R6) would cause him to identify almost too readily with other's distress, and he would dedicate himself (R6) to placing his very considerable financial expertise (R3 + R7) at their disposal. Ideally, with this combination of rays we would find a highly creative (R3), far–seeing (R3) philanthropist (R3 + R7), capable of designing in detail (R7 + R5) and administrating (R7 + R3) practical programs (R7) for the relief of those lacking sufficient financial resources. He would have abundant mental energy (R3 + R5), which, though creative and innovative (R3), would never become impractical (R7). His vibrant emotions (R6) would never allow his mind to stifle his feelings, nor practical considerations to dampen his emotional idealism (R6).

The Problem of the Disciple

The disciple with this ray chart would be an excellent thinker (R3 + R5) and practical executive (R7 + R3 + R5), but he would have to transmute not only his emotional nature (R6), but the physical appetites aroused by such a close relationship between his desire nature and his physical mechanism (R6). The purpose of the soul is to express a versatile (R3), mental creativity (R3) in practical (R7 + R5), commonsense ways (R5). From the point of view of the soul (R3), personality (R7) and mind (R5), all energies are aligned and under control, for they are all upon the same line of energy (1–3–5–7). The emotions (R6) and the physical nature (R6), however, are not, and further, their rebellion against well–planned higher purposes is fortified by the identity of their rays (both upon R6). Desperate emotional needs (R6), the recognition of which may often be supressed (R7 + R5), will have to be transformed into unselfish idealism (R6). Mind (R5) and emotions (R6) must be taught to work together. If the sixth and third rays worked in harmony, there would be a potential for tremendous productive activity, all well–organized and properly regulated by the personality energy (R7), and mental "matter–of–factness" (R5).

Example 4

```
         1
   IV  I  6
         7
```

General Character

This is the chart of a highly assertive (R1), self–confident (R1) creator of beauty (R4). The powers of synthesis (R4 + R1) are pronounced. The soul–inspired vision of unification and reconciliation (R4) is one that can and will be grounded (R1 + R7). Here is an individual equipped with abundant creativity (R4), and the unflinching determination (R1) to clear a path for its expression (R1 + R7).

Possible Vocation

An individual with this chart would make a powerful (R1) and influential (R1) artist (R4) – one who had faith in her ideas (R1 + R6), and the will to stick to them (R1) until they prevailed (R1). This combination shows powerful dramatic, or histrionic abilities (R4 + R1 + R6); it could be the chart of an actor (R4 + R6) with great projective power (R1) and emotional intensity (R6 + R4). She could also show marked abilities in the fields of mediation (R4) and conflict resolution (R4); this combination of rays, in fact, would very likely produce the accomplished "peace–maker" (R4 + R1). From the opposite point of view, soldiering and a military career could not be ruled out, for the fourth ray soul enters experience "loaded with the panoply of war," and in this case, the willful first ray and incendiary sixth ray accompany the fourth. Whatever the career, it would have to offer abundant opportunities for self-expression (R4 + R1) – a thrust (R1 + R6) which could not be denied.

Worst Case Scenario

At its worst, this is the chart of an individual in constant conflict with others (R4 + R1 + R6) – in fact, a provocateur (R4), happiest when battles are raging (R4). She might be extremely egoistic (R1) with greatly inflated sense of her expressive abilities (R4 + R1). As an artist (R4), she would constantly seek the "limelight" (R1), and have nothing but scorn (R1) and criticism (R1) for her competition. She would push her way through life (R1 + R6) in order to satisfy her professional ambitions (R1), and to cover up her very real insecurities (R4 + R6). Rather than serve art and beauty (R4), she would use them as a means of exalting her personal power (R1) and reputation (R1).

From another point of view, she could be hedonistic (R4) and totally ungovernable (R1), obeying no law but her own whim (R1 + R4). She would selfishly insist on beautiful adornment and apparel (R4 + R7), a luxurious environment (R4 + R7), and would look down upon people (R1 + R7) who did not have these things.

Best Case Scenario

At its best, this is the chart of a profoundly expressive (R4) and dynamic individual (R1 + R6) – an extraordinarily powerful artist (R4 + R1). She would have the strength of mind (R1) to pursue her artistic conceptions (R4) in the face of ridicule and despite any obstacles (R1). An uncompromisingly independent thinker (R1), she would remain true to her vision of the beautiful (R4 + R6); her work would always have a terrific impact (R1), forming an indelible impression (R1) upon the minds and hearts of all who come in contact with it. She would be a strong (R1) and idealistic servant of beauty (R4 + R6). She would understand life as a great drama (R4), and despite the raging conflict she everywhere perceived (R4), she would take her stand (R1) upon the principle of oneness and synthesis (R1 + R4). The many beautiful forms which she created (R4 + R7), would embody the theme of the heroic (R1 + R6) reconciliation of the opposites (R4). The full force of her vibrant interior life (R4) would be expressed powerfully through her personality (R1) and through everything she created.

The Problem of the Disciple

The disciple with this ray chart would be aware of a tremendous concentration of personal power (R1). She would have a great openness to ideas embodying beauty (R4), and an irresistable conviction (R1 + R6) as to the value of these ideas. She might be so assured (R1 + R6) of the value of her artistic vision (R4), that she would *demand* recognition (R1) for that vision (R4 + R6) – and for herself (R1). One big lesson indicated here is that of *artistic humility*. The soul seeks to create beauty for the world (R4), not for the glorification of the self (R1). She might have to learn to step back, off center stage (R1), and let her creative works speak for themselves (R4), rather than trumpet their value so loudly (R1). Beauty is *attractive*, working as it does through love and harmony (R4); appreciation of it cannot be forced (R1). She would have to place her undisputed power (R1 + R6) in the service of the soul (R4), rather than use it to promote herself personally (R1). Thus, a synthesis would be achieved (R4 + R1), and her creations would become both beautiful (R4) and startlingly potent (R1).

Example 5

```
        7
  V  4  2
        1
```

General Character

The individual with this ray chart would be unusual; two of the rays in the formula (the seventh ray mind and the first ray physical body) are not among those which usually qualify these vehicles.

The subject has both scientific (R5) and artistic (R4) leanings. This offers an opportunity for an singular synthesis, or for a cleavage between personality (R4) and soul (R5). The pursuit and verification of knowledge (R5) would be the fundamental "soul motivation" of his life, but an appreciation for color, beauty and excitement (R4) would run a "close second." The seventh ray mind is rare; it would introduce "patterning" as an important life theme, and this ability to register and understand patterns (R7) could serve with equal facility both scientific (R5) and artistic (R4) pursuits; in either case a mental vision of exact relationsips (R7) would be found. He would be calm and serene emotionally (R2), and this emotional quietude (R2) would tend to bring out the harmony (rather than the conflict) aspect of the fourth ray personality (R4A). Physically, he would have considerable stamina (R1), and the capacity to utilize the brain as a conductor of occult or highly refined energies (R1).

In this, as in a few of the hypothetical formulae, the deviations from the norm indicate that the individual must, at the very least, be an "awakening disciple", for a variation in the usual choice of rays is never undertaken by the soul unless the personality has reached this relatively advanced stage upon the Path.

Possible Vocation

We are dealing here with an individual who may well be a scientist (R5) with a flair for the artistic presentation (R4 + R7) of scientific discoveries (R5). Technical skills (R5 + R7) are highly accentuated, as is the ability to manage sophisticated equipment (R5 + R7). A profession requiring precise thought and action (R5 + R7) as well as an appreciation for beauty (R4) would be desirable; crystallography would be one such. In any case, the scientific/intellectual dimension (R5) would not be sufficient to provide complete vocational satisfaction – the interpersonal (human) dimension (R4 + R2) would have to be fulfilled. This individual could be an excellent liason (R4 + R2) between the scientific (R5) and the lay communities. He would definitely be an "expert,"

(R5) but he would understand how to relate (R4 + R2) his expertise attractively and helpfully.

Worst Case Scenario

At its worst, this chart could represent a rigidly, specialized individual (R5 + R7), incapable of integrating his personal (R4) and emotional (R2) needs with his reclusive scientific and experimental pursuits (R5). He could be moody (R4) and fearful (R2) – lacking confidence (R4), and feeling like a misfit (R7) (which, given his unusual combination of rays, is quite possible). He would be desperate to relate to others (R4 + R2), and yet his rigid and unadaptable thought patterns (R7 + R1), and unusually technical, specialized pursuits (R5) would make it very difficult for him to find those with whom he had anything significant in common. He would be awkward (R5), unstable (R4) and unpredictable (R4) in interpersonal situations, and would run the risk of becoming stagnant or crystallized (R7) in his areas of special focus (R5). He could be someone most uncomfortable with himself.

Best Case Scenario

At best, this chart represents an individual with strikingly diverse abilities. On the one hand he could be an accomplished research scientist (R5) with an exceptionally good grasp of the structural principles of matter (R7 + R5). The design of the material world would stand revealed to him (R7 + R5), and he would very capable of bringing his discoveries into manifestation (R7 + R1). On the other hand, artistic sensitivity (R4) would be his; he would be very responsive to the many patterns (R7) of beauty (R4) surrounding him. In fact, he would strive to create such patterns (R4 + R7), and with his well developed sense of form (R7) and color (R4), his creations would be beautiful indeed (R4 + R7). He would be a congenial person (R4 + R2), capable of interacting harmoniously with others (R4 + R2); no matter how unusual and technical his realizations and interests (R5 + R7), he would be capable of making them seem natural and approachable (R4 + R2). For him, science (R5) and art (R4) would be united; he would see great similarities between the patterns revealed by science (R5 + R7) and those revealed by the aesthetic sense (R4 + R7). The two types of patterns would blend and merge (R5 + R4 + R7). His approach to life would be both analytic (R5) and "holistic," (R4 + R2) and his perception would be unusually clear (R7 + R5 + R2).

The Problem of the Disciple

The disciple with this ray chart would be faced with an interesting problem of integration (R5 + R4). Both the technical/mental (R5 + R7) and vibrant/experiential (R4) potentials are strongly pronounced. The soul (R5) is intent upon the acquisition of knowledge (R5), and the revelation of the structure of the natural world (R5 + R7). Further the soul (R5) seeks to implement that revelation in practical, dynamic, and probably technical ways (R5 + R7). So this disciple would be inclined to relate to mechanism and instrumentation (R5 + R7); but another part of him (R4) would want none of it. His challenge would be to bridge the worlds of technology (R5) and humanity (R4) – to unite within himself the technocrat (R5) and the humanist (R4 + R2). This he could do through his potential to realize *beauty of pattern* (R4 + R7) in both fields of interest (R5 + R4).

He would have to guard against rigidities of thought (R7); one aspect of himself would like everything utterly planned and predictable (R5 + R7), but the other aspect would need to stay flexible and spontaneous (R4). This disciple would be a study in contrasts, but if integration is successful he could blend the qualities which make the human being truly human – the clear light of knowlege (R5), and a mediating, harmonizing position between the higher and lower kingdoms of nature (R4).

Example 6

```
         2
VI  3    1
         3
```

General Character

This formula, like the one preceeding it, carries two unusual ray placements – a ray two mind and a ray one astral nature. The entire combination suggests a strongly mystical (R6 + R2) and yet, paradoxically, a somewhat worldly orientation (R3). The sixth ray soul inclines towards idealism and a religious orientation. This tendency is furthered by the presence of a non–discriminating ray two mind, which is likely to focus abstractly and non–verbally upon subtle or intangible things. The personality, however, is upon the active, materialistic third ray, as is the physical body and brain. Although there is a strong subjective, introspective orientation (R6 + R2), the outer person may appear very much "of this world" (R3). The combination of the one sixth ray and two third rays augments the activity level; this is definitely an activist, however, the *mind* is not active (R2), raising the prospect of much action (R3) unguided by thought (R2). This person will be an idealist (R6), intent upon putting her vision (R6) into action (R3). There is the possibility of a lack of emotional sensitivity (R1), or at least some difficulty relating to others easily on the feeling level (R1). This liability may adversely effect the degree to which she can make her vision (R6) a reality.

Possible Vocation

The vocation of religious activist (R6 + R3) immediately comes to mind. This individual would feel driven (R6 + R1) to manifest her ideal (R6) in some form of very tangible activity (R3). She would be one who would feel that the religious or idealistic vision (R6) simply had to be externalized (R3). Motivational work (R6) within the business field (R3) is another possibility; there are many "gurus" (R6) in the economic sector (R3), who blend the power to arouse people's aspirations for self–improvement (R6) with an understanding of money (R3). Even politics (R6 + R1) and "special–interest" activities (R6 + R3) should not be excluded. This is definitely the chart of a "promoter" (R6) proceeding on intuitive "feel" (R2) rather than carefully thought–out plans (since the mind is on a even–lined ray – R2).

Tapestry of the Gods

Worst Case Scenario

At its worst, this is the chart of a fanatical (R6), fuzzy–minded (R2) opportunist (R3), manipulating every circumstance (R3) to push her point of view (R6 + R3). For this person, the end would definitely justify the means; she would not be adverse to whatever emotional bullying (R1) were required to set her plans in motion (R3). And yet the plans would be ill–conceived (R2), unrealistic (R6 + R2) and impractical (R6 + R2); she would lose herself in her schemes (R3) and aspirations (R6). She would produce a virtual frenzy of activity (R3), but her mind (R2) would hardly keep pace with what she was doing (R3). In fact, she would not really realize what she was doing (R2), but would keep doing it anyway (R6 + R3). She would set an example for unintelligent action (a R3 tendency, when unguided by careful thought), and for the ineffectual scattering of energy (R3). But no matter how well people might try to advise her, she would not "hear them" (R3), and would continue to drive herself forward (R6 + R1) – "spinning her wheels" (R3), doing anything she could to maintain the illusion of *action* (R3) even if it were only *motion*. Both maya and glamor (correlated most with the third and sixth rays) would have her in their grip; From her perspective, her ideals would seem so worthy (R6), and her plans so reasonable (R3) that she would not stop to question herself. She would, in short, have no intelligent understanding of her condition. She would resemble a human "perpetual motion machine" (R6 + R3) – talking and running around far more than she should (R3) – rarely stopping to "get clear" (R6 + R3).

Best Case Scenario

At its best, this is the chart of a high–minded (R6), extremely intuitive (R2) idealist (R6) who has the intelligence, adaptability (R3) and emotional fortitude (R1) to successfully weave (R3) those ideals (R6) into diverse situations (R3). Here is a person who would simply *know* what was right (R2 + R6); cogitation and reasoning would would be unnecessary (R2). The vision would always be there (R6), as would the sense of how to keep up with current happenings (R3) in order to make the vision a reality (R6 + R3). With two third rays, she would be at home in the world of business, realizing that even "otherworldly" ideals (R6) have to have an economic basis (R3) if they are ever to be more than dreams (R6). She would be "on" virtually all the time (R6 + R3), ever ready to seize an opportunity (R3) to advance the cause which means everything to her (R6). No one could ask for a more active (R3), enthusiastic (R6), true–believing (R6) advocate.

The Problem of the Disciple

The disciple with this ray chart would definitely have to learn the lesson of wise activity. In the early stages, through the personality (R3) and physical nature (R3), there would be a tendency to indulge in activity for its own sake (R3), oblivious to the sense of vision and direction which the soul seeks to impose (R6). The mind (R2), however, would align far more easily with the idealism and mysticism inspired by the soul (R6), than with the more materialistic personality energy (R3). As the Tibetan has pointed out when discussing a second ray astral vehicle and a third ray physical vehicle, there is an innate inharmony between the second and third rays – they work in fundamentally different ways. The individual with this ray chart would experience this difference acutely. Whereas the third ray impels rapid movement, the second ray does not. A slow-moving mental elemental (R2) in a rapidly moving personality (R3) creates a difficult situation. Thus, the mind of this disciple (R2) would not be well-suited to monitoring the many activities instigated by the personality (R3). Eventually, an accommodation with the ideal (R6) and the real (R3), the visionary (R6) and the mundane (R3), would have to be reached. One part of her energy system (R6) is active upon the vertical arm of the cross, and the other (R3) upon the horizontal. It is wisdom that is required to blend the two orientations (R6 + R3), but the activity (R3) and urgency (R6) levels must subside somewhat before the voice of wisdom (to which the ray two mind may have some access) can be heard.

Example 7

```
        4
VII  2  2
        7
```

General Character

This is an example of a chart which one might find frequently during the "New Age," especially since the seventh ray will be so prominent. As the formula demonstrates, the individual will be very well balanced. Both the seventh and second rays are repeated in two positions, and the fourth (or balancing) ray, occupies the midway point. He will be a very loving person (R2), well equipped with organizational skills (R7), and able to act as an agent of harmonization in most circumstances (R4). Patience and wise action will be his hallmarks (R2 + R7). His effect upon others will be clarifying (R2 + R7), soothing (R2) and even healing (R2 + R7). He has the potential to be a well-loved (R2), responsible (R7 + R2), up-standing (R7) individual – a skillful facilitator of all social and group undertakings (R7 + R2).

Possible Vocation

The individual with this ray chart is ideally suited to work in a group or organizational setting, perhaps in personnel or, management, or, better still – corporate training; always the humanitarian (R2), he would nevertheless have an excellent grasp of organizational structure (R7) and the ways in which it is necessary for people to relate when involved in corporate enterprise (R7 + R2). His vocation simply must have a social dimension; he is the quintessential "team player" (R7), and the ideal representative of the "corporation with a human face" (R7 + R2).

This individual would also be well-suited for any kind of community work or social work, especially when responsibilties include administration, coordination and "net-working" (R7). He would be an excellent facilitator of community and social action, an individual unusually capable of promoting cooperative group work (R7 + R2).

He would also make an excellent physician or healer. The second and seventh rays are the two primary "healing" rays, and in this formula they each appear twice.

Worst Case Scenario

At its worst, this is the chart of timid (R2) conformist (R7), who seeks to do everything correctly (R7) in order to "fit in" (R7) and be well liked (R2). Fear (R2), worry (R4), and the tension (R7) which afflicts those who are always seeking approval (R2), are likely traits of character. He would find it very difficult to initiate action (R2), and would agonize constantly (R4) about whether he were performing correctly (R7) or in accordance with some external, artificial standard (R7). This is an individual who would "run" with a certain social set (R7); he would feel uncomfortable unless he were just like all the other members (R7). He might be a "nice–enough" person (R2), but quite standardized and uninteresting (R7) – without a sense of his own center (R7) and lacking a strong sense of individual identity (R7).

Best Case Scenario

At its best, this is the chart of the consummate group worker (R7 + R2). He would be warm and outgoing (R2), ever able to harmonize the inevitable differences arising between contrasting personalities (R4), and extremely capable of creating orderly, rhythmic, cooperative interaction among those who must work together (R7). The energies of his ray chart are eminently *peace-making*; through skillful organization (R7), loving understanding (R2) and a facility for mediation (R4), he would be capable of averting the various frictions (R4) which lead so frequently to energy-wasting conflict. His is the ability to bring emotional clarity (R2) to any situation. Because of his facility for reducing turmoil (R4 + R2 + R7), making people "feel good about themselves (R2)," and "setting things straight" (R7), he would be a very *productive* individual. His energies would be used wisely (R7), and he could teach people to do the same (R2). He would excel in almost any position of teaching (R2) and training (R7).

The Problem of the Disciple

The disciple with this ray chart would constantly be faced with the need to differentiate between personal (R2) and organizational (R7) values. He would be an innately kind and loving person (R2), easily attached to others (R2). But his soul (R7) would constantly lead him into large group settings in which a respect for law (R7) and organizational rules (R7) would take precedence over his personal desires, comforts and attachments (R2). Within the larger group (and, especially, when one has important responsibilties within that group) a high degree of impersonality is required (R7). The integrity of the organization (R7) comes before the personal welfare of the individual members (R2) – though, of course, they are inextricably interrelated. The second ray personality and emotional nature are soft, accommodating and permissive. They would be willing to bend the law (R2), and to extend tolerance (R2) beyond the limits necessary to maintain a well-functioning organization (R7). If the personality (R2) were indulged, discipline might become lax (R2), and group members (and the disciple himself) might lose the will to "toe the line" (R7). This disciple would perpetually face a dilemma (R4) as he attempted to balance the welfare of the group organism (R7) against the personal welfare of the individual member (R2). The battle would be fought out within the field of the fourth ray mind, which, naturally, would seek a righteous compromise reconciling the two (R4). But, since the seventh ray is the soul ray, the direction of spiritual growth would require more discipline (R7), more impersonality (R7), and more conformity to group policy and law (R7); the permissiveness of the second ray would have to be "reined in" (R7).

THREE HYPOTHETICAL INDIVIDUALS AND THEIR RAY CHARTS

Thus far we have provided a detailed analysis of the seven rays. We have examined them individually, in relation to each other, in relation to each of the five human "force fields," and in relation to the process of soul/personality integration. We have also interpreted a numer of hypothetical ray charts in the abstract. Now, we will undertake an examination of the five-fold ray chart as it relates to both hypothetical and actual individuals. As students continue to study this section of the book, it should become increasingly easy to identify the rays in the complex fabric of "real-life" situations. Knowledge of the seven rays, both in isolation and in interaction, will therefore become a practical psychological tool for the more complete understanding of self and others.

There follow three brief character sketches describing certain aspects of the lives of three imaginary people. A particular ray chart was chosen in advance before creating each of the three characters, and each character description was then created to express that particular ray chart. As you read these vignettes, see if you can determine the ray configuration upon which each character has been created. The presence of certain rays will no doubt emerge fairly quickly; others may not be as obvious. The skill lies is assigning each ray to its appropriate position within the five-fold constitution of the human being: the soul, personality, mind, emotional and etheric-physical fields. Since these character sketches are of imaginary people, there is no one "right" answer. You may be just as correct as the author, and the justification for your choice of rays and their positioning may be just as valid as his.

This exercise is intended to illustrate some of the principles and problems of ray assessment, and to highlight some of the more important variables of which the "ray-assessor" must be aware if his results are to be at all accurate.

John: Age 54

John is a warehouse foreman. He runs the warehouse and he doesn't like his subordinates to forget it. As long as his employees massage his ego, he's very agreeable and easy going – a man with a colorful sense of humor. But he gets "touchy" and drops his familiar manner immediately if he feels that his men are forgetting "who's boss." With John, flattery is the one thing that always works. Despite his determination to "stay in charge," he's really not very sure of himself, and wants, almost desperately, to be appreciated. Consequently, whoever builds him up is well rewarded with special privileges. It's easy for John to treat his men like one big family, as long as he can always play the role of "father." He frequently takes new employees "under his wing," in a fatherly sort of way, and tells them how he likes to see things handled. He also advises them to "come directly to me if there's ever any problem." John doesn't share power very well, and he insists on making all the decisions (for which he has no great ability). He likes to think of himself as a benevolent dictator – someone who always knows what's best for people – someone who tells others what to do for their own good.

While he wants to be obeyed without question, he also wants to be well-liked, and this presents him with his biggest problem. Although John tries not to show it, he often feels weak and ineffective, and has lots of trouble making up his mind. But he won't let others see him that way because he fears that if he shows his weakness, he'll lose his authority and the respect of his men. If he has the least suspicion that he's being seen as uncertain or indecisive, he compensates by becoming almost aggressive, even though it really bothers him to "put people off."

John is a very active person, with a "hands on" approach to managing warehouse business. When he's feeling good about himself, he gets right in there and works alongside his men. He's usually "all over" the warehouse, and only rarely in his office. He has incredible stamina – a strong body and a determination never to quit until the job is done. He loves to eat, and almost nothing puts him in a better mood than a good meal, but when there's work to be done, something within him won't let him rest until the work is finished – even if it means missing a meal, or even two.

John really believes in the importance of what he's doing and has an emotional investment in doing a good job; he becomes emotionally upset if anyone even suggests that things aren't going well. He worked his way up the hard way – always ready to step into the shoes of the man above him, but never shoving anyone aside. Opportunity usually came, and even now he has ambitions to move higher. He would like to be in charge of all five of his company's warehouses, but (though he doesn't realize it) the prospects aren't all that good, because the position is a desk job requiring more organizational tasks than John can handle – at least, that's what his superiors think. In the eyes of those in charge, John does best on his feet, and is just where he belongs.

When his superiors say things are going well, John always takes the lion's share of the credit. Later, when describing the praise he has received, he exaggerates every positive remark (just as he is inclined to exaggerate the negative if he senses disapproval from anyone). After he's been complimented, his men find it very easy to get along with him. Basically, John is a generous person (as long as he's appreciated and unchallenged). He doesn't stand on formality. He knows how to get things done – keep things moving – and, really, he's quite fair-minded. He actually would have very few problems if it weren't for the authority issue, and his seeming inability to decide how to handle the conflict between his need to be loved and his even stronger need to be "boss."

Susan: Age 37

From a very early age Susan was interested in literature and the arts. She also seemed to have a nice way with people and especially with children. No one advised her to become a teacher, but she decided as soon as she could really think for herself to pursue a teaching career, and never deviated from her intention. Always self-reliant and independent, she left home early, insisted upon putting herself through college (although her parents would gladly have financed her education), earned her teaching certificate in highschool education, and has taught English literature at the highschool level for the past fifteen years.

Susan is a very approachable person whose inner strength and integrity are seldom recognized at first. She is usually perceived as being kind and patient, calm and even-tempered, but students (and faculty) turn to her immediately whenever difficult situations arise. She always keeps her head in emergencies, acting as a source of serene strength and confidence in troubled circumstances. She is known as one to be relied upon – someone who won't cave in under pressure. People are always amazed that such an apparently mild-mannered person can handle stress – her own, and the stress of others – so good-naturedly and effectively. She never makes snap judgements about who is right and who is wrong, but deliberates carefully, basing her decisions upon the firm principles from which she never deviates. She is one of those people who sets an example – working long hours (often without a break), inspiring others, and always preserving an attitude of tranquility no matter how hard she drives herself.

Recently, Susan has been inwardly troubled, though she is not the type to burden others with her personal difficulties. She used to think she would be content to teach English literature until she retired, but having reached the age of thirty seven she finds herself somewhat restless and feeling rather confined by her teaching responsibilities. When her closest friends, noting signs of her growing dissatisfaction, enquire regarding the problem, Susan never has any complaints about her students or her fellow teachers. Her experiences with students have been very positive; her classes are consistently well attended and she is one of the most popular teachers in the school. Her colleagues, also, hold her in high regard and, have been, almost without exception, helpful and cooperative. Her restlessness seems to arise from subtle changes taking place within herself.

When Susan searches her motives deeply, she realizes that teaching, per se, is no longer all that attractive to her. She has always done a splendid job, but her heart is no longer in it. At the same time she is firmly convinced that the future of her country depends upon the quality of its educational programs, so she has absolutely no intention of leaving the educational field.

What she does want to do is change things! She has always been an apparently patient person, unwilling to push others or force her opinions, but she has no such reservation about pushing the whole educational system forward. Susan simply believes that the educational process in this country is moving too slowly, encumbered by useless baggage inherited from less enlightened times. She sometimes almost frightens herself by the strength of her growing demand for immediate change within the system. Such radical thoughts are very new to her, and she is actually surprised by what she considers their sudden appearance and insistence. Being one who always acts upon her beliefs (however tactfully in interpersonal situations), she is quietly and deliberately planning to acquire a position of authority and influence where she can really make a difference, and on a large scale. To those who know her very well, this comes as no surprise. They recognized her determination long ago (perhaps, even before Susan, herself, realized the strength of her convictions).

During the past Spring semester, Susan wrestled with the decision of whether to renew her contract for the coming school year; she finally decided to take the risk of cutting loose. She realized, of course, that, from one point of view, she would be sacrificing her security, but her conscience informed her in no uncertain terms that concern for comfort and security could not be allowed to determine the course of her destiny. Her intention is to travel throughout the country, independently, talking to educators, observing the functioning of educational systems at first hand, and then, to go straight to Washington with a list of "hard-hitting" proposals based upon her experiences. She will insist upon the need for change.

Susan has been told that once she is no longer part of the "establishment" it will be more difficult to be heard by those in power, but she thinks that just the opposite is true. In any case, she seems to have no doubts or reservations about her ability to connect with those who can push hard for educational reforms. She has confided to a few, that within a year she intends to be appointed to a position of authority, so she can do more than merely suggest changes; she intends to be the executive force behind those changes. Those who know her well believe that her good humor, personal magnetism and unrelenting determination will help her accomplish whatever she decides to do. Susan's only real regret is leaving behind the students and colleagues with whom she has formed such productive and meaningful relationships. However, at this point, she has left the stage of wavering far behind. Deep down, she is anything but sentimental; it has long been her conviction that the future must always be better than the past, and, therefore, she faces that future eagerly and unafraid – determined to make a difference.

David: Age 42

Ever since he was a small boy, David seemed to know that he was immortal. His parents, themselves students of the Ageless Wisdom, marvelled at his interest in death and his composure in the face of death. When his Grandmother died, David's parents were greatly upset, despite the many words they had previously spoken about the reality of the other "worlds." It was David who had to remind them, rather sternly, about the inappropriateness of their grief, which was, he said "holding Grandma back from where she needed to go." He shocked everyone when he demanded that his parents (along with everyone who had gathered at their home) "stop crying immediately." Such was the force of his words that everyone did precisely that. As for David, his parents cannot remember an instance when he cried.

David's parents could not help but realize that their son was unusual – gifted in ways that are not easily described. It was not so much that he was highly intelligent – he was, or that he could, from a very early age, speak and converse virtually as an adult. It was something else – his unusual preoccupation with death, and the complete authority and certainty with which he expressed himself on the subject. There was no way that anyone could tell him anything about death and the process of dying. He already seemed to know, and offered, spontaneously and in his own words, ideas and descriptions of experiences about which his parents had read (or would later read) in the most trustworthy books on death and its mysteries.

In other ways, David seemed to lead almost a normal, if precoscious childhood. He loved music and poetry. His mother, a talented musician, would sing him songs in many languages, and David would memorize them immediately, and sing them back to her – faultlessly, in a clear and beautiful voice. David's mother knew French and German well enough to make simple conversation; she would sometimes speak to him in the attempt to familiarize him with these languages. David always seemed to understand her. One day when David was eight she was amazed to find him writing beautiful poems in both French and German. When she asked him how he knew what to write, he simply said, "I remembered." The theme of the poetry was death – the unreality of death.

David was, from the first a loving child, with a deep core of reserve, which even his parents found unfathomable. To all appearances, his nature was gentle, and, he seemed to have many friends, but, in the last analysis, it was impossible for his friends to really understand him. When he was in their company, he was quiet and good–natured, usually seeming to enjoy himself, but more often preferred to keep to himself. When David chose to be alone, his friends and even his parents hesitated to interrupt him; hours might pass during which he sat motionless, his eyes closed, apparently wrapped in thought. His parents were, at times, greatly concerned, but, nevertheless, they found it extremely difficult to disturb him during these periods of isolation. It was as if he were surrounded by a presence impossible to penetrate.

From his earliest years, David's parents had to learn to accustom themselves to his unusual behavior and its consequences, but they were completely surprised and frightened one day when David's school principal telephoned them both and insisted that they come to the school immediately; it seems there had been a fight, and David, they knew, *never* fought. When his parents arrived at the school office, they were relieved to find David sitting calmly, and deep in thought; his clothes were dirty and disheveled, but otherwise, he appeared peaceful and undisturbed. The principal asked them to step into his office and close the door. He explained that four boys were being treated in the school infirmary for rather serious injuries, and that David was to blame. It soon emerged that the four were members of a neighborhood gang with a reputation for brutality. As they were all at least five years older than David, who had always been a gentle boy, scrupulously kind and considerate, David's father insisted that there must have been some mistake. The principal, however, assured him that David alone had been responsible for the injuries.

It seems, the principal went on to describe, that David, while standing with some friends, had noticed the four beating a younger boy who was unable to defend himself. David's friends, apparently, started to move away quickly, because they knew they were no match for the older boys, but David, without a moment's hesitation walked right into the midst of the fight and quietly demanded that the four leave the younger boy alone, warning them of the consequences if they did not. As the principle started to describe what happened next, David interrupted him, politely but firmly, saying "I think I can speak for myself." "The four," said David, "not only refused to stop beating my friend, but started to attack me as well. I did what I had to do. Nothing more – nothing less. Their injuries will heal." The exasperated principal went on to say that David, apparently, had overpowered them, but that no one understands how he could. "The gang members," said the principal, "are accusing your son of using some kind of weapon, but we can't find anything." David again interrupted the principal. "There was no weapon. I warned them. I have never tolerated injustice and I never will." Then, turning to his parents he said, "Please understand. This little incident is nothing compared to dangers I have survived." After this, he refused to say anything further.

This episode took place when David was not quite thirteen years old and is significant because of its relation to his extraordinary behavior seven years later during some of the bloodiest fighting of the Viet Nam War. David was drafted shortly after he completed high school. He knew that he could have avoided the draft simply by continuing his education, which his parents pleaded with him to do, but he repeatedly said that he had no need for education of the kind to be found in colleges and universities, and that, in any case, he was not afraid. David served a two year tour of duty, during which he was wounded several times. Because he refused to carry a gun, he was trained as a medic. It is reported that he was absolutely fearless under fire, and would invariably insist on accompanying the most dangerous missions. He assumed the responsibility of protecting the men in any company to which he might be assigned, repeatedly risking his life in order to pull the wounded to safety; he excelled at rescue. No one could understand how he continued to survive. David simply said, "Death and I are old friends." Stories grew up around his daring behavior and his amazing ability to save lives. There were many occasions when those who were given up as mortally wounded survived, almost miraculously, when David tended to them. When David approached and spoke to those who were in the agony of their last moments, they became strangely peaceful and began to welcome death.

Today, David is the president of the Institute for the Conquest of Death, an organization which he founded in the face of tremendous ridicule. He leaves the desk work as well as the Institute's excellent educational program to others whom he has personally trained, although it is said that he can be an inspiring teacher. Instead, he travels constantly for nine or ten months a year, visiting hospices, hospitals and war zones, around the world bringing strength, assurance and tranquility to those facing death. At such times, he says very little, but the power of his presence gives people the strength to actually welcome their passage. Those who have seen him work say that he is filled with compassion and a radiant strength, and that, never once, does he allow the dying the weakness of self-pity. As he did with his parents when he was just a child, he refuses to countenance fear or grief in the presence of death; in his presence no one weeps. Instead he seems to fill the dying with a strange and powerful vitality, after which, in many cases, they immediately, and almost eagerly, pass on.

Analysis

Now that you have given each "story" some consideration, and have determined which ray energies appear to be active in the life of each character, it is important to disclose an *additional purpose* to this little exercise. It must have become obvious that each story depicts a person at a *distinctly different stage of evolution*. John has not yet reached the stage of solid personality integration. While his point of evolution is certainly not as low as the "pre-spiritual phase" (described earlier in Volume II, Section V, where the soul/personality integration process was discussed), spirituality, per se, and the conscious use of soul energy in service are not, by any means, significant themes in his life. Susan, on the other hand, is very definitely a successful, integrated personality, and the soul is exerting its pressure irresistably – so much so that a radical change of life–orientation is in process. David, as must be obvious, is a very "old soul." Soul influence was apparent from his earliest years, and directed his destiny undeviatingly. Almost from the moments of his first conscious acts, David was a completely soul–infused personality – an initiate. Of course, these are only three evolutionary stages among *many possible*, but they will serve to illustrate an important point: *When attempting to assess the ray structure of an individual, it is of the utmost importance to understand the individual's point in evolution.* This statement will take on added meaning when it is revealed (as some may have suspected) that *each of these three stories is intended to depict an individual with essentially the same ray structure*! The basic ray energies are intended to be the same (with some variation in the emotional vehicle), as are the rays which condition four of the five vehicles or fields, but naturally, *these rays function in a widely diverse manner because of the different stage of evolutionary attainment achieved by each of the characters*. Those major differences between these three hypothetical individuals which are not related to their stage of evolutionary unfoldment can be accounted for by the following:

a. the inherent uniqueness of each individual

b. the unique reincarnational "history" of each individual

c. differences in astrological makeup, quite apart from the similarity of ray structure

d. differences in physical heredity and environment

The ray structure intended to characterize each of the three is as follows:

Soul Ray: 1–the Ray of Will or Power

Personality Ray: 2–the Ray of Love–Wisdom

Mental Ray: 4–the Ray of Harmony through Conflict

Emotional Ray: 6–the Ray of Devotion and Idealism
(being transmuted in the Ray of Love–Wisdom)

Physical Ray: 3–the Ray of Active Intelligence

In the case of Susan, the sixth ray emotional vehicle is frequently pervaded by second ray energy, and in David's case, the emotional vehicle is completely transformed from a sixth to a second ray quality.

Analysis of Each Character

Let us consider each of the characters individually in order to bring various principles and problems of ray assessment to light.

Analysis of John's Ray Structure

As we read a description of John's life, we immediately discover first ray qualities – tinged with egotism. During the earlier stages of evolution, the first ray reinforces the individual's sense of self-importance; but during the later stages, the first ray is intimately related to the sacrificial will, and leads to heights of selflessness. John, however, is definitely going through the stage when the little self (the personal ego) – its power, its prominence, and its uncurbed expression – is the primary focus of the consciousness. There is almost nothing of what might be called conscious soul emphasis, for even his altruistic gestures arise only after he has received ego reinforcement. John is primarily motivated by the ambition to achieve power and position, as well as by the desire to be loved (a second ray motivation). His eyes are always upon himself.

If there is almost no clear soul expression, and so much expression of the self-absorbed personality, how can the first ray, which is expressing itself so prominently (and so negatively, overall) be the ray of the soul? Would it not be more justifiable to say that the first ray was conditioning the personality or the mind? For clarity on this difficult matter it is necessary to consider all pertinent factors in context.

For one thing, it is necessary to realize, as has been amply pointed out in the chapters on the integration process, that *the soul ray does not always express positively*. The personality (even when not completely integrated) can *appropriate soul energy and distort it*. This is what is happening in John's case. His *deepest* motive (not just an obvious personality motive, even though it manifests *through* the personality) is to "run things," to exercise power, authority and control, but because John has not reached the evolutionary stage when the *altruism* of the soul becomes the dominating factor, soul quality expresses itself selfishly, reinforcing that center of force called the personality. It is sometimes difficult to discriminate between a personality ray and a misappropriated soul ray expressing negatively through the personality. When attempting to determine the soul ray, one must look not only for the most evident motivation but for the *deepest* motivation. Sometimes, in early stages, the deepest motivation will not be the clearest, and secondary motivations will appear stronger. The intuition is needed for discrimination.

It must also be remembered that altruism (the pure love of others) is a fundamental quality of the soul no matter what may be the soul ray; there are seven distinct types of altruism corresponding to the seven rays. Equally, selfishness (or some form of self-accentuation or self-reference) is the quality of the unspiritualized (or "un-solarized") personality, again, no matter what the personality ray may be. For instance, it is indeed possible to have a selfish second ray personality, even though the second ray quality is usually associated with altruism. The character of John was created with a personality upon the second ray, and some of his most distinguishing traits are a product of the second ray type of selfishness or self-centeredness. The point is, that the soul is not all "good" and the personality all "bad"; there are usually shades of grey. When distinguishing soul and personality rays, it is the *depth* of the quality which makes the difference.

So, above all, John wants to be "boss." This is a personality distortion of the soul's "will-to-power." John's deep and impelling desire is to exercise more and more power, to achieve wider and wider control, within the context of circumstantial limitations. He desires to be in charge of "all five of his company's warehouses." This may seem a relatively small personality objective, but, given his present vision, it represents to him a peak achievement, and would widen the scope of expression for the expanding first ray urge which is demanding expression – even if in a rather 'ego-cramped' fashion.

Unfortunately, where his ambitions are concerned, (or, perhaps, fortunately), John has an abundance of second ray energy (especially the *love* aspect of the second ray). This manifests in his desire for familiarity with his men, his tendency to take new employees "under his wing," his usual pleasant, jovial, easy-going manner, and, above all, in his need to be loved and appreciated. Further, there is his feeling of weakness, insecurity and ineffectiveness – all linked to the glamors of the second ray. From a personality point of view, John craves intimacy, and warm fellow-feeling, but his drive to excel and to be highly respected as a man who "gets the job done" nips his softer second ray tendencies in the bud. At the same time the second ray personality (combined with his deep-seated need to be "number one") renders him vulnerable to flattery, and to those who have learned to manipulate him by "massaging" his ego.

Clearly, in John's energy system, the first and second rays are not working in an integrated manner, nor are the disparate forces within his personality well-coordinated (i.e., integrated). He is obviously troubled by the two major conflicting aspects of his nature (rays one and two), and the conflict has repercussions within both his mental and emotional nature. John's mental body is conditioned by the fourth Ray of Harmony through Conflict; through his mind he seeks, most often unsuccessfully, to reconcile the opposing pulls of his first and second ray energies. His mind, therefore, is often in a conflicted state, which contributes to the indecision in which he so frequently finds himself. His mind is also an *exaggerating* mind, so often found when the fourth ray conditions the mental vehicle. John's tendency to think of himself and his work in terms that are either too optimistic or too pessimistic has a reaction upon his volatile emotional nature, which, because it is easily upset, is clearly upon the sixth ray. John's sixth ray emotional body inclines him to be devoted to his work, and further, devoted to maintaining an elevated image of himself.

John's physical body is upon the third ray, giving him his physical strength, his constant activity, his desire to be "on his feet" and "all over the warehouse," and contributes to his ability to keep going until the job gets done, even if it means missing meals. It would be hard for a seventh ray body to keep up such a constant rate of activity and endure the violation of its regular rhythms.

It might be said that John's first ray soul is polarized or focused in his third ray physical body and brain. He has the will and the drive (if not always the skill) to complete whatever is required of him, and to be very effective upon the physical plane. His sensitive second ray personality is focused in his emotional sixth ray astral body, and this inclines him to react emotionally whenever he is feeling insecure or personally vulnerable. The fourth ray mind acts as the arbiter between these two often conflicting combinations of energy, but as things now stand, John has not really achieved mental equilibrium. Once a degree of mental balance and poise is achieved, and he can clearly *see* the cleavage in his nature, he will be able to control his emotions more successfully, reduce his insecurities, detach his love nature from its control by egotistic impulses, integrate his conflicting personality forces, and, eventually, blend love and will within his nature.

For those who may be interested in astrology, the influences of the signs Leo, Cancer and Capricorn can be readily discerned in the description of John's character.

Analysis of Susan's Ray Structure

In the case of Susan, we have an individual who has left far behind the glamors which prevented John from being a truly integrated personality. There can be no doubt that Susan has integrated the forces within her personality, and has used them successfully in her productive career. Although Susan may know nothing of technical esotericism or occultism, she is clearly a spiritual aspirant (and even a disciple) – one who is seeking to create a better world no matter what the costs may be to her personally.

The structure of this sketch of Susan's character allows us to understand her somewhat from a developmental perspective. Her early interest in literature and the arts suggests the presence of the fourth ray. There are several possibilities: the fourth ray may have been simply a legacy ray, perhaps the ray of the personality during Susan's last incarnation; or the fourth ray may be *both* a legacy ray *and* a ray now present in one of Susan's personality vehicles in this incarnation – often, a legacy ray will seem to "slide down" the hierarchy of positions in a ray chart, with, for instance, the personality ray of the previous incarnation appearing as the mental or emotional ray of the present incarnation; or, the fourth ray may simply and solely be the mental ray, the evidence and quality of which may appear early in the life. At any rate, the fourth ray seems to be a relatively *early* influence, and though its quality appears at various times in this character sketch, it does not seem, by any means, to be the most determining energy in Susan's life.

We learn also that Susan, from the time she was able to think for herself, decided to pursue a teaching career. It seems clear that in previous lives, Susan had achieved a relatively high degree of personality integration, for, from a relatively early age, she was able to *think for herself* and direct her life forward according to a self-chosen plan. Personality integration, technically considered, only occurs when an individual is *mentally polarized*, and is able to live purposefully; Susan is definitely mentally polarized and purposeful. It is important to remember, that once the stage of personality integration has been achieved over the course of several past lives, it becomes a stage which is relatively *easy to recapitulate*, regardless of the "new" rays which have to be integrated into a unified personality during the present incarnation. Thus a fair degree of personality integration can manifest much earlier than expected in the case of advanced individuals. Because the second ray qualities began to emerge once Susan began to "think for herself," it seems wise to assume that the second ray is the personality ray, emerging at an early age because of the momentum of mental polarization and personality integration well-established in past lives. With such people, the quality of the personality ray may, indeed, emerge early, *and* the clarity of personality ray qualities will continually increase with maturity. As a second ray mental body occurs only rarely it is, statistically, at least, unlikely; moreover, Susan seems too "sharp" and "clear" to possess a mental field conditioned by the second ray, for people with second ray minds are said to have difficulty clothing their thought in words, and Susan seems a very articulate person.

It is also interesting to note that an unmistakable quality of self-reliance and independence has been with her from the first. She decided upon a teaching career and did not deviate from her decision. She depended upon herself from the time she left home, and *insisted* (despite her parents' protests) upon putting herself through college. The qualities of the will are very strong, and seem to come from a *deep level* – although, it is still too early to say from how deep a level. When a ray quality emerges strongly in the life of the young child, it may, in fact, only be a legacy ray (which might be called a '*ray of personally generated momentum*'), however, in the case of a relatively advanced person, a ray of early emergence may also be a '*ray of spiritually generated momentum*' – i.e., the soul ray. It must not be forgotten that the soul ray remains relatively constant throughout thousands of years of individual history, and in the case of the advanced person, will definitely begin to condition and blend with the personality life. The quality of the soul ray will, then, merge with the personality qualities which are carried over from life to life as what the Buddhists call "skandhas" or "tendencies."

At any rate, the progress of a ray of early emergence will have to be followed as the life unfolds to determine its place within the human energy system; a ray that is simply a legacy ray will begin to fade out; a ray which is the soul ray will only grow stronger, provided the individual is living a positively oriented life.

Again, as in the case of John, we discover that the first and second rays are the two major rays conditioning the incarnation, but in Susan's case they are well integrated and functioning constructively. Susan has many positive second ray qualities – kindness, patience, calmness, even-temperedness, mildness, goodnaturedness, tranquility etc. In fact, those who do not know her really well perceive these second ray qualities before they perceive her strength. But then, a little exposure to Susan reveals the importance of the first ray: keeping her head in emergencies, steadfastness under pressure, confidence in stressful and troubled circumstances, the firm upholding of principles, etc. In general, Susan seems to display a quality of peacefulness, which is conferred when both the first and second rays manifest positively together. Actually, there is what might be called a *balancing* of the first and second rays. Until the present, neither ray has really predominated, even though Susan has invested fifteen years in what is clearly a second ray profession – teaching.

The second paragraph of the sketch, incidentally, reveals qualities which can be related to Susan's mental and physical rays. Her refusal to make snap judgements and her deliberative attitude point to the presence of the fourth ray on the level of mind – reinforcing the idea that her early love of literature and the arts arose from more than simply a legacy ray. Her long hours of work without a break, again, as in the case of John, suggest a third ray physical body driven by a first ray soul. A sixth ray emotional vehicle also adds "drive.".

When we reach the third paragraph, we discover that Susan is experiencing what might be called a "spiritual crisis," even though the spirituality of the issues which concern her have none of the usual religious connotations. In her case, spirituality is simply the urge to better conditions. Further, experiencing spiritual crisis does not mean that she is "going to pieces," or that she is emotionally distraught; her personality integration is too strong for such loss of mental and emotional control, and the will energy emanating from her first ray soul accentuates her ability to exercise self-control. But she is definitely experiencing conflict (strongly focused in the mind), and, as in all spiritual crises, the conflict is soul-induced.

As Susan's story unfolds, we begin to notice important hints about her ray structure. Earlier, we may have wondered whether the second ray could not, in fact, be the soul ray, for Susan is a successful teacher, and (via the promptings of a devoted sixth ray emotional vehicle) has been totally dedicated to that profession for fifteen years. But now we learn that "teaching, per se, is no longer all that attractive to her." The second ray is, as we know, the teaching ray; if the second ray is Susan's soul ray, it should be *growing stronger* in the life, instead of weaker, especially since she is an advanced individual. With a second ray soul, Susan would at least, feel impelled to continually strengthen the second ray influence in her life. But such is not the case. Instead, she is feeling inwardly compelled, to think in terms of dramatic change. The "wise use of slow action," so characteristic of the second ray, is no longer appealing to her. She is becoming impatient (a first ray quality). An internal energy is driving her to seek power and authority so that she can bring about constructive change. The usual second ray concerns for comfort and security are not allowed to stand in the way. She "wrestles with the decision" (an indication of her fourth ray mind) but she finally decides to "cut loose" and take very real risks by leaving the establishment and independently undertaking the role of self-styled "troubleshooter."

There can be no doubt that we are witnessing the emergence into dominance of a first ray soul. Susan's age, thirty seven, shows that she is ripe for what is popularly known as a "mid-life crisis." In advanced people, such a crisis occurs when the will of the soul becomes insistent, often upsetting the way of life established by the integrated personality. Because the first ray is emerging so powerfully at this crucial point in Susan's life (and because she is obviously an advanced person) we can dismiss the possibility that the first ray is merely a legacy ray, or even the ray of the personality. Thinking back upon her childhood and adolescence, we now feel even more certain that the early appearance of strong first ray qualities was a reflection of a powerfully established soul momentum which could not help but manifest long before the soul influence became a conscious factor in Susan's life. It would appear, then, that the soul (Solar Angel), prior to Susan's birth, chose a second ray personality elemental, in order to bring her into the field of education where great changes were needed, and to equip her with those magnetic and attractive qualities which would enhance her capacity to become an agent for catalyzing successful change. The personality ray must always be considered a subray of the soul ray, and is chosen by the soul to effect certain ends. It must also be remembered that the Ashrams strengthen and support one another by "loaning" certain souls to one another for the sake of creating balance. One has only to think of the significant number of first ray souls who were involved in the Alice Bailey work (a patently second ray enterprise); these souls were "on loan" to the Tibetan from a first ray Ashram (usually the Ashram of the Master M.) and were assigned to participate in such educational work, not only for their own instruction and to build in qualities which they may have lacked, but to *strengthen second ray activities with first ray qualities.* This is all by way of saying that Susan need not necessarily be a second ray soul just because she is involved with the educational field; it is her *function within the field* of education which must be examined, and that function is clearly tending towards the executive – a first ray function. The mysteries involved in vocational assignments may eventually be shown to be related to certain configurations of subrays, Triadal rays and even to the Monadic ray. Until there is greater understanding of these subtle aspects of the human energy system, it seems the part of wisdom to admit that we simply do not know enough about human nature to account for all forms of behavior.

In Susan's life then, the balance between soul and personality has been upset, and the soul has moved into a dominant position. The imbalance is temporary, however. The problems caused by the emerging soul urge were resolved through the balancing deliberations of the fourth ray mind, and once the decision was made, there were no obstacles to the course of action charted by the soul. The integrated personality nature was then ready to accommodate itself to the soul directive. Thus, in Susan's case, not only do we have an integrated personality, but, from every indication, there is an increasing integration between soul and personality, which promises to lead rapidly to the state of soul infusion.

Considering the matter of polarization, it is likely that the first ray soul is polarized or focused within the fourth ray mind, and that the second ray personality is focused with the emotional nature. Susan is a mentally polarized individual; the pressure exerted by the soul was experienced first in the realm of mind, and handled there until a decision had been made. Even while experiencing the dissatisfaction caused by the mounting urge to be an agent of dynamic change, Susan carried on with her teaching responsibilties, and maintained her close and productive relations with her students and fellow teachers. The second ray is the ray of attachment, and to some extent, Susan is attached to students and colleagues; leaving them behind is her only real regret. Susan's emotional nature is now probably upon the second ray. Though it was less true during her first twenty–five years, emotionally she is now calm, loving, and largely non–reactive. It is very likely that the resonance between her second ray personality and this largely second ray emotional vehicle contibutes to her feelings of attachment. But the first ray is not sentimental. Her personality and emotions may be fond of preserving her personal relationships, but her soul, with the acquiescence of her mind, insists upon the freedom to experience the new, and to work free from ties, no matter how satisfying those ties may be.

It is interesting that Susan chose to build upon her past rather than abandon it completely, for she intends to remain in the field of education, but with an entirely new emphasis. This building upon past experience and bridging towards the future is related to the linking qualities of her fourth ray mind and her second ray personality.

When considering polarization, it is not a foregone conclusion that polarization always occurs along similar ray lines. For instance a personality along the 1–3–5–7 line need not always be focussed in a personality vehicle which is also along the 1–3–5–7 line. The same is true for the soul. A careful reading of the instructions to the disciples in *Discipleship in the New Age* will reveal this to be the case.

If Susan's life were to be examined from an astrological angle, the sign of reformation Aquarius and the sign of inauguration, Aries, would probably be found dominant. Taurean energy, bestowing the qualities of illumination, stability, steadfastness, and financial productivity is also a strong possibility.

Susan's case is similar to the challenge facing many aspirants and disciples today. The life of the personality has ceased to satisfy, and the life of the soul is coming in on a full tide. As a result there is crisis, handled successfully or not according to the degree of mental stability, the degree of continuous fiery aspiration, and the degree of personality integration attained. The life of the soul will have its way, and it is the responsibility of the personality to adjust to the inevitable changes of both goals and affiliations.

Analysis of David's Ray Structure

David is obviously a highly advanced soul, almost certainly an initiate of the third degree, born with a deep connection to both his soul purpose and his reincarnational past. It would be fair to say that from his early childhood, David was conscious of being an immortal spiritual entity. This is the story of what might be called a fully conscious incarnation, the divinely intended theme of which was clear almost from the beginning. There are such people, though at this stage of human evolution, they are rare.

The outstanding themes of David's life are the realization of the illusory nature of death and the realization of the soul's immortality. David is what might be called, a "conquerer of death." His proccupation with the "life in death" relates him to the first Ray of Will or Power. The first ray is the great liberating energy, and death is the great liberator. David's approach is authoritative, clear, unsentimental, straight to the point – all first ray qualities. He *demands* (a first ray approach) that people recognize the essential unreality of death; he will not allow people to succumb to the illusion of death. In this respect, David is identified with the "life principle," and, using the first ray energy, it is his soul–inspired purpose to negate the great negation – death.

In David's case the presence of the first ray seems to overwhelm all other rays in his makeup. However, it must be remembered that there is no true first ray type at present in incarnation within the human family. The first ray is really the first subray of the great ray of Love–Wisdom. David, a fully conscious soul, expresses the innate love of the soul (for *all* souls are love) with the dynamism and unfettered power of the first ray.

Given David's stage of evolution, and the high degree of spiritual integration achieved, all the various rays in his makeup are consciously utilized subrays of his first ray soul. David, in fact and in consciousness, *is* a soul. The fourth ray mind gives him his love of music and poetry, and his creativity as a poet. It would seem that the fourth ray could very easily have been the personality ray of his previous incarnation. The second ray, too, is present in his gentleness, modesty, his quiet, unassuming nature. But it is the first ray which emanates from the very depths of his being, and it is the first ray which was responsible for the intensity of his hours of isolation, and for the "presence" which seem to form a psychospiritual barrier, virtually impenetrable to interruption by well-meaning intruders.

When we examine the conflicts in David's life, we see that they were of an *external* nature. Despite the presence of the fourth ray mind, such was the advanced stage of his evolution that inner psychospiritual conflicts had already been resolved. As is so often the case with advanced individuals upon the first ray, the purpose of their soul compels them to thrust themselves into external conflict, in which they attempt (often, initially, through battle) to act as agents of resolution and peace.

Whether we point to the conflict at school or the far greater conflict during the war, the first ray quality of *fearlessness* is unmistakable. This fearlessness, judging from David's cryptic remarks to his parents, apparently arose from a long history in which first ray energies had been applied in life-threatening situations. Fearlessness is a quality of the first ray soul.

Beautifully integrated with David's intrepid first ray qualities are the energies of love, accentuated by his second ray personality. Both in school and during the war, he assumed the role of protector – one who guards and shields others from harm. The perfect blending of his first and second ray qualities became *heroism* – the union of indomitable courage and self-effacing humility. The theme of self-sacrifice is certainly pronounced; for David there is no thought of self. Clearly, we have here a life lived solely for others – a life in which David's convictions (that death is an illusion) are consistently *put to the test* under the most harrowing conditions, so that he can serve as living example of his message.

David's present calling, as founder and president of the Institute for the Conquest of Death, demonstrates how totally he is *identified* with the life force. David is clearly a "disciple of Shamballa," a man of *peace* in the profoundest sense of the word. His major purpose has been to demonstate the indestructability of *life*, through victory over death. The first ray, life, death, peace, will and Shamballa are all inextricably interrelated.

The other rays, while clearly present in David's life, are all absorbed into the great first ray. In the earlier stages of evolution, the rays of the various vehicles often function quite independently of each other, and even work at cross purposes. As evolution proceeds, the hierarchy of rays becomes effective – each lower ray becoming the obedient subray of the ray immediately superior to it.

In terms of polarization, it seems clear that David's first ray soul is focussed in his third ray physical body and brain: all soul impulse is to be translated immediately into action. David was impelled from the outset to demonstrate his understanding of life and death *concretely*, upon the physical plane. His second ray personality was focused in his fourth ray mind, uniting the impulses of love and beauty – first noticed in his musical and poetic activities, and later, in the beautiful and probably poetic words of loving affirmation spoken to the dying.

Given David's advanced stage of evolution, which may be that of an individual active in the process of the "great renunciation" (the fourth initiation), it may be permissible to speculate upon the quality of the monadic ray. In David's case, the monadic ray may well be the second – through which emanates the energy of *salvation*, from Shamballa.

Astrologically, the presence of the sign Scorpio, with its focus upon death and dire testing, and of the sign Pisces with its emphasis again upon death, but equally upon renunciation and salvation, would both be highly likely, and both are ruled by the planet Pluto, the "lord of death." Again Aries, the foremost distributor of the energy of the first ray and linked to the Shamballa force (thus generating the qualities of courage, daring and fearlessness) would probably be found accentuated in the chart.

Conclusion

As suggested at the outset of this exercise, the interpretation offered is certainly not the only one possible. Perhaps you can find a more convincing justification for alternative ray structures. One's facility for understanding the rays in action is increased by proposing and justifying (if possible) alternative ray structures for a given individual. The main point of such exercises as this, however, is to become accustomed to analyzing and then synthesizing the various energy–strands of the human character, all the while cultivating a particular sensitivity to the *spiritual purpose* (and, hence, the major ray energy) lying behind the many lesser inclinations impulsed by secondary energies (i.e., those of the personality and its vehicles)

It is not easy to analyze successfully, or "take–apart" the fabric of human character – and then put it back together. Life processes in manifestation are complex and do not have neat, clearly defined boundaries. Character is very much a synthesis of qualities in which "threads of energy" often become lost and difficult to distinguish. But major "strands of character" do exist, and if they can be detected and "tracked" through the complexity of circumstance, the ray (and astrological) energies which are responsible for conditioning these strands can be determined with a fair degree of accuracy. Thus is human identity clarified, and human purpose revealed.

SEVEN BIOGRAPHICAL RAY ANALYSES
Annie Besant
Born, October 1, 1847 – Died, September 20, 1933

Annie Besant was a remarkable women. Her's was a career of outstanding accomplishment in a fascinating diversity of fields. Among students of the Ageless Wisdom she is, perhaps, best known as President of the Theosophical Society from 1907 until her death in 1933, and as the author of many excellent theosophical text books. But she did not become a Theosophist until the age of 42, at which time she was already widely known as a militant freethinker, a Fabian Socialist, a strike leader, a member of the London School Board, a crusading feminist, and (no matter what the particular "cause célèbre" to which she was *temporarily* dedicated), as a prolific journalist and great orator. Always interested in the politics of social welfare, her greatest political triumphs occurred *after* she rose to prominence in the Theosophical Society. After years of crusading for "home rule" in India, she was in 1917, at the age of 70, elected President of India's National Congress. The wide range of her activities drew upon a number of ray energies which we will now explore.

Note: It should be said in this, as in every one of the brief biographies which follow, that, for a complete understanding of the individual, the astrological chart should be consulted in depth. This is beyond the scope of this first volume in the *Tapestry* series, and so astrological references will occasionally be mentioned, but held to a minimum.

Rays in Evidence

The Presence of Ray One

Annie Besant was a powerful women. Her life, lived bravely and often fearlessly, demonstrated a steady acquisition of power, until, at length, she founded the Indian Home Rule League and was elected President of the Indian National Congress.

During her early years, she gave little indication of her prodigious mental and moral strength and great psycho/physical stamina. In her very conventional, Victorian upbringing, opportunities for dynamic expression were lacking. But even from her girlhood years, she saw herself as *leading* some great cause. As she grew into womanhood, her powerful will and capacity to organize soon emerged. She became a woman known for energy and courage of an extraordinary order.

From the first, Besant was *militant*. She would tolerate no halfway measures. These qualities pertain, perhaps ever more to ray six than to ray one, but in her character these two energies are so closely intertwined that they are difficult to differentiate. Her Aries ascendant with Uranus in the first house (both of which act as conduits for the first ray) are indications of the power of the first ray in her life. In addition, Mars, one of the rulers of Aries, is a sixth ray planet, and so one sees some of the interconnections between rays one and six.

Annie Besant's courage and militancy began to emerge as her marriage to Frank Besant disintegrated. Through relentlessly logical thinking, she was losing her Christian faith, and refused to disguise her doubts. She refused to submit to her husband's demand that she take communion (against her will), even though her refusal meant the end of the marriage and, eventually, the loss of her children. Annie Besant would not compromise her *principles* – an outstanding quality of those upon the first ray (especially when combined with the sixth).

Living strictly according to these principles, she soon became a militant atheist, and close associate of Charles Bradlaugh – head of the Freethought Movement and leading luminary of the National Secular Society. Whatever organization she joined, Annie Besant *always rose to prominence*, as is so often the case with those stongly endowed with the first ray. She always emerged as the courageous champion of some worthy cause, and took the rough treatment which is accorded those who have the temerity to place themselves squarely on the firing line in defense of progress. Let us remember that in Victorian England, as far as respectable society was concerned, atheism, contraception, socialism, feminism and militant radicalism were *all* unpopular causes (no matter what their ultimate humanitarian value might be), and certainly not fit avenues of expression for a 'decent' *woman*. We must realize the personal fortitude required to espouse such causes, so vocally. Annie Besant was an individual who did as she pleased, and went her own way, always with the highest motives. While her Libran energy inclined her to seek partnership in her various ventures, she always maintained a fierce (though polite) independence. Once she determined to do something, she become extraordinarily one–pointed and single–minded – virtually unstoppable.

Besant's many causes were not without physical danger, and she did not hesitate to expose herself. Whether it was leading a strike of "match girls" in London, or leading a funeral cortege of a comrade who fell during the "Bloody Sunday" riots, or stepping into the center of volatile Indian politics, she always "saw action at the front." Her persistent willingness to brave danger in the fight against what she perceived as evil, demonstrates the strength of her first ray nature.

Another of her first ray qualities was her prodigious capacity for work. Of course, the sixth ray enters the picture, but nevertheless, she was untiring in her ability to carry forward her projects and causes. Bradlaugh's daughter Hypatia comments on these qualities:

> **Tireless as a worker, she could both write and study longer without rest and respite than any other person I have known; and such was here power of concentration that she could work under circumstances which would have confounded almost every other person.**

The first ray is the ray of power, strength and endurance. Those upon this ray persist when others fall by the wayside.

Politics, of course, is the favorite arena of first ray individuals. Although those upon the sixth and seventh rays are also trained through political work, the area of government remains, predominantly, a first ray field. Annie Besant always wielded *power*

– on a smaller scale in early life, and on a global scale once she had reached the age of 44. For 40 years she was a leader of the Theosophical Society, and for 26 of them she was its President. This was extraordinarily demanding work, for the Theosophical Society was an an international organization with thousands of members and large centers in Europe, America and India. The ability to retain power (and admiration) for such a long period bespeaks the presence of the first ray. And of course, any woman who could, in the words of one biographer, "draw up a constitution for a continent," and become the focal point for the political aspirations of millions upon millions of India's people, *must* have been animated by the first ray. Upon her centenary one of her Indian colleagues expressed his assessment of her character in words which succinctly describe her first ray nature: "A great woman, a strong woman...a person we cannot forget easily."

The aspect of the will conveyed by the first ray is the Will to Initiate. This was one of the most dramatic themes in Annie's life. She was forever hurling herself forward into uncharted territory, undertaking new projects. She was a great pioneer, as her Aries Ascendant indicates. She 'burned her way through' one cause after another, always exhausting what they had to offer her, always moving forward towards greater promise and greater freedom. She was definitely a representative of that quality of *motion* associated with the first ray – "progressive motion...*driving forward through space.*" (cf.*A Treatise on Cosmic Fire*, pp. 41–2)

Finally, in attempting to justify the presence of the first ray in Annie Besant's energy system, we must consider her relationship with Madame Blavatsky, whom we know was a great first ray soul. H.P.B. respected few mortals, but she *did* respect Annie Besant. During an initial interview with her, H.P.B. spoke "with a yearning throb in her voice": "Oh, my dear Mrs. Besant, if you would only come among us!" On another occasion H.P.B. said to her: "You are a noble woman. May Master bless you." Whose Master? H.P.B. was a chela of the Master Morya (a great first ray Master), and in these words, it is hard to refuse the implication that "Master" (as she called Him) was also Annie Besant's Master. H.P.B, it seems, *recognized* Annie Besant as an Ashramic brother. Other writings, including Annie Besant's autobiography, leave no doubt of her close relation to the Master Morya. Again, this stands as a confirmation of her relationship to the first ray!

The Presence of Ray Six

From her earliest years, the life of Annie Besant was powerfully colored by the sixth ray. She was a passionate, militant crusader for noble causes. Periodically, she was subject to startling 'conversions' – drastic changes of allegiance, dramatic life–reorientations, which led many to question her integrity (and her psychological stability)! An understanding of the psychology of the sixth ray places these sudden realignments in proper perspective.

During her mid–teens, Besant was a passionate Christian who flagellated herself and fasted dutifully. She prayed ardently for a life of suffering for some great cause – a life of martyrdom. She longed to become a saint, a prophetess. Her marriage, at twenty, to a young clergyman, Frank Besant, would, she thought, offer her great opportunity for self–sacrifice. As a clergyman's wife she could fulfill her passionate longing to do good:

> All that was deepest and truest in my nature chafed against my easy, useless days, longed for work, and yearned to devote itself, as I had read women saints had done, to the battling against sin and misery.

It was impossible, however, for her powerful and restless spirit to be contented with such a limited, and often mindless role. Her mind and soul rebelled. She left her husband, and before long became a convert to militant atheism. She threw herself into the atheistic cause with the same passion and fervor she spent on evangelism. This, of course, is characteristic of those upon the sixth ray. It makes no difference if the sequence of causes they espouse seem contradictory; while they believe in a cause, they believe in it utterly, and nothing can dissuade them *until* they drop the 'old' cause for a new. The following panegyric from one of her articles in a Freethought pamphlet, lauds the atheist as a man beyond compare, and plainly reveals Annie Besant's extraordinarily idealistic nature. Describing the true atheist she writes:

> In form strong and fair, perfect in physical development as the Hercules of Grecian art, radiant with love, glorious in self-reliant power; with lips bent firm to resist oppression, and melting into soft curves of passion and of pity; with deep, far-seeing eyes, gazing piercingly into the secrets of the unknown, and resting lovingly on the beauties around him; with hands strong to work in the present; with heart full of hope which the future shall realize; making earth glad with his labour and beautiful with his skill – this, this is the Ideal Man, enshrined in the Atheist's heart.

These words alone can stand as sufficient evidence to the power of the sixth ray in Annie Besant's nature. Although these were *written* words, they also reveal the exalted oratory of which she was capable. She was, in fact, a brilliant orator, charismatic, inspiring and gifted with a sonorous, musical voice. We recall that D.K. said of the sixth ray man that "he may be a great preacher or orator" (*Esoteric Psychology, Vol. I*, p. 209).

Subsequently, there were other conversions, equally dramatic, equally dismaying to colleagues she left behind. Her conversion to Fabian socialism was startling but could be explained in terms of the development of her thought. Her conversion (and it was a *conversion*) to Theosophy took even some of her closest and dearest friends by surprise. Once again, it was a radical turn-around, though in the larger sense, it can be seen as *synthesis* relating to the *thesis* of militant Christianity and the *antithesis* of militant atheism. Despite the essential logic to this progression, the actual conversions occurred in a manner characteristic of the sixth ray.

This sixth ray quality is, again, plainly in evidence in Besant's second encounter with H.P. Blavatsky. She had just filled in her application to join the Theosophical Society. She found Mme. Blavatsky alone. She writes:

> ...I went over to her, bent down and kissed her, but said no word, 'You have joined the Society?' 'Yes.' 'You have read the report?' 'Yes.' 'Well?' I knelt down before her and clasped her hands in mine, looking straight into her eyes. 'My answer is, will you accept me as your pupil, and give me the honour of proclaiming you my teacher in the face of the world?

Annie Besant had found her guru.

There are many other incidents in her life declarative of the sixth ray. Her close and devoted relationship to C.W. Leadbeater is a case in point. She seemed to have implicit faith in him, although much of his work may have been glamored or erroneous. She believed in him, and his supernormal powers, entirely. He was a controversial character (though, according to D.K. a man of considerable attainment). She, apparently, was blind to his faults. Sixth ray people will, we realize, overlook the foibles of those they believe in. Even when Leadbeater came under suspicion of pedophilia, she remained loyal, though the evidence was virtually irrefutable. Throughout her career, in fact, she *believed* many things which, perhaps, she should not have. After H.P.B.'s death, she received letters, apparently in H.P.B.'s hand, (really penned by W.Q. Judge), and not only did she believe them to be authentic, but she announced to the world that they were. This is typical of a sixth ray individual. She simply had the will to believe, and needed, at times, (as sixth ray people often do) better discrimination.

Another point of interest relating to the sixth ray is Annie Besant's utter sincerity, bordering, often, on humorlessness. More than any ray type, sixth ray individuals need a sense of humor. They are often so earnest in their beliefs, that they think humor a sign of disrespect or an evidence of the weakening of their faith. While there are many esotericists who know how to have fun at their own expense, and can see the humor in their 'unusual' way of life, Annie Besant was not one. At one point, H.P.B., understanding Annie Besant's streak of humorlessness, wrote to W.Q. Judge, preparing him for Besant's impending visit. H.P.B. advised that there must be no irreverence about Theosophy and no deviation from the strict truth. She "is [wrote H.P.B.] the soul of honour and uncompromisingly truthful...and filled to the brim with pure, unadulterated Theosophy and enthusiasm."

The Presence of Ray Five

The above thoughts touching on Annie's utter truthfulness, bring us to a consideration of the fifth Ray of Concrete Knowledge and Science. The fifth ray confers the qualities of lucidity and extreme truthfulness. There was an uncompromising *logic* to Besant's thinking. It was this, in fact, which led her away from evangelical Christianity and into militant atheism. She had discovered historical discrepancies among the four Gospels. This sowed the seeds of doubt, and set her upon the road to questioning every aspect of Christianity. Although her various conversions were apparently sudden and dramatic, in every case, she *thought her way* into her new orientation before she declared it. Of her conversion to Socialism, she writes: "Slowly, I found that the case for Socialism was intellectually complete and ethically beautiful." If she was to believe in something (and, given her nature, she *had to*), then that something had to *make sense*. Her mind was logical. She was never satisfied with easy answers, and questioned everything carefully. Before assuming firm and uncompromising positions (as she was wont to do), she reasoned her way into them; thus, she used the energy of the fifth ray to pave the way for the full expression of the sixth. The reason, for instance, that she could not be shaken from her passionate Theosophical convictions (and George Bernard Shaw used all his wit, guile and persuasion to shake her), is because those convictions were based upon careful study and logical thought. They made perfect sense to her. If her convictions had been purely emotional beliefs, she might have been dissuaded by the intense pressure brought to bear from numerous quarters.

It is interesting to realize, that in many respects, Annie Besant was literal-minded. This, we know, is a quality conferred by a prominent fifth ray. She did not look at things symbolically. When she analyzed the Bible for discrepancies, she was looking for specifics. This love of specific detail is found in many of her Theosophical writings, such as *A Study in Consciousness*. Even though the theme of that book is extraordinarily abstract, it is filled with intricate descriptive detail. At times, she seemed to have been a master of occult minutiae. Her researches with C.W. Leadbeater produced a number of books, most of which had the same *descriptive* quality. As researchers, they were simply describing what they saw on the inner planes. A book like *Occult Chemistry* is a case in point. The construction and interactions of chemical atoms and molecules are described meticulously.

For all this, Besant was well prepared. Shortly after custody of her children was awarded to her husband on the basis of her unfitness as a mother, she threw herself into an intense study of the sciences. She acquired certificates qualifying her to lecture on chemistry, botany, mathematics, physiology and basic physics. She passed her examinations with honors, achieving first-class honors in botany. Besant describes her attitude towards her studies and the compensations they offered her in the following manner:

> ...let me say to anyone in mental trouble, that they might find an immense relief in taking up some intellectual recreation of this kind.

After her many court struggles, Besant "found it the very greatest relief to turn to algebra, geometry and physics, and forget the harassing legal struggles in wrestling with formulae and problems." It appears, then, that this type of thinking came somewhat naturally to her, for she found it *recreational* and she handled it very well. All this seems to confirm the presence of fifth ray energy in her ray chart.

The Presence of Ray Seven

Rays one, six and five seem to be dominant in the character of Annie Besant, but certain seventh ray qualities also appear. Of course, astrologically the seventh ray enters via the zodiacal signs in which her Sun, Moon and Ascendant are placed, as well as via the planet Uranus. Clearly, Annie Besant was an excellent organizer and administrator. It must be remembered, however, that the seventh ray is, from one point of view, a lower manifestation of the first Ray of Will and Power, and that organizational and administrative abilities are *also* associated with the first. There is no doubt that she was a Uranian *reformer*, and thus utilized *both* first and seventh ray energies. However, she lacked the *moderation* usually associated with the seventh ray. She drove herself incessantly, and seemed not to understand the value of rhythm and interludes. She was what we now call a "workaholic." Nevertheless, she appears to have had a fine sense of order, and the logical and sequential treatment of subjects (especially in her Theosophical writings) reflect this. Probably we are looking at a combination of the fifth and seventh rays within her personality vehicles. Her body-type, and descriptions of the way she dressed ("neat dark dresses with a touch of white"), especially earlier in her life, suggest the presence of the seventh ray, at least in the physical vehicle. There is also her great love of Masonry, and her extensive contributions to the Co-Masonic Order. Annie

Besant was a ritualist. At sixteen, she had discovered the beauties of church ritual while visiting Paris, and later in life, she committed much time and energy to writing rituals for Co–Masonry. Masonry is primarily a seventh ray discipline, although it is an important field of training for those who are upon the first ray. There can be no doubt that she utilized seventh ray energy in her considerable organizational work. We must decide, however, whether this energy was primary in her energy system, secondary, or, rather, the result of astrological influences which acted as 'conduits' for the seventh ray. Even if we decide the seventh ray energy to be principally astrological, it is still extremely significant. It must consistently be remembered that, in one way or another, *everyone has all the rays*. We are simply attempting to determine the ray emphasis in any one life. The important but difficult matter of distinguishing between the *purpose* (not the strength) of 1) rays within the ray chart, and 2) rays which enter the life strictly via planets and constellations (but which are *not* represented in the ray chart), still needs much exploration.

Proposed Ray Chart

```
            5
    I   6  6   L:  6
            7
```

Commentary

The two rays which manifest most prominently in the life of Annie Besant are the first and the sixth. There is, we realize, much similarity between them, though, on the whole, the first ray induces behavior which is far more "centered" and far less emotional. It is likely, then, that one of these rays is the soul ray and one the personality ray.

When attempting to distinguish the soul from the personality ray the major purpose of the life must be considered. Annie Besant was both a leader (R1) and a follower (R6), but above all, she was a *leader*. She loved power, and to her credit, she sought to wield it in the interests of humanity and in cooperation with Hierarchy; she succeeded. In every organization she joined, she rose to prominence. Despite the fact that Mme. Blavatsky was closely associated with W.Q. Judge, and Colonel Henry Olcott prior to Annie Besant's interest in Theosophy, she rightly considered Besant her natural successor as leader of the Theosophical Society. Blavatsky understood their ashramic link as initiate disciples in the ashram of the Master M.

In a life so rich in accomplishments, it is difficult to single out those that are most striking, and most reflective of the purpose of the soul. It would seem that Annie Besant's 26 year presidency of the Theosophical Society, and her daring efforts on behalf of independence and home–rule for India, would rank as her foremost contributions. Even from the time of Blavatsky's death in 1889 (some eighteen years before her election as President of the T.S.) Besant was very much its *focal point* and inspiration. The same might be said of her role in India's independence movement (prior to the rise of Mohandas Gandhi). It is the function of first ray souls to provide strength and vital inspiration to all those with whom they are affiliated. They are the very *heart* of the group, or of the organization. Annie Besant fulfilled this role superbly and with almost superhuman strength. It is hard to imagine how an individual could become (and successfully remain) president of a great international organization, as well as an internationally regarded stateswoman, and *not* be a first ray soul.

Those whose souls are upon the sixth ray (especially type [6B]) can also handle power, but their work is often less political than religiously inclined. Further, ray six souls are not, necessarily, dynamic leaders. They can inspire many, but their capacity for organizational and administrative work is less than that of those upon the first ray; in such work, Annie Besant excelled.

There can be no question that Annie Besant was profoundly influenced by the sixth ray, but it was strongest in the first half of her life. Her sixth ray orientation was with her, almost from the beginning, as evidenced by her very real "martyr complex" during her mid to late teens and early twenties, whereas her dynamic first ray influence gradually gathered strength throughout her life, culminating in her exemplary execution of the most demanding kind of leadership responsibilities. Although, in the case of an advanced human being, the soul energy *can* be detected in early life, it tends to grow in power as life progresses. As for the personality energy, it may also, with advanced people, become noticeable at an early age, but it will, at length, be *overtaken by the soul energy*. This was the case in Annie's life. Her sixth ray personality (driven by the first ray soul) led her from one idealism to the next, until her conversion to Theosophy (which was her final conversion, and the end to that particular sixth ray dynamic). In Theosophy, her ideal was fulfilled and her faith never waivered. At such a point of irrevocable commitment, she could no longer go on looking for ever–higher ideals. She had to "settle in", and assume *leadership responsibility*. Instead of racing forward in search of new and still more exciting projects, she had to "hold the center". Instead of racing off after a new vision of reality, she had to empower the vision she had embraced. These are entirely different dynamics: vitalization from the center, rather than pursuit.

Of course, the first and sixth rays were almost inextricably interwoven in her life. It is even likely, given some of her early and ardent religious responses, that the sixth ray had been her previous personality ray, as well as the personality ray of the present incarnation. This often occurs. The soul chooses the same personality ray for more than one life (perhaps for a series of seven lives), in order to build in some necessary quality. But always, *behind* the sixth ray stood the power of the first. This accounts for the dramatic intensity and frequency of her startling conversions. It was the first ray that drove her into and *through* her many sixth ray allegiances, always forcing her to emerge "on the other side" into greater freedom. Annie Besant's deep and abiding love (always an indication of soul quality) was *liberty* – the release and liberation from form which are perpetually stimulated by the first ray. She insisted upon freedom for others, and, of course, for herself. But the sixth ray, it must be remembered, is more a ray of *attachment* than of freedom. Sixth ray individuals may be attached to the *ideal* of freedom, but they have far more difficulty cutting ties and actually *achieving* liberation than do the true first ray types. Besant, however, consistently liberated herself from outworn attachments (even when great pain was involved). Her sixth ray grip was always tenacious, but when the time came, she knew how to let go – irrevocably – and move forward.

It seems clear, then, that for all its strength and prominence, the sixth ray was, for Annie Besant, a secondary ray – her personality ray. As a person she was an idealistic, militant, passionate, one-pointed crusader for many noble causes. Not only did she attach herself to great ideals, but (in typical sixth ray fashion) she attached herself to certain people as well, and with them she worked in close [and not always *discriminating*] partnership. Her sixth ray allowed her to make very rapid progress, for once she attached herself to a cause she clung to it until she exhausted it, and was then free to move on to the next (and greater) cause.

It must also be pointed out that Besant's close relation to the Master M. confirms her as a first ray soul. Those upon the sixth ray are related to the Master Jesus, and while this may have been so (in a very general, Christian way) in her earliest years (for the Master Jesus has much to do with the stimulation of the Christian Church), it was definitely not so, once she knew who she was. Further, sixth ray souls transfer to a second ray ashram following the third initiation (and, sometimes, even before). Given the nature of her life, it seems clear that Annie Besant had reached that particular point in her evolution, but there was little to suggest the growing presence of the second Ray of Love-Wisdom. She was entirely too dynamic and full of fiery power. Although her mind was excellent, she was on the Path of the Director rather than that of the Teacher/Scholar.

The fifth ray is present, but certainly not as powerfully as the first or sixth rays. This means that it probably qualifies the mental field. Besant was a logical thinker, and used her mind scientifically in both the orthodox and esoteric fields. Many of her Theosophical writings have a decidedly fifth ray character. They are clear, precise, descriptive, and deal at length with details of form (even though the form may be upon one of the subtler planes of nature). The fifth ray, therefore, seems a logical choice as the mental ray.

And yet, Annie Besant was a magnificent orator and spoke beautifully. These are qualities we more normally associate with the fourth ray mind. She was also, as is clear from her glowing estimation of the ideal atheist, given to exaggeration, which is another quality associated with the fourth ray mind, although, those with a strong sixth ray will exaggerate regardless of the nature of the mental ray.

These reservations notwithstanding, the fourth ray does not seem a good choice for the mind. Annie Besant was not a divided person. She did not suffer from mental agonies and conflicts. Her mind was *logical* and one-pointed, and even during so agonizing a process as the renouncing of her Christian faith, she kept a cool and logical head, reasoning her way inexorably towards her decision. Her mind could always work independently of her emotions, which is rarely the case with the fourth ray mind. Further, she had little humor, was quite literal, and could not really see the absurd and funny side of life. (Although closely related to George Bernard Shaw, a character with a great deal of fourth ray, she understood his humor very little).

We are, however, left with a problem. Do an individual's words reflect the quality of his mind? The answer must be *yes*, except that they *also* reflect the quality of his personality and his soul! Emotions, also, have their effect. Annie Besant the orator, was not Annie Besant the scientific thinker. From the podium Annie spoke not only from her mind, but from the deeper levels of her being, and with plenty of emotion as well. The mind was only part of it, and probably not the greater part. Her purpose was to arouse and inspire, for which the combination of the first and sixth rays were far more suitable than the fifth. But, when studying the sciences, when writing her books about the nature of man and the subtle dimensions in which he lives, the mind *itself* was very much more in evidence. She was sticking to the facts. She had no purpose other than the elucidation of truth. Consequently, it is at such moments that the fifth ray emerges through her words in *purity*, undisguised by the more powerful influence of the first and sixth rays. These are important points, and indicate the necessity of understanding an individual from many angles before judging his ray configuration. Certainly, a single piece of writing cannot be selected as all-sufficient evidence of the quality of the mental ray.

As regards the emotional ray, it seems to be the sixth. Annie Besant *was* emotional and passionate, though these qualities were disciplined and channeled by her powerful first ray nature. She was intense rather than calm. She emanated devotion rather than serene and gentle love, however deep and encompassing her true and essential love nature undoubtedly was (for all rays, even the first, are subrays of the great, essential Ray of Love-Wisdom).

Her physical nature seems to have been the seventh. Early photographs reveal a refined, poised, graceful and slender body. The ray of the etheric-physical field is very important, as it is also the ray of the etheric-physical brain. Annie was an excellent organizer, highly efficient and effective upon the physical plane. This is attributable to the combination of the first ray soul and seventh ray brain. It seems unnecessary to search for the seventh ray in a position higher than that of the etheric-physical nature. Annie Besant was altogether too driving and driven to have had a seventh ray soul or personality. The seventh ray was powerful not only because of its probable rulership over the etheric-physical mechanism, but because it was conveyed into her energy system via certain constellations and planets. A full discussion of these astrological factors, though fascinating, is beyond the scope of these first two volumes of *Tapestry of the Gods*.

The motto of the Theosophical Society is, "There is no Religion higher than Truth". This might, with justification, be considered the motto of Annie Besant as well. Throughout her life she pursued truth fearlessly, passionately, and with uncompromising logic. This pursuit is thus colored by the combination of her three major rays (excluding the Monadic) – namely, the first, the sixth and the fifth. Let us close with a passage from her writings which illustrates the power, high-mindedness, and purity of her quest:

> **That one loyalty to Truth I must keep stainless, whatever friendships fail me or human ties be broken. She may lead me into the wilderness, yet I must follow her; she may strip me of all love, yet I must pursue her; though she slay me, yet will I trust her; and I ask no other epitaph on my tomb but, 'SHE TRIED TO FOLLOW TRUTH.'**

Note: The sources used for all direct quotations by or about Annie Besant were: *Annie Besant*, by Rosemary Dinnage, Viking Penguin, Inc., New York, Copyright 1986; and the *Encyclopedia Britannica*, fifteenth edition.

Albert Schweitzer

Born, January 14, 1875 – Died, September 4, 1965

Albert Schweitzer was one of the greatest men of the twentieth century. Highly accomplished as a theologian, philosopher and musician, his achievements in any one of these fields would have merited world attention. But his true greatness lay in his humanitarianism, his moral authority, and his devotion to the preservation of human civilization.

His story is well known. A man rich in gifts of mind, heart and vitality, he utilized them all in the service of those far less fortunate than himself. Renouncing his prominent position in European society as a licenciate in theology, concert organist, and respected author in the fields of theology, philosophy, and music theory, he entered medical studies at age 31 in preparation for the life of a medical missionary in French Equitorial Africa, and seven years later, upon the completion of his medical training, embarked for Lambaréné, where he established a hospital for the native Africans of the Ogowe river basin. Despite incredible obstacles from man and nature, he continued his medical missionary work at Lambaréné until his death in 1965. His hospital had grown from the tiny, squalid chicken–house (which was the only building he found upon his arrival) to a facility with 40 buildings, beds for 350 patients, three doctors, six nurses, 10 native assistants, and a small asylum for the mentally ill.

Today Schweitzer is a legend. His name evokes the image of all that is finest in the human spirit. His life was an example of the heights which can be attained by an individual who is animated by a love of his fellow human beings, and the irresistible *will* to live self–sacrificially. Albert Schweitzer's work was a tremendous spiritual victory, both for himself, and for the millions of people he inspired. His life of selfless service stands as a constant reminder of what one *conscientious* individual can do when motivated by the moral imperative – *"reverence for life"*.

Rays in Evidence

When dealing with an individual of Albert Schweitzer's spiritual, moral and intellectual stature, all of the seven rays will emerge noticeably. Schweitzer was clearly what the Bible calls a "rich young man." The Tibetan informs us that this phrase is a technical appellation referring to an initiate of the third degree – a soul–infused personality, one who has attained the initiation of the Transfiguration. (Fittingly, his Sun sign was Capricorn – the sign of the initiate.) For one who is thus "rich" in spirit, the accumulated mental, emotional and moral faculties of his most recent incarnations are quite accessible. At such a relatively high stage of evolution, the immediately preceding lives have been lives of significant achievement, and these achievements "carry over" into the present incarnation. The individiual is, therefore, "rounded–out," with capabilities far beyond the ordinary. This accounts for the multiple talents frequently seen in those who are initiates of the third degree (or approaching this point of attainment), and their ability, seemingly, to live several lives in one.

It is to Schweitzer's great credit, however, that he took the incredibly difficult next step *beyond* soul–infusion, and *renounced* all his possessions in order to serve humanity – and the most needy members of the human family, at that. Here was a "rich young man" who was able to pass through the proverbial "eye of the needle," because he was willing to take nothing with him except that which was necessary to meet the overwhelming need. The extraordinary thing, however, is that once he had (with earnestness and deliberation) sacrificed *all* to follow Christ, he found that his riches were restored to him. He learned, in fact, that it was his duty to *use* those riches to enhance his service to humanity and to the "Kindgom of Heaven." In short, his great abilities as an author, lecturer, and organist were the principal means (at least for many years) by which he could financially support his hospital and medical missionary work. Further, his life of philosophical thought and musical sensitivity gave him the *strength* to withstand the almost superhuman demands which his new life placed upon his mind, emotions and body.

Schweitzer's status upon the Path of Initiation (shared by one or two others for whom biographical ray analysis has been attempted) make an analysis of his rays at once more interesting and more difficult. Nevertheless, there are certain ray tendencies which are most prominent, and focusing upon them we can, perhaps, arrive at a fairly convincing ray chart.

The Presence of Ray Two

Schweitzer was a great *sensitive*. From his earliest years he was deeply distressed in the presence of pain. He had what is called in German, "mitleid" – translated as "sympathy," but meaning, more literally, "the capacity to *suffer with* others." This is the compassion which is found in all great exponents of the second ray, of whom the greatest are the Buddha and the Christ. Schweitzer's compassion and sensitivity to pain evolved into a profound "reverence for life" – his foremost ethical principle. Actually, the phrase loses something in translation. "Ehrfurcht vor dem Leben," is more than *reverence* for life. "Ehrfurcht" suggests the sense of awe, shuddering wonder and great blessedness. It is a mystical sense of life's divinity shared by all great pantheists. It is a pity and compassion so deep that the individual is compelled to change the world in order to save all living things from suffering. It is clear that this is the motivation of all the "world saviors," who are living examples of the Vishnu or "Preserver" aspect of divinity. It is this quality which, over and above all his many impressive accomplishments, gave Schweitzer his hold upon the conscience of the world. He was a man who demanded of himself an intense devotion to each little flickering flame of life. To him, every leaf, every insect, every animal was sacred. He found life, even in ice–crystals and demanded that no one should break them, nor should grasses be needlessly trodden on, or twigs needlessly bent. To him the smallest was as the greatest. Like all great exponents of the second ray, he sought to *preserve life in form*. Thus, for all his flaws of character, he was a man of love, a man who *lived love* under such brutal conditions that it demanded incredible resolve simply to act like a decent, civilized human being.

The second ray, however, is not simply the ray of love – it is the ray of Love–Wisdom. Often an individual will demonstrate one aspect of this dual ray more than another. In Albert Schweitzer's case, he demonstrated both, potently. The wisdom aspect of the second ray often produces great scholars, and Schweitzer was a great scholar. He was a man of prodigious learning. In each of his three special areas of academic focus, he produced important scholarly works. His masterpiece in the field of theology was his comprehensive *Quest for the Historical Jesus*; as a philosopher he sounded a dire warning to modern humanity in *The Philosophy of Civilization*; and as a musicologist and organist he produced his erudite two–volume study on Bach. He worked the way all second ray scholars do, carefully gathering as much information as possible on his subject, and synthesizing it into a comprehensive presentation. He would leave libraries with armfuls of books, and his writing room would be heaped with great piles of them. He had the second ray scholar's love of completeness, and his major writings are lengthy, as one might expect of one conditioned by a ray which stimulates a love of "meticulous entirety."

When looking for other evidences of the second ray in Schweitzer's life, we must remember that he was a "religious" man. Like his father, he was a Christian pastor, and his relation to the absolute ethic of Christ determined his destiny. From an esoteric perspective, it might be said that Albert Schweitzer was affiliated with the second Department of Hierarchy – the Department of Religion, inspired and supervised by the Christ. Naturally, this Department is principally qualified by the second ray, and contains in its ranks all those whose foremost purpose is to illumine and to heal. Of course, healers are found upon all the rays, but those drawn to healing by great pity, compassion, and *sensitivity to pain* are found, primarily, upon the second ray. From the time he was a boy, seeing someone in pain drove him to the edge of madness. He was inwardly compelled, at any cost, to assuage pain – as was the World Teacher and Savior, the Christ. Christ was also the great Healer, and to the extent that Albert Schweitzer was capable, he attempted to follow in the footsteps of the great Exemplar.

Schweitzer was a philosopher in the truest sense – he loved wisdom. He hoped that philosophy would show humanity the way to a nobler life.

> **I believe there must arise a philosophy profounder and more living than our own, one possessed of greater spiritual and ethical power. In the terrible age through which mankind is passing, all of us, both in the East and the West, must watch for the coming of a more perfect and healthier form of thought which will conquer men's hearts and compel all people to acknowledge its sway. And it must be our aim to bring this philosophy into existence.**
> *Indian Thought and Its Development*

Philosophy, we know, is found primarily upon both the second and third rays. Although the strong Capricorn influence in Schweitzer's astrological chart would confer considerable third ray influence, it does not seem to have been a principle conditioning energy in his life.

Third ray philosophy is more purely mental, more related to mathematics and to the processes of understanding the mind and the nature of knowledge. Second ray philosophy is more concerned with wisdom, with ethics and the edification of the human being. It has a pedagogical purpose, and is intended to evoke the human soul. This is a simplification of course, but it might be said that second ray philosophy has more "heart" in it, and is more concerned with the principles of thought which *unify* humanity, both with itself and with divinity. For all of Schweitzer's mental acuity, he was an exponent of the second kind of philosophy, closer to wisdom than to pure intellect. He concerned himself principally with *ethics* – or, as the Tibetan might say, with "right human relations."

The Presence of Ray One

There is often a myth surrounding great individuals. The myth surrounding Albert Schweizter (based partially on truth) portrays him as a mild and kindly humanitarian figure, all gentleness, all "sweetness and light." It is this view which has prompted some ray analysts to assign him *both* a second ray soul and second ray personality. This is a false characterization – fortunately for both Schweitzer and the world.

In actuality he was a man of daemonic energy – a powerful man, often gruff and commanding. He was to the natives of Ogowe river basin a great patriarch, and it was in his nature to be so. His will was law, and he tolerated no opposition. He also had a terrible temper, brutal impatience, great stubbornness, tenacity and intransigence. An authoritarian, and strict segregationist, he was dogmatic and categorical in his views. Above all, he *refused* to give in. Refusal was a salient dynamic in his character; he would not countenance defeat. He pushed and punished himself to the utmost, thriving upon a work schedule which would have destroyed those of lesser stamina, never allowing himself more than four or five hours sleep a night. Without these first ray qualities, he never would have succeeded.

It is important to realize the sheer *strength* – physical, psychological and spiritual – demanded by the task which Schweitzer set for himself. The odds were constantly against him. He had to contend for many years with utterly primitive working conditions, an enervating and insidiously unhealthful climate, no assistance except for his wife and a former patient who became his helper, the ignorance and laziness of the native Africans who sought his help (albeit, a good one), and even the cruel interference of the French (since during the period of two wars, he was a German national in a French colony). In fact, Schweitzer and his wife were removed from Lambaréné and imprisoned in France at the close of the First World War. When, at last, he had regained his health, and sufficient finances and was able to return to Lambaréné seven years later, the hospital had vanished, overcome by the jungle; he had to rebuild everything.

From the very first day in Lambaréné, Schweitzer's work load was crushing. He was forced to work to his fullest capacity – actually, beyond his capacity. Often on his feet from morning to night, he had to deal with a never-ending stream of Africans suffering from the most appalling array of ailments. Even though he was a man of exceptional physical power, he frequently suffered from nervous exhaustion, his strong body attacked by anemia, ulcers and abscesses which could hardly be avoided given the inhospitable climate and the conditions under which he forced himself to work. All this is to say, that Albert Schweitzer was a *powerful* man, and he had to be!

In many ways he was *two* people, as is so often the case when both the second and first rays are prominent in the energy system. He *was* gentle, kindly, and intensely sympathetic – a man of heart. But, if one studies his physiognomy, one can see the great strength: the shaggy eyebrows, the strong nose, the powerful chin. The power of the first ray was absolutely required if he was to succeed in carrying out his mission of love and healing.

He always appreciated the beauty of the jungle, but it was his enemy as well. He had to clear a way for civilization, and he did so by main strength. He was a prodigious worker, and drove his laborers, often harshly. So much of his earlier life had been given to abstract and cultured thought, and the cultivation of refined sensibilities, but in the jungle he was forced to confront primitive realities. His hospital was ever in danger of being overcome by the natural forces of rain, wind, flood, erosion, disease and the relentless growth of the jungle. He had to fortify the hospital's physical plant against such encroachments, and it required constant and intense concentration upon the most concrete level of reality in order to do so. There were certain periods during his more than fifty years at Lambaréné when he was unequivocally 'man against the jungle.' Although, those who saw what he was attempting (such as the building of a new hospital in record time) thought he would collapse under the strain, he triumphed (bear in mind his Scorpio Ascendant, for Scorpio is the sign of *triumph*).

Like so many first ray individuals, he was not one to delegate authority. He kept all power in his own hands, and was "on site" for all changes. He was architect, foreman, builder, and task–master, and a hard master he was – though just.

Albert Schweitzer's great mentor was the poet/philosopher/novelist Goethe – a great German initiate. It was Goethe who had written the mighty first ray affirmation: "In the beginning was the *deed*" – a call to direct and fearless action from which Schweitzer took constant inspiration. When faced with that which apparently could not be done, he took matters into his own hands and did it. Though, himself, a great example of the flowering of European Civilization, he was forced to become an entirely practical, *elemental* man, in order to fulfill his spiritual mission. He was, in many respects, a "man of iron," and his astrological chart, with a powerful emphasis upon Capricorn and Scorpio (two of the *toughest* zodiac influences) supports this. A man of peace, yes, but in every respect a fighter, as his Scorpio ascendant and Mars upon the Ascendant strongly indicates. In typical first ray fashion, he was hard on many people, but hardest of all upon himself.

Finally, a word must be said about Schweitzer's personal austerity, his innate reserve and his love of isolation. He was in many respects an extremely private man, gathered into himself. Though his fame spread throughout the world, and though the life to which he committed himself demanded constant contact with others, he was essentially a lone, solitary figure. He was not one with whom it was easy to become "familiar." As a man of love and wisdom, committed to the supreme ethic of the Christ, he was approachable, but as an olympian, who placed uncompromising demands upon himself and others, he was not. The isolative qualities of the first ray can easily be recognized.

The Presence of the Fifth Ray

Schweitzer was as an excellent scholar and his methods of research were more than thorough. Individuals characterized by the combination of the second and fifth rays are often numbered among the finest scholars because, not only is their approach comprehensive and learned, but they are sure of their facts, patiently verifying the many details they invariably include in their presentations. Schweitzer's monumental works on *The Quest for the Historical Jesus*, and on the life and music of Bach were prepared with extraordinary meticulousness. For instance, it took him four years to write the study on Jesus. This undertaking involved an examination of *all* the lives of Jesus which had appeared in the last three centuries. He introduced 67 separate lives in the first edition, and added twelve more in the next. A number of the volumes he studied were truly massive (one was 2700 pages), and he worked through them diligently. The scope of his researches led him down many obscure trails, but he doggedly persisted, assembling a great number of quotations and other pieces of information. He sifted through all these interpretations comparing them with each other, and against his own ideas, and finally presented a refined interpretation which is among the most convincing ever offered. It is this method of working which is characteristic of the fifth ray – patient, thorough, meticulous, factual, non–exaggerative, taking nothing on trust, examining everything, and in no hurry to come to conclusions. In his *The Philosophy of Civilization* his style is often pedantic and somewhat dull, but impressive for the learning and depth of thought conveyed. Schweitzer valued truth and clear–speaking highly and was anything but "light-minded."

There are other evidences of the presence of the fifth ray. From his early years in school he showed an affinity for the natural sciences and this interest blossomed when he entered medical school. His interest in the world of medical facts was so pure and all–absorbing, that he almost forgot to go through the rather artificial process of "cramming" for examinations. He became completely fascinated by the "garment of God."

Albert Schweitzer was also a man of reason. In his childhood he questioned his father continually about certain Biblical accounts which did not seem to make sense. This was the enquiring tendency which led him into his Biblical researches for the 'true' Jesus – the "historical Jesus." Here we see the fifth ray refusal to be satisfied with myth, anecdote and hearsay. He wanted to know who this great man *actually* was, and he patiently and laborious pursued his questions until satisfied that he had arrived at the truth. Even in his youth, Schweitzer rebelled against the idea that reason was blind, and must be silenced before the mysteries of faith. It seemed to him that there was no limit to the power of reason, and that even the most exalted religious concepts must bow to its ordinances. One wonders if his most recent incarnation had been taken during the "Age of Enlightenment."

Before becoming a medical doctor (a discipline strongly related to the fifth ray), Schweitzer was a philosopher, a theologian and a musician. Interestingly, the Tibetan relates the philosophical impulse not only the second and third rays, but to the fifth as well (*see The Rays and the Intitiations*, pp. 601–2). Theology, too, is associated not only with the third ray but with the fifth, for under the fifth ray, concrete and rationalistic explanations of the nature of divinity are formulated. Further, the fifth ray "operates in connection with the Law of Cleavages," and cleavage (between man and man, and religion and religion) has been one of the outstanding results of theological argument. As regards Schweitzer's musicianship, he was an outstanding organist and his interpretations of Bach rank among the best, but he considered himself a music theorist. Music theory, as is well known, relies heavily upon analytical skills so often associated with the fifth ray.

Throughout his life, Albert Schweitzer acquired factual knowledge about a great many fields. He was always learning. When imprisoned during World War I in a camp which contained scholars in all branches of learning, he availed himself of the opportunity, studying hard, and learning all he could about banking, architecture, factory building, the growth of cereals, and, even, how to build a furnace! At Lambaréné he was far more than a physician, surgeon, psychiatrist and pharmacist; he became an architect, builder, carpenter, farmer, and engineer, responsible for designing and maintaining the physical plant. He was also a good mechanic (an almost sure sign of the presence of the fifth ray), and when things needed fixing (tools, pumps, refrigerators, etc.) he could fix them. Thus, he avidly acquired knowledge about many *concrete* matters, utilizing every opportunity to make sure that he was well-informed, and then applying what he had learned.

Fifth ray energy can also induce dogmatism, and when combined with the first ray, it is almost sure to appear. Once Schweitzer determined the best way to do something, there was no changing his approach, and no arguments were tolerated. As previously mentioned, he insisted upon segregation between blacks and whites. Whatever we may think of the value of this policy, it is significant given the association of the fifth ray with the Law of Cleavages. The first ray, too, can be separative. He summed up his attitude to the native Africans in the following way: "Admitted I am their brother, but it must be clearly understood I am the elder brother."

Finally, it must be mentioned that Albert Schweitzer was an expert in the art of organ building. He made a comprehensive and detailed study of this complex and demanding craft, just as he studied theology and the works of Bach. His approach, as might be expected, was "hands on." Not content, merely, to play the organ beautifully, he had to "get inside" it and find out how it worked. He understood the intricate mechanism, and would frequently be seen cleaning pipes and making various mechanical adjustments. This is another example of the fifth ray ability to work concretely and intelligently with the *things* of the material plane.

The Presence of the Sixth Ray

Schweitzer was animated by a tremendous idealism, and a stern and stoic sense of duty. He was utterly dedicated to the great Christian ethic which demanded that he be his "brother's keeper." He was driven by an unforgiving conscience to embody his consummate ideal – "reverence for life." He would not allow himself to compromise his principles. This tendency is fortified by the combination of the first and sixth rays (and the sign Capricorn). On matters of ethics and morality, he was unbending.

In many ways the sixth ray was expressed more in his *orientation* than in obvious traits of character. His quest was for the *historical* Jesus, and Jesus, we know, is the Master upon the sixth ray. Further, Schweitzer was a preacher, a pastor, one committed to carrying forth the Word of God, and this, of course, suggests a strong relation to the sixth ray. But his character, though imbued by many of the higher qualities of the sixth ray (probably the ray upon which his soul had been found for many lives before transferring to the second) was broader and far more encompassing than the character of those whose soul or personality is qualified by ray six. Further, Schweitzer was an utterly practical "man of the world," and the sixth ray, when prominent, introduces certain tendencies towards unreality and "otherworldliness." He was one of the most idealistic of men, but his idealism embraced all of humanity, human civilization, and the necessity of global peace. It must be remembered that the second ray (especially in the case of highly developed disciples) really *includes* the sixth ray, for the sixth ray resolves into the second ray, following the point of Transfiguration, and, sometimes, even before this initiation. Although certain astrologoical factors (Mars in Scorpio in the first house) bring in a strong sixth ray, it is reasonable to suggest that Schweitzer's life was an example of sixth ray devotion and idealism widened, transformed and *sublimated* (i.e., made more *sublime*) into a broad and embracing second ray compassion.

The Presence of the Third Ray

The third ray was not a pronounced influence (especially in the vehicles of the energy system), but it was present. Schweitzer was an extremely active person; it seemed at times as if he were endowed with the gift of perpetual motion. He was master of many trades, and a "jack" of many more. He had an unusual adaptability upon the physical plane (more so, it seems, than upon the mental). He was constantly beset with the challenges of his jungle environment, and he proved to have the flexibility, mobility and resourcefulness to meet them intelligently.

The Presence of the Fourth Ray

The fourth ray is suggested primarily by Schweitzer's deep dedication to music and the proficiency he achieved as an organist. This, alone, however does not necessarily indicate that the fourth ray was part of his ray chart. The fourth ray seems best placed as a 'legacy ray,' contributing in his youth to his extreme sensitivity to pain, his dreamy and imaginative nature, and his early love of harmony as expressed through music. His musical skills seemed to be in the nature of a "recapitulation," in which a line of activity, started in the past, is brought to the level achieved in a former incarnation, cultivated further, and then raised to a still higher level of accomplishment. The level of attainment was indeed high, but, when assessing the primary theme of Schweitzer's life, it must be realized that music and artistry (along with several other of his "gifts") formed a *support* for his life purpose, and were not the purpose itself. It should also be realized that the second ray has much to do with musicianship. The Master K.H. (reputedly, the former Pythagoras [to Whom music was so very important] is said, today, to be a consummate musician, and is occulty called "the Lord of music and the dance."). Again, it is important to remember that the fourth ray, like the sixth, can resolve into the second ray.

On a more personal level, the uncertainties and blatant inconsistencies associated with fourth ray influence, were more prominent early in his life, and faded with time. As a mature individual, Schweitzer had none of the debilitating instabilities associated with the fourth ray. He was, of course, multifaceted like many other gifted individuals, and those facets would, at times, war with each other, but this indicates more the "human condition" than the prominence of the fourth ray in the ray chart. In addition, Schweitzer was not an especially accommodating individual, nor particularly adept in the art of compromise. His intense love of harmony related principally to music, and later (and most profoundly) to global peace. Nor did he demonstrate the well–developed sense of color which is associated with the fourth ray. Even in European days, his clothing was austere, out–dated, and often ill–fitting. When the fourth ray is found prominently within the energy system, such lack of concern for dress and appearance is not usually found (especially, when the seventh ray is also present).

In one other *deeply subjective* respect, however, the fourth ray was present. As suggested, Schweitzer's life shows every evidence of that stage in evolution known as the "Great Renunciation," or, in more Christian terms, the "Crucifixion." Fourth ray energy is powerfully involved in this process, for there necessarily arises a conflict between the powerful and "gifted" personality, and the inner spiritual demand that all gifts be sacrificed to the Will of God. Interestingly, his Ascendant, Scorpio, is the constellation through which the fourth ray primarily reaches the earth, and so, in a profoundly subjective way, the fourth ray was potently active. This is a different matter, however, to the presence of the fourth ray in the ususal five–fold ray chart.

Proposed Ray Chart

```
            5
    II  1   6   L: 4
            3
```

Commentary

From all that has gone before it seems obvious that Albert Schweitzer, as a soul, emanated along the second ray line of love–wisdom. Both aspects of this ray energy were highly developed in his life. When an advanced individual becomes a world disciple (as Schweitzer undoubtedly was), it is the quality of his soul ray that shines forth. Schweitzer was known throughout the world as a great humanitarian, a healer, and a great moral force for peace. From the esoteric point of view, he is clearly upon the Path of the World Saviors, and has already made many strides. This incarnation was, in many respects, an archetypal second ray manifestation. Obviously, the weakness and timidity, so often found in the character of those upon this ray (and, indeed, found in Schweitzer's early years) had been totally transformed into positivity and assurance.

Similarly, the first Ray of Will and Power seems the proper choice for the ray of the personality. When contemplating his life (especially from the time he went to Lambaréné), one question which always comes to mind is, "How could any one individual accomplish so much under such adverse conditions?" Without the fortitude provided by the first ray, such accomplishment would have been impossible. The first ray, then, can be considered the sub-ray of the second ray soul. It was the ray chosen by the soul, prior to birth, in order to make possible an unusually arduous life-program.

As might be expected, there was an ongoing battle in Schweitzer's life between the beneficence of the second ray, and the harshness of the first. This is a powerful combination for good, but does present its definite problems. His "heart" brought him into the jungle, but without the power and daemonic energy of the first ray, his mission would never have survived, and his intended benevolence would have come to nothing. Of course, Schweitzer had his flaws of character, as do all human beings, and these were mostly along the first ray line: arrogance, temper, impatience, authoritarianism, stubbornness, wilfulness, dogmatism, and, quite simply, harsh behavior. From a study of esoteric psychology, we realize that the *personality* is the energy primarily (though not exclusively) responsible for the problems of character which thwart (or at least, complicate) the purposes of the soul. Schweitzer, was the great patriarch, the ruler. This was his first ray persona, hiding a painfully tender nature. This duality of energies is symbolically revealed in his photographs. The great mustache reinforces the image of rugged determination and elemental power, but it covers a mouth which is far softer and gentler than one might expect, and far more expressive of second ray quality.

The fifth ray seems the best choice for the mind. His was a gifted mind, of course, and at his stage of evolution, the quality of the soul definitely permeates the processes of the concrete mind, which would, therefore, be qualified by a blend of the fifth and second rays. Further, there would be a strong link between the lower mind and the abstract mind, which, generically, carries the quality of the third ray. But in light of his persistently clear and careful thinking, his love of research, and his patient, dogged methods of investigation, his uncompromising love of truth, his quiet and chiseled philosophical prose, his ability to understand the technicalities of many disciplines, and his ever-present interest in the natural and applied sciences, the fifth ray seems an inescapable choice. He gave far too much attention to detail for a first ray mind, and he was far too interested in accuracy to have a mind upon the fourth ray. Further, his writing was scholarly and factual, devoid of the colorful, picturesque and playful qualities so often found in connection with the fourth ray mental field. As for the possibility of the third ray mind, there was a simplicity, straightforwardness, common sense and clarity in his thought which are not usually found when the mind is upon the third ray. While he understood abstract thinking, and was at home pondering the great German philosophers (many of whom, like Kant, were strongly conditioned by the third ray), his approach to thinking, writing and speaking simply lacked the complexity and involved quality characteristically associated wtih the third ray mind.

Given the nature of his temper, and his furious outbursts, as well as the relentless pressure under which he chose to live, there can be little doubt that Albert Schweitzer's emotion field was qualified by the sixth ray. Except, perhaps, in his later years, he was *not* a serene individual. Often nervous, irascible, and intensely irritable, he experienced many difficult moods – hardly the calmness, serenity, and gentleness associated with the second ray astral nature. He was also a man of focused, one-pointed devotion to duty, driving himself and driving others forward to accomplishment. These, of course, are qualities conferred by the sixth ray emotional body. There was nothing restful in his emotional life (especially during his hours of work).

The physical nature – strong, broad-shouldered, robust, stocky, brimming with vitality and incessantly active – was almost certainly the third ray, and its strength was augmented by the influence of his first ray personality. It is hard to imagine a more active human being – on his feet from morning to night, whether during surgery, or making his rounds to the patients, or supervising laborers in the many building and maintenance projects which were consistently underway. This was a body which did not rest unless rest was forced upon it. It did not take *interludes* as the seventh ray body so often finds itself compelled to do. In 1944, at the age of 69, he was often seen *running* from one end of the hospital grounds to the other. He did this, he said, for exercise and in order to keep control (R1) of the far-flung operations of the hospital. Given the kind of punishment which his work (and his conscience!) demanded, the third ray body, hardy and adaptable, was indispensable. Again, there are astrological factors which added to its strength.

A small point, but worth mentioning, relates to the "untidiness" which became almost a point of honor with Schweitzer. As a youth, he realized when contemplating a great altarpiece in the Colmar Museum, that if the Beloved Disciple (represented as a typical German student of the period, with limp, unruly straw-colored hair) did not comb his hair, there was no need for him to worry about combing his either. He was never one to value *appearances,* nor did he ever change his casual approach to dress. He cared nothing for clothes which matched, or for the well-pressed look. It will be realized that this kind of attitude is much more characteristic of those with a third ray physical nature than of those with a seventh.

These energies, then: a second ray soul, a first ray personality, a fifth ray mind, a sixth ray astral body and a third ray etheric-physical body (plus numerous important astrological energies) gave Albert Schweitzer the qualities he needed to fulfill, in an exemplary manner, the redemptive purposes of his soul. So successful was he in carrying out these purposes, and so luminous was the example he set, that he appears today as a man of heroic proportions. But Schweitzer certainly did not regard himself as a hero – certainly not in the conventional sense. In a telling statement which reveals a great deal about the stage of his spiritual attainment, he writes:

There are no heroes of action. There are only heroes of resignation and suffering.

This is a uniquely second ray view, uttered by one who placed everything he had and everything he was upon the altar of sacrifice, the better to serve the Christ, and the Christ spirit within the human heart.

Note: The sources used for all direct quotations by or about Albert Schweitzer were: *The Three Worlds of Albert Schweitzer*, Robert Payne, Thomas Nelson and Sons, New York, Copyright 1957; and the *Encyclopedia Britannica*, fifteenth edition.

Albert Einstein

Born, March 14, 1879 – Died, April 18, 1955

The name Albert Einstein has become synonymous with genius. He is universally recognized as one of the most intelligent individuals who ever lived, and his achievements in the field of theoretical physics stand as incomparable testimony to the extraordinary potentials of the human mind. Einstein's revolutionary theories forever changed humanity's understanding of time, space and the universe. He performed a tremendous service in helping to shatter the world–illusion, based in large measure upon mental limitation and prejudice which masquerade as common sense. Without intending to, Einstein substantiated the reality of the ancient Kabbalistic principle which affirms that the apparently material universe is, in fact, densified light, congealed energy. If his contributions are examined impartially, it will be understood that he did more to advance the cause of *scientific occultism* than the many thousands of spiritually and religiously–inclined individuals who fancy themselves esotericists and occultists. Einstein penetrated into the "Mind of God" and returned with an understanding which for the first time allowed humanity to glimpse the physical universe a little more as God Himself perceives it.

Rays in Evidence

The Presence of Ray Three

Of all the rays which shine through Einstein's life and thought, the third ray – the "Ray of Higher Mind" (as the Tibetan calls it) – is the most prominent. More than other rays, the third ray seems to contain great extremes, as has been demonstrated through a discussion of the traits associated with types (3A) and (3B). Einstein most certainly was an example of type (3A), the commercial and materialistic aspects of the third ray being very foreign to him.

When considering the Tibetan's analysis of the third ray (found in *Esoteric Psychology, Vol. I*, pp. 204–205), one is struck by how many of the characteristics apply directly to Albert Einstein:

> **This is the ray of the abstract thinker, of the philosopher and the metaphysician, of the man who delights in the higher mathematics but who, unless modified by some practical ray, would hardly be troubled to keep his accounts accurately. His imaginative faculty will be highly developed, i.e., he can by the power of his imagination grasp the essence of a truth; his idealism will often be strong; he is a dreamer and a theorist, and from his wide views and great caution he sees every side of a question equally clearly.**
>
> **One type of this ray is unconventional to a degree. slovenly, unpunctual and idle, and regardless of appearances.**

Tapestry of the Gods

> The method of approaching the great Quest, for this ray type, is by deep thinking on philosophic or metaphysical lines till he is led to the realisation of the great Beyond and of the paramount importance of treading the Path that leads thither.

Even a little familiarity with Einstein's life will demonstrate the amazing aptness of these descriptions.

First let us examine the question of abstraction. During the past half-century Einstein's Special Theory of Relativity and General Theory of Relativity have been presented, explained and re-explained in hundreds of books. The concepts involved have become common currency among the intelligentsia, and even in the mass mind are, at least, familiar. How frequently we hear the words: "It's all relative!" All such explanations, however, are great simplifications of the original concepts; "relativity theory," in its pure form, is difficult to understand correctly and requires powers of abstract thinking beyond the ordinary. Certainly, the mathematics involved are esoteric, and well beyond the comprehension of all but a very few highly trained mathematicians and mathematical physicists. It is clear that, in order to grasp his revolutionary theoretical concepts, Einstein's consciousness had to soar into the higher reaches of the abstract mind (a feat accomplished most easily by those who are well-endowed with the third Ray of Active [and *Abstract*] Intelligence).

The average human intellect (conditioned generically by the fifth Ray of Concrete Knowledge – the ray of common sense) understands only with the greatest difficulty thoughts which are truly abstract. Einstein's conceptions were profoundly abstract, and they bewildered not only the layman, but many of those who were well-established in the scientific community. Even today, more than eighty years after the appearance of the articles proposing the Special Theory of Relativity, there are many in the more *concrete* and *applied* branches of the sciences for whom Einsteinian concepts apparently remain irrelevant and poorly understood at best (even though their veracity and importance have [by now] been proven repeatedly through numerous sophisticated experiments). Therefore, one can well understand how scientists steeped in Newtonian physics received these theories when they first appeared. The results of Einstein's lecture to a group of engineering professors (as described by Professor Hyman Levy, then a research student at the university) offers some idea of a reaction which was all too common:

> And here was this man talking in abstract terms about space-time and the geometry of space-time, not the geometry of a surface which you can think of as a physical surface, but the geometry of space-time, and the curvature of space-time; and showing how you could explain gravitation by the way in which a body moves in space-time along a geodesic – namely the shortest curve in space-time. This was all so abstract that it became unreal to them. I remember seeing one of the professors getting up and walking out in a rage, and as he went out I heard him say, "Das is absolut Blödsinn" (That is absolute nonsense).

Clearly, the possession of good, sound common sense was insufficient to comprehend thoughts which, in fact, defied common sense. The great experimentalist, Ernest Rutherford when told that no Anglo-Saxon could understand relativity responded in a revealing manner: "No. They have too much sense." Rutherford was a consummate experimentalist strongly conditioned by the fifth ray.

According to the Tibetan, the third ray man is a "dreamer and a theorist"; Einstein was indeed the dreamer and theorist. His mind was focussed far above the mundane sphere, which he considered almost an irrelevancy. He could be far more practical than is usually assumed (when he *had* to be), but so often he considered the ordinary details of life mere distractions. His attitude was profoundly meditative. Once he seized upon a productive line of thought he was unable to let it go, even if it meant standing in a snowstorm obliviously, scribbling calculations in a notebook, or impulsively covering his host's tablecloth with arcane mathematical formulae which had occurred to him during dinner. On a deep and intuitive level his pursuit of truth continued incessantly no matter what the task in which he might outwardly be engaged. Objective life was as a dream; the inner world of thought was his reality.

Einstein brought an intensely *theoretical* approach to scientific thinking. His method suggested that the best procedure might not be that of observation followed by the induction of general laws, but the totally different process of *postulating a theory* and then discovering whether or not the facts fitted it. The current understanding of facts was never to be considered a limitation upon theoretization; theory could justifiably range far beyond present facts (while still accounting for them), and point to entirely new collections of facts, as yet undiscovered. Thus, Einstein, worked as Djwhal Khul suggests all esotericists should work – from the general to the particular. He was far from being strictly a fifth ray empiricist; he was far more an intuitive, third ray generalist, reasoning his way from profound a priori assumptions to the realization of new facts which could be scientifically tested. For instance, Einstein's virtual proof of the existence of molecules, invisible to the human eye, postulated by theory rather than produced by experimental evidence, was symptomatic of the line which he was to take throughout his career. The Zionist leader Chaim Weitzman succinctly described two great men of science (and the difference between the two most mentally–inclined rays as well) when he said: "Einstein all calculation, Rutherford all experiment...." In Einstein's own words: "I concentrated on speculative theories, whereas Rutherford, managed to reach profound conclusions on the basis of almost primitive reflection combined with relatively simple experimental methods." Einstein believed that speculatively constructed theories into which facts were later seen to fit were more likely to stand the test of time than theories constructed entirely from experimental evidence.

It is well known in "ray theory" that, whereas the fifth ray approach to the discovery of truth is dependent upon observation (utilizing the senses or their instrumental extensions), the third ray procedure is very different. Advanced individuals upon the third ray (while not ignoring the testimony of the senses) are not dependent upon the senses for the discovery of truth. Truth, they believe, can be discovered through thought alone. Einstein was once quoted as saying, "The Lord God may be subtle, but he is not malicious." With this thought he expressed his faith that, subtle though the laws of nature might be, they were still understandable by the human reason. Einstein needed neither laboratory nor equipment for his work; pencil, paper (his ever–present pipe, of course) and the leisure to sail, stroll or play his violin, were all he required.

Einstein did, however, conduct experiments in his own manner; they were called *thought experiments* (possible in theory, but ruled out by experimental difficulties). He would, for instance, imaginatively ride upon a beam of light, visualizing, from numerous hypothetical frames of reference, the changes of mass, space and time which might occur at (or approaching) the ultimate velocity; he would imagine experiments at the minute scale of atoms and molecules, and visualize the probable inter-molecular and inter-atomic dynamics. So great was the range of his mind, so profound its penetration, and so abstruse the dimensions in which he customarily thought, that to think empirically and only in terms of available experimental data would have been an insuperable limitation upon his mental creativity. Through the modality of thought experiments, he was able to *play* with the "dimensions" of space and time, creating (through the use of his imagination) conditions presently impossible at the 'macro-level' of existence, and observe the results. The thought experiment is essentially a third ray modality designed to *manipulate* variables which cannot (as yet) possibly be experienced in the normal, brain-conditioned consciousness. While the fifth ray individual usually operates in a manner very dependent upon the brain, the third ray individual (so often "lost in thought") enters the contemplative stage of meditation, and experiences levels of reality which are unconditioned by brain awareness – levels of *pure, abstract thought*.

When considering whether or not the third ray conditioned the life and thought of Albert Einstein, it is important to realize how closely this ray is related to the divine principle of *Activity*, i.e., motion. The third ray is, indeed, called the "Ray of Activity," and much of Einstein's most provocative thought was given to elucidating the changes in "space-time" which could be expected to occur with changes in the rates of activity.

Heraclitus' statement, "There is nothing permanent except change," is peculiarly relativistic. In Einstein's world, space and time are in a constant state of change or flux relative to one another. Einstein's theories destroyed Newton's absolute space and absolute time, offering instead, an infinity of ever-changing "frames of reference" all moving relative to each other, each "frame" characterized by its own space-time dimensions. In short, in Einstein's universe, "everything is relative" – at least at the level of *physical* reality. He did not attempt to transfer the concepts of relativity to the field of values and spirituality.

Even when we temporarily set aside the profound scientific and mathematical foundations of relativity, and, instead, focus upon mundane experience, we soon realize that even those upon the third ray who are not mathematical geniuses are no strangers to relativistic conceptions. Average third ray people, too, tend to view a given situation "from all the angles," as it were. They have an ever-shifting perspective, and are among the least categorical, absolutist and dogmatic of the various ray types. As D.K. says of the third ray individual, "...he sees every side of question equally clearly." He is inclined to answer all questions from a relativistic perspective, and with that most *uncertain* of all responses – "It all depends." By this response, he means that his assessment of any situation (or set of variables) depends upon his frame of reference, his point of view, his angle of vision, all of which are perceived to be constantly changing. Interestingly, individuals upon the third ray, with their constant activity, fluidity, and mental mobility seem to have less trouble understanding (and imagining) Einstein's relativistic conceptions than those upon the other rays.

Another quality of those upon the third ray (especially type [3A]) is their love of philosophy. It is interesting that Einstein always considered himself more a philosopher than a scientist – an opinion shared by some of those who knew him best. His philosophical quest (epitomized by his never-ending aspiration to formulate a "Unified Field Theory") was to understand the physical cosmos as a whole – as a great, thoroughly integrated system. He revered the pantheistic philosopher Baruch Spinoza (who, like himself, was a Jew, and – from the perspective of the religious authorities – a heretic, just as Einstein had initially been considered a heretic by those for whom Newtonian physics had become, virtually, a religion). Einstein was what might be called a 'systemic thinker'; he thought in whole systems, and his 'variables' were the great "categories of thought" (space and time) which are so implicit in all normal mental processes that they are usually taken entirely for granted.

Einstein's early interest in philosophy (as well as in science and mathematics) was greatly stimulated by Max Talmey, a medical student and friend of the Einstein family. He visited the Einstein household every week, giving young Albert books to read and problems to solve. Einstein's progress was rapid, and his genius apparent even then. In Talmey's words:

> **After a short time, a few months, he had worked through the whole book of Spieker. He thereupon devoted himself to higher mathematics, studying all by himself Lubsen's excellent works on the subject....Soon the flights of his mathematical genius was so high that I could no longer follow. Thereafter philosophy was often a subject of our conversations. I recommended to him the reading of Kant. At that time he was still a child, only thirteen years old, yet Kant's works, incomprehensible to ordinary mortals, seemed to be clear to him. Kant became Albert's favorite philosopher after he had read through his** *Critique of Pure Reason* **and the works of other philosophers.**

Thus, we can see how, from the first, higher mathematics and philosophy (both of which are peculiarly third ray "lines of approach") were closely related interests in Einstein's life, and how he excelled in both. His love of Kant is noteworthy, for surely, Kant (one of the most 'difficult,' abstract and rigorously systematic of all philosophers) was a third ray soul.

Einstein was, of course, the quintessential, "absentminded professor," (found most frequently, as might be expected, upon the third ray). Many humorous stories (most of them at least partially true) have grown up around his proverbial forgetfulness. Actually, he was absentminded only about the things which did not matter to him (which included most of the mundane affairs of daily living). While he never forgot to think, he often forgot the key to his apartment, and found himself locked out even on his wedding night. This was typical. The many amusing anecdotes in circulation all portray a lively, well-meaning man, with his "head in the clouds," and his 'feet in the air,' passing through life's ordinary experiences as if through a dream. On one occasion Einstein accompanied by a friend, invited two guests to lunch, only to discover (at the end of the meal) that he had no money. The situation was saved only by sleight-of-hand when his friend passed him a 100-franc note under the table. As many third ray people are, Einstein was a great walker and talker. A story from his Princeton days tells of him becoming so enrapt in conversation on the way to a dinner party, that he forgot both the name and address of his host and had to go knocking on doors for reorientation. Those who knew him well agreed with the assessment that "in all practical things he [was] absolutely impractical."

Certainly, in keeping with the Tibetan's description of one of the third ray types, Einstein was unconventional and "regardless of appearances." He almost always dressed in a casual (often untidy) "bohemian" manner, detesting as an unnecessary waste of time all kinds of formality. The "well–pressed look" was completely foreign to him; as a matter of fact, he often preferred wrinkled clothing, even in public. His refusal in later life to wear socks was totally in keeping with his determination to simplify his life, by avoiding energy–wasting complications at all levels. His great shock of hair, uncombed and unruly, became his trademark – the symbol of a man who cared far more for what was going on *inside* his head than for the appearance of what was growing on top of it.

All external trivialities aside, however, the qualities which most impressively linked Einstein to the third ray (called "the acute energy of divine mental perception") was his determination to fathom God's thought. "I want to know how God created the world," he said, thus expressing his link to the Brahma, or *Creator* aspect of divinity. The third ray has a special relation to what has been called the "blueprint" of the Divine Plan, the 'working–drawings' according to which God the Creator ("The Great Architect of the Universe") executes his designs. In response to the Jewish philosopher and theologian Martin Buber, who pressed him hard on the matter of his faith, Einstein replied: "What we [and by this 'we' he meant 'we physicists'] strive for is just to draw His lines after Him. To draw after – as one retraces a geometrical figure." Could there be a better description of the quest to understand the 'blueprints' of the Divine Plan as prepared by "The Great Architect of the Universe" (one of the names of the Lord of the Third Ray). It is also fascinating, in light of Einstein's major contribution to scientific thought, to realize that two other names of the great Third Ray Lord are "The Dispenser of Time," and "The Lord of Space."

The Presence of Ray Two

As the Einstein myth gathered momentum, he became known as a philosopher–saint, one of the kindest and gentlest of men. There is much truth in this, even though it glosses over the directness and, even, harshness with which he could attack people and practices he considered foolish or dangerous.

Einstein was a man of goodwill. "How I wish," he said, "that somewhere there existed an island for those who are wise and of goodwill! In such a place even I should be an ardent patriot." Despite the great difficulties involved in understanding his concepts, he impressed almost everyone as a good–natured individual. The following assessment of Einstein's character by the physicist Louis de Broglie is characteristic:

> **I was particularly won over by his sweet disposition, by his general kindness, by his simplicity, and by his friendliness. Occasionally, gaiety would gain the upper hand and he would strike a more personal note and even disclose some detail of his day–to–day life. Then, again, reverting to his characteristic mood of reflection and meditation, he would launch into a profound and original discussion of a variety of scientific and other problems. I shall always remember the enchantment of all those meetings, from which I carried away an indelible impression of Einstein's great human qualities.**

The human and humane qualities of the second Ray of Love–Wisdom are plainly in evidence, and seem (here, at least) to occur at a more superficial level of Einstein's energy system than the profound qualities of the third ray, which are also indicated in the above description.

Mirth, jollity, good cheer, geniality, a gentle and easy–going nature, relaxation, friendliness, informality, the love of good company, flirtatiousness (in the early days) – all these were indications of Einstein's second ray energy, focussing, almost certainly, at the level of personality. Even as his reputation grew, he continued his modest and unassuming ways, always enlivened by a playful sense of humor. In most personal matters he was equable and serene, outwardly very personable, inwardly detached, as if seeing the panorama of life from a great distance. In such an attitude we see the blending of the third and second rays.

Those upon the second ray have a strong streak of openness and egalitarianism. They do not think in terms of status; the greatest and the least are the same in their eyes. Einstein was like that. He was popular as a lecturer and teacher because of his unconventional, unpretentious style, his humor, and because of his great love of his subject. He was also unquestionably sincere in his desire to make sure that his students understood what he was talking about, so he openly invited students to interrupt him at any time if there was any point they failed to understand. (Even outside of class, he was equally ready to interrupt his work at any moment in order to receive a students.) During lecture breaks he was constantly surrounded by those who had questions, and he unfailingly answered them in a patient and friendly manner. Once in the early days of his teaching experience he remarked, "Teaching gives me great pleasure, chiefly because I see that my boys really enjoy their work." As long as the topic of conversation was physics, mathematics or the exciting new ideas in which he was truly interested, Einstein could be very social and gregarious. He cultivated many casual friendships with students, inviting them to accompany him to cafés after class in order to continue their discussions. He was always happy explaining the excitements of physics. Certainly, this is behavior characteristic of the second ray.

Einstein was also a unifier, an internationalist (both characteristic of the inclusive second ray, not to mention Piscean energy). Before the First World War he cultivated the friendship of physicists in a number of European countries, and valued every opportunity to correspond with them or, better, get together with them to discuss the latest developments. He was consequently appalled at the effect which the War had upon the already established lines of scientific communication. To him, nationalism was stupid and unforgiveable – a great obstacle to the advancement of human knowledge. Although a resident of Germany, Einstein harbored no hostility towards Germany's enemies, and after the Armistice, did all he could to reestablish friendly and productive relations between all European scientists. This was not an easy task. German aggression had started the War, and, at its conclusion, there was great distaste among the Allies for everything German – even German science. But the validity of the Theory of Relativity had been substantiated by an English Scientist, Sir Arthur Eddington, in 1919, and there was no denying its supreme value and impact, even if its creator had been a German scientist. Einstein was, therefore, invited by men of science to England, France, Belgium, the United States, and other nations with which Germany had been at war. His kindness and irrepressible goodwill did much to overcome hostilities, and reestablish intellectual and cultural relations between former belligerents.

Those upon the second ray hate fighting. Fourth ray individuals are also peace makers, but they are both willing and inclined to engage in a period of conflict and combat prior to harmonization and reconciliation. Second ray individuals prefer to avoid conflict altogether. From the first, Einstein was a pacifist. Even as a child he had a great aversion to militarism. When he was four he was taken to see the Royal Guards parade through Munich in their splendid uniforms. While most boys at that time dreamed of becoming soldiers, Einstein wept at the sight of grown men who were forced to wear ridiculous clothes and march in unison. As he grew, he cultivated a deep distaste for the "Prussian mentality" – rigidly disciplined, narrow, mechanical and aggressive. He even renounced his German citizenship in an effort to escape from the harsh repressiveness he perceived in the German character, especially as it manifested through the school systems. Thus, by the time Einstein was a mature individual, he was an avowed pacifist. He viewed the Biblical commandment, "Thou shalt not kill" as an injunction against all war. It was his firm opinion that, "He who cherishes the values of culture cannot fail to be a pacifist." Repudiating all fighting as cruel, stupid and barbaric, Einstein maintained his pacifistic stance even at considerable danger to himself. During the First World War (though technically a Swiss citizen) he carried on his functions as a university professor in Berlin. While so many of his scientific colleagues were swept up in the fervor of German nationalism, he worked openly for peace, secretly hoping for an Allied victory. He refused to sign the misguided Manifesto to the Civilized World, by means of which nearly one hundred German intellectuals attempted to justify Germany's aggressiveness, and instead, signed (with only one or two others) the unpopular Manifesto to the Europeans denouncing nationalism, and calling for an end to the war, and for the creation of a united Europe. Following the war, it was his reputation as a man of peace which allowed him to be such an ambassador of goodwill in a world which despised Germany.

Ironically, some years later, when he realized the extent of the Nazi threat, he abandoned pacifism, and dedicated himself, passionately, to the defeat of Germany. It was Einstein's letter, after all, which had alerted Franklin Roosevelt to the danger that Germany might be capable of building an atomic bomb; thus, a man committed entirely to peace found himself largely responsible for encouraging the government of the United States to create the most devastating weapon ever known. It must here be remembered, however, that the Tibetan (a second ray Master and certainly a Man of peace) has informed us that even the Spiritual Hierarchy of the planet was forced to "take sides" in the extraordinary conflict between the Forces of Light and darkness which manifested outwardly as the Second World War. During that conflict the Tibetan was anything but a pacifist, and let it clearly be known that uncompromising, idealistic pacifism was obstructing the Forces of Light. Einstein had his own version of this attitude. During the war he wrote to a conscientious objector saying that he had given up pacifism since he could maintain it only at the risk of allowing the whole world to fall into the hands of the most terrible enemies of mankind. Later he wrote, in reply to the Japanese journal *Kaizo* which had reproached him for involvement with nuclear weapons: "While I am a convinced pacifist there are circumstances in which I believe the use of force is appropriate – namely, in the face of an enemy unconditionally bent on destroying me and my people."

Carrying the theme of unification beyond Einstein's normal, daily activities and worldly thoughts, we discover that it related to what was probably the deepest motive of his life – the construction of a field theory uniting the forces of electromagnetism and gravity. Einstein gave an interview to the *Daily Chronicle* in which he explained in simple, nonmathematical terms, the nature and purpose of his Unified Field Theory:

> **For years it has been my greatest ambition to resolve the duality of natural laws into unity. This duality lies in the fact that physicists have hitherto been compelled to postulate two sets of laws – those which control gravitation and those which control the phenomena of electricity and of magnetism....Many physicists have suspected that two sets of laws must be based upon one general law, but neither experiment nor theory has, until now, succeeded in formulating this law. I believe now that I have found a proper form....The relativity theory reduced to one formula all laws which govern space, time and gravitation, and thus corresponded to the demand for simplification of our physical concepts. The purpose of my work is to further this simplification, and particularly to reduce to one formula the explanation of the field of gravity and of the field of electromagnetism. For this reason I call it a contribution to 'a unified field theory.'...Now, but only now, we know that the force which moves electrons in their ellipses about the nuclei of atoms is the same force which moves our earth in its annual course about the sun, and is the same force which brings to us the rays of light and heat which makes life possible upon this planet.**

When we hear Einstein speak in this way, one can only think of the second Ray of Love–Wisdom and the fourth Ray of Harmony Through Conflict (which can be considered an aspect of the second ray, as the souls of those upon the fourth ray resolve into second ray souls). (Perhaps, Monads upon the fourth ray [and, according to the Tibetan, such do exist] also resolve into second ray Monads.) The aspect of the Divine Will characteristic of the second ray is "The Will to Unify." The Word of Power for souls upon the fourth ray is "Two Merge with One." These phrases certainly suggest the deep underlying purpose of Einstein's pursuit of a Unified Field Theory, and further suggest that it would be reasonable to consider such a theory as an aspect of the great cosmic Law of Attraction, the second cosmic law, related to the second aspect (the love aspect) of divinity. The last sentence in Einstein's quotation above may be seen as even more closely related to the great Law of Attraction when we remember that the Tibetan has called love the great motive force behind creation and evolution. A single phrase from Dante's *Divine Commedy* makes this clear: "The Love which moves the sun and the other stars."

A final word is in order regarding the presence of the second ray; it focuses upon Einstein's fascination with *light*. He knew that although he had formulated certain laws which revealed a profound and unsuspected relationship between light and matter, he understood light hardly at all. If he had had more time, he would have bent his considerable mental/intuitive powers to its understanding. Significantly, it is the second ray which is most associated with the phenomenon of light, as the second ray word of power – "I See the Greatest Light" suggests. Very possibly the second ray was placed not only on the personality level, but in a far more profound position in Einstein's energy system.

The Presence of the Fifth Ray

Most people consider Einstein the greatest scientist who ever lived and, so, immediately associate him with the fifth ray. While it is true that he must have possessed within his energy system (whether as an aspect of his ray chart, or as a 'legacy' from the past) a good deal of the fifth ray energy, there was perhaps less of it than at first might seem obvious. At least, other rays were more central to his most important pursuits. We will consider a few examples which seem to suggest the presence of the fifth ray, reserving for the section in which Einstein's ray chart will be proposed a discussion of whether, and in what manner, the fifth ray should be included.

In attempting to dispatch the question of hereditary talent, Einstein, with characteristic modesty, stated, "I have no particular talent. I am merely extremely inquisitive." We recognize inquisitiveness as a classical fifth ray trait (though, to a certain extent, it pertains to the third ray as well). When discussing the fifth ray mind in *Esoteric Psychology, Vol. II*, p. 293, the Tibetan lists among its characteristics: "The tendency to enquire, to ask questions and to find out. This is the instinct to search and to progress, which is, in the last analysis, the urge to evolve." Once again, there is a similarity between the fifth and third rays, as the third ray is associated with the "will to evolve," "the power to evolve," and is considered "the cause of evolutionary growth." Whatever the source, Einstein's inquisitiveness never abated; he never ceased to pose the most profound and searching questions to himself, and to seek the answers in the depths of his consciousness.

His extremely unpleasant educational experience at the Luitpold Gymnasium taught him the virtues of skepticism, a quality particularly related to the fifth ray. He questioned all forms of authority and determined to learn the truth for himself. His youthful religiosity, which began with a study of the Proverbs of Solomon and the Talmud at the age of ten, came to an abrupt end at age twelve when, through the reading of popular scientific books, he became convinced that the stories in the Bible could not possibly be true. Under the influence of Max Talmey, he absorbed much scientific understanding, reading particularly in the physical sciences. It would seem that a certain amount of fifth ray energy would be required for him to absorb the physical sciences as rapidly as he did. Interestingly, in ordinary mathematics, Einstein was not an especially good calculator, always requiring more time to think (suggesting the third ray), though he was patient, persistent and gifted in problem solving. He had a great fascination for numbers, and seemed rather disconcerted that the biological sciences could not be expressed in mathematical formulae. He could not understand why the Creator had produced things which could not be quantified. Beause of his love of quantification, he focused upon the physical sciences, and by the time he was only sixteen, he was tackling one of the most hotly disputed of scientific subjects, the relationship between electricity, magnetism and the ether. Surely, a certain amount of fifth ray energy was required for this daunting task.

In his later teens Einstein prepared himself to become a teacher of mathematical physics. He attended the ETH, the Swiss Federal Polytechnic School. The four year program was rigorous – differential and integral calculus, descriptive and analytical geometry, the geometry of numbers, and the theory of the definite integral. He naturally studied physics, as well as astrophysics and astronomy. To courses such as gnomic projection and exterior ballistics, he added various philosophical, geological and business courses. From a consideration of these course titles, it is clear how valuable would be the possession of a prominent fifth ray.

As further confirmation of the presence of the fifth ray, we find Einstein drawn to the natural sciences. Quite in contrast to the time when he would point to his head as his laboratory and his fountain pen as his working tools, he spent most of his time in a physical laboratory, fascinated by direct contact with experience. Later, when the scope of his work far transcended the scientific revelations of the day, he would never cease to emphasize that his theories (far from being mystical) were entirely based upon *observed or observable facts*. Those who consider Einstein simply a theoretician rather than an empiricist will be interested in his early empirical efforts. According to a biography written by one of his step-sons:

> **He wanted to construct an apparatus which would accurately measure the earth's movement against the ether....He wanted to proceed quite empirically, to suit his scientific feelings of the time, and believed that an apparatus such as he sought would lead him to the solution of a problem of far-reaching perspectives which he already sensed. But there was no chance to build this apparatus. The skepticism of his teachers was too great, the spirit of enterprise too small.**

Einstein's work as a civil servant in the Patent Office in the Swiss city of Berne was very 'concrete' when compared to the abstract nature of the speculations in which he consistently indulged. It was a task calling for considerable technical skill. His position, at least initially, called for a critical reading of technical specifications and an understanding of the drawings which went with them. This work was an excellent training in observation and analysis, and required that he put into intelligible German the specifications for typewriters and cameras, engineering devices, and a great number of unusual appliances for which inventors wished to claim legal protection. According to Einstein, the experience was extremely valuable: "It taught me to express myself correctly." Einstein was good at his work, and learned to handle very difficult patent applications with the greatest success. His expertise was highly valued in the office. Nothing could be more *concrete* than this type of work, nor more unlike theoretical physics. Again, it was work closely related to the fifth ray rather than the third.

Einstein's scientific work was diverse, and at first had little to do with the theory of relativity upon which his fame rests. His first papers concerned the nature of forces which hold together the molecules of a liquid. "My major aim....," he wrote, " was to find facts which would guarantee as much as possible the existence of atoms of definite finite size." Einstein's paper, "On the Motion of Small Particles Suspended in a Stationary Liquid According to the Molecular Kinetic Theory of Induction," was, in fact, a successful attempt to quantify Brownian motion. Such feats of thought certainly required the presence in his ray makeup of the fifth Ray of Concrete Knowledge and Science.

From another perspective, the fifth ray may well have been the cause of Einstein's utter truthfulness and lucidity. During his lectures, students found him precise and clear. Although he rarely used notes, he never foundered as even the best extemporaneous lecturers can. Madame Curie, assessing Einstein after a physics convention to which they were both invited, "appreciated the clearness of his mind, the shrewdness with which he marshalled his facts, and the depth of his knowledge." This evaluation, coming from one richly endowed with the fifth ray, seems to point to its presence in Einstein's energy system. Doubts concerning the presence of the fifth ray stem not so much from his inability to function using the fifth ray, as from the fact that his greatest feats of intellect and intuition far transcended its use, focussed as he was far *above* the level of the concrete mind.

The Presence of the First Ray

It is most interesting to consider the presence of the first ray in Albert Einstein's energy system. The Einstein myth contains very little of it. He is seen, primarily, as the 'genius–saint,' but it must be remembered that he was also the iconoclastic thinker who *destroyed* the illusion of the absolute adequacy and accuracy of Newtonian physics. The destructive impact of Einstein's thought was truly incredible. This may well be due to the presence of Uranus as a singleton planet in (or in the immediate vicinity of) the third house of his horoscope – the third house symbolizing the lower, concrete mind, and the world of common sense. The presence of Mercury in the Martian sign Aries, and the Moon in the outspoken sign Sagittarius, must also have contributed to the forcefulness of his ideas, and to his insistence upon speaking his mind.

So much myth surrounds Einstein's schooling that it is difficult to separate fact from fiction. Several of his teachers thought him dull-witted and destined to amount to nothing. As we know, the reverse was magnificently the case, so it is not surprising to discover that a number of teachers were threatened merely by Einstein's presence in class. One such told him, "Your presence in class is disruptive and affects the other students." Another instructor informed him, "You're a clever fellow! But you have one fault. You won't let anyone tell you a thing." Einstein was, in fact, extremely independent, a dissenting (Uranian) spirit. One of his classmates, Hans Byland, described Einstein as an "impudent Swabaian whose original nobility distinguished him from all the others." According to Byland, Einstein was "sure of himself," a "restless spirit," "unhampered by convention," and the "sarcastic curl of his rather full mouth with the protruding lower lip did not encourage the Philistines to fraternize with him." Einstein gave the impression of being a "laughing philosopher" whose "witty mockery pitilessly lashed any conceit or pose," – one who "made no bones about voicing his personal opinions whether they offended or not." All this seems to carry the note of the first ray, one would think at the level of mind (though other explanations will be entertained). Einstein himself recalled that he had been "untidy and a daydreamer...aloof and discontented, not very popular," clearly a person who made no concessions to tact. As a young man, he did things quite as he pleased. He had an innate defiance of tradition and authority, and (fortunately for the world) the courage of his convictions, otherwise he might never have had the temerity to come forward with theories which flew so brazenly in the face of established knowledge, shaking the scientific world.

The first ray is also the influence which inclines the individual to search for the "big picture" and ignore, somewhat, the details. The following statement tends to affirm the first and third rays, and deemphasize the fifth:

> I'm not much with people, and I'm not a family man. I want my peace. I want to know how God created this world. I am not interested in this or that phenomenon, in the spectrum of this or that element. I want to know His thoughts, the rest are details.

For Einstein, it was not the small things which really mattered. He searched for the broad and basic themes of creation.

Those strongly influenced by the first ray search for *principles* rather than specifics. Einstein was not overconcerned with specific experiments or even with philosophy; he had a grander purpose – to penetrate the fog and discern more clearly the principles upon which the material world had been built. He did not write voluminously. His papers were all comparatively short (first ray brevity?), and all contained the *foundations* or basic principles of new theories, even though they did not elaborate upon them. The physicist Louis de Broglie describes these first papers as "blazing rockets which in the dark of the night suddenly cast a brief but powerful illumination over an immense unknown region." The terminology almost suggests the "electric fire" of the first ray. Einstein explained his approach to science to a friend:

> For me, interest in science is restricted to the study of principles, and this offers the best explanation of my work. That I have published so few papers derives from the same circumstance: a consequence of my ardent desire to understand the principles is that much of my time has been spent in fruitless efforts.

There was an almost desperate, relentless search for these foundational principles; Einstein simply had to put first things first, ruthlessly eliminating routine or mundane matters which could get in his way.

Einstein always felt that even the most abstruse concepts in theoretic physics could be explained clearly and simply to the layperson. Many have complicated the explanations of the theory of relativity. "Since the mathematicians have attacked the relativity theory," mused Einstein, "I myself no longer understand it any more." Indeed, compared to the attempts of others, Einstein's explanations had a breath-taking simplicity. One may attribute this, perhaps, to the lucidity of the fifth ray or the unadorned simplicity of the first. Certainly simplifying the understanding of natural law was one of Einstein's greatest purposes, as was clear from his explanation of his unified field theory, quoted earlier.

The quest for simplicity was absolutely foundational to Einstein's scientific outlook. "A theory," he wrote, " is the more impressive the greater the simplicity of its premises, the more different kinds of things it relates, and the more extended its area of applicability." When Einstein formulated a theory, it was intended to explain one of the major blueprints of nature. The principles and bold outlines were all-important; the details could be filled in later.

Once Einstein had discovered a principle, or determined its inner necessity, he did not relinquish it easily. He determined that the veracity of the Theory of Relativity could be proven by experiment. According to the theory, light was ponderable, and should be subject to gravitation. The theory could be tested, he said, by observing (during a solar eclipse) whether starlight passing close to the sun was displaced (or bent) by the sun's gravitational field. Einstein stated that the Theory of Relativity would stand or fall by experimental results. Of course, the results proved conclusively that the theory was correct; light was displaced almost exactly to the extent Einstein predicted. In this respect it might appear that he was functioning very much as a scientist upon the fifth ray might be expected to. However, even if the experiment had failed, Einstein would *not* have relinquished his inner assurance regarding the correctness of relativity theory. Writing his friend Besso well before the measurements were made he declared, "Now I am fully satisfied, and I no longer doubt the correctness of the whole system, whether the observation of the eclipse succeeds or not. The sense of the thing is too evident." Clearly, Einstein was prepared to hold firmly to his conceptions, trusting his intuition whether or not the evidence supported it. Fortunately for all involved, it did. This firm adherence to an intuitively derived principle suggests the presence of the first ray.

The Presence of Ray Four

The fourth ray plays an interesting though secondary role in Einstein's life. It served, in many respects, as his psychological "safety valve" when the pressures of abstract thought became too burdensome.

Einstein loved music passionately. As a boy, he wrote and set to music songs praising God, which he performed at home or in the street. He began studying the violin when he was six, and learned to play with skill and grace. At first, however, he learned by rote rather than inspiration, and seven years passed before he was aroused by Mozart into an awareness of the mathematical structure of music. His technique improved without systematic practice (note the absence of the seventh ray); he merely attempted to reproduce the beauty he sensed. "I believe," he said, "that love is a better teacher than sense of duty – with me, at least, it certainly was." For many years he carried his violin with him wherever he went, playing for his own satisfaction alone or with friends, and, on occasion, performing for the public. It is easy to see how, to many eyes, he appeared more the artist/philosopher than the scientist, or at least, "an artist in science." He also learned early in life to improvise at the piano – something he continued to do well into old age, even after he put his violin aside.

The fourth ray also emerged in others ways. Although (responding, no doubt to his Sun Sign, Pisces, and his Ascendant, Cancer) he was a solitary and dreamy child who preferred to play alone, he would on occasion join in the activities of other children, but chiefly as an arbiter or peacemaker who mediated their quarrels. He retained both his love of peace and his belief in mediation throughout his life; he demonstrated them much later when he became involved in the Zionist cause, and the settlement of Palestine. Even then Palestine was a troubled land, with the native Arabs strongly resisting what they saw was the encroachment of the Jewish settlers. Einstein was consistently anxious to conciliate the Arabs, whatever provocation they might offer. This arose partially out of his innate love of harmony, and partly out of his belief in the moral value of "turning the other cheek."

Einstein was also a man of many contradictions – droll, unpredictable, pranksterish, with a quirky sense of humor. He would occasionally engage in bizarre, clownish behavior, for his own amusement and the delight of others, and he loved surprises. All of these traits suggest the presence of ray four.

He also had a love of simile and metaphor. At an early age he learned the value of simple, homely analogies, and never tired of using them to explain the more abstruse aspects of relativity theory to those who could not possibly follow the mathematics. He was, for instance, fond of comparing the birth of new ideas to a chicken laying an egg: "Cheep – suddenly there it is!"

Einstein could hardly be called a poet in the usual sense of the word, but he did like to compose little verses, often with a humorous twist, but sometimes for serious occasions. On the occasion of a dinner with President and Mrs. Roosevelt in the White House he composed a little poem – eight lines of doggerel – which he wrote before leaving Washington.

The German original and the English translation are as follows:

In der Hauptstadt stolzer Pracht
Wo das Schicksal wird gemacht
Kämpfet froh ein stolzer Mann
Der die Lösung schaffen kann
Beim Gespräche gestern Nacht
Herzlich Ihrer wird gedacht
Was berichtet werden muss Darum sende ich diesen Gruss.

In the Capital's proud magnificence
Where destiny is made
Cheerfully fights a proud man
Who can provide the solution
In our conversation of last night
There were cordial thoughts of you
Which must be spoken
So I send this greeting

There is nothing profound about this little poem, and most of Einstein's poems were written in a similar manner. But the poem does illustrate a deeply ingrained style of expression, associated, it would seem, with the fourth ray, considered as a legacy ray.

The fourth ray, however, may be more deeply ingrained in Einstein's nature than in the personal almost superficial ways thus far mentioned. Einstein, in a response to a Rabbi enquiring about his faith, asserted that he believed "in Spinoza's God who reveals himself in the harmony of all that exists...." Further, asked how he had arrived at the theory of relativity, he "replied that he had discovered it because he was so firmly convinced of the harmony of the universe." Then, there are also reports that Einstein felt that the secret of a Unified Field Theory could be discovered through music. If this is so, his life–long love of the violin and piano take on added scientific significance. Someone as deeply imbued with both an understanding of cosmos and of music must surely have devised his own conception of "the music of the spheres." For Einstein, music and cosmos were inseparably linked as we discover from his unreserved praise of the work of Neils Bohr. Speaking of the situation in physics which prevailed before Bohr's discovery, Einstein said:

> **That this insecure and contradictory foundation was sufficient to enable a man of Bohr's unique instinct and tact to discover the major laws of the spectral lines and of the electron shells of the atoms together with their significance of chemistry, appeared to me like a miracle – and appears to me as a miracle even today.** *This is the highest form of musicality in the sphere of thought.* **(emphasis MDR)**

So there are, perhaps, unsuspected depths to the presence of the fourth ray within Einstein's makeup. We shall explore these presently.

The Presence of Ray Six

While the sixth ray was probably not prominent in Einstein's ray chart (very likely conditioning only the astral body), it was certainly prominent in his horoscope. His Cancerian Ascendant is esoterically ruled by Neptune (sixth ray) as is his Sun Sign, Pisces (when considered from the spiritual perspective). Further, his Moon is placed in the sign Sagittarius; the Moon has much to do with emotional responsiveness, and on the Tabulation of Creative Hierarchies to be found in *Esoteric Astrology*, p. 35, Sagittarius is correlated with those lives which animate the sixth or astral plane, closely correlated with the sixth ray. All of this prompted in Einstein a strong sense of idealism.

Einstein was passionate. He played music passionately; he was passionately committed to pacifism; his feelings for Jewish culture were deep and intense, and (once Hitler rose to power) Einstein's anti–Germanism was emotionally obsessive, with traces of paranoia. While Einstein had achieved equanimity, objectivity and a lofty philosophical perspective in so many respects, his hatred of what Germany had become was positively visceral.

Einstein was among the most idealistic of men – naïve and gullible some would say. Once he achieved fame, he lent his name (often foolishly) to any variety of 'good causes' which came to his attention. His great ideals (at various times in his life) were socialism, internationalism, pacifism and Zionism. During the First World War, he met with the great novelist and pacifist, Romain Rolland. During their discussions Einstein (with his repugnance for the German character) displayed an intensity of feeling which shocked Rolland. Where pacifism was concerned, Einstein's idealism was white hot (later to be tempered by his understanding of the inescapable realities of rampant evil).

From the early 1920's until his death, Einstein became an ardent Zionist. While he did not share the political aspirations of many more materially–minded Zionists, he was thoroughly committed to a renaissance of Jewish culture in Palestine. He gave freely of his time, and participated with Chaim Weitzman (the leading proponent of the Zionist movement), in numerous fund raising tours, dinners and other activities. Einstein was especially interested in the establishment of the Hebrew University in Jerusalem.

Einstein's idealism remained powerful even in the last few years of his life, which saw the rise and fall of McCarthyism in the United States. Long suspected of communism by McCarthy and his crew, Einstein courageously defied them all, outspokenly calling for civil disobedience of the Gandhian type, and openly advising a number of those who were called before the McCarthy investigation, allowing them to invoke his name in their defense whenever necessary. Einstein lent the full force of his thought and reputation to protect the artists, scientists, educators, entertainers and disseminators of news and information who came under attack because they were moulders of public opinion. He considered it his duty to stir the conscience of the public, and he did.

Proposed Ray Chart

TWO/FOUR $T_{Buddhic}$ III_1 2 $\begin{matrix}5\\6\\3\end{matrix}$ L: 4

This rather complicated formula is, of course, speculative. It proposes a Monadic ray, a point of polarization within the Spiritual Triad (T), a sub–Ashram within the great third ray Ashram, as well as the usual complement of five ray energies (soul, personality, mind, emotions and etheric–physical. The major purpose of proposing a ray formula of this type is to provoke thought rather than to offer a definitive description of Einstein's rays. The Tibetan has only hinted at the effect of ray energies on the level of soul and above, but in the case of an advanced individual, the Monadic ray, the polarization within the Spiritual Triad, and the "dual ray of the soul" (*Esoteric Psychology, Vol. II*, p. 18) will inevitably be important.

It seems clear that Albert Einstein was a third ray soul. His ability to think abstractly was virtually unparalleled in the field of theoretical physics. His consciousness was focussed primarily within the realm of the higher mind, and it was there that his most creative work was accomplished. Preoccupied as he was with the great concepts and relationships to be found within the "Mind of God," he had some difficulty 'touching down,' and gave the impression of one disengaged and 'abstracted' from the normal preoccupations of life. The power of the sign Pisces, related as it is to the planet Neptune, contributed to this "dreamy" impression. Einstein's greatest contribution – his soul purpose, one might say – was to wrest certain great formulae from the Mind of God (accessed through the higher levels of the manasic plane), and to present such formulae to humanity so that it might align its consciousness more properly with divine understanding.

Humanity has always suffered (and still suffers) from the "Great Illusion." This Illusion is inherent in the limitations of the concrete mind, the consciousness of which is bounded and distorted by the limitations of the brain and the five senses. The senses themselves, though utterly necessary and useful, act as veils upon reality. Einstein, whose assaults against sense–conditioned mind (i.e., common sense) aroused both intense admiration and intense hostility, played a significant role in the lengthy process of shattering that Illusion, and thus in providing humanity with a truer world view. In this respect he was a philosopher leading human beings closer to a correct understanding of the cosmos and their place within it. His gift to humanity was the revelation of a truer understanding of God's physical creation – the physical cosmos.

The second ray qualities in Einstein's make-up were so strong that many have considered him a second ray soul. The second ray, however, seems far better placed within the personality, and explains his innate kindness, good humor, gentleness, congeniality, his relaxed informality, as well as his serenity and equanimity. Einstein's *essential pursuits* were entirely too mental and abstract to emanate from a second ray soul, and as he himself said, "I'm not much with people." In one way, he did care for people, and certainly he cared for humanity en masse, but working closely and intimately with people and their problems (which the second ray soul is inclined to do) was not his approach. When searching for the soul ray, one must determine the *essential animating motive* which, in Einstein's case, was not to teach, nurture, guide, save, heal, study, etc. His inner work was not directly related to the Department of Religion (that Department of Hierarchy over which the Christ specifically presides). As a worker within the Mind of God, his efforts were far more closely related to the Department of the Mahachohan, Who works more with manas than with buddhi or atma. It may well be that the second ray is indeed the most profound ray within Einstein's energy system, and this we will discuss presently, but when looking for the soul ray, one must not look *too deep*. The soul ray refers to man as an *individual* –a spiritual or spiritualized individual, of course, but an individual nonetheless. The soul ray determines the orientation of the spiritualized human being as he works out his destiny in the three worlds of human evolution. The soul ray does not determine man's work as a superhuman entity, one who has released himself from the planes of outer manifestation. It is far more likely that the Monadic ray is related to such inner work. Once the causal body is destroyed, a human being is no longer obliged to 'return' to the sphere of physical manifestation, and does so, if at all, only by choice and for service purposes. The Monadic ray, while detectable to the eye of the Master even in early stages of evolution, only gains in power and prominence after the third initiation, and cannot be considered the primary conditioning ray until after the fourth initiation. Only at the fifth initiation does it truly reign supreme. By that time, the entity is no longer, *strictly speaking*, a human being, and is, instead, a member of the fifth kingdom of nature. Though the entity may have a vehicle of manifestation upon the physical plane (i.e., a physical body), the majority of work is *inner* work. This is all by way of saying that the Monadic ray is, in comparison with the soul ray, *remote,* and that its effects within the three worlds of human evolution (and especially upon the physical plane) are far less noticeable than the effects of the soul ray. When influenced principally by the soul ray, the individual is still very 'human.' At that point in evolution where the Monadic ray conditions the entity most powerfully, the strictly human stage has been transcended.

Thus far, we are proposing that Einstein was a third ray soul with a second ray personality. Amazed by the enthusiastic and affectionate welcome he received wherever he went, Einstein once asked the question, "Why is it nobody understands me, and everybody likes me?" The proposed ray structure – a third ray soul and second ray personality – answers the question.

Let us quickly dispense with the rays of the emotional and physical vehicles before we enter more difficult areas. Everything points to a sixth ray emotional body, gradually being transformed into a second ray vehicle. Einstein was a fervent idealist. His Ascendant is in the emotional sign Cancer, and is ruled exoterically by the 'watery'

Moon which is placed in the 'fiery' sign Sagittarius (closely related to the sixth ray). All things being equal, this would be a "signature" pointing to a sixth ray astral nature. Perhaps when most identified with the abstracting power of his third ray soul, Einstein could achieve that emotional equanimity characteristic of the second ray emotional vehicle. Certainly, in his later years he was able to look on at the foibles of the human race more tranquilly, but he never lost his interest in supporting idealistic causes. At various times in his life that idealism, reputedly, burned white hot. There were also certain causes and circumstances which aroused in him an intense emotionality – pacificism was one, and Zionism another. His feelings regarding Hitler and Hitler's Germany were also extremely turbulent. If hate (an emotional attitude more readily associated with the sixth ray than with the second) could affect someone of Einstein's spiritual calibre, it did so only in this one area of his life.

When considering the transformation of the astral nature from the sixth to the second ray, it must be realized that the transformation does not occur suddenly, and that there will be certain moments when the astral nature is more influenced by the sixth ray, and other moments when the second ray is predominant. The soul (no matter what the ray upon which it may be found) is *love,* and when its influence pervades the personality, the emotional nature is swept by the energy of love.

The physical body and brain are almost certainly upon the third ray. Few people were less inclined to respect physical plane order. Einstein was careless in every way regarding appearance and mundane details; they simply meant nothing to him. The physical body always needed disciplining, which is rarely the case when it is qualified by the seventh ray. Janos Plesch, a friend of Einstein's and a medical doctor, summed up Einstein's approach to physical plane living in a way which should leave little doubt about the presence of ray three and the absence of ray seven:

> As his mind knows no limits, so his body follows no set of rules; he sleeps until he is wakened; he stays awake until he is told to go to bed; he will go hungry until he is given something to eat; and then he eats until he is stopped.

Nothing could be clearer. Additionally, Einstein possessed the body type usually associated with the third ray, robust and active.

When we reach the area of the mind there is some ambiguity. There is no doubt that Einstein was extremely involved in scientific and mathematical technicalities, and that he mastered them with ease. Everyone speaks of the lucidity of his mind, and the clarity of his presentations. He had a unique ability to explain abstractions in a very concrete manner. On the surface it would seem that the only possible choice for the mental ray would be the fifth Ray of Science and Concrete Knowledge, as proposed. But there are other qualities to his thought process which are very unlike the fifth ray mind, and must be mentioned.

Einstein was always ready to agree that imagination and intuition (the stuff of artistry rather than science) played a serious role in his work. Responding again to Janos Plesch, who commented upon the close relation between mathematics and fiction, both of which shared the characteristic of 'inventing' realities, Einstein replied:

Tapestry of the Gods

> **There may be something in what you say. When I examine myself and my methods of thought I come to the conclusion that the gift of fantasy has meant more to me than my talent for absorbing positive knowledge.**

Here, Einstein seems to be speaking for the primacy of the intuitive first or fourth rays over the more linear, detailed fifth ray. We know that the fifth ray, when it qualifies the concrete mental vehicle, is not especially visual, imaginative or intuitive – certainly not especially artistic. And we also recall Einstein's determination to focus upon principles rather than the details of science – details which the fifth ray mind would wish to entertain. We realize, as well, that Einstein always sought to "see the picture whole," and had an incredibly *synthetic* mental capacity. Nor was he especially empirical, even though he insisted that his theories were devised to account for observable facts. It seems clear that although he could function well within the usual domain of the fifth ray, it served a secondary rather than a primary function (a situation very different from that of the great empiricist, Ernest Rutherford).

We must also consider Einstein's strong tendency to be outspoken, and to hold firmly to his opinions even in the face of conflicting evidence. His thought had a decidedly intrusive and disruptive character. It was not simply that he added facts and evidence to the store of knowledge, as the fifth ray mind can be expected to do; rather he assailed the existing scientific situation by proposing new and revolutionary principles. This is the way the first ray mind functions.

Thus, there are a number of difficult questions to be answered, and several possible ways of resolving the uncertainties. The most likely solution, it would seem, would assign the fifth ray to the lower mental vehicle (for certainly Einstein, in the earlier part of his life, was heavily involved in all manner of scientific and mechanical technicalities which could only be easily handled by the fifth ray). Early evidences of the first ray might be attributable to Mercury in Aries, the Moon in Sagittarius (often blunt in its truthful response), and most importantly, to the singleton planet Uranus focused in the area of the astrological chart correlated with lower mind. Uranus is the great disrupter and reorganizer. Uranus is also (from the highest point of view) definitely a first ray planet; an individual with a high focus Uranus will always challenge the status quo.

While it can in no way yet be proven, it may be that *certain astrological positions account for the subrays to be found within the ray chart*. If such is the case, Einstein's mental vehicle (proposed as being upon the fifth ray) would have a subcoloration of the first ray; the first ray would be considered a subray of the fifth. This solution seems to make more sense than various alternative solutions. For instance, although the fourth ray clearly had a conditioning effect upon Einstein's energy system, it was almost certainly a legacy ray. (There may, of course, be more than *one* legacy ray. Any prominent combination of forces carried forward into the present incarnation, can be considered legacy rays. Usually, the legacy ray is the ray of the personality, but one can imagine that the momentum of a strong personality ray in combination with a strong mental ray could exert a powerful *dual influence* in the present). Einstein's early musicality, his song writing and versification, none of which were ever *central* to his life purpose, suggest that the fourth ray influence was a "background consideration," a quality originating in the past and serving as a comfortable means of psychological retreat and refreshment. It is unlikely that the lower mind was conditioned by the fourth ray because, intuitive though Einstein was, his thought process was far too lucid and precise to be fourth ray in character. Still another alternative solution might place the first ray as a legacy ray, but everything in Einstein's early childhood runs counter to that hypothesis. He was a gentle and dreamy child, and his early relationships were based primarily on the use of the "love–line" of energy. A certain amount of first ray energy comes through Pisces and may have (when blended with Cancerian energy) given him his inclination towards solitariness, but the usual 'carry–overs' of the first ray seem to be missing.

The first ray, however, seems to be profoundly important. In his search for the laws and principles of creation, Einstein seemed to be functioning under the first subray of the great third Ray of Creativity. This mode of functioning would place the first ray at a level *deeper* than that of the concrete mind; it would be a more fundamental placement and would be likely to last for a number of lives (i.e., for as long as the entity was associated with that particularly subsidiary Ashram in the great third ray Ashram). Einstein was not searching out all the details of knowledge as one might expect to find upon the third or fifth subrays of the third ray; nor was he seeking loving or philanthropic application of assembled information as one might find upon the second or sixth subrays of the third ray. Certainly there was no attempt at creating a physical pattern (seventh subray), nor did his Ashramic task involve artistic expressivity (fourth subray) – even though such expressivity was part of his personality nature). The "*two* soul rays" relate to the *Ashramic task* and not to any form of personality expression for its own sake. Instead he sought the *essential principles* which guide divine thought, the *laws* which all creative processes are compelled to obey.

Einstein, who was in some respects a materialist (one who focuses upon the 'material' aspect of divinity), a determinist, and one who did not believe in the reality of an individual soul which survives death, would never have phrased his quest in the terminology of classical esotericism, but he comes very close. Any man who says of God, "I want to know his thought," is imbued with a deep sense of the divine. Einstein certainly seems to have believed in a superior Intelligence, responsible for creation (though he may not have thought of this Intelligence as a Deity in the usual sense of the word). Einstein was searching for the organizing principles of the universe, the forms of thought which God continues to think in order to uphold and administer His Creation, the manifested world. It is for this reason that it may be most reasonable to think of Einstein as a third ray soul, affiliated with that subsidiary third ray Ashram in which first ray processes hold sway (Ashram III_1) – the Ashram which focuses upon the laws and principles in conformity with which the Divine Creative Intelligence functions.

Again, it must be stated that all this is highly speculative. One might argue convincingly that Einstein's ashram should be III_5, but it would seem that such an ashram would be more concerned with discovery and *application,* whereas Einstein was concerned with enunciation of principles rather than their concrete application. Further, not all the 49 Ashrams are yet formulated, nor does the Tibetan state (definitively, and in relation to all of the seven basic types of Ashrams) which ones are and which are not. Such fine points of understanding will have to await a fuller development of ray science.

At this point, the best that can be done is to suggest possibilities and potentially fruitful lines of enquiry.

It is for the most part useless to suggest Einstein's possible Triadal polarization and Monadic ray. We do know, however, that for an entity of his spiritual standing, these remote influences were probably making their presence felt. His thought was leading him into those realms where mysticism, science, religion and art all converge. His quest (lasting over half a century) for a Unified Field Theory seems to have had a distinctly *buddhic* quality. The buddhic plane (the plane of intuition) is that level of being upon which unification is first realized. The unification Einstein sought dealt purely with physical processes as one might expect of a third ray individual untrained in (and unaccepting of) occultism, but it was unification nonetheless. Though Einstein was frustrated in his attempt to bring through the equations and applications of a Unified Field Theory, he was responding to a deep intuitive realization that *duality cannot be an essential reality*. It is well to remind ourselves that the buddhic plane is the fourth plane and thus related to the fourth ray for which the word of power is "Two Merge with One." While Einstein may have eschewed the title 'mystic,' he certainly was a great scientific mystic (more properly, occultist), and one can imagine that his future work will lie in *proving the fundamental unity of creation*, not simply upon the physical plane but upon many dimensions – certainly, he will transcend seeking a purely physical unification.

What is suggested here, is that Einstein's motives for unification may have come from a very deep level of his energy system. Perhaps the impulses towards divine artistry and divine love *were* (and, will be) absolutely fundamental to his nature. Einstein's relationship to the Jewish people may illustrate this point.

Einstein was intimately identified with the Jewish people, and as his life progressed, the identification intensified. He became, in the eyes of many, the archetypal, ideal Jew – brilliant, 'touched' by the Divine Intelligence, and filled with a sense of universal harmony. The Tibetan gives the rays of the Jewish people as the first and the third (a first ray soul and a third ray personality), and then hints that the fourth ray is profoundly involved in the Jewish makeup. Interestingly, the Jews are said to be the *bridge* between the previous solar system and the present one, and all bridges, we know, are 'ruled' by the fourth ray. Given Jewish preeminence in the arts, given their tremendous suffering throughout the ages, and given certain "conflicted" aspects within their racial psyche, it may not be too far afield to presume that the Monadic ray of the Jewish race is the fourth Ray of Harmony Through Conflict. This would explain at a profound level many aspects of Jewish life and psychology that are difficult to account for otherwise.

But even if we grant the possibility that the Monadic ray of the Jews may be the fourth, it is quite impossible, at this stage of knowledge, to say that all those who are closely associated with that group of what might be called 'inter-systemic travellers' would be fourth ray Monads; some may be, and some may not. The thought, however, is suggestive. In Einstein's case, so deep was his love of music (deeper by far than simply playing the violin or improvising at the piano would indicate), that music (the quintessentially fourth ray art) may have held (and, in the future, may hold) the key to his *ultimate* motivation, the motivation which led him to formulate and enunciate the

Theory of Relativity – the determination to discover and understand *harmony within the universe*.

Certainly, Unified Field Theory is (in the language of the fourth ray) an attempt to *reconcile* two kinds of forces, gravitational and electromagnetic. No doubt there are higher correspondences to these forces. Perhaps one force correlates more closely with the energy of the first solar system, and the other with the energy of the second. At any rate, Einstein thought that two great dynamics (two great pairs of opposites) which seem to be separated, are really aspects of the same unifying 'something.' Perhaps the "mathematical torment" which he experienced as he sought to discover the equations with which to express a Unified Field Theory, relates to the arduous process of reconciling apparently contrasting forces – a reconciliation to be achieved at the very highest, abstract levels of the mind. It should be remembered at this point that the fourth ray is "the ray of mathematical exactitude."

Einstein firmly believed in the possibility (even the necessity) of reconciling and unifying the two kinds of force. His consciousness was firmly rooted in that intuitive world, and he *knew* with intuitive certainty the underlying reality of unity. But his task was to express that realization through mathematical formulae, thus expressing buddhic intuitions through the appropriate forms of abstract thought. This was an extraordinarily difficult task to achieve, and he did not succeed. Perhaps the time for such a revelation had not come.

One thought that stands out boldly and clearly was that *Einstein was a Triadal worker*. The major focus of his attention was not at all in the personality, but in the world of the Spiritual Triad, which is to the Monad what the personality is to the soul. The solutions he sought were impersonal and universal. For him, *mind* did not mean concrete, personality mind at all; mind was buddi–manas. This, perhaps, explains his abstracted attitude. In one way, he was not "of this world."

One last speculative point deserves mentioning. Just as the fourth ray can be considered an aspect of the second ray, and as the fourth ray soul can be considered (essentially) a second ray soul, so it may be (time will tell) that the fourth ray Monad can be considered essentially a second ray Monad. Upon the Monadic level the *will* is supreme. The aspect of will expressed through the second ray is "The Will to Unify." In searching for the profoundest theme in Einstein's life, one would have to identify it as *The Will to Unify*. When considering Einstein's life and his deepest aspirations, it becomes clear that what he has done for humanity is as nothing compared with what he will be enabled to do when his abiding *urge towards unification* is at last fulfilled.

Note: The sources used for all direct quotations by or about Albert Einstein were: *Einstein, The Life and Times*, Ronald W. Clark, The World Publishing Company, New York and Cleveland, Copyright 1971; *Einstein in America*, Jamie Sayen, Crown Pulishers, Inc., New York, Copyright 1985; and the *Encyclopedia Britannica*, fifteenth edition.

Tapestry of the Gods

Michelangelo Buonarroti

Born, March 6, 1475 – Died, February 18, 1564

Michelangelo Buonarroti was a "Renaissance man," one of the greatest sculptors, painters and architects in the history of humanity, and an accomplished poet as well. The word "Renaissance" (from the Italian word "rinascita" meaning *rebirth*) was coined to characterize the extraordinary flowering of the fine arts under the influence of Michelangelo and Raphael. During this period, there was a vast influx of fourth ray souls into incarnation, and *humanism* was reborn. Again, as in ancient times, human beings were accorded a value commensurate with their true value in the divine scheme of things; man was realized to be a "temple of the living God." The fourth ray (the soul ray of humanity) rose in power, and began to balance the sixth ray of idealism and devotion which had for so many centuries held sway. Mortal man was no longer seen to be merely an abject and pitiable creature, ever falling short of his ideal, and wretched in the eyes of God. The humanists saw man as "God incarnate," – man the great masterpiece of the Creator, and a reflection of His divinity. Michelangelo took incarnation at a time when it was possible for him to glorify the beauty of the human form, and express through his artistic treatment of that form more of man's ideal divinity than had ever been revealed.

Rays in Evidence

The Presence of Ray Four

Michelangelo lived for the expression of beauty. His incomparable pieces of sculpture, his massive, dramatic paintings in the Sistine Chapel, his celebrated architectural designs (including the great dome of St. Peter's Cathedral in Rome) and his creation of hundreds of poems, sonnets, madrigals and quatrains, attest to a passionate love of beauty which drove him to express through many media. While we know that the artist is found upon all the rays, the fourth ray is indispensable in the creation of the greatest art. When an individual is utterly consumed by the artistic impulse; when his artistic creations rival and even surpass the greatest art of the ancient world; when that individual's masterpieces serve as an incomparable monument of artistic achievement and a constant source of inspiration to innumerable great artists for centuries after his death – then, the fourth Ray of Harmony, Beauty and Art must indeed be present in full force.

The fourth ray is the Ray of Harmony Through Conflict – a ray of reconciliation and unification. The reconciliations and unifications which Michelangelo achieved in his conflict–ridden life had far more than merely personal significance; they set historical precedents, profoundly affecting thereafter the social role and function of the artist and his art.

The fourth ray is the reconciler of polarities. The greatest and most challenging polarity to be reconciled in Michelangelo's lifetime arose from the confrontation of pagan Humanism and Christian orthodoxy and authority (the first mode of thought conditioned by fourth ray energy, and the second, by the energy of the sixth ray). Michelangelo's artistic creations reconciled these two conflicting and contradictory cultural streams. He was devoted to both Christianity and to Platonism. His sculpture and paintings abound with figures from Graeco–Roman mythology, such as Cupid, Ganymede, Bacchus, Tityus, as well as those from traditional Christian theogony, such as Jesus, the Virgin Mother, St. Paul, St. Matthew, St. Peter, etc. The most conspicuous example of the way in which Michelangelo excelled in bridging and unifying the two contrasting world views is the juxtaposition of Old Testament prophets and pagan sibyls on the vault of the Sistine Chapel. Contemplation of this dramatic feat of harmonization immediately calls to mind the fourth ray word of power, "Two Merge with One."

Another important reconciliation and unification concerned the fusion of three great art forms within the person of Michelangelo himself. Although his early life was devoted primarily to sculpture, he was constantly called upon as a painter and an architect. In his later life, he was able to say confidently, "Everyone knows I am a sculptor, painter and architect." It was Michelangelo's unifying embrace of Humanism, that led him to adopt as his personal emblem three circles interwoven, in order to demonstrate the dependence of each of these art forms upon the other two. Many of his comments shattered the rigid distinctions which others sought to maintain among the parallel arts. While such individuals as Leonardo da Vinci were stressing the dissimilarity of the arts, Michelangelo held consistently to the unitarian view. The fourth ray, of course, is one of the rays of synthesis; in Michelangelo's case, the presence of a strong first ray (also a ray of synthesis) encouraged his tendency towards fusion and unification.

When we consider Michelangelo's character, we discover a classical example of the combat between "tamas" (inertia) and "rajas" (fiery activity) to which the fourth ray individual is subject. Michelangelo's personality was often in the grips of a daemonic, obsessive energy; no one could work more furiously and aggressively than he when the 'fire' descended upon him. But his driven and compulsive behavior contrasted starkly with a strange passivity, a sense of being in the hands of God. Those who are familiar with the behavior of fourth ray individuals, will recognize in this contrast the signature of the fourth ray.

This duality, induced by the presence of fourth ray energy within his energy system, is reflected in many of his figures, which he tended to create in *pairs*, each figure displaying a sharply contrasting attitude or emotion. The vault of the Sistine Chapel is filled with such contrasting pairs. "God and Adam"; the *Dying Slave* in contrast with the *Rebellious Slave*; and also the pair of drawings of Tityus and Ganymede (the first torn by a great bird as a punishment for unbridled passion, and the other soaring in the embrace of a great bird, heavenward in an esctasy of Platonic love) particularly demonstrate the dynamically contrasting polarities. Michelangelo's individuality contained furious contradictions, and he expressed them without reservation through his art.

One of Michelangelo's greatest torments was the battle within his psyche between carnal and spiritual love. Although he was a Neoplatonist by mental conviction, his sensual desires were powerful. Throughout his life he struggled with physical passion, and yet many believe that he led a chaste and spartan life. It is clear from his sculpture and painting that he had an overwhelming love for the nude, male form, and that his desires, whether or not he actually indulged them, were strongly homosexual. And yet the two great loves affairs of his life were both idealized, *platonic* relationships; while one relationship was with a nobleman, Tommasso de' Cavalieri, and had blantantly homosexual undertones, the other relationship (paralleling the spiritual love which Dante held for Beatrice or Petrarch for Laura) was with the widowed Marchioness of Pescara, Vittoria Colonna, one of the outstanding women of the Renaissance, a woman of incomparably elevated spirit and calm wisdom. Michelangelo, it seems, was a man always in love, but torn over how he might express that love. His great artistic outpouring served as a means of sublimating his agony.

When we examine Michelangelo's sculptures and painted frescos, we note that one of the outstanding characteristics of the figures he created is their *torsion* – the dynamic, often violent and agonized 'twisting' of bodies in intensely emotional attitudes. For almost fifty years his art continued to express pyschic as well as overt conflict, and a strong sense of frustration. The fourth ray is, according to the Tibetan, the "ray of struggle." Michelangelo's fierce inner and outer conflicts were transferred to many of his struggling figures who literally writhed from inner and outer torments.

In one respect, Michelangelo was an outstanding dramatist. He understood the full range of human emotions, from the most infernal and tormented, to the most sublime and beatific. One has only to compare the facial expressions of the damned in *The Last Judgment* to the expression worn by the Virgin Mary in the *Pietà*. Just as, physically, his figures expressed an extraordinary range of movements and attitudes, their range and variety of emotions was equally extraordinary. It must be remembered that the fourth ray is more closely identified with the human family than any other ray, and that those strongly influenced by this ray understand humanity profoundly – not as a scholar or a scientist understands, but through shared experience and identification. Michelangelo's works demonstrate that there was no emotion he did not feel – and feeling, long to express.

"Genius is akin to madness," and Michelangelo, a man of ultrasensitive temperament, and almost always worried and vexed by something, was often half mad. He was frequently given to melancholia and depression, and he constantly refers to his "strange mental states." The Sun, Moon and Mars in the sensitive, impressionable sign Pisces, no doubt, contributed to this condition, as did the often gloomy sign Capricorn at the Ascendant. Again, however, Michelangelo's distressed psychological state is a signature of the power of the fourth ray in his nature. His personal life was constantly conflicted (though, of course, there were moments of respite and satisfaction); the harmony aspect of the fourth ray was, nevertheless, destined to find fulfillment in his art alone.

A close study of his sculpture, painting and poetry reveals a deep awareness of allegory and symbolism. This was, to some extent, characteristic of his times (the Renaissance, qualified strongly by the fourth ray) and his nation (Italy, possessing a fourth ray personality). Nevertheless, Michelangelo's works must be studied allegorically. As a fourth ray individual, he received his inspiration from the fourth (buddhic) plane. That inspiration arrives often in images; great ideas are embodied in such images. Rather than develop his themes through the use of many words, he expressed them with great economy through perfectly executed images. This is the manner in which the fourth ray reveals truth.

The most convincing testimony for the presence of the fourth ray is simply Michelangelo's undying love of beauty. He was enraptured by beauty in any form, a slave to beauty. His entire life was given to the celebration of beauty. Such an orientation distinguishes the fourth ray individual from all others.

The Presence of Ray Six

One of Michelangelo's outstanding qualities was his idealism – idealism in art, and idealism in love. His lifelong artistic ideal was the nude, male figure. It became for him an artistic obsession, and he devoted himself to portraying it in all manner of intensely expressive poses and attitudes. This devoted fascination suggests the compelling power of the sixth ray.

His attitude towards love was also far more characteristic of the sixth ray than of the second. When Michelangelo fell in love, he loved with intense, idealistic passion. He exalted the beloved, and his attitude was almost one of worship. In a draft of a letter to Tommasso de' Cavalieri (the great love of his life) he calls him "light of our century, paragon of all the world." In this case, the ardor of his devotion caused him to forget all sense of proportion – thus it is, frequently, with those who respond strongly to the sixth ray. "Co–measurement" is definitely not a distinguishing sixth ray quality.

Michelangelo seems all his life to have been in love with the *idea* of love (another example of his Platonism). It may be that he chose to (or was forced to) transmute frustrated sexual desire into lofty sentiment, but he insisted that his love was chaste. This may indeed be the case, as astrologically Saturn is placed near the seventh house cusp, and squares Venus in Aries which is the ruler of the fifth house of love affairs. In earnest defense of the purity of his love, he felt compelled to write:

> **Therefore, alas, how will the chaste wish**
> **That burns my inward heart ever be heard**
> **By those who always see themselves in others?**

Accordingly, his love poetry is usually spiritualized. In another sonnet to Tommasso Calvalieri he wrote:

> **If a chaste love, if an excelling kindness,**
> **If sharing by two lovers of one fortune,**
> **Hard lot for one the other one's concern,**
> **Two hearts led by one spirit and one wish,**
> **And if two bodies have one soul, grown deathless...**
> **Neither loving himself, but each one each....**

All this carries the lofty quality of the sixth ray, which rises above physicality and seeks a mystical union with the beloved, a "marriage of souls." But beneath it all, a passionate fire was burning. The highly charged emotionality of the sixth ray, as expressed in the following lines cannot be denied.

> I burn, I consume myself, I cry
> Nearby you set me on fire, and parting, murder.

When, in later life, he became enamored of Vittoria Colonna, it was her poetry, her mind, and her religion he loved. With Cavalieri the attraction was violently physical – even if (under the uplifting, sublimating influence of the sixth ray) chaste.

Michelangelo's idealism and devotion in love were apparent even in his religious aspirations. His *Pietà*, depicting the Virgin Mother holding upon her lap the dead Christ, is one of the most sublime pieces of sculpture in all of Western art. In the *Pietà* he embodied his purest and most holy religious aspirations. But he was strongly criticized for creating a Virgin so young – of an age comparable to that of her Son. His answer to this criticism reveals the quality of his devotion to the Virgin (and, in a deeper sense to the Virgin Mother as an idealization of woman):

> Do you not know, that chaste women retain their fresh looks much longer than those who are not chaste? How much more, therefore, a virgin in whom not even the least unchaste desire that might work change in her body ever arose? And I tell you, moreover, that such freshness and flower of youth besides being maintained in her by natural causes, it may possibly be that it was ordained by the divine power to prove to the world the virginity and perpetual purity of the Mother....Do not wonder then that I have, for all these reasons, made the most Holy Virgin, Mother of God, a great deal younger in comparison with her Son than she is usually represented.

These words reveal an extraordinary, sixth ray idealism.

Another story related by the famous goldsmith, Benvenuto Cellini, shows to what an extent Michelangelo was passionately and unreservedly devoted to beauty and to love. According to Cellini, Michelangelo fell in love with the singing of one Luigi Pulci, who later became a poet and Latin scholar:

> When this Luigi had been a boy in Florence it used to be the custom on summer evenings to gather together in the streets: and on those occasions, he used to sing, improvising all the time, among the very best voices. His singing was so lovely that Michelangelo Buonarroti, that superb sculptor and painter, used to rush along for the pleasure of hearing him whenever he knew where he was performing....

Michelangelo explained the reason for his enthusiasm:

> I am a man more inclined than anyone who ever lived to care for people. Whenever I see anyone possessed of some gift which shows him to be more apt in the performance or expression of anything than others, I become, perforce, enamored of him and am constrained to abandon myself to him in such a way that I am no longer my own, but wholly his.

Certainly, this surrender of self to beauty, and to those who create beauty, arises through the influence of the sixth ray (cojoined, in this case, with Piscean energy).

Michelangelo's devotion to religion was intense. He was a man of great faith, and considered faith "the gift of gifts." Yet he lived in fear of damnation, and was preoccupied by a sense of his own unworthiness to stand before God on the Day of Judgment. The emotions of fear and terror (so often characteristic of those strongly influenced by the sixth ray) pervade his masterpiece *The Last Judgment* – perhaps the most arresting and compelling of all his creations. Michelangelo had the artistic power to inspire terror, awe, and an overwhelming sense of the omnipotence of deity; his contemporaries called it *"terribilità"* – a combination of terrifying power and divine sublimity. Obviously, a strong resonance with the first ray is necessary in order to evoke this quality, but sixth ray *awe* in the presence of overpowering majesty or grandeur is an equally important factor. As Michelangelo grew older, his religious passions grew even more intense, as did his striving for purity. This is revealed in a large corpus of confessional and mystical poetry of astonishing sincerity.

Michelangelo drove himself obsessively; he was a driven man. He lived life with the focused intensity characteristic of the sixth ray. When he wrote to his brother Buonarroto, "I'm being pressed in such a way that I haven't time to eat. God willing, I can bear up," he was describing not an isolated incident, but a way of life. When in the grips of the creative process (which was almost always), he was oblivious to all else. When Michelangelo worked, he worked in a fury. A furious driving of oneself (and others) is even more characteristic of sixth ray influence (especially type [6B]) than of first. His driving, daemonic, ferocious energy is clearly illustrated by the following remarks from a French visitor who reported that Michelangelo, even though old and in frail health, could

> ...hammer more chips out of very hard marble in a quarter hour than three young stonecarvers could do in three or four, which has to be seen to be believed, and he went at it with such impetuosity and fury that I thought the whole work must go to pieces, knocking off with one blow chips three or four fingers thick, so close to the mark that, if he had gone even slightly beyond, he ran the danger of ruining everything.

Clearly there is more than a little of the first ray here, but the unrelenting intensity of it (attacking the marble like one 'possessed') is definitely a signature of the sixth ray. The likelihood of this probability is reinforced by the presence of Mars (a sixth ray planet) in Pisces conjuncting both the Piscean Sun and Moon in Michelangelo's astrological chart.

It should also be pointed out that Michelangelo lived a spartan life and was a man of ascetic habits (as might be expected from a union of sixth ray, Capricornian and Piscean energy). He counted all as lost if he did not achieve his artistic objectives; oblivious to everything except that which lay before him to do, he worked at a furious pace. Because his work totally consumed him, he was able to ignore many mundane matters (like eating and sleeping!), though he had more than his share of frustrating mundane problems to overcome in the execution of his commissions. Supervising the quarrying of marble for months at a time, dealing with hostile workmen, journeying hastily from city to city (often in flight of a patron's wrath), painting upon his back for four years upon scaffolding high above the floor of the Sistine Chapel – all this took incredible (almost fanatical) tenacity, dedication, devotion and a willingness to forego those ordinary comforts of life which most people consider indispensable.

It is interesting to consider in Michelangelo the powerful combination of Pisces and the sixth ray, the two predominating potencies of the Christian Era. He had both Sun and Moon in Pisces; Pisces is a consummating influence, being the last of the twelve zodiacal signs, and a great sign of synthesis. It is said of Pisces, "Pisces takes from all the signs" (*Esoteric Astrology*, p. 334). Michelangelo was living at the climactic point of the great Piscean Age. The apotheosis of the sixth ray impulse had already been reached, and a little more than fifty years after his death, the sixth ray began passing out of manifestation. Michelangelo, in his best work for the Church (the vault of the Sistine Chapel, and *The Last Judgment*), brought to consummate expression the great themes of the Piscean Age (salvation through surrender to the Will of God), as well as the predominating cultural themes which arose under the influence of the sixth ray (ascension to God through idealism and devotion).

The Presence of Ray One

It seems very unlikely that Michelangelo could have produced such a great number of remarkable works over the course of his long (89 year) life without the support of the first Ray of Will and Power. Quite apart from the presence of the first ray in his ray chart, his Sun sign, Pisces, and his Ascendant, Capricorn, both introduce first ray energy: Pisces through its esoteric ruler, Pluto, and Capricorn as one of the transmitting constellations of the first ray. Let us, however, consider the evidence for ray one.

One of the outstanding features of Michelangelo's art is its overwhelming *power*. His figures are generally larger than life, and some of them (the *David* and *Hercules* [now lost]) of imposing size. (In fact, he longed to carve a true colossus overlooking the sea, which, in emulation of the ancient *Colossus at Rhodes*, would serve as a landmark for sailors.) All of the male figures and even some of the women are broad and heavily muscled, conveying the impression of great strength. Such figures are infused with a dynamic intensity reflective of Michelangelo's own daemonic energy. His *Moses* is the very image of *terribilità* – austere, invincible, infused with divine power. Moses, the Law-Giver, was doubtlessly an archetypal embodiment of first ray energy, and Michelangelo's representation of this great Biblical figure is absolutely charged with the potency of the first ray.

Michelangelo conceived boldly and upon a grand scale; his artistic intentions almost always outran the time available for their execution. His completed masterworks are monumental. When one stands before *The Last Judgment*, or beneath the vaulted ceiling of the Sistine Chapel, one is overcome by the impression of divine *might* – the awesome, inescapable power of God, the Creator and Destroyer. The effect of *The Last Judgment* was overwhelming from the first. Pope Paul III, at its unveiling, reportedly fell to his knees, crying "Lord, charge me not with my sins when thou shalt come on the Day of Judgment." One is compelled to agree with Georgio Vasari, one of Michelangelo's first biographers, that "*The Last Judgment* must be recognized as the great exemplar of the grand manner of painting, directly inspired by God and enabling mankind to see the fateful results when an artist of sublime intellect infused with divine grace and knowledge appears on earth."

It was typical of the evolution of Michelangelo's designs to begin with a conception for complex groupings of smaller figures and gradually develop them into simpler combinations of larger, more expansive, less specific forms. One of the characteristics of his development as an artist was his constant search for simplification of means, a reduction in ornament and detail, and an emphasis upon single figures or architectural members. Thus, drastic simplification and an enlargement of the essential focus within any composition, were two of the most distinguishing features of his art. Although he was capable of exquisite technical virtuosity (as he demonstrated in his *Pietà*), he became increasingly impatient with what he considered extraneous detail, and reduced everything to essentials. He is quoted by Ralph Waldo Emerson as having said, "Beauty is the purgation of all superfluities." Clearly this statement reveals the presence of first ray energy.

As Michelangelo matured as an artist, he showed a growing reluctance to finish his sculptures. He was far more attracted by a new challenge or idea than by the task of actually completing what he had begun. Under the influence of the first ray, the individual is impressed by the importance of asserting the essential idea rather than laboriously bringing the idea through into a refined and polished expression. Michelangelo worked with tremendous speed and assurance, brought his concept to the point of emergence, and then, with typical first ray impatience, raced on, seized by the desire to bring forth the next revelation. It may be that his Platonic view of art, as something preordained by God and implanted within the marble or pigment to be "perceived" by the artist, allowed him, consciously and in good conscience, to leave many of his sculptures unfinished. Interestingly, even during his lifetime, his unfinished statuary came to be highly valued, because it showed the great artist's idea in the process of finding objective form. Increasingly, for Michelangelo, it was the emergence of the new *idea* which he valued, and not its perfected manifestation.

Although Michelangelo constantly deprecated his efforts as a poet, he was, undoubtedly, one of the most immediate and basic interpreters of Renaissance civilization among the Italian lyric poets. His poetry, however, was passionate and rough like his unfinished sculptures, very far from the elegant "petrarchan" style of the professional literary men of his period. According to Enzo Girardi, the modern editor of Michelangelo's poems:

> **Unlike the others, without exception, he is not closed in his own little world: he does not portray a place or a manner, does not celebrate a literary fashion, taste, or style; he does not tell in verse his own personal life, or not it alone. His thoughts are the great thoughts of the century: art, beauty, love, death; his drama is the great drama of that era, fought between heaven and earth, flesh and spirit, love of life and the cult of death, Plato and Christ. That, writing of these things, he could have written 'better', may well be; but it is worth remembering that no one else, writing 'well', wrote of them at all.**

Here we are reminded of the Tibetan's statement that, "The literary work of a first ray man will be strong and trenchant, but he will care little for style or finish in his writing." As with his sculpture and painting, it was the essence which Michelangelo valued, the great and central themes which he emphasized.

Michelangelo was direct and outspoken; he did not mince words even with those in the highest ranks of authority. Before Marcello Cervini became Pope Marcellus II, Michelangelo had often disputed with him, ordering him not to interfere with the activities in the Vatican workshop and to "keep the money coming in and keep it out of the hands of thieves, and as for the planning of the building, leave that to me!" He even had gruff words for Pope Julius II, a man of the sword who could not lightly be defied. Michelangelo's rigidity and assertiveness is revealed by certain phrases in his letters: "I am firm in my opinion"; "I don't contradict myself"; "I'll abide with my original opinion." This direct language (characteristic of so many of his letters [except when he was under the influence of love]) is another confirmation of the presence of the first ray.

The Presence of the Seventh Ray

Michelangelo was a master of the perfected form. When he chose to exercise it, his technique was faultless, even in the execution of the tiniest details. His supreme, technical virtuosity is most apparent in his *Pietà*, created when he was still a very young man. The perfected expression of idea through form is, we know, one of the gifts of the seventh ray.

Michelangelo was preoccupied by a fascination with the human body, especially the male body. Leonardo Da Vinci called him an "anatomical artist," and there is some truth to this. His knowledge of human anatomy was extraordinarily accurate, and well it should have been, for in his passion for a true and exact understanding of the bodily form, he spent many hours studying and dissecting corpses whenever they were made available to him. Thus his work expresses an intense physicality, even in the portrayal of the most sublime and transcendent themes. The seventh ray is, par excellence, the ray of form, and under its influence there is frequently found a great interest in the body.

A consummate sense of design and composition are also signatures of the seventh ray. Michelangelo's placement of figures, the relationship of all elements within his sculptural groups and paintings, the precision of his architectural conceptions – all these suggest the presence of the seventh ray, the "ray of accurate arrangement." The fourth ray alone (although the motivating impulse behind all the fine arts) cannot alone account for surpassing excellence in the field of design; the fourth ray can convey drama and color, but its sense of form is sometimes weak; the seventh ray is needed to complete an artist of Michelangelo's stature.

One more small example of Michelangelo's mastery of form is his beautiful and regular handwriting. Exquisite penmanship is most often found when the physical body and brain are conditioned by the seventh ray.

Michelangelo's understanding of form and his ability to express himself through various media seems to have been innate. He claimed no teacher; in fact, he claimed to have been self–taught. Clearly he was evoking well–established talents from the past – especially his talent as a sculptor.

Proposed Ray Chart

$$\begin{array}{cccc} & & 1 & \\ \text{IV} & 6 & 6 & \text{L: } 7 \\ & & 7 & \end{array}$$

Commentary

If Michelangelo was not a fourth ray soul, it is hard to imagine who, if anyone, could claim that distinction. He was, in the eyes of most, the greatest artist of the modern Western world, the "artist–laureate of Christendom." At this moment in history there are very few fourth ray souls, and art has, for the time, apparently lost its way as a vehicle for the expression of Divine Beauty. But Michelangelo was a God–inspired man, both a devoted Christian and Platonist, who sought to wrest from the plane of divine ideas the great images which would embody the union of God with man. The third injunction to the great Lord of the Fourth Ray (*see, Esoteric Psychology, Vol. I*, p.72) reads: "Lower the thread. Unfold the Way. Link man with God. Arise." It was Michelangelo's supreme task to "Link man with God,", to reveal the Beauty of God through the beauty of man. His artistic purpose lay far beyond any merely personal outpouring; his creative powers glorified the Creator, and expressed, incomparably, the divine drama of human living in all its splendor and terror.

We now await a new Renaissance; after the first quarter of the 21st century a fresh influx of fourth ray souls is anticipated. Michelangelo embodied in his art the consummation of the Piscean ideal, but the art of the 21st century (and beyond) will unite man with God in a new way inspired by Aquarian idealism. It is hard to imagine that the soul who manifested as Michelangelo will not play a pivotal role in that destined reunion of human art and Divine Beauty.

Some may think it possible that Michelangelo was a seventh ray soul, so great was his understanding of form, and so intent was he upon expressing inspiring images through form. Indeed, the fourth and seventh rays are the two "practically artistic rays." But in his manner, his emotionality, and his exuberant approach to expression there is very little to suggest the seventh ray. Moderation, decorum, balance – these were qualities quite missing from his life demonstration. And if the seventh ray had been more conspicuous in his energy system, he might not have left so many pieces unfinished (many of them deliberately so). But above all, it was his *Humanism* – his profound identification with every type of human experience and his ability to express through his art the thoughts and emotions which all human beings share – which identify him as a fourth ray soul. The formal perfection he achieved was entirely secondary to the revelation of the ecstatic and tortured human psyche vibrating through the forms he created. A seventh ray soul would have expressed with greater restraint and formality, and emotionality would have been less accentuated.

Michelangelo's personality was almost certainly upon the sixth or first ray. The sixth ray has been chosen because of his uncompromising idealism, his idealization of love and of the human form, his intense emotionalism, his violent, all–consuming attachments to those he loved, and his great yearning for salvation (which, especially later in his life, he conceived in strictly Christian terms). He was a man of unflagging devotion – devotion to his art, to his father and brothers, to his friends and lovers, to his faith, and to his God. When he loved, he gave himself over wholly, passionately, immoderately. He was an extremist in every respect, obsessed by the power of love. It is unlikely that a first ray personality would be given to such blatant emotionalism, nor would the first ray personality idealize and exalt the beloved as Michelangelo consistently did. The upward thrust of the life was too great, and suggests the sixth ray rather than the first.

Of course, as discussed, the first ray was powerfully present. The most fitting placement for it seems to be at the mental level. Michelangelo was a man of great ideas. His artistic conceptions were bold, broad, even magnificent. He thought in terms of great, essential themes, and had no time for inconsequential details. His mental processes were synthetic and intuitive rather than analytical; he knew his own mind, had the courage of his mental convictions, and ruthlessly eliminated all superfluity. His mind was gifted with the power of simplicity. Working with speed and certainty, conceiving the end from the beginning, and clearly and simply revealing in every one of his creations its animating *idea*. The manner of his expression was most often direct and forceful, and frequently biting and caustic. His mind was formidable. One can see that a first ray mind would be extremely valuable as a point of cooperation with his fourth ray soul. It would add great power and impressiveness to the wealth of his intuitively grasped ideas. Further, the combination of the sixth and first rays would give him the speed, one-pointedness, concentration and total self-investment in the task-at-hand which his supremely arduous work required.

Emotionally, there can be little doubt that the sixth ray was the conditioning energy. Michelangelo was in all things intense and passionate. While his fourth ray soul (and his Piscean energy) allowed him to understand and express languor and lassitude, these were not his usual emotional states. "Rajas" was far more dominant than "tamas." He usually worked as one driven by a 'daemon' – ferociously, obsessively, tenaciously. His dissatisfactions and worries were constant, and his complaints frequent. Though self-assured in artistic conception, he lacked serenity and equanimity in his personal life. He could express through his art the gentler emotions – indeed, he could express them *all*, but he could not live serenely. His emotional intensity, sixth ray in nature, was too great. If his strongly devotional and aspirational tendencies are also considered, no doubts about the quality of his emotional ray can remain.

The sculpted likenesses of Michelangelo reveal him to be a rather spare man, as one might expect of an individual with a Capricorn Ascendant. Georgio Vasari gives us a description of the artist as he appeared in the 1550's and 1560's:

> I must record that Michelangelo's constitution was very sound, for he was lean and sinewy...he could always endure any fatigue and had no infirmity, save that in his old age he suffered from dysuria and gravel...His face was round, the brow square and lofty, furrowed by seven straight lines, and the temples projected considerably beyond the ears, which were rather large and prominent. His body was in proportion to the face, or perhaps on the large side; his nose was somewhat squashed, having been broken...his eyes can best be described as being small, the colour of horn, flecked with bluish and yellowish sparks. His eyebrows were sparse, his lips thin...the chin well formed and well proportioned with the rest, his hair black, but streaked with many white hairs and worn fairly short, as was his beard, which was forked and not very thick.

The description seems to suggest a seventh ray body, though the possibility of the first ray (or at least, a first physical subray cannot be overlooked). The bodily strength is attributable in part to the presence of Mars so closely cojoined with the Sun and Moon in his nativity. The Ascendant is a point in the chart often associated with the physical body as well as, esoterically, with the energy leading to soul fulfillment. Interestingly, Capricorn, as a constellation, is the foremost conduit of seventh ray energy into our planetary scheme.

Quite apart from Michelangelo's physical attributes, his preoccupation with the physical form suggests a seventh ray physical body and brain. He worked constantly with his hands (one of the chief characteristics of the seventh ray physical nature) and his entire life was concerned with the creation of form. One wonders how this could be so, unless the seventh ray quality was working in cooperation with the fourth ray.

It is interesting to realize that Michelangelo felt himself to be in constant artistic competition, not so much with his contemporaries, as with the sculptors of the ancient world – ancient Greece, especially. Considering how readily and naturally he took to sculpting (being self–taught), and how deeply he admired and respected ancient Greek culture, it is not difficult to imagine that *he himself* was a product of that ancient time, and that, long before he took incarnation as Michelangelo, he had already achieved great things in the art of sculpture. Thus his rivalry with the ancients can be understood as a rivalry with his earlier accomplishments. Should this be true, it would account for the hypothesis that the seventh ray was his 'legacy ray.' Whereas the seventh ray ability to sculpt was virtually instinctive, he did not, at first, consider painting and architecture his preferred art forms. Later, he mastered them and included them in his quiver of accomplishments; we can (in no small part) attribute his realization that the three were inescapably interrelated to the synthesizing power of his first ray mind.

While it is definitely too early to ascertain the truth from the horoscope as now understood, the power of Vulcan, the "blacksmith of the gods" (and, primarily, a first ray planet), may have been a very important influence in Michelangelo's character. Vulcan is related to all apects of the mineral kingdom (and may convey the seventh and fourth rays as well as the first). Vulcan, the "fashioner" of matter according to Divine Design, stimulates the creativity of those who mould matter to embody Divine Beauty. There are two points in Michelangelo's horoscope from which such an influence could have entered powerfully – the Sun, Moon, Mars conjunction, and the Capricorn Ascendant. This is not the place to enter into a detailed discussion of these possibilities, but there may come a time when we are able to understand Michelangelo's deepest, spiritual purpose (a purpose even deeper than his soul purpose) in relation to the planet Vulcan.

There is little to suggest what Michelangelo's Monadic ray may have been. The influence of the Monadic ray may come in as early as the period following the second initiation (cf. *Letters on Occult Meditation*, p. 267), or as late as the fourth initiation, for in *Initiation Human and Solar* p. 181, we read that "the last two [initiations – fourth and fifth] are taken upon the ray of the Monad. Transference from a Ray of Attribute may also occur prior to the third initiation (cf. instructions to I.S.G.–L. and H.S.D. in *Discipleship in the New Age, Vols. I and II*) or "eventually, after the third initiation" (cf. *Esoteric Psychology, Vol. I*, p. 402). In *A Treatise On Cosmic Fire*, p. 176, we read that "after the third Initiation all human beings find themselves on their monadic ray (which, presumably is one of the three rays of aspect [or a subray of a ray of aspect), but in *Letters on Occult Meditation*, pp. 15–19, we learn of *seven* different ways in which the causal body is destroyed at the fourth initiation, which implies that even as late as the fourth initiation, the Ego may *still* be upon any one of the seven rays. The matter is most intricate, and certainly we are not in any position to make definitive judgments about either an Egoic ray–transference from a ray of attribute to a ray of aspect, or the gradual growth in power of the Monadic ray to the point at which it dominates the Egoic ray.

We do know that Michelangelo was an ardent Platonist as well as an ardent Christian. In *The Externalisation of the Hierarchy*, p. 298, we learn that Plato emerged upon "the *second ray* line of energy, in the department of the Christ." The second ray is the "Ray of the Divine Pattern" and Platonic archetypes are aspects of that Divine Pattern. Michelangelo's art was guided partially by Platonic *ideals*, and partially by mystical Christian thought. In any case, he was infused with a sense of the Love of God, and it would seem that any change of energy emphasis, whether the transference of the soul to another ray, or the growing dominance of the Monadic potency, would involve the great second Ray of Love–Wisdom. As a fourth ray soul, Michelangelo was able to embrace both the Platonic and Christian worlds, and reconcile them. If, as a soul, he remained upon the fourth ray, until the fourth initiation (and, possiblly beyond [cf. *A Treatise On Cosmic Fire*, p. 1247]), he would probably be considered an initiate of the "fourth order" (cf., *Ibid.*, p. 1259) and, like the Egyptian Master and the Master Jesus, would prepare to follow the Path to Sirius. He would then be a "Lord of Compassion" in the process of acquiring the qualities of "cosmic rapture and rhythmic bliss." (Intuitively, considered, this seems very likely.) On the other hand, if, as a soul, he transferred to the second ray, following the third initiation, and followed more Platonic pursuits, perhaps it would be less likely that he would follow the Fourth Path.

Given our present level of understanding, it is impossible to tell at this point, but the subject is raised in order to point to the various possibilities which lie open to a highly developed individual whose soul is upon one of the rays of attribute. A transference to a ray of aspect is, apparently, unavoidable, but the timing of the transference appears to vary greatly. It may, apparently, occur even before the third initiation *or* much later, and may, in some cases, be delayed until the fifth initiation altogether, so that the initiate appears to remain upon a ray of attribute even after the destruction of the causal body. This can be explained in terms of Hierarchical need, and the fact that each Monadic ray has its subrays which correspond to all of the seven. Thus, for service purposes, the initiate may choose to emphasize a Monadic subray which is a ray of attribute, and thus, *appear* never to have transferred to a ray of aspect, as normally happens. In any case, the decision regarding that transference, and its timing, may have much to do with the eventual *destination* of the initiate concerned.

Note: The sources used for all direct quotations by or about Michelangelo Buonarroti were: *Michelangelo*, Howard Hibbard, Harper & Rowe, Publishers, Copyright 1974, second edition; and the *Encyclopedia Britannica*, fifteenth edition.

Louis Pasteur

Born, December 27th, 1822 – Died, September 28th, 1895

Louis Pasteur was a world famous chemist and microbiologist. His scientific contributions were among the most varied and valuable in the history of science and industry. Among the most extraordinary of his accomplishments were: providing proof that micro-organisms were the cause of fermentation and disease; developing and utilizing vaccines for rabies, anthrax, and chicken cholera; pioneering investigations in the field of stereochemistry; devising the purificatory process now known as pasteurization; and (even) coming to the rescue of the beer, wine and silk industries of France and other countries.

Rays in Evidence

The Presence of Ray Five

There can be no question but that Pasteur's energy system was strongly colored by the fifth ray of Concrete Knowledge and Science. In fact, he is virtually an archetype of fifth ray expression. From the time he reached maturity, his life was given to constant scientific research of the most exacting and productive kind. It was his one great passion, and through it, he became a great benefactor of humanity. Some of his own words are eloquent testimony to the influence of the fifth ray in his life:

> Never make any assertion which cannot be simply and decisively proved.

> If you wish to be ranked among *scientific* minds – the only minds which count – you must get rid of *a priori* notions and arguments and confine yourself to rigorous inference from observed fact; you must have nothing to do with inference from mere hypotheses.

> Pay all due concern, I beg of you, to those sacred edifices which are known, so expressively, as *laboratories*. Demand that they be numerous and as fine as possible; for they are the temples of the future...It is in them that men grow to full stature and become better beings; in them, that men learn to decipher the works of nature, works of universal progress and harmony, whereas men's own works are all too often at once the fruit and the cause of barbarism, fanaticism and destruction.

> Any scientist who allows himself to be lured by the prospect of industrial applications automatically ceases to be the servant of pure science; he clutters up his life and thinking with preoccupations which paralyse his faculty for discovery.

> Science should never concern itself with the philosophical consequences of its investigations.

> I have no theories – only facts, and conclusions which are adequate to the facts.

From the above can be gauged the depth of Pasteur's commitment to science. There are also hints which demonstrate that the third ray (in both its utilitarian as well as theoretical, philosophical aspects) did not play a significant part in his motivations, despite the presence of six planets in Capricorn, a constellation ruled by Saturn, the primary distributor of the third ray.

The Presence of Ray Four

In his youth Pasteur showed very little interest in anything but drawing, and produced a number of pastels and portraits of his parents and friends. His pastels are very well executed – lifelike and realistic. Even as he entered his scientific researches, his aesthetic sensitivity was apparent. He was fascinated by crystallography, "attracted by the subtle and delicate methods used in studying these beautiful crystalline forms."

However, in other respects (and especially as his life progressed) the qualities of the fourth ray were conspicuously missing. He lacked the ability to create harmony, and many controversies and disputes swirled around him. In the words of M. René Vallery-Radot, "He lacked the arts of dissipating a difficult situation with a word in season, or nipping dissension in the bud with a smile." The capacity to avert conflict relates to the harmony aspect (i.e., [4A]) of the Ray of Harmony through Conflict. Neither did he have the personal instabilities and mood swings associated with the conflict (4B) aspect. He was not a man given to compromise. The fourth ray seems to have been represented only through aesthetic appreciation and an early artistic expressivity.

The Presence of Ray One

Pasteur was often harsh and laconic, especially with his assistants. He did not make life easy for himself or for them, ruling them severely, but justly (Capricorn for severity, and his ascending sign, Libra, for justice). One of his most highly esteemed assistants, Duclaux, said, "He keeps us at a distance from his thoughts." Pasteur maintained what appeared to be an "Olympian silence," assigning tasks "curtly and without elaboration." Pasteur's lack of interest in the people working for him created an isolating barrier so often found in those qualified by first ray energy. This was not the result of egoism or pride; he was simply a man utterly intent upon his purposes, with no time for 'non-essential' niceties.

Pasteur was capable of maintaining a punishing work schedule. He drove himself with no respect for his physical needs or limitations – even forgetting to eat and drink. He was a highly disciplined individual. In a letter to his sisters he ennunciates the gospel of "hard work":

> An individual who gets used to hard work can thereafter never live without it. And work is the foundation of everything in the world. Knowledge raises us high above our fellows. Work depends on determination; moreover, it nearly always leads to success. In these three things, work, determination and success, lies the sum of human life; determination opens the door to a brilliant and prosperous career, hard work carries one over the threshold, and in the end comes the crown of success.

It is said that the first ray man will "come to the front in his own line," and Pasteur's credo certainly indicates this. Those familiar with astrology will also recognize the peculiarly Capricornian, Saturnian coloration of this credo; both Capricorn and Saturn distribute (among other energies) the energy of the first ray.

Pasteur was completely straightforward – and, most often said exactly what he thought. Modesty was not one of his virtues; he could be arrogant at times, but he was not proud or egotistical. He simply knew his worth, and was honest enough not to disguise it. Nevertheless, he often appeared rather cold and withdrawn.

He was also an authoritarian, and he almost invariably came down on the side of established authority. He was strict in this regard and would not tolerate what he considered insubordination – especially to those who were firmly established in power and authority.

Louis Pasteur was an ambitious and, at times, impatient man, determined not to be defeated by circumstances. Intent upon the advancement of science, he was also a careerist equally eager to advance himself. He was determined to emerge victorious from every encounter which life might bring; his was not a long-suffering temperament. When he threw himself into scientific disputes (and this he did frequently), he could be dogmatic as well as highly combative. In the battle to disprove the validity of the hypothesis of "spontaneous generation", he launched an impetuous assault upon its advocates. He had no patience with those who maintained what he considered scientifically untenable positions, and would confront them with unusual boldness, courage, (and harshness). In fact, anyone within the scientific community who contradicted him could expect this direct and aggressive response. Later in his life he apologized for "sometimes disturbing the calm of the Academies," but he excused himself saying, "it was simply that I wanted to defend the cause of truth."

One more point is worth mentioning, and of considerable interest. Pasteur's researches frequently concerned morbidity, putrefaction, decay, fermentation and a study of deadly diseases (both of men and animals). He focused upon the destructive and deadly effects of microbes, and how to counteract them. On a microscopic level, he was very much concerned with life and death, and there was no small danger in much of the research he performed. In an unusual manner, these themes suggest the presence of ray one.

The Presence of Ray Six

While reading the paragraphs describing the presence of ray one, the reader may have noticed certain ray six qualities. These were clearly present, and in strength. By now, it is apparent that ray one and ray six have much in common, and can be confused on a number of points.

Pasteur was an ardent, fiery man, with an unabashedly devotional streak. (Those familiar with the dynamics of the Capricornian Sun sign might call it "fawning" upon those in authority.) Not only could he become patriotic, but positively chauvinistic. During the Franco–Prussian war Pasteur indiscriminately condemned the entire German nation, and overlooked the errors in judgement of Napoleon III and his advisers. Of that conflict, he said:

> I want to see France resisting to the last man and the last defense–work. I want to see the war prolonged into the depths of winter, so that, with the elements rallying to our side, all those vandals confronting us shall perish of cold and hunger and disease. All of my work, to my dying day, will bear as an inscription, 'Hatred towards Prussia! Revenge! Revenge! Revenge!'

This demonstrates more than a little trace of destructive fanaticism, and is a blend of the sixth and first rays.

Excerpts from the following letter express what can only be called a quality of unabashed devotion – especially to those in authority:

> My father brought me up always to admire the great man [i.e., Napoleon I] and to hate the Bourbons....To him, the Emperor was a superhuman being....He was right. I naturally inherited these feelings, which are part of the indispensable foundations of the power of the present dynasty. It was those same feelings which inspired the immortal campaign of 1814 and brought a chorus of applause from all France at the time of the return [of Napoleon I] from Elba....
> A ruling house which has these memories to draw upon, memories of glory and greatness, and which is, moreover, strengthened by such a reign as that now unrolling before our eyes, is unshakeable....Courage such as this is fit to fill a nation with exalted pride, especially a nation like ours, which, in all Europe, is the one which most loves to feel that it is *being ruled by an outstanding personality* [emphasis, MDR].

Here, we definitely see the sixth ray as work, and perhaps, a tuning–in on the astrological sign of Leo (a sign distributing the first ray), which is the personality sign of the French nation.

A few more thoughts further reveal the fiery, devotional element:

> I should like to be younger, so as to devote myself with new ardor to the study of new diseases.

> All I want to be is a citizen, a worker devoted to my country.

> Enthusiasm is the God within, who leads to everything.

> Keen your enthusiasm, but let strict verification be its travelling companion.

In so saying Pasteur showed how the fifth and sixth rays 'travelled' together in his own life. His advice was a reflection of the way he lived, devoting himself with immense enthusiasm to science and its applications to medicine, agriculture and industry.

The Presence of Ray Seven

For all his revolutionary strides in science, Pasteur was a conventional and, at times, narrow individual. Narrowness is furthered by the fifth and sixth rays, but the seventh can definitely be implicated, because it renders a person satisfied with the established form. Pasteur was, in many respects, a complete conformist, and his conformity was reflected in his political, social, patriotic and religious views. He strove to become a model public servant, a model citizen and head of a family – a well–respected person with a model character. He virtually worshipped the established order, and defended it with severity. Even a very sympathetic biographer concludes that "Pasteur was a conservative of the most unenlightened kind...a conformist with an opportunistic streak."

In his more violent and uncompromising traits of character, we sense the presence of rays other than the seventh, but the undeviating support of the "establishment" is certainly a seventh ray quality (more specifically, a quality of the conservative [7A] aspect of the seventh ray). Such characteristics are, additionally, a reflection of the extraordinary six–planet "stellium" in Capricorn, a sign which, more than any other, induces conformity and conventionality. Capricorn, further, is the main constellational distributor, at this time, of the seventh ray.

Pasteur was from an early age, an excellent draughtsman. This ability emerged in his drawings; he had a conspicuous talent for creating realistic forms, rendering them with great clarity and precision. It is also interesting that he was fascinated by crystalline structures, and that his first scientific studies and investigations were in crystallography. Crystals and crystalline formations (as is well known) are closely related to the seventh ray of *order* - the ray of "accurate arrangement."

In all his scientific investigations, Pasteur was extremely methodical, moving through the experimental process in orderly, sucessive stages. This is partially a fifth ray characteristic, but the presence of the seventh ray is undoubtedly influential. In matters of method and procedure, the fifth and seventh ray have much in common.

Proposed Ray Chart

```
            5
V     1     6     L: 4
            7
```

Commentary

There can be little doubt that Pasteur was a fifth ray soul. Science was his great passion, and the field in which he made his greatest contribution to the welfare of humanity. It was the work of his heart and the source of all his enthusiasm. An advanced individual who achieves recognition is usually known for his soul quality, and all other qualities, as important as they may be in the conduct of his life, are secondary.

Pasteur fulfills the description of the fifth ray soul as given by the Tibetan under "Distinctive Methods of Ray Service" in *Esoteric Psychology, Vol. II*, p.143:

> **The servers on this ray are coming rapidly into prominence. They are those who investigate the form in order to find its hidden idea, its motivating power, and to this end they work with ideas, proving them either true or false. They gather into their ranks those whose personalities are on this ray and train them in the art of scientific investigation....**

This fits Pasteur exactly – the scientist above all.

It is when we reach the area of *personality* that the picture becomes less clear. There is, it seems, more than one reasonable option for the personality ray. First of all, let us dispose of the fourth ray – a ray which was almost certainly a "legacy ray." His strong artistic leanings, expressed through his drawings, paintings and pastels, lasted only during his youth, and ended before he began his serious studies. The fourth ray quality, it seems, was carried into his life by momentum from the past, and promptly faded out when his true soul purpose seized him. His often severe and gruff, reclusive, steady and intensely persevering manner, certainly does not resemble the lively, vivacious and unstable fourth ray personality. Pasteur, we remember, had no talent for compromise; he was not used to accommodations, and he certainly did not care about reconciliation with his opponents (all of which are distinguishing fourth ray characteristics). Although, interestingly, since Libra (the sign of peace and balance) was his Ascendant, he mellowed as he grew older, and did apologize for the commotion he caused. Only in his fighting spirit could he be said to resemble the fourth ray personality [in its (4B) aspect], but again, he was far too stable, level, regular and well-disciplined. Further, he fought only on principle, and to defend scientific truth, *not* simply for the love and exhilaration of conflict, which is so often the case with those affected by the dramatic (4B) aspect of the fourth ray.

The other rays which we can take more seriously as candidates for the personality ray are the sixth, the seventh and the first. There is no question that Pasteur was ardent and devoted in the cause of science – a man with great enthusiasm for research. He was also chauvinistic and narrow in his views. These are definitely sixth ray qualities, and Pasteur was abundantly equipped with sixth ray energy, but was it at the personality level? Although he was a religious "believer" he was certainly not a devotee or an extremist. Further he had a very strong sense of himself; he knew his own worth. His well-centered personality was not devoted to any 'exemplary' individual whom he strove to emulate. He retained a strong sense of personal power and did not "give it away" to others in the process of devotion. More importantly he tended to be isolated and detached (especially in work situations); the sixth ray on the personality level would stimulate attachment and a much more consistently animated persona. His persona was, in fact, rather severe and aloof. Rather than inspire and attempt to arouse enthusiasm in his subordinates, he ruled and disciplined them. Pasteur was, as well, a "down-to-earth" personality. So often when the idealistic sixth ray colors the personality, there is an unrealistic approach to living, or, at least, such an approach wars with the more grounded aspects of the nature. Pasteur had no such war, and was eminently at home upon the physical plane – something that can rarely, if ever, be said of the sixth ray personality. Further he had great discipline and restraint, and carried his experiements forward in a measured, deliberate manner. The sixth ray on the personality level would have difficulty restraining its emotional impetuosity, and might frequently lose self-control. He could, of course, drive himself forward and forget everything as he pursued his scientific objectives, but the first ray can do this as well – and especially when it is linked with the sixth (as was probably the case in Pasteur's life). So while the sixth ray was present, influential and motivating, there are strong reasons to conclude that it was not the personality ray.

The seventh ray also is a possible personality ray. Outside the scientific sphere, Pasteur was a most conventional man, and his respect for the established order was unvarying. These are qualities which correlate strongly with a pronounced seventh ray influence. However, he was a highly combative individual and he lacked tact and diplomacy – two qualities which the seventh ray personality possesses in abundance. Further, the seventh ray personality (when it fights) does not fight aggressively or boldly – it fights within the system, *using the system* to achieve its ends. It uses what the esoteric psychologist, Roberto Assagioli, used to call the "skillful will" rather than rely almost exclusively upon the "strong will" – as so many with first ray personalities seem to do. Pasteur, relied upon strong will; he confronted his opposition boldly and in person, speaking plainly, even bluntly, and criticizing his opposition frontally. From the personality point of view he was harsh rather than subtle, suave and polished (as the seventh ray personality often is). Further, a personality upon the seventh ray is a model of moderation. It loves work, but it respects rhythm and cycles; in short, it knows when to work and when to rest. It does not drive itself mercilessly forward. Pasteur could not stop working; it was relentless overwork which probably precipitated a paralytic stroke in his forty-sixth year. Many times, throughout the latter part of his life, he forced himself forward through sheer will. His determination would not let him capitulate to illness or circumstantial opposition. Therefore, while the seventh ray is doubtlessly a strong factor in his makeup, it does not seem to characterize his persona as a whole. More likely, it is a result of the heavy Capricorn influence, and is, probably, the ray governing his etheric–physical nature.

Having eliminated the sixth and seventh rays from consideration, we are left with the first ray as the probable personality ray. Many of Pasteur's first ray characteristics have already been discussed. This ray seems to exemplify the fortitude with which he lived. It should, however, be considered as a sub-ray of the fifth ray soul. Pasteur was a revolutionary in the field of microbiology. He was a fighter. In his fight against deadly diseases, and deadly misconceptions, he needed tremendous strength and the power to promote and defend his provocative new thoughts. The first ray, considered as the chief instrument of expression for the fifth ray, gave him this strength.

When we consider the ray of the mind, the fifth ray seems the most reasonable choice. This choice introduces the possibility that Pasteur's mental and soul ray were both the fifth Ray of Concrete Knowledge and Science. Although the mental ray is not *usually* the same as the ray of the soul (cf. *Glamour: A World Problem*, p. 58), even among the Tibetan's disciples–in–training, the two rays were *sometimes* the same. Pasteur's mind was far too precise to be qualified by the fourth ray and far too matter–of–fact and unphilosophical for the third ray. The first ray can be considered a possibility, except that the first ray mind tends not to immerse itself in the investigation of detail. Rather than a questioning, investigative mind, it tends to be quite sure of its own opinions – dogmatically so at times. Pasteur's mind was every curious, questioning, *probing minute details*, and ever ready to revise opinion when evidence indicated the necessity for doing so. His strong first ray personality naturally permeates every personality vehicle – including the mind – and this would tend to stiffen mental reactions and make the pronouncements of the mind more authoritative. The problem of ray 'overlays' must always be remembered in ray–assessment. However, it is reasonable to suppose that, in Pasteur's case, there was a close and powerfully focussed alignment between soul and mind; the driving soul urge to discover the mysteries of nature expressed itself through a lower, concrete mind ideally suited to the task.

Pasteur's emotional body was undoubtedly upon the sixth ray. His ardor and passion for science were constantly in evidence. He was impetuous, and threw himself into the fray, fired by devotion to the cause of scientific truth. A close reading of D.K.'s many descriptions of the sixth ray emotional body (especially in the case of disciples – and Pasteur was certainly an advanced disciple) show how really powerful and influential such a vehicle can be. If this ray analysis is valid, the emotional field would have been the only one through which the energy of the 2–4–6 line of energy had access to his energy system. Among D.K.'s disciples, this is the case in seven instances, and it is through the emotional vehicle that an adequate counterbalance to the 1–3–5–7 line of energy must come. Pasteur could certainly be emotional – more "fiery" than "watery" – and his devotion was easily aroused.

The physical body and brain would appear to be upon the seventh ray. Certain photographs and sketches of him as a young man suggest the seventh ray body type. His strong sense of form, as reflected in the excellence of his draughtsmanship, also suggests the seventh ray. In the early part of life, the ray of the physical body, (and, of course, the emotional body) as well as the ray of the previous incarnation are conspicuous. One can see how a fourth ray 'legacy' working in cooperation with seventh ray body and brain (and a Moon in Gemini – a sign contributing to manual dexterity and the power to delineate) could combine to produce his early inclination towards artistic expression.

In some photographs of Pasteur, one can see some characteristics described (hypothetically) under the fifth ray body. There is a compactness, a density, an elusive "gnome–like" quality. It is not possible to say whether the fifth ray qualified the physical body to any extent (as a subray, for instance), but it is suggested by the Tibetan that the soul ray will leave its physical imprint. Certain unusual aspects of Pasteur's appearance might also be attributed to the Capricorn stellium.

In summation, Louis Pasteur, it would seem, fulfilled the mission of his soul. His work emanated from the fifth ray ashram and, along that line, his contributions were extraordinary. His ray chart shows the great contrast between a revolutionary and liberated mind, and a rigid, unyielding personality. His personality liabilities, however, were easily overcome by the strength of his scientific quest, and he was able to use the power of the first ray, the ardor of the sixth, and the upright stability of the seventh to reinforce his soul purpose. From the fifth ray point of view, his life can be seen as an example of soul–infusion, and towards his latter days, the broad and general love of humanity (which one might think rare in the fifth ray type) emerged into beautiful expression.

Note: The sources used for all direct quotations by or about Louis Pasteur were: *Louis Pasteur: the Man and his Theories*, Hilaire Cuny, translated by Patrick Evans, the Camelot Press Ltd., London and Southampton, Copyright 1963; and the *Encyclopedia Britannica*, fifteenth edition.

Joan of Arc

Born, January 6, 1412 – Died, May 30, 1431

Joan of Arc is perhaps the most heroic figure to be found in the annals of French history. For over five hundred years her life has served as an inspiration not only to French patriots but to patriots of every persuasion throughout the world. Her brave example far transcends national boundaries and historical periods. Such was her incredible courage and conviction that some of the world's greatest authors have been inspired to tell her story.

When the life of Joan of Arc is viewed from a broad, esoteric perspective, it seems clear that she was chosen by divine agencies to play a role in world history far greater than she could possibly have imagined. There is good reason to believe that she was used as an instrument of divinity to reverse the trend of the Hundred Years' War by rallying the French royalist army so that France might be reunited as a nation, and thus be enabled to fulfill its proper destiny among the nations. Joan of Arc was instrumental in helping to restore a degree of balance between France and England.

Such great and weighty purposes are seldom achieved except through sacrifice. There exists an analogy here between Joan's sacrifice and the sacrifice of Jesus the Christ who pronounced the words, "I, if I be lifted up, will draw all men unto me." On a smaller scale, and in her own way, Joan of Arc was "lifted up," first onto the pyre, and then into the ranks of the saints to become a radiant *ideal* to all those who hate tyranny and feel called to give "the last full measure of devotion" to preserve the integrity of the country they love.

Rays in Evidence

The Presence of Ray Six

Joan of Arc was a mystic and militant visionary – a young woman utterly committed to a heroic, spiritual mission. It is well known that sixth ray individuals are strongly responsive to *guidance*, and from the beginning Joan's guidance was of the most extraordinary kind. When she was only twelve years old, she began to hear "voices," and then to see visions. The first voice she heard prophesied for her an amazing future:

> Joan, you are destined to lead a different kind of life and to accomplish miraculous things, for you are she who has been chosen by the King of Heaven to restore the Kingdom of France, and to aid and protect King Charles, who has been driven from his domains. You shall put on masculine clothes; you shall bear arms and become the head of the army; all things shall be guided by your counsel (*Procès de condamnation et de réhabilitation de Jeanne d'Arc*, by Jules Qucherat – as cited in *Saint Joan of Arc*, by Vita Sackville-West).

Many luminous figures or "spirits" appeared to her during the four and a half years which elapsed between her first otherworldly encounter and the time she set off upon her mission. The three spirits who constantly appeared to her and conversed with her were (at least in her estimation) the Archangel Michael, St. Margaret and St. Catherine. Frightened at first, Joan gradually came to trust her guidance implicitly. Her story is one of unwavering fidelity to the sources of her inspiration. She might argue with them, or protest that she was inadequate to carry out their behests, but never (except for her brief recantation when faced with the full terror of the Inquisition and the English army at the moment of her official, public condemnation) did she relent from following the course of action dictated by her guidance and her conscience. Once that miserable (and understandable) moment of weakness passed (as it did within three days), she asserted herself with renewed courage and steadfastly reaffirmed her faith in her "voices," even though she realized that to do so meant a certain and fiery death as a "relapsed heretic."

To Joan, as to all those powerfully conditioned by the sixth ray, the execution of her mission was an imperative, all-consuming obsession; nothing could stop her. Her voices, apparently, told her exactly what she had to do. Her task was incredibly demanding for a girl of seventeen (or for anyone!). It was at that age she left her native town of Domremy, never to return. Her mission as she understood it was twofold: to raise the siege at the city of Orleans (the English had contained the French within the city for many months), and to conduct the Dauphin, Charles VII, to Reims for his coronation as King of France. Joan believed herself to be the savior of the French nation. Some might call this "glamor of special selection," (to which those upon the sixth ray are very susceptible), but it does indeed seem that Joan *was* selected. Her presence had an almost magical effect upon the troops under her command, and her remarkable exploits did, in fact, signal the turning point in the Hundred Years' War.

Joan, with that quality of one-pointed determination so characteristic of those upon the sixth ray, did exactly what she determined to do (at least initially while responding to the first great wave of inspiration which carried her forward). Her unquestioning sixth ray faith in her destiny was her strength. In order to make her way to the Dauphin who was holding court in the city of Chinon, she had to persuade relatives, soldiers, governors, priests, courtiers, etc., first, that she was not simply some lunatic visionary and, second, that she was not a witch. Such was the purity of her motive, and her sturdy and simple piety (not to mention her commonsense) that she consistently prevailed over the skepticism she inevitably and invariably encountered.

Like so many sixth ray individuals, Joan was impatient, importunate and impetuous. She was entirely self-assured. With single-mindedness (and some might say with simple-mindedness) she always *knew* what needed to be done and would hear of no alternatives. Aided by the powers of heaven, she would confront the English, raise the siege of Orleans, and prevail over the enemy in one battle after another. The Dauphin, Charles VII, would be crowned as King. She would drive the English back across the Channel, and France would be united under his rule. Charles VII, however, was a weak, vacillating man, timid, overly cautious, and little-inclined to heroic thought and action. Joan was far more eager for his coronation that he himself, and, consequently, he (almost unconsciously) placed many tests and barriers in her way. Joan, however, overcame them all, proving herself to the satisfaction of both her courtly and ecclesiastical examiners. Finally, Charles, his court and his churchly advisors succumbed to her unrelenting insistence, and an army was assembled to attack those who were laying siege to Orleans. Joan, the visionary, holding firmly to her vision, had manifested the first phase of her plan.

Joan had a extraordinary effect upon her troops – not only upon their prowess in battle, but upon their morals. The sixth ray, we realize, is concerned with piety and purification. Joan sought to make her troops godly. She would tolerate no profanity or heavy swearing (though she herself used –and allowed to be used– one or two innocuous oaths). She insisted that her soldiers attend mass whever possible and repeatedly ordered them all to confession. Further, she demanded that all camp–following women of ill repute be banished from the army's retinue. At one point, so great was her moral fervor, that she reputedly broke her famous sword, *Fierbois*, over the back of a courtesan. There was no question that under Joan's leadership, the French royalist army was to be transformed into an army of God.

Joan was not a trained soldier. She relied, in military matters upon the inspiration (and sometimes, direct instruction) from her guidance, and not upon military tactics. Her method was always courageous, direct, heroic pursuit, augmented in its effectiveness by the incredible tenacity of the sixth ray. She was seriously wounded at the battle of Orleans (an arrow above her breast, six inches into her flesh), but after the wound was treated, and following a brief rest, she returned courageously to the field of battle. Because of her tenacity, and her refusal to retreat until her vision of victory was fulfilled, she was able to rally her troops and carried that most important day against great odds. She was, above all, an *inspiration* to her army – the army of France. It was her indomitable presence which inspired her soldiers (exhausted though they were) to fight as they had never fought before. Carrying her standard, she threw herself into the fray, persistently riding into the most dangerous and exposed positions. Yet, essentially, her's was a moral and spiritual force. Many of her soldiers believed her to be a saint sent by God to raise France from defeat. Their belief in her, and her own belief that the power of divinity was on their side proved decisive at the pivotal battle of Orleans. The French were inspired, and the English (at first disdainful and mocking) were terrified and forced to retreat. Though the French army was to suffer a number of reverses, the tide of the war had turned. Through the uplifting power of the sixth ray, their morale had been restored.

Certain events which followed the victory at Orleans also demonstrate Joan's profoundly sixth ray nature. The English army at Orleans was badly beaten and, both militarily and psychologically, in a disadvantageous position. The major victory had been won on a Saturday night, but the next day, when the French commanders wished to pursue the retreating English and destroy them, Joan restrained the entire army, simply *because it was Sunday*. She was so pious and devout a Catholic that she would not let her army attack on the Sabbath (although, with her usual commonsense, she said they might defend themselves if attacked). Thus, a tremendous tactical, military advantage was sacrificed to Joan's religious values – a clear indication of the preeminence of the sixth ray over the first and third. Her decision was not by any means an isolated incident;

many such tactical mistakes were made in deference to her ideals. For instance, it was agreed by all the French commanders (and even the English) that Joan should have pursued her advantage after the major victory at Orleans by moving swiftly to storm the walls of Paris. But again, a dutiful following of her mission (to see the Dauphin crowned at the Cathedral at Reims) was uppermost in her mind, and she one-pointedly pursued this end despite its eventual, unfavorable military consequences. Like many a sixth ray fanatic, she could not be deflected from the pursuit of her goal, nor was she open to reason if reason conflicted with her idealistic intentions.

Joan was also very emotional (a trait commonly found in those strongly conditioned by the sixth ray). She would weep frequently and copiously, and often for the wounded enemy – above all for their souls, especially if they met death unconfessed.

The qualities of devotion, so much a part of Joan's character, extended not only to her heavenly visitors, but to France and to the weak Charles, whom she helped so much (and who helped her so little). Complete faith and freedom from doubt were also numbered among her outstanding qualities. Once she had become accustomed to her voices and her apparitions, she never for a moment doubted their veracity and heavenly inspiration. Neither did she doubt the role which God, the "King of Heaven" (as she called Him) intended for her to play on behalf of France. Nor did she doubt the Dauphin Charles' rightful claim to the throne of France (though there was good reason to believe that he was, in fact, a bastard). She remained utterly committed to him even though his vacillations and double-dealings were inexcusable – in fact, treacherous. Even during her trial at Rouen she would allow no insult to be spoken of him, though he made absolutely no effort to ramsom her after she was captured by the Burgundians (allies of the English). It might be said of Joan, as is true of so many sixth ray people, that she was *credulous*. Her devotion was as unwavering as it was blind.

The sixth ray is the ray of *piety*. Joan's pious flame remained unextinguished throughout her life. She was pious as a child; pious in her acceptance of a mission that would have made the strongest commanders quake; pious in her command of armies; pious even during her outrageously unfair trial (the damning result of which was a foregone conclusion); and pious to the end, when on the pyre she asked that a priest hold the crucifix aloft so that she could always see it through the flames. A clear and simple note of sincerest piety was one of her outstanding virtues.

Although Joan was humble before God, she was anything but meek before men. When under direct inspiration, she was a fiery being – a fiery visionary, undaunted military captain and martyr to her cause. In this connection it is interesting that the Tibetan, when discussing the destruction of the causal body for the individual upon the sixth ray, states:

> ...he bends every faculty and every effort to the contemplation of what is required, and in sacrifice for that person or ideal lays even his causal body on the flames of the altar. It is the method of divine fanaticism that counts all lost apart from the vision, and that eventually sacrifices joyously the entire personality. The causal body is destroyed through fire, and the liberated life streams upward to the Spirit in divine beatification (*Letters on Occult Meditation*, p. 18).

Joan's fiery death (which she could have avoided had she been willing to relinquish her principles) was just the kind of self-sacrifice frequently experienced by advanced disciples upon the sixth ray. Throughout her trial, she was subjected to cruel and relentless physical and psychological pressure; the entire power of the Inquisition and of the English army in France was ranged against her, attempting to destroy what she stood for and, through her destruction, to discredit Charles VII and his claim to the throne of France. Had she finally succumbed, and sought to save her life, her highest spiritual purpose would have remained unfulfilled, and the inspiration which her name has given to the world for five hundred years would have been lost to history. But instead, she gave all, choosing the path of immolation rather than betray her divinely inspired mission. Certainly, Joan of Arc stands as one of humanity's greatest exponents of sixth ray energy.

The Presence of Ray One

One of the remarkable qualities which stands in bold relief throughout the amazing career of Joan of Arc is her incredible courage, and the apparent fearlessness she displayed in every kind of encounter – interpersonal, political, ecclesiastical and military. How could a girl, not yet twenty, have had the fortitude, confidence and charisma to throw herself into the most dangerous circumstances and alter the destiny of a nation? It is scarcely conceivable, and certainly must have required an ability to draw upon the strength of the Ray of Will or Power.

Interestingly, Joan's earliest years appear to have been very normal. She was said to have been a hard-working, dutiful, responsible child, as one might have expected with the Sun placed in the sign Capricorn. However, she was also extraordinarily self-contained. From the time she was twelve, she held a dreadful and awesome secret. In her own mind, the fate of France rested upon her shoulders, and yet she never divulged her mission to a soul, until, in January of 1419 she set off to the town of Vaucouleurs seeing permission to be sent to the Dauphin. What fortitude it must have required to keep that secret to oneself: what unusual discipline! Such qualities are distinctive evidence of first ray energy; individuals strongly conditioned by this ray have an instinctive reserve and know how to hold their tongue. The Scorpio Ascendant usually assigned to Joan (thus strengthening the power of the first ray planet Pluto), and emphasizing the strength of an elevated Mars in the tenth house (Mars bringing in both the sixth and first rays), is a further indication of the power of the first ray in her life.

The mission which Joan accepted from her voices, called for a dramatic and total break with her past way of life. She had been a humble peasant, a young girl whose principal duty was to watch over sheep and cattle, and to help her mother with heavy farm work. Her destiny, however, demanded that she leave all that behind and sever her connection with everyone and everything familiar. It is, of course, the first Ray of Will and Power that confers the ability to detach completely from those who are near and dear and from one's customary environment. It is the first ray which confers the initiative to plunge into the unknown. Because of the nature of her mission, Joan was unable to confide in anyone, especially her parents. Without the comfort and warmth of a true leave-taking, she simply had to depart – quietly and irrevocably. This required the great fortitude and the at least temporary suppression of her emotions in deference to a higher purpose. In short, it required the use of first ray energy.

Once she stepped into the "man's world," she had to demonstrate convincing strength and capacity or be immediately discounted and repulsed. She was, after all, saying and demanding 'preposterous' things. Only her great sincerity (a sixth ray trait) and her first ray ability to speak firmly and with utter directness allowed her to impress and bring to her aid those who usually would merely have laughed at the absurdity of what she was proposing.

We must remember too, that the first ray can be considered the masculine archetype, just as the second ray is naturally associated with the feminine. Joan not only was stepping into a man's world; for all intents and purposes she had to 'become' a man. While she is said to have had a very womanly voice, and while she easily gave way to tears (a behavior far more associated in the public mind with women rather than men), she nevertheless had to deal with some of the roughest and most powerful men in the kingdom. She did not do it by inspiration alone. It is true that many fell under the spell of her goodness and sincerity, and looked up to her with a devotion bordering almost on idolotry. With other stronger and less sentimental characters, however, she had to prove herself by her strength – and she could!

Apparently, she had the endurance of a man, and certainly the strength of her will was greater than that of most men (or women). At first she was certainly not the commander of the royalist army. She was regarded warily by the seasoned captains who plotted military strategy without her knowledge. Whether through intuition or guidance, she quickly became aware that she was being excluded from planning sessions or deliberately misled as to the real intentions of the army's strategists. She would not tolerate this, and insisted on having a voice in the proceedings – actually a *controlling* voice. She was certainly no sweet and amiable young girl (especially on the field of battle) but a militant captain made of the sternest stuff. Her approach to her soldierly comrades was peremptory and brutally frank; it was a first ray approach.

In so many of Joan's replies to those who would interrogate her or question her intentions (whether her interrogators were of the court or of the Church), she displayed a harsh directness, a sharp tongue. In the city of Poitiers she was closely questioned by doctors of the Church to see whether she should be trusted in her plans to raise the siege at Orleans. Some of the churchmen were rather condescending to her, but they got more than they bargained for. In the *Procès* which is the source of so much that is known of her life, it was reported that a certain professor of theology asked her in what language her voices spoke. He received a sharp reply: "A better language than yours." Persisting, he asked her, naively, if she believed in God. "Yes, and better than you," she responded. Still insistent, he advised her that they simply could not take her word that she was trustworthy, but that she would have to give them some proof or they would not advise the Dauphin to supply her with men–at–arms. At this, Joan apparently lost her temper: "By God's name," she said, "I have not come to Poitiers to perform signs. Lead me to Orleans, and I will show you the signs for which I am sent." Here is unabashed first ray directness: fearless speech in the presence of those who normally inspired fear (or at least a subdued and respectful manner) in those they interrogated.

Joan's superb audacity (actually, arrogance) was even more evident in her first letter to the English. Apparently there came a moment when she became utterly exasperated with her examiners, blurting out, "I cannot tell A from B, but God has sent me to raise the siege of Orleans and to get the Dauphin crowned at Reims. Have you paper and ink? Write! I will dictate to you." Let us remember that Joan was speaking in this manner to some of the most august members of the Catholic Church in France! Then in the most peremptory tones she dictated this letter:

> **Jhesus Maria. King of England, and you, Duke of Bedford, calling yourself Regent of France; William de la Pole, Earl of Suffolk; John Lord Talbot, and you Thomas Lord Scales, calling yourselves lieutenants of the said Bedford....Deliver the keys of all the good towns you have taken and violated in France to the Maid who has been sent by God the King of Heaven....Go away, for God's sake, back to your own country; otherwise, await news of the Maid, who will soon visit you to your great detriment."**

After this resounding opening, the letter became a little more reasonable, and more idealistic, but the power of the first ray is unmistakably present. Joan was either naive (a sixth ray quality) or truly fearless (probably a mixture of both) to call to account (and in such a high-handed manner) such powerful individuals – sworn enemies, some of whom would soon have the power of life and death over her.

Whether towards friend or foe, Joan was always direct – especially when the fate of the Kingdom of France was in question. In quieter more private moments she displayed a good sense of humor and love of fun, but such was the urgency of her mission that these moments were infrequent. If she spoke with deference at all, it was only to God in her frequent prayers (performed on her knees at every opportunity), to her familiar voices, and to Charles VII. She would importune him and hasten him, but she would never allow herself to verbally assault him as she did all others – even the English and the members of the Holy Inquisition *after* her capture.

During the course of her trial which lasted over five months, she was constantly subjected to intimidation, trickery, temptation and deceit. The English wanted her burnt. The Bishop of Beauvais who was in charge of conducting the trial (and who had been greatly inconvenienced, even threatened, by Joan's military victories) was convinced that she was either a witch or a heretic and, in any case, an enemy of Church authority. To him (and to many of his closest associates in the conduct of the trial) her guilt was a foregone conclusion, a matter of certainty even before the trial began. It was just a question of establishing it in a thorough and irrefutable manner, because Joan was an incredibly popular figure and had to be discredited in the eyes of the people before being destroyed. Joan had no counsel, and, intelligent and shrewd as she was, could not read. So unfair were the proceedings, that those few judges and members of the Inquisition who may not have been entirely sure of her guilt were forced to do or say nothing that might benefit her. Against this overwhelming opposition, intent upon her death or recantation, she responded with remarkable strength and fortitude. Using the power of her first ray energy, she would not allow herself to be intimidated. In fact, it was frequently she who became intimidating, and a cause of frequent consternation among that august body of righteous 'defenders of the faith.' Throughout her brief life, Joan was always willing to take risks. Her greatest victories were largely achieved through the display of the first ray qualities of courage and audacity. Where others showed fear, she did not, and many were the occasions in her life when fear might have been the normal response. Even her capture by the Burgundians at Compiègne resulted from her insistence upon leading a very risky, poorly reinforced sortie into the enemy's ranks, and from her courageous insistence upon staying behind to protect the rear flanks of her soliders when they were forced to retreat. It might be said that Joan thought she was invincible. Apparently she firmly believed that the King of Heaven and her familiar saints would protect her in all encounters, and that, basically, she had nothing to fear because of that protection. If this were so, perhaps she was not as courageous and fearless as it might at first seem. However, by the time of her capture she had already been told repeatedly by her voices that she must be taken – that her imprisonment was inevitable. The *moment* of capture was not prophesied – only its inevitability. Thus we see that Joan acted with bravery and daring, even though she felt convinced that fate or the Will of God was against her continued success upon the field of battle.

This first ray daring, audacity, even arrogance did not abandon her even when faced by a formidable array of hostile and often treacherous judges. Their questions were devious; their purpose was to trap her, to discover inconsistencies in her answers. She did not understand the tortuosity of their minds, yet she realized she was in mortal danger. Her answers were almost always direct, and surprisingly bold. From the testimony given by those who were questioned during the rehabilitation proceedings instituted by the Pope almost twenty years after her death, it appeared that she never allowed herself to be intimidated, and spoke in a bold and forthright manner which her judges at times found very impertinent and even unsettling. She could joke in the midst of solemnity. She betrayed no fear.

At the beginning of the proceedings, in typical first ray manner, she *refused* to take the required oath on the terms in which it was given. When Joan was asked to swear on the Gospels that she would answer nothing but the truth, she replied that she did not know what it was they wanted to ask her. "Perhaps," she added, "you may ask me things I will not tell you." She would not in any case promise to tell them everything about the revelations which God had made to her, even if they were to cut off her head. Realizing that her intransigence was a firm and permanent attitude, the court was forced to allow her to swear an oath in a modifed form and on her own terms. Further, when she felt disinclined to answer certain questions, she simply refused to do so. She even went so far as to confront her judge the Bishop of Beauvais (Pierre Cauchon) with the following challenge:

> **You say you are my judge; I do not know if you are or not; but be very careful not to judge me wrongly, for you would be putting yourself in grave danger. I am warning you of it now, so that if our Lord punishes you for it, I shall have done my duty in telling you.**

These daring words were completely consistent with her style. In similar terms she had challenged the English, each time warning them of the consequences of persisting in their ways. History, of course, has been the judge of Bishop Cauchon.

During her interrogation she also frequently refused to answer the questions of her judges, brazenly telling them that particular questions had nothing to do with their case, or simply saying that she was not allowed to answer. Sometimes she said that she had already answered such questions when interrogated by churchmen at Poitiers, before being allowed to lead the Dauphin's troops to Orleans. But most often she would answer directly and honestly. It should be said, though, that Joan was very wary. She instinctively knew when her interrogators were setting traps, and her answers (though biting and often ironical) were amazingly shrewd and cautious; one would expect this with a Capricorn Sun sign and a Scorpio Ascendant. The following exchange recorded at the trial will give some idea of the verbal tightrope she had to walk, and the cleverness *and* the directness with which she walked it. The interrogator is focusing upon the saints who, according to Joan, came to her regularly:

Q: In what shape do you see them?

A: I see their faces.

Q: Have they any hair?

A: C'est a savoir! (That would be nice to know)

Q: Is their hair long and hanging down?

A: I do not know. I do not know whether they have any arms or other members.

Q: If they had no members, how could they speak?

A: I refer that to God.

Q: Does Saint Margaret speak English?

A: Why should she speak English, as she is not on the English side?

Q: What did Saint Michael look like when he appeared to you?

A: I did not see any crown, and I know nothing about his garments.

Q: Was he naked?

A: Do you think our Lord has nothing to dress him in?

Q: Had he any hair?

A: Why should it have been cut off?

It is clear that Joan had the ability to turn questions back on her interrogators, at once avoiding their traps and making them look foolish.

In the minds of the Inquisition there was a very clear distinction between the Church Triumphant (God and His heavenly host) and the Church Militant (God's *sole* representative of the Church Triumphant). Perhaps Joan's greatest 'heresy' was her insistence upon submitting first to God and his saints (the Church Triumphant) and only *then* to the Holy Catholic Church (the Church Militant). This attitude was considered a tremendous threat to the spiritual and temporal authority of the Church, and could not (given the ecclesiastical mind–set of the day) be allowed to pass unchallenged and unchastised. Let us remember that the rays of the Catholic Church given by the Tibetan are a first ray soul, and a third ray personality and a sixth ray mind!

Joan's responses were unorthodox. In exemplary first ray manner, they cut clean through the magnificent edifice of authoritarianism carefully (and sometimes craftily) erected by the Church during the hundreds of years it spent invalidating the authority of the individual seeker after the mysteries of God. A simple exchange recorded in the trial reveals the crux of the matter:

> Q: Will you submit yourself in all your words and deeds, either good or evil, to the determination of our holy mother, the Church?
>
> A: I love the Church, and would uphold it with all my strength for the Christian faith. It is not I who ought to be prevented from going to church or from hearing Mass!
>
> Q: Will you submit yourself in all your words and deeds, either good or evil, to the determination of our holy mother, the Church?
>
> A: I refer myself to God who sent me, to Our Lady, to all the blessed saints in Paradise. As I see it, God and the Church are one and the same thing, and you ought not to make difficulties over that. Why do you make difficulties about it?

Why indeed? But Joan, who was perceiving an obvious synthesis (another of the foremost qualities of the first ray) had to confront those whose material interests were best served by preserving a schism between the Church Triumphant and the layperson – a schism, moreover, which could and 'should' (according to the Inquisition) only be bridged by the Church Militant. To the individual strongly conditioned by the first ray (especially when that ray is reinforced by the sixth) there should be no difficulties, no complexities and intricacies in the matter of the relationship of man and God. But the Church's third ray tendencies, abetted by its closed and separative sixth ray mind, and its drive for power (a distortion of its first ray soul quality) would not allow itself to be bypassed. A simple and direct approach to God was not to be permitted.

Treated in a direct and often disrespectful manner over the course of many days, the inquisitors became exasperated and began to threaten dire things: torture and the gruesome death of being burnt alive. To the threat of being punished by the ordeal of water, and by the stretching of the limbs with cords, Joan replied:

> Truly, even if you were to tear my limbs asunder and drive my soul out of my body, I could not speak otherwise; and, if I did say anything, I should always say afterwards that you had forced me to it.

And to their threats of the stake, Joan proudly affirmed:

> I will say no more about that. Were I to see the fire, I would still say all that I have said, and would not do otherwise.

Later when pressed further, she said that even if she were actually *in* the fire, she would hold to everything she had said, even to the death. Certainly, there can be no doubt of the power and presence of the first ray in her nature.

The Presence of Other Rays

In assessing what is known of the life of Joan of Arc, the sixth and first rays are far and away the most prominent. There may have been certain moments when other rays were in evidence. At times certain aspects of the fourth ray seem to have appeared, for, once in court she is said to have loved finery and dressing in lively colors, but surely there are other explanations. As a peasant girl in Domremy, she apparently showed none of these tendencies, but was a sober, dutiful and pious child (Capricorn, with rays six and one). Riding on the crest of the wave of her new-found popularity as the liberator of Orleans, it was only natural that Joan (who never had the opportunity as a child) should give expression to her enthusiasm and her anticipation of victory through the wearing of bright colors and a love of pagentry. It is significant that in every other way, the fourth ray seems to be missing from her makeup. She never hesitated (that was the province of the scandalously indecisive Dauphin, Charles VII); nor did she seek to harmonize. Her straight, direct and often abrasive manner demonstrated that the completion of her mission was far more important to her than adjusting to the likes and dislikes of those she felt herself responsible for mobilizing. Characteristically, when it was suggested that a truce or peace be made with the Duke of Burgundy (who had sided with the English), she insisted that such a peace could only be made at the end of a lance. Not much there to suggest a fourth ray love of reconciliation! To her the English and the Burgundians were the enemies of France, and only their *total* defeat could save the kingdom. No halfway measures would do. In this we see the sixth ray refusal to compromise (strengthened by the presence of the first ray). The fourth ray is nowhere to be seen.

In some respects there seems to be a bit of the third ray present. In most cases Joan was utterly direct and without guile. During her entire trial, there was no attempt to distort the truth or to deal in ambiguities as those with a strong third ray often will. When she could not answer, she would not; no subtle strategems were deployed. And yet she could be shrewd when necessity demanded. In the earliest days of her adventure, she knew that to pursue her mission she first had to conceal it from her parents and all friends (even, presumably, from her confessor in her village); and during her trial, she had to anticipate the strategems of her accusors. It seems, however, that these abilities were conferred more by the subtlety and silence of Scorpio, and the cautious prudence of Capricorn, than by the third ray in her ray chart. Capricorn, of course, is a conduit of the third ray, and its ruling planet, Saturn, is the primary distributor of the third ray. Pluto, as one of the rulers of Scorpio, may be somewhat associated with the third ray (which, symbolically, weaves the 'web' of the Scorpionic/Plutonic spider). There is little else, however, to suggest a prominent third ray placement. Certainly Joan relied upon inspiration and fortitude rather than strategy. The Tibetan tells us of the third ray soldier that "he will work out a problem in tactics at his desk, but is seldom great in the field." This is exactly the reverse of how Joan proceeded. She cared little for preplanning her strategy and she was *always* great in the field. Further, her utter simplicity and sincerity (uncomplicated by confusion or too many considerations), if anything, deny the presence of the third ray – at least in any prominent position (though, perhaps, it was the ray of her very strong and sturdy physical body).

The second ray, too, can probably be dismissed. The broad and gentle, inclusive love of the second ray was not characteristic of her nature. Joan's love was passionate and one-pointed; it was a love of God, his saints, and her country, France. It was also a love of her sovereign, Charles VII. But it was not an inclusive love. She could not love the *person* of her enemies, though she wept for their souls. Joan was altogether too militant, through and through, to be conditioned by the second ray. She was an activist and a firebrand. Second ray methods were too slow and apparently ineffective for her. Instead of "the wise use of slow action," she insisted upon the inspired use of impetuous action. It seems important here to raise the point that all sixth ray souls, at length, transfer onto the second ray; (or sometimes the third) but, even if we assume that Joan was a sixth ray soul (which is a rational assumption), there is almost nothing about her life which would suggest that a transition to the second ray (or third) was in progress.

The presence of the fifth ray is also doubtful. First of all, the fifth ray tends to reduce and individual's magnetism, perhaps due to fifth ray detachment and objectivity, and to the refusal to allow the emotions to rise at the expense of the mind. In any case, Joan was nothing if not charismatic. Everywhere acclaimed, she became the idol of the French; people were drawn to her irresistibly. Certainly her mind seldom, if ever, restrained her emotions (though her *will* did so when necessary). It was far more characteristic to see her in fervent prayer (and in tears) than deep in thought. Also, while it is true that Joan possessed commonsense, it was not the fifth ray variety of commonsense. It is important to remember that she did have five planets in earth signs (giving practicality and commonsense), and that her ruling planet Mars was in Virgo, one of the most down-to-earth of the zodiacal influences. Further, Joan was a French peasant. Everything about her upbringing promoted a matter-of-fact, commonsense approach to living. Those conditioned by the first ray, too, are *also* known for their commonsense, their direct no-nonsense approach. Those upon the sixth ray, however, are usually just the opposite, and typically, Joan did many apparently foolish things (especially militarily) because of her high-minded idealism and piety. Nor was Joan the careful and meticulous student. Rays two and five together give great studiousness. Her first interrogation at Poitiers demonstrated that Joan saw no need to *prove* who she was by using reasoning or logical proofs; her proofs lay in action. She was an intuitive. She did not (as so many fifth ray types do) doubt and question her divine sources. She accepted them uncritically, at face value, and did not analyze their origins. One of her biographers, Vita Sackville-West, in *Saint Joan of Arc*, offers a clear assessment of the situation: "her intellect was nil, though her genius was great."

This leaves the seventh ray to consider. Except, perhaps, for the love of fine clothes, floating standards and shining armor (all of which she developed, quite naturally, *after* she had been accepted into the court of the Dauphin), there is little to suggest a strong seventh ray in her make-up, except perhaps, on the physical level (though the third ray is a more likely choice). It might be argued, also, that Joan realized the value of these outer symbols as a source of inspiration for her followers. Above all, she knew that her purpose was one of inspiration, and given the practicality of her Capricornian energy, it was only natural that she would use all means at her disposal to be effective. Of course, Capricorn does bring in the seventh ray, as well as the first and third; in fact, it is the constellation through which the seventh ray is primarily focused. Some seventh ray energy must definitely have been present as a result, and it would seem that in the repetitious duties of her life as a peasant girl, seventh ray energies would have found expression. But there is little in her conduct, once she emerged into the wider world, to suggest the presence of that ray. Suppose, for instance, that the seventh ray had been her personality ray (for certainly it could not have been her soul ray). Such a placement would have induced a significant degree of moderation, politeness and conformity to custom. Joan, however, was consistently impatient, importunate, and often, rude, by courtly standards. She pressed forward constantly, and when she could not, she "chaffed at the bit," so to speak. Certainly, she did not display a refined and courtly manner; she had no time for such things. She was a one-pointed missionary to whom most matters of form were impediments to her goal. Certainly, when considering the manner in which she addressed even those who were her closest companions in arms, seventh ray politeness, consideration, tact and timing were completely missing. She did nothing but insist, demand, push people forward, and arouse – hardly the approach of the seventh ray type who considers right timing and a respect for cyclic activity so important. The seventh ray usually tempers fanaticism. This is evident when we compare the qualities of the sixth ray age, now ending, with the age of the seventh ray, now emerging. But Joan, divinely inspired though she was, was the quintessential fanatic. She had a vision, and counted all as lost should that vision not be achieved.

Proposed Ray Chart for Joan of Arc

Just as the life of Joan of Arc demonstrated the simplicity and clarity of a single theme, so her chart (at least as conceived by this author) does the same. The sixth and the first rays are, it would seem, completely dominant.

$$
\begin{array}{ccc}
 & 1 & \\
\text{VI} & 1 & 6 \\
 & 3 &
\end{array}
$$

This may seem an extreme kind of chart, but even among the Tibetan's group, two disciples, I.S.G.-L. and H.S.D. possessed this very chart, with modifications only on the level of the physical vehicle. It is clear from the Tibetan's advice to these two disciples, that it was important for them to learn moderation, restraint and rhythm. Interestingly, each of these disciples (albeit born some 650 years after Joan), was in the process of tranferring from the sixth to the second ray). This cannot convincingly be said of Joan.

There is little doubt Joan of Arc was a sixth ray soul. Her entire orientation was towards the higher worlds. She was a mystic and visionary with a divine mission to carry out upon the Earth but, truly, she longed for the realms where her familiar saints dwelled. She would often weep because, after coming to converse with her, they would not take her with them.

One of the most significant distinctions between sixth and first ray individuals is the tendency of the former to find their source of strength apparently *outside* themselves.

They project their strength onto others, who then become the source of their inspiration. First ray individuals, however, feel themselves to centers of power; even when more spiritually sophisticated, and thus realizing that personal power is extremely insignificant, they *identify themselves* with the source of divine power. Through the process of identification they see no separation between that source and themselves. Joan was definitely of the former persuasion. Her voices and her saints were (as she conceived it) the cause of her strength, and when they were silent, or seemed to abandon her, her strength and her inspiration seemed to falter. Her orientation was always up and out, rather than deep within.

When attempting to determine the priority of the sixth or the first ray in Joan's ray chart, it must be said that Joan was not a ruler by choice. The first ray field of government, per se, was not her most definite *calling*, her vocation. True, in order to achieve her mission – the rallying of the French nation which had become almost resigned to an English victory – she had to step into a commanding position, but once her task was completed, she would not have wanted to govern. She did not really have the temperament for it; she was too intense, too urgent, and her greatest longings related to the other world. After the coronation of Charles VII had been brought about through her tireless efforts and constant insistence, she confided to the Archbishop of Reims that she hoped to go home once again to tend her parent's flock (not that this would have been a psychologically valid option). Perhaps she felt that there she would have greater peace to commune with her angelic and saintly companions. They (Whoever they were) had no such intention.

When attempting to assess the soul ray of Joan of Arc, her relationship to the Master Jesus comes into focus. From all appearances it was the relationship of Master to chela. Perhaps it was through a subconscious identification that Joan usually began the letters she dictated with the words "Jhesus Maria." As a good Catholic, she would, of course, pray to Jesus (for, in those days, who but conscious initiates could have known of the distinction between Jesus and the Christ as revealed through the Ageless Wisdom?) When she died in flames, so the story goes, she called repeatedly at the top of her voice upon Jesus until her head sank forward.

Some of the Tibetan's earliest words about the Master Jesus (found in *Initiation, Human and Solar*, pp. 56–57, reveal an Individual Who can easily be seen as Joan's "role model" – not at all Jesus, the sweet and kindly sufferer:

> **The Master Jesus, Who is the focal point of the energy that flows through the various Christian churches....He is upon the sixth Ray of Devotion, or Abstract Idealism, and His pupils are frequently distinguished by that fanaticism and devotion which manifested in earlier Christian times amongst the martyrs. He Himself is rather a martial figure, a disciplinarian, and a man of iron rule and will....He is distinctively the Great Leader, the General, and the wise Executive....**

Is this not, in a way, the very picture of Joan? Cannot her essential quality be sensed in this description of the One who stands to her as an archetype? It may be that upon reading of Joan's exploits, bravery, courage, and fortitude on the field of battle some might insist that she would have to have possessed a ray one soul. But upon reading the Tibetan's description of the Master Jesus, such qualities are present as well upon the sixth ray. Students will by now be familiar with the idea that the first and sixth ray are closely related in certain respects, just as desire and will are related. The planet Mars, which is a sixth ray planet, and brings about a militant attitude in those it influences, is *also* a first ray planet. Of the Teachers who work on Mars, the Tibetan writes: "They work under the first logoic aspect and train those whose work is *along the lines of the destroyer*" [emphasis MDR], (*Esoteric Astrology*, p. 694). Is it not fascinating that Mars is the most elevated planet in the horoscope of Joan of Arc? Not only is it the ruler of her Scorpio Ascendant, but it is placed in the sign Virgo, the sign of the "Virgin." What could be a more graphic description of the militant Virgin – "la Pucelle," as she was known throughout France? Certainly, sixth ray Mars is Joan's most essential planet, not only in a personality sense, but in a far deeper respect.

There is one more point which should be discussed in this question of whether Joan was a sixth ray soul or a soul upon the first ray. During her trial, important questions arose concerning the standard which she carried into every battle. Upon her standard were painted the world supported by two angels, the lilies of France and, most importantly, the image of Jesus accompanied by the words *Jhesus Maria*. Her inquisitors found the standard most reprehensible and blasphemous, and Joan did not help her case by insisting that "Our Lord" (meaning Jesus), through the agency of St. Margaret and St. Catherine, had commanded her to create the standard in that manner. But when Joan was asked which she loved more – her standard or her sword – her response clearly indicated the priority of her values, and conclusively settles the question of which ray was preeminent in her life (the first or sixth). Although she loved her sword, "Fierbois," because it had been found in the Church of her beloved Saint Catherine, she loved her standard far better – "forty times better." When asked why she carried her standard into battle, she simply responded that doing so made it possible for her to avoid killing anyone with her own hands; she added that she had never killed any man.

The symbolism is clear. The sword has always been considered one of the outstanding symbols of the first Ray of Will and Power, and the standard (or flag) one of the preeminent symbols of the sixth Ray of Devotion and Idealism. The sword brings death and detachment, and the standard (held aloft) arouses and inspires the devoted so that they may may lift themselves to the highest pinnacle of aspiration and commitment. The first ray Word of Power – "I ASSERT THE FACT" – is a mantram embodying the concept of the "Sword of Truth." The sixth ray word of power – "THE HIGHEST LIGHT CONTROLS" – suggests the highest possible 'standard' of values to which the aspiring sixth ray individual seeks ever to conform, and according to which he controls his life demonstration within the three worlds of human evolution. Clearly then, Joan of Arc was a sixth ray soul – archetypally so.

Having decided the most important question of the soul ray, the conclusion that Joan had a first ray personality seems inescapable. She was a woman of undeviating purpose. Once her vision was clear, nothing and no one – the provincialism of family and peasant tradition, the obstructiveness of royal courtiers and jealous prelates, the disbelief of friends, and the ridicule and treachery of enemies – could keep her from performing the task to which she had committed herself. In true first ray manner, she acted essentially *alone*. Upon the physical plane, at least, she was the sole initiator of her immense project (the rallying of the French nation), and (rightly or wrongly) she took the entire responsibility for its success squarely upon her own shoulders. Her incredible hardiness and fearlessness; her obstinacy and determination; her rough manner and rude tongue; her ability to stand with battle-hardened soldiers as an equal (and even a superior); and her success in preserving both her dignity and integrity when facing (alone and without counsel) the entire force of the 'Holy' Inquisition and its English instigators, all point to a first ray personality. Joan was a great visionary, who had the strength, courage, singleness of intent, and sufficient of what might be called the 'conviction of invincibility' (which is certainly a first ray quality) to *force* her vision into history.

Its seems probable that the mental ray was the first as well. Her words were brief and often biting. She could spar verbally with the most sophisticated thinkers because she could cut right through their complexities to the essential point. She spoke the plain truth without hesitation to both friend and foe alike. Where matters of principle were concerned she spared no one's feelings. Her's was a great simplicity of mind (though she was far from simple-minded). Rather, her vision was one of great clarity, if not of subtlety. She had no time for niceties of speech. In fact, she usually spoke in the peremptory tones of one who sees exactly what must be done and expects others to seek likewise and act accordingly (and immediately). The outstanding feature of Joan's mental process was her *certainty*. When she knew something, she simply *knew*. No appeal to reason or caution could reverse her firmly held view. She was a natural intuitive. She did not piece information together and draw logical conclusions (as she would have had her mind been upon the fifth ray), nor were there any hesitation, indecision, vacillation, or uncertainty as are so commonly found when the mind is colored by the fourth ray. Futhermore, any woman who could say to the royal and powerful Bastard of Orleans – "...In God's name I order you to let me know as soon as you hear of Fastolf's coming [the English commander Sir John Fastolf], for if he passes without my knowledge, I promise you that I will have your head off" – certainly could not have had a second ray mind, or, for that matter, a sinuous, circumspect mind upon the third ray. In fact, only one with a first ray mind could speak as she spoke.

The ray of the emotional vehicle had to have been the sixth. Joan was capable of the most intense devotion – to God, to her saints, to Charles VII and to France. We recall the Tibetan's comment that the sixth ray manifests through the emotional vehicle as devotion, and through the personality vehicle as idealism. Further, Joan was emotionally spontaneous and excitable (and more often, volatile and irritable). Despite the presence of strong first ray energy, she seldom appears to have restrained herself emotionally. Her frequent tearful outbursts – whether weeping in frustration, pious contrition, or over the fate of the fallen enemy – are all indications of the emotionalism of the sixth ray astral body. Neptune, "God of the Waters" (and one of the planets distributing the sixth ray) is frequently associated with the lachrymal glands and with tears. The second ray astral nature is, we know, relatively calm and patient; but everything about Joan was impatient and importunate. Once she was launched upon her destined path, she lived with urgent, emotional intensity. Had the astral vehicle been upon the first ray, she would not have been capable of such spontaneous emotionalism, nor would people have found her so emotionally responsive. The line of energy extending from the sixth ray soul to the sixth ray astral vehicle created a combination of energies capable of inspiring ardent aspiration, but equally capable of emotional extremes. It must be remembered that Joan of Arc was above all an *inspiration*. She inspired not by the power of her thought, but by her unconquerable ardor in the cause of liberating France. She had a powerfully purifying, uplifting, and transformative effect upon the emotions of her soldiers. She aroused and focused their desire to prevail. Through strict and pious disciplines she elevated the emotional tone of the armies she led, restoring their enthusiasm and increasing their moral (and physical) strength. A vibrant and intensely devoted sixth ray emotional vehicle was one of her most powerful gifts.

Because no truly reliable likenesses of Joan have survived (if, indeed, there ever were any), it is difficult to assess with confidence the ray of the etheric–physical body. Through circumstantial evidence, however, it seems likely to have been upon the third ray. Certainly, Joan was sturdy – capable of supporting the weight of full armor for days at a time, which suggests the mesomorphic, third ray body. She also could go for long hours with little sustenance; she apparently did not have the need to eat and sleep with regularity, as is so often the case with those who have seventh ray etheric–physical bodies. Also, it seems clear that Joan did not stand on ceremony. There was no time in her life to cultivate courtly formalities and observances. She was adaptable upon the physical plane (as she would have to be, camping with and fighting alongside rough soldiers in crude and inhospitable conditions). From all indications, however, she was fairly oblivious to the rigors of such conditions, and to the crudeness of her military companions; refinement was not a concern. While it is said that Joan loved pageantry, and was not adverse to cutting a good figure in handsome armor (suggesting at least some presence of the seventh or fourth rays), she easily grew restive with the repetitive routines of court life, and longed to be in the field fighting the enemy. It seems that her activity level was very high and that routinization held little appeal for her. Even her attendance at Mass and her confessions were not done so much regularly and rhythmically as more spontaneously, with as much frequency as possible (sixth ray influence), and whenever the spirit moved her.

As a final point of interest, there is a little stone statue in the museum at Domremey, France (Joan of Arc's place of birth), which may well be, if not an authentic likeness of Joan, at least close. It seems to be a reproduction of a section from a sculptural group created some thirty years after her death. It shows a young girl kneeling in prayer. She is short, plain, sturdy (even a little on the stocky side) – the very image of a solid French peasant. Everything about this little statue suggests a third ray physical vehicle rather than a seventh. It should be realized, that until the akashic records can be reliably read for verification on such matters, hypotheses such as these must remain inconclusive. The weight of evidence, however, seems to be on the side of the third ray.

Conclusion

Although very much a historical figure, Joan of Arc has become a hero of almost mythological proportions. In the process of myth–making truth often suffers, and the character of the one mythologized becomes at once simpler and less credible as a real individual. Fortunately, in the case of Joan of Arc, the delineation of her true character is well–preserved because of the meticulous care with which her trial was recorded. We know a great deal about her short life – where she was on certain dates, what she did and what she said. Yet in all this well-documented chronicle, the simplicity of her life and her utter singleness of purpose are radiantly clear. She was, above all, the very archetype of the human being with a *mission*. From the time she agreed to follow her heavenly guidance (as presented by her voices and her saints), her life was as a straight line leading inexorably to the realization of her vision, and to the fulfillment of her awful (yet glorious) destiny. There are no rays more suited to the successful execution of an arduous mission than the combination of the first and sixth. It is clear that Joan of Arc's mission was, literally, *inspired from above*. She was the instrument of a dual purpose in alignment with the Divine Plan: a *national purpose* (the restoration and unification of the French nation) and, still more importantly, a *global purpose* – (the establishing of an extraordinarily high standard of heroism for all humanity, and especially for those whose destiny it would be to achieve spiritual liberation by following the sixth ray path of sacrificial *self-immolation*).

Note: The sources used for all direct quotations by or about Joan of Arc were: *Saint Joan of Arc*, Vita Sackville-West, Doubleday, Doran and Company, Inc., Garden City, New York, Copyright 1936; and the *Encyclopedia Britannica*, fifteenth edition.

Sir Francis Bacon

Lord Chancellor of England; Baron Verulam; Viscount St.Albans

Born, January 22, 1561 – Died, April 9, 1626

When studying the life of Sir Francis Bacon, we are confronted with a unique situation. In *Initiation Human and Solar*, under the section entitled "The Lodge of Masters," the Tibetan has informed us that the great soul who is now the Master Rakoczi (occupying the hierarchical post of the Mahachohan, or Lord of Civilization) was, in former incarnations, the Comte de St. Germain, Roger Bacon, and Sir Francis Bacon. Each of these illustrious personages was, therefore, a manifestation of the same great *spiritual individual*, and so it should be possible (to the extent that historical information allows) to trace, somewhat, the development of certain great themes and ray tendencies which animated each of these incarnational *appearances*.

A study of esoteric psychology reveals that if and when the soul ray changes, it does so according to certain laws, and only very infrequently – usually at the point when the soul begins incarnating in a new root race. In the case of those whose soul is upon one of the "rays of attribute" (rays four, five, six or seven), the soul ray often changes to one of the "rays of aspect" (rays one, two or three) immediately prior to the third initiation (and *inevitably* does so, sooner or later, after the third initiation). Today, because quite a number of individuals are on the threshold of that initiation, we can expect such changes of soul ray to occur more frequently (cf. *Discipleship in the New Age, Vol. I*, p. 572–3 and *Esoteric Psychology, Vol. I*, p. 402). Thus, we are living through a very fluid, transitional period, when certainty in matters of ray analysis is difficult to achieve.

The Master R. is known primarily as a seventh ray Master. It is known that recently, in order for Him to assume the office of the Mahachohan, or Lord of Civilization, His Ashram was shifted from the seventh Ray of Ceremonial Order to the third Ray of Active Intelligence, though He, Himself continues to remain very active along the seventh ray line. This change from the seventh to the third ray (a ray, which, because it synthesizes the four rays of attribute, naturally *includes* the seventh ray) cannot, in the usual sense, be called a change of soul ray, for it appears that the Master R. was, indeed, *already a Master* (an initiate of the fifth degree) when the change occurred, and, thus, He had moved far beyond that point in the evolutionary progress of the soul (i.e., around the time of the third initiation – sometimes preceding it, though often following it), when a soul upon a ray of attribute would be transferred to, or shifted onto, a ray of aspect. In fact, it would seem that (when considering the ray of a Master) it would be the *Monadic ray* that would be of paramount significance, since this "primary ray," which begins to be influential around the time of the third initiation, is, certainly, powerfully influential by the time the fifth initiation has been attained. Identifying the *true* ray of any Master, however, is somewhat complicated by the fact that Masters assume (or work upon) *various rays* as hierarchical need arises. The ray upon which a Master is presently functioning, therefore, may, or may not, be the soul ray upon which He for aeons evolved – though it would seem, that in order to respect the Law of Economy, there should be, at least, a close relation between the two.

All this is by way of saying that although the Master R. is *now* functioning upon (or, at least, with direct access to) the third ray (which may, indeed, be His Monadic ray), He was for many years focussed upon the seventh ray. It was (it seems reasonable to conjecture) his *soul ray*. This means that his preceding incarnations as Francis Bacon, Roger Bacon, (Paracelsus?), and the Comte de St. Germain (though "the Count" may have been Master R. in disguise, rather than a *separate* incarnation) *were strongly conditioned by the seventh Ray of Ceremonial Order and Magic.*

The Tibetan has not fully developed the fascinating subject of how the soul ray (when it is one of the four rays of attribute) is "shifted to," or 'translated' or sublimated into the appropriate ray of aspect. Nor has He discussed, to any great extent, the meaning of the growing power of the Monadic ray from the period following the second initiation (cf. *Letters On Occult Meditation*, p.267), to the point at which the fifth initiation is attained (at which point the Monadic ray is in full expression). It stands to reason, however, that in those cases when the soul is upon one of the rays of attribute, the quality of that ray of attribute does not simply 'vanish' when the shift begins, or when the Monadic ray begins to be influential. That soul ray (of attribute) must (it would seem) remain a *strongly conditioning ray* – at least a subray of that particular ray of aspect which begins to condition the soul when the shift occurs (whether preceding third initiation or sometime after it). Further, when the time comes for the destruction of the causal body, it is not reasonable to believe that the quality of the ray, which has for aeons conditioned the soul, simply 'evaporates,' giving way entirely to the Monadic ray. It must be remembered that, although the causal body is destroyed at the fourth initiation, the Spiritual Triad remains, and that the ray of the manasic permanent atom of the Spiritual Triad (which is the nucleus atom upon which the construction of the causal body is based) is the *same as the ray of the causal body* – i.e., the same as the soul ray. According to the Tibetan, the causal body "is...gradually built up of particles of matter belonging to the same quality and type as its nucleus atom..." (*Esoteric Psychology, Vol.I*, p. 169).

These ray dynamics are definitely relevant to the behavior and life demonstration of the initiate of the third degree. There can be little doubt that Francis Bacon *was* an initiate of the third degree, and, there is reason to believe he was more advanced still. If we realize that the Master R. is now a Chohan of the sixth initiation, and that the Master Jesus (also, now a Chohan) took the fifth initiation as Apollonius of Tyanna in the first century A.D., the progress of these two great initiates would have to have been extraordinarily unequal *unless* Roger Bacon, and, certainly, Sir Francis Bacon, were initiates of high degree – in Francis Bacon's case, a fourth degree initiate, or *perhaps*, even, an initiate of the fifth degree. Certainly, the Comte de Saint Germain, active 150 years after Francis Bacon's death, gives every indication of having been an initiate of the fifth degree – a Master of the Wisdom.

These thoughts are all an attempt to put our subject somewhat into perspective. We are attempting the ray analysis of one who is no ordinary individual, and for whom the Monadic ray must play an important role, even though the soul ray continues to be prominent. An individual such as Francis Bacon had reached a 'point of synthesis' far beyond the attainment of the average disciple, and, although strictly human qualities (and failings) apparently still manifested, the very highest sort of energies were also influencing the life. For instance, in Francis Bacon's case (especially during his maturity) it would be useful to be able to identify *the polarization within the Spiritual Triad* (*see A Treatise on Cosmic Fire*, p. 177.) Was it a manasic or buddhic polarization? If buddhic, it would account for the great "wisdom" in a man so mental. Such questions as these, however, will have to remain unanswered until more is given out upon the dynamics of those rays which condition the "higher reaches" of the human energy system.

With all the foregoing thoughts in mind, let us attempt to discover the rays which qualified the vehicles of the present Mahachohan (the Master R.) when He appeared during the 16th century as Francis Bacon.

Sir Francis Bacon – the Man

Sir Fransis Bacon was a brilliant individual: lawyer, courtier, royal counsellor, Lord Keeper of the Royal Seal, Attorney General, Lord Chancellor of England, educator, historian, scientist, visionary, utopian, and reformer. It is clear that he was in training for the responsibilities he would later assume as Lord of Civilization, for the scope of his interests and concerns encompassed all those things upon which civilization is based. He envisioned the potential of the human mind, and sought to initiate those great transformations which would liberate human thinking from its slavery to false "idols." For all his tremendous imagination, he was an eminently practical man who sought and enacted practical, concrete changes in numerous areas of daily living. But his great genius lay in his ability to glimpse the pattern that might be if humanity were willing to begin anew. He called his predominating life-theme, *Instauratio Magna*, the "Great Instauration," the conscious *renewal* of the most important aspects of human civilization – especially, the renewal of the life of the mind. As they study his life and his thought, students of esotericism will recognize great anticipations of the Age of Aquarius – an Age, in which it is promised that human civilization will be renovated and magically transformed under the impression of the incoming seventh Ray of Ceremonial Order. Fittingly, Sir Francis Bacon was born with the Sun in Aquarius, and the seventh ray was, almost certainly, his soul ray. Today we are experiencing many of the extraordinary changes which he envisioned. The patterns of civilized living are changing with incredible rapidity, and even the most prescient individuals do not know exactly where it will lead, except that it *will* lead to the Great Instauration which Francis Bacon rightly anticipated as humanity's greatest need. The study of the seven rays and the birth of a new psychology are an important part of this Great Instauration, for they are necessary if the work of the great and coming Seventh Ray Avatar is to be successfully accomplished (*see, Esoteric Psychology, Vol. II*, p. 282). With these thoughts in mind, let us begin our review of a few of the more significant factors of the life of Francis Bacon (i.e., from the point of view of ray analysis), admitting at the outset that much of paramount importance may presently be hidden from the enquiries of historians and biographers.

Rays in Evidence

The Presence of the Seventh Ray

Francis Bacon was a seventh ray soul (regardless of the Triadic and Monadic alignments which may have been occurring during his life). He was, in many respects, an archetypal embodiment of seventh ray energy at its most progressive, and also, interestingly, in its more conservative aspects. The seventh ray "Word of Power" is: "The Highest and the Lowest Meet." Quintessential seventh ray activity concerns the manifestation of the divine archetype (i.e., the "Highest") upon the physical plane (i.e., the "Lowest"). Under the influence of the planet Uranus, which is (at this time) the principal distributor of the seventh ray, obstructive patterns are *restructured* so that they *conform* to the descending Divine Archetype. This restructuring, reordering, renovation, renewal – this was Francis Bacon's impelling motivation (despite his deep conservatism in many political matters). His mind was vast, and ranged over an extraordinary number of subjects; whatever he thought about, he sought to reform – sometimes moderately, and, most often, drastically.

It must be remembered that the seventh ray is associated with the seventh plane – the plane of concrete manifestation. Bacon could handle abstract thought brilliantly, but his *soul*-concern was to initiate the manifestation of the archetype. He believed that the best ideas must be made to manifest as actualities. He thought Aristotelianism (especially as interpreted for centuries by the impractical, scholastic mind) useless,

> **...being a philosophy only strong for disputations and contentions, but barren of the** *production of works* **[emphasis, MDR] for the benefit of the life of man.**

Notice Bacon's preference for the practical humanitarianism of the seventh ray, as opposed to the strictly abstract intellectuality of the third.

As a lawyer he wished to recast the entire body of English Law, and to this end, set forth a little book called *Maxims of the Law* – a clear and incisive restatement of basic legal principles. This practical, little book remained in use more than two centuries after his death.

It was, however, chiefly as a "natural philosopher" (the modern term is "scientist") that he attempted his greatest reformation – the reformation of the human mind's orientation to reality. He sought to break free from the chains of the futile and arid scholasticism which dominated the universities of his day, and create an entirely new approach to knowledge and its acquisition – an empirical, scientific approach, which emphasized observation, experimentation and inductive thinking.

This was a tremendous departure from the prevailing pattern of thought; knowledge of the "real" world (i.e., the physical world) and its application were held in low esteem by rulers, the churchmen, scholastics, and 'gentlemen,' whose lifestyle would be challenged by the rapid growth of illumination. Bacon realized, however, that man would never be master of Creation, unless he came to terms with "things as they are." His purpose, then, was to *reorient* human thinking, to present the intelligent people of his day with an entirely new paradigm for understanding (and then restructuring) the physical, tangible world. As is characteristic of one whose soul is upon the seventh ray, he had a complete and detailed plan (complete in his mind, if not yet completely developed on paper) for this undertaking, and, in terms of the prevailing thinking of his Age (the close of the Renaissance) it was *revolutionary*.

Thus, we see that Bacon was, from one point of view, an inveterate reformer. Especially on matters touching the intellectual life of humanity, his plans for change raced far ahead of anything that was immediately possible. But, interestingly, Bacon was also a staunch royalist conservative. In his own words: "No man can say, but I am a perfect and peremptory royalist." As a seventh ray individual, he honored the principle of *hierarchy*, in matters both human and divine. He placed the monarch (his sovereign) at the very apex of the national/social hierarchy; this he considered a necessity to preserve law and order – clearly seventh ray themes. Thus, he deemed the power of the throne (though embodied by imperfect monarchs) absolute, and the Queen or King, necessarily, above the law. He expressed his attitude succinctly: "Let the judges be lions, but lions under the throne." Thus, he was closely identified with preserving royal prerogatives in the English legal system, and this practice created powerful enemies who, later, were only too eager to precipitate his dramatic fall.

When looking for the presence of the seventh ray in Bacon's energy system, it must be remembered that his father (the Lord Keeper of the Royal Seal under Queen Elizabeth) had been a lawyer, and that Francis Bacon's principal profession (regardless of his amazing diversity) was the law. Practical, legal matters (especially from the time his fortunes began, at last, to improve under the sponsorship of King James I), consumed a tremendous amount of his time. His principal service to the king was based upon his extraordinary knowledge of the law; his many other interests were neither understood, nor much appreciated in court. The law, we know, is a manifestation of first and seventh ray energies. Bacon, it seems, had very little of the first ray within his energy system; his approach was usually indirect, non–combative, and there were important moments in his life when he seemed helpless, vulnerable and unable to defend himself. Thus, his deep involvement with the law, must be understood from a seventh ray perspective.

Bacon learned to be the consummate courtier. When speaking of the individual upon the seventh ray, the Tibetan informs us that "the good type of the ray is absolutely determined to do the right thing and say the right word at the right moment; hence great social success" (*Esoteric Psychology, Vol. I*, p. 211). It had not always been so in Bacon's life, and often he had let his intellectual brilliance and spontaneity run away with him. After reaping the painful consequences of several severe mistakes, however, he began to study utilizing the "right word" and "right timing," and he studied so diligently, that he mastered the art. His notebooks (especially his *Promus of Elegancies*) are filled with phrases which he believed would prove advantageous either in writing or in conversation. These phrases are set down meticulously, and one can imagine that in private he *rehearsed* these phrases so they would be ready to the tongue at just the right moment. The quality of behavior which attempts to routinize 'correct' or appropriate responses (thus leaving nothing to chance) is closely associated with seventh ray influence.

Bacon also loved to write and speak in aphorisms (most often, in impeccable Latin). It was a form he found congenial. "This delivering of knowledge in distinct and disjointed aphorisms," he wrote, "doth leave the wit of man more free to turn and toss." He was capable of creating clean and spare, perfectly balanced phrases. Another great seventh ray soul, Benjamin Franklin, also enjoyed expressing himself in maxims and aphorisms: "Early to bed and early to rise, Makes a man healthy, wealthy and wise"; "Little strokes fell great oaks"; "There never was a good war or a bad peace"; etc. Bacon's aphorisms are far more learned and elegant, but, a similar *balance* is always present. Aphorism is a form which requires great precision of utterance; a good aphorism is a 'jewel of thought'; great powers of condensation are required, and the patience to polish a thought until it shines. Thinking and writing in aphorisms calls for the highest quality of verbal craftsmanship, and the seventh ray is the ray most associated with *craftmanship* – the creative power of the 'hand' (or of the 'five fingers' of the mind). The appeal of the aphoristic process to seventh ray individuals will, thus, clearly be seen.

The aphoristic form, is, also, something of a "magical formula" – a particularly concise and powerful means of presenting thought so as to achieve maximum results. One can recognize the ultrasophisticated use of the aphoristic style in the advertising industry. The message is condensed, balanced and delivered as an unforgettable 'slogan,' the impact of which, 'magically' causes the intended result – in most cases the purchase (or support) of that which is advertised. Mantrams and affirmations (both closely associated with the seventh ray) work on the same principle. Aphorisms, maxims, mantrams, affirmations, slogans, etc., are short and can be *repeated* until they "sink in," becoming part of the individual's *conditioning*. Through their use, the individual's response pattern becomes restructured or rearranged, and his behavior changes *manifestly*.

Bacon was what is now called a "networker." In his own choice words, he "rang the bell to call the wits together." He envisioned great cooperative enterprises for the advancement of learning, and the improvement of the life of humanity. He was a group-conscious Aquarian, of course, but it is also the seventh ray which is particularly related to the institution of well-organized group work. The seventh ray disciple creates or participates in "movements," great "team efforts" which are so much more powerful than the work of as many individuals working independently. Bacon foresaw the possibility of assembling the best talent in any number of fields, and engaging them fully and cooperatively in the execution of his transformative plans. He understood the seventh ray principle that *the well-organized whole is greater than the sum of its parts*.

Francis Bacon was also a man who loved the physical senses. The seventh plane is the plane directly related to the physical senses, and those upon the seventh ray are called realistic because they are alert to all that these senses convey. In the four-part psychological typology suggested by Carl Jüng, the characteristics of the individual which he calls the "Sensation Type" correlate most closely with the characteristics of the seventh ray. Francis Bacon, then, was *sensuous* (though not sensual). He loved his gardens, in their rich array; when he meditated indoors, he liked to have music playing in the next room; he dined elegantly; he dressed in beautiful clothes of the finest textures.

For all his flights into the empyrean, he was a man intensely *present* to life upon the physical plane, and *ordered* all things to increase the quality of that life.

Bacon was fond of pomp, pageantry, and great ceremonial displays; when his 'star' ascended under James I, he had the opportunity to indulge this fondness. He wished to look as well as play the part of a great man, and so he spent great sums on the *appearance of things* – his homes, his gardens, his clothes and the livery of his servants. As an interesting sidelight, the color purple (the color most often associated with the seventh ray) was his favorite, and he wore it upon very important occasions. On the occasion of his marriage, for instance, "he was clad from top to toe in purple...."

Conventional biographies of Bacon do not delve into his Rosicrucianism, and his reputed involvement with the "Mysteries of the Ancient Temple," but it is clear he understood the meaning and value of magic. Those who have studied his life from the esoteric perspective, suspect that Bacon was the leader of an inner circle of occultists (some of the greatest "lights" in Elizabethan society), whose purpose it was to transform their nation, and civilization as a whole – in fact, to create a "New Order of the Ages" to be established on the new continent, the "New Atlantis" – America. According to this point of view, Bacon was thus, even at that time, intimately involved in the process we now call the "Restoration of the Mysteries." It is fascinating, considering the Master R.'s interest in Masonry, and the Masonic origins of the government of the United States, to detect Masonic references in Bacon's *New Atlantis*. "Solomon's House" (or the "College of the Six Days Works") found upon Bacon's imaginary continent, certainly alludes to King Solomon (an earlier incarnation of the Master M.). It is sometimes suggested that the Master R. [i.e., Francis Bacon, etc.] was the great architect, Hiram Abiff, who cooperated with King Solomon in the building of Solomon's Temple). If this is true, and Francis Bacon had any memory of that earlier incarnation, his *New Atlantis* can be seen as a work dealing with universal themes of great importance for the evolution of the entire human race, for, as esoterically learned Masons will confirm, the building of Solomon's Temple is none other than the "Great Work" which every human being must, at length, accomplish; it is, in fact, the building of the causal body, the "Temple not made with hands, eternal in the heavens." Masons are known as *builders,* and one upon the seventh ray is also called a "builder." It is the function of Masonry to help all human beings *build the temple*, and to do this, the *house of the Temple* must be restored – i.e., there must be a "restoration of the Mysteries of Initiation." This, in fact, may have been the true and vitally important esoteric work upon which Francis Bacon, and his "secret society" were embarked – a work which peculiarly belongs to those whose soul is upon the seventh Ray of Order and Ceremonial Magic.

The Presence of Ray Three

Francis Bacon was one of the most brilliant intellects in the long history of the human race. He was an exemplary representative of what the Tibetan has called "the acute energy of divine mental perception" – the third Ray of Active (Abstract or Creative) Intelligence. He had that versatility of mind which was able to discourse on abstruse points of philosophy or the most concrete empirical data with equal facility. Dr. Willian Rawley, a close friend and admirer of Bacon's remarked:

> **I have been induced to think, that if there were a beam of knowledge derived from God upon any man in these modern times, it was upon him. For though he was a great reader of books, yet he had not his knowledge from books but from some grounds and notions within himself.**

The source of the knowledge of which Rawley writes is the abstract level of the mental plane, with which all initiates strongly animated by the third Ray of Active Intelligence are in the closest rapport.

Bacon was a complex man, both intensely practical, and (at least from the conventional perspective), impractical. With many who had been exposed to the ambitious reach of his thought process, he had the reputation of being a purely speculative man, unfit for the more mundane side of life. He was, indeed, one who asked of himself the greatest questions, and responded with a high-flying speculativeness which, though often technically inaccurate, was nevertheless filled with amazingly prophetic thought; in a number of instances, he anticipated discoveries which would only be made centuries later. Strongly conditioned as he was by the third Ray of Active Intelligence), he searched for the widest possible views on all manner of enquiries – scientific, philosophical and governmental. For all his capabilities in worldly affairs, he was undoubtedly an *intellectual*. His mental brilliance and precocity attracted a great following among those who loved the mind and its potentials, but it did not endear him to the sober, practical and often pedestrian men whose responsibility it was to manage affairs of state.

There was a great warfare in Bacon's nature between what he termed "the ambition of the understanding," and "the ambition of the will." Under the stimulation of the first ambition, writing to his uncle, William Cecil, the great Lord Burghley, he states:

> **I confess that I have as vast contemplative ends as I have moderate civil ends, for I have taken all knowledge to be my province.**

This is an extraordinary statement, showing the scope of Bacon's intellectual ambition (and, interestingly, anticipating his eventual duties as the Mahachohan, who, indeed, has all *knowledge* [upon the five rays of *manas* as they affect human civilization] as His province). Bacon sought the building of a new educational and intellectual empire in which learning would be advanced far beyond anything conceivable in his day. It is interesting, that esoterically considered, the entire Department of Education in Hierarchy can be classified under the aegis of the third ray (even though the second ray is the ray of the "teacher.") Today, in keeping with this classification, educational institutions, great and small, reflect, primarily, the quality of the third ray and its subsidiary fifth ray.

Returning to the implications of Bacon's statement to Cecil, we see that he deemed his "civil ends" as "moderate." This was only partly true. He fluctuated greatly at different periods of his life, often attempting to make a marriage of the two, but never really succeeding. From the point of view of the rays involved, his ambition of the will can be seen related, primarily, to the seventh ray, which is, indeed, a ray of will (being a more concretized expression of the first ray); his ambition of the understanding is more closely related to the third and fifth rays, both of which seem to have been prominent in his nature, with the third ray being, it would seem, *extremely* important. These two sets of rays, though related along the 1–3–5–7 line of energy, pulled him in opposing directions and brought much stress to his life.

Ray interrelationships are often complex, but it is necessary to explore the many possible connections. The fifth ray is not the *only* ray connected with scientific investigation. The student would be well advised to study the extraordinary phrases from the *Old Commentary* found in *Esoteric Psychology, Vol. I*, pp. 69–87. In this section, the seven Ray Lords address each other with certain statements and "requests," and various little-suspected qualities of the Ray Lords are revealed. After each phrase ('spoken' by a Ray Lord), the Tibetan lists a *quality* which epitomizes the phrase. The fascinating thing is (in this context, at least) that the quality of "scientific investigation" is associated with the *third* Ray Lord – the Lord of the Ray of Active Intelligence:

> **Produce the garment of the Lord; set forth the robe of many colours. Then separate that robe from That Which hides behind its many folds. Take off the veiling sheaths. Let God be seen. Take Christ from off the cross.**
> **Quality....scientific investigation.** *Ibid., p. 69*

These are words (so one would think) which should be reserved for the Lord of the fifth Ray of Concrete Knowledge and Science, but it is not so. Indeed, many great scientific investigators (especially those who were involved extensively in broad theoretical considerations, and in the philosophy of science) may have been colored (on a soul level or beyond) by the third ray. Although the fifth ray soul is said to transfer to the first ray (see *Discipleship in the New Age, Vol. I*, p. 573), there does seem to be a sense in which the third ray is the higher octave of the fifth ray, carrying scientific investigation into the realms of abstraction, which realms are the motivating causes of the concretions usually studied by the fifth ray type. At any rate, the ambition to take "all knowledge" as one's province is typically third ray, augmented, in this case, by Bacon's obvious fifth ray influence, entering 1) astrologically through Aquarius, 2) from earlier incarnations (especially his incarnation as the deeply scientific Roger Bacon [and, perhaps, as Paracelsus], and 3) through his energy system and ray chart – at least it seems a reasonable conjecture).

We have explored some of the higher qualities of the third ray as manifested in the life of Francis Bacon, but there are also numerous other evidences of a more mundane and human kind. Bacon, we know, was an extraordinary conversationalist, according to Thomas Fuller, a historian of the period, "...the eloquentest that was born in this isle." According to Ben Jonson, "the fear of every man that heard him was, lest he should make an end." Mercury, has been called "the god of eloquence," and it was a planet "ascending" in Bacon's astrological chart. Mercury is also closely associated with the three aspects of the mind (the concrete mind, the Son of Mind, and the higher [or abstract] mind), and quite possibly with rays three, four and (perhaps even) five. But focussing for a moment upon ray three, we know that it is the ray which, primarily, conditions the throat center. When pronounced in the ray chart or energy system of an individual, it gives the power to formulate speech and induces a great flow of words. Bacon was a great talker, and a great writer. The Tibetan informs us that "...the third ray man...under the fifth [i.e., under the influence of the fifth ray]...will be a master of the pen" (and, it would seem reasonable to conclude, of the spoken word as well). Hence, one possible explanation of Bacon's remarkable conversational abilities.

Bacon was ever disciplining himself, and, it might be said, *forming and re-forming* himself to more properly conform to the design which he conceived as his destiny. This 'sculpting of the self,' of course, is a seventh ray characteristic, but certain behaviors which he sought to correct bear the stamp of the third ray. For instance, his manners were marred by overeagerness, a tendency to interrupt others, and a tendency to stutter when excited. He resolved to himself that he must

> **suppress at once, my speaking with panting and labor of breath and voice. Not to fall upon the main topic too sudden....To compose and draw in myself.**

Admittedly, his Moon was in the impulsive sign Aries, but the above qualities are also associated with the *hyperactivity* of the third ray. Frequently, individuals strongly conditioned by this ray think and speak too rapidly, often because (given their great fertility of mind and natural abundance of thought) they have too much to say for the time allotted in which to speak. It is interesting that the third and sixth rays are closely related numerically ($2 \times 3 = 6$), and that those who are conditioned by these rays share the tendency to press a great deal of activity into a small amount of time (especially types 3B and 6B). Each of them needs stillness and restraint; they must *check* their feverish or frantic motion, and, quite plainly *moderate* their "presentation of self."

One more interesting characteristic relating to Francis Bacon's style of conversation, indicates the presence of the third ray: when he would converse with others he had the habit of looking upwards, away from the person addressed; his eyes were upon ideas. This is clearly an act of third ray *abstraction*.

While Bacon's manner was often impulsive and over-eager, he was also a man of *calculation* (many said, of self-interest). His cautious premeditation was a quality which did not endear him to all. Alexander Pope called him the "wisest, brightest, meanest of mankind." Lord Macaulay carried the insult further by naming Bacon "treacherous to his friends, a time-server, magnificent of intellect and cold of heart." We can see in these criticisms a focus upon the negative qualities of the third ray, and, to some extent, those of the seventh. The famous scientist William Harvey said of him, that "He had a delicate, lively, hazel eye, like the eye of a viper." Bacon's eyes, reputedly, had a certain "darting quality," and even in a terra-cotta bust made of him when he was a boy of ten, the expression of the eyes is indirect, his glance sidelong and evasive. The historian Henry Hallam made the serpentine comparison in a somewhat more polite form, when he said that Bacon possessed "adroitness and incomparable ductility." In the words of his biographer Catherine Drinker Bowen,

> **The sinuous mind could indeed twist and turn, loop and reloop, slide, untie and recover. The clear cold passionate eye could see two ways at once, could see three ways and beyond; the agile mind could coil and curvet before it struck.**

These descriptions relate to the subtle and sinuous quality of the third ray, which prefers to approach circumambiently, from numerous angles, rather than in a direct manner. These were not characteristics which Bacon always displayed, but, apparently, they were a part of his character.

Bacon was always eager for advancement. By every means conceivable, he sought to rise, and this alone, seems to suggest an Ascendant in later Capricorn rather than early Aquarius. Rarely was one more worthy of rank and responsibility, and rarely was one more denied and frustrated. At length he did succeed, becoming a man of great wealth and power, but, from the point of view of ray analysis, it is the *methods* by which he sought to rise which are of interest.

Always there was plot, contrivance, intrigue, craft and cleverness. Bacon *was* a calculating man with a long-range view. He was positively driven to rise in station, but his was not the way of the warrior or the fighter. He proceeded shrewdly and with subtlety. Behind the scenes he persistently wrote letters of self-advancement to those in power (such as his Uncle, William Cecil, or his cousin Robert Cecil) hoping (in vain) that they would arrange for his preferment. He joined the service of Elizabeth's handsome, spirited and unstable favorite, the Earl of Essex, not because of any great devotion to Essex, but because he knew it would be politic and useful for his career in government; it appears that Bacon understood expediency, and was, on occasion, opportunistic. Later, many accused him of duplicity and treachery, of abandoning his friends in order to further his relation to the crown. Apparently, he had, during Essex's trial for treason, quite unexpectedly called his former patron severely to account, siding staunchly with Essex's accusors. Did he do this to ensure Elizabeth's continuing favor? Years later, in a similar situation, he was conspicuously involved in the summary trial and execution of Sir Walter Raleigh – a man who had openly and generously praised his talents.

Bacon had a talent for strategy. As his status slowly improved under James I (Elizabeth had persistently blocked his rise), he sought by elaborate strategems to improve it further. In a brilliant piece of maneuvering, he became Attorney General by subtly recommending to King James that his (Bacon's) archrival, Edward Coke, be 'elevated' to the relatively powerless position of Chief Justice, thus clearing the way for Bacon's advance. Later, he was instrumental in providing the king with irresistible reasons for Coke's removal from office. In modern terms (and terms peculiarly suggestive of the third ray in its more material aspect) Bacon was ever *angling* for power and position. Over the course of many years, as he sought to advance his career, he frequently sounded what might be interpreted as a note of servility. In one letter of entreaty, he urged the king to use him as a "chessman" (a peculiarly third ray image): " I will be ready as a chessman to be wherever your royal hand set me." He was, so it seems, willing to be *used*, manipulated, moved about, albeit in the service of the crown. His views about how to manage government (despite his great utopian ideas) had something of the Machiavellian in them, and he gave James much shrewd (but sound) advice which could only have come from one who had a subtle understanding of the many possible implications and contingencies which can arise from various courses of action. There can, therefore, be no doubt, that there were (connected probably with his *personality* demonstration) certain powerful third ray traits. To his enemies these made him appear "slippery," self-interested, opportunistic, and manipulative in the cause of his own advancement. To his friends, these qualities appeared as brilliance, subtlety, and wisdom in the ways of the world.

All powerful men, of course, have many enemies, and the various indictments leveled at Bacon, while probably based upon some germ of truth, may have been exaggerated, and certainly pale before the transcendent qualities of his soul and mind. They do, however, interestingly, bring to light the "shadow side" of the third ray.

Looking further for evidences of the presence of the third ray, we must mention Francis Bacon's frequent financial difficulties. He was, it seems, a poor manager of (his own) money. He was forever borrowing on the promise of future advancement, and at least twice was arrested for debt, and almost imprisoned (his friends and relatives always intervened in time). In many respects the third ray should bring financial astuteness, especially in combination with the seventh, but it must be remembered that the Tibetan, speaking of the third ray man wrote:

> **This is the ray of the abstract thinker, of the philosopher and the metaphysician, and of the man who delights in the higher mathematics, but who, unless modified by some practical ray,** *would hardly be troubled to keep his accounts accurately* **[emphasis, MDR]**.

Francis Bacon was simply too busy learning, conversing, and doing an amazing diversity of things, to be concerned with small matters like accounting for his money, or repaying debts. With respect to his own financial affairs he was persistently impractical, and even careless (one of the pronounced traits of those upon the third ray who are focused too much in the realm of ideas), but when it came to giving others advice, he was invariably cautious, prudent, and far-seeing. Many of his concerns at court were financial, and had he applied to his own personal finances the same cautious counsel he made available to the king, he would not have experienced acute financial embarrassment so often.

This leads to a consideration of Francis Bacon's level of activity. It has been said of him, "Never was mortal man so busy." His *Commentarius Solutus* reveal a scope of activities which is truly staggering. Matters such as his income and his debts, his own gardens and plans for building, philosophical speculations, his health (including his symptoms and medications), the king's revenues, problems of the church, the desirability of annexing the Low Countries, Bacon's business in the law courts, ideas for future books to be written, ideas for founding a "College for Inventors," the names of men who might be set to work in the conducting of experiments, notes of ways to increase his law practice, maneuvers by which King James might control the Puritain common lawyers, and a welter of other concerns and plans of action were all set forth, often in painstaking detail. As we know, a ready response to third ray energy often leads the individual to "spread himself too thin," or to have "too many irons in the fire." The sheer multiplicity of Bacon's interests, duties and activities, the many loose ends, the many works begun but not completed – all suggest that he was powerfully conditioned by the third Ray of *Activity*.

One other point of interest and some amusement is worth mentioning. We have learned from the Tibetan that "the literary style of the third ray man is too often vague and involved...." Francis Bacon, of course, was extraordinarily eloquent, a master of the pen, but he could be a master of innuendo and indirection when he chose to be, and he did love great and complex words (often of his own fabrication) – words like "assentorily," or the term "sequacious," by which he meant to indicate a manner of thinking which made "words to follow ideas, instead of making ideas wait upon words."

When he wished to indicate that a man wrote obliquely and cunningly, he referred to "the more subtle forms of sophisms with their *illaqueations* and *redargutions*" (emphasis, MDR). When he wished to speak of a man's overconfidence he spoke of his "plerophoria." Bacon's plain-spoken mother was often at a loss to interpret what she viewed as her son's "enigmatical folded writing." Francis Bacon was, in fact, a master of *cipher*, which, reputedly, he utilized in his more occult and secretive activities. In the choice of such words and phrases we see a love of intellectual virtuosity which is characteristic of that most purely intellectual of rays, the third; in the secretiveness of cipher, cryptically attempting to conceal the truth, and leading prying eyes astray from the true meaning, we see a combined influence of both the seventh and the third rays.

During the last five years of his life (in the period immediately following his disgrace and fall from power) Bacon embarked upon a frantic attempt to bring his many intellectual projects to fruition. He began a *Digest of the Laws of England*, a *History of the Reign of Henry VII*, a body of natural history, a philosophical romance – *New Atlantis*, the treatise *De Augmentis Scientarium* (or, a Latin translation of his *Advancement of Learning*), a joke book called *Apophthgems*, the writing of numerous essays, and the attempt to carry out, single-handedly, a great variety of scientific experiments. He knew he could never finish the immense task to which he had committed himself, but proceeded eagerly, cheerfully, and with as little rest as possible. Again, he was driven by the activity aspect of the third ray.

The Presence of Ray Five

Francis Bacon advanced upon the road to knowlege by "submitting his mind to *Things*." He was a philosopher, yes, but an empiricist above all. Knowledge was to be acquired and mistakes of reasoning corrected, not by logic alone, as the Aristotelians of the past would claim, but solely by means of *direct investigation*. He urged uncompromising enquiry upon all sincere seekers of truth; never were they to be satisfied until they had discovered the truth of things for themselves. "Those who aspire not to guess and divine," wrote Bacon, "but to discover and know...who propose to examine and dissect the nature of this very world itself [should] go to facts themselves for everything." That which he urged upon others, he perfomed himself; he patiently and tirelessly carried out a wide range of experiments upon all manner of things.

Bacon, however, did not belong strictly to the company of scientists. He failed to appreciate the significance of some of the most important scientific discoveries of his day: Harvey's theories on the heart as a pump for the circulation of the blood; Gilbert's new understanding of the magnet; Galileo's conception of the cosmos. Certainly, there were scientists and technicians with far more technical skill than he. This demonstrates that he was not a fifth ray soul; he produced no significant scientific discoveries of his own. But he was a great *prophet* of science – one who saw, *en large*, what science could become, and its meaning for the transformation of the mind and civilization (which were his first concerns). It was the vast *scope* of his enquiry which made Bacon great, and his ability to inspire a change of orientation in human thinking. He knew that he was thinking and writing for future generations, for in his will, he bequeathed his "name to the next ages, and to foreign nations."

This is not to say that Bacon did not observe and experiment. He did, persistently and patiently, publishing the results of some of his observations, experiments (and speculations) in such works as the *History of the Winds, Of Dense and Rare, Of Hot and Cold, Of the Ebb and Flow of the Sea*. But, of course, there was much inaccuracy in these works, though much, as well, that was prophetic of future discoveries. He rightly conceived heat as "a motion expansive, restrained and acting in its strife upon the smaller particles of bodies....Heat itself, in its essence and quiddity is Motion and nothing else." Bacon also had initial glimmerings concerning the velocity of light. He writes of a:

> **strange doubt; viz. whether the face of a clear and starlight sky be seen at the instant when it really exists, and not a little later; and whether there be not, as regards our sight of heavenly bodies, a real time and an apparent time...So incredible did it appear to me that the images or rays of heavenly bodies could be conveyed at once to the sight through such immense space, and not take rather a perceptive time in travelling to us.**

His program of enquiry was so wide, however, that it would have taken cadres of investigators and numerous well-stocked laboratories to complete the experiments he proposed. He was creating a plan of action to be followed by *many* enquirers engaged in *many* experiments. He knew his limitations and how little he could accomplish without adequate assistance. Toward the end of his life, realizing that the many experimenters he needed would not be forthcoming, and using the full potential for activity with which he was endowed by third ray energy, he desperately plunged into a wide array of observational and experimental work alone and virtually unaided, breathlessly attempting to do what he knew could not be done. Dr. Rawley, commenting of Bacon's situation, wrote:

> **I have heard his Lordship speak complainingly that his Lordship (who thinketh he deserveth to be an architect in this building) should be forced to be a workman and a labourer, and to dig the clay and burn the brick; and more than that (according to the hard condition of the Israelites at the latter end) to gather the straw and stubble over all the fields to burn the bricks withal.**

His last deliberate scientific enquiry led directly to his death; he was suddenly moved to see whether flesh might be preserved if it were frozen. With his own hands he stuffed an exenterated hen with snow, was seized with a violent chill, contracted pneumonia or bronchitis and died two or three days later. Symbolically and actually, he died *actively* serving the cause of science.

In one of the few passages where Bacon speaks specifically of himself and his abilities, he presents an image of his thought process. One is struck by the fifth ray quality of his description.

> **For myself, I found that I was fitted for nothing so well as for the study of Truth; as having a mind nimble and versatile enough to catch the resemblances of things (which is the chief point), and at the same time steady enough to fix and distinguish their subtler differences; as being gifted by nature with desire to seek, patience to doubt, fondness to meditate, slowness to assert, readiness to consider, carefulness to dispose and set in order; and as being a man that neither affects what is new nor admires what is old, and that hates every kind of imposture. So I thought my nature had a kind of familiarity and relationship with Truth.**

In this accounting of his nature, he has listed some of the most important characteristics of the fifth ray mind. It is the fifth ray, with its love of *verification*, that engenders the love of truth.

This fifth ray love of truth, arouses the will to preserve truth from the predations of ignorance; this leads to scientific skepticism. Bacon encouraged skepticism and doubt.

> **The sinews of wisdom are slowness of belief and distrust...The entry of doubts are as so many suckers or sponges to draw use of knowledge...If a man will begin with certainties he shall end in doubts, but if he will be content to begin with doubts, he shall end in certainties.**
>
> **A faculty of wise interrogating is half a knowledge.**

Thus we read, in his own word, of his commitment to the questioning, doubting, skeptical attitude which is one of the most important ingredients in the search for truth – especially of the fifth ray approach to that search.

It is the function of the fifth ray to separate truth from error. In his *Novum Organum*, Bacon lists four "idols" (*idola*) which are deep fallacies of the mind, or general classes of errors into which the human mind is prone to fall: 1) "idols of the tribe," which are fallacies incident to humanity or to the race in general; 2) "idols of the cave," which are errors incident to the peculiar mental or bodily constitution of each individual, because the individual's view of things is based upon his state of mind; 3) "idols of the market place," which are errors arising from the influence exercised over the mind by mere words; and 4) "idols of the theatre," which are fallacious modes of thinking resulting from received systems of philosophy and from erroneous methods of demonstration. An attempt of this nature, to clarify the instrument of thought so that truth may be more readily apprehended, derives from a useful combination of fifth and third ray energies.

Lastly, it might be said, that Francis Bacon was a man of great *common sense*. He was known for his "levelheadedness," especially if his own finances were not concerned. His intellectual speculations were vast is scope, but they always bore the stamp of the practical, scientific mind. His enquiries revolved around the possible, the feasible, things that could be proven or verified by experiment. Like so many of those strongly influenced by ray five, he had little time for nonsense (unless at play); he was, essentially, a great realist and pragmatist.

The Presence of Ray Two

This is not a ray which seems to have played a great role in Bacon's life, but there are suggestions of its presence. It seems that Bacon, for all his problems of state and of health, was frequently a cheerful man. He had, in debate, an unflagging good humor, which can be related to the positivity of the second ray. Of course his command of ideas and words made him very sure of himself in such situations, and this allowed good humor to emerge. At other times, however, he betrayed an unexpected sensitivity, fearfulness, helplessness and vulnerability. When he was most attacked, he seemed least able to defend himself. In such cases he seemed to absorb the hostility leveled against him rather than return it. As the full fury of impeachment proceedings assailed him, he became ill and submissively confessed to every charge, although (given prevailing standards) they were manifestly unjust.

For many years in his young adulthood, he had lived without adequate funds. Arrested for debt on at least two occasions, he showed a certain *helplessness* about his situation; what money he had, simply flowed through his fingers. When at last he rose to wealth and prominence under James I, he indulged all of his tendencies towards largesse; he did for others what he wished had been done for him in earlier years. He was endowed with a Jupiterian quality (probably through Aquarius; Jupiter, the esoteric ruler of Aquarius is the primary distributor of the second ray at this time in human evolution). Jupiter bestows the attitude of generosity, and Bacon became a great spender, a giver and patron. In fact, in his private life, he became excessively *permissive*. Servants freely took money from his coffers by the handfuls. When questioned by one incredulous guest who had witnessed such a scene, Bacon almost apologetically explained, "Sir, I cannot help myself" – again the old helplessness, so often associated with the 2–4–6 line of energy, and especially with ray two. In this one area of his personal life (*not* his governmental life, or his life of the mind) Bacon was simply too free and easy. He never knew how much money he had or where it went.

As a further evidence of second ray energy, it seemed that Bacon was incapable of holding a grudge, even against his nemesis Edward Coke. He never seems to have remembered that his enemies truly hated him, and he would naively lay himself open and vulnerable to their attacks. But, perhaps the most important second ray indication is the nature and quality of his friendships. Bacon, was an Aquarian, and the advanced Aquarian knows how to value friendship above all else. As a prophet, he no doubt caught glimpses of the Aquarian Age – an Age, ideally, of brotherhood and universal friendship. He had that cohesive, magnetic quality which enabled him to "sound the bell" and call "the wits together." It was not only his mind that attracted and held the great men he numbered among his friends, but the quality of the man himself.

The second ray, we know, is the most inclusive of all. Any man who takes "all knowledge as [his] province" must be animated by the spirit of inclusiveness. It does not seem that the second ray conditioned the (usually considered) higher aspects of Bacon's energy system, but there was in his approach a buddhic quality of synthesis, a search for *unity in nature* – the same kind of unity which Einstein (as a third ray soul, most probably polarized Triadally within his buddhic vehicle) sought.

The Presence of the Fourth Ray

Again, the fourth ray, does not appear to be one of the most prominent rays in Bacon's makeup (and perhaps it was not a part of his ray chart), but there were numerous instances suggestive of its quality. Perhaps this is inevitable when an individual has the planet Mercury rising in the first house of his astrological chart.

It is Francis Bacon's *eloquence* and verbal imagery which most suggest the presence of the fourth ray. Of course, we must remember that he was living in an age when many fourth ray souls were in incarnation. Further, Elizabethan society was, essentially, a late Renaissance society, much colored by the quality of the fourth ray. But there was something in his speech and writing (although, he professed that he was not a poet) which was *beautiful*. Although he wrote and spoke beautifully, he advised against a too "affectionate study of eloquence," which causes men

> **to hunt more after words than matter, and more after the choiceness of the phrase, and the round and clean composition of the sentence, and the sweet falling of the clauses, and the varying and illustration of their works with tropes and figures, than after the weight of matter, soundness of argument, life of invention or depth of judgment.**

But even in warning against eloquence, he could not help himself – he waxed eloquent!

Could one without access to fourth ray energy, humor King James I in difficult moments when the House of Commons was presenting its most serious Petition of Grievances? What sort of energy was present in Bacon's conciliatory words to his sovereign?:

> **Excellent sovereign! Let not the sound of grievances, though it be sad, seem harsh to your princely ears. It is but *gemitus cloumbae*, the mourning of a dove, with that patience and humility of heart which appertaineth to loving and loyal subjects....**

And when Bacon presented the apologia to the 97 legal aphorisms found in his *De Augmentis*, what quality of energy did it suggest?:

> **This treatise of mine, seems to me not unlike those sounds and preludes which musicians make while they are tuning their instruments, and which produce indeed a harsh and unpleasing sound to the ear, but tend to make the music sweeter afterwards. And thus have I intended to employ myself in tuning the harp of the muses and reducing it to perfect harmony, that hereafter the strings may be tended by a better hand or a better quill.**

Always there is great style, a polishing of phrases, perfect cadences. Much may be rightly attributed to ray seven, but Bacon was gifted with the *art* and *charm* of felicitous verbal expression.

From another point of view, we remember that Bacon, in his own estimation was gifted with *both* the ability to "catch the resemblances of things (which is the chief point), and at the same time steady enough to fix and distinguish their subtler differences." Both fourth and fifth ray qualities are found here, for although all thinking people can see similarities and differences, it is the peculiar ability of those influenced primarily by the the fourth ray mind to see similarities (i.e., "resemblances"), and of those influenced, primarily by the fifth ray to see "differences." Now, there are some critics who believe that, although Bacon was a great advocate of science, he was no great scientist, largely because of what these critics call his habitual *inaccuracy* (a trait associated with both the fourth and the third rays). Bacon's greatest and most comprehensive biographer, James Spedding, felt that he suffered from an intellectual imbalance; his mind so quick to note likenesses was not equally ready to distinguish differences. This is most interesting, for it shows a tendency to prefer the functioning of the fourth ray over that of the fifth; Bacon himself, by using the phrase – *"which is the chief point"* – suggests that, to him, the ability to see resemblances was more important than the ability to see differences. Thus, Bacon's own testimony tends to confirm Spedding's assessment of his mental process.

Carrying this idea forward, Bacon was no friend of pure differentiation in the manner of the fifth ray. "Strife and friendship in nature," he says (sounding the note of both harmony and conflict) "are the spurs of motions and the keys of works...These fabulous divorces and distinctions...beyond what truth admits of, will be a great obstacle to true philosophy and the contemplation of nature." Bacon sought to see in the human mind, the marriage between the intuitive and rational faculties, "the unkind and ill-starred separation of which has thrown into confusion all the affairs of the human family." One can see that the fifth ray is strictly under control, and that the bridging, unifying quality of the fourth ray (aided by the synthesizing seventh) is pronounced.

There are other aspects of Francis Bacon's life which also suggest the fourth ray. He had a very keen nervous sensibility, a tendency to give way under pressure, and a penchant for sudden "about-faces." He was extremely improvident, and, often, impulsive beyond the bounds of common caution. (Of course, his Moon was in Aries.) He was one who would enter too fully into the moment for his own good. Especially in his early years, he was capable of rash and impolitic gestures, and once, so offended Queen Elizabeth, by (spontaneously and without warning) opposing a measure she strongly supported, that he almost permanently ruined any chances he might have had for political advancement. For one who calculated so carefully, there was a certain air of unpredictability, and an air of recklessness which might emerge unheralded, at any moment. He was also prey to strange bouts of melancholy, which came upon him in the afternoon (the *moods* so often induced by the fourth ray?). There was also something of the dandy about him. Frequently, this comes with the seventh ray, but the addition of the fourth ray emphasizes the tendency.

In the advice he gave to two sovereigns, he displayed a talent for conciliation, for the harmonizing of conflicting demands. And when he was appointed Lord Chancellor, one of his first gestures was to establish harmony between himself and a number of judges who had viewed him with apprehension and suspicion.

But at last, we must return to the style of his language – elegant, perfectly balanced in his aphoristic utterance (the fourth ray in addition to the seventh?), and his dry, witty, ironic sense of humor. Shelly, a great fourth ray poet, commenting on the writing of Bacon wrote:

> **Lord Bacon was a poet. His language has a sweet and majestic rhythm which satisfies the sense....**

Bacon was a great artist in the fashioning and expression of words.

Proposed Ray Chart(s)!

To assess the rays of one so highly advanced as Sir Francis Bacon – one who was doubtlessly manifesting the accumulated benefit and ray quality of several previous lives of high distinction – is extremely difficult. We know from reading the Tibetan how prominent the ray quality of the previous incarnation(s) can be, and in Bacon's case, his illustrious life as Roger Bacon (and Paracelsus?, not to mention the fabled Merlin?!) was surely influential. Rather than draw hard and fast conclusions, two (very similar) ray charts will be proposed, and some justification given for each. Students may judge for themselves, which of these charts (if any) seem most appropriate.

```
              5                             4
THREE VII 3  2  L: 4    THREE VII 3  2  L: 5
              7                             7
```

Commentary

Let us begin with the soul ray, of which we may be assured. It is the seventh. The unrelenting alchemical and magical interests of *Roger* Bacon (probably the previous incarnation of Francis Bacon, if Paracelsus be discounted) suggests in the strongest possible terms that the seventh ray was Roger Bacon's soul ray. One of the names of the seventh Ray Lord is "The Divine Alchemical Worker." Francis Bacon, as well, was reputedly associated with Rosicrucianism (filled with seventh ray ritualism and alchemical symbolism), and, perhaps, with an occult society of his own making. He seems to have followed many secret practices associated with the seventh ray, and certainly, his more prophetic writings, have that coloration. Most importantly, he was intent upon the *transformation* of civilization, which is the foremost theme of those whose souls are upon the seventh ray.

The only reservation (and it is slight) which one might have in relation to assigning a seventh ray soul to Bacon is the issue of his elevated status upon the path of initiation. If, indeed, he were an initiate of the third degree (and this seems the very *least* that can be said of him), the soul ray might well have been in the process of transferring from the seventh to the first or the third ray. We know from D.K.'s writings that it is customary for the seventh ray soul to transfer onto the first ray line, but, to the knowledge of the writer, there is no section in which it is *explicitly* stated that the seventh ray soul can transfer onto the third ray (seemingly, a very logical type of transference). And yet, this latter type of transference seems *implied* in a number of passages in D.K.'s writings. Certainly the third ray is a synthetic ray which absorbs and synthesizes the seventh; the planet Uranus is a point of distribution for both the third and seventh rays; and the Master R. Himself, transferred his Ashram from the seventh to the third ray. (Presumably, His transfer, although something of a "special dispensation" did proceed along a line of least resistance.) There is little in Bacon's writings or behavior to associate him with the first

Ray of Will and Power – in fact, much to dissociate him. Thus, since it can be reasonably assumed, that he was at least an initiate of the third degree, *if* any transference of soul ray was in process, it would have to have been from the seventh to the third ray.

As stated earlier, however, even if such a transference did occur, there would be no reason to minimize the importance of the seventh ray, which would certainly preserve its strength and 'aeonial momentum' as a powerful subray of the third ray. There is, however, one other problem which seems to imply that no transference from the seventh ray soul was in process. Since the Master R. was upon the seventh ray *until very recently*, any transference from the seventh to the third in the life of Francis Bacon would suggest that, two or three centuries later, there would have to have been a transference *back* from the third to the seventh ray, and this seems unnatural, uneconomical, and contradictory. Thus, for our purposes, it seems sufficient to consider Bacon's soul ray the seventh, and leave the issue of exactly how and when soul rays of attribute become soul rays of aspect for another occasion – when we know more!

The third ray is indeed powerful in the life of this great Individual. Given the present, powerful third ray position of R. as Mahachohan, and the interesting resonance which Francis Bacon reputedly had with the Moon (the Moon being the *third* chain of our planetary scheme, and hence, closely associated with the third ray – since 75% of the Monads which individualized upon the Moon chain were third ray Monads), it is reasonable to think of Bacon as a third ray Monad. Speculatively, however, it might be said, that his polarization within the Spiritual Triad may have been buddhic, and thus keyed to the second ray, so great was his desire for an *inclusive synthesis of knowledge.* Also, the Master R. is presently involved with the formation of a new Ashram called the "*Wisdom* Ashram" – the quality of wisdom being related to the second aspect, and the second ray.

The third ray would be especially accentuated in the life of Francis Bacon if, in addition to being the Monadic ray, it were also the personality ray. Considering the foibles he may have had (though slander is always to be suspected when dealing with a man so great), and considering the extreme busyness of his life, the diversity and multiplicity of his personality activities, his great versatility, ductility, intellectual sophistication, his excellence as a strategist, his highly-stimulated throat center, and many other indications, the third ray seems the most appropriate choice for his personality ray. He certainly was not the devotee upon the sixth ray, nor was he sufficiently strong and assertive, personally, to have been upon the first ray. There was far too much activity and mobility for a second ray personality, and he was, by far, too magnetic, resilient, diverse and *eclectic* for a personality upon the fifth ray.

To assign a fourth ray personality *is* possible, but Francis Bacon was not a fighter, nor was harmonization (though he could be skilled at it) his goal. Further, unless one credits him with being the author of the Shakespeare plays (and there is the strongest possible evidence to suggest that he *was*, indeed, involved – at least in some manner), he was neither artistically inclined, nor (in his own estimation) a poet. (While it is probable that William Shakespeare was *not* the author, it is also probable that Bacon was not either, but, rather, that he served to assemble a group of superb dramatists [which may have included Ben Jonson, Christopher Marlowe and the Earl of Essex] to write the

Shakespeare plays.) It seems, given what we know of the hectic pace of his life, that he hardly would have had the time to write them himself. While there was a certain improvident streak in Bacon which suggests a fourth ray personality, overall, he was not unstable, and he was certainly far more calculating that a fourth ray personality ever would be. In addition, if he were a seventh ray soul and a fourth ray personality, one would certainly expect artistic production of a very high quality, for these two rays are the primary rays of artistry, and give an excellent sense of both form and color. As for the seventh ray, since it was his soul ray (*and* a ray of attribute), it can be discounted as the personality ray. Interestingly, with a seventh ray personality Bacon would have been far more acceptable to his more practical (and unimaginative) superiors, who resisted advancing him because of what they perceived as insufficient administrative skills, and an insufficient sense of responsibility (rarely lacking in a seventh ray personality). What Bacon actually did, was *work towards* the seventh ray, applying seventh ray disciplines to contain his overactive personality, and to this end, he *rehearsed* the many phrases and behaviors which he jotted down in his various notebooks. This was a clear example of the soul ray gradually exerting a controlling effect upon personality tendencies.

When we reach the ray of the mind, we have a problem. Given Francis Bacon's extraordinary orientation towards scientific discovery and experiment, plus his willingness actually to conduct experiments, there can be no doubt that the fifth ray formed an important part of his nature. Certainly, his own description of his thought process, makes him seem the exemplary fifth ray mind. The question is, would a fifth ray mind have such extraordinary eloquence? Granted that the combination of the third and fifth ray makes a man "a master of the pen," would this combination of rays also produce such charm, grace, imagination, imagery, and the beautifully turned and balanced phrases which spangled the writings and conversation of Francis Bacon? It is difficult to answer this question. There were times when Bacon's thought process was indubitably colored by the fifth ray. There were other times when great 'artistry' shone through, and, exulting in a use of picturesque image and metaphor, he expressed himself with exquisite aestheticism. Believing that he perceived in the thinking of advanced individuals *both* fourth and fifth ray qualities (i.e., both "right brain and left brain" qualities), Dr. Douglas Baker (a pioneer in ray thought and research) postulated that those who are extremely "gifted" could have *two* mental rays – both the fourth and the fifth, simultaneously. It is impossible at this point to say anything about the validity of such a hypothesis. We must first become more assured of our capacity to detect rays and determine their quality.

There is one thought, however, which, in the case of Francis Bacon, may prove helpful in gathering more information to solve the riddle. If one studies the life of his predecessor *Roger* Bacon, there is a powerful dominance of the fifth ray. Roger Bacon displayed prodigious energy and zeal in the pursuit of experimental science. He was far more the *scientist* than was Francis Bacon. Roger Bacon actually *practiced* far more science (even given the limitations of his Medieval culture). Thus, there would have been a powerful *legacy ray* conditioning the vehicles of Francis Bacon, whether or not the fifth ray was actually a part of his energy system. If we are among those who believe that the manifestation of Theophrastus Bombast von Hohenheim [i.e., Paracelsus] was *also* a manifestation of the entity who is now the Master R., then our argument is even strengthened, for the fifth ray energy of Paracelsus, like that of Roger Bacon was strongly emphasized. A study of the meaning of the scope and power of "legacy rays" must be made, but, at our present stage of evolution, we have sufficient knowledge for only a very superficial study.

It must also be said that the fifth ray is heavily represented in Francis Bacon's horoscope. In some proposed charts, Aquarius is *both* his Sun sign and Rising sign, and, let us remember, that the only ray presently coming through the constellation Aquarius to the Earth is the fifth ray. Even if Capricorn were his Ascendant, and Aquarius only his Sun sign, the influence would still be potent.

Just as we have to ask, could Bacon have had such eloquence if his mental ray were the fifth, we must ask, could he have had such an interest in science and concrete phenomena, and such mental acuity if his mental ray were the fourth? There will be no attempt to answer these questions at present. Suffice it to say, his mind seems to be upon either the fourth or fifth ray. Until we have an infallible, certainty of intuition in these matters (or an equally infallible instrumentation for measurement) the best policy is to try to "think things through."

There is one very recondite point which must be mentioned here, and which may, in a future phase of ray analysis, play a very significant role. There are 49 "fires of Brahma," and one day there will be 49 Ashrams in Hierarchy to correspond with these 49 fires. This is to say that each of the major ray ashrams is intended to have six subsidiary ashrams, in each of which the major ray and *one of the other six rays* will be the principal conditioning energies. For instance, according to this scheme, the major seventh ray ashram would be notated as 7_7, and each of the six subsidiary ashrams (though all are probably not yet formed) as 7_1, 7_2, 7_3, 7_4, 7_5, and 7_6. In *Esoteric Psychology, Vol. II*, p. 18, we learn that there is a "dual ray of the soul," and that there is also a ray which can be called "the highest of the soul rays." This has quite astounding implications, for it may mean that when attempting to assess the ray of the soul, *two* rays must always be taken into consideration, and that these two rays may well be the ray conditioning the major Ashram with which the soul is affiliated, *plus* the subsidiary ray which colors one of the six subsidiary Ashrams in which the soul may be placed. A close reading of the lives of Roger Bacon and Sir Francis Bacon will reveal that they were concerned with many of the same issues; there was a remarkable similarity of orientation; they sought to transform the world (alchemically and scientifically). Might this mean that their ashramic placement (at that time) was within the subsidiary seventh ray ashram denoted by the symbol 7_5? All seventh ray Ashrams are involved, ultimately, in the process of transforming the status quo by manifesting the archetypes embodied with the Divine Plan, but is it possible that individuals within the 7_5 ashram undertake this transformational process through the utilization of science? Whereas in the 7_1 ashram the transformation process would be more political, and in the 7_4 ashram more through the agency of art and beauty, etc.? Perhaps Marie Curie (according to the Tibetan, a seventh ray soul) was also a member of the 7_5 ashram.

If we accept this hypothesis as worthy of consideration, it might mean that an individual would remain associated with a particular Ashram for a number of cycles (who knows how many?) and that the two numbers conditioning his major spiritual service (i.e., his *two soul rays*) would remain the same no matter what the rays of the personality, mind, emotions, and etheric–physical body might be. Now, if the soul ray (since the soul is placed upon the mental plane) can strongly affect the quality of the thinking within the concrete mind, why should not the secondary soul ray do likewise? This secondary soul ray is *one* of the subrays of the soul, but not necessarily the *only* subray of the soul. The personality is *also* a subray of the soul (cf., *Esoteric Psychology, Vol. II*, p. 358).

Now, here is the point upon which this whole conjecture turns. There is no reason to believe that the subsidiary ashramic ray is *necessarily* the same as the personality ray. *Both would be subrays of the soul*, but the personality ray would, according to this way of thinking, change more often that the subsidiary ashramic ray (i.e., the subsidiary soul ray). Thus, for instance, someone like the entity who manifested as Roger Bacon and Francis Bacon could maintain the 7_5 conditioning *for many lives*, but might still change the personality ray for each of those lives! There is probably no exact numerical law here; much would depend upon the need of the Ashram and of humanity.

We must realize that this hypothesis necessarily introduces a new factor: *one more ray to consider*! – especially in those who are advanced souls and are definitely a member of an Ashram (for unless one were a member of an Ashram, such a secondary ray [at least as the secondary soul ray is here conceived] would not apply). The secondary ashramic ray would definitely be potent and conditioning, and would have definite effects upon the personality. It would affect orientation and behavior. Thus, in this case, we ask, might the fifth ray *not* constitute part of Francis Bacon's personality ray chart at all, but, instead, be a result of his identification with the 7_5 Ashram? The author is incapable of answering this question with any degree of assurance, but hopefully, a fruitful line of inquiry has been indicated, and, in the future, answers will be forthcoming. This matter of distinguishing the rays is simple in one respect, and 'devilishly complex' in others.

The astral nature, sensitive, often cheerful, often fearful, and basically non–emotional seems, justifiably, the second. The second ray astral nature would account somewhat for Bacon's vulnerability and his perplexingly non–assertive behavior when under attack.

The physical body is almost certainly the seventh. It was extremely sensitive; Bacon spent much time concerned with physical health. He had that "body–consciousness" so associated with the seventh ray etheric–physical nature. The physical body was certainly not capable of taking much abuse (unlike the third ray vehicle), but instead had to be ministered to constantly. He did, however, have a powerful nervous energy, which could be produced through an alignment of the seventh ray soul with the seventh ray brain and etheric–physical body. There was, also, a great love of order upon the physical plane. Further, he liked to dress well, cut a good figure, and there was a sensuous quality in his relationship to the physical plane which is often characteristic of the seventh ray etheric–physical vehicle, especially when reinforced by a seventh ray soul or personality. One has only to see certain of the paintings or likenesses of Sir Francis Bacon, erect, stately, poised, sensitive and vibrant, to sense the quality of the seventh ray in his etheric–physical nature.

Conclusion

This attempt to analyze the rays of the initiate Sir Francis Bacon, has involved more speculation and subtle inference than any of the other examples. His case presents an unusual opportunity to the ray analyst, because it is one of the few in which a reliable continuity of incarnations is presented, and in which we have reliable historical information about such incarnations. Even if we were to take the case of Cagliostro and Mme. Blavatsky, whole sections of their lives are shrouded in mystery, and it is far more difficult to obtain a clear picture.

In this process, we have explored an intricate problem from a number of perspectives, and students should have a fair idea of what kinds of questions have to be asked and how they might be approached for resolution. It is recommended that students undertake systematic ray analyses of contemporary and historical figures, as well as of those people whom they may know well.

The great entity, previously known as Roger Bacon, Francis Bacon, and the Comte de St. Germain, and presently known as the Master R. (or rather the *Chohan* R.), is very present to us at this unique time in history. Certainly, in this transitional period immediately preceeding the Aquarian Age, His plans and activities are of vital importance to all spiritually inclined men and women. He will be one of Those to externalize in the process of the Reappearance of the Christ, and his responsibilities for "restoring the Plan on Earth" will be enormous. Through numerical resonance, He is no doubt aligned with the efforts which the great and *coming* Seventh Ray Avatar is making on behalf of the planet and, incidentally, on behalf of humanity. If we wish to be of assistance to that Avatar, we need to understand the seven rays as well as we possibly can, so that we can help many people *know themselves* according to the ray paradigm.

Perhaps the time will come in the not so distant future, when we can consult with the Master R. about the nature of his evolution during the past 800 or so years. Perhaps, for our edification and illumination, He will explain the various rays He utilized during particular incarnations, His reasons for doing so, and the dynamics of His various ray transferences – dynamics which can appear so perplexing to those of limited mentality, like ourselves.

Note: The sources used for all direct quotations by or about Sir Francis Bacon were: *Francis Bacon: The Temper of a Man*, Catherine Drinker Bowen, Little Brown and Company in association with the Atlantic Monthly Press, Copyright, 1963; *Foundations Unearthed*, Marie Bauer Hall, Veritas Press, Glendale California, Copyright, 1940; and the *Encyclopedia Britannica*, fifteenth edition.

CLOSING REMARKS

We have entered into a deep consideration of many complexities. We have examined the intricate interweaving of energies from many perspectives. But ultimately, it is *simplicity* that counts. "Straight–knowledge" (as infallible, intuitive perception is called in the Agni Yoga Teaching given by the Master Morya) is worth far more than learned speculation and reasoning. Those of us who wish to help humanity by understanding and applying esoteric psychology, must develop the intuition and spiritual perception so that – *in all simplicity* – we actually *know* (without the mediation of the reasoning mind) the rays of the individuals we seek to aid.

It is, however, dangerous to abandon the mind prematurely. A subject of such depth and magnificence as the science of the seven rays must be *thought through* before the concrete mind and reasoning powers are relinquished in favor of what may (or may not) be true intuition. Intuition is, in a sense, a sublimation of the lower mind. That mind must be used to its full capacity before *unerring* intuition becomes constantly available.

The *Tapestry of the Gods* series is for those who have not yet abandoned the mind – those who still wish to *think* about what they *feel* may be true. It is for those who wish to put their assumptions to the test of reason and, eventually, experiment. This may be a slower way than direct, intuitive perception of the truth, but (given humanity's present deluded manner of thinking) perhaps a safer way.

It is clear to the author that this book must, necessarily, contain a number of errors, for much that is offered is speculative. But it is his hope that his efforts will stimulate sincere students of esoteric psycholgy and the science of the seven rays to search and search until the truth is found. An intense, sincere and intelligent search, *will* invoke the infallible intuition.

The Tibetan, a great esoteric psychologist, now *knows* with certainty all aspects of the science of the seven rays as that science applies to struggling humanity. There must have been a time, however, when He, too, had only partial knowledge and understanding. One day those of us who seek to understand and practice esoteric psychology can be as He is now – expert in the science of the seven rays – a science which is of the utmost importance to humanity's spiritual evolution. Towards that end, let us strive.

TAPESTRY OF THE GODS
VOLUME II

Section VII

APPENDICES AND GLOSSARY

APPENDIX I

Some Ray Tabulations From the Tibetan's Teachings

As Given in the Books of Alice A. Bailey

Words of Power

Ray I: I ASSERT THE FACT
Ray II :   I SEE THE GREATEST LIGHT
Ray III: PURPOSE ITSELF AM I
Ray IV: TWO MERGE WITH ONE
Ray V: THREE MINDS UNITE
Ray VI: THE HIGHEST LIGHT CONTROLS
Ray VII: THE HIGHEST AND THE LOWEST MEET

From *The Rays and the Initiations*

Integration Formulae

Ray I: Inclusion
Ray II: Centralization
Ray III: Stillness
Ray IV: Steadfastness
Ray V: Detachment
Ray VI: Restraint (proposed, MDR)
Ray VII: Orientation (proposed, MDR)

From *Esoteric Psychology, Vol. II*

Fusion Formulae

Ray I: Isolated Unity
Ray II: Inclusive Reason
Ray III: Presented Attributes

From *Esoteric Psychology, Vol. II*

The Rays In and Out of Manifestation

Ray I...... Not in manifestation.

Ray II.....In manifestation since 1575 A.D.

Ray III... In manifestation since 1425 A.D.

Ray IV... To come slowly into manifestation around 2025 A.D.

Ray V.... In manifestation since 1775 A.D.

Ray VI... Passing rapidly out of manifestation. Began to pass out in 1675 A.D.

Ray VII..In manifestation since 1675 A.D.

From *Esoteric Psychology, Vol. I*

Ray Methods of Teaching Truth

Ray I

Higher expression: The science of statesmanship, and of government.

Lower expression: Modern diplomacy and politics.

Ray II

Higher expression: The process of initiation as taught by the Hierarchy of Masters.

Lower expression: Religion.

Ray III

Higher expression: Means of communication of interaction. Radio, telegraph, telephone and means of transportation.

Lower expression: The use and spread of gold.

Ray IV

Higher expression: The Masonic work, based on the formulation of the Hierarchy and related to Ray II.

Lower expression: Architectural construction. Modern city planning.

Ray V

Higher expression: The science of the Soul. Esoteric psychology.

Lower expression: Modern educational systems.

Ray VI

Higher expression: Christianity and diversified religions. Note relation to Ray II.

Lower expression: Churches and religious organizations.

Ray VII

Higher expression: All forms of white magic.

Lower expression: Spiritualism in its lower aspects.

From *Esoteric Psychology, Vol. I*

Discipleship and the Rays

Ray I.......Force...................Energy................Action.............The Occultist
Ray II.....Consciousness....Expansion..........Initiation.........The true Psychic
Ray III....Adaptation.........Development....Evolution.......The Magician
Ray IV....Vibration...........Response...........Expression.....The Artist
Ray V.....Mentation..........Knowledge.........Science...........The Scientist
Ray VI....Devotion...........Abstraction.........Idealism.........The Devotee
Ray VII...Incantation........Magic.................Ritual.............The Ritualist

From *Initiation Human and Solar*

Certain Names of the Seven Ray Lords

The Lord of the First Ray

The Lord of Death

The Opener of the Door

The Liberator from Form

The Great Abstractor

The Fiery Element, producing shattering

The Crystallizer of the Form

The Power that touches and withdraws

The Lord of the Burning Ground

The Will that breaks into the Garden

The Ravisher of Souls
The Finger of God
The Breath that blasts
The Lightning which annihilates
The Most High

The Lord of the Second Ray
The Displayer of Glory
The Lord of Eternal Love
The Cosmic Magnet
The Given of Wisdom
The Radiance in the Form
The Master Builder
The Conferrer of Names
The Great Geometrician
The One Who hides the Life
The Cosmic Mystery
The Light Bringer
The Son of God Incarnate
The Cosmic Christ

The Lord of the Third Ray
The Keeper of the Records
The Lord of Memory
The Unifier of the lower Four
The Interpreter of That Which is seen
The Lord of Balance
The Divine Separator
The Discriminating Essential Life,
The One Who produces Alliance
The Three–sided Triangle

The Illuminator of the Lotus
The Builder of the Foundation
The Forerunner of the Light
The One Who veils and yet reveals
The Dispenser of Time
The Lord of Space
The Universal Mind
The Threefold Wick
The Great Architect of the Universe

The Lord of the Fourth Ray
The Perceiver on the Way
The Link between the Three and Three
The Divine Intermediary
The Hand of God
The Hidden One
The Seed, that is the Flower
The Mountain whereon Form dies
The Light within the Light
The Corrector of the Form
The One Who marks the parting of the Way
The Master
The Dweller in the Holy Place
The Lower than the Three, the Highest of the Four
The Trumpet of the Lord

The Lord of the Fifth Ray
The Revealer of Truth
The great Connector
The Divine Intermediary
The Crystallizer of Forms

The Three-fold Thinker
The Cloud upon the Mountain-top
The Precipitator of the Cross
The Dividing Sword
The Winnower of the Chaff
The Fifth great Judge
The Rose of God
The Heavenly One
The Door into the Mind of God
The Initiating Energy
The Ruler of the Third Heaven
The Guardian of the Door
The Dispenser of Knowledge
The Angel with the Flaming Sword
The Keeper of the Secret
The Beloved of the Logos
The Brother from Sirius
The Master of the Hierophants

The Lord of the Sixth Ray
The Negator of Desire
The One Who sees the Right
The Visioner of Reality
The Divine Robber
The Devotee of Life
The Hater of Forms
The Warrior on the March
The Sword Bearer of the Logos
The Upholder of the Truth
The Crucifier and the Crucified
The Breaker of Stones

The Imperishable Flaming One
The One Whom Naught can turn
The Implacable Ruler
The General on the Perfect Way
The One Who leads the Twelve

The Lord of the Seventh Ray
The Unveiled Magician
The Worker in the Magical Art
The Creator of the Form
The Bestower of Light from the Second Lord
The Manipulator of the Wand
The Watcher in the East
The Custodian of the Seventh Plan
The Invoker of Wrath
The Keeper of the Magical Word
The Temple Guardian
The Representative of God
The One Who lifts to Life
The Lord of Death
The Whirling Sphere
The Sword of the Initiator
The Divine Alchemical Worker
The Builder of the Square
The Orienting Force
From *Esoteric Psychology, Vol. I*

The Colors Associated with the Seven Rays

Ray I: red, orange and blue
Ray II: indigo and light blue
Ray III: green, yellow and black
Ray IV: yellow, creme and green
Ray V: orange, indigo and yellow
Ray VI: blue, silvery rose and red
Ray VII: violet and white

These colors are gathered from statements and tabulations in various of the Tibetan's books, notably *Letters On Occult Meditation*, and *Esoteric Psychology, Vol. I* They are not arranged in any particular order, nor are they here distinguished with respect to their exoteric or esoteric nature. The science of color is a profound study, and nowhere nearly so simple as it might seem. It is well–protected with occult "blinds." However, a knowledge of the ways in which colors relate to the rays will be an indispensable aspect of esoteric psychology. Philosophical and experimental research is encouraged.

APPENDIX II

A Brief Consideration of the Constellations and Planets from the Perspective of Esoteric Astrology as Presented in the Teachings of the Tibetan Master, Djwhal Khul

Volumes I and II of *Tapestry of the Gods* are *not* about astrology. The subject of esoteric astrology will be extensively developed in *Tapestry of the Gods, Vols. III and IV*. However, the science of the seven rays and the science of esoteric astrology are so inextricably interwoven, that it is impossible to avoid mentioning the contellations and planets when seeking to convey an understanding of the seven rays. Therefore, the following very brief exposition will serve to introduce students to a few of the essentials of esoteric astrology, so that the various references scattered throughout Volumes I and II (and especially within the biographical ray analyses) will be intelligible and meaningful.

The Twelve Zodiacal Constellations or Signs

Each constellation will also be given, as well as the three planetary rulers of each constellation – i.e., the orthodox ruler, the esoteric ruler and the hierarchical ruler, in that order. Orthodox rulers condition average humanity; esoteric rulers condition the transpersonally oriented individual; hierarchical rulers condition those of initiate status.

The rays which are (during this world period) associated with each constellation will also be given, as well as the three planetary rulers of each constellation – i.e., the orthodox ruler, the esoteric ruler and the hierarchical ruler, in that order. Orthodox rulers condition average humanity; esoteric rulers condition the transpersonally oriented individual; hierarchical rulers condition those of initiate status.

Additional mantrams, and words and phrases of significance are also given for each constellation:

1. The Spiritual Mantram emphasizes qualities which are intended to guide those who are attempting to increase the influence of the soul in their lives.

2. The Evolutionary Mantram emphasizes zodiacal qualities which have characterized the evolving human being *prior* to an interest in spiritual living.

3. The words or phrases for the *Undeveloped Man* indicate qualities which are characteristic of the human being who is in the early stages of human development.

4. The words and phrases for *Advanced Man* indicate qualities which are characteristic of the individual born in or under a particular sign, when that individual is an advanced person just beginning to aspire towards the spiritual life.

5. The words and phrases for the *Disciple or Initiate* indicate qualities which are characteristic of the individual born in or under a particular sign, when that individual has already been living the spiritual life for some time, and has, therefore, achieved discipleship or initiate status.

Note: A word about the difference between the meaning of the words "constellation" and "sign" should be included. So often these two terms are used interchangeably because, as far as humanity is concerned, their practical effect is indistinguishable. Regarding the real difference between the two, Djwhal Khul states, on p. 621 of *Esoteric Astrology*:

> **In the understanding of the significance of** *the distinction between the constellations as galaxies of stars, and signs as concentrated influences* **will come fresh light upon the science of astrology.**

It seems clear that the source of the zodiacal energies is the constellations, but that they are distributed to all life on Earth by means of the signs. The signs exist because of the unique relationship between the inclination of the Earth's axis and the ecliptic. For Alan Leo, the famous esoteric astrologer, the signs are twelve sectors of magnetic influence surrounding the Earth. If his theory is correct, it seems apparent that each of these sectors would be keyed to, or resonant with, *one* of the zodiacal constellations, and that the energy and influence of a particular zodiacal constellation would be transmitted *through* a particular sector.

This little bit of background on the contrast between these two frequently used terms is given to clarify any confusion that might arise. Of course, a thorough comprehension of the dynamics of the relationship between the two is beyond our understanding.

Sign I : Aries

The sign in which powerful mental impressions emerge from the Transpersonal Self, galvanizing the lower personal self into dynamic initiatives, as it attempts to respond to the transpersonal impulses. Aries is the sign in which the Transpersonal Self commences a new cycle of activity.

Positive traits: initiative, pioneering spirit, independence, assertiveness, leadership, dynamic energy, ideational power, power to originate

Negative traits: impulsiveness, aggressiveness, combativeness, impatience, lack of moderation, unrealistic estimation

The constellation Aries distributes ray one and ray seven. The planets associated with Aries are Mars (orthodox), Mercury (esoteric), and Uranus (hierarchical), distributing ray six, ray four and ray seven, respectively.

Spiritual Mantram: I come forth, and from the plane of mind I rule.

Evolutionary Mantram: And the Word said: Let form again be sought.

Undeveloped Man: Blind undirected experience. Instinctual reaction.

Advanced Man: Directed personality effort.

Disciple or Initiate: Recognition and work with the Plan. Will.

Sign II: Taurus

The sign in which the Transpersonal Self focuses special streams of illumination upon the lower personal self, helping to free it from lower desires and attachments.

Positive Traits: stability, endurance, strong sense of value, power to acquire, constructiveness, drive towards illumination

Negative traits: immobility, stubbornness, possessiveness, self-indulgence, routinization

The constellation Taurus distributes ray four. The planets associated with Taurus are Venus (orthodox) and Vulcan (esoteric and hierarchical), distributing ray five and ray one, respectively.

Spiritual Mantram: I see, and when the eye is opened, all is illumined.

Evolutionary Mantram: And the Word said: Let struggle be undismayed.

Undeveloped Man: Selfish desire. The light of earth.

Advanced Man: Aspiration. The Light of Love

Disciple or Initiate: Illumined living. The Light of Life.

Sign III: Gemini

The sign which promotes the communicative interplay between Transpersonal Self and personality.

Positive Traits: versatility, mental agility, inquisitiveness, communicativeness, awareness of duality, power to educate, fluid interplay between the transpersonal and personal self

Negative Traits: instability, superficiality, changeability, restlessness, diffusiveness, inconsistency

The constellation Gemini distributes ray two. The planets associated with Gemini are Mercury (orthodox), Venus (esoteric) and the Earth (hierarchical), distributing ray four, ray five and ray three, respectively.

Spiritual Mantram: I recognize my other self, and in the waning of that self, I grow and glow.

Evolutionary Mantram: And the Word said: Let instability do its work.

Undeveloped Man: Mutation of relation. "I serve myself."

Advanced Man: Orientation of "I serve my brother."

Disciple or Initiate: Right relation. "I serve the One."

Sign IV: Cancer

The sign in which the physical form for the full manifestation of the Transpersonal Self is prepared, provided, and illumined. A foundational base of operations for the illumed expression of spirituality is established.

Positive Traits: domesticity, nurturance, tenacity, protectiveness, rootedness, a well–developed 'common touch,' emotional sensitivity, realization of wholeness

Negative Traits: over–sensitivity, moodiness, fear and worry, timidity, over–retentiveness, retrogression, refusal to release, excessive self–protectiveness, inferiority feelings

The constellation Cancer distributes ray three and ray seven. The planets associated with Cancer are the Moon (orthodox) and Neptune (esoteric and hierarchical), distributing ray four and ray six, respectively.

Spiritual Mantram: I build a lighted house and therein dwell.

Evolutionary Mantram: And the Word said: Let isolation be the rule, and yet the crowd exists.

Undeveloped Man: The blind unit is lost. The Mass.

Advanced Man: The unit awakens to that which is around. The House.

Disciple or Initiate: The whole is seen as One. Humanity.

Sign V: Leo

The sign in which the personality becomes powerful and integrated, or in which there is a fully dramatized expression of the identity of the Transpersonal Self.

Positive Traits: dignity, self–confidence, generosity, warm–heartedness, dramatic power, magnanimity, power to rule and inspire, strong sense of identity with the One Self

Negative Traits: vanity, domination, extravagance, arrogance, 'show–offishness,' excessive pride

The constellation Leo distributes ray one and ray five. The luminaries and planets associated with Leo are the Sun (orthodox), Sun (esoteric – veiling Neptune) and Sun (hierarchical – veiling Uranus), distributing ray two, ray two/six, and ray two/seven, respectively.

Spiritual Mantram: I am That and That am I.

Evolutionary Mantram: And the Word said: Let other forms exist. I rule.

Undeveloped Man: The lower self. The hidden point.

Advanced Man: The Higher Self. The revealing point.

Disciple or Initiate: The One Self. The relinquished point.

Sign VI: Virgo

The sign in which all dimensional fields within the personality are refined and purified to make a fit and 'spiritually sanitized' receptical for the expression of the Transpersonal Self; the growing *presence* of the Transpersonal Self within the personality is nurtured.

Positive Traits: discrimination, meticulousness, purity and humility, practicality, capacity for hard work, power to heal through right diet and physical discipline, ability to nurture the inner light

Negative Traits: hyper-critical attitude, pettiness, perfectionism, fastidiousness, coldness, materiality

The constellation Virgo distributes ray two and ray six. The planets associated with Virgo are Mercury (orthodox), the Moon (esoteric – veiling both Vulcan and Neptune), and Jupiter (hierarchical) distributing ray four, ray four/one, and ray two, respectively.

Spiritual Mantrams: 1) I am the Mother and the Child. I God, I Matter am. 2) Christ in you, the hope of glory.

Evolutionary Mantram: And the Word said: Let matter reign.

Undeveloped Man: The germinating energy. The Mother.

Advanced Man: The creative force. The Protector.

Disciple or Initiate: The Christ activity. The Light.

Sign VII: Libra

The sign in which the Transpersonal Self and the personal self are united in 'marriage' – the so-called "marriage in the heavens."

Positive Traits: sense of justice, diplomacy, mutuality, harmony and equilibrium, dedication to peace, social consciousness, adherence to the "golden mean"

Negative Traits: indecision, over-compliance, hesitancy, appeasement, excessive love of pleasure, jugementalism, overly mannered and polite, over reliance on partnership

The constellation Libra distributes ray three. The planets associated with Libra are Venus (orthodox), Uranus (esoteric) and Saturn (hierarchical), distributing ray five, ray seven and ray three, respectively.

Spiritual Mantram: I choose the way which leads between the two great lines of force.

Evolutionary Mantram: And the Word said: Let choice be made.

Undeveloped Man: Unbalanced fiery passion. Human love.

Advanced Man: The weighing of the opposites. Devotion and aspiration.

Disciple or Initiate: Balance attained. Divine love. Understanding.

Sign VIII: Scorpio

The sign in which the Transpersonal Self wages a 'war' against the lower, personal self. This results in the metaphysical "death of the personality," which dies to any separative desire of its own.

Positive Traits: transformative power, penetrating perception, magnetic intensity, power to triumph, depth of character, power to regenerate, power to confront the "shadow self"

Negative Traits: destructiveness, repression, revengefulness, treachery, jealousy, self-destructiveness.

The constellation Scorpio distributes ray four. The planets associated with Scorpio are Mars (orthodox and esoteric) and Mercury (hierarchical) distributing ray six and ray four, respectively.

Spiritual Mantram: Warrior am I, and from the battle I emerge triumphant.

Evolutionary Mantram: And the Word said: Let Maya flourish and deception rule.

Undeveloped Man: Unity of selfishness. The Monster.

Advanced Man: Conflict with duality. The fighter.

Disciple or Initiate: Higher unity. The Disciple.

Sign IX: Sagittarius

The sign in which the vision of higher evolutionary possibilities is transmitted by the Transpersonal Self, and intuitively received by the focused, one-pointed consciousness of the individual personality. In this sign, rapid one-pointed progress is made towards the goal of initiation.

Positive Traits: goal-consciousness, straight truthfulness, foresight, expansiveness, lofty idealism, rapid intuition, adventuresome exploration, one-pointed focus, global vision

Negative Traits: tactlessness, exaggeration, blind optimism, recklessness, lack of restraint, wanderlust, fanaticism

The constellation Sagittarius distributes ray four, ray five and ray six. The planets associated with Sagittarius are Jupiter (orthodox), Earth (esoteric) and Mars (hierarchical), distributing ray two, ray three and ray six, respectively.

Spiritual Mantram: I see the goal. I reach that goal and see another.

Evolutionary Mantram: And the Word said: Let food be sought.

Undeveloped Man: Self–centredness. Experimental approach.

Advanced Man: One–pointedness. Directed approach.

Disciple or Initiate: The director of men. The controller of the Gate.

Sign X: Capricorn

The sign of "Initiation" in which the personality is transfigured through complete fusion with (and infusion of) the Transpersonal Self.

Positive Traits: discipline, responsibility, industriousness, conscientiousness, power to survive, power to achieve the peak of attainment, power to conform to the highest Law or Will

Negative Traits: pessimism, rigidity, isolation, conventionality, suppression, materialism, callousness

The constellation Capricorn distributes ray one, ray three and ray seven. The planets associated with Capricorn are Saturn (orthodox and esoteric), and Venus (hierarchical), distributing ray three and ray five, respectively.

Spiritual Mantram: Lost am I in light supernal, yet on that light I turn my back.

Evolutionary Mantram: And the Word said: Let ambition rule, and the door stand wide.

Undeveloped Man: The earthbound soul.

Advanced Man: The one who crosses the water. Fluid.

Disciple or Initiate: The Conqueror of Death. Initiated.

Sign XI: Aquarius

The sign of loving, impersonal service, in which the powers of the Transpersonal Self are distributed through the redeemed and transfigured lower personal self for the benefit of humanity.

Positive Traits: humanitarianism, ecumenism, spirit of sharing, progressivism, innovation, universality, group conscious spirit, power to pour forth in service for the benefit of all

Negative Traits: eccentricity, rebelliousness, aloofness, excessive extroversion, 'groupiness,' emotional superficiality, unfocused sense of individuality

The constellation Aquarius distributes ray five. The planets associated with Aquarius are Uranus (orthodox), Jupiter (esoteric) and the Moon (hierarchical – veiling either Neptune or Uranus) distributing ray seven, ray two, and ray four/six/seven, respectively.

Spiritual Mantram: Water of Life am I, poured forth for thirsty men.

Evolutionary Mantram: And the Word said: Let desire in form be ruler.

Undeveloped Man: All things to all men. The burden of the self.

Advanced Man: Dedication to the soul. The burden of humanity.

Disciple or Initiate: The Server of all men. The burden of the world.

Sign XII: Pisces

The sign in which the full powers of the Transpersonal Self pour through the liberated personal self in order to salvage and redeem humanity. Essentially, Pisces is the sign of the savior and of salvation.

Positive Traits: compassion, self–denial, sensitivity to impression, intuitive sensitivity, redemptiveness, gentle patience, poetic imagination, inclusiveness, power to save

Negative Traits: escapism or evasiveness, impracticality and dreaminess, illusion and delusion, sentimentality, helplessness, utopianism, aimlessness, hyper–sensitivity, gullibility.

The constellation Pisces distributes ray two and ray six. The planets associated with Pisces are Jupiter (orthodox), Pluto (esoteric and hierarchical) and, in a special sense, Neptune, distributing ray two, ray one and ray six, respectively.

Spiritual Mantram: I leave the Father's Home, and turning back I save.

Evolutionary Mantram: And the Word said: Go forth into matter.

Undeveloped Man: Responsiveness to environment. The medium.

Advanced Man: Sensitivity to soul. The Mediator.

Disciple or Initiate: Spiritual responsibility. The Saviour.

A close study of all the above will show that whenever certain of these signs are prominent in the astrological make–up of an individual, *the Transpersonal Self is attempting to accomplish certain purposes through the personality life*. Much depends upon the level of evolution at which the individual stands. The general quality of each sign can be applied accordingly.

Note: There are other rays distributed by each of the planets, a discussion of which will be fully undertaken in Volumes III and IV or *Tapestry of the Gods*.

APPENDIX III

A Brief Discussion of the Meanings of the Planets from the Perspective of Esoteric Astrology

The essential meanings of the zodiacal constellations (manifesting through astrological signs) have now been listed – especially the kinds of meanings which may be useful to esoteric psychologists as they attempt to facilitate the achievement of personality integration and eventual fusion of the personality with the Transpersonal Self. The qualities distributed by those great Entities known as planets (in the esoteric tradition, they are called Planetary Logoi) must now be briefly considered.

Sun: In esoteric astrology the effect of the Sun sign is known as "the potency of the Sun of Probability." The zodiacal sign in which the Sun is found at birth indicates that energy the use of which constitutes the personality's line of least resistance for a particular life cycle. For those individuals who are not yet aware of (or seeking to become aware of) the influence of the Transpersonal Self, the Sun is considered to be the focal point of the astrological chart. Symbolically, the Sun stands either for the personal or transpersonal will – in most cases, the former. Planetary aspects to the Sun give considerable information bearing upon the process of *personality integration*. In an important sense, the Sun represents the integrating center, through which flows the power integrating the various facets of the personality into a unified whole. On a higher level, the Sun is also a symbol for the Solar Angel, that radiant solar Being Who infuses each individual human being with transcendent light, love and power. The association of the Sun with the heart, and the heart with the soul (the Transpersonal Self) is also significant. In some mysterious manner the Sun may also be associated with the essential spiritual Self (the Monad).

The Sun is said to "veil" an undiscovered second ray planet. As ruler of the sign Leo, the Sun is active upon the orthodox, esoteric and hierarchical levels. On an esoteric level it veils Neptune and on the hierarchical level the Sun veils Uranus.

Moon: In esoteric astrology the Moon is literally a *dead planet* with no living emanation of its own. The effect sensed as coming from the Moon usually comes from the planets Vulcan, Neptune and Uranus. The other effect of the Moon arises from the nefarious influence of its decaying personality fields – analogous to the physical, emotional and mental fields of the human being. These decaying "lunar vehicles" exert an inhibiting and retrogressive effect upon the personality vehicles of each individual. Interestingly, these personality vehicles are, in the language of esotericism, called "*lunar vehicles.*" For the esoteric psychologist, the Moon represents all that is past, subconscious, automatic, habitual, residual and inhibiting of progress. The Moon is particularly associated with the physical body, which, in esotericism, is *not* a "principle," and which, in many respects, is an obstacle or impediment for the inner individual. Thus, wherever the Moon is found (sign and house position) there may be discovered a field of conflict in which the spiritual nature of the individual must compete with the lowest form of matter. This conflict is also due to the Moon's association with an undiscovered, non-sacred fourth ray planet – the planet representing the *'conflict aspct'* of the Ray of Harmony Through Conflict.

The Moon, with its endless succession of phases, also represents a repetitive rhythm which must be broken if psychologically transformative progress is to be made. In a more positive sense, lunar phases can be correlated with the cyclic phases of the growth process of all forms.

When the Moon acts as a "veil," obscuring or muting the influence of one of the three planets mentioned above, it serves to indicate the condition of the form (the personality, broadly considered), i.e. the condition of all that which must be subdued, controlled and infused by the Solar Angel, which is symbolized, in part, by the Sun. When the veiled planet is emphasized, rather than the Moon itself, the issue no longer concerns the obstruction which form represents, but how that form can be uplifted and spiritualized through the influence of the veiled planet. One looks at the Moon position for hints about how the spiritualization of the matter aspect of the life can be achieved – matter made brilliant through Vulcan, luminous through Neptune and electrically scintillating through Uranus.

The Moon (primarily interpreted as a fourth ray influence) is the orthodox ruler of the sign Cancer, the esoteric ruler of the sign Virgo and the hierarchical ruler of the sign Aquarius.

Ascendant: Although the Ascendant is not a planet, it is a powerful zodiacal "sensitive point" formed by the intersection of the individual horizon with the ecliptic. In esoteric astrology the Ascendent is known as the "Sun of Possibility, indicating that it is the energy which, when properly used, will bring the personal life into alignment with the will of the Transpersonal Self, thus making the incarnation a spiritual *success*. While the horoscope of the average, non-aspiring individual can be built up around the Sun sign (which, very likely, means erecting and interpreting the *solar chart* – with the Sun at the Ascendant), the horoscope of the individual seeking to live the transpersonal life is to be interpreted with reference to the Ascendant (or the Rising Sign, as it is often called). From the point of view of esoteric psychology, it can safely be said that *the Ascendant is the most important point or influence in the astrological chart*. With the soul ray, it gives the esoteric psychologist the most illuminating key to the *spiritual design* which the Transpersonal Self is intending to actualize through the personal life. When interpreting the chart of a spiritually inclined individual, the Ascendant must be given priority, and all other astrological influences must be rendered subservient to its quality. This is a major task requiring great understanding and ingenuity.

Vulcan: In the esoteric tradition, Vulcan is named as a real, though undiscovered, planet. Vulcan is closely identified with the Sun, the soul and the Transpersonal Self. Vulcan, the mythological "blacksmith of the gods," forges the bonds between the Transpersonal Self and the lower, personal self. Vulcan stabilizes, strengthens and confirms the channels of intercourse between the Transpersonal Self and the personality. This planet strengthens the spiritual will, and represents what might be called the 'grip of the soul.' Vulcan is intimately involved in the spiritualization of matter, *burnishing* matter to a high state of brilliance. There are a number of ephemerides for Vulcan, purporting to give its position in the astrological chart, but their accuracy has been unconfirmed. Generally, Vulcan is thought to be within eight degrees of the Sun, and thus, will frequently, though not always, be in the same sign as the Sun. Although Vulcan cannot, at this time, be accurately located in the chart, its qualities can be understood and applied – especially in the case of those in whom the first ray is strong, and those who are born in or under certain signs.

Vulcan, which acts as an agent of distribution for the first Ray of Will and Power, is active in the signs Taurus, where it is the esoteric and hierarchical ruler, and Virgo (where it is "veiled" by the Moon).

Mercury: Esoterically, Mercury is associated with all processes of communication, nervous transmission and thought formation. Mercury is particularly connected with the intuitive processes. Often called the "Star of Intuition,"" (as well as the "Star of Conflict") Mercury forms a bridge between the personal self and the Transpersonal Self. When seeking the manner and style of communication between the transpersonal and the personal fields, the esoteric psychologist/astrologer will have to consult the status of Mercury in the astrological chart. It is, par excellence, the *linking* planet, exerting a bridging influence (either horizontal, vertical or both) in the life of every individual.

Mercury, which acts as an agent of distribution for the fourth Ray of Harmony Through Conflict, is the orthodox ruler of Gemini and Virgo, the esoteric ruler of Aries and the hierarchical ruler of Scorpio.

Venus: Esoterically, Venus is especially associated with the life of the Solar Angel and the substance of the vehicle of the Transpersonal Self. For disciples and initiates, Venus relates to all that which has been through the refiner's fire of the personal life, and which, consequently, is of *quintessential value* (remember Venus' association with the number 5 and the fifth ray). All values extracted from personal experience while in incarnation are stored within the field of the Transpersonal Self - called by esoteric psychologists, the "Causal Body." In the astrological chart Venus is related to the mental and aesthetic faculties of the Transpersonal Self which evaluate and extract *quality* from the lower personal life. In certain respects, Venus represents the fashion in which the soul *beautifies* the lower, personal life, as well as the beauty inherent in the soul itself. The higher nature of Venus always exerts a refining influence on the individual and leads towards the fusion of the Transpersonal Self with the personal self.

Venus, which acts as an agent of distribution for the fifth Ray of Concrete Knowledge and Science, is the orthodox ruler of Libra and Taurus, the esoteric ruler of Gemini and the hierarchical ruler of Capricorn.

Mars: Mars is not a sacred planet, which means that it is more potent in, and representative of, the personal sphere than the transpersonal sphere. Mars is particularly associated with the passional nature and with the solar plexus and sacral centers in the vital/etheric force field of the human being. To the esoteric psychologist/astrologer, the position of Mars in the astrological chart indicates the way in which the blind, rebellious emotional nature is liable to interfere with the imposition of the will of the

Transpersonal Self. Mars can act as a divisive force within the personality and within the social milieu, but it can also indicate the strength of the personal aspiration towards the transpersonal life, once its energies are harnessed and directed. Esoterically, Mars represents a fiery power which can thwart or expedite the intentions of the Transpersonal Self as this higher center seeks to express through the lower personal self.

Mars, which acts as an agent of distribution for the sixth Ray of Idealism and Devotion, is the orthodox ruler of Aries and Scorpio, the esoteric ruler of Scorpio and the hierarchical ruler of Sagittarius.

Jupiter: Jupiter is a planet much associated with the growth of wisdom and the expansion of consciousness. Esoteric psychologists are always alert to ways of offering their clients avenues of growth, increased breadth of understanding, and the opportunity for a *fuller* life. The position of Jupiter in the astrological chart indicates the method by which the broad scope and vision of the Transpersonal Self may gradually replace the rather limited vision of the lower personal self. The influence of Jupiter expands the 'auric reach' of the individual, so to speak, and promotes the process of personal/transpersonal fusion by means of broadening the individual's perspective. Later, Jupiter promotes the fusion of the Transpersonal Self with the Monad. Esoterically, Jupiter always promotes *fusion*.

Jupiter, which acts as an agent of distribution for the second Ray of Love–Wisdom, is the orthodox ruler of Sagittarius and Pisces, the esoteric ruler of Aquarius and the hierarchical ruler of Virgo.

Saturn: Saturn is the planet which indicates one of the most important methods by which the Transpersonal Self *tests* the fitness of the personal self for the further reception of transpersonal influence – the method of *adversity* or *resistance*. The Law of Evolution demands that transpersonal quality be expressed effectively and concretely throughout the lower four personal fields. The influence of Saturn *grounds* that expression; it forces each individual to make real, concrete and practical all ideas and influences emanating from the transpersonal realm. The personality often experiences this grounding process as adversity and resistance. If, for instance, an inspiring idea has not been properly expressed in form, the continued infusion of further dynamic energies and inspiring ideas can only be destructive. Saturn, therefore, helps (virtually forces) the individual to create a solid, stable foundation of tangible personal accomplishment so that a fresh access of transpersonal influence will not be wasted. Saturn is also the agent of solar–systemic Law (applied through the will of the Transpersonal Self), forcing all individuals, at length, to *conform* – to keep themselves within divinely–determined bounds. Significantly, Saturn is closely associated with the Law of Economy.

Saturn, which acts as an agent of distribution for the third Ray of Active Intelligence and Adaptability, is both the orthodox and esoteric ruler of Capricorn and the hierarchical ruler of Libra.

Uranus: Uranus is the planet which indicates the power of the Transpersonal Self to shatter confining structures within the lower personal life. Under the lightning–like Uranian influence, the Transpersonal Self can restructure and transform the personal life so that it becomes a true reflector of transpersonal quality. The impact of brilliant, intuitive ideas from the higher mind reveals everything in a startlingly new perspective. Hence, Uranus is the lightning which illuminates the future, and demands that the individual initiate and create the new. Wherever Uranus is found in the astrological chart, the renovative impulse is to be given full sway.

Uranus, which acts as an agent of distribution for the seventh Ray of Ceremonial Order and Magic, is the orthodox ruler of Aquarius, the esoteric ruler of Libra and the hierarchical ruler of Aries.

Neptune: To the esoteric psychologist/astrologer, Neptune is the means by which divine compassion and universal love enter the lower personal sphere. In esotericism, the intuition is something different than what one might expect. The intuition is the faculty by which *unitive consciousness* is achieved – the state of consciousness well–understood by mystics of all ages and traditions. The intuitive faculty is called "buddhi" and is a faculty which, in its essence, lies *beyond* the field of the Transpersonal Self. It is Neptune which enables an individual to begin to coordinate the "buddhic vehicle," or intuitional force field. Further, Neptune represents that state of inclusiveness which dissolves all arbitrary boundaries created by the lower mental faculties. The mind, in one sense, is said to be the "slayer of the real." Neptune, subtly, slays the slayer by negating all arbitrary mental distinctions. On the highest turn of the spiral, there is a sense in which Neptune is the conveyer of transcendent beauty (thus representing the final quality in the trinity of the Good, the True and the Beautiful). Neptune is associated with the highest functions of the imagination, through which the individual can place himself in rapport with the transpersonal realm, and fathom its beauties.

Neptune, which acts as an agent of distribution for the sixth Ray of Idealism and Devotion, is not the orthodox ruler of any sign, though it has a special relationship to Pisces. Neptune is both the esoteric and hierarchical ruler of Cancer.

Pluto: In esoteric astrology, Pluto is not a sacred planet, and is, therefore, more related to the personal than the transpersonal sphere. Nevertheless, Pluto has great utility in executing the intentions of the Transpersonal Self, for it purges the lower self of all obstacles to soul infusion. Pluto is much associated with the *kundalini power* resident (according to esotericism) at the base of the spine. Once Pluto has purged the "realms of Tartarus" – the lower subconscious residues accumulated during many individual life cycles – it is instrumental in raising the extraordinarily powerful lower energies of the material aspect of the personality so that they become totally available to the Transpersonal Self. Pluto brings death to all ancient obstruction, and eliminates all poisons (physical or psychic) from the human energy system. The position of Pluto in the astrological chart indicates where drastic 'deaths' (detachments) and rebirths can occur; where the personal "hydra" may be encountered and slain; and where, consequently, the Transpersonal Self may find the way cleared of all personal 'garbage' and debris. Amazing re–energizings and revitalizations can take place as a result of Pluto's work within the personality.

Pluto, which acts as an agent of distribution for the first Ray of Will and Power, is not the orthodox ruler of any sign, but has a special relationship to the sign Scorpio. Pluto is both the esoteric and hierarchical ruler of Pisces.

Earth: Earth is rarely considered in exoteric, mundane astrological calculations, but it has pivotal importance in the life of all Earth beings. Because we are inhabitants of Earth, and intimately a part of its living system, it is somewhat more difficult to assess its astrological importance. Like Mars and Pluto, Earth is a non-sacred planet, and its influence is, therefore, rather more related to the personal than the Transpersonal Self.

In the astrological chart the Earth is frequently read as if it were found opposite the Sun. The status of the Sun in the chart is said to indicate the nature and condition of the individual's vitality; the Earth is very likely involved in this indication. The third ray personality of the Earth is directly associated with the principle of *activity*, which, itself, is a good measurement of vitality. There are, as we know from occultism, at least two great categories of prana – one more associated with the Sun, and the other with the Earth. Earth may well be associated with the splenic etheric center through which pranic vitality is accumulated. The condition of the Sun/Earth axis in the astrological chart may indicate the condition of an individual's personal (and, especially, physical) vitality. This is an important consideration when assessing the ease or difficulty with which the Transpersonal Self can express itself through the personality. Insufficient vitality, or excessive vitality poorly distributed, can thwart transpersonal intent. Abundant, well-regulated vitality is a definite boon to the fulfillment of the soul's archetypal design.

The Earth, which acts as an agent of distribution for the third Ray of Active Intelligence and Adaptability, is the esoteric ruler of Sagittarius and the hierarhical ruler of Gemini. It does not rule any constellation from the orthodox angle.

APPENDIX IV

The Personal Identity Profile and the Challenge of Ray Assessment

Although there exists a great deal of information about the seven rays, and although many worthy investigators have given considerable attention to the problem of *ray assessment* (i.e. the attempt to determine the ray chart or ray formula for an individual), *it is never an easy thing to determine an individual's ray make-up.* Starting with the very credible assumption that the seven ray paradigm is valid, a few psychologists, rayologists and esoteric astrologers have devised psychometric instruments which are intended to measure the relative strengths of weaknesses of the seven rays in the individual's energy system. James Davis (San Diego, CA) developed the *Self Search* questionnaire; working in cooperation with John Cullen, Ph.D., president of the I.A.M.O.P (the International Association for Managerial and Organizational Psychosynthesis), Lane Holt created the *T.P.P. – Types Personality Profile*; Judi Laws (Washington, D.C.) enlarged, codified and systematized an interview technique of ray assessment evolved by Douglas Baker, M.D.; Paul O'Neill, Ed.D. (Jackson, MS) devised the O.P.V.I. (the O'Neill Personal Values Inventory) designed to correlate human behavior patterns with chakra emphasis (a correlation definitely related to *ray* emphasis); etc. No doubt there have been other valuable questionnaire and interview techniques which have not yet come to the author's attention.

There are also methods of ray assessment which do not utilize the questionnaire (or 'statementaire') approach. David Tansley, D.C., (an excellent researcher and practitioner whose untimely, early death was a great loss to the systematic study of human energetics) utilized various methods related to the science of radionics in order to determine the ray structures of his patients and clients; Robert Gerard, Ph.D. (Los Angeles, CA) has been a pioneer in the field of ray assessment by trained groups (or assessment teams) which utilize psychoradiethesic methods (somewhat akin to the radionic methods) and also methods which, essentially, necessitate the development of a highly sensitive intuitive response on the part of the ray assessor. (For a fuller explanation, please see Robert Gerard's introductory *Commentary* to *Tapestry of the Gods*, Volume I.)

Thus, there are a number of serious investigators vitally interested in solving the many problems associated with accurate ray assessment. As valuable and productive as the many instruments and approaches may be, there is still no fool-proof method of ray assessment. The Master *knows*, infallibly and in every case; we, no matter how intelligent and resourceful we may be, do not – *yet*.

The Purpose of the Personal Identity Profile

The *Personal Identity Profile – Version 1* (or P.I.P.#1) is yet another attempt to bring added light to the challenges of ray assessment. It was created in 1985–1986 with the invaluable assistance of the members of the Seven Ray Institute. The Tibetan's books were thoroughly researched and all references to ray qualities were culled and systematized. Of the many qualities associated with each one of the seven rays, twenty of the most important were chosen, making 140 qualities in all. Then, 140 statements were carefully devised to embody each of the 140 qualities. The P.I.P. offers respondents the opportunity to indicate the degree to which each statement describes them or fails to describe them. On the basis of their 140 responses (and their responses to two other kinds of measures) a useful indication of the relative strength of each of the seven rays within their energy system can be derived.

P.I.P.#1 has been administered to approximately 1500 individuals over the course of the past three years, and the results have been most encouraging. Although P.I.P.#1 (like any other personality inventory) has its limitations, it has proven very useful in helping hundreds of individuals gain a fuller understanding of their ray structures.

What You Will Receive When You Take the Personal Identity Profile

1. A seven–color bar graph illustrating the relative strengths of the seven rays (and the various ray sub–types) within your energy system.

2. A four page computer printout containing numerous tabulations based upon your P.I.P.#1 responses. Correct interpretation of these tabulations will reveal important aspects of your identity and ray structure.

3. A "Personal Growth Formula" based upon the triangle formed by your Sun, Moon and Ascendant positions.

4. A 100 page *Personal Identity Profile Interpretation Manual* filled with valuable information needed to interpret your P.I.P. results and begin erecting your Ray Chart.

Procedure for Taking P.I.P.#1

If you are interested in taking P.I.P.#1:

1. simply write or telephone the Seven Ray Institute. The P.I.P.#1 questionnaire and answer sheet will be sent to you.

2. or you can utilize P.I.P.#1 [hereinafter included] and photocopy the answer sheet). After you complete the P.I.P., mail your answer sheet to the Institute.

Financing the P.I.P. Project and Ray Research

In order to partially defray the cost of processing your P.I.P., and to financially support further necessary research in the field of ray assessment, the Seven Ray Institute recommends **a tax deductible donation of $50.00 for each Personal Identity Profile processed.** You can expect to receive your P.I.P. results **about three weeks** after you complete and submit your P.I.P. answer sheet to the Seven Ray Institute.

The P.I.P. and the Seven Ray Institute's Seminar Program

Perhaps the *best* way to understand your P.I.P.#1 results is to enroll in a **Seven Ray Seminar.** This is not always possible for every individual, but the experience is strongly recommended. Such Seminars have been offered by the Seven Ray Institute throughout the United States (and internationally) for the past three years, and provide an ideal **group learning environment** for understanding how the science of esoteric psychology and the results of P.I.P.#1 relate to your psychospiritual unfoldment.

P.I.P.#1 and the Evolution of P.I.P.#2

It is clear from the name P.I.P.*#1* that a further development of the P.I.P. is intended. In fact, the research for P.I.P.#2 is well under way. The pool of over 1500 completed P.I.P.#1 tests provides a very respectable sample for statistical analysis. The attempt is being made to see if P.I.P.#1 can be refined and expanded to assess even more accurately the presence of the various rays as they condition the various vehicles of the human energy system. The psychometric researchers affiliated with the Seven Ray Institute are presently deeply involved in this project.

Although many readers of these volumes will have already taken P.I.P.#1, *it is included within the context of Tapestry of the Gods* for further study and deepened reflection, and so that those who may be new to the Personal Identity Profile may have the opportunity to utilize it in the investigation of their ray structure.

Note 1: P.I.P.#1 has been skillfully adapted by Dorothy J. Maver, Ph.D. for the use, primarily, of high school students (though some junior high and college students can also benefit greatly from this instrument). Dr. Maver's inventory is called the *S.I.P.* – the *Student Identity Profile.* The author strongly recommends the S.I.P. to all progressive educators as an excellent means of understanding their students more thoroughly.

Note 2: As you review P.I.P.#1, it is important to understand that it was devised to be taken by esotericists and non–esotericists alike, and, therefore, does not contain terminology which is explicitly esoteric or astrological.

The PERSONAL IDENTITY PROFILE: Version I

You are about to take the PERSONAL IDENTITY PROFILE, a self-assessment inventory designed to indicate the strength of the Seven Fundamental Qualities (and their subsidiary traits) in your personality structure. The Profile will help you explore and understand your personality in a very new way. The P.I.P. is not a *test*: there are no right or wrong answers. There is no such thing as doing well or badly, passing or not passing. You are the sole judge of the "right" way of responding to any of the (140) statements. The "right" answer for you is completely determined by how you think and feel about each statement.

The Purpose of the P.I.P.

The P.I.P. is designed to describe your personality in terms of seven major dimensions: the Seven Fundamental Qualities. Some of the most important similarities and differences between people are determined by the presence or absence of these Qualities. Actually, every individual has *all* of the Seven Qualities, but in differing degrees of emphasis. The statements in the P.I.P. are designed to determine which of the Seven Qualities are most strongly represented in your personality make-up, and which are not so strongly represented. The result of this assessment will be an IDENTITY PROFILE of your personality – a personal pattern or "energy picture" with broad implications for your self-understanding and for your approach to self-fulfillment.

Choosing your Responses on the P.I.P.

There are seven basic ways (1, 2, 3, 4, 5, 6, 7) for you to respond to each statement, ranging from (1.) = Very True –to– (7.) = Very False. Simply choose the particular response of the seven which *most adequately describes* how you think or feel about a statement.

A Way to Show How You Have Changed During the Course of Your Life

You also have the option of responding to each statement from the point of view of your development as a person over *time*. People are constantly changing and growing. Qualities which were very strong ten to twenty years ago may not be as strong today; conversely, Qualities which were absent or undeveloped earlier in life may be quite strong today. The Personal Identity Profile takes this dynamic into consideration, giving you the option of noting those statements for which your current response is significantly different from what it would have been earlier in your life. No attempt is made to set hard and fast time limits; the idea is simply to note *general* increases or decreases in the strength of any particular Quality. The results add an important tool for interpreting your P.I.P. with a greater degree of sophistication.

The P.I.P.'s Use of *General* Statements

You will notice that many of the statements in the P.I.P. are *general* statements. In many instances, the *specific* approach has been deliberately avoided. A wide diversity of people take the P.I.P.. People share similar Qualities *in general*, but the manner in which people apply or express these Qualities will differ significantly. So it will be up to you, as you think about the specifics of your particular life situation, to decide whether or not you possess a certain quality – **in general**.

If You Encounter the Sense of Uncertainty or Contradiction

You may also, at times, "be of two minds" about a statement. You may feel that a certain part of the statement is quite true of you, and that another part of the statement is quite false. This is entirely normal. People are very complex and have many different sides to their character. What you are asked to do, if such cases arise, is to allow counter–indications to *blend in your mind*; you will then come up with a **general sense or feeling** about the statement which will be a sort of "subjective average" of the counter–indications. Just trust your feelings (or intuition) in such cases and the results will be sufficiently accurate.

How to Take the P.I.P.

Those who have taken the Personal Identity Profile have found it to be a real adventure in self–discovery. Simply set aside some quiet time during which you will not be disturbed, and reflect upon who you are and who you have been. Take a look at yourself as if for the first time. As you get a "feel" for each statement, related "scenes" or memories from you life may come to mind. Let them appear, see what they are telling you about yourself, and then *circle the response which seems best to you.*

In terms of how long to take answering the P.I.P., you can take the Profile rapidly, or you can spend as long as you wish, pondering over it as you search for the responses which most represent who you "really are." Most people find that it can be finished in an hour or so.

Be Totally Honest with Yourself

Naturally, for the best results, it is important to be totally honest. Just about everybody realizes this, but human nature plays its tricks on even the most well–intentioned person. Evidence has shown that it is natural to want to *identify with all* character traits which are perceived as virtues – and there are many such in the P.I.P.. There is also a tendency to *avoid identifying* with those character traits which are perceived as deficiencies. This tendency is not very helpful for arriving at a true and accurate profile of identity. Although everyone has *all* the Seven Fundamental Qualities, not everyone has *all* the *traits* associated with these Qualities. The only way to determine which of the Qualities are strongest in your life is to respond with the greatest possible accuracy and honesty to the many, diverse character traits you will encounter in the P.I.P..

You may also recognize in the statements certain desirable traits of character you *wish* you had, and that you feel you *could have* if you just worked a little; **nevertheless**, it is important for you to choose the response that describes how you *actually are*, and **not** how you wish you were or think you could be. Similarly, you may come upon character traits that you *wish* you didn't have, and that you feel you *could get rid of* if you just worked at it a little. The same approach applies: **TRY TO SEE YOURSELF EXACTLY AS YOU ARE.** The more clearly you really see yourself, the more accurate and helpful will be your results.

Enjoy Your P.I.P Adventure

If you read the questions carefully and thoughtfully and, as you answer, imaginatively review your past thoughts, feelings and actions, an accurate and very useful Personal Identity Profile will emerge. Enjoy your adventure with the P.I.P.. It may help you understand yourself and your place in the world in an entirely new way.

PERSONAL IDENTITY PROFILE

SECTION I

Please respond to the follwing statements as truthfully and accurately as you can. This is not a test and there are no right or wrong answers. Simply indicate your choice according to how you think or feel about a given statement. Please read each statement **carefully** before responding. If you respond to the statements thoughtfully, a very useful picture of Seven Fundamental Personality Qualities will emerge. If, at first, you feel you do not know how to respond to a statement, just think it over, absorb the meaning of the words, and the best response will occur to you. The value of your P.I.P. results is directly related to how *clearly* you see yourself, so try to see yourself exactly as you really **ARE.**

HOW TO TAKE THE P.I.P.

For each statement, please circle **ONE NUMBER** from the list (1, 2, 3, 4, 5, 6, 7).

You also have the **OPTION** of circling either (x) or (y) if there has been what you consider a significant change, over the years of your life, in the way you now react to any particular statement.

THE MEANING OF EACH NUMBER

Circle **(1)** – If you think the statement is **very true** of you.

Circle **(2)** – If you think the statement is basically **true** of you with very few exceptions.

Circle **(3)** – If you think the statement is partially true of you and partially false, but basically **more true than false.**

Circle **(4)** – If you think that for you the statement is **as true as it is false.** In this case you would be "in between."

Circle **(5)** – If you think the statement is partially false for you and partically true, but basically **more false than true.**

Circle **(6)** – If you think the statement is basically **false** for you with very few exceptions.

Circle **(7)** – If you think the statement is **very false** for you.

Circle **(x)** – If you think that, over the course of your life, the basic Quality represented in the statement has **increased** to a significant extent.

Cirlce **(y)** – If you think that, over the course of your life, the basic Quality represented in the statement has **decreased** to a significant extent.

PLEASE NOTE: Responses of **(x)** and **(y)** are **not** a substitute for responses 1 through 7. Your P.I.P. cannot be properly scored unless you give a numerical response to **each** of the 140 statements. Your **(x)** and **(y)** responses are simply meant to provide you with *additional* useful information. **PLEASE CHECK OVER YOUR ANSWER SHEET BEFORE SUBMITTING IT IN ORDER TO INSURE THAT YOU HAVE RESPONDED TO EACH AND EVERY STATEMENT!**

The **SIMPLEST APPROACH** is, first, to make your choice of (1, 2, 3, 4, 5, 6, 7,) for each statement. Then, before moving on to the next statement, just think about yourself as you are **now** and as you were in the **past**; if you decide you are significantly more like the statement **now** than in the past, choose **(x)**; if you decide that you were significantly more like the statement in the **past** than you are now, choose **(y)**. If you think there has been no significant change, do *not* circle (x) or (y), and simply move on to the next question. **You** are the one who determines what **"significant"** means.

NAME: Last _____ First _____ Middle _____
ADDRESS: Street _____ City _____
State _____ Zip _____ Country _____
PHONE: (home) ( ) _____ (work) ( ) _____

For each statement on the Personal Identity Profile, please circle **ONE** number from the list (1, 2, 3, 4, 5, 6, 7) which most closely corresponds to the way you think and feel about the statement. You also have the **option** of circling **one** letter from the list (x,y) if you feel there has been a significant change, over the course of your life, in the way you currently respond to the statement.

You may complete the Profile rapidly, if you choose, or you may take as long as you like. The one thing that is important is that you think clearly and answer truthfully. To give the responses which will be most valuable in determining the profile of your identity, try to look at yourself very objectively and deeply.

THE MEANING OF EACH NUMBER AND LETTER

1 = Very True 2 = True 3 = More True than False
4 = In Between: As True as False
5 = More False than True 6 = False 7 = Very False

x = The Quality has increased over the years

y = The Quality has decreased over the years

1. 1 2 3 4 5 6 7 x y
2. 1 2 3 4 5 6 7 x y
3. 1 2 3 4 5 6 7 x y
4. 1 2 3 4 5 6 7 x y
5. 1 2 3 4 5 6 7 x y
6. 1 2 3 4 5 6 7 x y
7. 1 2 3 4 5 6 7 x y
8. 1 2 3 4 5 6 7 x y
9. 1 2 3 4 5 6 7 x y
10. 1 2 3 4 5 6 7 x y
11. 1 2 3 4 5 6 7 x y
12. 1 2 3 4 5 6 7 x y
13. 1 2 3 4 5 6 7 x y
14. 1 2 3 4 5 6 7 x y
15. 1 2 3 4 5 6 7 x y
16. 1 2 3 4 5 6 7 x y
17. 1 2 3 4 5 6 7 x y
18. 1 2 3 4 5 6 7 x y
19. 1 2 3 4 5 6 7 x y
20. 1 2 3 4 5 6 7 x y
21. 1 2 3 4 5 6 7 x y
22. 1 2 3 4 5 6 7 x y
23. 1 2 3 4 5 6 7 x y
24. 1 2 3 4 5 6 7 x y
25. 1 2 3 4 5 6 7 x y
26. 1 2 3 4 5 6 7 x y
27. 1 2 3 4 5 6 7 x y
28. 1 2 3 4 5 6 7 x y
29. 1 2 3 4 5 6 7 x y
30. 1 2 3 4 5 6 7 x y
31. 1 2 3 4 5 6 7 x y
32. 1 2 3 4 5 6 7 x y
33. 1 2 3 4 5 6 7 x y
34. 1 2 3 4 5 6 7 x y
35. 1 2 3 4 5 6 7 x y
36. 1 2 3 4 5 6 7 x y
37. 1 2 3 4 5 6 7 x y
38. 1 2 3 4 5 6 7 x y
39. 1 2 3 4 5 6 7 x y
40. 1 2 3 4 5 6 7 x y
41. 1 2 3 4 5 6 7 x y
42. 1 2 3 4 5 6 7 x y
43. 1 2 3 4 5 6 7 x y
44. 1 2 3 4 5 6 7 x y
45. 1 2 3 4 5 6 7 x y
46. 1 2 3 4 5 6 7 x y
47. 1 2 3 4 5 6 7 x y
48. 1 2 3 4 5 6 7 x y
49. 1 2 3 4 5 6 7 x y
50. 1 2 3 4 5 6 7 x y
51. 1 2 3 4 5 6 7 x y
52. 1 2 3 4 5 6 7 x y
53. 1 2 3 4 5 6 7 x y
54. 1 2 3 4 5 6 7 x y
55. 1 2 3 4 5 6 7 x y
56. 1 2 3 4 5 6 7 x y
57. 1 2 3 4 5 6 7 x y
58. 1 2 3 4 5 6 7 x y
59. 1 2 3 4 5 6 7 x y
60. 1 2 3 4 5 6 7 x y
61. 1 2 3 4 5 6 7 x y
62. 1 2 3 4 5 6 7 x y
63. 1 2 3 4 5 6 7 x y
64. 1 2 3 4 5 6 7 x y
65. 1 2 3 4 5 6 7 x y
66. 1 2 3 4 5 6 7 x y
67. 1 2 3 4 5 6 7 x y
68. 1 2 3 4 5 6 7 x y
69. 1 2 3 4 5 6 7 x y
70. 1 2 3 4 5 6 7 x y
71. 1 2 3 4 5 6 7 x y
72. 1 2 3 4 5 6 7 x y
73. 1 2 3 4 5 6 7 x y
74. 1 2 3 4 5 6 7 x y
75. 1 2 3 4 5 6 7 x y

76. 1 2 3 4 5 6 7 x y
77. 1 2 3 4 5 6 7 x y
78. 1 2 3 4 5 6 7 x y
79. 1 2 3 4 5 6 7 x y
80. 1 2 3 4 5 6 7 x y

81. 1 2 3 4 5 6 7 x y
82. 1 2 3 4 5 6 7 x y
83. 1 2 3 4 5 6 7 x y
84. 1 2 3 4 5 6 7 x y
85. 1 2 3 4 5 6 7 x y

86. 1 2 3 4 5 6 7 x y
87. 1 2 3 4 5 6 7 x y
88. 1 2 3 4 5 6 7 x y
89. 1 2 3 4 5 6 7 x y
90. 1 2 3 4 5 6 7 x y

91. 1 2 3 4 5 6 7 x y
92. 1 2 3 4 5 6 7 x y
93. 1 2 3 4 5 6 7 x y
94. 1 2 3 4 5 6 7 x y
95. 1 2 3 4 5 6 7 x y

96. 1 2 3 4 5 6 7 x y
97. 1 2 3 4 5 6 7 x y
98. 1 2 3 4 5 6 7 x y
99. 1 2 3 4 5 6 7 x y
100. 1 2 3 4 5 6 7 x y

101. 1 2 3 4 5 6 7 x y
102. 1 2 3 4 5 6 7 x y
103. 1 2 3 4 5 6 7 x y
104. 1 2 3 4 5 6 7 x y
105. 1 2 3 4 5 6 7 x y

106. 1 2 3 4 5 6 7 x y
107. 1 2 3 4 5 6 7 x y
108. 1 2 3 4 5 6 7 x y
109. 1 2 3 4 5 6 7 x y
110. 1 2 3 4 5 6 7 x y

111. 1 2 3 4 5 6 7 x y
112. 1 2 3 4 5 6 7 x y
113. 1 2 3 4 5 6 7 x y
114. 1 2 3 4 5 6 7 x y
115. 1 2 3 4 5 6 7 x y

116. 1 2 3 4 5 6 7 x y
117. 1 2 3 4 5 6 7 x y
118. 1 2 3 4 5 6 7 x y
119. 1 2 3 4 5 6 7 x y
120. 1 2 3 4 5 6 7 x y

121. 1 2 3 4 5 6 7 x y
122. 1 2 3 4 5 6 7 x y
123. 1 2 3 4 5 6 7 x y
124. 1 2 3 4 5 6 7 x y
125. 1 2 3 4 5 6 7 x y

126. 1 2 3 4 5 6 7 x y
127. 1 2 3 4 5 6 7 x y
128. 1 2 3 4 5 6 7 x y
129. 1 2 3 4 5 6 7 x y
130. 1 2 3 4 5 6 7 x y

131. 1 2 3 4 5 6 7 x y
132. 1 2 3 4 5 6 7 x y
133. 1 2 3 4 5 6 7 x y
134. 1 2 3 4 5 6 7 x y
135. 1 2 3 4 5 6 7 x y

136. 1 2 3 4 5 6 7 x y
137. 1 2 3 4 5 6 7 x y
138. 1 2 3 4 5 6 7 x y
139. 1 2 3 4 5 6 7 x y
140. 1 2 3 4 5 6 7 x y

Name:_____

Section II: TRAITS TO TRANSFORM

Most Significant _____ (number)

Next _____

Next _____

Section III: HIGHEST ASPIRATIONS

Highest Aspiration _____

Next highest _____

Next highest _____

HOLGRAPHIC PERSONAL GROWTH FORMULA

Please provide the following information which will be used to determine additional personal qualities and traits important to your self-understanding:

Present Occupation: _____

Former Occupations: _____

Place of Birth: City _____ State _____ Country _____

Date of Birth: Month _____ Day _____ Year _____

Exact Time of Birth: Hour _____ Minutes _____ am / pm (circle one)

Avocations or Hobbies: _____

_____

Favorite Subjects: _____

_____

Educational Majors: _____

Life Goals: _____

_____

Please enclose a recent photograph of yourself

STATEMENTS

1. Compared to others I am a powerful person – strength and steadfastness are two of my commanding virtues.

2. I'm constantly running here and there, busily filling my time with many things to do, say or think about. Settling down quietly and becoming still are simply not my line of least resistance.

3. Because disharmony always makes me feel extremely uncomfortable, I act immediately to restore harmony as quickly as possible.

4. It is easier for me than it is for most to establish warm and loving relationships with a wide variety of people.

5. I reason with careful logic about highly abstract, theoretical issues in which a complex web of abstract relationships must be clearly and exactly understood. (For example: higher mathematics, academic philosophy, economic theory, commodity and stock projections, historical trends, etc.)

6. I am animated by the spirit of scientific discovery, and derive enjoyment and satisfaction from the pursuit of scientific investigation.

7. I frequently experience strong feelings of devotion.

8. More than most people, my life has been filled with conflict (inner, outer, or both); very often I have felt torn between conflicting forces.

9. I like to read scholarly or technical publications which explain, in considerable detail, developments in certain specialized fields of enquiry.

10. I derive great satisfaction from devising or participating in thoroughly planned, highly structured programs of action, in which appropriate procedures are clearly detailed, and intended results are clearly defined.

11. I am one who directs others.

12. I focus with utter one–pointedness upon my ideal – always devotedly, often intensely, perhaps even militantly.

13. I am very well–organized, and approach my activities in a very orderly way.

14. Often, I feel a welling–up of sympathy and compassion for all people. At such special times, I love everybody unconditionally, no matter who they are, or what they may have done.

15. Whenever I'm faced with a major problem or challenge, I diversify; I exercise a number of different options, approach the solution from a number of different angles, and never "put all my eggs in the same basket."

16. I am firmly purposeful in almost everything I think or do.

17. I almost always identify (immediately and deeply) with people's feelings and states of mind – absorbing them as if they were my own.

18. I'm something of an expert in the fine art of compromise.

19. I place a very high value upon strict, factual accuracy – even when others might lose patience with such precision and exactitude.

20. I delight in mental gymnastics and the demonstration of intellectual virtuosity.

21. I frequently write and speak in colorful words and picturesque images.

22. I truly idealize certain individuals; because I admire them so greatly, I frequently quote them or talk about them.

23. I attach real importance to the manner and style in which a thing is done. I'm a great one for doing everything "in good form."

24. I enjoy tinkering, and taking things apart (pieces of equipment, mechanical devices, various objects, etc.) to see how they are put together, how they work, and how they can be repaired.

25. I desire to give myself totally to a worthy or an ideal cause.

26. I have no real difficulty terminating or discarding things. In fact, it often exhilirates me – especially when something old and outworn has to be eliminated so that something fresh and new can take its place.

27. Calmness, long–suffering patience and a serene temper are some of my most characteristic qualities.

28. Rhythm (in at least one of its many forms of expression) is very important to me – whether rhythmic dance, rhythmic exercise or body movement, rhythmic speech, rhythmic music, or participation in some other rhythmically organized activity.

29. I am a builder of networks (whether large or small); I'm highly skilled at organizing people with diverse abilities into well–integrated, closely–linked systems of cooperative enterprise.

30. My intellect is precise, highly analytical, and sharply focused on factual knowledge and specific, concrete issues.

31. My usual approach to doing things is characterized by bursts of incessant activity, followed by nearly equal periods of complete lethargy during which (even though I feel I should be active) I just can't get myself to do a thing. Then, suddenly, my mood changes, and again I fly into action.

32. I love to worship God, and am filled with reverence for great saints and sages who exemplify His Ways.

33. Even though an idea *seems* to be true, I do not accept it as true unless it has been *verified* by what I consider to be a reliable experimental procedure.

34. I often approach sensitive situations with 'creative indefiniteness'; I frequently find it is the most prudent policy to hint, infer, or say things in an indirect manner, rather than openly discuss the specifics of a situation.

35. I have a deep–seated need to nurture and comfort people.

36. Not only am I irresistibly drawn to the creative arts, but I express and release my emotions through some form of artistic creativity.

37. I especially enjoy those aspects of any business enterprise which call for me to arrange transactions cleverly and creatively.

38. I don't bother with lengthy pondering and analysis; I determine my objective, then accomplish it swiftly and directly.

39. When I arrange things, I am more particular than most people about making the arrangement exact, accurate or "just so!"

40. I draw people together through warmth and magnetism, and my love helps to hold them together.

41. For whatever reasons, I am strongly inclined to be dominant. I do not shrink from imposing authority.

42. I will follow my vision wherever it may lead.

43. I prefer to focus upon a field of specialization, achieving intellectual and technical expertise within that field, rather than spread my attention over a number of fields.

44. I'm a habitual time–scheduler and list–maker; that's how I make sure I do everything I have to do, at the time it should be done, and in the time I have to do it.

45. My "heroes" and "heroines" are very important to me, and I am filled with the aspiration to follow in their footsteps.

46. I fight, then make–up – fight again, then make–up again. It seems I enjoy doing both!

47. I am a tactician and strategist – a person who always likes to have a "game plan."

48. When I explain something, I make certain I am extremely lucid, logical and specific (offering concrete examples to illustrate my point), so my listener can grasp every single detail with complete clarity.

49. The feeling of being "down" and discouraged comes over me frequently, but the mood soon lifts and I'm "up" and ready to try again.

50. Often, I ponder deeply, and at length, on how to attain wisdom and understanding.

51. Detachment is my way; I will not sacrifice my freedom and independence by attaching myself too closely to people and circumstances.

52. I am something of an "absent–minded professor"; I often entertain such interesting thoughts that I don't focus much on my immediate physical environment. For example, I am forever forgetting where I put things.

53. I give close, detailed (yet intuitive) study to even the broadest of subjects; my aim is to achieve *complete* comprehension, becoming so thoroughly familiar with the subject that I absorb it entirely.

54. I'm one for "straightening things up," and "sorting things out." "A place for everything and everything in its place" is my motto.

55. Something in me just loves to preach.

56. I am prepared, equipped and inclined to force matters and issue ultimatums whenever I think it necessary.

57. I am usually the power at the center of things; it is a position that is completely natural for me.

58. I am *very* fluid and adaptable; I quickly and easily change my position or alter my approach to suit varying circumstances.

59. I'm very good at entertaining and amusing people with sparkling, imaginative conversation, but I'm just as likely to be introspectively silent.

60. I always seek to develop a *complete* understanding of people – a deep, intuitive, "heart to heart" understanding.

61. I seldom move directly towards a single goal; I'm usually "spread out," (or "spread thin") moving rapidly and energetically towards many diverse goals at the same time.

62. Being intent on distinguishing one thing from another, I seek to discover or learn the correct classification or name for anything I examine, so that I can know exactly what a thing is and what it isn't.

63. I am a "crusader."

64. I simply love color and have a highly developed color sense which I express, in one way or another, at every opportunity.

65. I am actively involved (vocationally or avocationally) in one or more of the "exact sciences," such as physics, chemistry, astronomy, biology, electronics, computer science, etc., or their many combinations, extensions or applications.

66. I am almost always extremely careful about handling even the smallest details; I want things done *properly*.

67. I have the strength and independence to stand alone; I require the support and company of others far less than most people do.

68. Whenever my cherished ideals are challenged, I zealously rise to their defense.

69. In almost everything I do, the most natural thing is for me to develop a routine or personal ritual – a regular pattern of action which works efficiently for me, and which I like to repeat.

70. I am very attracted to religion, but only when it is broadly tolerant and ecumenical in spirit.

71. More than many people, I like to "play with money" – speculating and using my *wits* to generate profit.

72. When I am in a personal or professional situation which should not continue as it is, I prefer drastic and liberating adjustments which end the old conditions abruptly.

73. I have a highly developed ability to perceive clearly and with intuitive foresight. This ability is especially keen when applied to understanding people – their potentials, motives, problems and relationships.

74. Creating beauty in everything I do is absolutely indispensable to me; I seek to become the "artist of my life."

75. I feel at home in laboratories, and would enjoy working in some kind of laboratory setting, where knowledge is pursued and confirmed experimentally.

76. I'm good at "pulling all the right strings"; I'm adept at arranging circumstances, and influencing all parties concerned so that everything goes according to plan.

77. Making choices is a demanding process for me, because I usually oscillate for some time between the alternatives before arriving at a decision.

78. I live my life with undimmed faith and unflagging optimism no matter how dark, frustrating or hopeless things may appear.

79. I have an innate understanding of how labor should be apportioned within organizations and groups, and I find it easy to fulfill my proper function, in my place, and in concert with my co-workers. I believe that people should always make a point of being clear about their place and function.

80. I am particularly good at applied mathematics – the kind of mathematics which calls for rapid, accurate calculations and for skill in various arithmetic operations that can be applied to the solution of practical problems.

81. I hold fast to certain lofty ideals which I frequently and enthusiastically reaffirm to myself and emphasize to others. These ideals are my "guiding star," and by them I chart my course in life.

82. I am a natural leader.

83. Some people find it easy to terminate familiar conditions or relationships when it should be done, but for me it seems especially difficult.

84. When I am responsible for deciding upon a course of action, I make very sure that it is in accordance with the established laws, rules and precedents of the context in which I am working.

85. I focus a good deal of attention on the body – on rules and regimens to keep it vitally healthy, or on programmes for cultivating its full potential.

86. In analyzing my approach to speaking and writing, I am, above all, factually correct.

87. While many people like music, my life is deeply influenced by it; I spend a great deal of time either listening to it or expressing myself musically; melodies often run through my mind, and I go around humming, singing or whistling tunes.

88. I often vow to myself (or to others) that I will uphold some high standard.

89. I have an insatiable curiosity for understanding specific causes and specific effects; I carefully follow causes to their effects, and carefully trace effects back to their causes.

90. I operate on the premise that truth can be reached without experimentation, simply by using rigorous, logical, deductive thinking – provided one's premises are correct and one's reasoning is sound.

91. Because it does my heart good to see people grow and develop, one of my greatest pleasures is to be a teacher.

92. I love being dramatic, and my life is filled with dramatic experiences and emotional contrasts.

93. My writing style is quite abstract, complex and rather involved. I enjoy elaborations and ramifications, and I extend my mind into numerous fields in order to combine many strands of thought.

94. Compared to others, I have an extremely strong will.

95. I love to shape, style, mould or design forms which express my ideas.

96. In all life situations, being inclusive is one of my highest priorities. For instance, I always make a special point of including everyone who wants to be included, and find it very painful to leave anyone out.

97. I have a striking ability to initiate action, galvanizing others into activity. I deliver the hammer stroke which sets things vibrating.

98. I'm a firm believer in loyalty, which I consider an indispensable virtue. I require it of myself, and look for it in others.

99. I enjoy thinking up technical improvements, and finding inventive ways to express new ideas mechanically or through some form of instrumentation.

100. I'm a skillful and efficient administrator, who enjoys coordinating the many practical details involved in the management of a complex enterprise.

101. I always hold those I love very close to me; I feel utterly devoted to them and inseparably attached.

102. I don't worry about saying or doing the opposite of what I have just said and done. I find it much more exciting to improvise and do the unexpected, even if it means appearing inconsistent or illogical.

103. I enjoy creating elaborate plans with a great many contingencies.

104. Whenever I conduct a study, I do so rigorously and systematically – thoroughly mastering all the factual detail of my subject.

105. I have lived my life soaring to the heights and plumbing the depths of human experience.

106. When I am afraid, it is usually because I am a very sensitive and vulnerable person, and because I sense the vulnerability of those I love, and fear for their welfare.

107. I am well-endowed with the dynamic power to smash through obstacles – and I do!

108. I enjoy "figuring the odds" – speculating and conjecturing on the probabilities.

109. I give my permission easily; saying "No!." and sticking to it, is almost always difficult for me.

110. I think appearances are very important; I invest considerable energy promoting good appearance in all aspects of my life and circumstances.

111. I often long to be where everything is pure and perfect; call it utopia or call it paradise.

112. I'm determined to "reach the top" in virtually everything I do.

113. Participating in the establishment and/or execution of governing principles – whether on the national, state, civic, community, corporate or smaller-group levels – is one of my major priorities.

114. I talk a great deal – more than most people. My mind is almost always filled with many interesting thoughts, and I just have to give them verbal expression.

115. I love to create appealing ensembles, compositions or mixtures by imaginatively making a unity out of things which are not usually found together.

116. My line of least resistance is to become closely and lovingly attached to people; throughout the attachment, I maintain an attitude of faithfulness, forgiveness, and sympathetic understanding.

117. My distinctive way of working is to reach afar (and selectively) for a diversity of things, people or thoughts – gather them all, and weave them together.

118. I generally have a very objective attitude, arising from a cool, dispassionate, highly mental and analytical examination of life situations.

119. Whenever I "go for" something, I go for it passionately, with unbounded, unrelenting enthusiasm.

120. My usual way of writing and speaking is to express my thoughts with "feeling" – freely, spontaneously, often poetically.

121. Not only do I enjoy doing research, but I have the patience and perseverence to track the smallest fact to its source in order to ensure the accuracy of my research.

122. I enjoy viewing or participating in ceremonial events, in which uniforms or some sort of formal apparel (as well a formal protocol) are required. (For example: graduation, wedding or state ceremonies; religious, masonic, or organizational rituals; parades, processions, formal affairs, etc.)

123. Even when the risks are great, I will fight for my own rights and freedoms, and for the rights and freedoms of those who are weaker than I am.

124. I pray in complete trust that my prayers are always answered, and in humble willingness to accept whatever answers I receive.

125. I am constantly restructuring the existing order of things, rennovating and re–designing the practical aspects of daily living – whether in my own personal and professional sphere, or in a much larger context.

126. It is most natural for me to approach any important goal patiently and sensitively. I accomplish much through tact, considerateness, and the wise use of slow action.

127. The unusual flexibility and fertility of my mind make it easy for me to modify and adapt ideas in all kinds of ways; I'm very good at helping people see things from a variety of novel angles, thereby multiplying their options.

128. Although fear is a natural human emotion, I have achieved almost complete mastery over the fear response.

129. I persistently pour forth all the knowledge and wisdom I have attained for the benefit of others.

130. Whenever tension builds up, I almost always say or do something humorous to release the tension.

131. I frequently approach problems or tasks through "quantification." I analyze or evaluate a problem or task in terms of numbers, and determine a solution accordingly.

132. I spend a great deal of time communicating a broad range of ideas and information through whatever means are available to me – whether word–of–mouth or the many types of media.

133. I'm always finding myself "in the middle" – a mediating bridge and an agent of reconciliation between contradictory opinions and contending forces.

134. Whenever I find myself in a difficult or uncertain situation, I consistently seek and follow a trusted source of guidance.

135. The ranking and positioning of all things is a structural necessity in the natural order, and I am strongly convinced that social and organizational hierarchies are equally necessary.

136. I approach problem–solving through first–hand observation, carefully examining all the particulars. Then I begin experimenting methodically, using a "trial and error" procedure, and I don't stop until I've prove to myself that I have a solution which really works.

137. I shun compromise, especially in matters of faith and belief.

138. When I determine what must be done, I absolutely refuse to let sentiment or emotions prevent me from fully executing my intention.

139. I continually pursue complete enlightenment and absolute truth – even though such exhaustive understanding may not have an immediate, practical application in present circumstances.

140. I enjoy designing and building structures (material structures or less tangible ones); I conceive the idea, make detailed plans, assemble the necessary elements, and systematically construct the form.

TRAITS TO TRANSFORM

Associated with each one of the Seven Fundamental Qualities (Rays) are a number of traits which we should transform as we grow towards our full potential. Recognizing the traits we *most* need to transform is an important key to our personal development and to identifying our major Qualities.

Each of the twenty-one traits is numbered below. First choose the **three** which most pertain to you, and then list their numbers on the answer sheet. At the top of the list, place the trait which you consider to be the **greatest obstacle** to the realization of your highest potential.

Please choose **exactly three traits**. If you think this list does not include the traits which challenge you the most, choose the traits which come closest. You don't have to be entirely subject to a trait to include it among the three; a noticeable **leaning** towards a particular trait is sufficient. If you feel that you have already overcome most, if all of these traits, list the ones which formerly needed the most work.

1. **Over-concern for rules and regulations**
2. **Uncontrolled enthusiasm**
3. **Too much skepticism**
4. **Too many "highs" and "lows"**
5. **Wasted energy through overactivity and restlessness**
6. **Giving-in too easily**
7. **Willfulness**
8. **Desire to dominate and control others**
9. **Fear because of over-sensitivity**
10. **Manipulativeness and deviousness**
11. **Over-eagerness for compromise**
12. **Intolerance of ideas which don't fit in with established knowledge**
13. **Over-eagerness to trust and believe**
14. **Subservience to habit and routine**
15. **Over-concern for orderliness and detail**
16. **Over-leaning on others**
17. **Too much intellectual analysis and dissection**
18. **Tendency to fight and be contrary**
19. **Intellectual pride**
20. **Too much study without taking action**
21. **Unrelenting ambition for power**

YOUR HIGHEST ASPIRATIONS

The following is a list of phrases expressing the **highest aspirations** associated with the Seven Fundamental Qualities. Recognizing your highest aspirations is an important clue to identifying your Most Important Quality.

First choose three phrases which best express your highest aspirations. Each phrase has a number associated with it. On the answer sheet, put the number of the phrase which is most important to you in the space labeled **"Highest Aspiration."** Then, list the numbers for the other two phrases **in descending order of their importance to you.** It may be that you aspire to many of these goals, but choose just the three which are **most** descriptive of your highest aspirations.

1. I aspire to become a dynamic, powerful and benevolent leader, serving the highest good.

2. I aspire to a deep, intuitive, loving-understanding of people, so that I can nurture them and help them to unfold their highest potential.

3. I aspire to great mental agility and resourcefulness, so that I can apply them creatively to intellectually challenging enterprises.

4. I aspire to express great artistry in every aspect of my life, thereby inspiring others to increase their sensitivity to beauty.

5. I aspire to become vitally involved in discovering solutions to Nature's mysteries through scientific research and experimentation.

6. I aspire to live with complete faith and commitment – true to my highest "Vision of the Right."

7. I aspire to bring rhythmic order out of the chaos of human living by "grounding" progressive ideas in practical activity and seeing them through to perfected expression.

8. I aspire to liberate people from all forms of bondage.

9. I aspire to a wise and complete understanding of life so that I can teach and illumine others.

10. I aspire to arrive at truth through the power of deep thinking and careful reasoning.

11. I aspire to be a mediator – a reconciler of human conflicts and an instrument of peace.

12. I aspire to invent or develop those mechanisms, instruments, or technical improvements which will transform and uplift the quality of human life.

13. I aspire to serve God, or the "highest ideal," with complete faith and utter devotion.

14. I aspire to take a practical, administrative role in redesigning and transforming the patterns of human civilization, so that a "New World Order" may emerge.

APPENDIX V

Search for the Soul Ray

A Meditative Technique
to Assist in the Determination of the Soul Ray

Perhaps the most important question which arises in the study of esoteric psychology is: "How can the ray of the soul be accurately determined?" We may be uncertain about a number of the other energies in our Ray Chart, but if we know our soul ray and its function within the "nature of things," we will be in an excellent position to take our next step ahead. We will know our *essential energy*; to express it fully is joy and fulfillment.

A study of the Tibetan's books (and of various other books on the rays, including *Tapestry of the Gods*) may incline an individual to believe that his soul is found upon a particular ray, but, in the last analysis, some *doubts* may still remain. The Personal Identity Profile (in its present form) does not indicate the soul ray (or any other ray position) with certainty – as helpful as it may be in establishing relative ray strength. Perhaps no personality inventory of this nature will ever be able to do that, though P.I.P.#2 intends to achieve a closer approximation to this desirable aim. But, given what we do have, how can we become as certain as possible?

Some individuals simply *know* what their soul ray is. They have such a strong *intuitive* conviction that they believe there is no reason to *reason* – no need to double check. Quite often, they may be entirely correct. Most others, however, are far less sure. They can, with a fair degree of certainty, identify ray qualities within their energy system, but they are not sure "where everything goes" and, sometimes, they identify strongly with more rays than there are vehicles to which to assign such rays!

The Three Strongest Rays

After quite a bit of experimentation utilizing the P.I.P. in counseling and seminar settings, there is good reason to believe (especially for those who are on the Path of spiritual transformation) that among the three rays which score the strongest, the soul ray can be found. For those who have not taken the P.I.P., the soul ray will (most probably) be found among the three rays with which the individual identifies most closely. After having narrowed the field to three rays, it is often quite possible to reason and infer with a considerable degree of accuracy which of them is most probably the soul ray. Inference, however, is basically a strictly *mental* process, and thus subject to certain limitations. It is important to realize that there are other ways to proceed – ways which are equally reliable, if not more so.

Using, then, the three strongest rays on the P.I.P. (or the three rays with which one most identifies) one can devise certain meditative or imaginative exercises which give a real intutiive feel for the importance or *essentiality* of a ray. Here is how one might proceed.

Ray Meditation Exercise

1. Achieve physical comfort, emotional poise, and mental stillness.

2. Align yourself with your Higher Self, your transpersonal center, your soul. Realize that whatever imaginative or thought procedures you now follow will all be accomplished *in the Light*.

3. Think of the meaning of any one of the three rays you have chosen to consider. *Feel* the quality of this ray. Mentally, repeat its name (or names) slowly to yourself. Feel yourself imbued with the quality of this ray.

4. Visualize yourself going through a few of your characteristic daily activities imbued with the quality of the ray you are considering. See yourself immersed in this quality as you perform every action and participate in every relationship. Feel the quality pervade you, permeate you.

5. Now, visualize yourself performing a number of the kinds of activities which you know are characteristic of the ray you are working with. (For example, for R1, you would see yourself as a leader, director, governer, etc., having to confront situations which call for great will power, firmness, decisiveness and the ability to face difficult and even dangerous situations without fear, etc.) Allow this fantasy to go where it will. Take plenty of time. Gain distinct impressions. Then, for a moment or two, without really leaving the meditative state, allow your consciousness to be strongly impressed by these thoughts and images, or write down a few of your impressions to *ground* them.

6. Follow exactly the same procedure with the second of the three rays you have chosen to work with – beginning with naming the ray to yourself (either audibly or inaudibly).

7. Follow exactly the same procedure with the third of the three rays you have chosen to work with.

(You can work with the three rays in any order you choose.)

8. Now, imaginatively, re–enter the Light, and see a stream of light descending from the soul center above your head, and permeating all the "fields" within your personality – your mental field, emotional field, and etheric–physical field.

9. Once you are securely, and sensitively established in the Light, think back upon what you just experienced internally. Ask yourself:

   a. What ray gave me the greatest feeling of joy?

   b. What ray made me feel most inspired?

   c. What ray promoted images that completely captured my interest – images that I could have entertained for a long while?

   d. During the use of which ray did my imaginative activities feel most meaningful and, even, sacred?

e. Through the use of which ray could I make my greatest *contribution* to the welfare and spiritual transformation of humanity?

   f. Which imaginative ray activites resonated most closely to my "heart's desire?"

10. **Allow** a decision to be made. The concrete mind does not make the decision. It is an intuitive decision, made in the light of the soul. Once the decision has been made, allow yourself to become imbued with that ray — your most important quality — and see yourself several years in the future, using that ray to fulfill your deepest dreams, your heart's desire. See yourself contributing, joyously and completely, to others, helping and uplifting them through the quality of your soul ray, which you express with great skill, beauty and finesse.

11. Now imaginatively call upon your other two ray qualities. Realize that although they are subordinate to your soul ray, they can serve as vehicles to aid in its expression.

12. See yourself successfully performing many beautiful, worthy and valuable deeds using the combination of your soul ray and the two subsidiary rays.

13. Write your impressions of your experience.

You can probably see the potential in this sort of exercise. Just make sure that you have plenty of time to do it, as it may take a while and you should not be interrupted. Those who have performed this exercise during a Seven Ray Seminar, may wish to repeat it on their own one or more times, allowing themselves a good deal more time than it was possible to spend during the seminar. This is literally an exercise in *soul searching* and must be performed without any sense of rush or hurry.

There are a number of possible variations, based upon this basic approach, which can be devised. It is possible to position the other rays of your energy system in a similar way. For instance, beginning with the three strongest rays on your P.I.P. (or the three rays with which you most identify), you could look for the ray which tends to emphasize your *separative personhood*, and which makes it most difficult for the soul ray quality to take precedence. This would be the ray which expresses your particular variety of "selfishness," if you will, just as the soul ray expresses your best form of "selflessness." A number of rays could be imaginatively reviewed in this way, and the one which seemed most convincing could well be your personality ray.

Also, you could imagine yourself *thinking* in various ways, each characterized by a certain ray quality. You could visualize yourself solving a problem of your own imagining. How do you go about it now? How would you do it if you had a R1 Mind, a R3 Mind, a R4 Mind a R5 Mind, and so forth?

In Volume V of *Tapestry of the Gods*, the development of these kinds of active visualizations will be undertaken, so that there will be proposed a battery of "experiential" strategies for determining ray placement. Using such strategies is one of the best ways to work towards that intuitive conviction which everyone desires. First *reason*; then, *intuitive conviction*; then, the *confirmation of the Master*. If we start with the first, and work our way to the second, the third will surely follow.

APPENDIX VI

Recommended Reading on the Subject of Esoteric Psychology and the Seven Rays

The following books by Alice A. Bailey and the Tibetan Master, Djwhal Khul, contain information upon esoteric psychology, the seven rays and the astrology of the seven rays. They are recommended to all earnest students for serious study:

Initiation, Human and Solar

Letters on Occult Meditation

A Treatise on Cosmic Fire

A Treatise on White Magic

Discipleship in the New Age, Vols. I and II

The Destiny of the Nations

Glamour: A World Problem

Telepathy and the Etheric Vehicle

Education in the New Age

The Externalisation of the Hierarchy

Esoteric Psychology, Vol. I

Esoteric Psychology, Vol. II

Esoteric Astrology

Esoteric Healing

The Rays and the Initiations

The books of Alice A. Bailey are available through the:

Lucis Publishing Company
113 University Place, 11th Floor
New York, New York 10003

Further Recommended Reading

Abraham, Kurt. *Psychological Types and the Seven Rays.* Cape May, New Jersey: Lampus Press, 1983.

Abraham, Kurt. *Threefold Method for Understanding the Seven Rays.* Cape May, New Jersey: Lampus Press, 1984.

Abraham, Kurt. *Introduction to the Seven Rays.* Cape May, New Jersey: Lampus Press, 1986.

Abraham, Kurt. *The Seven Rays and Nations: France and the United States Compared.* Cape May, New Jersey: Lampus Press, 1987.

Baker, Douglas. *Esoteric Psychology.* Essendon, Herts., England: Little Elephant, 1975.

Baker, Douglas. *Esoteric Astrology, Vol. I.* Essendon, Herts., England: Little Elephant, 1975.

Baker, Douglas. *The Seven Rays: Key to the Mysteries.* New York: Samuel Weiser, 1977.

Baker, Douglas. *Esoteric Astrology, Vol. II.* Essendon, Herts., London: Little Elephant, 1978.

Burmester, Helen. *The Seven Rays Made Visual.* Marina del Rey California: Devorss & Company., 1986.

Davis, James and Raifsnider, John. *Astrology of the Seven Rays.* Lakemont, Georgia: CSA Press, 1977.

Eastcott, Michal. *'I' the Story of the Self* Wheaton, Illinois: Theosophical Publishing House, 1980.

Eastcott, Michal. *The Seven Rays of Energy.* Tunbridge Wells, Kent, England: Sundial House, 1980.

Gerard, Robert. All articles, monographs and papers as listed in the "References" section of his introductory Commentary to *Tapestry of the Gods.* (*See* Volume I).

Hodson, Geoffrey. *The Seven Human Temperaments.* Adyar, Madras: The Theosophical Publishing House, 1952.

Lansdowne, Zachary F. *The Rays and Esoteric Psychology* York Beach, Maine: Samuel Weiser, Inc., 1989.

Laws, Judi. *Esoteric Psychology: The Science of Human Energetics.* Washington, D.C.: Amethyst, 1982.

Oken, Alan. *Soul–Centered Astrology.* New York: Bantam, Doubleday, Dell, 1989.

Pugh, Stephen Douglas. *A Treatise on the Greater Zodiac.* (To be published in 1989).

Tansley, David. V. *Chakras, Rays and Radionics.* Saffron Walden, Essex, England: C.W. Daniel Company Limited, 1984.

Tansley, David. V. *Radionics: Science or Magic?* (second printing). Saffron Walden, Essex, England: C.W. Daniel Company Limited, 1985.

Tansley, David. V. *Ray Paths and Chakra Gateways: An Approach to Spiritual Psychology Through Radionics.* Saffron Walden, Essex, England: C.W. Daniel Company Limited, 1985.

Wood, Earnest. *The Seven Rays* (Sixth printing). Wheaton, Illinois: The Theosophical Publishing House, 1972.

Note: The eight issues (to date) of the *Journal of Esoteric Psychology* contain many articles specifically upon the subjects of esoteric psychology, the seven rays, and the astrology of the seven rays, and will be a source of valuable information to the serious student.

The University of the Seven Rays offers an M.S.E. Degree (Master of Science in Esotericism) in the field of Esoteric Psychology. Degree programs are also available in a number of other disciplines vital to the spiritual transformation of humanity. Those interested in the newer forms of group–oriented spiritual/academic training may write to the publisher for further information.

GLOSSARY

Much of the terminology used throughout *Tapestry of the Gods* is similar to that found in the books of Alice A. Bailey and in the major Theosophical works. Therefore, the *Theosophical Glossary* by H.P. Blavatsky (as well as the glossary found in her *The Key to Theosophy*), the *Occult Glossary* by G. de. Purucker, and the glossary to be found at the end of Alice Bailey's *Initiation Human and Solar* would be very useful to students of *Tapestry*. However, since it cannot be assumed that all students of *Tapestry* will be familiar with the Bailey and Theosophical works, or with the glossaries associated with them, it was thought wise to include a glossary which would define some of the esoteric or specialized terms used with frequency throughout the first two volumes of the Tapestry series. Definitions drawn directly from the Blavatsky, Bailey or Purucker glossaries (or their works) will be cited accordingly.

Ageless Wisdom: That secret teachings of all ages which embodies the core of Divine Truth from which all the great world religions, philosophies and sciences draw their inspiration.

Ain Soph: The "Nameless ONE. The boundless or limitless Deity. The "One Without a Second."

Alignment: The psychospiritual process by means of which the incarnated "I" (the *soul in incarnation*) first controls the semiautonomous tendencies of its personality vehicles, and then comes into direct rapport with the overshadowing Solar Angel.

Antahkarana: The "rainbow bridge" of mental substance connecting the mental unit with the manasic permanent atom. For the disciple, the antahkarana is the self–constructed path by means of which consciousness escapes from the confines of a limited individuality into the expanses of a relative universality – i.e., into identification with the Mind of God.

Arhat: An initiate of the fourth degree. One who has passed through the Great Renunciation or the Crucifixion, as it is called in the West.

Aspirant: A person who is beginning to transmute desire into aspiration, and has thus set foot upon the Path of self–conscious spiritual evolution.

Astral body: The vehicle or "field" of sentient energy. That part of the human constitution which is the seat of the emotions, feelings, and desires. The most powerful of the three "lunar lords" (un–self–conscious, involutionary, semiautonomous, elemental lives) comprising the personality of the human being.

Atma: "The Universal Spirit; the divine Monad; the seventh Principle; so called in the septenary constitution of man." (*IHS* Glossary) Atma is considered the seat of the spiritual will.

Aura: "A subtle invisible essence or fluid which emanates from human and animal bodies, and even from things. It is a psychic effluvium, partaking of both mind and body. It is electro–vital, and also electro–mental." (*IHS* Glossary)

Avatar: Usually, an advanced spiritual being Who intervenes in the process of human evolution in order to bring to bear a divinely necessary energy or influence. Certain highly evolved human beings have been called avatars because of their extraordinarily beneficial effect upon the human race. Actually, any beneficent intervention acting from a higher sphere upon a lower can justifiably be called *avataric*. There are planetary avatars, systemic avatars and also cosmic avatars.

Bio–field: A term drawn from the lexicon of Integral Psychology, founded and developed by Dr. Robert Gerard. The bio–field is roughly equivalent to what theosophists call the etheric vehicle – the subtle, vital–electric matrix surrounding, interpenetrating and moulding the dense physical body.

Bodhisattva: "Literally, he whose consciousness has become intelligence or buddhi. Those who need but one more incarnation to become perfect buddhas. As used in these letters the Bodhisattva is the name of the office which is at present occupied by the Lord Maitreya, Who is known in the occident as the Christ. This office might be translated as that of World Teacher. The Bodhisattva is the Head of all the religions of the world, and the Master of the Masters and of the angels." (*IHS* Glossary) The consciousness of all Bodhisattvas is characterized by a profound compassion for humanity and a determination to defer spiritual gratification in order to save struggling human beings.

The Buddha: "The name given to Gautama. Born in India about B.C. 621 he became a full buddha in B.C. 592. The Buddha is one who is the 'Enlightened,' and has attained the highest degree of knowledge possible for man in this solar system." (*IHS* Glossary) The Buddha is the primary distributor to our planet of the Wisdom aspect of the Ray of Love–Wisdom. He is known as the Lord of Light, just as the Christ is known as the Lord of Love.

Buddhi: "The Universal Soul or Mind. It is the spiritual soul in man (the Sixth Principle) and therefore the vehicle of Atma, the Spirit, which is the Seventh Principle." In esotericism, buddhi, pure reason, intuition and love are essentially equivalent terms.

Causal body: A relatively permanent aspect of the human constitution which survives the cyclic deaths or disintegrations of all personality vehicles. It is created through the interaction of spirit and matter. Formed of the substances of the highest mental subplanes, it is created through the cooperative interaction of the human Monad and the Solar Angel. The causal body is the material organ through which the "ahamkara principle," the principle of individuality (or "I–ness") manifests. It is also the repository for all higher qualities and values garnered by the incarnating soul during the entire sequence of incarnations. The causal body is alternatively known as the "soul body" and the "Egoic body."

Center: A term denoting a vortex of force to be found in specific locations within each of the three personality vehicles (the mental, emotional and etheric). Such centers are also called "chakras" which is a Sanskrit term generally signifying "wheel," because the centers or chakras are always found in various states of rotary motion. In the present literature of esoteric psychology the centers referred to are most frequently those to be found within the etheric field. There are seven such centers, each corresponding to one of the major ductless glands of the physical body. The major chakras or centers are: the head center, the center between the eyebrows, the throat center, the heart center, the solar plexus center, the sacral center, and the center at the base of the spine.

Centering: The psychospiritual process of abstracting the attention from the fluctuations of the personality fields, and fixing it first upon the "I," which is the *center* of personality awareness, and then upon the inner Self or Higher Self, which is a still more essential phase of identity. Ultimately, centering means SELF-realization as a Monad – an essential unit of *life*.

Centrifugal personality tendencies: Actions and impulses within the personality leading the "I" or incarnated soul towards identification with fluctuating personality states, rather than disidentification from such states.

Centripetal personality tendencies: Actions or impulses within the personality leading towards disidentification from fluctuating personality states, and the establishment, first, of a centered "I-consciousness," and then of a consciousness of the Higher Self.

Chain (Planetary): An aggregation of seven planetary globes, each composed of a distinct quality of energy/substance. During the course of planetary evolution, the planetery life wave proceeds sequentially from globe to globe in a manner timed according to cyclic law.

Chohan: An initiate of the sixth degree. One who has passed through the Initiation of Decision.

The Christ: The World Teacher. The Leader of the Spiritual Hierarchy of the planet Earth. The term "Christ" refers more to an *office* of spiritual responsibility than to any particular individual. At present the office of the Christ is held by the Lord Maitreya, that great Individuality who overshadowed the Master Jesus in Palestine some two thousand years ago. When the present Christ has completed His mission of service, the office of the Christ will be fulfilled by yet another great spiritual Individuality. The present Christ is the embodiment of *pure love*, the second Divine Aspect. He is considered "the eldest in a great family of brothers," and the "first flower" of our Earth humanity. He is also known as the "World Savior," "the Daughter of Sanat Kumara," and "the Teacher alike of angels and of men."

Clairaudience: An inner sense giving the capacity to hear subtle sounds originating on planes of nature higher than the physical.

Clairvoyance: An inner sense giving the capacity to register subtle visual impressions emanating from planes of nature higher than the physical.

Complex: A psychological term denoting an aggregation of well-established, seminautonomous energy forms within the mental/emotional fields of the personality. Complexes are most often unconscious, but not necessarily so; they condition behavior potently until recognized, neutralized or mastered by the "I" – the soul-in-incarnation.

Conscience: Conscience is essentially the voice of the soul. It is the guiding influence of the Transpersonal Self as that Self seeks to impose its values and standards upon the unit of consciousness submersed within the personality fields, i.e., upon the soul–in–incarnation. Sensitivity to the voice of conscience often arises because of painful experiences accrued during former incarnations.

Consciousness: Soul *is* consciousness. Consciousness is awareness of and sensitivity to impact. In the triplicity of the Knower, the Knowing and the Known, consciousness is the process of *Knowing*; it is always the *relation between* the subject and the object. Essentially, and on a high level, consciousness and love are equivalent terms. Concsiousness in its fullness can only be experienced in the fullness of love. All is known because all is embraced; nothing is excluded. Consciousness and awareness have similar meanings, but consciousness is an intensification of awareness; in a truly conscious state, the center from which consciousness emanates (i.e., the subject) is in high focus, as is the object to which the subject is relating. Actually, the two (subject and object) merge and become indistinguishable.

Constitution of man: The physical and *meta*physical anatomy of the human being. The structure of the human energy system includes (beginning with its 'lowest' aspects) the physical vehicle, the etheric vehicle, the astral vehicle, the lower mental vehicle, the causal vehicle, the spiritual Triad, and the Monad.

Deva (or Angel): "A god. In Sanskrit a resplendent deity. A Deva is a celestial being, whether good, bad or indifferent. Devas are divided into many groups, and are called not only angels and archangels, but lesser and greater builders." (*IHS* Glossary) Devas comprise an evolution which parallels that of the human evolution. The esoteric psychologist seeks to employ those measures which make it possible for the human being to master the lesser (i.e., lunar) devas comprising his personality nature.

Dimension: A "plane" or distinctive range of vibratory frequencies within the spirit/matter continuum. Normal human evolution is concerned with three such dimensions: the etheric–physical, astral and lower mental dimensions – the so–called "three worlds of human evolution." Progress through the higher levels of human evolution demand mastery of the higher mental plane as well as two other dimensions: the plane of intuition (the buddhic) and the plane of spiritual Will (the atmic).

Disciple: Literally, a "learning boy." In modern esotericism the term "disciple" refers to a mentally polarized server of humanity who is coming increasingly under the influence of the overshadowing soul.

Disidentification: The process by which the incarnated "I" detaches itself from the personality vehicles and becomes conscious of itself, first, as a center of pure awareness, and then as an aspect of the expanded, inclusive consciousness of the soul on its own plane.

ego: The lower personal ego. A sense of self which is confined to the personality and its vehicles. The perception of self–identity which results when the soul–in–incarnation identifies with the personal form.

Ego: The Higher Self; the soul on its own plane. The causal "egg." The state of consciousness which is identified with the causal field rather than with the personality field. On a still higher turn of the spiral, the term "EGO" can refer to the "Monadic egg" and the state of SELF-awareness which results when man has become *in consciousness* the Monad.

Elemental: " The Spirits of the Elements: the creatures involved in the four kingdoms, or elements, Earth, Air, Fire and Water. Except for a few of the higher kinds and their rulers they are forces in nature rather than ethereal men and women." (*IHS* Glossary) Elementals 'inhabit' various of the lower planes or dimensions. The etheric-physical, emotional and lower mental vehicles of the human energy system are actually so many elementals.

Emanation: The projection or outflow of a ray from a source upon a higher plane of nature to a destination upon a lower plane. Such a ray is identical in *essence* with the source from which it flows or is projected, though not identical with that source in *appearance* once it has reached a lower plane. The form of its manifestation upon the lower plane varies from the form of its manifestation upon its 'plane of origin' due to the lower vibratory conditions upon the lower plane which inhibit the expression of the ray in its pure and original vibratory state. Upon each descending plane of nature emanations are "stepped down" to conform to progressively inert conditions. An emanation descending through the substance of a lower plane is automatically *clothed* in the substance of that plane.

Energy: The dynamism of the One Life – God-in-action. The term *energy* is frequently used to describe the manifold qualities of the One Energy. There are many different kinds and qualities of energy, but they are all subdivisions of the One Energy, differentiated movements within the One Movement of the One Creator.

Entity: A unit or subdivision of the One Being. Every entity is rooted in "Be-ness," and is thus indefeasibly part of the One Life. The endless emanatory subdivisions of the One Being are the cause of *entification,* although the ultimate *One* (which the Tibetan calls by the name "SPACE" may with some justification be called an ENTITY as well.

Esoteric: That which is too subtle to be registered by humanity's organs of registration in their present state of sensitivity. These organs of registration are not only the five etheric-physical senses, but the astral and lower mental vehicles in their average, brain-limited range of sensitivity. That which is esoteric is always relative to that which is readily known and perceivable. What the normal human being regards as esoteric is common knowledge to the Masters of the Wisdom. The Masters, however, regard the knowledges and ranges of sensitivity of the Planetary Deity as highly esoteric. No knowledge is esoteric in and of itself. Everything depends upon the degree of development of the entity which is attempting to register the knowledge.

Esoteric psychology: That branch of occult psychology which deals in a highly technical and precise manner with the nature and dynamics of the *true psyche* (the Transpersonal Self or soul upon its own plane) and the relationships existing between that Higher Self and the psychomental dynamics of the specifically human psyche of the incarnated "I" – the soul-in-incarnation. From another perspective, esoteric psychology is a technical study of the dynamic interrelationships between that great entity known as a Solar Angel and the Monad of the human energy system. It details the dynamics which occur when (symbolically speaking) Mercury (Monad), Venus (Solar Angel/Transpersonal Self) and Earth (Personality) become interdependent.

Ether: In relation to man, the microcosm, the ether is a rarefied physical dimension of substance composed of various grades of electro–vital fluid. The higher four subplanes of the systemic physical plane are composed of ether. From the perspective of the Planetary Logos, the higher four planes of the cosmic physical plane (the buddhic, atmic, monadic and logoic planes) are also considered etheric.

Etheric body: "The physical body of a human being is, according to occult teaching, formed of two parts, the dense physical body and the etheric body. The dense physical body is formed of matter of the lowest three subplanes of the physical plane (the dense, liquid and gaseous). The etheric body is formed of the four highest or etheric subplanes of the physical plane." (*IHS* Glossary) The etheric body (also called the etheric double and the vital body) is the conductor of prana or vital energy to the physical body.

Evolution: The progressive unfoldment of all aspects of every being (whether macroscopic or microscopic) within Kosmos, with the purpose of expressing an ever–fuller measure of essential spiritual potentiality. Traditionally, the term evolution has referred to the improvement and refinement of the physical form of the human race. According to the Ageless Wisdom, however, the evolution or unfoldment of the consciousness *within* the form is far more important and is, in fact, the cause of the beneficial changes to be noted within the form itself.

Field: In esoteric psychology, a fundamental subdivision of the human aura composed of energy/substance vibrating within a specified frequency range and serving as the vehicle for one of the seven human principles or faculties.

Glamor (or Glamour): An emotionally induced distortion of perception and apperception producing distorted values and, thus, wrongly oriented desires and behavior. Glamor is characterized by a combination of distortion–generating exaggeration and minimization which renders a true and clear picture of reality impossible. When desire becomes the servant of a soul–illumined consciousness, spiritual detachment results and glamor ceases.

Group consciousness: An inclusive quality of consciousness which characterizes the soul or Solar Angel upon the higher mental plane, and will increasingly characterize the evolving human soul–in–incarnation as it comes under the influence of the Solar Angel. A group–conscious entity preserves its own sense of individuality but loses any sense of separateness or isolation from other entities. This quality of consciousness is characterized by the realization that all entities have emanated from the same divine Source and are, therefore, *one in essence*.

Guide: One of the names (and principle functions) of the psychotherapist in the process of psychospiritual counseling. The term "guide" connotes an educational rather than a strictly therapeutic or rehabilitative function for the counselor.

Guru: "Spiritual Teacher. A Master in metaphysical and ethical doctrines." (*IHS* Glossary)

Human soul: The "I" as opposed to the overshadowing soul (or Solar Angel) on its own plane (i.e., the higher mental plane). The human soul is the incarnated soul, an emanation or projected *ray* of the Monad (which is for all practical purposes the irreducible, essential identity of the human being).

Hylozoism: The philosophy that everything within the universe is *alive* – that nothing is inanimate (or without soul).

"I": A pure point of self-awareness. The apparent core of identity within the personality. It is an attenuation of that *ray* of the Monad which informs the causal body, and, secondarily, persistently incarnates through the personality vehicles.

"I-consciousness": In its pureset sense, that state of consciousness which is achieved by the human being when, through the process of disidentification, he realizes that he is the "I", the dweller *within* the personality vehicles.

Identifcation: A twofold process (depending upon whether the consciousness is focused involutionarily or evolutionarily) leading either to the obscuration of the "I" (the soul-in-incarnation) by the personality vehicles, or, later, to the complete liberation of the "I" from all sense of limitation by form. Mistaken identification is the process through which the "I" comes to believe itself to be that which it is not. It fails to distinguish between itself and the not-self, and therefore loses its sense of "I-consciousness." True *I*dentification (often capitalized) occurs when the "I" realizes itself to be, essentially, an emanation of the Monad, thus realizing its essential *sameness* with all that *Is*.

Illusion: An inadequate apprehension of reality based upon the limitations of the lower concrete mind, and the inadequate functioning of the unifying intuition. Illusion arises when the symbol which is intended merely to indicate the "thing-in-itself" is mistaken for the "thing-in-itself." Illusion results when there is a failure to see reality as it is because of the interference of thoughtforms.

Incarnation: The process through which the "I" gains experience upon the etheric-physical, astral and lower mental planes. It is also the process through which the personality evolves and the causal body is enriched with quality and potency. Incarnation is literally the immersion of the "I" into "flesh." The word "flesh" denotes the substance of the personality vehicles.

Individual: Usually, a human being who has reached the stage of distinct personhood – i.e., an integrated personality. In a more general sense, however, the term is simply used as a means of referring to a person, although the term hardly applies unless the person has emerged from the mass of humanity and has developed, therefore, certain unique characteristics. In a deeper sense, the true individual is the soul – i.e., the indivisible, 'un-dividable' identity, which is the true source of any distinctness found in its (the soul's) appearance, the personality.

Initiate: One who, having demonstrated a degree of mastery over a given phase of spiritual development, has entered a new and succeeding phase with the purpose of eventually mastering that phase as well. Every initiate is one who is commencing a new task having satisfactorily completed a previous one. Technically, an individual is called an initiate once he has undergone what is called in Christian terminology "the Birth of the Christ in the Cave of the Heart" – i.e., the first initiation. From the perspective of Hierarchy, however, no individual is considered a true initiate until he has become a completely soul–infused personality, and has, hence, attained the third initiation – the initiation of the Transfiguration.

Inner: A general term pertaining to the subtle or subjective planes of nature and the fields of the human energy system which are composed of the substance of those planes. "Inner" is obviously a relative term.

Inner god: The Solar Angel. A highly developed spiritual entity which supervises over aeons the evolution of the incarnated human being.

Integrated personality: A condition of interactive harmony between all aspects of the personality, and their purposeful and efficient coordination and management by the soul–in–incarnation.

Involution: The descent of spirit into matter. The phase of involution characterized by the tendency of spirit to *in–volve* itself (i.e., "wrap itself up" in matter), precedes the phase of evolution in which spirit gradually frees itself from the material sheaths or fields it has painstakingly appropriated.

Kama–manas: Desire–tinged mind. An admixture of the principle of *kama* (desire) and the principle of *manas* (mind) producing a non–objective thought process – a thought process strongly influenced by the astral body with its emotional and feeling states.

Law of Correspondences: A Cosmic Law in accordance with which the structure of any entity upon any level or dimension of nature *corresponds* significantly to the structure of any other entity upon any other level or dimension. Therefore, every entity within Kosmos is built and functions according to structural principles which are *essentially similar* (however different in detail). *Analogy*, consequently, becomes the premier instrument of interpretation when seeking to understand the structural relationship existing between any microsystem and the macrosystem which includes it. The essence of the Law of Correspondences is expressed in the Hermetic Axiom: "As above; so below."

Light: The radiance which results when the One Life enters manifestation. Light is the result of the union of spirit and matter. From one perspective, light *is* manifestation; in the unmanifested state of spirit/matter there is no light. All material forms (however gross or attenuated) are condensations of primal Light.

Light of the soul: Essentially the soul *is* light. From the perspective of the unit of consciousness immersed within the personality vehicles the light of the soul refers to the illuminating influence of superconscious energies playing upon the personality vehicles. Soul light irradiates the personality vehicles increasingly as contact between the personality and soul is strengthened.

Logos (Planetary): "The term is generally applied to the seven highest spirits corresponding to the seven archangels of the Christian. They have all passed through the human stage and are now manifesting through a planet and its evolutions, in the same way that man manifests through his physical body. The highest planetary spirit working through any particular globe is, in reality, the personal God of the planet." (*IHS* Glossary)

Logos (Solar): A term referring to a great Being or Entity Who is the informing Life of a solar system. A Solar Logos is the all–inclusive IDENTITY of a solar system just as a human Monad is the true and essential identity of man, the human unit. When the terms "*the* Solar Logos," or "*our* Solar Logos" are used, they refer to that great solar deity Who informs our particular solar system. This great Being, according to the Tibetan, is to be found upon the Cosmic Ray of Love, and functions as the heart center in a still greater Being known only as "The One About Whom Naught May Be Said."

Lower man: The fourfold personality: the physical field, etheric field, sentient (astral) field, and lower mental field.

Lower Unconscious: The Freudian unconscious. It contains, according to Dr. Roberto Assagioli, "(a) the elementary psychological activities which direct the life of the body; (b) the fundamental drives and primitive urges;(c) many complexes charged with intense emotion; (d) dreams and imaginations of an inferior kind; (e) lower, uncontrolled parapsychological processes; (f) various pathological manifestations, such as phobias, obsessions, compulsive urges and paranoid delusions." It is the "hell" of psychological life, and its phenomena emanate from the lowest strata of the astral and mental planes.

Lunar lords: The lesser builders. The entities responsible for creating the lower aspects of the human being. The personality nature of man is comprised of several lunar lords – the involutionary elementals which constitute the major aspects of personality.

Macrocosm: "The great universe, literally; or God manifesting through His body, the solar system." (*IHS* Glossary) The term "macrocosm," again, is a relative term, and refers to a great, embracing Unity which contains a multitude of lesser unities (microcosms) which are, essentially, reflections of the Unity which embraces them. The macrocosm is the prototypical pattern for all microcosms which it contains and through which it expresses. The human kingdom, for instance, is the macrocosm to the animal, vegetable and mineral kingdoms; however, the human kingdom is merely *micro*cosmic when compared to the Heavenly Man (the Planetary Logos of the planet Earth), Who, in turn, is *micro*cosmic compared to the Grand Heavenly Man (the Solar Logos of our particular solar system), etc.

Mahatma: A great soul. An advanced spiritual teacher.

Mahamanvantara: "The great interludes of time between two solar systems. This term is frequently applied to the greater solar cycles. It implies a period of universal activity." (*IHS* Glossary)

Manas, or Manasic Principle: "Literally, the Mind, the mental faculty; that which distinguishes man from the mere animal. It is the individualising principle; that which enables man to know that he exists, feels, and knows. It is divided in some schools into two parts, higher or abstract mind, and lower or concrete mind." (*IHS* Glossary)

Mahachohan: "The Head of the third great department of the Hierarchy. This great being is the Lord of Civilisation, and the flowering forth of the principle of intelligence. He is the embodiment on the planet of the third, or intelligence aspect of deity in its five activities." (*IHS* Glossary) These five activities are correlated with the third ray and the four subsidiary rays of which the third ray is considered the synthesis.

Mantram, pl., mantra: "A form of words or syllables rhythmically arranged so that when sounded certain vibrations are generated." (*IHS* Glossary) More loosely, a mantram is an affirmation – a verbal formula which facilitates the "grounding" or manifestation of transpersonal energies through the personality. Mantra yoga is the practice of the divine science of sound.

Manu: "The representative name of the great Being Who is the Ruler, primal progenitor and chief of the human race. It comes from the Sanskrit root 'man' – to think." (*IHS* Glossary) The Manu wields the Will of Sanat Kumara, and is one of the foremost representatives upon our planet of the first Ray of Will and Power.

Manvantara: "A period of activity as opposed to a period of rest, without reference to any specific length of cycle. Frequently used to express a period of planetary activity and its seven races." (*IHS* Glossary)

Maya: A basically etheric condition characterized by the dominance of chaotic forces which impulse spiritually purposeless activity.

Meditation: Prolonged concentration leading to the transcendence of the lower concrete mind. For the spiritual aspirant and disciple, meditation is that means of mental culture through which the influence and control of the Solar Angel are established in the life of the personality. Meditation is also practiced by entities far in advance of the human being. It is always a means of penetrating into new dimensions of consciousness and of being.

Mental body: The chitta or mind–stuff. That part of the human constitution through which the soul–in–incarnation formulates concrete thoughts or thoughtforms. The mental body is the most creative aspect of the threefold personality, and is definitely responsive to the guidance of the personal (and, later, transpersonal) will.

Microcosm: "The little universe, or man manifesting through his body, the physical body." (*IHS* Glossary) The microcosm is often regarded as the threefold human system considered as a unit: personality, soul and Monad.

Middle Unconscious: "This is formed of psychological elements similar to those of our waking consciousness and easily accessible to it. In this inner region our various experiences are assimilated, our ordinary mental and imaginative activities are elaborated and developed in a sort of psychological gestation before their birth into the light of consciousness." (*Psychosynthesis*, Roberto Assagioli)

Monad: "The One. The threefold spirit on its own plane. In occultism it often means the unified triad – Atma, Buddhi, Manas; Spiritual Will, Intuition and Higher mind, – or the immortal part of man which reincarnates in the lower kingdoms and gradually progresses through them to man and thence to the final goal. (*IHS* Glossary) "Monads are spiritual–substantial entities, self–motivated, self–impelled, self–conscious in infinitely varying degrees, the ultimate elements of the universe." (*Occult Glossary*) Within this planetary manifestation, the human Monad can be considered the irreducible spiritual SELF.

Monism: "A view that there is only one kind of ultimate substance. The view that reality is one unitary organic whole with no independent parts." (*Webster's New Collegiate Dictionary*)

Not–Self: Within man the microcosm, the not–Self denotes all aspects of the human energy system with the exception of the essential spiritual Self, the Monad. More frequently, all aspects of the human personality. In a larger sense, the not–SELF includes all aspects of the universe with the exception of the essential IDENTITY, the ONE LIFE. The not–SELF is the one *Object* in relation to which the SELF is the one Subject.

Noumenon: The subjective, abstract, causal pattern which, precipitated upon any of the planes of form, becomes a phenomenon.

Numerical resonance: A structural characteristic of Kosmos as a result of which a given entity whose essential nature is closely related to a given number will bear certain structural or functional similarities to another entity whose essential nature is closely related to the same number.

Old Adam: A biblical term referring to the personality and its consciousness before they come under the influence of the Solar Angel. The union of the personality and its consciousness with the Solar Angel results in what is often called the "new man in Christ."

The One Life: The ultimate, indivisible Ground of All Being – THAT from which all entities emanate.

Overshadowing: The psychospiritual process by which a nonphysical entity becomes an influential presence in the personality life of an incarnated entity of lesser evolutionary development. Some prefer to call this process "over–lighting."

Overshadowing soul: The Solar Angel, once it begins to become actively involved in the guiding of the human personality which it has under supervision. The Solar Angel becomes an influential, communicative presence once the soul–in–incarnation within the personality begins to disidentify from the personality vehicles and turn its attention towards the spiritual Source from which it emanated.

Pairs of opposites: Any of a great number of dualities, each of which are characterized by energies of contrasting polarities. As far as humanity is concerned the most important pairs of opposites are spirit and matter; soul and personality; and the many diametrically opposed tendencies to be found within the astral body and upon the astral plane.

The Path: The lengthy sequence of rightly–oriented thoughts, feelings and acts which are required to lead the human being from darkness to light, from the unreal to the real, and from death to immortality. From another perspective, the *sutratma* ("thread soul") and the *antahkarana* (bridge of light) can also be considered the Path, as they unite the higher principles of the human being with the lower. The Path is sometimes called the Path of Return or the Path of Evolution.

Permanent atom: "Those five atoms, with the mental unit, one on each of the five planes of human evolution (the mental unit being also on the mental plane) which the monad appropriates for purposes of manifestation. They form a stable centre and are relatively permanent. Around them the various sheaths or bodies are built. They are literally small force centers." (*IHS* Glossary)

Personality: Usually regarded as the lower quaternary consisting of the physical, etheric, astral and lower mental bodies, plus the incarnated "I" which is separable from these bodies (though temporarily immersed within them). The personality is considered the "mask" of the soul. It is at once the soul's primary instrument of expression and also that which often stands in the way of the manifestation of soul energy.

Phenomenon: A phenomenon is an event precipitated within the three worlds of human evolution (the lower three planes) and deriving its impetus and essential structure from a subjective, archetypal pattern (found upon the so-called "formless planes") which is its noumenon.

Personal psychosynthesis: The harmonization and coordination of the personality around an integrating center – the "I" (or soul–in–incarnation). Strictly personal psychosynthesis is a preliminary phase in the psychosynthetic process, and does not require that the influence of the Transpersonal Self be consciously related to the various aspects of the personality undergoing integration.

Physical body: The lowest and most familiar of the four personality vehicles. It is composed of matter in its densest form, and is essentially an automaton, completely conditioned by the energies and forces which flow through the etheric body. According to the Ageless Wisdom the etheric body is the true physical vehicle of man.

The (Divine) Plan: The hierarchically–conceived sequence of activities by means of which the Purpose of our Planetary Logos is executed. While the Plan is flexible, the Purpose is not. The Plan is like a great "blueprint" (frequently modified as need arises) which details the type and sequence of evolutionary steps necessary for all beings upon all planes of our planetary manifestation.

Plane: "From the Latin *planus* (level, flat), an extension of space, whether in the physical or metaphysical sense, *e.g.*, a 'plane of consciousness.' As used in Occultism, the term denotes the range or extent of some state of consciousness, or of the perceptive power of a particular set of senses, or the action of a particular force, or the state of matter corresponding to any of the above." (*Theosophical Glossary*) A particular range of vibration in the One Substance.

Point of Tension: An intense focalization of consciousness by means of which impressionability is heightened, and penetration into higher levels of consciousness or being is expedited.

Prana: "Usually translated 'life'; but rather the psycho-electrical veil or 'psycho-electrical field' manifesting in the individual as vitality. Commonly called the 'Life-principle.'" (*Occult Glossary,*) For practical purposes, prana can be considered the vital energy which is conducted through the etheric body and which vitalizes and animates the physical body.

Precipitation: The condensation or congealing of energy into a more "material" state. This is brought about by a reduction of vibratory frequency which results in a densification of energy/substance. Hence, precipitation is the transition of energy/substance from a state of relative formlessness into a state which, relatively considered, is one of form.

Psyche: In general, the combined emotional and mental fields which determine the nature and quality of the psychological life of the average individual. More accurately, the true psyche is the soul functioning through the higher three mental subplanes – i.e., consciousness functioning through the causal body. Even after the destruction of the causal body, *psyche* persists. Psyche is essentially the *subjective sensitivity* of any self-conscious entity.

Psychosynthesis: An eclectic system of psychotherapeutics the purpose of which is the recognition, coordination, harmonization and integration of all aspects of the human being. Psychosynthesis is usually divided into two phases: personal psychosynthesis and spiritual psychosynthesis. Psychosynthesis was pioneered by the Italian psychiatrist (and esotericist) Roberto Assagioli.

Ray: An emanation which is continuous in essence with its source. For instance, the Monad projects itself into all systemic planes lower than its own by emanating a ray (not to be confused with the "monadic ray" – 1st, 2nd, 3rd, etc.) which incarnates in these kingdoms by means of appropriating a single atom of substance cosubstantial with each such plane (i.e., a permanent atom). The Monad thus creates 'outposts of its own identity' upon each of the 'sub-Monadic' planes. This ray (which might be called the 'identity ray of the Monad' and is 'the *I* in essence' arrives at the self-conscious stage of development in the human kingdom.

The (Seven) Rays: The primary universal septenate. Within our local cosmosystem the seven rays are the seven qualitative emanations of those seven great Beings known as the "Seven Rishis of the Great Bear." These seven emanations are the primary conditioning streams of energy which qualify all entities within the ring-pass-not of That Entity Whom we may (with justification given our limited stage of evolution) regard as the macrocosm – namely, "The One About Whom Naught May Be Said."

"The seven rays are the sum total of the divine Consciousness, of the universal Mind; They might be regarded as seven intelligent Entities through Whom the plan is working out. They embody divine purpose, express the qualities required for the materialising of that purpose, and They create the forms and are the forms through which the divine idea can be carried forward to completion....They are the conscious executors of divine purpose; They are the seven Breaths, animating all forms which have been created by Them to carry out the plan." (*Esteric Psychology, Vol. I, p.60–61*)

Rays of Aspect: The primary trinity of energies consisting of the first, second and third rays. These three rays correspond to the three essential divisions of every entity. In the human being they correspond archetypally to the Monad (ray one), the soul (ray two) and the personality (ray three). From the combinations and permutations of these three rays are derived the four Rays of Attribute.

Rays of Attribute: The four subsidiary rays (rays four, five, six and seven) derived from all possible combinations of the three Rays of Aspect.

Reincarnation: "Rebirth; the once universal doctrine, which taught that the Ego is born on this earth an innumerable number of times. ...the putting on of flesh periodically and throughout long cycles by the higher human Soul (Buddhi–Manas) or *Ego* is taught in the Bible as it is in all other ancient scriptures, and 'resurrection' means only the *rebirth* of the Ego in another form." (*The Key to Theosophy* Glossary)

Ring–pass–not: "This is at the circumference of the manifested solar system, and is the periphery of the influence of the sun, both esoterically and exoterically understood. The limit of the field of activity of the central life force." (*IHS* Glossary) Every entity, great and small, has its particular ring–pass–not, which is capable of extension as the potency of the entity's life nucleus increases. In the human family, every initiation signifies the achievement of a significant extension of the initiate's ring–pass–not.

Scheme (Planetary): An aggregation of seven planetary chains within the ring–pass–not of a Planetary Logos. Each chain (consisting of seven planetary globes) is qualified by one of seven distinct qualities. Each chain, as well, functions as one of seven major centers or chakras within the energy system of the Planetary Logos.

Self: According to the convention used in *Tapestry of the Gods,* when this word is spelled with a capital, it usually refers to the soul, Solar Angel, Higher Self, or Transpersonal Self. When written in the lower case, the word "self" generally refers to the incarnated human soul within the personality. When all letters are capitalized (as is SELF), the term generally refers to the Identity of the One Life – the One Universal SELF, from Which (or from Whom) all other selves emanate.

Shamballa: The supreme state of spiritual tension upon our planet. This state (though in some respects it may also be considered a locale) is usually called "the Center where the Will of God is Known." In terms of the energy structure of our Earth and its various planes, Shamballa is considered the planetary head center. Shamballa is the 'residence' of Sanat Kumara (the Lord of the World, the Ancient of Days, the One Initiator, the "Father" to Whom Christ often addressed Himself, as recounted in the various Biblical narratives).

Sheath: A term referring to a "body" or vehicle of consciousness on any of the seven systemic planes found upon the cosmic physical plane. The seven sheaths are seven fields of substance/energy differentiated by seven distinct ranges of vibration. Each sheath is, essentially, a vesture of consciousness.

Solar Lords: Great entities Who, in contradistinction to the lunar lords, constitute the relatively immortal aspect of the human energy system – i.e., the causal body and the Egoic lotus upon the abstract levels of the mental plane. According to *A Treatise on*

Cosmic Fire, Solar Lords (Agnishvattas) of varying ranks and grades come together to create the Egoic manifestation.

Soul: When it is called "the soul," this term usually refers to that highly developed entity (at least, from the human perspective) known as the Solar Angel, Higher Self, Transpersonal Self, or Ego (with a capital *E*) aeonially associated in a supervisory capacity with every human being. More generally, soul refers to the factor of sensitivity, sentiency, or consciousness underlying all manifestation. On all levels of manifestation, and within all systems great and small, there is but *One Soul*, one great sensitive, responsive Consciousness which is the *essential consciousness* of the countless multitude of conscious units. Soul or consciousness is, ultimately, *indivisible*, even though the multitudinous differentiations of form produce in the mind of man the illusion of separate consciousnesses, and separate souls.

Soul–infused personality: A transfigured personality which, consequently, offers no resistance or obstruction to the radiance of the overshadowing soul. When the personality is soul–infused, the soul is manifesting its nature, which, essentially, is Love–Wisdom, through a purified and prepared personality instrument.

Soul–in–incarnation: The incarnated "I" (i.e., the attenuated projection of the Monad) in its state of temporary, cyclic association with the personality vehicles.

Spirit: The Monad. "The spirit is the immortal element in us, the deathless flame within us which dies never, which never was born, and which retains throughout the entire Maha–manvantara its own quality, essence, and life, sending down into our being and into our various planes certain of its rays or garments or souls *which we are*. The divine spirit of man is linked with the All, being in a highly mystical sense a ray of the All." (*Occult Glossary*)

Spiritual growth: The gradual manifestation of the soul and later the Monad through the human personality. Spiritual growth necessitates the expression of the higher principles of man through his lower principles.

Spiritual Hierarchy: The heart center of the planet, the nucleus of which is a group of enlightened and perfected human beings called the Masters of the Wisdom. The leader of this group is the Lord Maitreya – the Christ. The Spiritual Hierarchy is responsible for guiding the human family according to the Plan of the Planetary Logos. In the process of this guiding, human free will is never infringed.

Spiritual Master (more simply, Master): An enlightened human being known also as a Master of the Wisdom. A Master has overcome the usual personality limitations (and the limitations of human individuality) and is consecrated to carrying forward the Divine Plan, which, as far as earth beings are concerned, is the Plan of the Planetary Logos. A relatively small number of the Masters are directly responsible for teaching and guiding the human family.

Spirit–Matter: "Homogeneous or undifferentiated primordial substance." (*Occult Glossary*)

Spiritual psychosynthesis: The integration of the personality with the will and influence of the overshadowing soul. When the soul or Transpersonal Self is able to fully express itself within and through the personality, a spiritual psychosynthesis has been achieved.

Spiritual Triad: That aspect of the constitution of the human being which stands to the Monad, as the etheric–physical, astral and lower mental vehicles stand to the personality. The Spiritual Triad is a synthesis of the faculties of *atma*, *buddhi* and *manas*. Triadal consciousness is planetary in nature and transcends the spiritual individuality of causal consciousness. Those who have attained Triadal consciousness have entered to a significant extent into the mind, love and will of the Planetary Logos. From one important point of view, the Spiritual Triad is not only a state of being and a level of consciousness, but an *entity* as well.

The Subconscious: During a given incarnation the subconscious contains the memories of all personal experiences which have fallen below the threshold of consciousness. The subconscious, however, contains *all* memories of *all* previous incarnations. Such memories can be deliberately evoked for review once a high stage of spiritual unfoldment has been attained.

Sub–personality: A semiautonomous constellation of personality elements forming a relatively enduring personality pattern. Each such pattern within the personality reacts in a manner consistent with its own nature. Each such pattern develops from the individual's attempt to satisfy a particular need or a particular constitutional tendency. Certain sub–personalities may be legacies of previous incarnations and will be distinguished by the quality of a certain ray or rays.

Substance/energy: Light. Energy considered as the primordial substance and appearing in a vast continuum of vibratory states. The lower states of vibration result in what is perceived by the human consciousness as a condensation or crystallization of energy (i.e., the world of concrete objects). The higher states of vibration are perceived as rarefaction, attenuation and pervasiveness. Even in relation to the dense physical plane, the new physics has informed us that matter is essentially energy, and that energy is matter.

Superconscious: The higher unconscious. The "region" from which man receives his "higher intuitions and inspirations – artistic, philosophical or scientific, ethical 'imperatives' and urges to humanitarian and heroic action. It is the source of the higher feelings, such as altruistic love; of genius and of the states of contemplation, illumination and ecstasy. In this realm are latent the higher psychic functions and spiritual energies." (*Psychosynthesis*, Roberto Assagioli)

Theosophy: "A compound Greek word: theos, a 'divine being,' a 'god'; sophia, 'wisdom'; hence divine wisdom. Theosophy is the majestic Wisdom–Religion of the archaic ages and is as old as thinking man." (*Occult Glossary*)

Transcendent personality: The true *individuality*, the human consciousness as it expresses itself through the causal body. The qualities of the transcendent personality are the result of the accumulation or harvest of the best qualities of all personality cycles or incarnations. It is characterized by the wisdom which the individual has 'won' for himself through aeons of personal labor; the fruitage of this experience is stored as quality in the substance of the causal body in semipermanent form.

Transpersonal Self: The Solar Angel. A highly evolved being Who mastered the human stage of evolution in another solar system. The Solar Angel has undertaken responsibility for the supervision and guidance of the evolving "I" or *Monadic projection* within the personality. The Transpersonal Self (sometimes called the "Angel of the Presence" is an ontological reality capable of experiential verification, and can be contacted by the individual largely through the processes of meditation. From another point of view, the state of consciousness and selfhood which results when the "I" (which is essentially a Monadic projection or emanation) manifests consciously through the causal body (and thus directly under the inspiration of the Solar Angel) can justifiably be called the state of Transpersonal Selfhood.

The Unconscious: All the subtle states and planes of nature which are not (for various reasons) immediately cognizable by the soul–in–incarnation.

Vehicles of consciousness: The bodies of man; the fields through which the soul–in–incarnation functions. Vehicles are the means by which the "I" can contact the various planes of nature.

Vibration: An oscillation of a unit of primordial substance, the frequency of which determines the degree of condensation or rarefaction of that substance.